Auditing Toolbar

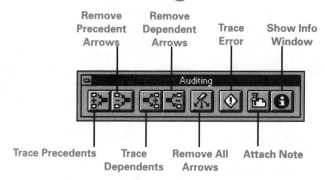

Remove Precedent Arrows

Remove Dependent Arrows

Trace Error

Show Info Window

Trace Precedents

Trace Dependents

Remove All Arrows

Attach Note

Drawing Toolbar

Line   Ellipse   Freeform   Arrow   Filled Rectangle   Filled Arc   Create Button   Bring to Front   Group Objects   Reshape   Pattern

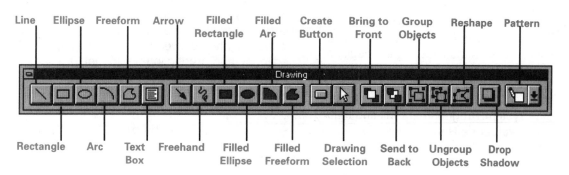

Rectangle   Arc   Text Box   Freehand   Filled Ellipse   Filled Freeform   Drawing Selection   Send to Back   Ungroup Objects   Drop Shadow

Query and Pivot Toolbar

Pivot Table Field   Group   Show Detail   Refresh Data

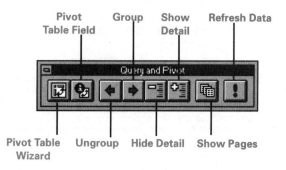

Pivot Table Wizard   Ungroup   Hide Detail   Show Pages

FOR EVERY COMPUTER QUESTION,
THERE IS A SYBEX BOOK THAT HAS THE ANSWER

Each computer user learns in a different way. Some need thorough, methodical explanations, while others are too busy for details. At Sybex we bring nearly 20 years of experience to developing the book that's right for you. Whatever your needs, we can help you get the most from your software and hardware, at a pace that's comfortable for you.

We start beginners out right. You will learn by seeing and doing with our **Quick & Easy** series: friendly, colorful guidebooks with screen-by-screen illustrations. For hardware novices, the **Your First** series offers valuable purchasing advice and installation support.

Often recognized for excellence in national book reviews, our **Mastering** titles are designed for the intermediate to advanced user, without leaving the beginner behind. A **Mastering** book provides the most detailed reference available. Add our pocket-sized **Instant Reference** titles for a complete guidance system. Programmers will find that the new **Developer's Handbook** series provides a more advanced perspective on developing innovative and original code.

With the breathtaking advances common in computing today comes an ever increasing demand to remain technologically up-to-date. In many of our books, we provide the added value of software, on disks or CDs. Sybex remains your source for information on software development, operating systems, networking, and every kind of desktop application. We even have books for kids. Sybex can help smooth your travels on the **Internet** and provide **Strategies and Secrets** to your favorite computer games.

As you read this book, take note of its quality. Sybex publishes books written by experts—authors chosen for their extensive topical knowledge. In fact, many are professionals working in the computer soft-ware field. In addition, each manuscript is thoroughly reviewed by our technical, editorial, and production personnel for accuracy and ease-of-use before you ever see it—our guarantee that you'll buy a quality Sybex book every time.

To manage your hardware headaches and optimize your software potential, ask for a Sybex book.

FOR MORE INFORMATION, PLEASE CONTACT:

Sybex Inc.
2021 Challenger Drive
Alameda, CA 94501
Tel: (510) 523-8233 • (800) 227-2346
Fax: (510) 523-2373

Let us hear from you.

Talk to SYBEX authors, editors and fellow forum members.

Get tips, hints and advice online.

Download magazine articles, book art, and shareware.

Join the SYBEX Forum on CompuServe®

you're already a CompuServe user, just type **GO SYBEX** to join the BEX Forum. If not, try CompuServe for free by calling 1-800-848-8199 d ask for Representative 560. You'll get one free month of basic rvice and a $15 credit for CompuServe extended services—a $23.95 lue. Your personal ID number and password will be activated when u sign up.

Join us online today. Type **GO SYBEX** on CompuServe.
If you're not a CompuServe member, call Representative 560
at **1-800-848-8199**.

(outside U.S./Canada call 614-457-0802)

Mastering Excel 5 for Windows™
for Windows™
Special Edition

Second Edition

Thomas Chester

San Francisco ▲ Paris ▼ Düsseldorf ▲ Soest

SYBEX®

ACQUISITIONS EDITORS: Joanne Cuthbertson, Kristine Plachy
DEVELOPMENTAL EDITOR: Richard Mills
EDITORS: Doug Robert, Armin Brott
PROJECT EDITOR: Michelle Khazai
TECHNICAL EDITORS: Tanya Strub, Bob Schmidt
BOOK DESIGNER: Helen Bruno
DESKTOP PUBLISHERS: Ann Dunn, Dina F Quan
PRODUCTION COORDINATOR: Janet K. Boone
PRODUCTION ASSISTANT: Kate Westrich
INDEXER: Ted Laux
COVER DESIGNER: Design Site
COVER PHOTOGRAPHER: Mark Johann
PHOTO ART DIRECTION: Ingalls + Associates

SYBEX is a registered trademark of SYBEX Inc.

TRADEMARKS: SYBEX has attempted throughout this book to distinguish proprietary trademarks from descriptive terms by following the capitalization style used by the manufacturer.

Every effort has been made to supply complete and accurate information. However, SYBEX assumes no responsibility for its use, nor for any infringement of the intellectual property rights of third parties which would result from such use.

First edition copyright ©1994 SYBEX Inc.

Library of Congress Card Number: 94-69305
ISBN: 0-7821-1602-7

Manufactured in the United States of America

10 9 8 7

Contents at a Glance

Table of Contents

►► INTRODUCTION

Spreadsheets started out as electronic versions of hard copy accounting worksheets with one major purpose: simple row-and-column arithmetic. These programs have evolved dramatically over the past decade, and are now one of the most widely used categories of software products. Excel has long been the leading graphical spreadsheet, and Microsoft has released a major upgrade with version 5.0.

►► *How Excel Is Used in the Workplace*

Excel is used for a wide variety of applications.

► *Basic Use*

Even though Excel is a multifaceted tool, a considerable percentage of users still use it as an electronic replacement for the hardcopy accountant's worksheet. In this capacity, Excel can be used to help automate financial statements, business forecasting, transaction registers, inventory control, accounts receivable, accounts payable—the list of potential applications is endless.

► *Financial Modeling*

Financial models can be created that let you play what-if. By changing one or more variables, the model recalculates, and a new set of results can be presented in tabular and/or graphical format. Multi-level roll-ups can be performed automatically. For example, cost centers can roll up into departments, which roll up into divisions, which roll up into company summaries.

▶ Scientific & Engineering

While spreadsheets are usually thought of as tools for business, Excel provides many statistical, analytical, and scientific functions. It is used in many scientific and engineering environments to crunch numbers and present findings.

▶ Presentation Graphics

Excel is a powerful, flexible graphical presentation tool. Worksheets can include charts and graphs, and can be formatted for high-impact presentations.

▶ Database Management

Excel is a highly adept data management tool. For many database requirements, users find that Excel's interface allows them to get up to speed very quickly in comparison to "real" database management programs. It is very easy to enter, edit, sort, and filter databases in Excel.

▶ Database Front-End

Excel database manipulation is simple, yet spreadsheets inherently lack certain features found in actual database management programs. By using Excel as a database *front-end*, you can realize the best of both worlds. Excel is able to access data stored in a wide variety of database formats, and is an ideal tool to analyze and manipulate data, and to create high-impact reports and graphical presentations.

▶ Custom Applications

Excel is a powerful application development tool. Many of the world's largest corporations have utilized Excel to create serious, large-scale custom applications. It is the first Microsoft product to include *Visual Basic, Applications Edition* (VBA), the language that will eventually drive all of Microsoft's programmable applications.

▶▶ *Roadmap*

The book is divided into seven parts.

▶ *Part One—Getting Started*

This part of the book is important for beginners, but even veterans can learn about some important new features.

- Chapter 1 explains the elements of the Excel workspace, including new user-interface features such as tabbed dialog boxes and submenus.

- In Chapter 2 you'll learn about the new workbook interface, and get an introduction to such basic skills as saving your work.

- Chapter 3 is essential for novices. It explains how to enter and edit information, how to navigate the worksheet, and how to copy and move information.

▶ *Part Two—Basic Skills*

Here is where you learn many of the most important basic skills.

- In Chapter 4, learn how to enter formulas and functions. You can also get a clear explanation of a topic that sometimes confuses new users—cell references.

- Chapter 5 covers the many different ways you can format cells.

- Learn about the nuances of printing in Chapter 6.

- Chapter 7 provides a number of productivity tips. You will probably learn some important skills, regardless of how much Excel experience you have.

▶ *Part Three—Tapping Excel's Power*

This section of the book provides important insights on how to get the most out of Excel.

- Using names is vitally important, and Chapter 8 provides a thorough discussion of this topic.

- Chapter 9 provides a comprehensive discussion of the handful of worksheet functions considered essential for serious Excel users.

- Don't skip Chapter 10! Templates are an important topic, and this chapter explains not only how to use them, but why.

- Chapter 11 explains how to audit, protect, and document workbooks and worksheets.

▶ *Part Four—Graphics and Charts*

You might have a lot of fun in this part of the book.

- Chapter 12 shows you how to place graphics on worksheets, and how to format them.

- Learn all of the important charting skills in Chapters 13 and 14.

▶ *Part Five—Working Effectively with Databases*

This part of the book is vitally important, even if the problems you are trying to solve do not appear to be database problems.

- Chapters 15 and 16 show you how to work with internal databases (or *lists*)—data that resides on a worksheet.

- Arguably, pivot tables are the most important new feature in Excel 5, and they are covered in depth in Chapter 17.

- Excel is a powerful tool for accessing external databases, and Chapter 18 explains how to do it.

▶ *Part Six—Customizing Excel*

Excel is easy to customize, so don't be put off if you are not a programmer.

- In Chapter 19, learn how to place controls, such as list boxes and option buttons, on worksheets. (It's easy!) You'll also learn how to create custom dialog boxes.

- Chapter 20 provides an introduction to macros, and shows you how to use the macro recorder effectively.

- Create a powerful, graphical custom application, start to finish, in Chapter 21.

▶ Part Seven—Solving Real-World Problems

This part of the book covers many special skills to help you solve real problems.

- Consolidation, a vital topic, is covered in Chapter 22.

- Chapter 23 shows how to use three important what-if features: Goal Seek, Solver, and Scenario Manager.

- Learn how to work with add-ins in Chapter 24, including View Manager, Report Manager, and the Analysis ToolPak.

- If you think OLE is just a buzzword, read Chapter 25 to learn how to employ this important (yet simple) technology. You will also learn how to import and export data, and how to transition from Lotus 1-2-3.

- Learn some key skills in Chapter 25, such as custom AutoFill, customizing toolbars, and array formulas.

▶▶ What's New in Excel 5

There are a lot of new features in Excel 5 that you will want to explore.

▶ Everything Is a Workbook

Workbooks were first introduced in Excel 4. In Excel 5, workbooks are no longer an option. All Excel 5 worksheets reside in workbooks, with tabs used to navigate the sheets. See Chapter 2 for in-depth coverage of this key structural change.

▶ *Charting Overhaul*

Many users will welcome the major overhaul of Excel's charting engine. Some of the key new features are:

- Simplified interface for creating, modifying, and customizing charts
- Drag and drop data onto a chart to add a data point or data series
- New Error Bars and Trendlines
- Flexible combination charts

See Chapters 14 and 15 for in-depth coverage of the new charting features.

▶ *Simplified Interface*

The Excel interface has received a facelift. Several new interface features are covered in Chapter 1:

- Submenus, also known as cascading menus
- Tabbed dialog boxes
- Tear-off palettes

▶ *TipWizard*

The new TipWizard, covered in Chapter 7, provides shortcuts for tasks that you perform, as you perform them.

▶ *In-Cell Editing*

This feature will be welcome news to those with eye fatigue after squinting at the formula bar for hours on end. Chapter 3 explains how to edit cells in-place.

▶ *Format Individual Characters within a Cell*

Excel has long provided a rich variety of cell formatting options. Now, you can format *individual characters* within a cell. See Chapter 5.

▶ *Database Management*

Excel has always provided powerful database manipulation features, but a lot of learning was involved in order to harness this power. Excel 5's major overhaul of the database features is one of the most important improvements to Excel. Sorting and filtering have been vastly simplified. See Part 5 to learn about managing and analyzing data.

▶ *Pivot Tables*

For many users, Pivot Tables will be the most important new feature in Excel 5. Pivot Tables provide a very flexible and powerful way for users to view and pivot data. If you are considering using Lotus Improv as an analytical tool, it will serve you well to explore Excel's Pivot Table before taking the Lotus plunge. See Chapter 17 for coverage of this powerful new feature.

▶ *Simplified Access to External Databases*

A large percentage of Excel users, particularly those in the corporate environment, use Excel to access information stored in external database systems such as dBASE, Paradox, FoxPro, SQL Server, and Oracle. A new tool, Microsoft Query, has vastly simplified access to external databases. See Chapter 18 for a primer on Microsoft Query.

▶ *OLE 2 Support*

Excel now supports the second version of the object linking and embedding specification (OLE 2). This means it will be easier to work with embedded objects from other applications, such as a word processor or graphics program, in your Excel documents. (See Chapter 25.)

▶ *Visual Basic, Applications Edition*

Excel 5 is the first Microsoft application to adopt Microsoft's common macro language, which is based on their highly successful programming language, Visual Basic. This will be by far the biggest news for application developers. See Part 6 for an introduction to VBA.

▶▶ *Conventions Used in this Book*

- Toolbar shortcuts are indicated with an icon in the left margin, as pictured here.

- Menu commands are expressed using the following convention: File ➤ Print.

- The plus sign is used to indicate when one key is held down while another key is pressed. For example, Shift+Tab means to hold down the Shift key while pressing the Tab key.

- At the beginning of each chapter is a *Fast Track*, which provides quick coverage of the most important topics covered in the chapter.

Getting Started

PART ONE

▶ ▶ **I**n *Part One* you will get an overview of the Excel landscape, which consists of cells, worksheets and workbooks, windows, dialog boxes, and toolbars. If you have worked with previous versions of Excel this will be familiar terrain, but it's well worth your while to skim through Part One and check out new features in Excel 5, such as workbooks, in-cell editing, and drop-down tool palettes.

► ► **CHAPTER** **1**

The Excel
Environment

▶▶ FAST TRACK

▶ ***A worksheet consists of 16,384 rows and 256 columns.*** **16**

They are all available—whether you use them or not.

▶ ***To display or hide a toolbar*** **17**

Choose View ➤ Toolbars, select checkboxes for the toolbars to display, and click OK.

▶ ***To learn a tool's function*** **18**

Point at the tool with the mouse. A pop-up tool title will be displayed below the tool (if tool tips are turned on), and an explanation will be displayed in the status bar.

▶ ***To reshape a toolbar*** **19**

Drag the toolbar borders.

▶ ***To get help*** **23**

Choose the Contents, Search, or Index command from the Help menu. Or, press F1 for help on a selected menu command or for the active dialog box. Or, click the Help tool, then click the item you want help on.

▶ ▶ *T**his** chapter provides an overview of the Excel workspace, with an emphasis on new and changed features:*

- *How to start Excel*
- *The menu system*
- *Tabbed dialog boxes*
- *Workbooks and worksheets*
- *Cells*
- *Toolbars*
- *Charts*
- *Getting help*

▶ ▶ *How to Start Excel*

Excel's setup program installs all of the required files on your hard disk and adds several icons to your Program Manager desktop. Once Excel has been installed, there are several ways to start the program:

- From Program Manager, double-click the Excel icon. You will find the Excel icon in the Microsoft Office group if you have Microsoft Office installed, or in the Excel group if you have Excel installed alone, or sometimes in a custom group if a copy of the icon has been pasted there.

- From File Manager, double-click the file EXCEL.EXE (located in the directory that you specified when setting up Excel).

- From File Manager, double-click any Excel file (for example, SALES.XLS or STATS.XLS). Excel will start *and* the file will be opened. (If this doesn't work, you need to *associate* the .XLS extension with Excel, using the File ➤ Associate command in File Manager.)

The first time you run Excel, you are given the opportunity to take a guided tour. If you decline, you can later choose the Help ➤ Quick Preview to get an interactive tour of the Excel environment.

 ➤ ➤ N O T E

> **Because Excel 5 can be easily customized by the user, the screen you see when you first start up the program will probably not look exactly like the screen you might see on your coworkers' machines. Excel's default appearance is based on settings that were chosen when the program was installed and various settings that are available from within Excel.**

➤ ➤ *How to Exit Excel*

There are several ways to exit Excel, all of which will be familiar if you have used other Windows programs:

- Choose the File ➤ Exit command.

- Choose the Close command from the Control menu.

- Double-click the Control menu box in the upper left corner of the Excel window.

- Press Alt+F4.

▶▶ The Windows Interface

Excel runs under Microsoft Windows, and adheres to Windows interface standards. If you have used other Windows programs, you will see many familiar controls, such as the application controls, window controls, menu bar, and scroll bars (see Figure 1.1). These controls work the same way as other Windows programs. If you are new to Microsoft Windows, refer to the introduction for pointers on getting up to speed on the Windows interface.

FIGURE 1.1 ▶

The Excel Workspace

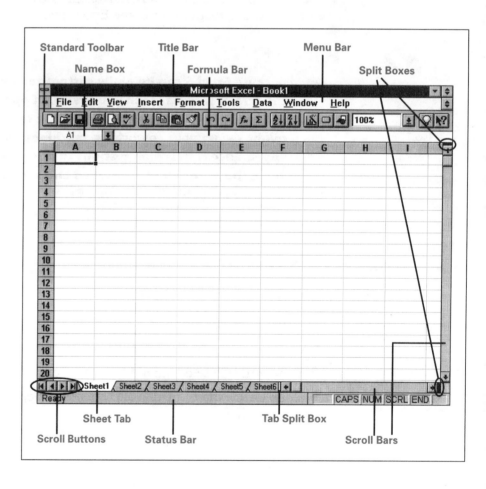

THE STATUS BAR

The status bar (see Figure 1.1) displays a variety of status messages and other information that can be very useful—especially if you are new to Excel. For example, the status bar usually says Ready, which means that the workspace is ready for new activity. When you click on a menu or command, or point to a tool, the status bar displays a brief description of what the menu, command, or tool does. If you want to know the function of a tool you don't recognize, just point to the tool and look at the status bar.

When Excel is carrying out certain activities, such as saving a workbook, the status bar tells you what is happening behind the scenes. If Excel is performing a lengthy operation, such as opening a file with lots of links, you might think Excel has forgotten about you because nothing is happening on the screen. But if you look at the status bar, you will see a message such as "Link:" followed by a time-line that measures the progress of the operation.

Sometimes the status bar displays instructions on what to do next. For example, when you cut or copy cells, the status bar instructs you to "Select destination and press ENTER or choose Paste". On the right side of the status bar are boxes that display the on/off status of several keyboard modes, like Caps Lock, Number Lock, and Overwrite mode.

▸▸ *The Menu System*

In Excel 5, the menus have been completely reorganized, and veterans of previous releases will require some adjustment to the new structure (see Figure 1.1). The simplification of the menu system is achieved with *submenus* and *tabbed dialog boxes*. (Appendix A provides a cross-reference between the Excel 4 menu system and the Excel 5 menu system.)

▶ *If You Know One Windows Application*...

Perhaps the most beneficial aspect of Microsoft Windows is its *common user interface*, often referred to as CUI. What this means is that some of the most often used commands, such as File ➤ New; File ➤ Open; File ➤ Close; File ➤ Save; Edit ➤ Copy; and Edit ➤ Paste; are similar, if not identical, from program to program. If you have used other Windows programs, these commands will be familiar when using Excel. Microsoft has taken the common user interface a step further with Microsoft Office, the suite of products that includes Excel, Word, PowerPoint, and Access (Access is included in the Office Professional bundle). The menu structure of these programs is very similar, so that once you learn any one of them, it is relatively easy to learn another. Other similarities between the Office programs include toolbars and shortcut keys.

▶ *Submenus*

An important improvement to the Excel interface is *submenus*, sometimes referred to as cascading menus. The submenu displays more choices which *cascade* to the right of the menu command when selected. You then choose a command located on the submenu. Commands that display submenus are indicated by the triangle symbol:

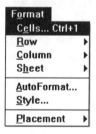

For example, the Format ➤ Row command, when selected, displays a submenu with several options from which you can select:

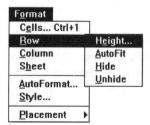

▶ *Keyboard Shortcuts*

Many menu commands have keyboard shortcuts, which appear to the right of the command. For example, Ctrl+C is the shortcut for the Edit ➤ Copy command, and F5 is the shortcut for Edit ➤ Go To, as you can see in the Edit menu. You can learn these shortcuts just by observing the menu commands as you use them.

Edit	
Undo Clear	Ctrl+Z
Repeat Clear	F4
Cut	Ctrl+X
Copy	Ctrl+C
Paste	Ctrl+V
Paste Special...	
Fill	▶
Clear	▶
Delete...	
Delete Sheet	
Move or Copy Sheet...	
Find...	
Replace...	
Go To...	F5
Links...	
Object	

▶ *Commands with Checks*

Some menu commands, such as View ➤ Status Bar, have a checkmark next to the command:

View	
Formula Bar	
✓ Status Bar	
Toolbars...	
View Manager...	
Full Screen	
Zoom...	

These commands are toggles—the checkmark is an indicator specifying whether the setting is on or off. For example, consider the View ➤ Status Bar command on the next page.

- When checked, choosing the View ➤ Status Bar command hides the status bar and unchecks the command.

- When unchecked, choosing the View ➤ Status Bar command displays the status bar and checks the menu command.

▶ Dimmed Menu Commands

A dimmed menu command is a command that, for one reason or another, is unavailable for use. For example, the Window ➤ Unhide command in the following menu is available only when there is a hidden window; otherwise it is dimmed:

▶ Quick Explanations of Menu Commands

The status bar (refer to Figure 1.1) displays a brief explanation for menu commands. The description is displayed when the command is *selected* but not *issued*. To select a command with the mouse, click on it but don't release the mouse button. An explanation of the selected command will appear. For example, when the Insert ➤ Cell command is highlighted, the status bar reads: Insert row, column, or selected cells.

▶ Which Commands Stop for Input?

Menu commands that display dialog boxes have an ellipsis (...) after the command. For example, the View ➤ Toolbars... command in the View menu pictured earlier displays a dialog box, whereas the View ➤ Formula Bar command takes immediate action.

There are exceptions to this interface convention. Some commands are immediate in certain situations and display a dialog box in others. For example, when saving a file that has never been saved, the File ➤ Save command displays a dialog box. Otherwise the command acts immediately. Such commands do not include an ellipsis.

WORKING WITH SHORTCUT MENUS

One of the most convenient ways to choose commands is to use *context-sensitive menus*, also referred to as *shortcut menus*. A shortcut menu is a menu you can display by clicking the right mouse button. The shortcut menu will contain frequently-used commands that pertain to the object you clicked on. Suppose you hide and display toolbars regularly. It takes four mouse-clicks to display a toolbar using the View menu, but only two mouse clicks using the toolbar shortcut menu. To display a toolbar using the shortcut menu, right-click on any toolbar that is already displayed, then click on the name of the toolbar you want from the shortcut menu

Suppose you have a large workbook containing 50 worksheets—it takes a long time to scroll through all those sheet tabs to find the sheet you want. Instead, you can use an often-overlooked shortcut menu for the sheet tab scroll buttons. Right-click the sheet tab scroll buttons at the left side of the sheet tabs (see Figure 1.1), then click on the sheet name you want to display. Perhaps the most useful shortcut menu is the one displayed when you right-click a cell. Commands like Cut, Copy, Paste, and Format are available. To get rid of a shortcut menu, press Esc or click elsewhere on the worksheet. Chapter 7 lists many of the shortcut menus available in Excel 5.

▶▶ *Tabbed Dialog Boxes*

 An important new feature used in Excel is the *tabbed dialog box*. Tabbed dialog boxes group related dialog boxes under one roof. A good example is the dialog box displayed by the Format ➤ Cells command, pictured in Figure 1.2.

FIGURE 1.2 ▶

A tabbed dialog box is like a stack of manila file folders.

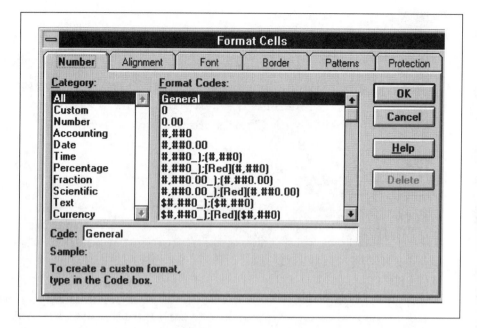

All the cell formatting commands are grouped together in the Format Cells dialog box. Click the tabs on top of the dialog box with the mouse to display the desired dialog box. Tabbed dialog boxes remember which tab was last used—when you redisplay the dialog box, the last tab used is the active tab.

▶▶ *Workbooks*

An Excel document is a *workbook*. Workbooks are containers for one or more *worksheets* (and other types of sheets, as you will later discover).

- Think of a workbook as a binder.
- Think of every worksheet as a page in the binder.

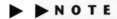 **N O T E**

> **Whereas workbooks were an option in Excel 4, *all* Excel 5 documents are workbooks. Also, there is no longer a concept of bound and unbound worksheets. All worksheets in an Excel 5 workbook are automatically bound.**

Upon starting up Excel, the first thing you typically see is a workbook named *Book1* (see Figure 1.1). Book1 is a new, unsaved workbook that is displayed by default.

▶ *Opening Worksheets Created in Earlier Versions of Excel*

Worksheets that were created in earlier versions of Excel can be opened using the File ➤ Open command. When opened, the old worksheet automatically becomes a workbook containing just one worksheet. When you save the file, Excel asks if you want to convert to Excel 5 format. If you answer no, the file stays in the older format, though any formulas and formats you may have used that are new to Excel 5 will not be saved (see Figure 1.3).

FIGURE 1.3

When you save a file created in an earlier version of Excel, you will be asked if you want to save it in the previous version or update it to Excel 5 format.

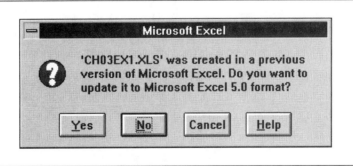

►► **T I P**

> **If users within your organization are still using an older version of Excel, you can still transfer files back and forth. Just remember *not* to update the file to Excel 5 format. See Chapter 2 to learn about workbooks and worksheets.**

►► *Worksheets within Workbooks*

Worksheets are the pages within a workbook. A worksheet consists of a grid of *cells*, very similar to a hardcopy accounting worksheet. Cells, which are oriented in rows and columns, are used to store numbers, text, and formulas. Worksheets are not limited to numbers and text—they can also contain graphical objects, such as charts, arrows, and pictures.

By default, a workbook includes 16 worksheets, named *Sheet1* through *Sheet16*, though there is no limit to the number of worksheets other than available memory. Typically, you would store related worksheets in a single workbook to keep them together. For example, you might keep regional sales projections in one workbook, with information for each region stored on individual worksheets. Another worksheet within the same workbook might be used to consolidate the regions.

At the bottom of the workbook are tabs, which are used to activate the worksheets within that workbook. Activating a worksheet is the equivalent of opening a book to that page. See Chapter 2 for more information on worksheets.

►► *Cells*

Each worksheet is comprised of a tabular grid of *cells*. There are 16,384 rows of cells, numbered 1 through (you guessed it) 16,384 along the left margin of the worksheet. There are 256 columns along the top margin of the worksheet. Usually these columns are labeled alphabetically as A through IV using a single-letter then a double-letter alphabetization scheme. (Columns can also be labeled with numbers by changing the cell reference style, as noted in Chapter 4.)

This means that every worksheet contains over 4,000,000 cells. Text, numbers, and formulas can be entered into cells.

▶ Cell References

Cells are referred to using the column label followed by the row number. For example, the cell coordinate A2 would refer to column 1, row 2. In spreadsheet terminology, a cell's row and column coordinates are called the *cell reference*. See Chapter 4 to learn about cell references.

▶ The Active Cell

When you select a cell by clicking it with the mouse, or moving to it using the keyboard, it becomes the *active cell*. The *Name Box*, on the left of the formula bar (see Figure 1.1), displays the reference of the active cell.

▶▶ Toolbars

Toolbars provide shortcuts for many of the most common commands. There are many different toolbars, each of which contains several individual *tools*. The *Standard toolbar* is displayed by default (see Figure 1.1).

▶ Displaying and Hiding Toolbars

The View ➤ Toolbars command displays the toolbar dialog box, which controls which toolbar or toolbars are displayed and allows them to be customized (see Figure 1.4). The toolbar names have checkboxes next to them—check the box to display the toolbar, or uncheck the box to hide the toolbar.

FIGURE 1.4 ▶

*The View ▶ Toolbars
dialog box*

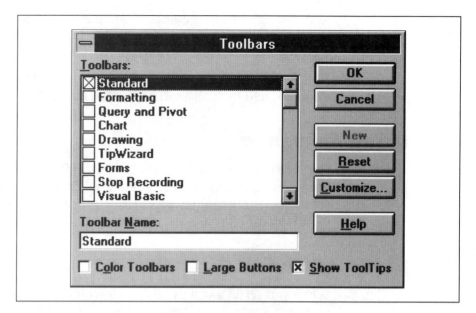

 ▶ ▶T I P

A quick way to display the toolbar dialog box is to point at a toolbar, click the right mouse button, and choose Toolbars from the shortcut menu that appears. You can also choose the toolbar you want from the toolbar shortcut menu.

▶ *Getting Pop-up Tool Explanations*

The function of a tool is sometimes hard to determine by looking at the toolface. The Show ToolTips setting (see Figure 1.4), when checked, causes the title of a tool to be displayed when the tool is pointed at with the mouse. Regardless of the Show ToolTips setting, a brief explanation of the tool is displayed on the status bar when the tool is pointed at with the mouse.

▶ *Controlling the Size of the Tools*

By default, tools are relatively small, and, depending on your monitor, it may be difficult to clearly discern the toolface. Choose the Large Buttons setting (see Figure 1.4) to display large tools.

▶ *Moving Toolbars*

By default, toolbars are "docked" underneath the menu bar. To move a toolbar, point at the bar (i.e., without actually pointing at any single tool) and drag it to a different location on the Excel window. If the toolbar is dragged to the top, bottom, left, or right edge of the workspace, it is docked on that edge of the screen. If it is dragged anywhere inside the workspace, it is said to "float" (see Figure 1.5). You can also resize toolbars by dragging their borders.

One advantage of floating versus docked toolbars is that you gain a larger workspace. However, a floating bar will always obscure some part of the workspace.

FIGURE 1.5 ▶

A floating toolbar

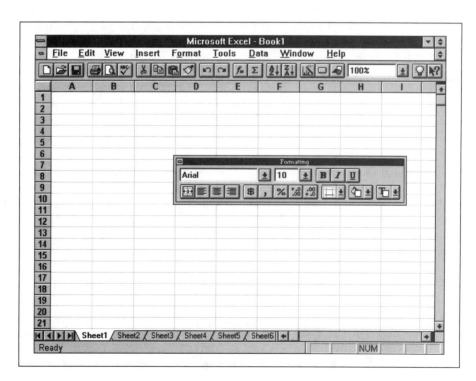

▶ *Drop-down Palettes*

Some tools have an arrow button next to them. An example is the Borders tool shown at left, found on the Formatting toolbar. You can click the arrow to display a drop-down palette of choices:

To tear the palette away from the toolbar, click on the palette with the mouse, then hold the mouse button down and drag the palette away from the toolbar. After being torn away, the palette behaves just like a floating toolbar (except that you cannot dock it again—you must click its control box to close it instead).

▶ *What the Tools Do*

Table 1.1 describes the functions of the tools on the Standard toolbar. Toolbars and tools can be customized—see Chapter 26, "Advanced Productivity Tips," to learn how.

▶ **TABLE 1.1:** *Standard Toolbar Tools*

Tool	Command Equivalent	Function
	File ➤ New	Opens a new workbook
	File ➤ Open	Opens an existing workbook
	File ➤ Save	Saves an active workbook
	File ➤ Print	Prints an active workbook
	File ➤ Print Preview	Previews what printed pages will look like

▶ **TABLE 1.1:** *Standard Toolbar Tools (continued)*

Tool	Command Equivalent	Function
ABC✓	Tools ➤ Spelling	Checks spelling
✂	Edit ➤ Cut	Moves selected cells
🗐	Edit ➤ Copy	Copies selected cells
📋	Edit ➤ Paste	Pastes cut or copied cells
🖌	n/a	Format Painter—Copies formatting between cells or objects (see Chapter 5)
Σ	Insert ➤ Function ➤ Sum	AutoSum—Enters SUM function in selected cells (see Chapter 4)
fx	Insert ➤ Function	Starts FunctionWizard
↺	Edit ➤ Undo	Undoes last action
↻	Edit ➤ Repeat	Repeats last action
A↓Z	Data ➤ Sort Ascending	Sorts selected cells in ascending order
Z↓A	Data ➤ Sort Descending	Sorts selected cells in descending order
📊	Insert ➤ Chart	Starts ChartWizard (see Chapter 14)
📄	n/a	Draws text box (see Chapter 13)

▶ **TABLE 1.1:** *Standard Toolbar Tools (continued)*

Tool	Command Equivalent	Function
	View ➤ Toolbars ➤ Drawing	Displays Drawing toolbar
`100%`	View ➤ Zoom	Reduces/enlarges worksheet magnification
	n/a	Starts TipWizard
	Help	Displays Help pointer (see Help section in Chapter 1)

▶▶ *Charts and Graphics*

Excel worksheets are not limited to numbers and text. Charts and other graphical objects can be placed on worksheets, allowing you to create high-impact graphical presentations.

- There are several ways to create charts, but the *ChartWizard* is the quickest and easiest. The ChartWizard, accessed by clicking the ChartWizard tool shown at left, gives you a variety of basic chart types to work with, as shown in Figure 1.6. The ChartWizard tool can be found on the Standard toolbar.

- Charts are usually linked to data stored on worksheets, and change automatically when the data on the worksheet changes.

- Excel is a capable drawing program in its own right. The drawing tools allow various objects to be drawn on worksheets (covered in Chapter 12).

- Graphics from other programs can be pasted onto a worksheet. See Chapters 12 and 25 to learn how to incorporate graphics from other programs.

FIGURE 1.6 ▶

Some of the chart types available through the ChartWizard

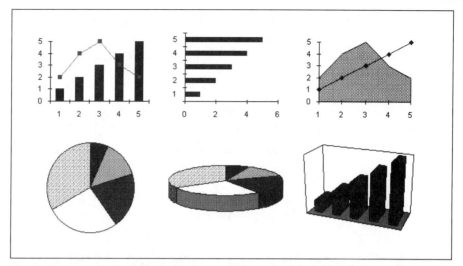

- Many formatting options can be applied directly to cells, such as fonts, borders, and colors. See Chapter 5 to learn how to format cells.

▶▶ *Using Online Help*

Excel's online help system is extensive, and there are a number of ways to access it, as explained in the following paragraphs.

▶ *The Help Menu*

The Help menu provides several entry points into the online help system.

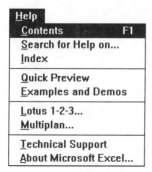

- Help ➤ Contents displays a table of contents for the on-line help system.

- Help ➤ Search for Help lets you search for help on a certain topic.

- Help ➤ Index displays an index for on-line help.

- Help ➤ Examples and Demos accesses various samples of worksheets and charts, in a tutorial format.

- Help ➤ Quick Preview provides a tutorial-like preview of Excel.

- Help ➤ Lotus 1-2-3 provides help for Lotus users.

- Help ➤ Multiplan displays a dialog box that provides help for Multiplan users.

▶ Getting Help on a Specific Menu Command

Help can be easily displayed for any menu command. Follow these steps:

1. Using the mouse, select the command *but don't release the mouse button*. (Or, using the keyboard, select the command without pressing Enter.)

2. Press F1.

▶ SEARCHING FOR A TOPIC IN HELP

What if you want to check the spelling in a worksheet, but you can't quite remember how to do it? There are a couple ways to get on-line help about a specific subject. You can choose Help ➤ Contents (or press F1) and sort through layers of overview information until you locate specific help about consolidation, but the quickest way to get help on a specific topic is by searching. To search for help, choose Help ➤ Search For Help On. Begin typing the topic. As you type, Excel moves through the list of help topics, getting closer to the topic you want with each letter you type. In this case, you only have to type spel to get to the list of spellcheck topics. Double-click a topic (for instance, *spelling checking*), or click the Show Topics button. Specific help topics will be listed in the lower half of the Search dialog. Double-click a topic that looks useful, or select the topic and click Go To.

In the Help and How To windows, you will see words or phrases with broken (as opposed to solid) underlines. Click on the broken-underlined word or phrase to display a definition. Other phrases will have solid underlines. When clicked, the solid-underlined phrases will jump you to a related help topic.

Suppose you have jumped to a related topic, and now you want to see the previous Help window? If you are looking at a How To window, click the Close button. If you are looking at a Help window, click the Back button. To return to a Help topic you selected earlier, click the History button and double-click a topic in the list (the History dialog lists all the Help topics you have seen during the current Help session).

▶ *Using the Help Tool*

Another way to get help is with the Help tool shown at left. It lets you get context-sensitive help by pointing and clicking on different areas of the workspace.

1. Click the Help tool. The mouse pointer will now have a large question mark attached to it (as seen below), and is now called a *help pointer.*

2. Point and click on the part of the window you want help for. Excel will display the Help window with text explaining how to use the selected item.

3. To cancel the help pointer, click the Help tool again or else press Esc.

▶ Getting Help for Dialog Boxes

Online help is available for every dialog box. Click the Help button in the dialog box, or else press F1 while the dialog box is displayed.

▶ ▶ ▶ CHAPTER **2**

Managing
Workbooks, Worksheets,
and Windows

—

▶▶ FAST TRACK

*T*his chapter provides the essential skills needed for working with workbooks, worksheets, and windows:

- *Opening, closing, and saving workbooks*
- *Managing worksheets within workbooks*
- *Arranging and navigating windows*
- *Controlling how things are displayed*

▶▶ Workbooks

Unlike previous versions of Excel, *all* Excel 5 documents are workbooks. Think of a workbook as a binder. This binder contains one or more sheets, which can be thought of as pages within the binder. Workbooks can contain:

- Worksheets (covered in this chapter)
- Chart sheets (covered in Chapter 15)
- Macro sheets, modules, and dialog box sheets (covered in Part Six)

When you start Excel, a workbook named Book1 is automatically displayed. Book1 is a new, unsaved workbook that is ready for input.

NOTE

In earlier versions of Excel, the first thing many users did after starting Excel was close the automatic new worksheet. (Opening old documents is no doubt a more common activity than creating new ones.) In Excel 5, if the first thing you do is open an existing workbook, Book1 is closed automatically—no need to close it on your own.

▶ *Creating New Workbooks*

Choose the File ➤ New command to create a new workbook. Each workbook you create during an Excel session is automatically named using a sequential number, i.e., Book1, Book2, and so on. The first time a workbook is saved, you can assign it a name of your choosing (within DOS file naming limitations). The keyboard shortcut for creating a new workbook is Ctrl+N.

TIP

You can create a new workbook by dragging a worksheet tab out of the workbook window and dropping it on the Excel desktop (resize the workbook window so there is room on the Excel desktop to drop the sheet icon).

▶ *Opening Existing Workbooks*

Choose the File ➤ Open command to open a workbook that has been previously saved to disk (see Figure 2.1). This dialog box is very similar to other File ➤ Open dialog boxes you may have used in other Windows programs. You can select the file from the list of files, or type in a file name. You can type a full path to a file that is not located in the current directory, i.e. C:\BUDGET\EAST.XLS.

FIGURE 2.1

File ➤ Open dialog box

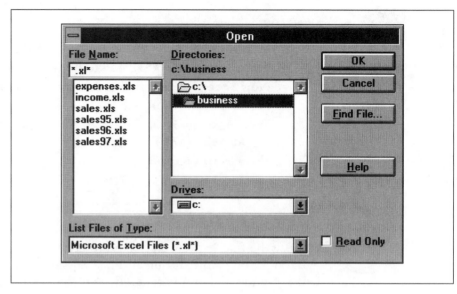

Finding Workbooks

Click the Find File button in the File ➤ Open dialog box (see Figure 2.1) to search for a workbook based on name, location, title, subject, author, keywords, time created, or time last saved. More details on the Find File feature are in Chapter 11, "Auditing and Protecting Your Work."

Opening Files Read-Only

Check the Read Only setting in the Open dialog box if you want to open the file *without* the ability to save changes. Opening a file read-only does not prevent you from making changes—it prevents you from *saving* the changes to a file with the same name. The read-only option serves several useful purposes:

- You can open a workbook as read-only to avoid accidentally changing a file that you don't want to change.

- A read-only workbook may be shared by more than one user on a network; if opened as read-only, another user can still open it, change it, and save it.

- If another user on the network has a file open with write permission (in other words, not read-only), you will still be allowed to open it as read-only.

▶ ▶ **TIP**

What if you make changes to a read-only workbook, and want to save the changes? Answer: Choose the File ➤ Save As command to save it to a different file name.

WHEN ANOTHER USER ON THE NETWORK HAS YOUR FILE OPEN

What if someone else on the network is using a file you need, and you require read/write access to the file as soon as possible? You can try to open it every few minutes, which is aggravating, or you can have Excel notify you as soon as the file becomes available.

When you attempt to open a file which is in use by someone else on the network, the File Reservation dialog will be displayed. Click the Notify button to ask Excel to alert you when the file is available for read/write access. The file will be opened read-only, and as soon as the file becomes availble, a dialog will be displayed notifying you that the file is available for read/write access. When you click the Read-Write button, the file is automatically closed and then re-opened. Remember not to make any changes to the file until you have read/write access.

Workbooks and Worksheets

▶ ▶
Ch.
2

Many Types of Files Can Be Opened

The List Files of Type list in the File ➤ Open dialog box determines which files are displayed in the File Name list box. It serves to filter the file names just as you can at the DOS prompt, using an asterisk as a wildcard. You can open files created in Lotus 1-2-3, dBase, QuattroPro, and text files. See Chapter 25, "Working with Other Programs," for more information on the types of files Excel is capable of working with.

Opening More than One File at a Time

The list box in the File ➤ Open dialog box is a multi-select list box. Using the mouse, you can select more than one file by holding down the Ctrl or Shift keys while selecting from the list.

- To select non-contiguous files, hold down the Ctrl key while clicking each file name with the mouse.
- To select a contiguous range of files, click the first file, then hold down Shift and click the last file. All files in between will be selected.

To select files using the keyboard, type the file names in the File Name box, separated by spaces.

When you click OK, all selected files are opened.

If the Workbook Is Stored on a Network Drive

If you are already logged on to a network, no problem—just open the file using one of the approaches discussed above.

If you are not already logged on to the network—that is, if your machine is physically connected but you haven't logged on, click the Network button, and a dialog box is displayed allowing you to make the network connection to the disk drive containing the workbook.

Opening Recently Used Files

Excel keeps track of the last four files used, and displays them on the bottom of the File menu:

```
File
  New            Ctrl+N
  Open...        Ctrl+O
  Close

  Save           Ctrl+S
  Save As...
  Save Workspace...

  Find File...
  Summary Info...
  Print Report...

  Page Setup...
  Print Preview
  Print...        Ctrl+P

  1 SALES95.XLS
  2 INCOME.XLS
  3 EXPENSES.XLS
  4 SALES.XLS

  Exit
```

Choose the file name from the File menu to open it.

▶ *More Than One Workbook Can Be Open*

As implied above, Excel supports what is known as the *multiple document interface*, or MDI. You may have more than one workbook open at a time. Each time you create a new file using File ➤ New, or open an existing file using File ➤ Open, another workbook is added to the workspace. The Window menu

will list all open workbooks at the bottom, with a checkmark next to the *active* workbook. The active workbook is the workbook that you are working in. Select a different workbook from the Window menu to activate it.

 ▶ ▶ **T I P**

Excel supports a special type of workbook known as a template, which can be used as a form or starting place for creating more complex documents. Templates are usually designated with the default .XLT suffix. When you open a template, a copy of the template is opened instead of the original file. If you need to make changes to the original template, hold down the Shift key while opening the file. (See Chapter 10 to learn more about templates.) Depressing the Shift key can also be used to suppress the execution of an Auto_Open macro.

Workbooks and Worksheets

▶ ▶
Ch.
2

▶ *Saving Your Work*

Once changes are made to a workbook, choose the File ➤ Save command to save it to disk. The first time you save a workbook, Excel displays the Save As dialog box (Figure 2.2) so you can give the file a name.

FIGURE 2.2 ▶

File ➤ Save As dialog box

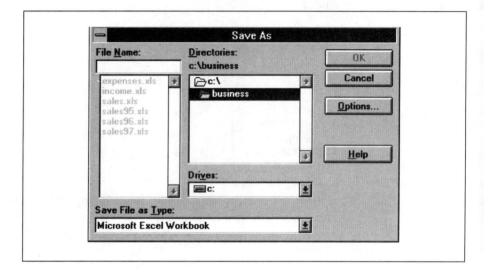

Subsequent File ➤ Save commands automatically use the current file name to save the file.

The file name is subject to DOS file name limitations. You are not required to use the default .XLS suffix, though it certainly makes it easier to identify the file in the future.

Save As...

The File ➤ Save As command allows you to save a file under a different name. The command's dialog box is identical to the one displayed the first time you save a file (see Figure 2.2).

Creating Different Types of Files

The Save File as Type drop-down list lets you save the file in one of many different file formats. See Chapter 25, "Working with Other Programs," to learn how to work with different types of files in Excel.

Options

Click the Options button in the File ➤ Save As dialog box to access a variety of save options:

The File Sharing options in this dialog box provide protection for the workbook, and are covered in Chapter 11, "Auditing and Protecting Your Work." Check the Always Create Backup setting to make Excel automatically create a backup of the file each time it is saved. See Chapter 7, "Productivity Basics," to learn more about this setting.

▶ Closing a Workbook

Choose the File ➤ Close command to close the active workbook. If there are unsaved changes, you will be asked if you want to save.

 ▶ ▶ T I P

> To close all workbooks with one command, hold down the Shift key, then choose the File menu. The Close command will be changed to Close All. In the same manner, the Shift key can be used to suppress the execution of an Auto_Close macro.

▶▶ *Worksheets within Workbooks*

Worksheets are the pages within a workbook. A workbook can contain one worksheet or hundreds of worksheets, memory allowing. Typically,

Workbooks and Worksheets

▶ ▶

Ch.

2

worksheets within a workbook are related to one another. For example, you may create one worksheet for each department, or one for each month, or a collection of sheets pertaining to a scientific experiment.

▶ Activating Worksheets

To activate a worksheet using the mouse, click the worksheet tab on the bottom of the workbook.

To activate a worksheet using the keyboard:

- Press Ctrl+Page Down to activate the next worksheet.
- Press Ctrl+Page Up to activate the previous worksheet.

The active worksheet is indicated by the highlighted tab.

▶ Scrolling the Tabs

Only several worksheet tabs are visible at a given time. Use the tab scrolling buttons pictured in Table 2.1 to scroll the tabs. These four buttons control which tabs are displayed, but they do not change the active worksheet.

▶ **TABLE 2.1:** *Tab Scrolling Buttons*

Click this button:	To display:
◀	First tab in workbook
◀	Previous tab (left)
▶	Next tab (right)
▶	Last tab in workbook

You can change the number of visible tabs by moving the Tab Split Box (see below). Point to the tab split box, and slide it to the left or right.

▶ Printing a Worksheet

To print a worksheet, choose the File ➤ Print command, then click OK. Chapter 6, "Printing," covers the many different settings and options related to printing.

▶ Inserting a Worksheet

To insert a worksheet into the active workbook, choose the Insert ➤ Worksheet command. Or, right-click a tab, then choose the Insert command from the shortcut menu.

▶ Deleting a Worksheet

To delete a worksheet from a workbook, activate the sheet, then choose the Edit ➤ Delete Sheet command. Excel will display a dialog box confirming the deletion. Or, right-click the tab, then choose the Delete command from the shortcut menu that appears.

▶ Copying and Moving Worksheets

Worksheets can be moved or copied —within a workbook or to a different workbook.

Moving a Worksheet within the Same Workbook

Activate the worksheet.

- With the mouse, click the worksheet tab, then drag and drop it to a new location along the row of worksheet tabs.

- Or, from the keyboard, choose the Edit ➤ Move or Copy Sheet command (the Move or Copy dialog box is displayed; see Figure 2.3).

FIGURE 2.3 ▶

Move or Copy dialog box

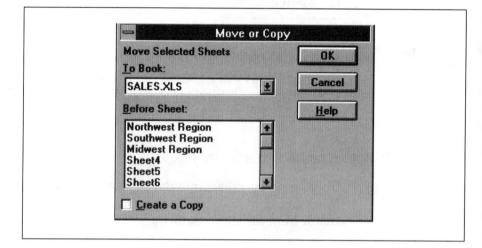

Copying a Worksheet within the Same Workbook

Follow the procedure for moving a worksheet (above), except:

- With the mouse, hold down the Ctrl key while you drag and drop the tab.
- Or, with the keyboard, check the Create a Copy check box on the Move or Copy dialog box. A copy of the worksheet is inserted.

Moving or Copying to a Different Workbook—The Easy Way (Mouse Method)

The simplest way to move or copy a sheet to a different workbook is to use the same procedure that you use within one workbook: drag and drop. Both workbooks must be open and visible. (The discussion on windows later in this chapter will explain how to make more than one workbook visible at the same time.) To move a sheet, drag and drop the tab to the row of tabs on the destination workbook. To copy, hold down Ctrl while you drag and drop.

Moving or Copying to a Different Workbook—The Hard(er) Way (Keyboard Method)

If you do not want to rearrange workbooks to make them both visible, or if you want to move/copy to a *new* workbook, use this procedure: Choose the Edit ➤ Move or Copy Sheet command, and the Move or Copy dialog box is displayed as in Figure 2.3.

The To Book drop-down list lets you specify the destination workbook. All open workbooks will display in this list, as will a (new book) choice. The Before Sheet list lets you specify where in the destination workbook the sheet will be placed. Check the Create a Copy setting to copy the sheet, or uncheck it to move the sheet.

▶ Manipulating More than One Worksheet at a Time

The procedures described above for copying, moving, and deleting a sheet can be performed on more than one sheet at the same time. This is accomplished by selecting more than one sheet before performing the desired operation. Selecting multiple tabs involves a procedure that is similar to selecting multiple items in a multi-select list box:

- To select and deselect tabs individually, hold down the Ctrl key while clicking tabs.
- To select adjacent tabs, hold down the Shift key. If you click Sheet1, then hold down Shift while clicking Sheet4, the tabs for Sheet1 *through* Sheet4 will be selected.

Here is how to copy two sheets using drag and drop:

1. Click the tab of the first sheet to be copied.
2. Holding down the Ctrl key, click the tab of the second sheet to be copied.
3. Release the Ctrl key.
4. Holding down the Ctrl key, now drag and drop.

Workbooks and Worksheets

Ch. 2

To cancel multiple tab selection, do one of the following:

- Click a tab that is not selected.
- Or right-click a tab, and choose Ungroup Sheets from the shortcut menu that appears.

► ►**T I P**

> **Multiple worksheets can be edited and formatted simultaneously, by selecting more than one tab. This technique is explained in Chapter 7, "Productivity Basics."**

► *Using Meaningful Worksheet Names*

You are not required to use Excel's default worksheet names. Worksheet tabs become a very useful interface for navigating a workbook when sheets have names like *Sales Analysis* and *Forecast* instead of Sheet1 and Sheet2. Choose the Format ➤ Sheet ➤ Rename command to specify a meaningful name for the active sheet. Or, you can:

- Right-click a sheet tab, then choose the Rename command from the shortcut menu.
- Double-click the sheet tab.

A worksheet name is limited to 31 characters, including spaces.

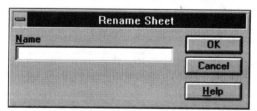

► *Controlling the Default Number of Worksheets in New Workbooks*

By default, there are 16 worksheets in a new workbook. This number conveniently accommodates one sheet per month, plus one summary sheet per quarter, but you might not need to work with that number of sheets every time you open a new workbook. To change the number of worksheets shown by default in a new workbook, choose the Tools ➤ Options command, and select the General tab in the dialog box. This displays the General options available from the Options dialog box, as shown in Figure 2.4.

FIGURE 2.4

The General dialog box in the Tools ➤ Options dialog box

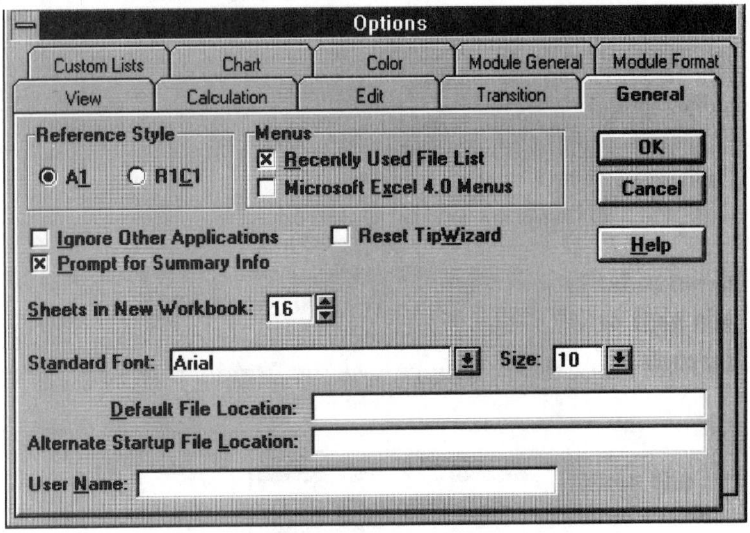

Change the Sheets in New Workbook setting according to preference. Although there is no limit to the number of sheets that can be added other than that imposed by available memory, the default Sheets in New Workbook setting has a maximum limit of 255.

►► *Windows in Excel*

It comes as a surprise to many users to learn that "windows" and "workbooks" are not synonymous. One workbook can be displayed in more than one window. (If you are just learning about workbooks and worksheets, there is no compelling reason to tackle the windows topic

Workbooks and Worksheets

Ch.
2

right away—you may want to get comfortable with workbooks and revisit this section later.)

► *Displaying a Workbook in More than One Window*

Assume that the active workbook is Book1. Choose the Window ➤ New Window command to create a second window for Book1. There will then be two open windows: Book1:1 and Book1:2. These are windows into the same workbook. One particular benefit to multiple windows is the ability to view two or more worksheets in the workbook simultaneously.

► *Arranging Windows*

There are several ways to quickly arrange multiple windows so that you can see them. To understand all the options, try this short exercise. Create three or more windows by choosing Window ➤ New Window a few times, then choose the Windows ➤ Arrange command. The following dialog box is displayed:

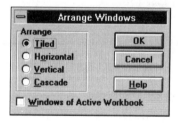

Now choose one of the Arrange options from the dialog box:

Tiled	Each window is made fully visible, and Excel decides how to arrange them based upon the number of open windows.
Horizontal	Each window is made fully visible, and arranged horizontally.

Vertical	Each window is made fully visible, and arranged vertically.
Cascade	Windows are overlapped, with the title of each window visible.

Arranging the Active Workbook Only

If you have more than one workbook open, and multiple windows have been created for each workbook, you can use the Windows of Active Workbook checkbox to limit the arranging of windows to the active workbook only:

- If checked, only the windows of the active workbook are arranged.

- If unchecked, all windows of all open workbooks are arranged.

▶ Moving between Windows

There are various ways to move from one window to another in Excel:

- The bottom of the Window menu lists all open windows—choose the one you want to activate.

- If the windows are arranged so that more than one is visible, click on the window you want to activate.

- Press Ctrl+F6 to activate the next window, or Ctrl+Shift+F6 to activate the previous window.

▶ Closing Windows

The File ➤ Close command is *not* necessarily the way to close a window—if the workbook is displayed in multiple windows, *all* of the windows will be closed. Instead, you must use the Close command on the Control menu for the specific window. The active window's Control menu is opened by clicking the control box on the left side of the window's title bar, as shown in Figure 2.5.

To close just one window, click the window's control box, then choose Close from the menu. Or just double-click the window control box. (The commands on the window Control menu are Microsoft Windows conventions, and not specific to Excel.)

FIGURE 2.5 ▶

Click the active window's control box to display its Control menu.

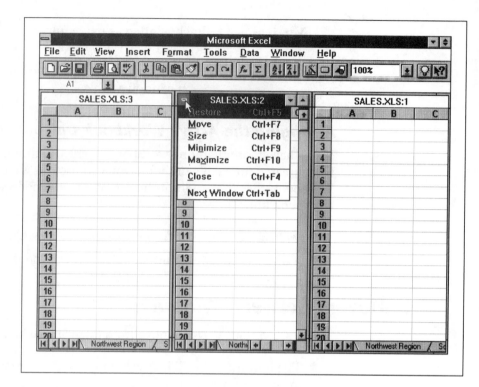

▶ *Hiding Windows*

You may want to temporarily hide a window to unclutter the workspace. Choose the Window ➤ Hide command to hide the active window, and choose the Window ➤ Unhide command to unhide a window.

 ▶ ▶ **N O T E**

Remember, workbooks and windows are not necessarily synonymous—one workbook can be displayed in multiple windows. If a workbook is displayed in only one window, then the window and workbook are virtually synonymous—closing the window closes the workbook.

▶▶ *Controlling the Display*

There are many different settings that control how things are displayed, and these settings apply at different levels: workspace, workbook, worksheet, or window.

▶ Controlling How the Workspace Displays

Workspace level settings are global to the entire Excel workspace, and are not specific to any workbook or worksheet.

Hiding the Formula Bar and Status Bar

There is one primary reason for hiding the formula and status bars: gaining additional screen real estate.

- Use the View ➤ Formula Bar command to hide or display the formula bar.
- Use the View ➤ Status Bar command to hide or display the status bar.

Excel "remembers" these settings from session to session. If you hide the formula bar and exit Excel, the formula bar will still be hidden the next time you run Excel.

Full Screen Display

The View ➤ Full Screen command maximizes the Excel workspace. A full screen display yields extra screen real estate. It is often used when doing an overhead presentation. Excel remembers this setting from session to session.

▶ Controlling How the Workbook or Window Displays

Workbook settings are saved with the workbook. If you change any of these settings and then save the workbook, close the workbook, and later reopen it, the setting remains. These settings are accessed by choosing the Tools ➤ Options command, then choosing the View tab (see Figure 2.6).

FIGURE 2.6 ▶

The View tab in the Tools ➤ Options dialog box

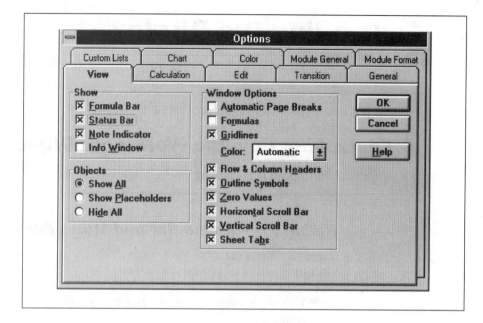

Horizontal Scroll Bar/Vertical Scroll Bar Horizontal and/or vertical scroll bars can be displayed or hidden using the settings pictured in Figure 2.6. (In Excel 4, there was only one scrollbar setting, and it applied to the workspace, not to the workbooks or windows themselves.)

Sheet Tabs This option controls the display of the worksheet tabs at the bottom of the workbook. You may want to hide the tabs if you are distributing a workbook with multiple sheets but only one sheet is intended to be viewed. Use the Sheet Tabs checkbox pictured in Figure 2.6.

▶ Controlling How the Worksheet Displays

Worksheet settings are applied only to the active worksheet, and are saved only for that worksheet. Worksheet settings, like the settings for controlling the display of workbooks and workbook windows, are accessed by choosing the Tools ➤ Options command, then choosing the View Dialog box tab (refer to Figure 2.6).

Row & Column Headings If this setting is checked, row and column headings are displayed; otherwise they are hidden.

Gridlines If this setting is checked, gridlines are displayed on the worksheet. If unchecked, gridline display is turned off for both the screen worksheet and the printed worksheet. Gridlines are not the same as cell borders—gridlines are an all or nothing proposition, whereas cell borders can be applied selectively. Cell borders, covered in Chapter 5, are far more effective when gridlines are turned off. Use the Gridlines setting in the dialog box shown in Figure 2.6.

Gridlines Color A different gridline color can be selected from the drop-down Color list in Figure 2.6. Try experimenting with a light gray color to create less obtrusive gridlines.

Automatic Page Breaks If this setting is checked, automatic page breaks are displayed as broken lines along the gridlines where page breaks occur. If unchecked, page breaks will not be displayed until the page is printed. (Page break lines only show on the screen—they do not appear on the hardcopy printout.)

Zero Values If this setting is checked, cells containing zero values display zero; otherwise they display as blank. Remember, this setting applies to the entire worksheet. Chapter 5 shows some formatting techniques to suppress zeroes selectively.

Workbooks and Worksheets

Ch. 2

WHEN YOU CLICK THE XL5GALRY.XLS

The first time you choose the Tools ➤ Options command during an Excel session, you may notice that a file named XL5GALRY.XLS is opened before the dialog appears (observe the status bar). XL5GALRY.XLS is a hidden workbook that is used to store custom chart autoformats—it is located in Excel's XLSTART directory. (See Chapter 14 to learn more about custom chart autoformats).

If you delete XL5GALRY.XLS, or the file becomes corrupted, you will lose all previously created custom chart autoformats, and Excel will create a new XL5GALRY.XLS the next time you create a custom chart autoformat or save a chart as the default chart format.

To Split Window Panes

Windows can be split into *panes*, resulting in either two or four separate scrollable regions on the window. One common reason for splitting panes is to create row and/or column headings that do not scroll out of view. Another reason is to simply view two different regions of the sheet at the same time.

To split windows into panes, first select the cell(s) to represent the split point:

- Select an entire column to split panes vertically.
- Select an entire row to split panes horizontally.
- Select a single cell to split panes immediately above and to the left of the cell.

Then choose the Window ➤ Split command. Figure 2.7 shows a window with both vertical and horizontal splits. The four regions are *separately scrollable*.

FIGURE 2.7 ▶

Split windows

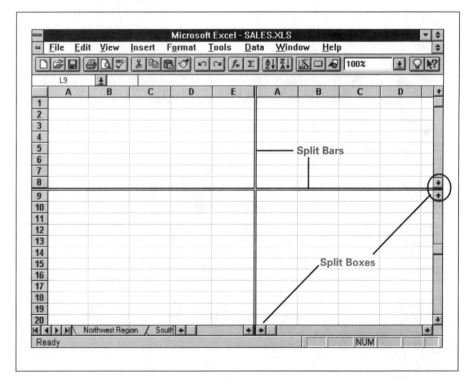

To Freeze Panes

If the purpose of the split panes is to freeze row and/or column titles in place, choose the Window ➤ Freeze Panes command to lock the split in place. At that time,

- The split bar or bars turn into solid lines;
- The pane above a horizontal split can no longer be scrolled;
- The pane to the left of a vertical split can no longer be scrolled.

The following exercise may help to clarify splitting and freezing panes.

1. Enter the following onto a blank worksheet:

	A	B	C	D	E	F
1	Dept	Qtr 1	Qtr 2	Qtr 3	Qtr 4	
2						
3						
4						
5						
6						
7						
8						

Book1

2. Select cell B2.

3. Choose the Window ➤ Split command. You should now have four panes, each of which is separately scrollable.

4. Choose the Window ➤ Freeze Panes command. Row 1 and column A are now frozen in place. When you scroll the worksheet, the headings stay in view.

  T I P

Another way to split panes is by dragging the split boxes with the mouse. Splits created using this method do not have to lie on the cell border. (Figure 2.7 points out the split boxes.)

Workbooks and Worksheets

Ch.
2

To Remove Splits

There are three ways to remove split windows:

- Choose the Window ➤ Remove Split command to remove both horizontal and vertical splits.

- If the window is unfrozen, double-click a split bar to join the panes. If the window is frozen, choose the Window ➤ Unfreeze Panes command first. Split panes can also be removed on unfrozen windows by dragging the split boxes all the to the top or left with the mouse.

To Zoom In and Out

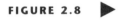

Choose View ➤ Zoom to display a dialog box to let you reduce or increase the magnification of the window display (see Figure 2.8). Zooming out is one of the handiest ways to step back and get the big picture of your worksheet model. Zooming in is a great way to avoid eye fatigue while working a particular section of the sheet.

FIGURE 2.8 ▶

The View ➤ Zoom dialog box

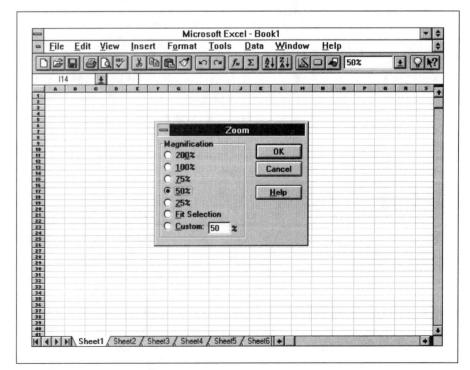

You can choose one of the several preset zoom settings in this dialog box, or you can specify your own magnification setting using the Custom option. If you choose the Fit Selection option, the selected range is zoomed to fill the window up to a maximum of 400%.

 ▶ ▶**N O T E**

Splitting panes, freezing panes, and zooming do not affect the printed document.

► ► CHAPTER **3**

Working inside Worksheets

▶ ▶ FAST TRACK

▶ ***To copy cells*** **75**

Hold down Ctrl while dragging the border of the selection to a new location.

▶ ***To insert cells*** **78**

Select the cells, rows, or columns where you want to insert, and choose Insert ➤ Cells, Insert ➤ Rows, or Insert ➤ Columns.

▶ ***To change column width*** **82**

Click and drag the border on the right side of the column header.

▶ ***To find a value*** **85**

Choose Edit ➤ Find and type the characters to find in the Find What edit box, then click Find Next.

▶ ▶ *T*his chapter covers the basics of working inside a worksheet:

- *Selecting cells*
- *Types of data that can be contained in a cell*
- *Entering and editing data into cells*
- *Navigating the worksheet*
- *Changing row height and column width*
- *Copying and moving cells*
- *Finding and replacing values*

▶ ▶ About Cells

The basic element of an Excel worksheet is the cell. Cells possess these basic properties:

- They can contain text or numbers.
- They can contain formulas, which are used to perform calculations.
- They can be formatted using a wide variety of formatting options, such as font, borders, color, and alignment of data within the cell.
- Every worksheet contains 16,384 rows and 256 columns, whether you use them or not, for a total of 4,194,304 cells.

▶ How Cells are Identified

Cells are identified by their position in the worksheet grid, with letters used to designate the column, and numbers used to designate the row.

For example, cell B4 is located at the intersection of the second column and fourth row. A cell address, such as B4, is called a cell *reference*.

▶ ▶ **N O T E**

Columns can be labeled with numbers by changing the cell reference style to R1C1 (choose Tools ➤ Options, and select the General tab to change reference style). You can learn more about reference styles in Chapter 4.

▶ The Active Cell

One cell is always the *active cell*. The reference of the active cell is displayed in the *Name Box*, on the left part of the formula bar (see Figure 3.1). One easy way to activate a cell is by clicking it with the mouse. Then, whatever you type is entered into the active cell.

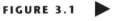

FIGURE 3.1 ▶

The Worksheet grid

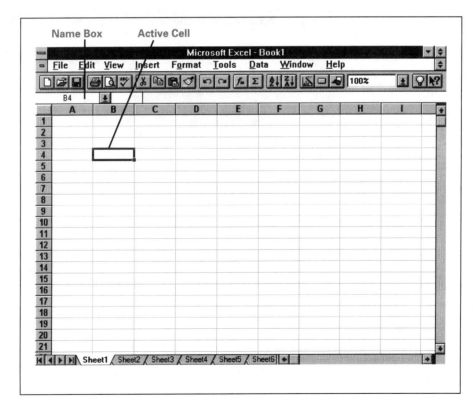

Working inside Worksheets

▶ ▶

Ch.

3

 ▶ ▶**N O T E**

> There are times when there is *not* an active cell, such as when a graphical object is selected. Macros you intend to be bulletproof need to take this factor into account.

▶ More than One Cell Can Be Selected

A *range* of cells can be selected. The easiest way to select a range is to click a cell with the mouse, hold down the left mouse button, drag the mouse pointer across several cells, then release the mouse button. From the keyboard, a range of cells can be selected by holding down the shift key and depressing one of the arrow keys. The selected cells are referred to as the *selection*. Even when a range of cells is selected, one cell is still the active cell.

In the selection shown here,

─			Microsoft Excel - Book1					▼	▲

□	**File**	**Edit**	**View**	**Insert**	**Format**	**Tools**	**Data**	**Window**	**Help**	⬍

	B2	⬍	

	A	**B**	**C**	**D**	**E**	**F**	**G**	**H**
1								
2								
3								
4								
5								
6								
7								
8								
9								
10								

- Cell B2 is the active cell.

- Just as one cell has a reference, so does a range of cells. The selection here would be referred to as B2:D5—the colon is shorthand for the word *through*.

▶ Types of Data

There are four distinct types of data that can reside in a cell: text, numbers, logical values, and error values.

Text

Text can include any combination of letters, numbers, and special characters.

- A cell can contain up to 255 characters.

- If column width prevents a text string from fitting visually in a cell, the display extends over neighboring cells. However, if the neighboring cells are occupied, the display is truncated.

Numbers

Performing numeric calculations is the most common thing that is done with spreadsheet programs, and over the course of the next several chapters, you will learn many ways to perform calculations, and to format numbers on the worksheet. Here are some important things to understand about the way Excel treats numbers:

- A number may be displayed using commas, scientific notation, or one of many built-in numeric formats. Do not confuse a number's *display format* with the *underlying value*. The *display format* is what you see in the cell, and the *underlying value* is the calculated value (which you can see in the formula bar). (Numeric formatting is covered in Chapter 5, "Formatting Cells.")

- Dates and times are numbers, but with special formatting.

- Excel tries very hard to guess the "meaning" of numeric input, and format it accordingly. If you try to enter **1-9** as a text string, Excel will interpret this as a date and display it as **9-Jan**.

- When an unformatted number does not fit in a cell, it is displayed in scientific notation.

- When a formatted number does not fit in a cell, number signs (####) are displayed.

Logical Values

The logical values TRUE and FALSE can be entered into cells. Also, there are many formulas that can return logical values. Chapter 10, "Using IS Functions For Data Validation," contains examples of logical values in use.

Error

Formulas, covered in Chapter 4, "Using Formulas and Functions," can result in errors. An error value is a distinct type of data. For example, if a formula attempts to divide by zero, the result is the #DIV/0! error value.

▶▶ *Entering, Editing, and Clearing Cells*

Here are the common procedures for entering data into cells, editing data in a cell, and clearing the contents of cells.

▶ *Entering Data into a Cell*

1. Select the cell by clicking it with the mouse.
2. Type numbers and/or text.
3. Press Enter (or select a different cell by clicking it with the mouse).

Notice that when you select the cell, the data contained in the cell is displayed on the formula bar. This will become more important later on when you start working with formulas. The formula bar displays the formula contained in the active cell, whereas the resulting value is displayed in the cell.

Entering Numbers

A numeric entry can include one or more digits and the special characters shown in Table 3.1. The underlying numbers which Excel supports can be as large as 9.99999999999999^{307} (roughly, 1 followed by 14 zeros, raised to the 307th power) and as small as -9.99999999999999^{307}.

▶ **TABLE 3.1:** *Common Characters Allowed for Numeric Entries*

Character	Function
0 through 9	Any combination of numerals
+	Indicates exponents when used in conjunction with E.

▶ **TABLE 3.1:** *Common Characters Allowed for Numeric Entries (continued)*

Character	Function
–	Indicates negative number
( )	Indicates negative number
, (comma)	Thousands marker
/	Fraction indicator or date separator
$	Currency indicator
%	Percentage indicator
. (period)	Decimal indicator
E	Exponent indicator
e	Exponent indicator
:	Time separator
(single space)	Separators for compound fractions (ex. 4 1/2) and date time entries 1/2/94 5:00

(Note: various alphabetic characters may also interpreted as parts of a date or time entry, ex. 4-Jan or 5:00 AM).

▶ ▶**T I P**

You can enter numbers with fixed decimal points by choosing Tools ➤ Options, then choosing the Edit tab. Check the Fixed Decimal checkbox, and select a number of decimal places. Accountants often prefer to work with two fixed decimals, because the decimal point does not have to be typed. If you are entering a long list of dollar values, you can type just the numbers (Excel inserts the decimal point).

Working inside Worksheets

Entering Numbers as Text

An inventory product code may consist of only numeric characters, yet you may not want Excel to treat such data as numeric. As in the above

Ch.
3

example, if you enter **1-9** intended as a product code, Excel displays **9-Jan**. To force an entry to be text, use an apostrophe as the first character. The apostrophe will not display in the cell, nor will it print out. It will display when you edit the cell, however. When you use an apostrophe to force a number to become text, the cell can no longer have number formats applied to it.

Entering Dates and Times

When you enter a number that Excel interprets as a date or time, the cell display will be formatted as such. (Date conversion is usually convenient, but at times it can drive you crazy!)

▶ ▶ **T I P**

> **By default, text is left-aligned within the cell, and numbers are right-aligned. This provides a quick visual cue as to whether Excel interpreted your entry as text or numeric.**

▶ Editing a Cell

There are two places where you can do your editing: on the formula bar or in the cell.

Formula Bar   Click the formula bar to begin editing.

In-Cell   In-cell editing is new to Excel 5, and will be much appreciated by those who have strained their eyes for years looking at the small font used in the formula bar. Double-click a cell to activate in-cell editing (see Figure 3.2).

Double-clicking to activate in-cell editing is a setting that can be turned on or off. Choose the Tools ➤ Options command, select the Edit tab, and set the Edit Directly in Cell checkbox. There are several advantages to turning off in-cell editing:

- Double-clicking a cell with a note displays the cell note dialog box (see Chapter 11 to learn about cell notes).

FIGURE 3.2 ▶

Double-clicking cell C6 here lets you perform in-cell editing.

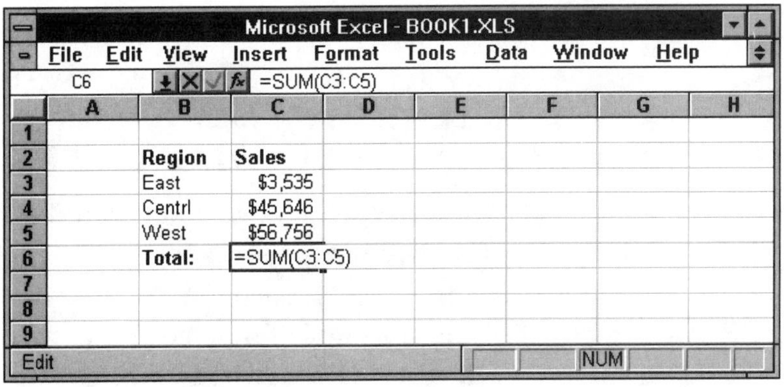

	A	B	C	D	E	F	G	H
1								
2		Region	Sales					
3		East	$3,535					
4		Centrl	$45,646					
5		West	$56,756					
6		Total:	=SUM(C3:C5)					
7								
8								
9								

- Double-clicking a cell that refers to other cells takes you to the other cells.

The techniques for editing cells are similar, whether in-cell or in the formula bar:

If Edit Directly in Cell Is Turned On   Double-click the cell. Or, select it and press F2. The insertion point is placed at the end of the cell contents.

Editing on the Formula Bar   Select the cell, then click in the formula bar. (This works regardless of whether Edit Directly in Cells is on or off.) The insertion point is placed into the formula bar.

Edit the cell contents using basic text editing techniques:

- Double-click a word to select it. Use the mouse to position the insertion point or to select text.
- Highlighted text is replaced by whatever you type.
- Press Home to go to the beginning, or End to go to the end.
- Use the left and right arrow keys to move left and right.
- While editing cell references in formulas, F2 toggles the meaning of the left and right arrow keys. The arrow keys can be used to edit the cell references by navigating the sheet, rather than navigating the formula.

Working inside Worksheets

Ch.
3

Press Enter or click the enter box on the formula bar to finish editing.

SELECTING DEPENDENT AND PRECEDENT CELLS

If you used Excel 4, you know that you could double-click a cell to select all of that cell's precedent cells (see Chapter 11 to learn more about precedent cells). You can still do the same thing in Excel 5, but only if in-cell editing is turned off. But what if you really like the new in-cell editing behavior in Excel 5, and still want the option to quickly select precedent cells?

Here are some keystrokes that give you the best of both worlds:

Control +[	Selects direct precedents
Control+Shift+{	Selects all precedents

Here are the keystrokes for selecting dependent cells:

Control+]	Selects direct dependents
Control+Shift+}	Selects all dependents

▶ Canceling Cell Entries/Edits

If you change your mind about an entry or edit while you are making it, you can undo it before moving on to the next entry:

- If you haven't yet pressed Enter while entering or editing, you can cancel your changes by pressing Esc or clicking the cancel button (the cancel button is only visible while you are editing a cell—it is the small button in the formula bar which has an "X" in it).

- If you've already pressed Enter, but haven't yet taken any other action, you can choose the Edit ➤ Undo command.

If, however, you've already performed another action after making an entry or an edit, you will be unable to undo the change. You will have to change the cell back manually, or close the file without saving.

▶ *Clearing a Cell*

Clearing a cell is like erasing a mistake. (Unlike deleting, which causes cells below and/or to the right to shift position.) Follow these steps to clear cells:

1. Select the cell(s) to be cleared.

2. The quickest way to clear the contents from the selected cell(s) is to press the Delete key. This clears the contents of the cell, but leaves formatting and cell notes intact. Choose the Edit ➤ Clear command if you want greater control over what exactly you are clearing:

    - To clear just contents, choose Contents from the submenu. This is the same as pressing the Delete key.
    - To clear just formats, choose Formats.
    - To clear just cell notes, choose Notes.
    - To clear everything (contents, formats, and notes) from the cell, choose All.

 ▶ ▶**T I P**

If you want to replace a cell's contents with a different entry, there is no need to clear the cell first. Select the cell and begin typing the new entry; the old entry will be replaced.

▶▶ *Navigating Worksheets Using the Mouse*

You can use some special mouse techniques for more efficient movement across the worksheet, as explained in the following paragraphs.

▶ Jumping to the Beginning or the End of the Block

A quick way to jump to the end of a block of filled or blank cells is by double-clicking the *cell border* in the direction you want to move. For example, to move to the bottom of a column of data, double-click the bottom border of the cell. To move to the end of a row of data, double-click the right cell border.

▶ How To Go Directly to Specific Cells

The fastest way to go directly to specific cells is to use the Name box:

- Click on the Name box and type a cell reference, then press Enter.
- If the cell is named, select the name from the Name box dropdown list (see Chapter 8 to learn about cell names). Click the dropdown arrow on the left side of the formula bar to drop down the Name box dropdown list.

Alternatively, use the *Go To* command:

1. Choose Edit ➤ Go To (or press F5).
2. Select a cell or range from the list of names, or type a cell reference into the Reference box.
3. Click OK.

Excel remembers the last four locations you selected using any of the methods described above and lists them at the top of the GoTo list in the dialog box (see Figure 3.3). Any named cells in the workbook will be listed below the last four locations.

▶▶ Navigating Worksheets Using the Keyboard

Table 3.2 explains the keystrokes for worksheet navigation. Make sure that Scroll Lock is off.

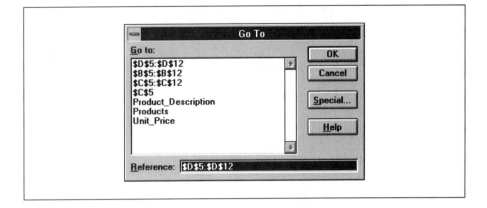

FIGURE 3.3

The Edit ➤ GoTo dialog box

▶ **TABLE 3.2**: *Moving with Keystrokes*

This Keystroke	Moves
Arrow keys	Right, left, up and down (one cell at a time)
Ctrl+arrow keys	To the edge of the *current data region* (region the cell is currently in)
Page Up, Page Down	Up or down one window
Home	To the beginning of row
Ctrl+Home	To cell A1
Ctrl+End	To lower right corner of worksheet
End, Arrow key	By one block of data, within current row or column
End, Enter	To the last cell in current row
End (with Scroll Lock on)	To the lower right corner of window
Home (with Scroll Lock on)	To the upper left corner of window

▶ *Moving within a Range of Cells*

You can select a range of cells, and then use the keystrokes in Table 3.3 to navigate the selected range.

Working inside Worksheets

▶ ▶

Ch.

3

▶ **TABLE 3.3:** *Moving within a Selection*

To Move	Press
Down one cell	Enter
Up one cell	Shift+Enter
Right one cell	Tab
Left one cell	Shift+Tab

▶ ▶**TIP**

If you scroll to a distant area of the worksheet using the mouse and scrollbars, you can return to the active cell quickly by pressing Ctrl+Backspace.

▶▶ *Selecting Cells Using the Mouse*

There are several ways to select cells using the mouse, as explained in the following paragraphs.

Dragging a Range

1. Click on a cell, but don't release the mouse button.
2. Drag the mouse to select the range.
3. Once the desired range is selected, release the mouse.

▶ ▶**NOTE**

While selecting a range of cells, the Name box displays the dimensions of the selected range. If the selection is four rows by two columns, 4R X 2C will appear. These dimensions only display *while selecting*—as soon as you release the mouse button, the dimensions are replaced with the active cell reference.

Selecting a Large Range without Dragging

Selecting a very large range by dragging the mouse can be cumbersome. Here's another way to do it:

1. Click a cell in one corner of the range.

2. Hold down Shift and click the cell in the opposite corner of the range.

Other Ways to Select with the Mouse

Table 3.4 illustrates the variety of ways cells can be selected using the mouse.

▶ **TABLE 3.4:** *Selecting Cells with the Mouse*

To Select	Do This
One Row	Click on row number at left side of worksheet
Multiple Rows	Click and drag up or down through row numbers
Non-contiguous Rows	Hold down Ctrl while selecting row numbers
Columns	Same as rows, but click column letters
Entire Worksheet	Click Select All button on upper left corner of worksheet (see Figure 1.1)
Multiple Ranges	Hold down Ctrl while selecting
Current Data Region	Select cell within data region, click Select Current Region tool

▶▶ *Selecting Cells Using the Keyboard*

Table 3.5 defines the keystrokes for making a wide variety of cell selections.

Working inside
Worksheets

▶

Ch.
3

▶ **TABLE 3.5**: *Keystrokes for Selecting Cells*

This Keystroke	Selects
Ctrl+Spacebar	Entire column
Shift+Spacebar	Entire row
Ctrl+Shift+Spacebar	Entire worksheet
End, Shift+Arrow keys	Extends selection to end of data block
End, Shift+Home	Extends selection to lower right corner of worksheet
End, Shift+Enter	Extends selection to last cell in current row
Ctrl+Shift+* (asterisk)	Current data region
F8, Arrow keys	Same as holding down Shift while using arrow keys

KEYBOARD SHORTCUTS FOR SELECTING REGIONS OR ARRAYS

Quite often you will need to select an entire region of adjacent cells to do something, such as copy the table, chart a PivotTable, apply an outline border, or format a range of cells. New users typically use the mouse to select the region by dragging, which is usually efficient. But what if the region is larger than the window? The fastest way to select an entire region of adjacent cells is to press Ctrl+Shift+*. There are two other ways to select the current region—if you don't want to remember keystrokes, place the Select Current Region tool on a toolbar, and click the tool to select the current region (see Chapter 26 to learn how to customize toolbars). Otherwise, bring up the Go To dialog box from the Edit menu (press F5), click the Special button, and then select the Current Region option.

Suppose you need to edit an *array* (see definition and discussion in Chapter 26) that resides in a range of cells? If you need to change any part of an array, you must select the entire array, which means you have to figure out which cells are included in the array. You could look at cell formulas individually, and try to remember which cells contained the array formula that you want to edit, but that's slow and inefficient. A better way is to select any cell within the array, press F5, click the Special button, and select the Current Array option. But the fastest way is to select a cell in the array and press Ctrl+/.

▶▶ *Moving and Copying Cells*

Cells can be copied and moved using drag and drop, or using menu commands.

Moving Cells Using Drag and Drop

1. Select the cells you want to move (the range must be contiguous).

2. Point to an outside border of the selected range using the mouse. The mouse pointer will turn into an arrow.

▶ ▶ W A R N I N G

> The lower right corner of the selected cells has a special marker called the *fill handle*. When you point at the fill handle, the mouse pointer becomes a black cross. When dragging and dropping, be sure not to accidentally use the fill handle. (See Chapter 7, "Productivity Basics," for information about the fill handle and AutoFills.)

3. Click the mouse button, drag the cells to a new location, then release the mouse.

Copying Cells Using Drag and Drop

Copying via drag and drop is the same as moving, except the Ctrl key is held down during the procedure. The cursor arrow will have a plus (+) near it as a visual indication that you are copying rather than moving.

 ▶ ▶ N O T E

> The drag and drop feature can be turned on or off by choosing the Tools ➤ Options command, selecting the Edit tab, and checking or clearing the Allow Cell Drag and Drop setting.

Using the Drag and Drop Shortcut Menu

If you hold down the right mouse button while dragging and dropping cells, the following *shortcut* menu will be displayed when the cells are dropped:

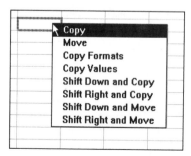

Copy
Move
Copy Formats
Copy Values
Shift Down and Copy
Shift Right and Copy
Shift Down and Move
Shift Right and Move

The commands on this shortcut menu are described in Table 3.6.

▶ **TABLE 3.6:** *Drag and Drop Shortcut Menu Commands*

Command	Function
Copy	Copies cells
Move	Moves cut cells
Copy Formats	Copies formats only
Copy Values	Copies values only
Shift Down and Copy	Inserts copied cells, shifts existing cells down
Shift Right and Copy	Inserts copied cells, shifts existing cells right
Shift Down and Move	Inserts cut cells, shifts existing cells down
Shift Right and Move	Inserts cut cells, shifts existing cells right

▶ Copying and Moving Using Menu Commands

Drag and drop is very efficient when cells are being copied or moved short distances. Menu commands (and toolbar shortcuts) may prove more effective when the target cells are a long distance from the source cells.

Moving Cells Using Menu Commands

1. Select the cell(s) to be moved.
2. Choose the Edit ➤ Cut command.
3. Select the upper left cell of the region where the cells are to be pasted.
4. Choose the Edit ➤ Paste command.

Copying Cells Using Menu Commands

1. Select the cell(s) to be copied.
2. Choose the Edit ➤ Copy command.

Working inside Worksheets

Ch.
3

3. Select the upper left cell of the region where the cells are to be pasted.

4. Choose the Edit ➤ Paste command.

▶▶ *Inserting and Deleting Cells*

The following procedures explain how to insert and delete cells, or entire rows and columns.

▶ *Inserting Cells*

To insert cells,

1. Select the cell(s) where you want to perform the insertion. This can be one cell, a range of cells, entire rows, or entire columns. If you select two rows, Excel will insert two rows, and so on.

2. From the Insert menu, do one of the following:

   • Choose the Rows command to insert entire rows.

   • Choose the Columns command to insert entire columns.

   • Choose the Cells command to insert a range of cells. The Insert dialog box is displayed, asking how the insertion should occur.

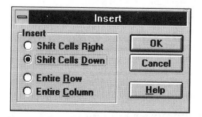

The number of rows and columns in a worksheet is fixed—inserting does not actually create new cells, but rather shifts cells. An insertion will not cause data that is located at the end of the worksheet to "fall off the edge." For example, if there is data in cell IV2 (the second row of the *last* column) and you insert a column, Excel displays a warning and will not allow the insertion to occur.

 ▶ ▶**N O T E**

> **Inserted cells will assume the formatting of the region into which they are inserted.**

▶ *Inserting Cells That Have Been Cut or Copied from Another Location*

Cells that have been moved or copied can be inserted into existing data using either menu commands or drag and drop.

Inserting Using Menu Commands

To insert cut or copied cells using menu commands:

1. Select the cells, then cut or copy them.

2. Select the cell where the insertion is to occur.

3. Choose the first command on the Insert menu. (The command will be either Copied Cells or Cut Cells, depending on which operation you performed in Step 1.)

4. The Insert Paste dialog box (pictured below) will display, letting you specify how to insert.

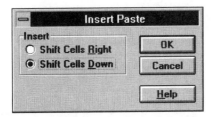

Inserting Using Drag and Drop

To insert cut or copied cells using drag and drop, use the same procedures as when cells are moved or copied with drag and drop (covered earlier in this chapter), but hold down the Shift key while dragging the cells. A gray insertion marker will display. The keystroke combinations get confusing when copying—here are the precise steps for a copy-insert:

1. Select the cells to be moved or copied.

Working inside Worksheets

▶ ▶

Ch.
3

2. Point to the edge of the range until the mouse pointer becomes an arrow. Click the mouse and drag the cells to their new location.

3. Hold down Shift while dragging the cells. You'll see a gray insertion bar between rows and columns instead of a range outline. Then, to insert *copied* cells, hold down Ctrl+Shift when dropping.

► Deleting Cells

When you delete one or more cells, the cells beneath or to the right shift position. (*Clearing* cells, on the other hand, does not cause other cells to shift position.)

1. Select the cell(s) that you want to delete. This can be one cell, a range of cells, entire rows, or entire columns.

2. Select the Edit ➤ Delete command:

   - If an entire row or column was selected, the row or column is deleted immediately.
   - Otherwise, the Delete dialog box (shown below) is displayed, giving you the opportunity to specify what to delete.

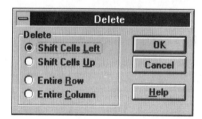

► DELETING CELLS VS. CLEARING CELLS

New users are often confused by the difference between clearing cells and deleting cells. *Clearing* a cell means emptying a cell of its contents (or formatting or notes). Clearing a cell does not affect the worksheet structure. *Deleting* a cell removes the cell from the worksheet, like pulling a single brick out of a brick wall. Unlike a brick wall, deleting a cell does not leave a hole in the worksheet.

> Cells below or to the right of the deleted cell shift to fill in the hole. Confusion is compounded by the fact that the Delete key does not delete cells—it clears cells by deleting the cells' contents.
>
> If you want to delete selected cells from the worksheet, choose Edit ➤ Delete. If you want to clear a cell of its contents, choose Edit ➤ Clear, or press the Delete key. Don't make the mistake of typing a space in a cell to erase the cell's contents—Excel considers the space a character, even though you can't see it, and the cell is not blank. This can create problems with worksheet functions and database commands, and is difficult to uncover.

▶▶ Controlling Row Height and Column Width

You can change row height and column width in several ways.

▶ Setting Column Width Using Menu Commands

Select any cell(s) in the column you want to resize. Then choose the Format ➤ Column command. The following options are provided on the submenu:

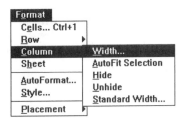

Table 3.7 explains the commands available on the Format ➤ Column submenu.

▶ **TABLE 3.7:** *Format* ➤ **Column Commands**

Command	Function
Width	Displays dialog prompting for column width
AutoFit Selection	Sizes column(s) according to the widest entry within selected range
Hide	Hides selected column(s) from view
Unhide	Unhides hidden columns
Standard Width	Sets column to default column width

▶ ▶**T I P**

Since a hidden column cannot be selected, how is it un-hidden? If column B is hidden, select columns A through C, then choose the Unhide command. Nothing happens to columns A and C since they were not hidden to start with, but column B becomes unhidden. Alternatively, use the Name box to go to a cell in the hidden column (hidden cells can be selected even though the selection can't be seen), and choose the Unhide command.

▶ Setting Column Width Using the Mouse

To use the mouse to change the column width:

1. Point to the line between column letters. The mouse pointer becomes a two-way arrow.

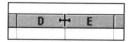

2. Click and drag to resize the column. (While dragging, the new width is displayed in the Name box.)

You can size several columns at once with the mouse. Select the columns you want to size (hold down Ctrl to select non-contiguous columns), and drag the border of any *one* of the selected columns.

Best Fit

The mouse can be used to quickly perform the same function as the Format ➤ Column ➤ Autofit command. Double-click the right border between column headings. The column will be sized according to the widest value within the entire column.

If you see ##### in a cell, it means the column is too narrow to display the number. Use the double-click technique described above to instantly size the column so all values will fit.

▶ Row Height

Row height works just like column width, except that rows will automatically increase in height to account for changing font size or wrapped text. Select a row or a cell in the row, and choose the appropriate Format ➤ Row commands to specify height or to hide/unhide rows. Row AutoFit is based on the largest font or wrapped text in the row.

▶ ▶ **T I P**

> **You can unhide a hidden row or column using the mouse. To unhide a column, place the mouse pointer just to the right of the column header where the column is hidden, so that the pointer becomes a split double arrow (rather than the solid double arrow you usually see between column headers). Drag the split double arrow to the right to unhide the column. To unhide a row, place the mouse pointer just below the row header where the row is hidden (so that it becomes a split double arrow), then drag the split double arrow downwards.**

▶▶ *Searching and Replacing*

The Edit ➤ Find and Edit ➤ Replace commands are used to search the worksheet for user-specified values, and, optionally, to replace them with a different value. For example, suppose you have a worksheet which keeps track of payroll information, and employee Jane Smith changes her name to Jane Jones. Excel can search for every occurrence of *Jane Smith* and replace it with *Jane Jones*.

The Edit ➤ Find command displays the dialog box pictured in Figure 3.4.

FIGURE 3.4 ▶

The Find dialog box

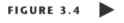

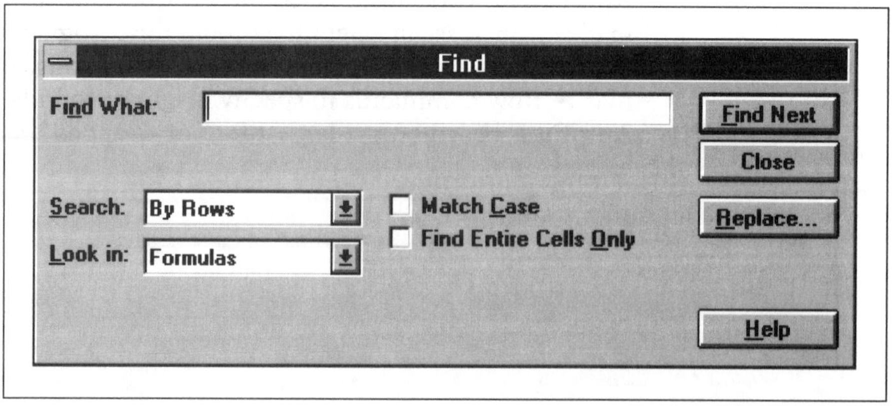

▶ *Finding a Value*

To find a value:

1. Choose the Edit ➤ Find command.

2. Type the characters you want to find in the Find What box.

3. Use the Look In list box to specify where to search:

    - Select Value to search cell values.
    - Select Formula to search formulas.
    - Select Note to search cell notes.

4. Specify the row or column search sequence using the Search list.

5. Checking Match Case will limit the search to text strings that match the Find What entry in upper and lower case (for instance, if you search for *Bill*, the search will ignore *bill*).

6. Checking Find Entire Cells Only will limit the search to exact matches. For example, if you are searching for *Rob*, the search will find *Robert* and *Robin*, but if you check Find Entire Cells Only, only *Rob* will be found.

7. Click Find Next to find the next cell containing the search value.

▶ *Using the Replace Option*

The Replace option works like Find, but allows you to replace the found value with another value. Try the following exercise:

1. Enter the following on a blank worksheet:

	A	B	C	D	E
1					
2		Jane Smith	Smith & Jones		
3		Bob Smith	Smithsonian		
4					
5					
6					
7					

Book1

Working inside Worksheets

Ch. **3**

2. Choose Edit ➤ Replace to display the Replace dialog box.

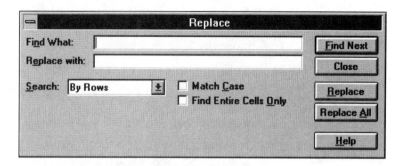

3. Type **Smith** in the Find What box.

4. Type **Jones** in Replace With.

5. Click Replace All to replace all instances of *Smith* with *Jones*.

▶ Specifying the Search Range

You can search an entire worksheet, a range of cells, or multiple work-sheets within a workbook. Before choosing the edit or replace command, do one of the following:

- Select only one cell to search the entire sheet.
- Select a range of cells to search the range.
- Select multiple sheets to search multiple sheets (see Chapter 2).

▶ Using Wildcards

The question mark (?) and asterisk (*) can be used in your search text as wildcard characters.

- The asterisk represents one or more characters—a search for *A*Z* will find *ABZ* and *ABCZ*.
- A question mark represents only one character—a search for A?Z will find *ABZ* and *ACZ*, but not *ABCZ*.

T I P

If you want to search for a question mark or asterisk, precede these characters with a tilde (~). For example, to search for the string *QUIT?* and not find *QUITO*, enter *QUIT~?* as the search string.

Basic Skills

PART TWO

▶ ▶ **I**n **Part Two** you'll be introduced to simple formulas and functions, and learn how cell references and links behave. You'll learn to format worksheets for a professional appearance, and how to print your work. Finally, you'll get lots of tips and techniques to help you work more productively.

Using Formulas
and Functions

———

▶▶ Fast Track

▶ ***To freeze a value*** **102**

First,select and copy cells to be frozen. Then choose Edit
➤ Paste Special, select Values, and click OK.

▶ ***To change cell reference type*** **108**

Place the insertion point in the formula so it touches the
cell reference, then press F4 to cycle through reference
types.

▶ ***To change a link*** **115**

Choose the Edit ➤ Links command. Then select the
source file to be changed and click the Change Source button. Finally, select a new source file and click OK.

▶ ***To use the Function Wizard*** **123**

Choose Insert ➤ Function, or click the Function Wizard
tool on the Standard toolbar.

▶ ***To switch calculation mode to manual*** **126**

Choose Tools ➤ Options, then select the Calculation
tab. Choose the Manual option.

►► **T***his* chapter covers some of the most important topics for new Excel users:

- *Performing calculations with formulas*
- *Understanding cell references*
- *Linking workbooks*
- *Introduction to functions*
- *Controlling worksheet calculation*

►► *Performing Calculations with Formulas*

In Chapter 3 you learned about entering text and numbers into cells. In this chapter, you will learn how to do calculations using *formulas*. Formulas provide the real power when doing analysis and *modeling*—creating functioning spreadsheet systems—in Excel. You can perform a wide variety of numeric calculations, including addition, subtraction, multiplication, and division. You can manipulate text, and look up values in tables. By using formulas, entering a single number into a single cell can cause a ripple effect throughout a complex model.

A formula is essentially a sequence of values and operators that begins with an equal sign (=) and produces a new value. Excel comes with several hundred built-in formulas, called *functions*, which are designed to perform many different kinds of calculations. The SUM function provides a simple demonstration of how formulas work, and is easily entered using the AutoSum tool on the Standard toolbar.

▶ *Using the AutoSum Tool*

The SUM function is probably the most often used function, and the AutoSum tool makes it very easy to enter SUM functions. Try the following exercise to see how it's done in a very simple case:

1. Enter the following:

▬	BOOK1.XLS	▼ ▲
	A	**B**	**C**	
1	12			
2	456			
3	98			
4	253			
5				
6				
7				

2. Select cell A5.

3. Click the AutoSum tool on the Standard toolbar.

4. Press Enter (or click the Enter box in the formula bar).

Excel determines which cells you want to sum—the formula in cell A5 sums cells A1:A4 (the answer is 819). The AutoSum tool is not limited to a single cell. Suppose there are numbers in cells A1:C3. If you select A4:C4, then click AutoSum, sum formulas will be entered for all three columns.

▶ ▶ **T I P**

> **You can enter sum totals across the bottom of an entire table of numbers with one click. First, select the entire table range. The fastest way to select the entire table range is to select a cell in the range and click the Select Current Region tool (or press Ctrl+Shift+*). Then click the Autosum tool.**

▶ Entering a Formula

Next, you will learn how to enter formulas manually. To enter a formula into a cell, try the following as an example:

1. Select cell A1 on a blank worksheet.

2. Enter **=1+2** then press Enter. The resulting value, 3, displays in the cell.

▶ Basic Properties of Formulas

Formulas in Excel share some basic properties:

- All formulas begin with an equal sign.

- After a formula is entered, the *resulting value* is displayed in the cell.

- When a cell containing a formula is selected, the underlying formula displays in the formula bar.

▶ Editing Formulas

The procedure for editing formulas is the same as for editing numbers and text, which was covered in Chapter 3. You can use the formula bar, or you can edit directly in the cell. When you double-click a cell containing a formula, the formula is displayed in the cell.

 ▶ ▶ T I P

Do you want to see all of the formulas on a worksheet at once, instead of viewing them one by one in the formula bar? Press Ctrl+` (Ctrl plus the grave apostrophe, usually found to the left of the exclamation point) to switch back and forth from displaying formulas to displaying values on the worksheet. This is useful if you want to know which cells contain values and which contain formulas, or if you want to document the formulas used in the worksheet.

FORMATTING FORMULAS WITH TABS AND LINE BREAKS FOR READABILITY

Long formulas are often difficult to decipher. Suppose you have a long formula that just can't be shortened—how can you make it easier to read? You can insert tabs and line breaks into the formula. Here's a long formula:

=(A1+A2)*5-(A3+A4)/12-A5+2

The same formula with tabs would look like this:

=(A1+A2)*5   -(A3+A4)/12   -A5+2

The same formula with line breaks might look like this:

=(A1+A2)*5

-(A3+A4)/12

-A5+2

To enter a tab in a formula, press Ctrl+Alt+Tab. To enter a line break, press Alt+Enter.

▶ *Arithmetic Operators*

Table 4.1 lists the arithmetic operators Excel supports in formulas:

▶ **TABLE 4.1:** *Arithmetic Operators Supported in Formulas*

Symbol	Function
+	Addition
-	Subtraction
*	Multiplication

▶ **TABLE 4.1**: *Arithmetic Operators Supported in Formulas (continued)*

Symbol	Function
/	Division
^	Exponentiation
%	Percent when placed after a number

The following examples display some formulas utilizing arithmetic operators:

=1+1	Add 1 plus 1
=4/2	Divide 4 by 2
=2*2+10	Multiply 2 times 2, then add 10
=3^2	Square 3
=435.67*10%	Multiply 435.67 times 10%

▶ *Order of Calculation*

It is very common for formulas to include more than one operator. Table 4.2 explains the order in which operators are evaluated:

▶ **TABLE 4.2**: *Order of Evaluating Operators*

Order	Operator	Function
1	–	Negation
2	%	Percent
3	^	Exponentiation
4	* and /	Multiplication and division
5	+ and –	Addition and subtraction
6	&	Joining text (covered below)
7	=<>, <=, >=, <>	Comparison

Following the order of precedence shown in the table, you can see that the multiplication operator is evaluated before the addition operator; therefore, the formula

=1+2*5

yields 11 (1 plus the result of 2 times 5), not 15 (the sum of 1 plus 2, which equals 3, times 5).

When there is more than one operator with the same priority level, the operators evaluate from left to right. For example, since multiplication and division are at the same priority level, the formula

=10/5*2

yields 4 (10 divided by 5, times 2), not 1 (10 divided by the product of 5 times 2).

Changing the Evaluation Order

Parentheses can be used to group expressions within a formula. An expression within parentheses evaluates *before* all arithmetic operators.

=1+2*3   Yields 7

=(1+2)*3   Yields 9

▶ Joining Text

The ampersand character (&) joins text—a process referred to as *concatenation*. Concatenation is useful, for example, in client invoices. You can enter a formula in cell F25 which totals fees (suppose, in this case, the value in F25 is $10681). In a different cell, the formula

="Your balance due is"&~F25

evaluates to **Your balance due is $10681**.

▶ ▶**N O T E**

Though earlier versions of Excel supported the & operator, calls to Microsoft's help line indicated that users didn't know where to find it in the manual. The Excel 5 CONCATENATE function adds nothing that the & operator doesn't already provide; it was simply added so that users could find it more easily.

▶ *When Formulas Return Errors*

When there is a problem with a formula, an error value is returned. One of the most common errors occurs when attempting to divide by zero. Enter the formula **=1/0** into a cell. The error **#DIV/0!** is returned. Table 4.3 explains the different errors that can result from an errant formula.

▶ **TABLE 4.3:** *Error Values*

Error Value	Cause
#DIV/0!	Divided by zero
#N/A!	Different meanings depending on circumstance (usually means no value available or inappropriate argument was used)
#NAME!	Reference to an invalid name
#NULL!	Reference to intersection of two areas that do not intersect (e.g. if named areas January and Profits do not intersect, **=January Profits** returns #NULL!)
#NUM!	Incorrect use of a number (unacceptable numeric argument, such as SQRT(-1), or formula returns a number too large or too small to be represented in Excel)
#REF!	Invalid cell reference
#VALUE!	Usually caused by incorrect argument(s) or operand(s)

WHAT IS A CIRCULAR REFERENCE (AND WHAT CAN I DO ABOUT IT?)

Suppose you have entered the formula =B1+C1 into cell A1. You press Enter, and are surprised by an alert that says "Cannot resolve circular references." What's a circular reference, and how did it get into your formula? A circular reference is a reference that refers to itself, either directly or indirectly. It is a formula that depends on its own value. After clicking the OK button on the alert (which is your only choice at this point), look at the status bar. It says *Circular: C1*, for example, which means that C1 is the cell which contains the circular reference.

Usually circular references happen by mistake, and you can fix the problem by editing the formula. But occasionally, circular references are a valid approach to solving a problem, and Excel can resolve them if you set calculation to use Iterations. To turn on Iterations, choose Tools ➤ Options. Select the Calculation tab, and check the Iterations checkbox. By default Excel allows a maximum of 100 iterations, or repeated calculations. This means that Excel recalculates the formulas 100 times, and each time gets a little closer to the correct value. The getting closer process is called convergence. Excel keeps track of how much the value changes with each iteration, and when the amount of change is reduced to the *Maximum Change* (or the maximum number of iterations is reached), Excel stops converging.

You can change the Maximum Iterations and Maximum Change values in the Tools ➤ Options ➤ Calculation dialog box. You can make the calculation faster by setting fewer iterations and a larger maximum change value, or you can reach a more accurate solution by setting more iterations and a smaller maximum change value. You may want to set *Calculation* to Manual when you set Iteration—otherwise Excel will recalculate the circular references each time you make a cell entry. Iteration and convergence are also the means by which Solver and Goal Seek solve problems. You can learn more about Solver and Goal Seek (and iteration and convergence) in Chapter 23, "Performing What-If Analyses."

► How to Freeze Values

There are times when you will want to "freeze" a range of cells by replacing formulas with values. For instance, you might print a report that is distributed to other people in your organization. Later, it may be important that you see exactly what was contained on the original report—formulas make it all too easy to change the report. Follow this procedure to freeze a range of cells:

1. Select the cell(s) you want to freeze.

2. Choose the Edit ➤ Copy command.

3. Choose the Edit ➤ Paste Special command.

4. Select the Values option, then click OK.

All formulas in the range are replaced with constant values.

►► *Understanding Cell References*

Each of the sample formulas presented so far in this chapter contains text and numeric *constants*. But a formula with only constants is not very useful. You can use *cell references* to incorporate *variables* into formulas, as demonstrated in the following examples.

=A1*2	Multiplies the value in cell A1 by 2
=A1*B1	Multiplies the value in cell A1 by the value in cell B1

="ABC"&A1	Concatenates the characters ABC and the value in cell A1
=A1&B1	Concatenates the value in cell A1 and the value in cell B1

Try this simple exercise on a blank worksheet:

1. Enter the number **2** in cell A1.

2. Enter the number **4** in cell A2.

3. Enter the formula **=A1+A2** in cell A3 (the value returned is **6**).

4. Change the value in A1 to **8**, and watch the value in A3 change automatically to **12**.

You have just observed one of the basic features of a spreadsheet program—automatic recalculation of formulas as cell values change. As you become familiar with more of Excel's built-in functions, automatic recalculation lets you perform powerful what-if analysis. Once your needs progress beyond the most simplistic calculations, it becomes vital that you fully understand every nuance of cell references.

 ▶ ▶ N O T E

> **A cell that has a formula which refers to another cell is called a *dependent cell*—meaning it depends on the value in another cell. A cell that is referred to by another cell's formula is called a *precedent* cell.**

▶ *A1 and R1C1 Reference Styles*

Excel supports two styles of cell references:

- **A1 Style** This is the Excel default. Columns are labeled with letters A through IV, allowing for the maximum 256 columns. Rows are labeled by number, 1 through 16384.

- **R1C1 Style** Rows and columns are both referred to by number. For example, R3C2 in this system is the same as B3 in the other system.

For better or for worse, A1-style references are the *de facto* standard for almost all spreadsheet products, including Excel. There is no compelling reason to work with both reference styles, and the inclusion of both styles in the Excel manuals only serves to further complicate an already complex subject. This book focuses exclusively on A1. Once you understand A1, it is easy to go back and understand R1C1 if so desired.

▶ There Are Three Ways to Reference, and You Need to Know All of Them

You have just read about the two reference styles—A1 and R1C1. Regardless of which style you use, there are also three *types* of cell reference. A cell reference can be *relative*, *absolute*, or *mixed*. To explain, we will use a street address analogy:

Relative Reference Refers to cell(s) relative to a given position, such as "go one street down and two houses over."

Absolute Reference Refers to a specific cell or cells. In this analogy, a specific home address, such as 123 Elm Street.

Mixed Reference One of the coordinates is absolute, but the other is relative. "You're on the right street, but Ms. Jones lives three houses down."

 ▶ ▶**N O T E**

> Excel supports three-dimensional cell references, which are used in conjunction with functions. 3-D references are covered later in this chapter.

▶ Relative References

The lack of a dollar sign in front of the cell coordinate denotes a *relative* reference. Use relative references to refer to cells *relative to the cell containing the formula*. The formula =A1, entered into cell B1, actually means "the contents of this cell are equal to the contents of the cell that is now one to the left" (A1 being one to the left of B1). Furthermore, since the formula uses a relative reference, the reference automatically adjusts when the cell is copied to another location.

Try this example:

1. Enter **=A1** into cell B1. This gives B1 the same content as A1, its neighbor directly to the left.

2. Copy and paste cell B1 to B2.

The formula in cell B2 automatically changes; Excel has adjusted it to read: =A2, giving B2 the same content once again as its neighbor directly to the left (in this case A2).

Try another example:

1. Enter numbers in cells B2, B3, C2, and C3.

2. Enter **=B2+B3** into cell B4.

3. Copy and paste B4 to C4; the formula in C4 reads **=C2+C3**.

NOTE

Unlike copy/paste, if you *cut* and paste a cell with relative references, the references will not change.

▶ Absolute References

A dollar sign in front of the cell coordinate denotes an *absolute* reference.

$A$1 is an absolute reference to cell A1.

$B$2 is an absolute reference to cell B2.

An absolute reference does not change when copied to another cell. The following exercise will demonstrate this:

1. Enter **=$A$1** into cell B1.

2. Copy and paste cell B1 to B2.

The formula in cell B2 is unchanged; it still reads =$A$1.

▶ When to Use Absolute or Relative References

Here is an example that will illustrate the difference between absolute and relative references. Enter the constants in Figure 4.1 on a blank worksheet:

FIGURE 4.1 ▶

Column D is intended to extend (multiply) the numbers in columns B and C.

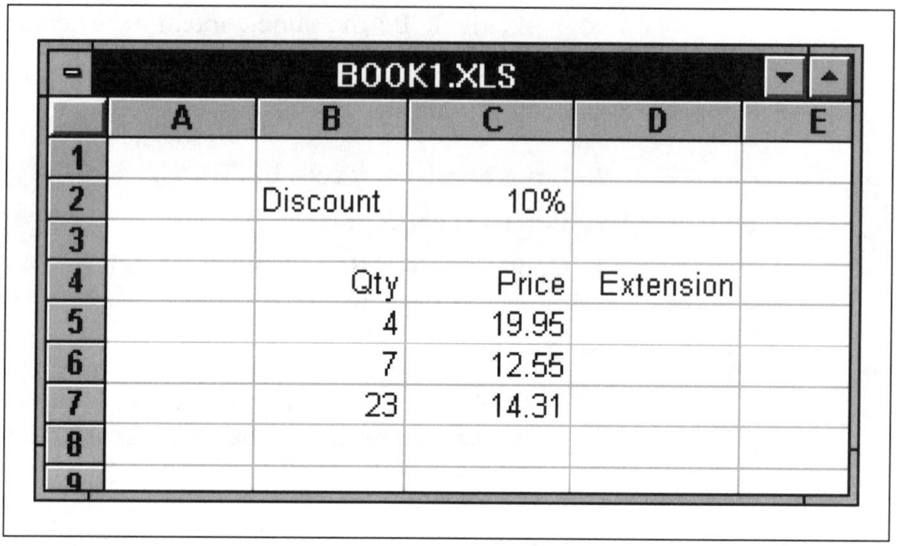

	A	B	C	D	E
1					
2		Discount	10%		
3					
4		Qty	Price	Extension	
5		4	19.95		
6		7	12.55		
7		23	14.31		
8					
9					

An Example of Doing It the Wrong Way

1. Enter the formula **=$B$5*$C$5** (absolute references) into cell D5.
2. Copy the formula in D5 to cells D6 and D7.

Since absolute references were used, cells D6 and D7 mistakenly extend (multiply) the figures on row 5—not what we intended.

An Example of Doing It the Right Way

1. Enter the formula **=B5*C5** (relative references) into cell D5.
2. Copy the formula in D5 to cells D6 and D7.

Since D5 contains relative references, Excel automatically adjusts the references when copied, and the extensions are now correct.

Now we will add an absolute reference to the equation. Assume that the discount in cell C2 (see Figure 4.1) applies to each row:

1. Enter the formula **=(B5*C5)-((B5*C5)*$C$2)** into cell D5. In English, this formula says "The contents of this cell equals Extension minus Discount." Notice that cell C2 is being referred to absolutely.

2. Copy this formula into cells D6 and D7. Excel will adjust the relative references, but leave the absolute reference alone.

▶▶**N O T E**

The formula in step 1 above has extra parentheses that were added to enhance the readability of the formula. They do not affect the order of calculation.

▶ *Mixed References*

You have now used absolute references (with a dollar sign in front of the coordinate), and relative references (with no dollar sign). A *mixed reference* has one absolute coordinate and one relative coordinate. A$1 and $A1 are both examples of mixed references. To illustrate, enter the following constants on a blank worksheet:

	A	B	C	D	E	F	G
1							
2		Freight	Red Widgets		Blue Widgets		
3		Per Unit	Units	Freight$	Units	Freight$	
4	North	11.95	5		9		
5	South	12.55	12		4		
6	East	13.52	6		2		
7	West	9.75	23		11		
8							
9							
10							

BOOK1.XLS

In this scenario, the freight calculation for red widgets and blue widgets are both based on the Freight Per Unit in column B. Formulas are required in columns D and F to calculate freight. The following paragraphs offer two ways to solve the problem.

An Example of Doing It the Less Efficient Way

1. Enter the formula **=B4*C4** in cell D4, and copy it to cells D5 through D7.

2. Enter the formula **=B4*E4** in cell F4, and copy it to cells F5 through F7. (If the formula in D4 is copied to column F, it would be *incorrect* due to the use of purely relative references.)

No problem, right? Not exactly. Using a mixed reference, the *same formula* can be used in columns D and F. This may seem like a trivial saving of time and energy, but this is a simple example. Anytime you can get away with using the same formula, a lot of time and hassle can be saved when the formula is originally entered, and when you go back later to change it.

An Example of Doing It the More Efficient Way

1. Enter the formula **=$B4*C4** in cell D4. $B4 is a *mixed* reference—the first coordinate is absolute and the second coordinate is relative.

2. Copy D4 to cells F4 through F7.

Check out the formulas in columns D and F after you have copied them. Excel has adjusted the relative portion, but left the absolute portion alone.

 ▶ ▶**T I P**

> **The use of names can greatly simplify references. Names also add clarity: a formula that reads =Sales– Cost makes a lot more sense than =$B$25–$B$47. See Chapter 8 to learn about naming.**

▶ Shortcut for Changing Reference Type

Instead of constantly typing and deleting dollar signs to switch reference type, the F4 key can be used to quickly change a reference.

1. Enter the formula **=A1** into cell B1.

2. In the formula bar (or in the cell), place the insertion point anywhere within the cell reference.

3. Press the F4 key repeatedly—the reference type will cycle through each of the ways the reference can be expressed.

▶ *Referring to Multiple Cells*

In all of the examples so far, references have been made to *single cells*. A cell reference can also refer to a *range of cells*. In the cell reference A1:A3, the starting cell is A1, the colon means *through*, and A3 is the ending cell. References to ranges of cells will take on greater significance when you start to work with formulas later in this chapter. In the meantime, here is a simple illustration:

1. Press F5 (the shortcut for Edit ➤ Go To)

2. Enter **A1:A3** as the reference, then click OK.

The range of cells A1 through A3 will be selected.

▶ *You Don't Have to Type Cell References*

Fortunately, it is not necessary to actually type cell references when entering or editing formulas. References can be entered into formulas by pointing and clicking. Try this:

1. Enter numbers into cells A1 and A2 on a blank worksheet.

2. Select cell A3. Type an equal sign to start a formula.

3. Click on cell A1 with the mouse. Notice in the formula bar that the cell reference A1 has been added to the formula.

4. Type a plus sign.

5. Click on cell A2 with the mouse to add it to the formula.

6. Press Enter to complete the formula, which adds cells A1 and A2.

▶ *Referring to Other Worksheets within the Same Workbook*

In all of the examples so far, references have been made to cells located on the same worksheet. You can also refer to cells that are located on different worksheets. Let us return to the street address analogy: Instead of saying *123 Elm Street*, you must say *123 Elm Street, Chicago* because the address is located in another town. The same is true with references to other worksheets. Try this exercise in a new workbook:

1. On Sheet1, enter **10** into cell A1.
2. Activate Sheet2 by clicking its tab.
3. Enter an equal sign into cell B1 to begin a formula.
4. Activate Sheet1 by clicking its tab—notice that the formula is still being built.
5. Click cell A1 to add it to the formula.
6. Press Enter to complete the formula.
7. The formula in cell B1 (on Sheet2) will read =Sheet1!A1 and the number 10 will display in the cell.

Notice that the cell reference is preceded by the sheet name and an exclamation point. (The exclamation point separates the sheet name from the cell reference.) Don't be confused by references to other worksheets—they are essentially the same as references to the same sheet. All of the same rules apply.

If a worksheet name has a space in it, references to the sheet from other sheets must enclose the sheet name in single quotes, as in

='Sales Forecast'!B3

However, if a space is added to a sheet name *after* references have been made to the sheet, Excel automatically places single quotes in dependent cells for you.

Why Refer to Other Sheets?

Referring to cells on other worksheets is a very common practice. A workbook might contain departmental forecasts, with one worksheet for each of four departments. A fifth sheet might be used to summarize the departments, and this summary sheet might refer to cells on each of the four departmental sheets.

▶ *Referring to a Worksheet in Another Workbook: External References*

A reference to another workbook is called an *external reference*. In our analogy, the address is not only located in another town, but in another state. And of course, the state must become part of the address. Try this exercise:

1. Create two new workbooks, Book1 and Book2. Arrange them horizontally using the Window ➤ Arrange command.

2. On Sheet1 of Book1, enter **Hello** into cell A1.

3. On Sheet 1 of Book2, enter an equal sign into cell B1 to begin a formula.

4. Activate Book1 by clicking anywhere on the workbook.

5. Click cell A1 (on Sheet1, Book1) to add it to the formula.

6. Press Enter to complete the formula.

7. The formula in cell B1 (Sheet1, Book2) will read:

   =[Book1]Sheet1!$A$1

   and *Hello* will display in the cell.

The reference begins with the book name, enclosed in square brackets. (Notice that the reference defaults to absolute.)

▶ *What Happens to References As Cells Are Moved?*

Various things can happen to cell references when cells are moved, depending on how and where they're moved.

Same Sheet	When you move a cell to a different location on the same worksheet, cells that refer to that cell (*dependent cells*) are automatically updated to point to the new cell reference, regardless of the method you use to move the cell. This is true even if the dependent cell is located in a dependent workbook— but only if the dependent workbook is open when the cell is moved.

Different Sheet   When you cut and paste a cell to a different worksheet (in the same workbook or a different workbook), dependent cells are left with **#REF!** (a reference error).

Dependent Cell   When you move a dependent cell, it will still point to the same cell(s) it originally pointed to, regardless of the method you use to move the cell. This holds true even if the dependent cell is moved to a different worksheet or workbook.

▶ ▶ **N O T E**

If you are new to cell references, you may want to absorb what you have learned so far before reading about the next topic: *links.* **Links are very important, though—make sure to come back to this discussion.**

▶

R1C1 REFERENCE STYLE

Although the A1 reference style is the style you will most likely use, and is the style used throughout this book, you may want to know a bit more about the R1C1 style.

You have already learned the A1 style refers to cell addresses by column letter and row number, and you can see the column letters and row numbers on your worksheets. R1C1 style refers to cell addresses by row and column *numbers*, and you can see numbered rows and columns on your worksheets if you choose the Reference Style as R1C1 in the Tools ➤ Options dialog, General tab. If you change the reference style in the Tools ➤ Options dialog, all the A1-style references in your workbook will change to R1C1 references.

As with A1 style, R1C1 style has both relative and absolute reference types. The absolute cell address R2C2 is equivalent to $B$2—it refers to a specific row/column intersection. Relative cell addresses are defined by their relationship to the cell containing the formula, rather than by worksheet coordinates. For example, the relative cell address R[-2]C[3] means "the cell 2 rows up and 3 columns to the right." Positive row and column numbers indicate rows down and columns right. Negative row and column numbers indicate rows up and columns left. No number indicates "this row" or "this column."

▶▶ *Understanding File Links*

When an external reference is entered, something special happens—a file *link* is automatically created. A file link always involves two workbooks:

- The workbook containing the external reference is dependent on the other workbook—it is called the *dependent workbook*.

- The workbook that is referred to by the external reference contains the source cell(s)—it is called the *source workbook*.

The dependent workbook is *linked* to the source workbook. The source workbook is not linked—it has no idea that one or more dependent workbooks may be linked to it.

▶ *Why Use Links?*

Linked workbooks are used quite commonly—even in relatively simple models. Linked workbooks provide several key advantages compared to using multiple worksheets in one workbook:

- Workbooks can be edited concurrently by different users. The manager of the western region can be editing WEST.XLS while the manager of the eastern region is editing EAST.XLS.

● An entire model does not have to be opened at once, making opening, recalculating, and saving of workbooks faster. Also, a large model stored in one workbook may not "fit" in memory.

● Multi-level rollups (e.g. rolling up, or consolidating, data from several corporate levels into a single summary) can be achieved using multi-level linked workbooks.

▶ Excel Keeps Track of the Full Path

Excel tracks the full path of the source book, and when the source book is closed, the full path appears in the external reference. For example, an external reference to a source workbook named SALES.XLS, located in a directory named FILES on the C drive, would look like this:

When source is open:

=[SALES.XLS]Sheet1!$A$1

When source is closed:

='C:\FILES\[SALES.XLS]Sheet1'!$A$1

▶ There Can Be Lots of Links in Lots of Directions

Although a particular link always refers to a single workbook, a workbook can be linked many times, in many ways:

● One workbook can be linked to many different source workbooks.

● One source workbook can have many dependent workbooks.

● Workbook A can be linked to workbook B. Workbook B can be linked to workbook C. In other words, one workbook can be a dependent book *and* a source book.

● Two workbooks can be linked to each other, in which case each is dependent on the other.

▶ *Changing a Link*

One way to change a link is by editing the formula containing the external reference. But what if a dependent workbook contains dozens of external references? Choose the Edit ➤ Links command to display the Links dialog box pictured in Figure 4.2.

FIGURE 4.2 ▶

The Links dialog box lists all source workbooks for the active workbook.

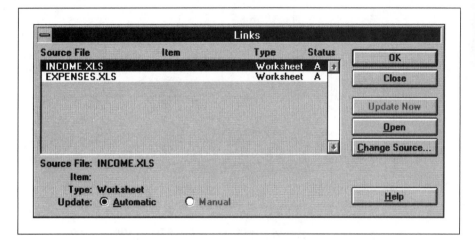

Select the source file you want to change, then click the Change Source button to display the Change Links dialog box (Figure 4.3).

The Change Links dialog box looks and behaves very similarly to the File ➤ Open dialog box. You can navigate the file system to find the workbook you want to link to. Once you have selected a new source file to link to, all affected external references are automatically changed in one fell swoop. Assume you have changed the source file EAST.XLS to WEST.XLS. Every external reference in the dependent workbook is automatically changed to WEST.XLS.

▶ *Opening a Dependent Workbook*

Excel behaves differently depending on whether the source workbook is opened or closed at the time the dependent book is opened.

- If the source workbook is already open, the dependent workbook recalculates automatically (unless you are in manual calculation mode).

FIGURE 4.3 ▶

The Change Links
dialog box

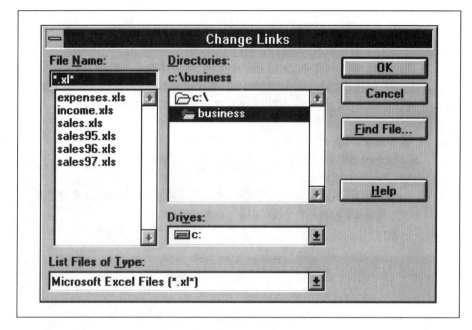

• The source workbook does *not* have to be open for the dependent
book to retrieve values from the source book. Excel will display the
following dialog box. Click Yes to update the external references.

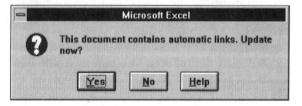

 ▶ ▶TIP

As you may have noticed, formulas can refer to cells in
closed workbooks. When such formulas recalculate,
current values are retrieved from disk, from the closed
workbook, without the workbook being opened. These
formulas can even use functions such as SUM and
INDEX. However, some functions, such as OFFSET and
VLOOKUP, do not work when the source workbook is
closed—these functions are too complex.

▶ *Linking to Unsaved Workbooks*

Linking to a workbook that has *never* been saved is not a good idea; if you close the source workbook without saving it, the dependent workbook is linked to a workbook that does not exist. In general, it is good practice to save source workbooks before saving dependent books.

▶ *When Workbooks Become Inexplicably Large*

Behind the scenes, dependent workbooks invisibly save values contained in source workbooks (external values). For example, if workbook A refers to A1:A999 in workbook B, all 999 values are saved inside workbook A. There is one problematic manifestation of this feature: Sometimes a seemingly small workbook consumes an inexplicably large amount of disk space. A workbook can be set to *not* save external values by choosing the Tools ➤ Options command, then selecting the Calculation tab. The Save External Link Values setting, shown in Figure 4.4, controls this behavior. If you uncheck this setting, the source workbook must be recalculated when it is opened, otherwise the dependent cells will contain errors.

FIGURE 4.4 ▶

The Tools ➤ Options Calculation dialog tab

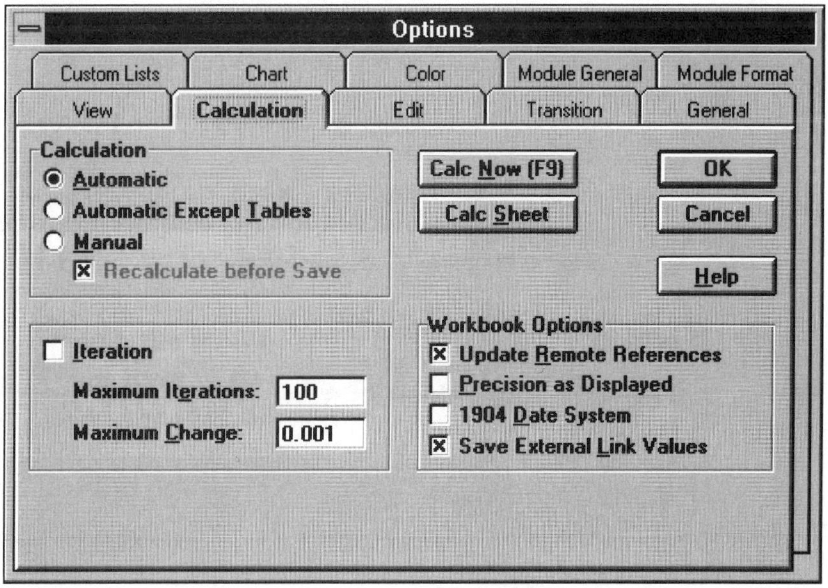

▶ **AVOIDING THE UPDATE LINKS ALERT**

When you open a workbook which contains external or remote references, an alert will be displayed which says "This document contains automatic links. Update now?" This alert causes a great deal of confusion for novice users. Answering "Yes" will update all the links in the newly-opened workbook. Answering "No" means formulas that contain external or remote references will not re-calculate with current data.

There is a way to prevent the question from being asked, so that links are always updated automatically: Choose Tools ➤ Options, click the Edit tab, and clear the Ask to Update Automatic Links checkbox. This is a global setting, and cannot be applied to individual workbooks. Another way to avoid the alert is by opening the source workbook before opening the dependent workbook.

▶▶ *Using Functions*

Picture a worksheet with numbers in cells A1 through A9, and these numbers need to be summed. You could enter the formula:

=A1+A2+A3+A4+A5+A6+A7+A8+A9

This method is tiresome when summing nine cells, but becomes downright impossible if thousands of cells needed to be summed. The same result can be achieved using the SUM function:

=SUM(A1:A9)

The SUM function is one of several hundred built-in functions. These built-in functions provide the real power when it comes to the manipulation of text and numbers in Excel. A function can be used by itself, as with the SUM function above, or can be used as a piece of a complex formula. Formulas using functions must adhere to the following rules:

- All formulas must *begin* with an equal sign. (A function is *not* preceded by an equal sign unless the function is at the start of the formula.)

- Most functions need to be provided with one or more pieces of data to act upon, referred to as *arguments*. The arguments are enclosed in parentheses following the function name. If there are multiple arguments, they are separated by commas. The argument to the SUM function above is A1:A9.

▶ MATCHING CLOSING PARENTHESIS INSIDE FORMULAS

When you are first learning to write formulas (and even when you get to be an expert), getting all the parentheses matched up correctly can be quite a chore, particularly in long formulas. Sometimes Excel figures out what you want and does it for you. For example, in simple formulas, like a SUM or an INDEX function with no nested functions, the closing parenthesis can be omitted.

When you press Enter, Excel adds the closing parentheses automatically. In more complex formulas, Excel will not close the parentheses for you. Instead, an alert will be displayed which says "Parentheses do not match", and the offending portion of the formula will be highlighted. When you enter a closing parenthesis, the matching opening parenthesis will be highlighted briefly.

Even more helpful is this trick for finding all the matching pairs of parentheses in a formula: use the arrow keys to scroll through the formula character by character. Each time you cross a parenthesis, both parentheses in the pair will be highlighted briefly.

▶ Exercise—Using Functions in Formulas

The following exercise will demonstrate the application of several critical skills:

- Entering functions with arguments.
- Using *nested functions*, where one function serves as an argument for another function.
- The use of the IF function, used to calculate a value conditionally.

 ▶ ▶ **N O T E**

The functions used in this exercise do not have special significance—they are intended to illustrate the general syntax of functions within formulas.

1. Enter the following constants onto a blank worksheet.

	A	B	C	D	E
	\multicolumn{5}{c}{BOOK1.XLS}
1	Full Name	Last Name	Score 1	Pass	
2	Smith, Joe		80		
3	Jones, Mary		92		
4	Dunn, Sam		64		
5	Roberts, Jill		76		
6					
7		Average:			
8					
9					

2. Enter the following formula into cell C7 to calculate the average score:

=AVERAGE(C2:C5)

This averages the values in cells C2 through C5. The range C2:C5 is the argument for the AVERAGE function. (Remember, ranges don't have to be typed—they can be entered via point and click.)

T I P

Enter functions in lower case. If entered correctly, they automatically revert to upper case.

3. Enter the following formula into cell B2 to calculate the student's last name:

=LEFT(A2,SEARCH(",",A2)-1)

This is an example of *nested* functions, which are evaluated from the inside out. In order to calculate the last name, the LEFT function is used, which takes two arguments:

- Text string found in cell A2.
- Number of characters in the last name. We have to search for a comma, which is the separator between the last and first names, using the SEARCH function. The expression

SEARCH(",",A2)-1

translates to "get the position of the comma within the name, then subtract one."

This entire expression is the second argument to the LEFT function, and evaluates to 5.

In simplified form, **=LEFT("Smith, Joe",5)** evaluates to Smith.

T I P

Expressions within a formula can be independently evaluated by selecting the expression (in the cell or formula bar), then pressing F9. Remember to cancel the change, or else the value will replace the expression in the formula. Try it: Select the entire expression SEARCH(",",A2) and press F9—then press ESC.

4. Copy the formula in cell B2 to cells B3 through B5.

5. The following formula, entered into cell D2, will display No if the student failed, or Yes if the student passed:

=IF(C2<65,"No","Yes")

This is an example of the all important IF function, which breaks down into five pieces:

IF	**Function keyword**
C2<65	Condition
"No"	Value if condition is true
~,	ELSE clause (implied with a comma)
"Yes"	Value if condition is false

In English: "If the score is less than 65 then *No*, otherwise *Yes*."

6. Copy the formula to cells D3 through D5. If the formulas were entered correctly, the worksheet will appear as follows:

	A	B	C	D	E
				BOOK1.XLS	
1	Full Name	Last Name	Score 1	Pass	
2	Smith, Joe	Smith	80	Yes	
3	Jones, Mary	Jones	92	Yes	
4	Dunn, Sam	Dunn	64	No	
5	Roberts, Jill	Roberts	76	Yes	
6					
7		Average:	78		
8					
9					

► Checking Complex Conditions

In the above exercise, the IF function was used to apply conditional logic in a formula. The AND and OR functions allow more complex conditions to be tested.

AND Checks If More Than One Condition Is True

The general syntax of AND used with IF is as follows:

=IF(AND(Expression1, Expression2),Value if TRUE,Value if FALSE)

There can be up to 30 expressions as arguments to the AND function, and *all* must evaluate true for the AND function to evaluate true. On the following worksheet, it is OK to leave cells B1 and B3 blank. But, if a first name is entered in B1, a last name must be entered into B3.

	A	B	C	D	E
1	First Name	Smith			
2					
3	Last Name		Must enter last name		
4					
5					
6					
7					

BOOK1.XLS

The following formula, entered into cell C3, will remind the user to enter a last name if a first name has been entered:

=IF(AND(ISTEXT(B1),ISBLANK(B3)),"Must enter last name","")

In English: If there is text in B1 *and* B3 is blank, display a reminder or else display nothing. (The empty quotes represent null text.)

OR Checks If One Condition Is True

The AND function required that *all* expressions be true. The syntax of the OR function is identical, but with one fundamental difference: only *one* of the expressions must be true for the OR function to evaluate true.

▶ Creating Formulas with the Function Wizard

Excel includes over three hundred built-in functions, and no one—not even the most advanced user—is familiar with each and every one. The Function Wizard is a great way to explore, learn, and build functions. It automates and goof-proofs the creation of formulas using functions by guiding you through the arguments and syntax required by each function. Try the following exercise:

1. Enter **Smithers** in cell A1.

2. Select cell B1 and choose Insert ➤ Function (or click the Function Wizard tool). You'll see the following dialog box:

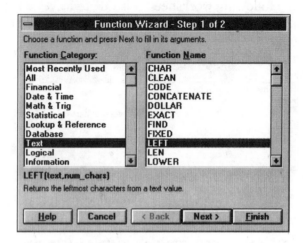

3. From the Function Category list, select Text.

4. From the Function Name list, select LEFT.

5. Click the Next button.

▶ ▶ **T I P**

If you click Finish at this point, you can skip the rest of these steps. The argument placeholders are entered in the formula bar, where you can finish the formula without the Function Wizard.

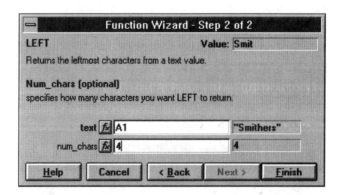

6. Click on cell A1 to place its reference in the first argument. The value in the cell appears next to the argument.

7. Type 4 in the *num_chars* argument.

8. Click Finish. Cell B1 returns the value **Smit**.

▶ ▶**T I P**

You can nest functions using the Function Wizard. To nest a function, click the Paste Function button (the *fx* button next to the argument window). A fresh Function Wizard dialog box will be displayed for the nested argument—when you complete the nested function, clicking Finish will return you to the previous level.

▶ *3-D Cell References*

3-D cell references are used to reference cells in multiple, adjacent worksheets within a workbook. The following exercise demonstrates the use of a 3-D cell reference to sum cells spanning workbooks:

1. Create a new workbook.

2. Enter a number into cell A1 on Sheet1, Sheet2, Sheet3, and Sheet4.

3. Activate Sheet1. In cell B2, type **=SUM(**

4. Select Sheet1 through Sheet4 as a group (select Sheet1, hold down Shift and select Sheet4).

5. Select cell A1.

6. Type) and press Enter.

This formula sums cell A1 on sheets 1 through 4. You can also type the reference into the formula as follows:

=SUM(Sheet1:Sheet4!A1)

▶▶ *Controlling Worksheet Calculation*

By default, Excel calculates worksheet formulas when changes to cell values so require. Automatic calculation is possibly the single most important feature of a spreadsheet program, and it is important to understand how to control it. To set calculation mode, choose the Tools ➤ Options command, then select the Calculation tab (Figure 4.5).

FIGURE 4.5 ▶

Calculation Settings

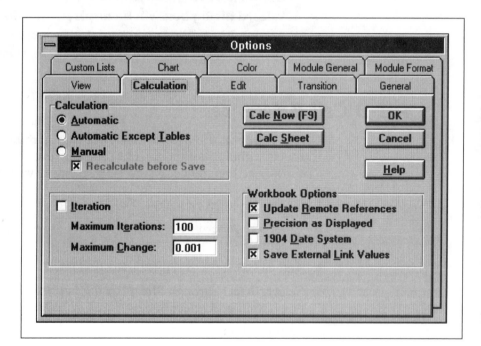

▶ *Calculation Modes*

Calculation mode is a setting that is global to the workspace—it is not a workbook setting.

- **Automatic Calculation** is the default mode. Calculation automatically occurs if a cell value is changed and there are formulas referring to the changed cell. While calculation is taking place, a message is displayed on the status bar indicating what percentage of the calculation is complete.

▶ ▶ T I P

> **You can continue to work while Excel is calculating, though the calculation process pauses until you stop working.**

- **Manual Calculation** is used to speed up response time. When working with a large model, it will make your life easier if you turn off automatic calculation until after you've entered all the data. The word *Calculate* will display on the status bar as a reminder that recalculation is required. Press F9 to perform a one-time calculation, yet remain in manual calculation mode. Click the Calc Sheet button pictured in Figure 4.5 to calculate just the active worksheet rather than the entire workspace.

- **Automatic Except Tables** is a special mode that recalculates everything except data tables. (Data tables are pretty obscure, and are discussed briefly in Chapter 23, "Performing What-If Analyses".)

▶ *Precision as Displayed*

The value that appears in a cell is not necessarily the same as the actual value stored in the cell. Excel stores numbers with 15-digit accuracy, yet a cell may be formatted to display dollars and cents. (The formula bar always displays the actual underlying value.) Variation between formatted numbers and underlying values can cause incorrect results, which vexes accountants to no end. Check the Precision as Displayed setting, pictured in Figure 4.5, to recalculate based on the formatted values.

▶ ▶ W A R N I N G

> **This is a workbook setting that is saved with the workbook, unlike the automatic and manual calculation settings.**

▶▶ Putting Formulas and Functions to Work

This section will demonstrate how to use formulas and functions to create two simple but useful worksheets: a loan calculator and a loan amortization table.

▶ Creating a Loan Calculator

Suppose you are taking out a car loan, and want to analyze the various loan options that are available. This exercise will show you how to create a simple, reusable loan calculator to determine what the monthly payments will be based on the loan amount, interest rate, and term.

Enter the following information onto a blank worksheet:

Cell	Entry
B2	Loan Calculator
B5	Interest rate
C5	Term (months)
D5	Loan amount
G5	Monthly Payment
G6	=PMT(B6/12,C6,-D6)
B6	10.0% (be sure to type the % sign)
C6	24
D6	2000

You can play "what if?" by changing the interest rate, the number of monthly payments, and the loan amount.

▢			BOOK1.XLS				▼ ▲
	A	B	C	D	E	F	G	H

Loan Calculator

	Interest rate	Term (months)	Loan amount		Payment
	10.00%	24	2,000		$92.29

▶ *Creating a Loan Amortization Schedule*

The loan calculator tells you what the monthly payment is. Suppose you want to know how much interest is being paid in a given year. This exercise will add a loan amortization schedule to the loan calculator.

The basic calculations used in the table are:

Beginning balance (except for initial)   The ending balance from previous period

Interest (compounded monthly)   The annual interest rate divided by 12, multiplied by the beginning balance for the period

Principal   The payment less interest

Ending balance   The beginning balance less principal

1. On the same worksheet as the loan calculator, make the following entries:

Cell	Entry
B10	Amortization Schedule
B17	Period
C17	Beginning Balance
D17	Payment
E17	Interest
F17	Principal
G17	Ending Balance
B18	May-96

Cell	Entry
C18	=$D$6
D18	=$G$6
E18	=$B$6*C18/12
F18	=D18-E18
G18	=C18-F18
B19	Jun-96
C19	=G18
D19	=$G$6 (copy from D18)
E19	=$B$6*C19/12 (copy from E18)
F19	=D19-E19 (copy from F18)
G19	=C19-F19 (copy from G18)
C14	Totals
D13	Payments
E13	Interest
F13	Principal
D14	=SUM(D18:D378)
E14	=SUM(E18:E378)
F14	=SUM(F18:F378)

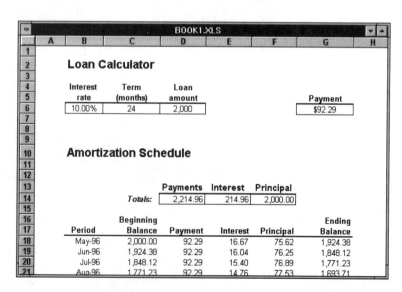

> **N O T E**
>
> **The SUM formulas in cells D14:F14 allow for up to 360 payments (monthly payments on a 30-year mortgage), so this template can be used to test much larger loans without recreating the SUM formulas. The formulas are placed above the table so that you can put unlimited rows into the schedule without overwriting the totals.**

2. Select cells B19:G41. Choose the Edit ➤ Fill ➤ Series command, select the AutoFill option, then click OK. (See Chapter 7 to learn more about AutoFill.)

3. Select cells C18:G41, then choose the Format ➤ Cells command and select the Number tab. Select Category Number and Format Codes #,##0.00 (See the next chapter to learn more about cell formatting.)

> **N O T E**
>
> **Excel performs these calculations with 15-digit precision, and will display the full precision unless you format the cells otherwise. Changing the format doesn't change the actual underlying cell value.**

▶ EXPANDING A SUM FORMULA TO INCLUDE INSERTED ROWS

Suppose you have values in cells A1:A10, and the formula =SUM(A1:A10) in cell A11. You want to add another value to the bottom of the list, so you insert a new row at row 11 (directly above the SUM function) and enter the new value in cell A11. But the new value is not included in the summed range. How can you insert a new value at the end of a list, and have the summed range expand automatically to include the new value? There are a couple of tricks to accomplish this.

First, you can leave a blank row at the bottom of the range (in this case, row 11) and include the blank row in the sum formula. The formula in this instance would be =SUM(A1:A11). Then insert a row above the blank row (row 11) whenever you want to add a value to the list, and the summed range will automatically adjust to include the new row.

As an alternative, you can use this formula to sum a range which always includes the cell above the formula:

```
=SUM(first_cell:INDEX(column:column,ROW()-1))
```

The argument *first_cell* refers to the first cell in the summed range (in this example, cell A1). The argument *column:column refers to the column being summed (in this example, $A:$A). In this case, the formula in cell A11 would be =SUM($A$1:INDEX($A:$A,ROW()-1)). See Chapter 9 to learn more about the INDEX and ROW functions.*

▶ ▶ **CHAPTER** **5**

Formatting Cells

▶▶ *F*AST *T*RACK

►► **S**ome people believe that the substance of a document is all that counts. Even if you are in this camp, keep in mind that much of the world is not. As a user of a graphically rich spreadsheet program, you probably appreciate how important a report's appearance can be. Fairly simple formatting practices can yield the following benefits:

- *Important information can be highlighted with formatting.*
- *Simple formatting procedures can greatly enhance overall readability of reports.*
- *Styles can be used to easily create a consistent look, and consistency enhances professionalism.*

►► Basic Formatting Procedures

This chapter will cover many formatting options, all of which follow the same basic procedure:

1. Select the cell(s) you want to format.
2. Choose the desired formatting command.

►► Fonts

In Excel, the font format property encompasses several aspects of the character:

- Typeface, such as *Times New Roman*, *Arial*, and *Courier*
- Size measured in points

- Bold and/or italic
- Color
- Underline
- Special effects—strikethrough, superscript, subscript

Three important new font formatting features have been added in Excel 5:

- Accountants will appreciate the support of underlining that adheres to rigid accounting standards.
- The scientific community will appreciate the addition of superscript and subscript as global font options.
- Everyone will appreciate that fonts can be applied to individual characters within a cell.

▶ *Applying Fonts*

Choose the Format ➤ Cells command, then select the Font tab to display the dialog box pictured in Figure 5.1. Select the font properties you want to apply and click OK.

FIGURE 5.1 ▶

The Format ➤ Cells, Font dialog box

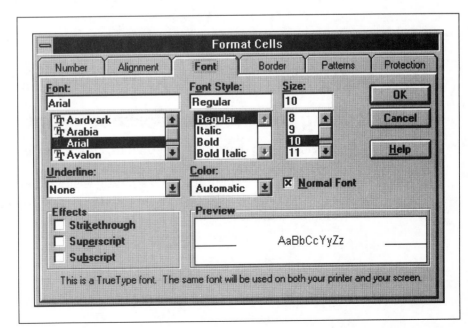

Font

- Available fonts are not specific to Excel—the list includes all fonts available under Microsoft Windows.

- TrueType fonts are indicated by a TT symbol next to the type-face—TrueType is a scalable font technology built into Microsoft Windows.

- Fonts available for the currently selected printer are indicated by a printer symbol next to the typeface.

Size

Font size is measured in points. There are 72 points per inch (measured from the top of the **b** upstroke to the bottom of the **p** downstroke), so a 12-point font is $\frac{1}{6}$th of an inch from top to bottom when printed.

Underline

- *Single* and *Double* underlines apply to all characters in the cell.

- *Single Accounting* and *Double Accounting* underline styles, when applied to a dollar format, underline only the digits, not the dollar sign (unlike normal underline styles, which underline the dollar sign as well).

Normal Font

Checking *Normal Font* resets font selections to default settings.

▶ Changing the Default Workbook Font

To change the default workbook font, choose the Tools ➤ Options command, then select the General tab. The *Standard Font* and *Size* settings determine the default font. This setting is applied every time you create a new workbook. (Excel must be restarted before changes in this setting take effect.)

▶ *Tools for Setting Fonts*

Table 5.1 describes the various font tools available in Excel. Note that the tools marked with ★ do not appear on a built-in toolbar—see Chapter 26 to learn how to display them by customizing toolbars.

▶ **TABLE 5.1:** *Font Formatting Tools*

Tool	Function
`Arial ▼`	Font (typeface)
`10 ▼`	Size (in points)
B	Bold
I	Italic
U	Single Underline
D	Double Underline ★
K	Strikethrough ★
A	Increase Font Size ★
A	Decrease Font Size ★
T	Font Color Palette (tearaway)
A	Cycle Font Color ★

►► *Borders*

Cell borders add clarity and organization to a worksheet, and when used judiciously are one of the most useful formatting options. To set borders, choose the Format ➤ Cells command, then select the Border tab to display the dialog box shown in Figure 5.2.

FIGURE 5.2 ►

The Format ➤ Cells, Border dialog tab

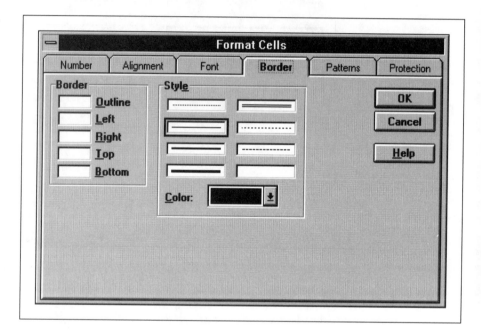

► *Understanding the Border Options*

The following list describes the options available in the Format Cells, Border dialog box:

- **Style** controls the line style of selected borders, including varied line weight, solid or broken, and single or double.

- **Color** controls the color of selected borders.

- **Border** controls which borders are applied to selected cells, and displays the *Style* and *Color* selected for each border.

▶ ▶ **N O T E**

If a *Border* is shaded grey, it means that the specific *Border* is applied to only some of the selected cells (or that different styles are applied to the selected cells). For example, select cell B2 and apply a left border. Now select cells B2:B3 and display the Border dialog box. *Border, left* is shaded grey because only part of the selection is left-bordered.

To remove a border, display the Border dialog box and click the Border you want to remove.

 ▶ ▶ **N O T E**

Sometimes when you remove a border, the border doesn't disappear from the cell. This happens because there are two borders applied to the gridline, and you must remove both. For example, select cells B2:C2 and apply left and right borders. Now try to remove the border between the two cells by removing the right border from cell B2. The border still displayed on the worksheet is the left border of cell C2. Remove the left border from cell C2, and the border between the two cells on the worksheet disappears.

▶ *Gridlines Are Not the Same as Borders*

Cell gridlines are not the same as cell borders. Gridlines are global to the worksheet, and they diminish the impact of borders. To remove gridlines:

1. Choose the Tools ➤ Options command, then select the View tab.

2. Uncheck the Gridlines option.

Formatting Cells

▶ ▶
Ch.
5

T I P

Light grey borders, or thin borders, can be less visually obtrusive, and provide a more professional look. The appearance of these effects will vary depending on monitor or printer resolution.

▶ *Tools for Applying Borders*

 The Border tool displays a palette of various border styles (see Chapter 1 to learn about tear-off palettes). Table 5.2 describes each tool on the Border tool palette.

▶ **TABLE 5.2:** *Border Formatting Tools on the Border Tool Drop-down Palette*

Tool	Function
	No border (removes existing borders)
	Bottom
	Left
	Right
	Bottom double
	Bottom heavy
	Top and bottom
	Top and double bottom
	Top and heavy bottom

► **TABLE 5.2:** *Border Formatting Tools on the Border Tool Drop-down Palette (continued)*

Tool	Function
⊞	Outline (each cell in selection)
⊡	Outline (around selection)
▣	Heavy outline (around selection)

►► *Patterns*

Patterns and colors can improve the appearance of a worksheet or emphasize specific information. To apply patterns and colors to selected cells, choose Format ➤ Cells, then select the Patterns tab.

- Select a color.
- Select a pattern and a pattern color from the Pattern drop-down.

Bright colors can be muted by mixing with a white pattern, or by applying the bright color as a pattern over a white background.

Make large tables easy to read across by shading every other row in a light color or grey:

	A	B	C	D	E	F	G
1	7180	5921	826	9781	8295	145	6480
2	1972	8060	4033	7807	6401	7591	3902
3	6170	1233	7893	4038	8415	3690	1710
4	5308	9073	7691	5232	7970	1592	7173
5	977	7395	1392	8186	647	535	1889
6	3204	824	5934	1473	1810	239	5114
7	1154	4232	7140	8979	8746	4792	8837
8	7242	4718	717	802	9785	7469	4818
9	8595	2072	1535	3314	7203	161	9272
10	968	4829	1564	8806	4164	3737	365
11	2368	6005	5305	7459	7588	6353	3723

EXPENSES.XLS

Formatting Cells

Ch. 5

▶ *Tools for Applying Colors and Patterns*

 The Color tool is found on the Formatting toolbar. When clicked, it displays a tear-off palette of colors. To tear the palette away from the toolbar, click on the palette and drag it onto the worksheet (where it will act like a floating toolbar).

 The Pattern tool is found on the Drawing toolbar, and also has a drop-down, tear-off palette.

▶▶ *Alignment*

Alignment refers to the positioning of characters within the cell. By default, text is left-aligned and numbers are right-aligned. To set alignment, choose the Format ▶ Cells command, then select the Alignment tab to display the dialog box in Figure 5.3.

FIGURE 5.3

The Format ▶ Cells, Alignment dialog tab

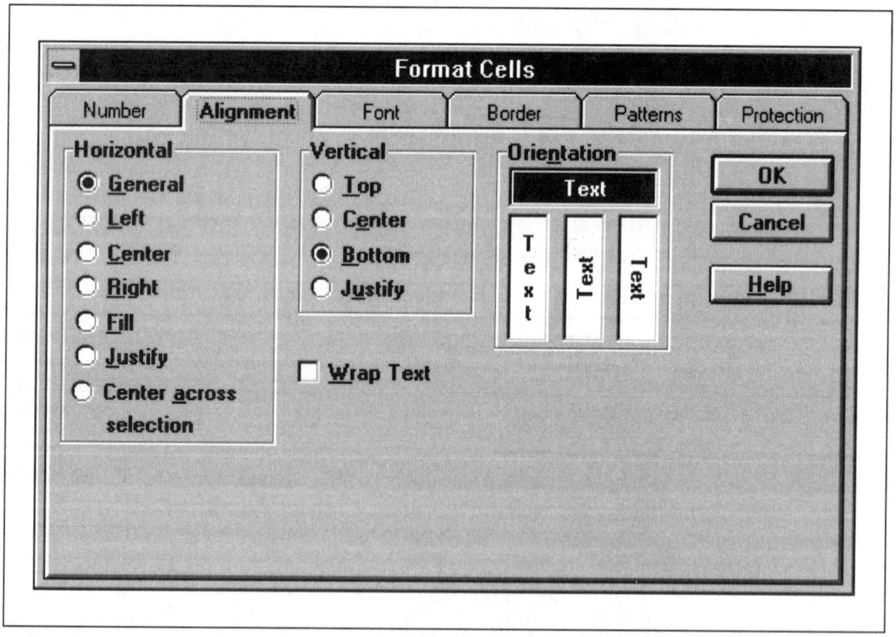

▶ *Horizontal Alignment*

The following describes the options for horizontally aligning the text:

General aligns text to the left, numbers to the right.

Left aligns cell contents to the left.

Center centers characters within the cell.

Right aligns cell contents to the right.

Fill fills selected cells evenly with a single character.

Justify aligns wrapped text right and left (text is automatically wrapped). Results are visible only with multiple lines.

Center Across Selection centers text across multiple columns.

Center Across Selection

The *Center Across Selection* option is very useful for titles, as it centers the text across the selected cells regardless of varying column widths. For example, suppose you want to center the title **1996 Quarterly Revenue** over columns A through D (in row 2).

1. Enter text in cell A2.
2. Select cells A2:D2.
3. Choose Center Across Selection from the Alignment dialog tab.

REAPPLYING THE CENTER ACROSS CELLS FORMAT

Suppose you have centered a worksheet title across six cells using the Center Across Cells format. Now you want to re-center the title across just five cells. The common mistake most users make is to select the five cells, then apply the Center Across Cells format. But this won't work, because when you apply the Center Across Cells format to a range, the format is applied to each cell in the range individually. The sixth cell will retain the center-across format until you specifically remove it.

The easiest way to change the centering is to select the sixth cell and remove the center-across format (click on the Center Across Cells tool to toggle the format *off*). To add a cell to the center-across range, apply the Center Across Cells format to the next cell on the right side of the range. To remove a cell from the center-across range, remove the Center Across Cells format from the last cell on the right side of the range.

Wrap Text

The *Wrap Text* option breaks a long line of text into multiple lines to fit within the cell. Excel breaks the lines to fit column width, but you can insert specific line breaks with Alt+Enter. Rows automatically heighten to fit multiple lines of text.

FILLING A CELL WITH A SINGLE CHARACTER

Suppose you are creating a form in which you want some cells to be filled in with a specific character, perhaps --------- or ####### or *$$$$$*. The Fill option, on the Format ➤ Cells, Alignment tab, will fill a selected cell or cells with a single character for you. You can also fill cells with a repeating string of characters, such as *abc* (the cell will fill with *abcabcabc*). You might think it simple to fill the cell by typing the character until the cell is filled, but what happens when you change the width of that column? If you have typed, for instance, nine characters, there will be nine characters in the cell, no matter what the width of the column is. But if you fill the cell using the Fill option, the cell will be filled with the character regardless of the column width.

You can also use the Fill option to fill several cells (or an entire row) with a single character, and the line of characters will look unbroken. If you typed characters to fill each cell, you would see discrete groups of characters, with spaces left for gridlines between cells.

To fill a single cell, enter the character or string of characters with which you want to fill the cell. Then choose Format ➤ Cells, the Alignment tab, and select the Fill option (under Horizontal). To fill several cells or an entire row, enter the fill character(s) in the leftmost cell, then select all the cells (or the row) and format them with the Fill option.

▶ Vertical Alignment

The vertical alignment settings control alignment between the top and bottom of the cell.

Top positions contents at the top of the cell.

Center centers contents vertically within the cell.

Bottom positions contents on the bottom of the cell.

Justify justifies lines vertically, from top to bottom of the cell, and automatically wraps text.

To demonstrate the effect of vertical alignment, try this:

1. Enter some text in cell B2.

2. Increase the height of row 2.

3. Change the vertical alignment in cell B2 to *Top*.

Notice that the vertical alignment in a cell is not apparent unless the row height is increased.

▶ Orientation

The Orientation settings control how the text is oriented within the cell. The four settings on the dialog box (see Figure 5.3) display what the text will look like.

 ▶ ▶**N O T E**

> **Row height automatically adjusts when the cell is oriented vertically or sideways. For instance, if you format a cell for vertical orientation, the row height will increase to fit the entire entry into the cell.**

▶ Alignment Tools

Table 5.3 lists and describes Excel's alignment tools. Note that the tools marked with ★ do not appear on a built-in toolbar—see Chapter 26 to learn how to display them by customizing toolbars.

▶ **TABLE 5.3:** *Alignment Tools*

Tool	Function
≣	Left-align
≣	Center-align
≣	Right-align
≣	Justify ★
←a→	Center across Selection
a b	Vertical orientation ★
ꙇ	Sideways (read bottom-to-top) ★
ꙇ	Sideways (read top-to-bottom) ★

Formatting Cells

▶▶
Ch.
5

▶▶ *Numbers*

Number formats control how numbers, including date and time, are displayed. Excel allows numbers to be displayed in a vast array of number, time, fraction, currency, accounting, and scientific formats, as well as a General or default format.

▶ *Using Number Formats*

1. Choose Format ➤ Cells, then select the Number tab (see Figure 5.4).

2. Select a Category of formats (to narrow the search for a formatting code).

3. Select a Format Code. (*Sample* displays the selected format applied to the data in the active cell.)

4. Click OK.

FIGURE 5.4 ▸

*The Format ➤ Cells,
Number dialog tab*

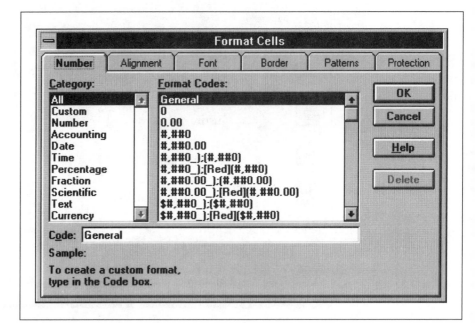

▶ Format Symbols

Excel's number formats are controlled by the use of format symbols. Format symbols can be combined to specify the appearance, length, and alignment of numbers, and even to add a text description to a number.

Excel's number format symbols are listed in Table 5.4.

▶ Date and Time Formatting Symbols

When a date or time is entered, it is recognized and displayed in a date or time format. Table 5.5 shows the variety of formats available for dates and times.

TABLE 5.4: *Number Format Symbols*

Symbol	Function	Remarks
0	Digit placeholder	Determines number of decimal places displayed; rounds to number of 0's right of decimal point, displays leading and trailing zeros
#	Digit placeholder	Same as 0; doesn't display leading or trailing zeros
?	Digit placeholder	Same as 0; insignificant 0's removed, spaces inserted to align numbers correctly
. (period)	Decimal point	Marks location of decimal point
%	Percent	Displays % sign, and treats number as percent
, (comma)	Thousands separator	Marks thousands position
_ (underscore)	Alignment feature	Skips width of character following underscore; aligns positives with negatives enclosed in ( ) so that numbers and commas remain aligned
E- E+ e- e+	Exponent indicator	Displays number in scientific format
: $ _ + ( ) - /	Characters	These characters displayed
/	Fraction separator	Indicates fraction
\	Text indicator	Character following is text
" "	Text indicator	Entry within quotes is text
*	Fill indicator	Fills remaining cell width with character following asterisk
@	Format code	Indicates where user-input text will appear
[color]	Color indicator	Displays characters in indicated color (black, blue, white, green, cyan, magenta, red, yellow)
[color n]	Color indicator	Displays characters in corresponding color from color palette (*n* is number from 0–56)
[condition value]	Conditional statement	Sets criteria for each section of number format; uses conditions **<,>,=,<=,>=,<>**, and numeric values

Formatting Cells

Ch. 5

▶ **TABLE 5.5**: *Date and Time Format Symbols*

Symbol	Display	Remarks
yyyy	1997	Year—four-digits
yy	97	Year—two-digits
mmmm	January	Month—full name
mmm	Jan	Month, abbreviated to three characters
mm	01	Month—number, leading zeros
m	1	Month—number, no leading zeros
dd	07	Day—number, leading zeros
d	7	Day—number, no leading zeros
h	1	Hour
mm	01	Minute (displays leading zeros)
ss	01	Second (displays leading zeros)
AM/PM	AM	AM or PM for 12-hr time format(if not included, times are displayed in 24-hour format)

Inexplicably, there is no built-in format to display a date in the format *January 7, 1998*. To display a date in this format, either enter it as text (by preceding the entry with an apostrophe), or create the custom format *mmmm d, yyyy*. Keep in mind that the date cannot be used in calculations if entered as text.

▶ ▶**T I P**

When you enter a fraction, such as 1/2, Excel interprets your entry as a date, and displays *2-Jan*. To "force the fraction," enter it as a mixed fraction: *0 1/2*.

N O T E

M or mm immediately following h or hh signifies minutes, not months.

▶ Samples

Table 5.6 shows some of Excel's many number-formatting options at work.

▶ **TABLE 5.6:** *Sample Built-In Formats*

Value	Format	Display
1234.335	0	1234
1234.335	#,##0	1,234
1234.335	#,##0.00	1,234.34
1234	0.00	1234.00
1234.335	# ?/?	1234 1/3
.1234	0%	12%
1234.335	0.00E+00	1.23E+03
June 11, 1998	m/d/yy	6/11/98
June 11, 1998	d-mmm-yy	11-Jun-98
June 11, 1998	mmm-yy	Jun-98
8:07 PM	h:mm AM/PM	8:07 PM
8:07 PM	h:mm	20:07
8:07:32	h:mm:ss	8:07:32

▶ ▶ T I P

When you enter a formula that refers to other cells, the cell inherits the number formatting of the first referenced cell in the formula (unless a specific format has already been applied to the cell containing the formula).

▶ CUSTOM NUMBER FORMATTING FOR ELAPSED TIME

Suppose you keep track of your daily work hours by recording start times and stop times. Every morning and evening you type Ctrl+Shift+: (colon) to enter the current time on your time worksheet—then you subtract the start time from the stop time to calculate the elapsed work time, and format the result as hours. You get 8 or 9 (or 10 or 12) hours worked daily—no problem.

Now you want to total up your work hours for the week—you sum the daily elapsed times and get 16 hours, even though you expected an answer of 40! This happened because Excel's standard time formatting allows for a maximum of 24 hours (and 60 minutes, and 60 seconds). Don't despair, it's easy to fix the formatting to display the full elapsed time in hours (or minutes, or seconds).

Special formatting is required to display an elapsed time value which is more than 24 hours, or 60 minutes, or 60 seconds. Enclose the time code in brackets to remove the limitation. For example, the custom format code *[h]:mm* will display a 40-hour work week as 40 hours (and a fractional hour as minutes). The custom code *[mm]* will display your 40-hr week as 960 minutes, and *[ss]* will display it as 57600 seconds.

▶▶ *Custom Number Formats*

You are not limited to the built-in number formats. Using the format symbols in Table 5.4 and Table 5.5, you can construct your own custom number formats.

▶ *Creating a Custom Number Format*

Suppose that you want to display numbers in thousands, without changing the values:

1. Select cell A1 and enter **1234567**.
2. Choose Format ➤ Cells, then select the Number tab.
3. Type **#,###,** in the *Code* box (be sure to type both commas).
4. Click OK. The number will display as **1,235**.

▶ *Applying Custom Number Formats*

Once a custom number format is defined, it is stored in the workbook and can be applied just like built-in formats. Custom formats will display in the Number dialog tab (see Figure 5.4) at the end of the appropriate category, the end of the All category, and in the Custom category.

▶ *Deleting Custom Number Formats*

Custom number formats are stored in the workbook in which they were defined. To delete them, activate the workbook, then follow these steps:

1. Display the Number dialog tab.
2. Select the Custom category.
3. Select the custom format you want to delete, then click the Delete button.

▶ *Number Formats Based on Cell Value*

Numbers can be formatted to display differently, based on cell value. For example, a cell can be formatted to display negative numbers red and positive numbers blue. Several of the built-in formats use this type of conditional formatting. Examples 1 and 2 are built-in formats, and are included as a first step in understanding the tedious, complex syntax involved.

▶ ▶**T I P**

> **There is one element common to all conditional formats: the different segments are separated by a semicolon.**

The easiest way to create a custom conditional format is to modify one of the built-in formats. Select the built-in format, then edit the format in the *Code* edit box (see Figure 5.4 earlier in this chapter).

EXAMPLE 1: **#,##0_);(#,##0)**

#,##0_)   Format for positive number—right parenthesis does not display; underscore causes format to skip width of right parenthesis, so positive numbers align properly with negative numbers displaying parentheses; value displayed as whole number with commas marking thousands

(#,##0)   Format for negative number—parentheses placed around number; value displayed as whole number with commas marking thousands

EXAMPLE 2: **#,##0_);[Red](#,##0)**

#,##0_)   Format for positive number, same as Example 1

[Red](#,##0)   Negative number displayed in red, in parentheses

Examples 1, 2, and 8 use *implicit* thresholds; the remaining examples include expressions that *explicitly* set the conditional value thresholds.

EXAMPLE 3: **[Red][<10]#,##0;[Green][>20]#,##0;[Yellow]#,##0**

[Red][<10]#,##0   Numbers less than 10 displayed red

[Green][>20]#,##0   Numbers greater than 20 displayed green

[Yellow]#,##0   All other numbers (from 10 to 20) displayed yellow

EXAMPLE 4: **[Red][<=10]#,##0;[Green][>=20]#,##0;[Yellow]#,##0**

[Red][<=10]#,##0   Numbers less than or equal to 10 displayed red

[Green][>=20]#,##0   Numbers greater than or equal to 20 displayed green

[Yellow]#,##0   All other numbers (between 10 and 20) displayed yellow

Examples 5 through 7 use text constants in place of number formats:

EXAMPLE 5: **[<10]"Few";[>100]"Many";"Some"**

[<10]"Few"   Numbers less than 10 displayed as *Few*

[>100]"Many"   Numbers greater than 100 displayed as *Many*

Some   All other numbers (from 10 to 100) displayed as *Some*

EXAMPLE 6: **[<-100][GREEN]"Too small";[>100][RED]"Too large";###0**

[<-100][GREEN]"Too small"   numbers less than –100 displayed as *Too small*, in green

[>100][RED]"Too large"   Numbers greater than 100 displayed as *Too large*, in red

###0   All other numbers (from –100 to 100) displayed as whole numbers, in default color; no comma marking thousands

EXAMPLE 7: **"Quantity: "#,##0**

"Quantity: "   Numbers display following this text string (e.g., *Quantity: 2,345*)

#,##0   Number format

A number format may contain up to four segments, separated by semi-colons. Up to three value ranges may be formatted (as you have seen in the preceding examples). If the value ranges are not explicitly specified

Formatting Cells

Ch.

5

(for instance, *[<100]*) then Excel assumes a syntax of

Positive values;negative values;zero values;text values

EXAMPLE 8 uses a fourth segment to specify the format for a text value:

Example 8: **#,##0;(#,##0);0;"Enter a number!"**

#,##0   Positive numbers displayed whole, with comma; no space-holder to align with parentheses around negative numbers

(#,##0)   Negative numbers displayed whole, with comma, in parentheses

0   zero values displayed as **0**

"Enter a number!"   Text values displayed as **Enter a number!**

WARNING

As you have seen, custom formats can be used to display information that is very different than the underlying cell value. This can be very confusing down the road when 2 + 2 does not equal 4. Look to the formula bar to see actual underlying cell values.

► *Some Useful Custom Formats*

Here are some custom formats which may come in handy, and will further illuminate format code syntax:

;;   Hides all numbers (but not text)

;;;   Hides all values (including text)

0;0;   Displays both positive and negative values as whole positive numbers; zero values as blank cells; text as entered

►

THREE WAYS TO HIDE ZEROES ON A WORKSHEET

Suppose you have assembled a worksheet which contains a lot of zeroes. A worksheet peppered with zeroes is hard to read because there is too much information on it. How can you hide the zeroes so that the worksheet will be easier to read? There are three ways to hide zeroes. The method you choose will depend on the circumstances in which you want to hide zeroes.

If you want to hide zeroes throughout the worksheet, choose Tools ➤ Options, select the View tab, and clear the Zero Values checkbox. The zeroes can be displayed again by checking the checkbox. If you only want to hide the zeroes in specific cells, you can format the cells to hide zeroes by adding a semicolon at the end of the format code. Choose Format ➤ Cells and select the Number tab, then customize the format code in the *Code* edit. Here are some sample "hide zero" format codes:

    #,##0_);(#,##0);

    #,##0.00_);(#,##0.00);

    $#,##0_);($#,##0);

If you want to hide zeroes that are the result of a formula, you can use an IF function. For example, say you have a formula which reads =A1-B1, and if the result is zero you don't want it to be displayed. You can nest the formula in an IF function to hide a zero result, like this: IF(A1-B1=0,"",A1-B1). This formula reads "if A1-B1 is zero, then display null text, otherwise display A1-B1".

▶▶ *Format Painter*

 A new feature in Excel 5 is the *Format Painter* tool, available on the Standard toolbar. Format Painter copies and pastes formats by "painting" them onto cells. To use Format Painter:

1. Select a cell containing formatting you want to copy.
2. Click the Format Painter tool.
3. Click and drag through cells where you want to apply the formatting.

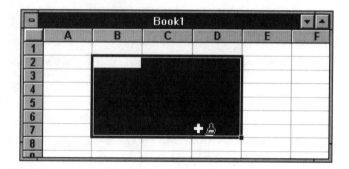

You can paint formatting repeatedly without clicking the tool each time if you double-click the *Format Painter* tool. The *Format Painter* cursor remains active until you click the *Format Painter* tool again.

 ▶ ▶ **T I P**

You can clear formats fast using Format Painter. Select an unformatted cell, then click Format Painter, then select (paint) the cells to be cleared.

▶▶ *AutoFormats*

An *AutoFormat* is a built-in table format which can be quickly applied to a range of cells. AutoFormats include formatting for numbers, alignment, font, border, pattern, color, row height, and column width.

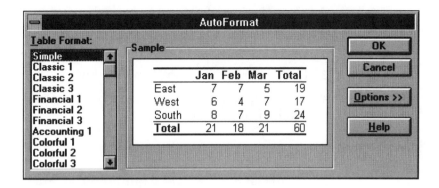

▶ *Applying an AutoFormat*

Follow these steps to apply an AutoFormat to a range of cells:

1. Select a range of data (either an entire contiguous range or a single cell within a range of data).

2. Choose Format ➤ AutoFormat.

3. Select an AutoFormat from the *Table Format* list.

4. Click OK.

▶ *Selectively Applying an AutoFormat*

An AutoFormat includes six attributes, but when you apply an Auto-Format you can elect to include only selected attributes, so that when the AutoFormat is applied it won't erase previously applied formatting. For example, suppose you want to apply an AutoFormat without changing the current row and column sizing on the worksheet:

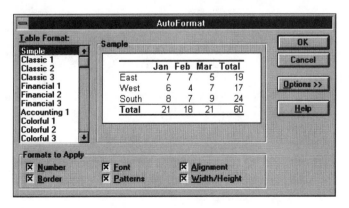

Formatting Cells

▶ ▶

Ch.
5

1. Select a range of data and choose Format ➤ AutoFormat.

2. Select an AutoFormat from the Table Formats list, then click the Options button.

3. Under Formats to Apply, uncheck the Width/Height option.

4. Click OK. The AutoFormat will be applied without any column width or row height attributes.

 ► ►**T I P**

> **Format Painter will paint an AutoFormat from one table to another (but without row/column sizing). Select the entire AutoFormatted range, click Format Painter, then select (paint) the entire range to be formatted.**

► ## MAKING CELLS LOOK THREE DIMENSIONAL

By using cell borders creatively, you can create 3-D effects that add a professional touch to worksheets that are viewed on the screen. (Depending on your printer, the effect will work for printed documents as well.) Notice that some of Excel's built-in table AutoFormats use a 3-D effect. Here, you see how to create the same effect selectively. The technique involves the creative use of cell borders. The following procedure shows how to make one cell appear raised, or embossed:

1. Format a range of cells (at least a 3 x 3 range) as dark grey. (On the color palette of the Patterns tab, use the grey on the second row, last column.)

2. Select a cell inside the grey range, choose Format ➤ Cells, and click the border tab.

3. **Apply a light grey border to the left and top borders (On the color palette, use the grey on the second row, seventh column.)**

4. **Apply a black border to the right and bottom borders.**

The cell will now appear to be raised. To make the cell look sunken, reverse the borders: make the left and top borders black, and make the right and bottom borders light grey. You do not have to use a dark grey background to achieve this effect. The cell borders simply have to be one shade lighter, and one shade darker, than the background color.

At first glance, the practical benefits of this technique may seem limited, but in fact there is an important benefit to be realized— the 3-D effect lets you highlight cells without using color. Users who are new to a graphical environment often go overboard with the use of color, instead of judiciously using color meaningfully.

▶▶ *Styles*

Picture a worksheet that has dozens of subheadings, each formatted Times New Roman, 12, Bold, with a bottom border. It can be time-consuming to apply four styles to dozens of subheadings, and more time-consuming if you decide to change all the subheadings to font size 14. But you can define a *style*, which is a named combination of formats, then rapidly apply the style to cells. If you change the style, all cells using the style change automatically.

Styles are vitally important when it comes to simplifying sheet formatting. The small amount of time it will take you to learn about styles will save you a lot of time and hassle in the long run. Some of the benefits of styles are:

• Time savings when developing sheets

- Time savings when changing formats later
- Establishment of formatting standards

For example, if standardizing the look of reports, you might want to define styles for section titles, total rows, subtotal rows, and column headings.

► Creating Styles by Example

When you create a style by example, you first format a cell, then define a style using the cell's formatting. (This is the fastest way to create a new style.)

1. Format a cell using desired formatting commands, and leave that cell selected.

2. Choose the Format ➤ Style command. The Style dialog box is displayed (see Figure 5.5).

3. Type a name for the new style into the Style Name box.

4. Click OK.

FIGURE 5.5 ►

The Format ➤ Style dialog box

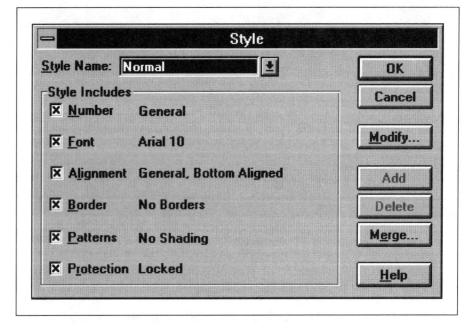

The new style will contain all the formatting characteristics of the selected cell.

▶ ▶**T I P**

You can create a new style by typing the name directly into the Style tool rather than using the Style dialog box. To use the Style tool, add it to a toolbar (see Chapter 26 to learn how).

▶ *Creating Styles Explicitly*

Previously, you learned how to create by example. The following procedure lets you define a style explicitly, using the options in the Style dialog box.

1. Choose the Format ➤ Style command.

2. Type a name for the new style in the Style Name box.

3. Click Modify. The Format Cells dialog box is displayed.

4. Select the formatting options you want from the dialog box tabs, then click OK.

5. The Style dialog box is displayed again:

   ● To apply the new style, click OK.
   ● To define the style without applying it, click Add, then click Close.

The Style dialog box displays a list of the six attributes a style can include (see Style Includes in Figure 5.5), and the settings for each attribute in the selected style. You can uncheck any attributes that you don't want to include. For example, you can create a style that doesn't include border or pattern attributes, so that the style, when applied, won't alter existing borders or patterns.

▶ ▶**N O T E**

Row height and column width are not part of the style definition.

▶ Changing a Style Definition

The steps involved in changing the style are very similar to creating a style:

1. Choose Format ➤ Style.

2. Select or type the name of the style you want to change.

- If you *select* the name, the existing style formats serve as the starting point for changes.
- If you *type* the name, the formatting of the active cell serves as the starting point for changes.

3. Click Modify, and change the formats using the Format Cells dialog box tabs.

4. Click OK. The Style dialog box is displayed again.

5. Click OK to apply the new style, or click Add to keep the Style dialog box open (to create or redefine more styles).

 ▶ ▶**TIP**

You can also change a style using the Style tool. Select a cell containing the style and change the formatting. Use the Style tool to reselect or reenter the same style name. Excel will ask if you want to redefine the style name based on selected cells—click Yes.

▶ Applying a Style

You have learned how to create styles. Here is the procedure for *applying* a style to one or more cells:

1. Select the cell(s) that you want to apply the style to.

2. Apply the style in one of two ways:

- Choose Format ➤ Style, then select a style from the Style Name list, then click OK.
- Select a style from the Style tool (see Chapter 26 to learn how to add the Style tool to a toolbar).

▶ *Deleting a Style*

Styles are stored inside the workbook in which they were created. To delete a style:

1. Activate the workbook containing the style.
2. Choose Format ➤ Style.
3. Select the style to delete from the Style Name list.
4. Click Delete, then click OK.

Any cells still defined with the deleted style will revert to normal style.

 ▶ ▶ **N O T E**

You can't delete the Normal style, but you can change its properties.

▶ *Merging Styles*

Styles are stored in workbooks, and are only available in the workbook where the style was created. Assume that you have created some styles in a workbook, and want to merge them into a different workbook without having to redefine them:

1. Open the *source* workbook containing the style(s) to be copied from, and the *target* workbook the style(s) are to be merged into.
2. Activate the target workbook.
3. Choose the Format ➤ Style command.
4. Click Merge.
5. Select the source workbook from the Merge Styles From list.
6. Click OK to copy the styles into the target workbook—all styles in the source workbook will be merged into the target workbook.
7. Click OK to close the Style dialog box.

▶ ▶ **N O T E**

If both workbooks have a style with the same name, Excel will prompt "Merge styles that have same names?". If you choose Yes, the incoming style (from the source workbook) will replace the style in the target workbook.

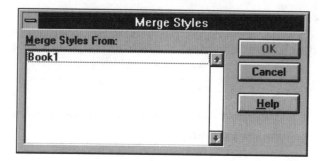

▶ ▶ **T I P**

Use styles in conjunction with templates to create standardized worksheet formats. See Chapter 10 to learn about templates.

▶ ## CHANGING BUILT-IN STYLES

There are a handful of built-in styles that come with Excel. The Normal style is one of these built-in styles—Normal is the default style for all cells in a new workbook, and is the style to which cells revert when you clear formatting. But what if the Normal style doesn't provide what you want? For example, you may want your worksheets to be created in the font Times New Roman 12 instead of Arial 10.

You can change the definition of Normal style in the active workbook the same way that you change any style definition. Choose Format ➤ Style, select Normal from the list of Style Names, then click the Modify button. Make the changes in the Format Cells dialog, then click OK to close the dialog. Click OK again to close the Style dialog.

Now you've changed the Normal style in one workbook. Suppose you want to use the new Normal style in all workbooks? You can re-define Normal style in every new workbook you create, but that's inefficient. You can change the Normal style for all new workbooks by re-defining Normal in a global workbook template. Name the template BOOK.XLT, and save the template in the XLSTART directory (see Chapter 10 to learn more about templates). All new workbooks will be created from this template, and will have the Normal style that you defined.

▶▶ *Copying Formats and Styles to a Different Workbook*

When you copy a cell from one workbook to another, the formatting moves with the cell. This is most beneficial with custom number formats and styles, since it can be time consuming to recreate the definitions.

To copy a custom number format or style to another workbook, select a cell containing the format or style and copy it to the new workbook. Custom number formats and styles will be added to the lists in the new workbook.

▶▶ *Design Tips*

Here are some simple tips for designing aesthetically pleasing and easy-to-use worksheets:

- **Keep it simple!** Too many fonts and colors can be overwhelming. Limit a given worksheet to one or two typefaces, with variations in size and style (bold, italic).

- **Use scalable fonts,** such as TrueType, to keep your figures sharp and clear on the screen.

- **Use color meaningfully,** to highlight information or focus the reader's attention. Use muted colors, like grey, for backgrounds.

- **Turn off gridlines,** and use borders for clarity.

- **Incorporate plenty of white space**—a lot of condensed data can be difficult to digest.

- **Incorporate graphic features** (charts, logos, etc.) to make the worksheet more visually appealing. See Chapter 12 to learn more about graphic objects.

▶▶ *A Formatting Exercise*

As an exercise, let's create the example worksheet shown in Figure 5.6 and then take the steps to format it differently. (Don't worry about having to enter all the numbers as shown here; in these steps you'll learn how to use a function that will fill in the number cells with random data.)

1. Open a new worksheet and enter the following:

Cell	Entry
B2	Northwest Athletic Wear
B3	Quarterly Sales - By Product
B6	Shoes
C7	Qtr 1
D7	Qtr 2
E7	Qtr 3

FIGURE 5.6

A typical hard-to-read worksheet

```
             Northwest Athletic Wear
           Quarterly Sales - By Product


      Shoes  Qtr 1   Qtr 2   Qtr 3   Qtr 4
             ------- ------- ------- -------
    Running    616     963     539     119
     Tennis     21     539     647     140
 Basketball    807     663     487     958
             ======= ======= ======= =======
   subtotal   1444    2165    1673    1217


     Shirts  Qtr 1   Qtr 2   Qtr 3   Qtr 4
             ------- ------- ------- -------
        Tee    106     321     853     728
       Polo    608     515     205     570
      Sweat    447     228     507     449
             ======= ======= ======= =======
   subtotal   1161    1064    1565    1747
             ======= ======= ======= =======
      Total   2605    3229    3238    2964
```

Cell	Entry
F7	Qtr 4
B8	Running
B9	Tennis
B10	Basketball
B11	subtotal
C11	=SUBTOTAL(9,C8:C10)
D11:F11	(copy formula from C11)

2. Apply the following formatting:

Cell	Formatting
B2	Bold, italic, 16 points
B3	Bold, italic, 12 points
B2:B3	Center across worksheet (select B2:F3; choose Format ➤ Cells, Alignment tab, *Center Across Selection* setting)
B6	Bold, italic, 11 points
B8:B11	Right-align
B11:F1	Bold
C7:F7	Bold, center-align
C8:F10	Thin, grey borders to left, right, top, and bottom
C11:F11	Grey double borders to top; built-in number format **#,##0**
C8:F10	Custom number format **[Red][<300]#,##0;[Blue][>600]#,##0; #,##0**

3. Turn the gridlines off.

4. Create a style for the title cells:

- Select cell B6.
- Choose Format ➤ Style, type **Title** in the Style Name edit box, then click OK.

▶ ▶ **N O T E**

If you change the properties of a style, all the cells using that style will change. This may seem a minor efficiency with only a few titles, but picture a worksheet with hundreds of titles. If the titles have been formatted using a style, a single change to the style will automatically change the formatting of all of the titles.

5. Create a second section by copying the first:

  - Select cells B6:F11.
  - Copy and paste to cell B13.

6. Change these values in the second section:

  - Enter **Shirts** in cell B13.
  - Enter **Tee**, **Polo**, and **Sweat** in cells B15:B17.

7. Enter the following function to enter random data:

  - Select cells C8:F10 and C15:F17 (hold down Ctrl to select both ranges).
  - Type **=INT(RAND()*1000)** and press Ctrl+Enter.

8. Freeze the random values:

  - Select C8:F10, Edit ➤ Copy, choose Edit ➤ Paste Special, select *Values*, and click OK.
  - Repeat this freeze procedure for cells C15:F17.

9. Create a Grand Total row:

  - Enter **Total** (right-aligned and bold) in cell B19.
  - Enter the formula **=SUBTOTAL(9,C8:C10,C15:C17)** in cell C19, then copy the formula to cells D19:F19 (see Chapter 9 to learn more about the SUBTOTAL function).

10. Apply a grey double border to the tops of the Grand Total cells.

11. Give the totals some visual separation from the data:

  - Select rows 11, 18, and 19.
  - Choose Format ➤ Row ➤ Height, and enter a row height of **19**.

When completed, the exercise worksheet should look like Figure 5.7.

Formatting Cells

Ch. 5

FIGURE 5.7 ▶

The worksheet from
Figure 5.6, newly
formatted

Northwest Athletic Wear
Quarterly Sales - By Product

Shoes

	Qtr 1	Qtr 2	Qtr 3	Qtr 4
Running	616	963	539	119
Tennis	21	539	647	140
Basketball	807	663	487	958
subtotal	**1444**	**2165**	**1673**	**1217**

Shirts

	Qtr 1	Qtr 2	Qtr 3	Qtr 4
Tee	106	321	853	728
Polo	608	515	205	570
Sweat	447	228	507	449
subtotal	**1161**	**1064**	**1565**	**1747**
Total	**2605**	**3229**	**3238**	**2964**

► ► **CHAPTER 6**

Printing

►► FAST TRACK

Despite trends toward the paperless office, hardcopy business reports and printed worksheets will likely be fixtures for the foreseeable future. Preparing and printing worksheets is one of the most common activities performed with Excel, according to Microsoft surveys. This chapter will cover:

- *How to select a printer*
- *Setting up headers, footers, margins, and pagination*
- *Printing color worksheets on a black and white printer*
- *Special printing problems*

▶▶ Selecting a Printer and Printing

Your computer may be connected to more than one printer. If so, the following procedure allows you to select which printer to use.

1. Choose File ➤ Print, then click the Printer button.
2. Select a printer from the list in the Printer Setup dialog box.
3. Click OK to close the Printer Setup dialog box.
4. Click OK to print (when Cancel is clicked, the print job is canceled, but the chosen printer remains in effect).

▶▶ *Setting Up Worksheets for Printing*

The File ➤ Page Setup command displays a tabbed dialog box which provides access to most print-related settings. The four tabs are: Page, Margins, Header/Footer, and Sheet.

▶ *Page Setup*

The Page tab, pictured in Figure 6.1, controls the basic layout of the printed pages.

On each of the four Page Setup dialog tabs, there is an Options button—this button displays the Setup dialog for the selected printer. Any changes you make in the Page Setup dialog boxes which affect the printer setup (such as changing paper size) will automatically be made in the printer Setup dialog box.

Table 6.1 describes the settings found on the Page tab.

The Scaling options allow you to enlarge or reduce the printed worksheet, without changing the size of the on-screen display. You can reduce the printed worksheet as low as 10% to fit more of the worksheet

FIGURE 6.1 ▶

*File ➤ Page Setup-
Page tab*

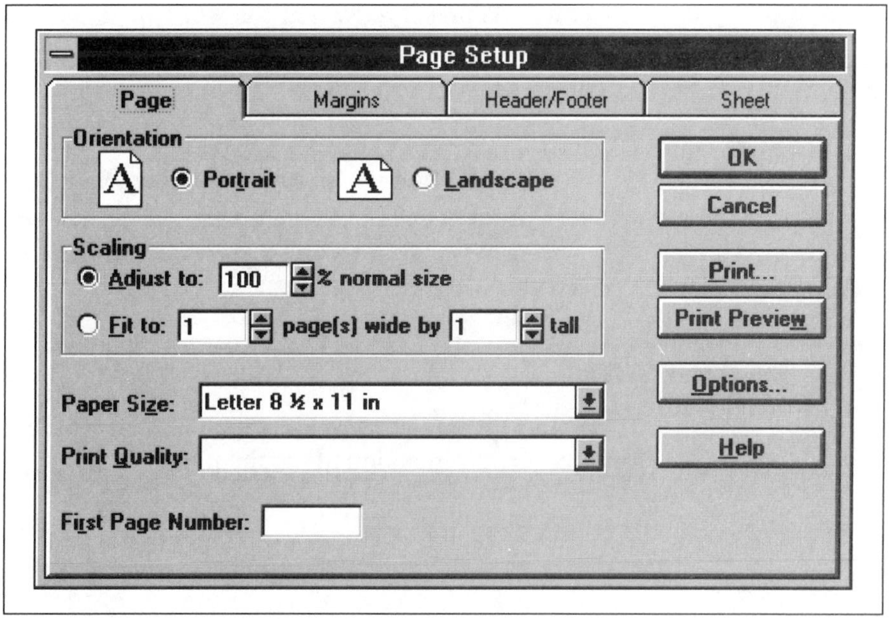

Printing

▶▶

Ch.
6

▶ **TABLE 6.1:** *Page Options*

Options	Remarks
Orientation	Select portrait (tall) or landscape (wide).
Scaling—Adjust To	Increases (magnifies) or decreases (shrinks) scale of worksheet to fit printed page.
Scaling—Fit To	Adjusts scale to fit specified number of pages.
Paper Size	Select paper size from drop-down list.
Print Quality	Select resolution (dpi) from list.
First Page Number	Begins numbering at specified page number.
Options button	Displays dialog box for settings on selected printer.

on a page, or enlarge up to 400% to enhance detail. To change the scale, select Adjust to:, then type or scroll to the magnification you want.

To fit a worksheet onto a specific number of pages, choose the Fit to: option, then select how many pages wide and how many pages tall you want the printed worksheet to be. The relative dimensions of the worksheet will be preserved when the worksheet is fitted to the specified number of pages.

▶ ▶ **N O T E**

If you choose the Fit to: option, Excel will ignore any page breaks you have set and fit the entire worksheet or print area to the specified number of pages.

▶ *Margins*

The Margins tab, pictured in Figure 6.2, is where margins, headers, and footers are positioned on the page.

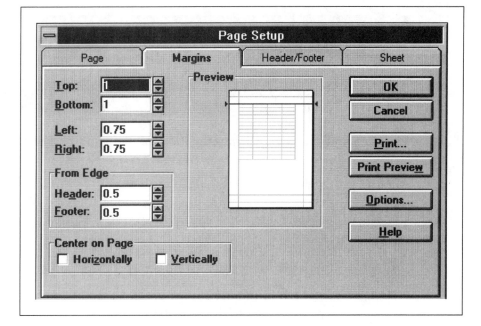

The settings on the Margin tab are described in Table 6.2. The Preview area on the dialog box indicates which margin is being set. (Select a margin, and the corresponding line on the dialog box Preview picture will be highlighted.)

▶ **TABLE 6.2:** *Margins Options*

Options	Remarks
Top, Bottom, Left, Right	Sets margins (inches from edge)
From Edge	Sets header/footer placement (inches from edge)—Should be less than top/bottom margins
Center on Page	Check to center vertically/horizontally within margins.

Printing

▶

Ch.

6

▶ Creating Page Headers and Footers

The Header/Footer tab, pictured in Figure 6.3, is where page headers and page footers are entered and formatted.

A header will be printed at the top of every page, and a footer will be printed at the bottom of every page. Headers are commonly used for company names and report titles (the default header is the filename). Footers are commonly used for page numbers and printout dates/times.

Headers and footers are not actually a part of the worksheet—they are part of the printed page—and are allotted separate space on the printed page. How much space the header and footer are allotted is controlled on the Margins dialog tab (the header occupies the space between the Header margin and Top margin, and the footer is positioned between the Bottom and Footer margins). See Table 6.2, Margins Options, for more information on worksheet and header/footer margins.

Headers and Footers work exactly alike—you can choose a built-in header/footer, or define a custom one.

FIGURE 6.3 ▶

*File ➤ Page Setup-
Header/Footer tab*

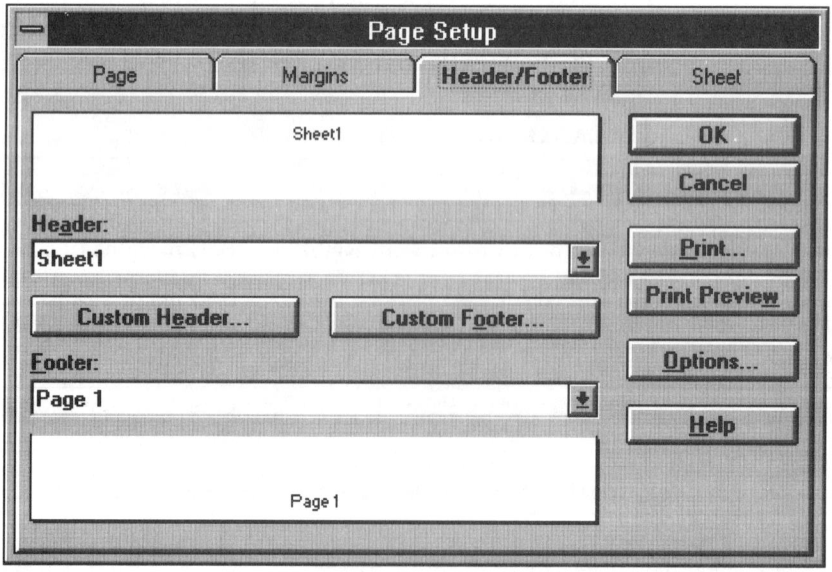

Using Built-in Headers/Footers

Select from a variety of built-in headers and footers using the respective drop-down lists on the Header/Footer tab. The lists include several commonly-used header/footer formats, such as the page number, worksheet name, user name, date, and combinations of these.

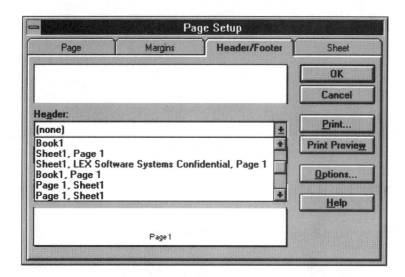

Creating Custom Headers/Footers

Click the Custom Header or Custom Footer buttons to customize headers/footers.

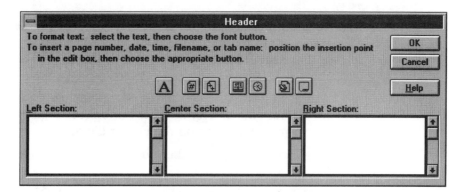

Click on the section (left, center, or right) where you want to place a header/footer. The left section is left-justified, the center section is centered on the page, and the right section is right-justified. Type text into any of these three sections. (Press Enter for a new line.) The buttons in the center of the dialog box, defined in Table 6.3, are used to format the text and to insert special values into the header/footer.

▶ **TABLE 6.3:** *Custom Header/Footer Buttons*

Click On:	To Insert:
A	Font format (Select text, click button, select formatting options.)
[#]	Page number
[#+]	Number of pages
[date]	Current date
[clock]	Current time
[workbook]	Workbook name
[worksheet]	Worksheet name

A common custom footer is (page #) of (# pages) (e.g., **1 of 12**), which is created by combining footer codes and text. Follow these steps to create this custom footer:

1. Choose File ➤ Page Setup, then select the Header/Footer tab.

2. Choose the Custom Footer button (see Figure 6.3), then click in the center section on the Footer dialog.

3. Click the Page Number button, then type a space, **of**, and another space.

4. Click the Number of Pages button. Click OK to close the Footer dialog box.

The preceding steps will insert the code *&[Page] of &[Pages]* into the center section of the Footer dialog box, and a preview of the footer will be displayed on the Header/Footer dialog tab. The code will also be added to the dropdown list of footers for the workbook.

N O T E

The ampersand (&) is a code symbol for headers and footers, and doesn't print. So what if you want to print an ampersand in your header (Brown & Brown, for instance)? Type two ampersands—enter Brown && Brown as the custom header.

▶ *Sheet Options*

The Sheet tab, pictured in Figure 6.4, allows you to specify a print area, print titles, and several other print options.

Table 6.4 describes the options found on the Sheet tab.

FIGURE 6.4 ▶

File ➤ Page Setup, Sheet Tab

Page Setup
Page / **Margins** / **Header/Footer** / **Sheet**
Print **A**rea: [   ]   **OK**
┌─ Print Titles ──────────────────┐ **Cancel**
Rows to Repeat at Top: [   ]
Columns to Repeat at Left: [   ] **Print...**
┌─ Print ──────────────────┐ **Print Preview**
☒ **G**ridlines   ☐ **B**lack and White
☐ **N**otes   ☐ **R**ow and Column Headings   **Options...**
☐ Draft **Q**uality
┌─ Page Order ──────────┐ **Help**
⦿ **D**own, then Across
○ **A**cross, then Down

Printing

▶▶

Ch.

6

▶ **TABLE 6.4:** *Sheet Options*

Options	Remarks
Print Area	Select area of worksheet to print (select or type reference).
Print Titles	Select or type rows/columns to print on every page.
Gridlines	Turns gridlines on/off (only affects printed pages).
Notes	Prints cell notes on additional pages. (To print references with notes, check Row and Column Headings.)
Draft Quality	Fewer graphics, no gridlines—reduces printing time.
Black and White	Prints all in black and white (no shades of grey for colors).
Row and Column Headings	Includes row and column headings on printed page.
Page Order	Select page order for multi-page worksheet.

 ▶ **T I P**

Turning off the workspace gridlines (on the Tools ➤ Options, View dialog tab) will automatically turn off the printed gridlines (on the File ➤ Page Setup, Sheet dialog tab), and vice-versa. But you can print gridlines without displaying them in the workspace if you *first* turn off the Gridlines setting on the Tools ➤ Options, View dialog tab, *then* check the Gridlines checkbox on the File ➤ Page Setup, Sheet dialog tab.

Setting a Print Area

To set a Print Area, click in the Print Area edit box, then select a range of cells using the mouse (or type in a cell range reference).

You can set a Print Area quickly by selecting the range to print and clicking the Set Print Area tool. This tool is not available on a built-in toolbar—see Chapter 26 to learn how to add it to a customized toolbar.

SETTING MULTIPLE PRINT AREAS ON THE SAME PAGE

Suppose you have a worksheet with several tables and you want to print each table sequentially on its own page. You can set lots of page breaks all over the worksheet, but what if the tables are different sizes and don't fit neatly between page breaks? Also, the pages you create with page breaks will print in the order defined on the Page Setup dialog box, on the Sheet tab (either across then down, or down then across—see Figure 6.4). What if you want to print the tables in a more random order, rather than in the order designated on the Page Setup dialog box? In Excel 5, you can set multiple print areas on a worksheet and the order in which they print.

To set multiple print areas, use the File ➤ Page Setup dialog rather than the Print Area tool (the Print Area tool can only set one Print Area on a worksheet). Choose File ➤ Page Setup, and select the Sheet tab. Click in the Print Area edit box, then select the first print area by dragging on the worksheet. Now, here's the trick for multiple areas: type a comma, then select the next print area. You can set as many print areas as you want by separating the print area references with commas in the Print Area edit box. You can set the print area references in the order in which you want them to print. The area you set first will print on page one, the second area will print on page two, and so on.

Printing

Ch.
6

T I P

You don't have to define a print area in order to print a certain range of cells. Select the cells to print, choose File ➤ Print, and choose Selection from the Print What options.

Setting Print Titles

When printing a multi-page document, you may want certain rows or columns to appear on each page.

For example, suppose you have a worksheet of scientific air-quality data, with a year's worth of daily readings from 150 sites. The worksheet is 365 rows (dates) long by 150 columns (sites) wide, and requires several pages to print. Each data point must be identified by date (down the left column) and by site (along the top row). A page containing, for example, data for Sites 95–106 in June must have appropriate dates and sites along the left and top of the page (as in Figure 6.5).

The page shown in Figure 6.5 is just one page out of 144 pages (the worksheet is 12 pages tall by 12 pages wide). Setting the Date column

FIGURE 6.5

A portion of a spreadsheet with data for 150 sites recorded every day for a year.

Site#	95	96	97	98	99	100	101	102
6/1/97	604	248	429	502	634	881	175	933
6/2/97	127	579	156	36	954	912	596	797
6/3/97	555	235	970	936	558	740	85	230
6/4/97	394	995	916	458	873	924	358	309
6/5/97	457	272	140	522	781	104	558	275
6/6/97	624	523	638	995	4	475	409	832
6/7/97	748	473	565	453	64	311	18	731
6/8/97	48	275	343	356	672	2	899	613
6/9/97	277	453	408	257	632	818	784	919
6/10/97	480	120	159	803	223	337	489	809
6/11/97	851	475	564	47	190	858	470	358
6/12/97	525	861	890	163	189	154	628	217
6/13/97	998	934	23	114	388	916	693	274
6/14/97	308	842	172	371	619	176	769	892
6/15/97	772	865	605	273	640	618	700	733
6/16/97	69	998	197	269	134	574	235	951
6/17/97	680	974	829	26	557	988	155	817
6/18/97	10	955	353	446	222	97	33	837
6/19/97	267	135	68	779	853	472	178	989
6/20/97	949	331	981	10	278	729	584	292

(Column A) and the Site row (Row 1) as Print Titles makes it possible to print any range of cells in the worksheet without having to paste in the identifying dates and sites (the appropriate date and site titles are printed automatically with whatever portion of the worksheet is printed).

NOTE

Print titles are not the same as page headers, though they can be used for similar purposes. A page can be set up for both print titles and page headers.

To set Print Titles:

1. Choose the File ➤ Page Setup command, then select the Sheet tab.
2. Click in the Rows to Repeat at Top edit box.
3. On the worksheet, select the rows to be repeated or type the cell reference.
4. Click in the Columns to Repeat at Left edit box.
5. On the worksheet, select the columns to be repeated. (Or type the cell reference.)
6. Click OK.

Deleting a Print Area or Print Titles

If a print area has been defined, and you want to print the entire worksheet, you must first delete the Print Area.

To delete the Print Area, choose the File ➤ Page Setup command, then select the Sheet tab and clear the Print Area edit box. To delete print titles, clear Rows to Repeat at Top and/or Columns to Repeat at Left.

When you set the print area or print titles, range names are automatically defined on the worksheet. Setting the print area causes the name *Print_Area* to be defined. Setting print titles causes the name *Print_Titles* to be defined. If you want to see either of these ranges, select them from the Name box. Because they are named ranges, they can be deleted using the Insert ➤ Name ➤ Define command. (See Chapter 8 to learn more about names.)

Printing

Ch.
6

▸▸ *Preview before Printing*

Choose the File ➤ Print Preview command to see what the printed pages will look like before you actually print them. There are also several settings that can be controlled while in print preview mode. Figure 6.6 displays the Print Preview workspace.

FIGURE 6.6 ▸

Print preview

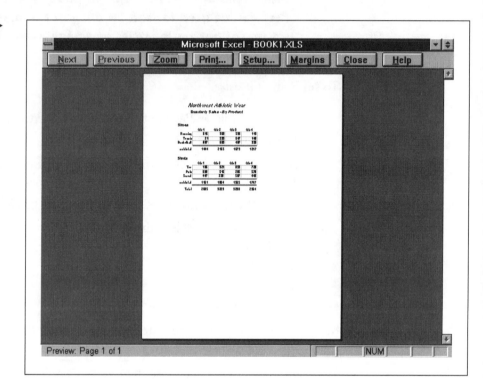

▸ *Zooming In and Out*

When in print preview, the mouse pointer becomes a magnifying glass. Click on the part of the worksheet that you wish to zoom in on. The sheet will be magnified, and the pointer becomes an arrow. Click on the worksheet again to zoom back out. (Alternately, use the Zoom button on the top of the window.)

▶ *Print Preview Buttons*

The following list explains the buttons that are displayed along the top of the workspace in print preview mode (see Figure 6.6):

Next   Displays the next page (dimmed when there is no next page).

Previous   Displays the previous page (dimmed when there is no previous page).

Zoom   Toggles between magnified and full page display.

Print   Displays the Print dialog box.

Setup   Displays the Page Setup dialog box.

Margins   Toggles on/off lines depicting page margins, header/footer margins, and column width (drag the lines to reposition).

Close   Closes the Preview window and returns to the worksheet.

The Margins button, which toggles the display of margin and column lines, is a particularly useful feature. When margin and column lines are in view, they can be dragged with the mouse to a new position. To reposition a line, place the mouse pointer on a margin line, a column gridline, or a handle at the edge of the page, and drag the line with the two-headed arrow (Figure 6.7). Margin settings (in inches) or column widths (in column width units) are displayed on the status bar while dragging margin/column lines. Sometimes it's easier to drag the lines if you zoom in first.

The inner horizontal margins are text margins; the outer horizontal margins are header/footer margins. The extra handles along the top of the page correspond to column lines.

▶▶ *Pagination*

When you print, Excel automatically creates page breaks where needed. If automatic page breaks cause a page break to occur in an undesirable place on the worksheet, you can insert manual page breaks.

Printing

Ch.
6

FIGURE 6.7 ▶

Dragging a column gridline.

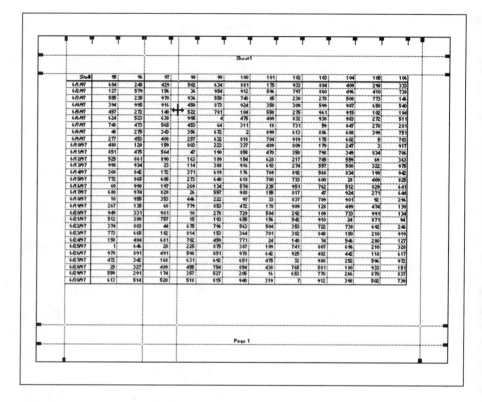

▶ *Automatic Page Breaks*

By default, automatic page breaks are not indicated on the worksheet until the sheet is printed (or print previewed) for the first time. To display page breaks, choose Tools ▶ Options, then select the View tab, and check the Automatic Page Breaks option. Automatic page breaks are indicated by broken lines which run along the gridlines.

▶ *Manual Page Breaks*

Suppose there is a multi-page worksheet with a table of numbers, and an automatic page break is occurring in the middle of the table (causing the table to print on pages two and three). But the table is only several rows tall, and if you place a manual page break just before it begins, the table will fit on a single page. The following paragraphs explain how to accomplish this.

REMOVING AUTOMATIC PAGE BREAK LINES

When you print (or print preview) a worksheet, automatic page break lines are displayed in the worksheet. Sometimes the lines are helpful, but often they are just annoying. You can remove them by choosing Tools ➤ Options, the View tab, and clearing the Automatic Page Breaks checkbox. The next time you print or print preview the worksheet, they will be displayed again—there is no way to turn them off permanently. Remember, this setting pertains to just the active worksheet.

Inserting a Manual Page Break

There are three ways to insert manual page breaks:

To insert:	Do this:
Vertical page break	Select column right of break, choose Insert ➤ Page Break.
Horizontal page break	Select row below break, choose Insert ➤ Page Break.
Vertical and horizontal page break	Select a single cell, choose Insert ➤ Page Break. (Breaks insert along top and left side of cell.)

Manual page breaks are indicated by heavier broken lines than automatic page breaks, as shown below. Automatic page breaks automatically adjust when manual page breaks are inserted.

 ▶ ▶ N O T E

If you attempt to print a worksheet and find your page breaks are ignored, you probably have the Scaling, Fit to: option selected. Choose File ➤ Page Setup, select the Page tab, and change the Scaling option to Adjust to:.

Printing

▶ ▶

Ch.

6

⊟			Book2			▼ ▲
	H	I	J	K	L	M	N
1							
2							
3	Automatic Page Break >>				<<Manual Page Break		
4							
5							
6							

Removing a Manual Page Break

Select a cell to the right of a vertical break or immediately below a horizontal break, and choose Insert ➤ Remove Page Break. (If the Insert menu doesn't list the Remove Page Break command, there is no manual page break at the selected cell.)

▶▶ *Worksheet Printing Options*

The File ➤ Print command displays a dialog box which offers options for printing selected cells, specific sheets or pages, or an entire workbook. To print multiple copies of your print selection, type the number of copies you want in the Copies edit box (or set the number using the spinner).

 ▶ ▶**N O T E**

The Print tool will begin printing immediately without displaying a dialog box. The default Print dialog box settings will be used (i.e., selected sheet, one copy, all).

▶ *Printing Sections of a Worksheet*

Often you won't want to print an entire worksheet. For example, you might have a year's worth of data accumulating in a given worksheet, and want to print just one month's worth, or perhaps you want to print it all but in small chunks.

1. Select the range of cells to print.

2. Choose File ➤ Print, and under Print What choose Selection.

Excel ignores any Print Area that has been set, and prints the selected range.

▶ Printing More than One Worksheet at a Time

To print several worksheets with one command, select all the sheets you want to print and choose File ➤ Print, then choose the Selected Sheet(s) option (the worksheets must be within the same workbook). See Chapter 3 to learn how to select multiple sheets.

▶ Printing a Few Pages

Follow these steps to print selected pages from a multi-page printout. This example will print only pages two and three:

1. Choose File ➤ Print.
2. Under Page Range, select Page.
3. Type **2** in the From: box, and type **3** in the To: box.

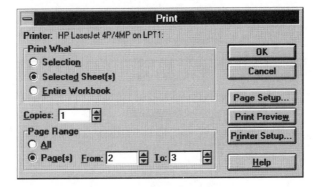

▶ ▶ **N O T E**

> If you want to print a single page, type the page number in *both* the From: and To: boxes. If, for instance, you want to print just page 3, and you enter 3 in the From: box but not in the To: box, Excel will print everything from page 3 on.

Printing

▶ ▶
Ch.
6

PRINTING RANGES FROM DIFFERENT WORKSHEETS ON THE SAME PAGE

Suppose you have four worksheets, each containing a small table that you want to print. Rather than printing four separate pages, each with a small table, you can trick Excel into printing all the tables on a single page. The trick is to place *pictures* of all four tables onto one worksheet:

1. Select the first table, then choose Edit ➤ Copy.

2. Activate the worksheet where you want to paste the tables, and select a cell where you want to paste the picture. Hold the Shift key down, and choose Edit ➤ Paste Picture Link.

3. Repeat steps 1 and 2 for each table.

4. You can use the worksheet grid to align the pictures with each other—hold down the Alt key while dragging to snap each picture into a cell grid position.

5. Choose File ➤ Print Preview to check the layout of the worksheet before you print.

By default, the pictures are linked to the source cells. When you select a linked picture, the source cell reference is displayed on the formula bar. You can edit the source reference on the formula bar, or clear the reference entirely. When the reference is cleared, the picture becomes static. See Chapter 12 to learn more about linked pictures.

The camera tool simplifies this procedure considerably (see Chapter 12 to learn about using the Camera tool); unfortunately, it is not on any of the built-in toolbars. See Chapter 26 to learn about customizing toolbars—the camera tool is located in the Utility section on the customize dialog.

▶ *Printing Formulas*

By default, a worksheet is printed as displayed on-screen. While the workspace normally displays formatted values instead of the underlying formulas, you can print the underlying formulas instead (to document the internal logic of the worksheet, or for audit or inspection). Follow these steps to print formulas:

1. Display the formulas by choosing Tools ➤ Options, then selecting the View tab, and checking the Formulas checkbox (or press Ctrl+').

2. Print the worksheet.

▶ ▶ T I P

Make the formula printout more useful by printing row and column headings. Choose File ➤ Page Setup, then select the Sheet tab and check the Row and Column Headings option.

	A	B	C	D
1	Full Name	Last Name	Score 1	Pass
2	Smith, Joe	=LEFT(A2,SEARCH(",",A2)-	80	=IF(C2<65,"No","Yes")
3	Jones, Mary	=LEFT(A3,SEARCH(",",A3)-	92	=IF(C3<65,"No","Yes")
4	Dunn, Sam	=LEFT(A4,SEARCH(",",A4)-	64	=IF(C4<65,"No","Yes")
5	Roberts, Jill	=LEFT(A5,SEARCH(",",A5)-	76	=IF(C5<65,"No","Yes")
6				
7		Average:	=AVERAGE(C2:C5)	
8				
9				
10				

▶ *Printing Info Windows*

An Info Window displays underlying information about a cell (see Chapter 11 to learn about Info Windows).

Printing

▶ ▶

Ch.
6

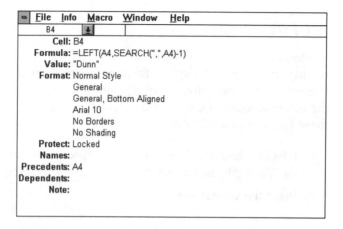

To print the Info Window for a cell:

1. Select the cell you want information for.

2. Display the Info Window by choosing Tools ➤ Options, selecting the View tab, and checking the Info Window checkbox.

3. Choose the Info menu, then select cell information to be displayed.

4. Choose File ➤ Print.

▶▶ *Using Colors*

Colors are invaluable for adding emphasis to certain points and increasing overall visual appeal and readability. There are a wide variety of colors for fonts, borders, backgrounds, and background patterns, limited only by what your printer is capable of printing. See Chapter 5, For-matting Cells, to learn about the options available for coloring cells and text.

▶ *Translating Colorful Worksheets into Black and White Reports*

To print a color worksheet in black and white (no shades of gray), choose File ➤ Page Setup, **then select the Sheet tab**, and check the Black and White checkbox.

▶▶ *Printing Problems*

If you have problems when trying to print worksheets, here are a few important details to check:

- There should be plenty of hard drive space (at least 5-6 MB) avail-able while in Windows. Windows creates temporary print files, and the space must exist on your hard disk.

- The printer should have at least 1 MB of memory, and preferably 2 MB or more for printouts that include a lot of graphics.

- Many print problems can be attributed to the printer driver. Make sure you have the most current driver for your printer. Sometimes, reinstalling a print driver can correct problems due to a corrupted driver file.

▶ ▶ **CHAPTER 7**

Enhancing
Your Productivity

———

FAST **T**RACK

▶ **To spell check a worksheet**   **214**

Select a single cell in the worksheet, then press F7 (or choose Tools ➤ Spelling).

▶ **To enter the current date**   **217**

Enter the current date with the keystrokes Ctrl+; (semicolon)

▶ **To enter the current time**   **217**

Enter the current time with the keystrokes Ctrl+: (colon)

▶ **To save the workspace**   **218**

Choose File ➤ Save Workspace.

▶ **To use AutoFill**   **225**

Drag the lower right corner of the cell selection up, down, left, or right to fill values or extend series.

▶ **To display a shortcut menu**   **225**

Right-click the item (cell, toolbar, sheet tab, object, etc.) for which you want the shortcut menu.

▶ **To reverse a reversible tool**   **228**

Hold down Shift while you click the tool.

▶▶ *his* chapter covers a number of skills, techniques, and shortcuts that will enhance your overall productivity. The tips are organized in the following categories:

- *Getting help*
- *Editing and navigating worksheets*
- *Working with workbooks, worksheets, and windows*
- *Using shortcut menus*
- *Working with AutoFill*
- *Using reversible tools*

▶▶ *Getting Help*

In Chapter 1, we discussed ways to get help on a particular topic, menu item, or dialog. The following paragraphs discuss additional ways to get and use help from Excel.

Getting Tips from the TipWizard

 The TipWizard is a tool which, when activated, can provide valuable productivity tips while you work. It "watches" you work, and displays a tip when there is a more efficient way to perform a given task. Click the TipWizard tool to activate this feature.

 The tips are brief in nature. But the Tip Help tool (on the right end of the Tip Wizard) will provide a fuller explanation by accessing Excel's online help.

Tip of the Day: To add a sheet to a workbook, choose Worksheet, Chart, or Macro from the Insert menu.

You don't have to notice the tip immediately. You can resume working, then later use the up and down arrows on the TipWizard to scroll through the tips at your leisure. When the TipWizard is displayed, the TipWizard button will hide it.

Keeping the Help Window in View

After accessing online help, you may want to switch back and forth between viewing your worksheet and the online help window. But if Excel is maximized, the help window is obscured when you switch back to Excel. To keep the help window in view as you work, choose the Help ➤ Always On Top command while help is displayed. You can reduce the size of the help window, and the help text will wrap automatically.

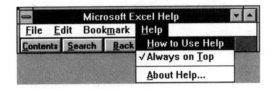

Placing a Bookmark in Help

Sometimes it takes a fair amount of searching to find the online Help topic you need. If it is a topic that you access often, such as the worksheet function reference, you can use a bookmark to speed up the search.

To place a bookmark into online help, find the topic that you want to mark, then choose the Bookmark ➤ Define command from the Help menu bar. Type your own name for the bookmark if desired, then click OK.

To use the bookmark, choose the Help ➤ Contents command. Select your bookmark from the Bookmark menu.

To delete a bookmark, choose Bookmark ➤ Define, select the bookmark to be deleted, and click Delete.

►► *Editing Cells and Navigating Worksheets*

The following paragraphs include a number of skills that will help you to effectively enter and edit formulas, fix mistakes, and navigate worksheets.

How to Undo Mistakes

Most things you do in Excel can be undone if you use the Edit ➤ Undo command from the menu *immediately* following the action you want to reverse. You can undo typing, editing, inserting, deleting, and many other tasks where errors often occur.

However, some things cannot be undone—either because of their inherent nature or due to memory restrictions:

- You cannot undo a File ➤ Save command or File ➤ Close command.

- If you change the formatting for a huge range of cells, you may have insufficient memory for Excel to "remember" the status of the sheet prior to the change. In these cases, Excel will issue the following warning:

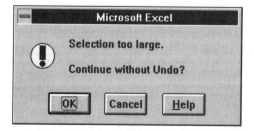

If a serious mistake is not noticed until it is too late to be undone, you can close the file without saving it, and then reopen it.

Repeating the Last Command Using Edit ➤ Repeat

The Edit ➤ Repeat command is used to quickly repeat the last command that you issued.

For example, you might format a cell, which takes several keystrokes. Then repeat the procedure on other cells using Edit ➤ Repeat.

The Quickest Way to Clear Cell Contents

The common task of clearing the contents of one or more cells requires only one keystroke:

1. Select the cells to be cleared (selection may be non-contiguous).

2. Press the Delete key.

▶ ▶NOTE

As you learned in Chapter 3, the Delete key clears cell contents, while the Edit – Delete command deletes the cell from the worksheet (and causes the surrounding cells to shift position).

Pasting Copied Cells with Enter

Copied cells can be pasted by pressing Enter rather than using a Paste command:

1. Copy cell(s).

2. Select the cell where you want to paste.

3. Press Enter.

You can also use the Enter key to fill a range. Copy a cell, select the range to fill, and press Enter.

Evaluating Expressions within a Formula

Often a formula refers to cells that are out of view. When entering, editing, or debugging such a formula, a lot of time can be spent scrolling the sheet to check the value of the cell(s) being referred to.

Instead, you can highlight the cell reference within the formula bar (or in-cell), and press F9. The cell reference is replaced with the cell value. This technique is not limited to cell references; you can highlight any expression, such as **(A1*B1)/C1**, and when F9 is pressed, the entire expression is replaced with the calculated value.

After evaluating an expression, remember to cancel the changes (press Esc). Otherwise, if you press Enter, the expression is replaced with the calculated value.

Quickly Selecting a Word within a Formula

Most standard text-editing techniques can be used when editing formulas. One of the most useful techniques is double-clicking words to select them, rather than painstakingly selecting the word with the mouse. This works whether editing is taking place in the formula bar or in the cell.

Entering the Same Formula into Multiple Cells

The following procedure allows you to enter the same formula (or constant) into multiple cells:

1. Select the cells (selections can be non-contiguous).
2. Type the entry.
3. Press Ctrl+Enter instead of Enter.

Quickly Creating a Table of Numbers

When you design a new worksheet model, whether simple or complicated, the model needs to be tested periodically as you build it. Sometimes actual data is not available, and test data is used instead. Test data can also be faster to enter than real data, which can save you a lot of time in the testing process. Here is a technique to help you quickly place a range of numbers onto a worksheet:

1. Select a range of cells.
2. Enter the formula **=RAND( )** then press Ctrl+Enter. This places the random number function into the range of cells.

To keep the RAND() functions from recalculating and returning new random values:

3. Select the range of cells.

4. Choose Edit ➤ Copy.

5. Choose Edit ➤ Paste Special, select Values, and click OK.

The numbers generated by the RAND function are fractions. Here are two variations to generate numbers bearing more similarity to the data you are emulating:

=RAND( )*1000	Creates random numbers between 1 and 1000
=INT(RAND( )*1000)	Creates whole random numbers between 1 and 1000

Entering Numbers with Automatic Decimal Places

Accountants typically prefer to enter numbers with two automatic decimal places. Excel can be configured for this type of data entry:

1. Choose Tools ➤ Options, then select the Edit tab (See Figure 7.1). Check the Fixed Decimal box.

2. Enter the desired number of decimal places.

Moving Down Automatically after Pressing Enter

By default, the active cell selection moves down one cell after pressing Enter. In some situations (entering a column of numbers, for instance) this behavior is very useful, while at other times it may be more efficient to prevent the active cell from moving when you press Enter. To change the active cell behavior, choose the Tools ➤ Options command, then select the Edit tab to access the Move Selection after Enter setting.

Moving from Corner to Corner in a Selection

The keystroke combination Ctrl+. (period) changes the active cell from corner to corner, clockwise, within a selected rectangular cell range.

FIGURE 7.1 ▶

The Tools ➤ Options-Edit tab

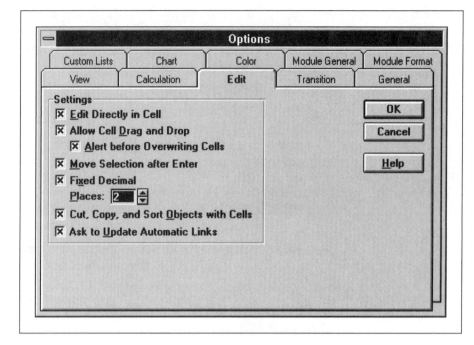

▶▶ *Using Spell Check*

To check spelling, choose the Tools ➤ Spelling command.

Table 7.1 explains the various items which can be selected for spell-checking.

▶ **TABLE 7.1:** *Spell-Checking Selections*

Select:	To Check:
A single cell	Entire worksheet, including headers, footers, cells, cell notes, text boxes, buttons
Multiple cells	Selected cells
One or more objects	Selected objects (text boxes and buttons only)
Multiple sheets	Contents of selected sheets
Formula bar	Entire formula bar
Words within a cell or formula bar	Selected words

▶ ▶ **N O T E**

Spell-checking checks hidden cells and cells in collapsed outlines; formulas and Visual Basic modules are not checked.

When Excel finds a word not in its dictionary, the Spelling dialog box is displayed:

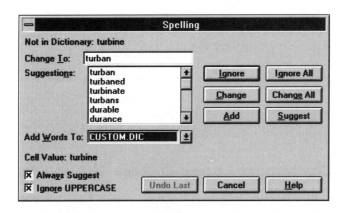

Table 7.2 explains the options on the Spelling dialog box.

▶ **TABLE 7.2:** *Spelling Options*

Dialog Option	Function
Change To	Replacement for unrecognized word (select or type)
Suggestions	Select replacement from list of suggestions.
Add Words To	Lists available custom dictionaries
Ignore	Leaves unrecognized word unchanged
Ignore All	Leaves unrecognized word unchanged throughout spell-check selection
Change	Replaces unrecognized word with Change To word
Change All	Replaces unrecognized word with Change To word throughout spell-check selection

▶ **TABLE 7.2**: *Spelling Options (continued)*

Dialog Option	Function
Add	Adds unrecognized word to dictionary in Add Words To
Always Suggest	If checked, Suggestions list is always displayed
Suggest	Displays Suggestions list when Always Suggest box is unchecked
Ignore UPPERCASE	Ignores words containing only capital letters
Undo Last	Undoes last change

If you only want to spell-check a certain range of cells, select the range before choosing the spell-check command.

Creating and Using Custom Dictionaries

If you use lots of technical words or acronyms, you may be spell-checking those same words repeatedly. Custom dictionaries save you the time of having to click the Ignore button over and over again. A custom dictionary is a separate file you create that contains words not in the default Excel dictionary—it contains only the words you add.

To create a custom dictionary, spell-check the worksheet. When Excel finds an unrecognized word, follow these steps:

1. Type a name for the custom dictionary in the Add Words To edit box.

2. Click the Add button. The following message will be displayed:

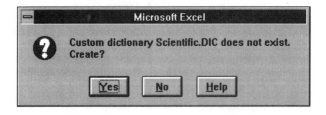

3. Click Yes to create the new dictionary.

To add a word to an existing custom dictionary, select the dictionary from the Add Words To list, then click Add.

Entering a Number as Text

Sometimes a number should be entered as text (for example, the zip code 07384, which will lose its leading zero if entered as a number). To enter a number as text, type an apostrophe first, such as: **'07384**.

Formatting Numbers to Retain Leading Zeros

Sometimes numbers need to be entered as numbers that retain their leading zeros (for example, inventory part number 00284). The solution is the custom number format **00000**, which retains leading zeros in a 5-digit number. To apply a custom number format to selected cells, choose the Format ➤ Cells command and select the Number tab. Type the format in the Code edit box.

Entering the Current Date and Current Time

The following keystrokes will place the current date or time into a cell, or into the middle of a formula:

Ctrl+;	(Ctrl+semicolon) Enters the current date
Ctrl+:	(Ctrl+colon) Enters the current time

▶▶ Working with Workbooks, Worksheets, and Windows

The following paragraphs will help you work more effectively with workbooks, worksheets, and windows.

Opening Several Files at Once

Select multiple files in the File ➤ Open dialog box by holding down Ctrl or Shift keys while selecting file names, then click OK to open all selected files at once. Hold down the Ctrl key if you want to select discontiguous files; to select contiguous files, hold down the Shift key.

Editing Multiple Worksheets Simultaneously

Workbooks often contain many similar worksheets. A lot of time can be saved by editing and formatting similar sheets simultaneously.

Select the group of worksheets that you want to edit. One way to select multiple sheets is to hold down the Ctrl key while clicking the worksheet tabs (see Chapter 2 for other ways to select groups of worksheets). All input, editing, and formatting are applied to each sheet in the group.

Saving the Workspace

Perhaps there are several workbooks you use regularly, and the process of opening each of them and arranging them on the screen is time-consuming. When you choose the File ➤ Save Workspace command, Excel "remembers" the names of all open workbooks, and how the windows are arranged. This information is saved in a workspace file with a .XLW extension. Later, when you open the workspace file using the File ➤ Open command, the individual workbooks are opened and arranged automatically.

 ▶ ▶ **W A R N I N G**

Workbooks are not physically stored inside the workspace file—only the workbook names and how the windows are arranged. Thus, saving a workspace file does not eliminate the need to save the workbooks (you will be queried about saving each workbook before it is closed).

Removing Add-Ins That Are Not Used

Add-ins are workbooks that add commands and functionality to Excel. An example is the Analysis Toolpak, which provides a number of engineering and financial functions.

When you install Excel, you are given the opportunity to install the many add-ins that are included with Excel. What the install program fails to point out is that the add-ins will not only be installed on your hard disk, but in some cases are automatically loaded into memory every time you start Excel. This uses up memory and system resources, and increases the amount of time it takes to start Excel.

To remove unused (or seldom used) add-ins from memory, choose the Tools ➤ Add-Ins command to display the Add-Ins dialog box (see Figure 7.2).

FIGURE 7.2 ▶

*The Tools ➤ Add-ins
dialog box*

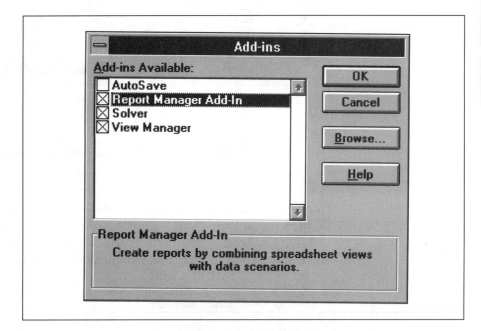

Clear the checkboxes next to the add-ins you want to remove, and click OK. The add-ins are not actually removed from your disk; rather, Excel's configuration is changed so that they will not load into memory automatically the next time you start Excel. You can still open the add-in on demand. (See Chapter 24 to learn more about these useful workbooks.)

Viewing Two Worksheets within the Same Workbook at the Same Time

Suppose you have a workbook with lots of details on one sheet and with summaries on another sheet. You want to be able to see the summaries and various details at the same time—the solution is to open two windows into the workbook, as shown in Figure 7.3.

FIGURE 7.3 ▶

*Two windows into the
same workbook*

REPORT97.XLS:1							
	A	B	C	D	E	F	G	H
2		Region	Product	Units	Dollars			
3								
4		Northeast	sofas	125	25,000			
5		Northeast	tables	234	46,800			
6		Northeast	chairs	135	27,000			
7		Southeast	sofas	134	26,800			
8		Southeast	tables	215	43,000			
9		Southeast	chairs	341	68,200			
10		Midwest	sofas	256	51,200			
11		Midwest	tables	214	42,800			

Details By Region / Summary

REPORT97.XLS:2								
	A	B	C	D	E	F	G	H	I
3		Region totals							
4		Northeast			98,800				
5		Southeast			138,000				
6		Midwest			127,600				
7									

Details By Region \ Summary /

To open a second window into a workbook, choose the Window ➤ New Window command. Then choose the Window ➤ Arrange command, and select an arrangement (check the Windows of Active Workbook setting if you want to arrange only the windows into the active workbook).

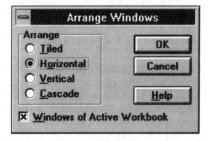

Using Automatic File Backups

You can choose a setting that automatically creates a copy of your file prior to saving it. Choose the File ➤ Save As command, click the Options button, then check the Always Create Backup setting.

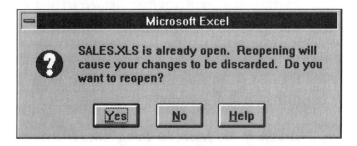

This setting provides an extra safety net. For example, say you make mistakes editing a file named SALES.XLS, the mistakes cannot be undone using Edit ➤ Undo, and the file is set to create backups. You can revert to an older copy of the file using one of these two methods:

- If the mistake was made *after* the file was last saved, choose File ➤ Open SALES.XLS. You will be prompted:

Click Yes. All changes made since the file was last saved will be lost.

- If the mistake occurred *before* the file was last saved, close the file without saving. File ➤ Open SALES.BAK. By default the Open dialog box displays only files with a .XL* extension, so you will have to type in the file name. (Since it is unwise to resume work on a file with a .BAK extension, save the file under a different name immediately.)

 ▶ ▶**WARNING**

> **Automatic backups are saved with a .BAK extension. If you have files named FINANCE.XLS and FINANCE.XLT in the same directory, and both files are set to create backups, both backups will be saved as FINANCE.BAK.**

▶ ▶**W A R N I N G**

Automatic backups in no way take the place of "real" disk backups (backup copies on floppy discs), which should be performed diligently.

▶▶ *Working Productively with Microsoft Windows*

The following tips are not specific to Excel. They are applicable throughout Microsoft Windows.

Switching to Another Application during a Lengthy Procedure

When Excel is maximized, and a time-consuming procedure is in process, the mouse cannot be used to switch applications. Press any of the following key combinations, Alt+Tab, Alt+Esc, or Ctrl+Esc as an alternative method for switching applications.

Adding an Icon to Program Manager to Open a Specific Workbook

Typically, after starting Excel, you use the File ➤ Open dialog box to open the file that you want to work with. This can be time-consuming, especially if the file is buried in an obscure subdirectory. Instead, you can place icons on Program Manager to start Excel and open the workbooks that you access most frequently. Follow these steps:

1. Start File Manager.

2. Resize File Manager and Program Manager so that they are both in view, as shown in Figure 7.4.

3. Use File Manager to locate the Excel workbook.

4. Click on the workbook, then drag it to Program Manager—drop it in the desired group.

FIGURE 7.4 ▶

*To place an icon for an
Excel workbook on
Program Manager,
arrange Program Man-
ager and File Manager
so that you can work
with both of them.*

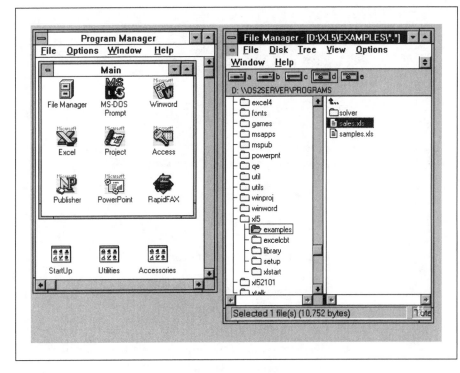

5. An Excel icon will be added to the group—you can change its description using Program Manager's File ➤ Properties command.

Remember, this procedure is not specific to Excel; it can be used for
files created by (most) other Windows programs.

WHAT TO DO WHEN YOU GET AN "OUT OF MEMORY" MESSAGE

Suppose you have recently upgraded your computer with 16 MB of
RAM. You begin work on a large Excel file, confident that your
memory problems are solved. Suddenly, an alert is displayed which
says "Out of memory," or "Not enough system resources to display completely." You have plenty of RAM—how can you be out of
memory?

The problem is not a shortage of RAM—it is a shortage of *system resources*, and can happen no matter how much RAM is on your system.

Here is a list of items that consume system resources:

- Chart elements such as legends, text boxes, custom markers, arrows, drop shadows, etc.

- Toolbars

- Cell borders, shading, and patterns

- Multiple fonts and font sizes

- Drawing objects (particularly ellipses)

- Pictures taken with the Camera tool

- Worksheet display elements such as status bar, scroll bars, formula bar, and window splits

- Multiple open windows

To solve the problem:

- Reduce as many graphics as possible.

- Close other applications that are not in use.

- Minimize the number of fonts you use.

- Close all applications (including Excel), exit Windows, then restart Windows. This allows Windows to start with a clean system resources memory heap.

- When possible, combine multiple workbooks into one workbook. Extra sheets within a single workbook do not consume additional system resources memory.

►► *Shortcut Menus*

The right mouse button is used to display context-sensitive shortcut menus. Here are the items in the workspace you can right-click to display a shortcut menu:

- Menu bar
- Toolbars
- Column/row headers
- Cells
- Sheet tabs
- Objects
- Charts—each element has a specific shortcut menu
- Tools—when the Toolbars or Customize dialog box is displayed

►► *AutoFill*

The AutoFill feature, explained in the paragraphs below, is an important feature that can save you countless hours of data entry.

Using the Fill Handle

The Fill Handle provides a shortcut for automatically filling a range of cells with a series of values. The fill handle is the small black square located on the lower right corner of the selected cell(s).

> ▸ ▸ **N O T E**
>
> **If the fill handle does not display on a worksheet, choose the Tools ➤ Options command, then select the Edit tab, and make sure the Drag and Drop setting is checked.**

Filling Months

Follow these steps to fill month names in a range of cells:

1. Enter **Jan** into cell A1.

2. Point to the fill handle with the mouse—the mouse pointer will become a black cross.

3. Click and drag through cell L1, then release the mouse button. **Jan** through **Dec** will be filled into cells A1 through L1.

More Simple AutoFills

This exercise will demonstrate some of the other types of data that can be filled:

1. Enter the following values:

	A	B	C	D
1	January			
2	Jan			
3	1/1/93			
4	Monday			
5	Mon			
6	Q1			
7	1			
8	9:00 AM			
9				
10				

Book1

2. Select cells A1 through A8.

3. Select the fill handle, and drag through cell L8.

Establishing an AutoFill Trend

In the previous exercise, each AutoFill was based on a single starting value. If two or more values are selected as the starting range for an AutoFill, Excel tries to determine a trend and AutoFills accordingly.

1. Enter the following values:

Book1			
A	**B**	**C**	**D**
2	4		
Jan	Apr		
Mon	Wed		
1995	2000		
1:00	1:15		

2. Select cells A1 through B5.

3. Select the fill handle, and drag through cell H5. The result will be:

Book1								
A	**B**	**C**	**D**	**E**	**F**	**G**	**H**	**I**
2	4	6	8	10	12	14	16	
Jan	Apr	Jul	Oct	Jan	Apr	Jul	Oct	
Mon	Wed	Fri	Sun	Tue	Thu	Sat	Mon	
1995	2000	2005	2010	2015	2020	2025	2030	
1:00	1:15	1:30	1:45	2:00	2:15	2:30	2:45	

AutoFill Based on Adjacent Cells

You can AutoFill a range of cells adjacent to a range of data by double-clicking the Fill Handle. This AutoFills the row or column where values are found in the adjacent row or column:

1. Type numbers into cells B1 through B4.

2. Enter **Q1** into cell A1.

3. Double-click the fill handle on cell A1. Cells A1 through A4 will be filled with **Q1** through **Q4**.

See Chapter 26 to learn how to create custom AutoFill lists.

▶▶ *Reversible Tools*

Many tools are reversible, meaning that one tool can perform two functions. A reversible tool:

- Performs an action when the tool is clicked
- Performs an alternate action when the Shift key is held down and the tool is clicked

For example, the Zoom In tool normally zooms in. But with Shift pressed, it changes to Zoom Out (the tool face and status bar description change to reflect the alternate function). The Zoom Out tool does just the opposite. By using only one of a pair of reversible tools, you can create space for more tools on a favorite toolbar. Table 7.3 displays pairs of reversible tools. Some of these tools are not available on any toolbar, but can be found in the toolbars Customize dialog box. See Chapter 26 to learn how to customize toolbars.

▶ **TABLE 7.3:** *Reversible Tool Pairs*

Tool Face	Action	Shifted Tool Face	Shifted Action
🔍	Zoom in	🔍	Zoom Out
🖨	Print	🔍	Print Preview
$/	Paste Formats	12	Paste Values
⬭	Clear Contents	$/	Clear Formats
A	Increase Font Size	A	Decrease Font Size
A↓Z	Sort Ascending	Z↓A	Sort Descending
.0→.00	Increase Decimal	.00→.0	Decrease Decimal

▶ **TABLE 7.3:** *Reversible Tool Pairs (continued)*

Tool Face	Action	Shifted Tool Face	Shifted Action
	Insert Cells		Delete Cells
	Insert Row		Delete Row
	Insert Column		Delete Column
	Group Objects		Ungroup Objects
	Bring to Front		Send To Back
	Draw Unfilled Rectangle		Draw Filled Rectangle
	Draw Unfilled Ellipse		Draw Filled Ellipse
	Draw Unfilled Arc		Draw Filled Arc
	Draw Unfilled Polygon		Draw Filled Polygon
	Draw Unfilled Freeform		Draw Filled Freeform
	Run Macro		Step Macro
	Group Selected Rows or Columns		Ungroup Selected Rows or Columns

► **TABLE 7.3:** *Reversible Tool Pairs (continued)*

Tool Face	Action	Shifted Tool Face	Shifted Action
	Trace Precedents		Remove Precedent Arrows
	Trace Dependents		Remove Dependent Arrows

PART THREE

►► **In Part Three** you will acquire invaluable tools for creating powerful worksheet models, including names and essential worksheet
functions. You will also learn to create and use templates, and learn
how to audit and protect worksheets and workbooks.

CHAPTER 8

The Power of Names

FAST TRACK

▶▶   *In* its simplest form, a name is a recognizable and memorable label for a cell or range of cells. For example, the name *Sales1995* is easier to recognize and remember than the cell reference B4:G18.

Using names is an important practice overlooked by many Excel users. If you are creating models of moderate complexity, or even simple models with linked workbooks, it is important that you learn basic naming techniques. This chapter covers the following topics:

- *Why use names*
- *Naming cells*
- *Naming constants*
- *Naming formulas*
- *Using names in formulas*
- *Advanced naming techniques*

▶▶ Why Use Names?

There are a variety of important benefits to knowing how to use names. They're outlined in the following paragraphs.

▶ Clarity and Documentation

Names add clarity to worksheets:

- Names make formulas easier to understand and maintain. The formula =Sales-Cost makes a lot more sense than =C3-B3, especially six months later when you need to revise the worksheet.

- Organization-wide naming conventions let users of shared workbooks better understand formulas.

▶ Integrity of External References

Referring to cells by name rather than by cell address can help ensure the integrity of cell references—in other words, a formula that uses the named cell **Sales** will *always* refer to the appropriate cell, even if cell **Sales** is moved on the worksheet, (or to another worksheet). The ability to maintain reference integrity is even more important when you work with external references. Consider the following scenario:

1. Two workbooks, DETAIL.XLS and SUMMARY.XLS, are open. SUMMARY.XLS has an external reference pointing to cell A3 on DETAIL.XLS.

2. The dependent workbook, SUMMARY.XLS, is closed.

3. A new row is inserted at the top of DETAIL.XLS. The value in cell A3 is now in cell A4.

4. When SUMMARY.XLS is reopened, the external reference incorrectly points to cell A3 instead of A4.

When a cell moves, its name moves with it. Had the external reference on SUMMARY.XLS been referring to cell DETAIL.XLS!A3 by name, there would be no adverse side effect caused by the insertion.

▶ Names Provide Added Power

Names are more than cosmetic! The advanced naming techniques covered in this chapter provide important *functional* benefits:

- Named formulas serve to centralize logic (as explained below), and can be used as powerful building blocks in complex formulas.

- Names can be used to create ranges that expand and contract depending on how many items are included.

▶ *General Productivity*

Names can help to make you more productive by speeding up worksheet navigation and by simplifying the entering of formulas:

- The Name box drop-down can be used to rapidly go to a named range.
- Names reduce errors caused by mistyped entries. A formula will accept any valid cell reference, even the wrong cell reference. But an error displays when a name is misspelled.
- Writing formulas is simplified by inserting names into the formula.

▶▶ *Valid and Invalid Names*

Here are the rules for defining names:

- A name can only contain the following characters: A–Z (upper or lower case allowed), 0–9, period, and underscore.
- The first character must be a letter or underscore.
- Names cannot be longer than 255 characters.
- A name cannot be the same as a cell reference, such as B3 or Y1998.

Here are some examples of valid and invalid names:

Valid Names	Invalid Names (reason)
Last.Year.Sales	95.Sales (starts with a number)
Profit_1995	Gross Profit (contains a space)
UnitPrice	A1 (same as a cell reference)
Labor	R2C2 (same as a cell reference)

▶▶ *Naming Cells*

The most common use of names is to name cells and ranges of cells. There are several ways to name cells: using the Name box, using the Define Name dialog box, and using the Create Names dialog box.

▶ *Using the Name Box*

Using the name box, found on the left part of the formula bar, is the quickest way to name cells:

1. Select the cell(s) you want to name.

2. Click in the Name box (not the drop-down):

3. Type the name, then press Enter.

▶ ▶**W A R N I N G**

The Name box won't let you accidentally overwrite a previously used cell name (the named cell will be selected), but it *will* let you overwrite a named constant or formula without warning.

▶ *Using the Define Name Dialog Box*

The Define Name dialog box lets you name cells, and will also be used later in this chapter to name constants and formulas:

1. Select the cell(s) you want to name.

2. Choose the Insert ➤ Name ➤ Define command, or press Ctrl+F3, to display the Define Name dialog box pictured in Figure 8.1.

FIGURE 8.1 ▶

*The Define Name
dialog box*

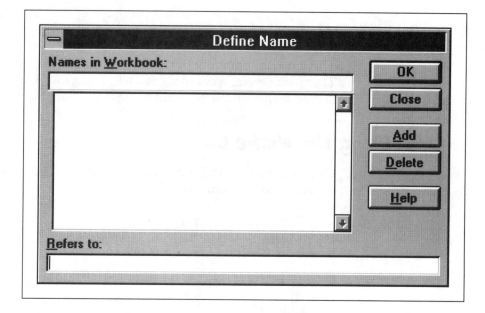

3. Type a valid name in the Name edit box.

▶ ▶ **T I P**

**Excel will suggest a name if the active cell or an ad-
jacent cell contains text, and the text is not already
used as a name.**

4. The Refers to: entry defaults to the current selection. (If not correct, enter a new cell reference—this is a range edit which can be
filled in by pointing and clicking on the worksheet.)

5. Click OK to finish, or click Add to accept the name without closing the Define Name dialog box.

▶ ▶ **W A R N I N G**

**The Define Name dialog box will let you overwrite
previously used names without warning, though
existing names are displayed in the Names in Workbook
list, and can be scanned to see if the name is in use.**

▶ *Using the Create Names Dialog Box*

The Create Names dialog box provides two key advantages over the
Define Name dialog box:

- You are warned if you attempt to overwrite an existing name.
- Many cells can be named with one command.

Choose the Insert ➤ Name ➤ Create command, or press Ctrl+Shift+F3,
to display the Create Names dialog box pictured in Figure 8.2.

FIGURE 8.2 ▶

*The Create Names dia-
log box*

The Power of Names

Ch.
8

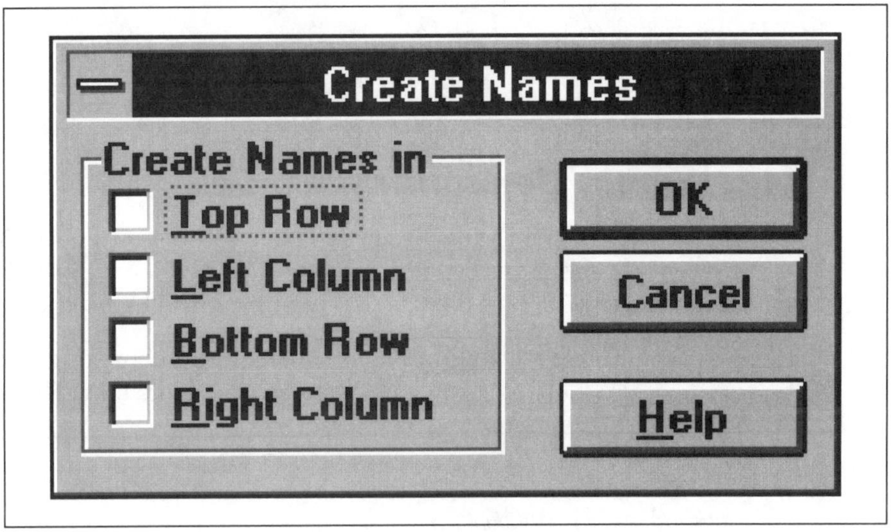

The Create Names dialog box lets you name cells based upon the contents of adjacent cells. The following exercise illustrates the procedure:

1. On a blank worksheet, enter the values pictured below.

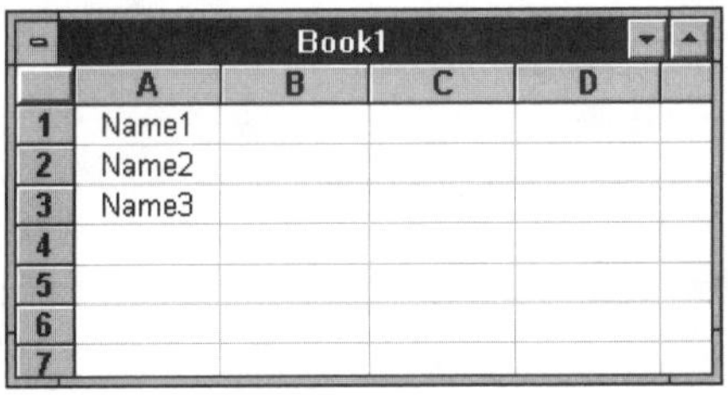

	A	B	C	D	
1	Name1				
2	Name2				
3	Name3				
4					
5					
6					
7					

2. Select cells A1 through B3, then choose the Insert ➤ Name ➤ Create command.

3. Only the Left Column setting should be checked.

4. Click OK. Cells B1, B2, and B3 have *each* been named according to the text in cells A1 through A3.

If a name is already used, the following warning is displayed:

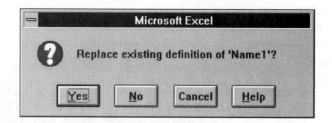

▶ Naming Noncontiguous Cells

A named range does not have to be contiguous. You can name non-contiguous ranges using the Define Name dialog box or the Name box (the Create Names dialog box cannot be used).

If you are attempting to name a range consisting of many non-contiguous sections, the Refers to: can become quite long. Be careful, because Refers to: is limited to 255 characters.

▶ Deleting Names

Follow these steps to delete a name, regardless of the type of name (cell, constant, formula):

1. Choose the Insert ➤ Name ➤ Define command to display the Define Name dialog box pictured in Figure 8.1.

2. Select the name you want to delete in the Names in Workbook list.

3. Click the Delete button.

⊚ ▶ ▶**W A R N I N G**

Any cell referring to a deleted name will display the #NAME? error, since the name will no longer be valid.

▶▶ *Referring to Named Cells in Formulas*

Very simply, a named cell, or range of cells, is an *absolute cell address*. The following formulas assume that cell $A$1 is named Profit and cells $B$1:$B$3 are named Detail.

=Profit	Equal to cell A1
=Profit*2	Multiply A1 by 2
=SUM(Detail)	Sum cells B1:B3
=AVERAGE(Detail)	Average cells B1:B3
=Profit+SUM(Detail)	Add A1 to the sum of B1:B3

Referring to cells by name is very simple. The cell name is used in place of the cell address in your formulas.

▶ *Inserting Names into Formulas*

While entering or editing a formula, names can be pasted into the formula rather than typing them. This is a helpful procedure if you forget the name, don't want to misspell the name, or are too lazy to type the name.

If the Name Is in the Same Workbook

Follow these steps to insert a name into a formula when the formula and named reference are in the same workbook:

1. Name cell A1 **GrossProfit** and enter **100** into it.

2. Select cell B1. Type an equal sign to begin the formula.

3. Use the Name box drop-down list, and select the name GrossProfit. The name will be added to the formula.

4. Type ***2** (to multiply by 2) then press Enter. Cell B1 will equal 200.

 ► ►**T I P**

The Name box only lists named cells and named ranges. To paste in a name that refers to a formula or constant, use the Insert ➤ Name ➤ Paste command.

If the Name Is from a Different Workbook

Assume that hypothetical workbooks SUMMARY.XLS and DE-TAIL.XLS are open, and DETAIL.XLS has a cell named Cost. Here's how you would enter a name from DETAIL.XLS into a formula in SUMMARY.XLS:

1. Activate SUMMARY.XLS, select cell A1, and enter an equal sign to begin the formula.

2. Activate DETAIL.XLS. (Use the Window menu, or click on DE-TAIL.XLS if visible.)

3. Use the Name box drop-down list, and select the name Cost. The name will be added to the formula.

4. Press Enter to complete the formula. SUMMARY.XLS is automatically reactivated.

► ## PASTING NAMES INTO FORMULAS

There are several ways to paste names into formulas—you can use the Name box, the Insert ➤ Name ➤ Paste command, or the Paste Name tool. To use the Name box, place the cursor inside the formula at the point where the name must be pasted, then select the name from the Name box drop-down list. Since the Name box only lists range names, it cannot be used to paste named constants or named formulas.

If you want the flexibility to paste any type of name into a formula, use the Insert ➤ Name ➤ Paste command, or the Paste Name tool. Both the tool and the command display the Paste Name dialog, from which you can choose any available name. The Paste tool is not on any of Excel's built-in toolbars—it must be added to a toolbar (see Chapter 26). The tool can be found in the Formula, Macro, and Utility categories in the Toolbars Customize dialog.

▶▶ *Referencing a Row-and-Column Intersection*

The Power of Names

Suppose you have a budget with columns labeled by month (January, February, etc) and rows labeled by category (supplies, utilities, etc). What if you want to refer to March Utilities, or October Supplies, but you don't want to name each and every cell in the worksheet? There is a special way to reference a cell that lies at the intersection point of a given row and column (for instance, Utilities and March)—use a space character. The *space character* implies an intersection. For example, the formula =C:C 2:2 is a roundabout way of referring to cell C2, and breaks down as follows:

▶▶
Ch.
8

C:C	Reference to column C
Space	Intersection operator
2:2	Reference to row 2

While an intersection reference does not require the use of names, its power is realized when used in conjunction with names:

1. Enter the following values onto a new worksheet:

	A	B	C	D	E
1					
2			East	West	
3		Gadgets	3897	4123	
4		Gizmos	9000	2721	
5		Widgets	8521	9699	
6					
7					
8					

Book2

2. Select cells B2:D5. Choose the Insert ➤ Name ➤ Create command.

3. The Create Names dialog box is displayed (see Figure 8.2). Check the Top Row and Left Column settings, then click OK. Five names have been created:

Name	Refers to:
Gadgets	C3:D3
Gizmos	C4:D4
Widgets	C5:D5
East	C3:C5
West	D3:D5

4. The following formulas can be used to refer to the intersection point of these names:

Formula	Refers to:
=East Gadgets	C3
=West Widgets	D5
=Gizmos East	C4

▶ Implied Intersection

Using the worksheet from the above exercise, enter the formula **=East+West** into cells E3, E4, and E5. Even though East and West are ranges, the formulas calculate correctly based on the values on the same row. This is due to an *implied intersection*. Now enter the formula **=East+West** into cell E6. The **#VALUE!** error will display because the names East and West do not extend to row 6.

▶▶ *Names Are Not Case-Sensitive, but They Are Case-Retentive*

Names are *not* case-sensitive. If you define the name SALES, then define the name Sales, the second name will replace the first. On the other hand, names *are* case-retentive. When a name is used in a formula, it will automatically revert to the same case used when the name was defined. If a name is defined as GrossProfit, and you enter the formula =grossprofit, the formula will automatically change to =GrossProfit when Enter is pressed.

 ▶ ▶ **T I P**

> **There is a benefit to always using mixed case in names. Formulas are typically entered in all upper or all lower case. Since names revert to their original case, you get immediate visual feedback if a name was misspelled—it will not revert to mixed case.**

▶▶ *Quickly Selecting Named Cells*

Names can be used to help navigate a workbook. Select a name using the Name box dropdown list. The named cell(s) will be selected. The Edit ➤ Go To command, or F5 key, provides the same functionality.

▶▶ *Applying Names after the Fact*

In the short run, it is easier to construct formulas by clicking cells. Using names requires that the names be defined, and then used. Here is how to work quick and dirty with cell references, and then quickly clean up later:

1. On a blank worksheet, enter the formula **=A1** into cells A2, A3, and A4.

2. Name cell A1 **TestApply**.

3. Choose the Insert ➤ Name ➤ Apply command; the Apply Names dialog box (Figure 8.3) is displayed.

4. Make sure **TestApply** is selected in the Apply Names dialog list. Click OK.

5. Look at the formulas in cells A2, A3, and A4—they now refer to cell A1 by name.

FIGURE 8.3 ▶

*The Apply Names
dialog box*

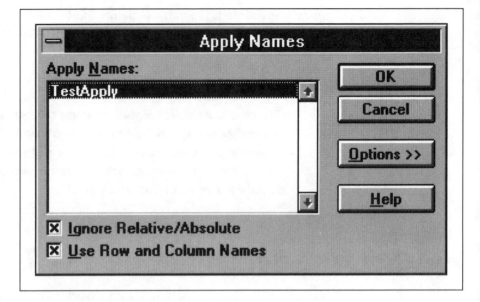

▶ *Ignore Relative/Absolute*

The Ignore Relative/Absolute checkbox toggles between two useful settings:

- If checked (default setting), replaces reference with name regardless of whether reference is relative, absolute, or mixed.

- If unchecked, will only replace absolute references with absolute names, relative references with relative names, and mixed references with mixed names.

▶ *Use Row and Column Names*

Use Row and Column Names uses intersection names (covered above) if an actual cell name does not exist. For example, if an unnamed cell sits at the intersection of a column named January and a row named Profits, this setting allows Excel to apply the name January Profits.

▶ *Advanced Options*

Click the Options button (see Figure 8.3) to expand the dialog box to include the options pictured in Figure 8.4.

FIGURE 8.4

Advanced Apply Names options

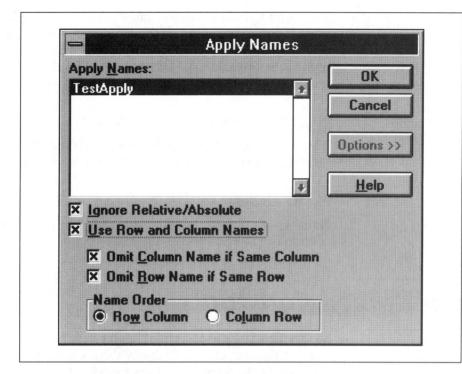

Omit Column Name If Same Column

In the worksheet pictured below, the columns and rows are named ranges. Profit is equal to Revenue less Expenses. Suppose you set up the profit formulas quickly, using point-and-click cell references (e.g., the formula in C5 is =C3-C4), and you want to replace the cell references with cell names:

	A	B	C	D	E	F	G	H
1								
2			Fiscal.96	Fiscal.97		*Named Ranges*		
3		**Revenue**	10000	13000		Fiscal.96	C3:C5	
4		**Expenses**	8000	7000		Fiscal.97	D3:D5	
5		**Profit**	2000	6000		Revenue	C3:D3	
6						Expenses	C4:D4	
7						Profit	C5:D5	
8								

BOOK1.XLS

The Power of Names

Ch.
8

The Omit Column Name if Same Column setting is checked by default. If you apply names without changing this setting, the formula in cell C5 will be =Revenue-Expenses. If you clear the setting and apply names, the formula in cell C5 will be =Fiscal.96 Revenue–Fiscal.96 Expenses.

Omit Row Name If Same Row

This is the same as the previous setting, but works on formulas which reside in the same rows as the cells referenced in the formulas.

Name Order

Name Order determines the name order for an intersection name: row-column or column-row.

▶▶ Named Constants

So far, the names used in this chapter have all been named cells. You can also name *constants*. Probably the most common reason for naming a constant is to discourage users from inadvertently changing values. Consider the following:

1. A commission rate of 12% is to be used throughout a sheet.

2. Knowing that the commission rate may change, you don't want to embed the 12% constant in formulas throughout the sheet.

3. If the 12% is stored in a cell, the user is invited to change it. A named constant provides the flexibility of a named cell, with some added security.

Use the Insert ➤ Name ➤ Define command, which displays the Define Name dialog box pictured in Figure 8.1.

1. Enter the name as usual.

2. In Refers to:, type in a constant value. The constant can be a number, text, logical (TRUE/FALSE), or even an array.

3. Click OK to add the name and close the dialog box. Click Add to add the name and keep the dialog box.

►►T I P

When you define a named constant, Excel automatically places an equal sign (and quotation marks surrounding text constants), in Refers to:. Remember, you do not have the type the equal sign or quotation marks—let Excel do it for you.

►► *Fixing #NAME? Errors*

The #NAME? error displays when a formula Refers to: a non-existent name. If this happens, check that:

- Name(s) in the formula are typed correctly.
- Function name(s) in the formula are typed correctly.
- The name is not enclosed in quotes.

►►N O T E

The remainder of this chapter deals with advanced naming techniques. You may want to revisit this section after becoming comfortable with the topics covered earlier in the chapter. You will also need to understand external references (covered in Chapter 4).

►► *Names That Refer to Cells on Other Worksheets*

A name can refer to cells on external workbooks. This technique is critically important when developing templates (see Chapter 10), and in

The Power of Names

►►

Ch.

8

worksheet development in general. Suppose that the names below are defined in Book1:

Name	Refers to:	Comments
Sales	=[XYZ.XLS]Sheet1! A1:A3	Refer by cell address
Profit_1	=[DEPT1.XLS]Sheet 1!Profit	Refer by cell name
YTD.Table	=SUM([SALES.XLS] Sheet1!A1:A3)	Refer by range

Formulas in Book1 can now use the names Sales, Profit_1, and YTD.Table as if the ranges were actually in Book1, without concern for the book name prefix. The following formulas are valid:

=SUM(Sales)

=ROWS(Sales)

=INDEX(Sales,2)

=Profit_1*2

To create a name that refers to an external reference:

1. Choose the Insert ➤ Name ➤ Define command.
2. Type in the name.
3. In Refers to, type **=[BOOK1.XLS]Sheet1!MyCell** (in this exercise, BOOK1.XLS is the name of the external workbook, and My-Cell is the cell reference, or cell name).

▶ Saving External Link Values

Any time you create names referring to other worksheets, you should be aware of the Save External Link Values setting, which determines whether the external data is saved inside the worksheet (though not visible). Consider the following:

1. The name YTD.Sales, created in Book1, refers to the external range SALES95.XLS!Database, which is 5000 rows by 20 columns.

2. The Tools ➤ Options ➤ Calculation Save External Link Values setting is checked by default. This causes the values from SALES95.XLS!Database to be stored, invisibly, in Book1.

3. When Book1 is saved, a huge workbook has been created because the external link values were saved.

Uncheck this setting if the external values do not need to be saved with the sheet. This will often be the case.

NAME EXTERNAL REFERENCES

You already know how to name a range of cells. But you may not know that a name can refer to a range of cells in a different workbook. This is a *named external reference*—an important construct if you are doing serious Excel modeling. A worksheet might have many references to a range in an external workbook. Such references are difficult to work with—they include the name of the source workbook. And, if the source workbook is closed, they include the full path as part of the reference. By naming the external range, your formulas become easier to enter, edit, and read.

Naming an external range is not much different than a "normal" named range. Just include the workbook name in the Refers to: edit box in the Define Name dialog. This can be accomplished by typing the reference or by pointing and clicking on the external workbook. Suppose that you want to create a name in workbook ABC.XLS that refers to a range in workbook XYZ.XLS, and that both workbooks are open. Activate ABC.XLS, then choose Insert ➤ Name ➤ Define. Type a name, then place the cursor in the Refers to: edit box. Use the Window menu to activate book XYZ.XLS.

The Power of Names

Ch. 8

▶

Select the range with the mouse, then click OK.

Now, instead of entering a formula like:

=SUM([XYZ.XLS!Sheet1]!$A$1:$A$3

...you can enter:

=SUM(Sales)

▶▶ *Centralizing Logic Using Named Formulas*

You are now accustomed to naming cells and constants. If you observe the syntax of defined names using the Define Name dialog box (see Figure 8.1), you will notice that the Refers to: for *all* names begins with an equal sign. *All names are essentially named formulas*—some more complex than others. Almost any formula that can be entered into a cell can also be defined as a *named formula*. One important way that named formulas are used is to centralize logic. Consider this problem:

- A complex formula is used to calculate the rate of return for an investment.

- This same formula is used in hundreds of cells on a sheet. The cells are not contiguous.

- The formula needs to be changed. You can do a find/replace, but there are other similar formulas that you must be careful not to overwrite.

This problem can be solved by defining a single named formula, and then referring to this formula by name. Because the Refers to: edit box in the Define Name dialog box is awkward to work with, it is easier to name formulas by first entering the formula into a cell, and then copying it into the Define Name dialog box. Follow this simple exercise:

1. Enter the following constants onto a blank worksheet:

	A	B	C	D	E	F
1						
2		Item	Qty	Price	Extension	
3		Widgets	7	22.95		
4		Gadgets	15	19.55		
5		Gizmos	11	8.98		
6						
7						
8						

BOOK1.XLS

2. Enter the formula **=C3*D3** into cell E3.

3. Select the formula (on the formula bar, or using in-cell formula editing), then choose the Edit ➤ Copy command.

4. Press Esc.

5. Choose the Insert ➤ Name ➤ Define command to display the Define Name dialog box.

6. Enter the name **Extension** (if Excel has not already entered it for you).

7. Clear the entry in the Refers to: edit box.

8. Choose the Edit ➤ Paste command to paste in the formula.

9. Click OK.

The named formula Extension has been defined, but has not yet been used:

10. Select cells E3:E5.

11. Type **=Extension**, then press Ctrl+Enter to place the formula in all three cells.

The Power of Names

Ch.
8

▶ ▶ T I P

> Select cell E3, display the Define Name dialog box, and select the name Extension. It will refer to =Sheet1!C3*Sheet1!D3. Close the dialog box, select E4, and look at the definition of Extension again. It will refer to =Sheet1!C4*Sheet1!D4. The definition depends on the active cell because it contains relative references.

▶ THE CELL-ABOVE TRICK

Suppose there are numbers in cells A1:A10, and the formula =SUM(A1:A10) in cell A11. You need to add another value to the list which must be included in the SUM formula. If you insert a row in the middle of the column, the SUM range expands automatically. But a common scenario is the need to add the new value to the *bottom* of the list—when you insert at row 11, the formula must be edited to include row 11. One way around this problem is to create a named formula, using a relative reference, that refers to the cell one above. In the following example, cell A2 is the active cell: Choose Insert ➤ Name ➤ Define and enter CellAbove as the cell name. In Refers to: enter =A1 then click OK. Now, you can enter the formula =CellAbove into *any* cell on the sheet (except row one) and it will refer to the cell one row up.

Back to the SUM problem the formula will read: =SUM(A1:CellAbove); which in English means: sum cells A1 through the cell one cell above the formula. You can insert rows immediately above the SUM formula, and the relative reference in the named formula causes the SUM to expand automatically.

▶▶ *Named 3-D References*

Three-dimensional references (references that refer to ranges on more than one worksheet) can be named. (See Chapter 4 for an explanation of 3-D references.) Consider the scenario pictured in Figure 8.5: a workbook has five worksheets, one for each of four regions (East, West, North, and South) and a summary sheet. Cell C5 on each of the regional sheets contains annual sales for the region.

 ▶ ▶**N O T E**

> **Figure 8.5 shows two worksheets from the same workbook in separate windows. This is accomplished with the Window ➤ New Window command.**

Cells B5, B8, D5, and D8 can each contain a formula referring to the 3-D range =East:South!$C$5. But if a new region sheet is added, and

FIGURE 8.5 ▶

Summary and Regional sheets

The Power of Names

Ch. 8

	A	B	C	D	E	F	G	H
1								
2		Regional Summary						
3								
4		Total Sales		Lowest Sales				
5		66,580		12,555				
6								
7		Regional Avg.		Highest Sales				
8		16,645						
9								
10								

CH08EX4.XLS:1

Summary / East / West / North / South

CH08EX4.XLS:2

	A	B	C	D	E	F	G	H	I
1									
2		Widgets	5,000						
3		Gadgets	7,500						
4		Gizmos	6,200						
5		Total Sales	18,700						
6									
7									
8									

Summary \ East / West / North / South

it is not placed between East and West, all formulas require modifications. Instead, define the name TotalSales to Refer to:

=East:South!$C$5

Then enter the following formulas onto Summary:

Cell	Formula
B5	=SUM(TotalSales)
B8	=AVERAGE(TotalSales)
D5	=MIN(TotalSales)
D8	=MAX(TotalSales)

These formulas never require modification. When a new region sheet is added, only the name TotalSales requires modification.

 ► ►**TIP**

> As you read about the different types of names explained in this chapter, remember that *all names* are essentially named formulas, even named ranges. Almost any formula that can be entered into a cell can also be named, including 3-D formulas and formulas referring to external workbooks.

► ► *Using Named Formulas to Create Dynamic Named Ranges*

Dynamic named ranges are ranges that automatically change based upon certain conditions. There is no formal dynamic named range construct; they are simply named formulas that refer to a range of cells. Consider the following problem:

- A range of cells is named Portfolio_Details.

- Various complex formulas and charts refer to the named range Portfolio_Details for the purpose of analyzing the portfolio.

- The need to analyze two portfolios emerges. Using traditional methods, a second set of complex formulas and charts can be created which refer to the second portfolio range. Since the model requires modification to accommodate a second portfolio, a design that will easily accommodate a third and fourth portfolio is highly desirable.

The problem can be solved using a dynamic named range—with no change to the complex formulas that refer to Portfolio_Details. User input will determine which portfolio is being analyzed. Follow this exercise:

1. Enter the following onto a blank worksheet:

2. Name cells B2:C6 **Portfolio1**.

3. Name cell E2:F6 **Portfolio2**.

4. Name cell D8 **Choice**. (User input into this cell determines which portfolio is analyzed.)

5. Choose the Insert ➤ Name ➤ Define command.

6. Enter **Portfolio_Details** as the name.

7. Enter the following formula in Refers to:

=IF(Choice=1,Portfolio1,Portfolio2)

8. Click OK.

Now test the dynamic name:

9. Enter **1** into cell Choice.

10. Choose the Edit ➤ Go To command. Type the name **Portfolio_ Details** in the Reference edit box, and click OK. The range Portfolio1 will be selected.

11. Enter **2** into cell Choice, then repeat step 10.

Suppose that, in the future, a third portfolio is added. All you need to do is add the portfolio data, name it **Portfolio3**, then change the definition of Portfolio_Details to refer to:

=IF(Choice=1,Portfolio1,IF(Choice=2,Portfolio2,Portfolio3))

▶ ▶ **N O T E**

Excel will not display dynamic named ranges in the Go To dialog box or in the Name box drop-down.

▶▶ *Named Array Constants*

Array constants are very useful, though awkward to construct. An array constant is similar to a range of cells, but it does not reside in rows and columns and thus is not easily visible. One use of array constants is to store tables of data out of view from the user of the worksheet. As with other named constants, array constants are defined using the Insert ➤ Name ➤ Define command, which displays the Define Name dialog box pictured in Figure 8.1.

An array constant stores multiple values which, like cells, are oriented in rows and columns. But since the array does not reside in the worksheet grid, the rows and columns are indicated by the use of two separators, as shown in Table 8.1.

In the following examples, the boldfaced entry indicates what would be typed into the Refers to: edit box of the Define Name dialog box to create the array to the right:

={2;4;6;8}   4 rows, 1 column of numbers

={"East",12,100;"West",15,135}   2 rows, 3 columns of text and numbers

={"A",TRUE,99.99}   1 row, 3 columns—text, logical, and number

Accessing the data in an array constant is similar to accessing data stored in cells. The INDEX function can be used to refer to an individual data element. The ROWS function will return the number of rows in the array, and the COLUMNS function will return the number of columns.

▶ **TABLE 8.1:** *Array Separators*

Separator	Meaning
Comma	Denotes new column
Semicolon	Denotes new row

▶ ▶ **T I P**

Application developers often store information in array constants, but the process of building the arrays is controlled programmatically. This allows the use of the construct, without the tedium of defining the names. Also, since names that are defined programmatically can be hidden, another layer of security can be achieved.

▶▶ *Names Can Be Workbook or Worksheet Level*

Names can be *global* to the workbook or can be *local* to a specific worksheet. This is a distinction that is very important to understand in order to use names effectively.

▶ *Global Names*

By default, all names are global to the workbook. This means that when cell B2, on Sheet1 in Book1, is named Total:

- The name Total can be referred to from any worksheet (in the same workbook) without having to specify the sheet name prefix— Sheet2 can contain the formula =Total.

- If the name Total is defined again, anywhere in the workbook, the new definition will replace the old definition.

- Regardless of which sheet is active, the name will appear in the Name Box drop-down.

- If a sheet from a different workbook with the global name Total is moved or copied to Book1, the original name on Sheet1 takes precedence—the name defined on the just-copied sheet is changed to a local name.

▶ Local Names

A local name is defined by including the sheet name as part of the name using the Define Name dialog box (see Figure 8.1), or the Name box. To create a local name Total on Sheet1:

1. Activate Sheet1.

2. Select cell(s) you want to name.

3. Enter name **Sheet1!Total** in the Name box—the sheet name is included as part of the name. After the local name is defined, it will appear in the Name box without the prefix Sheet1!, and it will only appear in the Sheet1 Name box (it will not appear in the Name boxes of any other sheets).

 ▶ ▶ **N O T E**

The Name box cannot be used to name constants or formulas, only cells, ranges, and objects. Also, the only names that will appear in the Name box are global cell and range names, and local cell and range names for the active worksheet.

The implications of the local name Total, defined on Sheet1, are as follows:

- Total can be referred to from any worksheet, but the sheet name prefix must be included (e.g., Sheet2 can contain the formula =Sheet1!Total).

- The formula =Total entered onto Sheet2 will return a #NAME? error.
- Total can be defined on other worksheets, and Sheet1!Total will *not* be overwritten (even if the new definition for Total is global).
- If Total is redefined on Sheet1 with the sheet name prefix omitted (as if it were a global name), it will still be a local name.

▶ ▶ **N O T E**

The explanations of global and local names above use named cells to illustrate the concept. The same rules apply for all other worksheet names, including named formulas and named constants.

▶

A SHORTCUT FOR DEFINING LOCAL NAMES

Since the Create Name dialog does not have an option for creating local names, there is no obvious way to quickly create local names without going through the painstaking process of defining them one at a time using the Define Name dialog. Consider the following scenario: suppose you have a worksheet with monthly data for January, and you have used lots of names on the sheet. Now it's February, and you want to create another worksheet in the same workbook, using the same names that were used on the January sheet. (And in subsequent months, the process must be repeated.) Make a copy of sheet January in the same workbook (hold down Option while you drag-and-drop the January sheet tab to a new position). A new worksheet will be created, with the name January [2]. Double-click the new sheet tab, then type the name February into the Rename Sheet dialog. The new February worksheet will contain the same names as the January sheet, but they will be local to the February sheet.

▶▶ Naming Conventions

Once you start to use names, you are apt to use them a lot. A complex model might contain hundreds of names, and the list of names in the Define Name dialog box can become unwieldy. Special prefixes and/or suffixes can be used to help document and manage the names. The naming conventions in the following examples are not intended to be used verbatim, but rather to provide ideas on how to create meaningful conventions that work for you.

▶ Convention Based on Type of Name

The naming conventions listed in Table 8.2 are based on the type of name created:

▶ **TABLE 8.2**: *Convention Based on Type of Name*

Prefix	Meaning
NF	Named formula
AC	Array constant
ER	External reference
DC	Database criteria
DB	Database table
DE	Database extract range
CR	Calculated (dynamic) range

▶ Conventions Specific to a Model

Naming conventions can also be specific to a worksheet model, as in the following examples:

- Several ranges on one sheet that are printed as separate reports—Use Report as a prefix, as in Report_Summary and Report_Detail.

- Worksheet contains data for multiple regions—use Region as a prefix, as in Region_East and Region_West.

- Worksheet used to track investments—use a prefix identifying type of investment, as in Stock.IBM, Stock.ATT, Bonds.Muni, Bonds.TB.

WORKING WITH HIDDEN NAMES

An important feature used extensively by application developers is the ability to define hidden names. Don't bother to look for this feature in the user interface—the only way to define a hidden name, or delete one, is programatically. (A hidden parameter can be set for the Names.Add function in the Visual Basic for Application language or the DEFINE.NAME function in the Excel macro language—see On-line Help or hardcopy documentation.)

Hidden names are often used to store information on a worksheet, and prevent the user from seeing, changing, or deleting the name. An example is the Data ➤ Get External Data command (covered in Chapter 18). This command is not part of the core Excel program. Rather, it is provided courtesy of the XLQUERY.XLA add-in, which comes with Excel. The last dialog displayed by the Data ➤ Get External Data command provides the option to keep the query definition. If this option is checked, the add-in defines several hidden names on the active worksheet that allow the query to be refreshed at a later time without having to redefine the query. The hidden names contain the SQL statement, the ODBC data source, and several additional settings.

The only difference between a 'normal' name and a hidden name is the fact that a hidden name is hidden. A hidden name can be a range name, a named constant, or a named formula.

▶▶ How to See All Names at Once

A complex workbook might contain hundreds of names. The Define Name dialog box only lets you view the definition for one name at a time. The Insert ➤ Name ➤ Paste command displays the following dialog box:

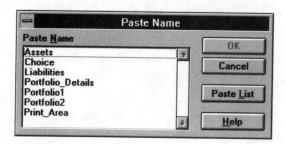

Click the Paste List button to paste all of the definitions onto the active worksheet, starting at the active cell. All global names are pasted, as are all local names that are defined on the active worksheet. Local names defined on worksheets other than the active sheet are not pasted.

 ▶ ▶ **W A R N I N G**

Since the names are pasted starting at the active cell, you must be careful not to overwrite data on the worksheet. One way to avoid this pitfall is to add a new worksheet to the workbook, then paste the names onto the new worksheet. Be aware, however, that the pasted list will contain all global names in the workbook, and local names only for the active worksheet.

OBJECTS CAN BE NAMED

When you place a graphical object on a worksheet, such as drawing objects, embedded charts, and on-sheet controls, Excel automatically names the object using the object type followed by a sequential number. For example, when you place a text box on a worksheet, it is named Text 1. Then draw an oval—it is named Oval 2. In earlier versions of Excel, there was no way to override these automatic names. Programmers will appreciate the fact that these objects can now be named, because macro code can then refer to meaningful object names.

- Objects are named using the Name box. To name an object, select the object. Click in the Name box, type a name for the object, and press Enter.

- The rules for naming objects are different than for naming cells—object names can contain spaces, and they cannot contain periods. For example, My Square and My_Square are valid object names, but My.Square is not.

- The name of a selected object is displayed in the Name box.

The Power of Names

Ch.

8

► ► CHAPTER **9**

Essential
Worksheet
Functions

———

►►►**F**AST **T**RACK

T_here_ are hundreds of built-in Excel functions, and it is a given that most users will learn the ones needed for basic worksheet arithmetic, such as SUM. But as you start to create more powerful models, the inherently dry nature of Excel's function reference becomes apparent—it fails to point out which functions are _essential_ for serious worksheet modeling and data analysis.

What makes a particular function essential? Even the most obscure functions are momentarily essential when required to solve a specific problem. But the functions covered in this chapter are important generic tools. A case in point is the OFFSET function—the thought of doing even simple modeling and analysis without OFFSET is literally inconceivable, yet few Excel users are even _aware_ of it.

This chapter covers the following worksheet functions:

Totals and Subtotals	**Sumif, Subtotal**
Lookup and Reference	VLOOKUP, MATCH, INDEX, OFFSET, INDIRECT, ROW, ROWS, COLUMN, COLUMNS
Counting	COUNT, COUNTA, COUNTBLANK, COUNTIF
Text	LEN, LEFT, RIGHT, MID, SEARCH, FIND
Date & Time	TODAY, NOW, DATE, DAY, HOUR, MINUTE, MONTH, WEEKDAY, YEAR

▶

USING FUNCTIONS THAT REFER TO CLOSED WORKBOOKS

In Chapter 8 you learned to write formulas that refer to closed workbooks. These formulas can include functions like SUM, IN-DEX, and SUBTOTAL. An example of a SUM function that sums cells in a closed workbook is

    SUM('C:\BUSINESS\[BUDGET.XLS]Sheet1'!$A$1:$A$5)

Functions that refer to closed workbooks are exactly the same as functions that refer to open workbooks, except that the full path of each external reference is written out. You can type the full path into the formula, but an easier way to enter the full path for the external reference is to open the referenced workbook, enter the external references into your formulas by pointing and clicking, then close the referenced workbook. Excel will append the full path for each reference for you. You can also name the external reference, and use the name rather than the full path in your function.

Most functions can refer to data in closed workbooks, which saves time and memory useage by not requiring additional workbooks to be opened. There are some formulas which, because of their complexity, cannot refer to closed workbooks. These include OFF-SET, COUNTIF, SUMIF, and INDIRECT.

▶▶ *Calculating Totals and Subtotals*

The SUMIF and SUBTOTAL functions are very important new additions in Excel 5, and serve to streamline two very common calculations: *conditional totals* and *nested subtotals*.

Worksheet Functions

▶▶

Ch.
9

▶ SUMIF

In previous versions of Excel, there were two ways to conditionally calculate a sum of certain of the cells within a range (based on specified criteria):

- Array formulas—powerful but inordinately complex
- Criteria ranges combined with the DSUM function—again, powerful but tedious to construct

Array formulas and criteria ranges still provide important functionality, but SUMIF provides simple solutions for common conditional summing problems.

Syntax

The following options are used with SUMIF:

SUMIF(CheckRange,Criteria,SumRange)

CheckRange   A range of cells being compared against the *Criteria*

Criteria   An expression specifying which cells in *CheckRange* meet the evaluation criteria

SumRange   A range of cells being summed—only cells that correspond to qualifying CheckRange cells are summed

Examples

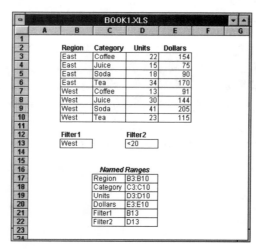

EXAMPLE 1:

=SUMIF(C3:C10,"Soda",E3:E10)

Returns *295*—total dollars for category Soda*EXAMPLE 2:*

=SUMIF(Category,"<>Tea",Dollars)

Returns *759*—total dollars for all categories except Tea*EXAMPLE 3:*

=SUMIF(Region,Filter1,Units)

Returns *107*—total units for region West

EXAMPLE 4:

=SUMIF(Units,Filter2,Dollars)

Returns *256*—total dollars for every row where units are less than 20

Notes

- Use the COUNTIF function, covered in this chapter, to count values conditionally.

- Use the SUBTOTAL function to place nested subtotals in a row or column.

▶ SUBTOTAL

The SUBTOTAL function is a long-overdue addition to Excel 5.

- Subtotals can be easily calculated using several calculation methods.

- Multiple levels of subtotals can be nested in a column, and a grand subtotal will ignore nested subtotals.

- Rows that are hidden as a result of a data filter (see Chapter 15) are not included in the calculation.

Syntax

The following options are used with SUBTOTAL:

SUBTOTAL(Type,Ref)

Worksheet Functions

Ch.
9

Type   A number from 1 to 11 that specifies type of calculation, as listed below:

1	AVERAGE	(arithmetic mean of values)
2	COUNT	(count numeric values)
3	COUNTA	(count non-blanks)
4	MAX	(maximum value)
5	MIN	(minimum value)
6	PRODUCT	(multiply)
7	STDEV	(standard deviation based on a sample)
8	STDEVP	(standard deviation based on entire population)
9	SUM	(add values)
10	VAR	(variance based on a sample)
11	VARP	(variance based on entire population)

Ref   The range being subtotaled

Examples

EXAMPLE 1:

The following exercise demonstrates the versatility of the SUB-TOTAL function:

1. Enter the following on a blank worksheet:

	A	B	C	D	E	F
1						
2		Region	Category	Units	Dollars	
3		East	Coffee	22	154	
4		East	Juice	15	75	
5		East	Soda	18	90	
6		East	Tea	34	170	
7		West	Coffee	13	91	
8		West	Juice	30	144	
9		West	Soda	41	205	
10		West	Tea	23	115	
11						
12						
13						
14						

BOOK1.XLS

2. Insert one row below the "East" rows (to make room for East subtotals).

3. Enter the following formulas to calculate subtotals and a grand total:

Cell	Formula
E7	=SUBTOTAL(9,E3:E6)
E12	=SUBTOTAL(9,E8:E11)
E13	=SUBTOTAL(9,E3:E12)

EXAMPLE 2:

The second part of this exercise makes the formulas dynamic, and demonstrates the versatility of SUBTOTAL:

1. Name cell F16 **CalcType**.

2. In each of the three SUBTOTAL formulas, replace the Type argument **9** with a reference to cell **CalcType**, for example:

=SUBTOTAL(CalcType,E3:E6)

3. Enter numbers from **1** to **11** in cell CalcType and watch the SUBTOTAL calculations change.

 **TIP**

The Data ➤ Subtotals command can quickly insert embedded subtotals, without the need to manually insert rows, and will create an outline in the process. See Chapter 16 to learn more about this command.

▶▶ *Lookup Functions*

A worksheet is one great big table, which typically contains one or more tables of data. Accordingly, the ability to access data stored in tables is an essential skill, regardless of the type of analysis and modeling you are performing. Functions such as INDEX, OFFSET, and VLOOKUP are some of the most important worksheet functions for serious users.

Worksheet Functions

▶
Ch.
9

▶ *VLOOKUP*

The VLOOKUP function is used to search the leftmost column of a range (or array) for a specific value, then return a corresponding value from a different column in the table.

- Use VLOOKUP for traditional table lookups requiring exact matches—retrieving a customer address by using a customer code, or retrieving sales figures using a product number.

- USE VLOOKUP to search for the closest value less than or equal to a search value, then retrieve a value from a corresponding column—for example, lookups into tax tables.

- The search is *not* case-sensitive.

Syntax

The following options are used with VLOOKUP:

VLOOKUP(LookupValue,LookupRef,ColumnNo,Nearest)

LookupValue   The value being searched for in the first column of LookupRef

LookupRef   A rectangular range or array

ColumnNo   The column number within the range containing the lookup value; must be a number greater than or equal to 1, and less than or equal to the number of columns in the table

Nearest   Specifies whether the search value must be an exact match to a value in the first column of LookupRef

- If Nearest is TRUE, the first column of LookupRef is searched for the closest value less than or equal to LookupValue in first column of *LookupRef*—The values in the first column of LookupRef must be sorted in ascending order, otherwise VLOOKUP will not work properly.

- If Nearest is FALSE, the first column of LookupRef is searched for an exact match to LookupValue—Values in first column of LookupRef do not have to be sorted.

Examples: Exact Lookups

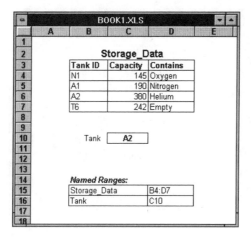

EXAMPLE 1:

=VLOOKUP("T6",B4:D7,2,FALSE)

Returns *242*—T6 is located in the fourth row, and 242 found in second column of range

EXAMPLE 2:

=VLOOKUP(Tank,Storage_Data,3,FALSE)

Returns *Helium*

EXAMPLE 3:

=VLOOKUP(Tank,Storage_Data,2,TRUE)

Mistakenly returns *#N/A* due to improper use of TRUE as the *Nearest* argument

Worksheet Functions

Ch.
9

Examples: Lookup Based on Closest Value

```
┌─────────────────────────────────────────────────┐
│ ▫            BOOK1.XLS              ▼ ▲          │
├───┬──────┬──────┬──────┬──────┬──────┬───────────┤
│   │  A   │  B   │  C   │  D   │  E   │           │
├───┼──────┼──────┼──────┼──────┼──────┤           │
│ 1 │      │      │      │      │      │           │
│ 2 │      │   Tax_Table │      │      │           │
│ 3 │      │Income│ Tax  │      │      │           │
│ 4 │      │10,000│ 12%  │      │      │           │
│ 5 │      │20,000│ 15%  │      │      │           │
│ 6 │      │30,000│ 18%  │      │      │           │
│ 7 │      │40,000│ 20%  │      │      │           │
│ 8 │      │      │      │      │      │           │
│ 9 │      │      │      │      │      │           │
│10 │      │Income│25,000│      │      │           │
│11 │      │      │      │      │      │           │
│12 │      │      │      │      │      │           │
│13 │      │Named Ranges:│      │      │           │
│14 │      │Tax_Table    │B4:C7 │      │           │
│15 │      │Income       │C10   │      │           │
│16 │      │      │      │      │      │           │
│17 │      │      │      │      │      │           │
│18 │      │      │      │      │      │           │
└───┴──────┴──────┴──────┴──────┴──────┴───────────┘
```

EXAMPLE 1:

=VLOOKUP(15000,B4:C7,2,TRUE)

Returns *.12* (12%)—10,000 is the closest value less than or equal to 15,000

EXAMPLE 2:

=VLOOKUP(Income,Tax_Table,2,TRUE)

Returns *.15* (15%)—20,000 is the closest value less than or equal to 25,000

EXAMPLE 3:

=VLOOKUP(5000,Tax_Table,2,TRUE)

Returns .*#N/A*—there is no value equal to or less than 5000 in the first column of Tax_Table

NOTE

There are two functions closely related to VLOOKUP: HLOOKUP and LOOKUP. The HLOOKUP function is identical to VLOOKUP, except that it searches a row for a given value, and returns a value from a corresponding row—once you understand VLOOKUP you will understand HLOOKUP. The LOOKUP function is not covered in this chapter because the sort requirements severely limit its usefulness.

▶ MATCH

Use MATCH when you have a known value, and you want to determine its position (first, second, third, etc.) in a one-dimensional list.

- Use MATCH for input verification, when an input value must exist within a list in order to be valid.

- Use MATCH to determine the exact position of a value within a list where the list may or may not be sorted.

- Use MATCH to determine where within a sorted list a given value falls (without the requirement for an exact match).

Syntax

The following options are used with MATCH:

MATCH(LookupValue,LookupRef,Type)

LookupValue The value being searched for

LookupRef The range, or array constant, being searched; the range or array must be one-dimensional (a single row or column)

Type   The type of match being performed, as listed below:

0	Search for an exact match—if match not found, returns #N/A
1	Search for the largest value that is less than or equal to the LookupValue; LookupRef must be sorted in ascending order; if all values in Ref are greater than LookupValue, returns #NA
-1	Search for the smallest value that is greater than or equal to LookupValue; LookupRef must be sorted in descending order; if all values in Ref are less than LookupValue, returns #NA

Examples: Exact Matches

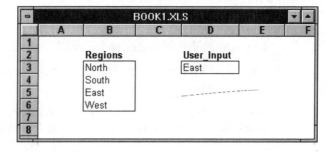

EXAMPLE 1:

=MATCH("South",B3:B6,0)

    Returns 2, because *South* is the second value within the range B3:B6

EXAMPLE 2:

=MATCH(User_Input,Regions,0)

    Returns 3, because cell User_Input is the third value within the named range Regions

EXAMPLE 3:

=MATCH("Central",Regions,0)

Returns #N/A, because *Central* is not found in the named range Regions

EXAMPLE 4:

=IF(ISNA(MATCH(User_Input,Regions,0)),"Invalid region!","")

Returns text string intended as an error message if the entry in cell User_Input is not found in the range Regions, otherwise returns null text

Examples: Match Closest Value

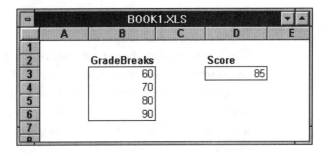

EXAMPLE 1:

=MATCH(92,B3:B6,1)

Returns 4, because the fourth value in the range is the largest value less than or equal to 92

EXAMPLE 2:

=MATCH(Score,GradeBreaks,1)

Returns 3, because the third value in the range is the largest value less than or equal to 85

EXAMPLE 3:

=MATCH(74,GradeBreaks,-1)

Returns #N/A. Since GradeBreaks is sorted in *ascending* order, this is an improper use of match type -1

Worksheet Functions

Ch. 9

▶ INDEX

The INDEX function is used to refer to a cell within a range of cells (or to an element within an array) when the position of the cell within the table is known.

- Use INDEX to refer to a cell within a range when the row and/or column is variable.
- Use INDEX in conjunction with MATCH to perform lookups.
- Use INDEX to refer into one-dimensional or two-dimensional ranges.

 ▶ ▶ **N O T E**

The Excel on-line function reference provides a thoroughly confusing treatment of this essential function. The distinction between two forms, array and reference, is confusing and inaccurate. Even in its simpler variations, INDEX is very powerful, fairly easy to use, and is a must-know function.

Syntax

The following options are used with INDEX:

INDEX(LookupRange,Coordinate1,Coordinate2,AreaNum)

LookupRange   The range or array being referred to

Coordinate1   If LookupRange is one-dimensional, specifies row or column number within range; if LookupRange is two-dimensional, specifies row number

Coordinate2   Column number within LookupRange; use this argument only when LookupRange is two-dimensional

AreaNum   LookupRange can include multiple noncontiguous areas, in which case AreaNum specifies which area number

Examples: One Dimensional Range

```
┌──────────────────────────────────────────────────┐
│ ═                    BOOK1.XLS                ▼ ▲ │
├──────────────────────────────────────────────────┤
│     A      B        C        D       E        F      G │
│  1                                                 │
│  2              Gadgets  Gizmos  Stuff   Widgets   │
│  3       North      5        2       3        4    │
│  4       South      2        1       7        6    │
│  5       East       6        9       5        8    │
│  6       West       7        4       3        9    │
│  7                                                 │
│  8                                                 │
│  9       RowNum     2                              │
│ 10       ColNum     4                              │
│ 11                                                 │
│ 12                                                 │
│ 13                                                 │
│ 14          Named Ranges                           │
│ 15       Regions   B3:B6                           │
│ 16       Products  C2:F2                           │
│ 17       Stats     C3:F6                           │
│ 18       RowNum    C9                              │
│ 19       ColNum    D9                              │
│ 20                                                 │
└──────────────────────────────────────────────────┘
```

EXAMPLE 1:

=INDEX(B3:B6,1)

Returns North, the first element of range B3:B6

EXAMPLE 2:

=INDEX(Products,RowNum)

Returns Gizmos, the second element of Products

EXAMPLE 3:

=INDEX(Regions,5)

Returns #REF!—there are only 4 cells in Regions

Examples: Two Dimensional Range

EXAMPLE 1:

=INDEX(Stats,1,3)

Returns *3*—the intersection of first row and third column of range Stats

Worksheet
Functions

Ch.
9

EXAMPLE 2:

=INDEX(Stats,RowNum,ColNum)

> Returns *6*—the intersection of second row and fourth column of range Stats

Referring to an Entire Row or Column

If zero is specified for either coordinate, the entire row or column is referred to.

EXAMPLE 1:

=SUM(INDEX(Stats,0,1))

> Returns *20*—the sum of the first column of Stats

EXAMPLE 2:

=AVERAGE(INDEX(Stats,RowNum,0))

> Returns *4*—the average of the second row of Stats

Examples: Range Consisting of Multiple Areas

On the following worksheet, the non-contiguous range C4:F7,C12:F15 is named Calls.

	A	B	C	D	E	F	G
1							
2			Service Calls - 1994				
3			Q1	Q2	Q3	Q4	
4		North	159	287	523	705	
5		South	378	777	20	219	
6		East	639	779	334	622	
7		West	928	559	977	68	
8							
9							
10			Service Calls - 1995				
11			Q1	Q2	Q3	Q4	
12		North	665	784	229	705	
13		South	192	707	947	910	
14		East	434	951	75	889	
15		West	91	178	184	99	
16							
17							
18							

BOOK1.XLS

EXAMPLE 1:

=INDEX(Calls,4,3,1)

Returns *977*—the intersection of fourth row and third column within the first area of range Stats

EXAMPLE 2:

=INDEX(Calls,4,3,2)

Returns *184*—the intersection of fourth row and third column within the second area of range Stats

 ► ► **TIP**

> **When used together, MATCH and INDEX can be used to do lookups similar to lookups performed by the VLOOKUP and HLOOKUP functions. MATCH and INDEX require more effort (two functions instead of one) but with more flexibility.**

► # EXPANDING A FORMULA TO INCLUDE INSERTED ROWS

Suppose you have values in cells A1:A5, and the formula =SUM(A1:A5) in cell A6. If you insert a row into the middle of the range A1:A5, the SUM formula automatically expands. But it is common to place new values at the bottom of the list, and when you insert at row 6, the SUM formula does *not* expand. Here's a trick to solve this problem: Use the INDEX and ROW functions to create a formula that always points to the cell immediately above the formula:

=SUM(first_cell:INDEX(column:column,ROW()-1))

The argument *first_cell* refers to the first cell in the summed range (in this example, cell A1). The argument *column:column* refers to the column being summed (in this example, A:A). In this case, the formula in cell A6 would be =SUM(A1:INDEX(A:A,ROW()-1)).

► ►

Ch.
9

▶▶ *Reference Functions*

The functions in this category are closely related to those in the Lookup category.

▶ *OFFSET*

OFFSET is arguably the single most powerful general-purpose worksheet function. It allows you to refer to one or more cells that are *offset* from a given starting point by a specified number of rows and/or columns (for example, you can refer to a cell that is two rows below and three columns right of the starting point).

Main points:

- Similar uses as the INDEX function
- Unlike INDEX, not limited to cells within a range
- Range referred to can be any height or width

Syntax

The following options are used with OFFSET:

OFFSET(AnchorRange,RowOffset,ColOffset,Height,Width)

AnchorRange   The position on the worksheet being offset from

RowOffset   Vertical offset, measured in rows, from upper left corner of AnchorRange:

- Positive number moves down
- Zero performs no vertical offset
- Negative number moves up

ColOffset   horizontal offset, measured in columns, from upper left corner of AnchorRange:

- Positive number moves right
- Zero performs no horizontal offset
- Negative number moves left

Height　The number of rows in the offset range; if omitted defaults to same number of rows in AnchorRange

Width　The number of columns in the offset range; if omitted defaults to same number of columns in AnchorRange

Examples: Referring to One Cell

	A	B	C	D	E	F	G	H	
					BOOK1.XLS				
1		DRAFT							
2		*Employees*	1990	1991	1992	1993	1994	1995	
3		**Sales**	19	23	24	31	28	35	
4		**Marketing**	4	9	16	12	16	18	
5		**Admin**	5	7	8	11	12	15	
6		**Technical**	19	31	25	34	42	49	
7		*TOTAL*	47	70	73	88	98	117	
8									
9									
10		**NoRows**	2						
11		**NoCols**	4						
12									
13									
14		*Named Ranges*							
15		Corner	B2						
16		Employees	C3:H6						
17		NoRows	C10						
18		NoCols	C11						
19									
20									

EXAMPLE 1:

=OFFSET(B2,1,3)

Returns *24*—one row down and three columns over from cell B2 (height and width default to 1—the same height and width of B2)

EXAMPLE 2:

=OFFSET(Employees,4,NoCols,1,1)

Returns *98*—four rows down and four columns over from upper left corner of range Employees

Worksheet Functions

Ch.
9

EXAMPLE 3:

=OFFSET(Corner,-1,0)

Returns *Draft*—one row up, same column as cell Corner

EXAMPLE 4:

=OFFSET(Corner,NoRows,-3)

Returns *#REF!*—there is no column three to the left of cell Corner

Examples: Referring to Range of Cells

EXAMPLE 1:

=AVERAGE(OFFSET(Employees,3,0,1,))

Returns 33.33—the average number of technical employees 1990 through 1995; refers to range offset from Employees three rows down and zero columns right, with dimensions one row high and six columns wide (defaults to six wide because last argument is omitted and Employees is six columns wide)

EXAMPLE 2:

=SUM(OFFSET(Employees,0,2,,1))

Returns *73*—the total number of employees in 1992; refers to range offset from Employees by zero rows and two columns right, with dimensions four rows high and one column wide (defaults to four high because fourth argument is omitted and Employees is four rows high)

EXAMPLE 3:

=OFFSET(Employees,3,1)

Returns #VALUE!—one cell cannot equal a range of cells; since last two arguments omitted, offset range is four rows high and six wide

▶ *INDIRECT*

The INDIRECT function allows a text string to be treated as a cell reference. You are better off if a problem can be solved *without* using INDIRECT because it is slower than other functions. But in special cases, INDIRECT provides unique, powerful functionality.

Main points:

- Used in template development when trying to achieve extraordinary modularity (see Chapter 10, "Using Templates")
- Used under the rare circumstances when a cell reference is only known in textual form

Syntax

The following options are used with INDIRECT:

    INDIRECT(Text)

Text   Text that is equal to a cell reference

Worksheet Functions

Ch.
9

Examples

□	BOOK1.XLS		▼	▲
	A	**B**	**C**	**D**
1				
2		ABC		
3				
4		B2		
5				
6		Sheet2!A1		
7				
8				
9				
10				

EXAMPLE 1:

=INDIRECT("B2")

   Returns ABC—the contents of cell B2

EXAMPLE 2:

=INDIRECT(B4)

   Returns *ABC*—since cell B4 contains "B2", this returns the contents of cell B2

EXAMPLE 3:

=INDIRECT("ABC")

   Returns #REF!—there is no cell reference ABC

EXAMPLE 4:

=INDIRECT(B6)

   Returns the value in cell Sheet2!A1—INDIRECT can refer to cells on other worksheets on the same workbook, or other workbooks

 ▶ ▶ **T I P**

In many cases, users solve problems with INDIRECT that could, and should, be solved with OFFSET and INDEX.

► *ROW and COLUMN*

The ROW function returns the row number of a given reference. The COLUMN function returns a column number. Though seemingly obscure, these functions can play a key role in your modeling strategies.

Syntax

The following options are used with ROW and COLUMN:

ROW(Reference)
COLUMN(Reference)

Reference   The cell reference or name

Examples

EXAMPLE 1:

=ROW(B3)

>   Returns *3*—the row number of cell B3

EXAMPLE 2:

=COLUMN(B3)

>   Returns *2*—the column number of cell B3

EXAMPLE 3:

=ROW(MyTable)

>   Returns the starting row number of named range MyTable

EXAMPLE 4:

=ROW()

>   When Reference omitted, row number of cell containing the formula is returned

EXAMPLE 5:

=COLUMN()

>   When *Reference* is omitted, column number of cell containing the formula is returned

▶ ROWS and COLUMNS

The ROWS function returns the number of rows in a given reference. The COLUMNS function returns the number of columns.

Syntax

The following options are used with ROWS and COLUMNS:

ROWS(Reference)
COLUMNS(Reference)

Reference   The cell reference or name

Examples

EXAMPLE 1:

=ROWS(B3:B4)

Returns 2—B3:B4 consists of 2 rows

EXAMPLE 2:

=COLUMNS(B3)

Returns *1*—B3 consists of 1 column

EXAMPLE 3:

=ROWS(MyTable)

Returns the number of rows in named range MyTable

Exercise

Whenever a range of cells is named, a question arises about whether to include a header row as part of the named range. Some functions are easier to use one way and some the other. Both ranges can be named, but if a row is inserted immediately under the header row and the named range does not include the header row, the data area will not expand. The following exercise uses the OFFSET and ROWS functions, used in a named formula, to automatically keep a named data range in sync with the data-plus-header range.

1. Enter the following onto a blank sheet:

	A	B	C	D
1				
2		Name	Dept	
3		Amy	D10	
4		Jane	D20	
5		Mark	D10	
6		Sam	D30	
7				
8				

BOOK1.XLS

2. Name the range B2:C6 Database

3. Use the Insert ➤ Name ➤ Define command to define the name Data to refer to:

   =OFFSET(Database,1,0,ROWS(Database)-1)

4. Test the name using the Edit ➤ Go To command, and type **Data** as the reference (it will not display in the list box). Cells B3:C6 should be selected.

5. Insert a row under the headings (at row 3). Go to Data again, and cells B3:C7 will be selected.

▸▸ *Counting Functions*

The various counting functions provide important generic functionality, and should be an integral part of your worksheet development strategy. They are often used as arguments in other functions, as you will see in later chapters.

▸ *COUNT (and COUNTA, COUNTBLANK)*

The COUNT function counts the numeric values found in a range of cells (or array).

Main points:

- Used to determine number of entries in a column or row
- Used as an argument to functions such as INDEX and OFFSET

Syntax

The following options are used with COUNT:

COUNT(Arg1, Arg2, etc.)

Arg1   There can be up to 30 arguments, each of which can be a constant or a range of cells

Examples

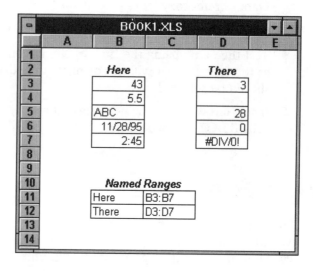

EXAMPLE 1:

=COUNT(B3:B7)

>Returns 4—every value is numeric except for ABC

EXAMPLE 2:

=COUNT(There)

>Returns 3—every cell is numeric except for blank cell and cell with error

EXAMPLE 3:

=COUNT(Here,There)

Returns 7—counts numeric values in both ranges

Notes

- The COUNTA function is identical to COUNT, except it counts nonblanks (any cell with text, number, or error value).

- The COUNTBLANK function is identical to COUNT, except it counts blank cells (and it takes only a single range as an argument). Cells that are empty and cells containing space characters or null text ("") are both considered blank.

Exercise

The following exercise uses the OFFSET and COUNTA functions in a named formula to create a dynamic named range that automatically expands based on the number of rows of data.

1. Enter the following values onto a blank sheet:

	A	B	C
1		North	
2		South	
3		East	
4		West	
5			
6			
7			
8			

BOOK1.XLS

2. Use the Insert ➤ Name ➤ Define command to define the name Regions as:

=OFFSET($B$1,0,0,COUNTA(OFFSET($B$1,0,0,9999,1)),1)

In English, *Regions* is defined to start at $B$1, and the number of rows is based on the number of values found in the first 9,999 cells of column B. (In other words, if there are five values anywhere within the first 9,999 cells of column B, Regions will contain five rows.)

3. Edit ➤ Go To Regions (the name will not appear in the list box)—if defined correctly cells B1:B4 will be selected.

4. Enter a value in cell B5.

5. Edit ➤ Go To Regions again—cells B1:B5 will be selected—the range has automatically expanded.

▶ *COUNTIF*

In previous versions of Excel, there were two ways to count conditionally:

- Array formulas—powerful but inordinately complex
- Criteria ranges combined with the DCOUNT function—again, powerful but tedious to construct

Array formulas and criteria ranges are still applicable for counts requiring multiple criteria. But COUNTIF is a far simpler solution for counts based on a single criterion.

- Use COUNT function to count numeric values (covered in this chapter).
- Use COUNTA to count non-blank cells (covered in this chapter).
- Use COUNTBLANK to count blank cells (covered in this chapter).

Syntax

The following options are used with COUNTIF.

COUNTIF(Range,Criteria)

Range The range of cells being counted

Criteria An expression specifying which cells in *Range* are to be counted

Examples

```
┌─────────────────────────────────────────┐
│  □           BOOK1.XLS          ▼ ▲      │
│      A      B      C       D      E       │
│  1                                        │
│  2                 Stuff                  │
│  3         12  Smith          0           │
│  4         20  XYZ          107           │
│  5         14           SMITH             │
│  6         37   7/4/96     235            │
│  7                                        │
│  8       Filter  <>Smith                  │
│  9                                        │
│ 10                                        │
│ 11       Named Ranges                     │
│ 12     Stuff   B3:D6                       │
│ 13     Filter  C8                          │
│ 14                                        │
│ 15                                        │
└─────────────────────────────────────────┘
```

EXAMPLE 1:

=COUNTIF(B3:B6,">30")

Returns *1*—the number of cells greater than 30

EXAMPLE 2:

=COUNTIF(Stuff,"Smith")

Returns *2*—the number of cells equal to *Smith*—notice that COUNTIF is *not* case-sensitive

EXAMPLE 3:

=COUNTIF(Stuff,Filter)

Returns *10*—the number of cells not equal to *Smith*

EXAMPLE 4:

=COUNTIF(Stuff,"<=20")

Returns *4*—the number of cells less than or equal to 20 (notice that the blank cell was not counted)

►► *Text Functions*

Excel has many powerful text-manipulation functions, most of which are very simple to learn and apply.

► *LEN*

Determines the length of a text string. (Often used as an argument in other functions.)

Syntax

The following options are used with LEN.

LEN(Text)

Text   Text string

Examples

EXAMPLE 1:

=LEN("ABCDE")

Returns 5—there are 5 characters in the text string

EXAMPLE 2:

=LEN(B2)

Returns length of text string in cell B2

EXAMPLE 3:

=IF(LEN(B2)>7,"Entry in B2 too long!","")

Displays error message if text in cell B2 is longer than 7 characters, or null text (" ") if less than or equal to 7 characters

► *LEFT (and RIGHT)*

Returns the leftmost characters of a text string.

Syntax

The following options are used with LEFT and RIGHT.

```
LEFT(Text,Chars)
RIGHT(Text,Chars)
```

Text   Text string

Chars   Number of characters—defaults to 1 if omitted

Examples

EXAMPLE 1:

=LEFT("ABCDE",3)

> Returns ABC—the left 3 characters of text string ABCDE

EXAMPLE 2:

=LEFT("ABCDE")

> Returns *A*—when Chars argument omitted it defaults to 1

EXAMPLE 3:

=LEFT("ABC",5)

> Returns *ABC*—if Chars is larger than length of *Text*, entire text string is returned

EXAMPLE 4:

=LEFT(A1,2)

> Returns the 2 left characters of text string contained in cell A1

The RIGHT function works identically to LEFT, except it returns the rightmost characters of a text string.

▶ MID

Returns characters from the middle of a text string

Syntax

The following options are used with MID.

Worksheet Functions

Ch. **9**

MID(Text,Start,Chars)

Text   Text string

Start   Starting character

Chars   Number of characters

Examples

EXAMPLE 1:

=MID("ABCDE",2,3)

   Returns BCD—three characters beginning with the second character

EXAMPLE 2:

=MID("ABCDE",1,2)

   Returns AB—two characters starting at the first character

EXAMPLE 3:

=MID("ABCDE",4,99)

   Returns DE—if Chars extends beyond length of Text, entire text string beginning with Start is returned

EXAMPLE 4:

=MID(A1,10,5)

   Returns 5 characters beginning at the tenth character of text string contained in cell A1

▶ SEARCH (and FIND)

Returns the position of one text string within another text string.

Main points:

- SEARCH is not case-sensitive
- Allows wildcard characters to be included in search text

Syntax

The following options are used with SEARCH.

SEARCH(SearchText,InText,Start)

SearchText text string being searched for—supports wildcards:

*	matches any sequence of characters
?	matches a single character

InText Text string being searched for an occurrence of SearchText

Start Character number within SearchText to begin searching at; if omitted defaults to 1

Examples

The following examples assume that cell A1 contains the text string Smith, Janet.

EXAMPLE 1:

=SEARCH("C","ABCDE")

> Returns *3*—C is the third character of ABCDE

EXAMPLE 2:

=SEARCH("Jan",A1)

> Returns *8*—Jan begins at the eighth character in cell A1

EXAMPLE 3:

=SEARCH("T",A1,8)

> Returns *12*—the twelfth character is the first occurrence of T after the eighth character

EXAMPLE 4:

=SEARCH("XYZ",A1)

> Returns #*VALUE!*—XYZ not found in cell A1

Worksheet Functions

Ch.
9

EXAMPLE 5:

=SEARCH("J?N",A1)

Returns *8*—question mark used as single-character wildcard

EXAMPLE 6:

=SEARCH("J*T",A1)

Returns *8*—asterisk used as multi-character wildcard

EXAMPLE 7:

=LEFT(A1,SEARCH(",",A1)-1)

Returns *Smith*—searches for comma and subtracts 1 in order to determine the last name

Notes

The FIND function is identical to SEARCH except:

- FIND is case-sensitive
- FIND does not allow wildcards

▶▶ *Date and Time Functions*

Working with dates and times is a common worksheet task, and Excel includes a rich set of date and time functions. First, it is important to understand how Excel works with date and time values:

- Date and time values are numbers, regardless of how the cells are formatted.
- Dates and times are stored as serial numbers—by default, Excel uses a 1900 date system in which serial numbers range from 1 to 65,380 corresponding to dates Jan 1, 1900 through Dec 31, 2078.
- In the serial number, digits to the right of the decimal point represent time of day (as a fraction of 24 hrs.); 12:00 PM is the equivalent of .5.

- The 1900 date system was employed for Lotus compatibility; a 1904 date system can be chosen (for Macintosh compatibility) using the Tools ➤ Options ➤ Calculation dialog box.
- Excel automatically formats the serial number with a date or time format. To see the serial number, format the cell as General using the Number tab on the Format Cells dialog box.

▶ TODAY

Returns the serial number of the current date. The TODAY function takes no arguments. It recalculates every time the worksheet recalculates.

Examples

EXAMPLE 1:

=TODAY()

Returns 35703 on 9/30/97

EXAMPLE 2:

=IF(DAY(TODAY())=15,"Check inventory today!","")

Displays message on the fifteenth day of the month

▶ ▶ **N O T E**

If you enter the formula =TODAY( ) into an unformatted cell, Excel will automatically format the cell using M/D/YY format. Do not confuse the formatted cell with the underlying value. This holds true for many of the date/time functions.

▶ NOW

Returns the serial number of the current date and time (unlike TO-DAY, which returns only the date). The NOW function takes no arguments. It recalculates every time the worksheet recalculates.

Worksheet Functions

▶ ▶

Ch.

9

Example

EXAMPLE 1:

=NOW()

  Returns 35703.57639 on 9/30/97 at 1:50 PM (35703 is the serial number for the date, and .57639 is for the time)

 ▸ ▶T I P

> **To freeze the date and time, use the Edit ➤ Copy and Edit ➤ Paste Special commands, then paste values.**

▶ DATE

Returns serial number of a date.

Syntax

The following options are used with DATE:

DATE(Year,Month,Day)

Year number from 1900 to 2078 (1904–2078 if 1904 date system is selected)

Month Number representing month of the year (can be greater than 12—see examples)

Day Number representing day of the month (can be greater than number of days in month specified—see examples)

Examples

EXAMPLE 1:

=DATE(97,9,15)

  Returns 35688, the serial number for 9/15/97

EXAMPLE 2:

=DATE(97,14,15)

Returns 35841, the serial number for 2/15/98 (month 14 of 1997 translates to month 2 of 1998)

EXAMPLE 3:

=DATE(97,9,35)

Returns 35708, the serial number for 10/5/97 (day 35 of September translates to day 5 of October)

EXAMPLE 4:

=DATE(A1,A2,A3)

Returns the serial number for the date defined by the year in A1, the month in A2, and the day in A3

▶ DAY

Calculates day of month (1–31) given date as serial number or text.

Syntax

The following options are used with DAY:

DAY(SerialNumber)

SerialNumber   The date as serial number or text

Examples

EXAMPLE 1:

=DAY(35688)

Returns 15—the day in 9/15/1997

EXAMPLE 2:

=DAY("9/15/97")

Returns 15

EXAMPLE 3:

=DAY("15-Sep-97")

Returns 15

Worksheet Functions

▶ ▶

Ch.
9

EXAMPLE 4:

=DAY(A2)

> Returns day of the date in cell A2

EXAMPLE 5:

=IF(OR(DAY(F2)=1,DAY(F2)=15),"Payday!","")

> Displays message if date in F2 is first or fifteenth of month

► HOUR

Converts serial number to an hour.

Syntax

The following options are used with HOUR:

HOUR(SerialNumber)

SerialNumber   The time as serial number or text

Examples

EXAMPLE 1:

=HOUR(0.75)

> Returns 18—0.75 times 24 hours equals 18 hours

EXAMPLE 2:

=HOUR("1:50 PM")

> Returns 13—the hour, using 24-hour clock, of the given time

EXAMPLE 3:

=HOUR(35688.75)

> Returns 18—the hour, using 24 hour clock, of 9/15/97, 6:00 PM

EXAMPLE 4:

=HOUR(NOW())

> Returns hour of the current time

EXAMPLE 5:

=IF(HOUR(C9)>8,"Enter reason for late arrival","")

Displays message if time in C9 is later than 8:00 am

▶ MINUTE

Converts serial numbers into minutes, displayed as an integer from 1 to 59.

Syntax

The following options are used with MINUTE:

MINUTE(SerialNumber)

SerialNumber   The time as serial number or text

Examples

EXAMPLE 1:

=MINUTE(0.3)

Returns 12—0.3 times 24 hours equals 7.2 hours, which equals 7 hours, 12 minutes

EXAMPLE 2:

=MINUTE(35688.3)

Returns 12—the minutes of 9/15/97, 7:12 AM

EXAMPLE 3:

=MINUTE("1:50:36 PM")

Returns 50—the minutes of the given time

EXAMPLE 4:

=MINUTE(B3)

Returns minutes of the time in cell B3

▶

CONVERTING TIME TO DECIMALS

Suppose you calculate the payroll for your company, and one of your jobs is to translate timesheet times into decimal format to calculate hourly wages. An easy way to accomplish that is to use the formula =(time-INT(time))*24. *Time* is the time in hours and minutes (e.g. 6:30) that you want to convert to a decimal (e.g. 6.5). As an example, enter time worked (using hour:minute format) into cell A1. In cell B1, enter the formula =(A1-INT(A1))*24. The result is shown in decimal format, and can be used to perform calculations.

▶ MONTH

Converts a serial number to a month.

Syntax

The following options are used with MONTH:

MONTH(SerialNumber)

SerialNumber   The date as serial number or text

Examples

EXAMPLE 1:

=MONTH("15-Sep")

　　Returns 9—the month number of the given date

EXAMPLE 2:

=MONTH(35688)

　　Returns 9—the month number of the given date

EXAMPLE 3:

=MONTH(B5)

Returns month number of date in cell B5

EXAMPLE 4:

=IF(MONTH(B5)=4,"Tax Time!","")

Displays message if date in B5 is in April

▶ *WEEKDAY*

Converts serial number to day of the week.

Syntax

The following options are used with WEEKDAY:

WEEKDAY(SerialNumber,ReturnType)

SerialNumber   The date as serial number or text

ReturnType   Number which determines type of return value:

1	Returns 1 through 7 representing Sunday through Saturday
2	Returns 1 through 7 representing Monday through Sunday
3	Returns 0 through 6 representing Monday through Sunday

 ▶ ▶ **N O T E**

If you omit the ReturnType argument, the result is the same as if you entered 1—i.e., it returns 1 through 7 representing Sunday through Saturday.

Examples

EXAMPLE 1:

=WEEKDAY("9/15/97")

Returns 2—date is a Monday, ReturnType omitted

Worksheet Functions

▶ ▶
Ch.
9

EXAMPLE 2:

=WEEKDAY(35687)

Returns 1—date is a Sunday, ReturnType omitted

EXAMPLE 3:

=WEEKDAY(35687,2)

Returns 7—date is a Sunday, ReturnType is 2

EXAMPLE 4:

=IF(WEEKDAY(A1,2)>5,"Entry must be weekday!","")

Displays error message if entry in A1 is not a weekday

► YEAR

Converts serial number to a year.

Syntax

The following options are used with YEAR:

YEAR(SerialNumber)

SerialNumber   The date as serial number or text

Examples

EXAMPLE 1:

=YEAR("9/15/97")

Returns 1997

EXAMPLE 2:

=YEAR(35688)

Returns 1997

EXAMPLE 3:

=IF(YEAR(A1)<>YEAR(NOW()),"Entry must be in current year.","")

Displays error message if date in A1 is not in the current year

► ► ► **CHAPTER 10**

Using Templates

▶▶ **F**AST **T**RACK

▶ *If a template named CHART.XLT is saved in the XLSTART directory* **324**

All newly created charts will be based on CHART.XLT.

▶ *To modify a template* **325**

Hold down the Shift key while opening the file. This opens the original template rather than a copy.

▶ *To validate data entry* **326**

Use IS functions (ISTEXT, ISNUMBER, etc.).

A *carpenter* uses templates as reusable guides to produce the same identical item over and over again. This simplifies tasks, saves time, and avoids mistakes. You can use workbook templates in the same way to create reusable workbooks and worksheets, thus saving time and in the following distinct areas:

- *Control the appearance of new workbooks, worksheets, and charts.*

- *Create business forms, such as purchase orders, time sheets, and expense reports.*

- *Standardize the look of your reports.*

- *Use templates as modular building blocks in the development of complex models—for instance, a template can be used to "slice and dice" data from a variety of sources without having to reinvent the wheel every time.*

▶▶ What Is a Template?

This chapter will deal with templates using two distinct definitions of the word:

"Official" Excel Definition The official definition of a template in Excel is "a special workbook you can use as a pattern to create other workbooks of the same type." What makes the workbook special is that it is saved as a *template* (rather than as a workbook).

There is a file-save option that allows you to save a workbook as a Template. Very simply, this kind of template has one special characteristic: when opened, a copy of the template (instead of the original) is placed in memory. The first part of this chapter is dedicated to explaining the simple task of creating and using such templates.

Broader Definition Generally speaking, the word *template* implies a re-usable form or model. Reusability is not limited to *official* Excel templates. Any workbook can perform a template-like function (though without the special characteristic of official templates described above). Gradually, this chapter will expand the topic of templates and explain how to create powerful reusable worksheets that can be used as building blocks in worksheet development.

▶▶ *Creating Templates*

Any workbook can easily be made into a template:

1. Create a new workbook, or open an old one.
2. Enter constants, formulas, and formatting (anything goes—a template can include charts, macros, and dialog boxes).
3. Choose the File ➤ Save As command.
4. Use the Save File as Type drop-down list to select Template.

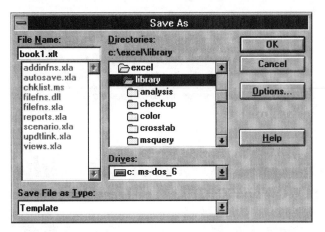

 ▶ ▶**N O T E**

> **Excel will change the file suffix from .XLS to .XLT. As with any workbook, you can override the suffix. However, the .XLT suffix serves as a visual reminder that the workbook is a template.**

▶▶ *Opening a Template*

Open a template just as you would a normal workbook. A copy of the template is opened rather than the original. This prevents users from accidentally changing the original template. Assume that you have just opened a template named REPORT:

- The workbook in memory will be an unsaved file, similar to new workbooks created with the File ➤ New command (though it will contain all of the data, formulas, and formatting from REPORT.XLT).

- The unsaved workbook will be named REPORT1.

- If you open the template again (during the same Excel session) the workbook in memory will be named REPORT2. (There can be multiple copies of the same template opened at the same time.)

- Saving REPORT1 is no different than saving any new workbook—by default, it is saved as a workbook with a .XLS suffix.

 ▶ ▶▶ **W A R N I N G**

Never link other workbooks to a template. The link breaks when copies of the template are opened (since the name of the template is different when opened). However, templates can be linked to other workbooks.

▶▶ *Making Templates Readily Available*

Templates that are placed in the XLSTART directory or the *alternate startup* directory automatically appear as options when you choose the File ➤ New command (they will appear after you restart Excel). For instance, if two templates named REPORT.XLT and INVOICE.XLT were saved in the XLSTART directory, the New dialog box would display as follows:

Selecting Report or Invoice from the list is simply a shortcut for opening the templates using the File ➤ Open command.

N O T E

The *alternate startup directory* is separate from XLSTART. You may want to specify an alternate startup directory if you want a private startup directory that is separate from your network. You can specify the alternate startup directory using the Alternate Startup File Location edit box on the Tools ➤ Options dialog, General tab.

► ► *Creating Autotemplates*

You can control the characteristics of *all* new workbooks and worksheets with special templates called *autotemplates*. An autotemplate is a template placed into the XLSTART or alternate startup directory, and which has been named using one of the special names listed in Table 10.1.

If there is a template named BOOK.XLT in XLSTART (or the alternate startup directory), the File ➤ New command will cause BOOK.XLT to be opened. If there is a template named SHEET.XLT in XLSTART, the Insert ➤ Worksheet command will cause SHEET.XLT to be inserted.

▶ **TABLE 10.1:** *Template Names*

Name	Controls
BOOK.XLT	All new workbooks
SHEET.XLT	All newly inserted worksheets
CHART.XLT	All new chart sheets
MODULE.XLT	All newly inserted VBA modules
DIALOG.XLT	All newly inserted dialog box sheets
MACRO.XLT	All newly inserted .XLM-macro sheets

▶ ▶ **N O T E**

All of the autotemplates other than BOOK.XLT control individual sheets; these templates should contain only one sheet.

The following AutoTemplate possibilities are not necessarily recommendations—they are just ideas to show what is possible with autotemplates.

New Workbooks (BOOK.XLT)

If you want all your new workbooks to open, for instance, with grey-shaded cells and no gridlines, you can accomplish it using a workbook autotemplate. Here are some more possibilities for customizing new workbooks:

- Customize the names of worksheet tabs, or hide tabs entirely
- Uncheck the Save External Link Values setting
- Change the standard colors
- Change page setup settings
- Add a company logo

New Worksheets (SHEET.XLT)

Here are some possibilities for customizing new worksheets. Remember, if you create a workbook autotemplate with special worksheet formatting, you will want to create a similar worksheet autotemplate so that inserted worksheets will match those already in the workbook.

- Hide gridlines
- Sheet formatting (fonts, borders, styles, etc.)

New Charts (CHART.XLT)

Here are a couple of possibilities for a chart autotemplate.

- Define chart type
- Chart formatting (colors, fonts, etc.)

 ► ► **T I P**

Programmers can use MODULE.XLT and/or MACRO.XLT to include basic code framework used in all modules and/or macro sheets.

► ► *Modifying a Template*

When a template is opened, a copy of the template is opened into memory. However, you may want to edit the original template. To edit the original template, follow these steps:

1. Choose the File ➤ Open command.
2. Select the template in the file list (do not open it yet).
3. Hold down Shift and click OK—the original template will be opened.
4. Modify and save.

T I P

A common mistake is to open a copy of a template when you intended to open the original template, then not notice the mistake until after changes have been made. To avoid losing changes, save the copy on top of the original—you must *explicitly* save it as a template in this circumstance.

▶▶ Using IS Functions for Data Validation

Input verification is a common requirement for templates. You can place formulas on a template (or any worksheet) to display error messages when data entry is invalid. There is a family of functions, all beginning with IS, that check the type of data that is in a certain cell. Table 10.2 lists all of the IS functions:

▶ **TABLE 10.2:** *IS Functions*

Function	Returns
ISBLANK	TRUE if value is blank
ISERR	TRUE if value is any error value except #N/A
ISERROR	TRUE if value is any error value
ISLOGICAL	TRUE if value is logical value
ISNA	TRUE if value is #N/A error value
ISNONTEXT	TRUE if value is not text
ISNUMBER	TRUE if value is number
ISREF	TRUE if value is a reference
ISTEXT	TRUE if value is text

An IS function can be used to display error messages when invalid input occurs. For example, assume that cell C3 requires the text input, as in Figure 10.1:

FIGURE 10.1 ▶

User input is required in column C.

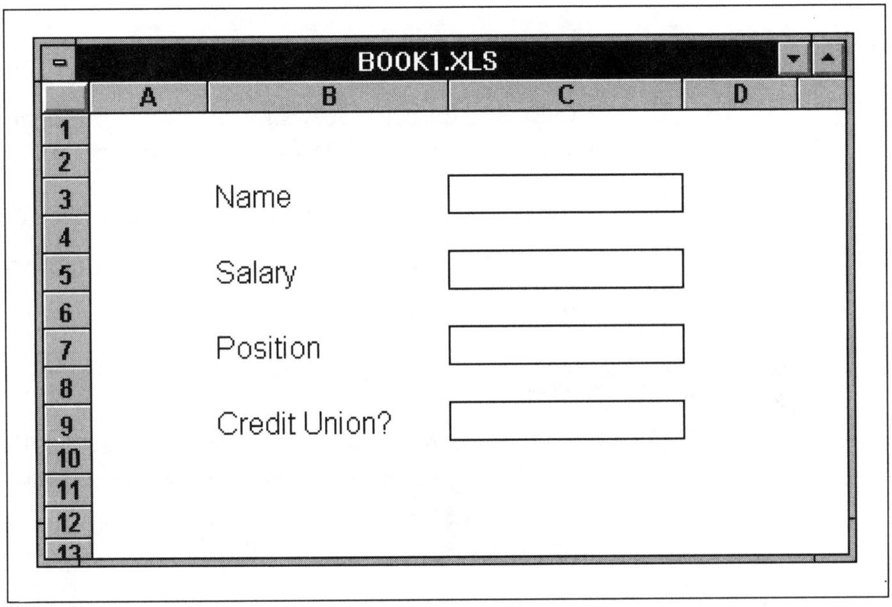

Enter the following formula in D3:

> =IF(ISTEXT(C3),"","Enter name.")

Translates to: If there is text in C3 then null text (two quotes), else message.

The following formulas are examples of various IS functions; they are used to validate data entered onto the worksheet pictured in Figure 10.1:

- The following formula displays a message if cell C5 does not contain a number:

    =IF(ISNUMBER(C5),"","Enter a salary.")

- The following formula displays a message if cell C7 contains a non-text entry:

    =IF(OR(ISBLANK(C7),ISTEXT(C7)),"","Enter position")

- The following formula displays an error message if cell C9 does not contain either "True" or "False":

=IF(ISLOGICAL(C9),"","Enter true or false")

▶▶ *Invoice Template Exercise*

The following exercise draws upon several important skills in the creation of an invoice template for a fictitious consulting firm:

- lookups into a database using the VLOOKUP function
- using the NOW function to suggest a unique invoice number
- input verification using IS functions

▶ ▶ **NOTE**

The exercise instructs you to save the file as the final step—you may actually want to save your work from time to time as you progress.

1. Create a new workbook consisting of three worksheets (see Chapter 2).

2. Name the sheets **Invoice**, **Clients**, and **Consultants**.

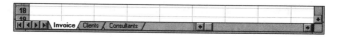

3. Enter the following information onto the Clients sheet:

	A	B	C	D	E
1	Code	Name	Address1	Address2	Address3
2	ARGUS	Argus Industries	123 Industrial Way		Seattle, WA 98023
3	BC	B&C Paper Products	456 Cedar Lane	Suite 1105	Seattle, WA 98105
4	SALTY	Salty Dog Chandlery	12 Marine Drive		Everett, WA 92654
5	TALLY	Tally-Ho Clothing, Inc.	11205 First Ave	Suite 121	Seattle, WA 98102
6	GREEN	Greentrees Nursery	521 Rose Lane		Cle Elum, WA 95642
7					
8					
9					

BOOK1.XLS

4. Name the range A2:E6 **ClientData** (see Chapter 8 to learn about naming).

5. Enter the following information onto the Consultants sheet:

	A	B	C	D
1	Code	Name	Level	
2	BG	Ben Gomez	SR	
3	ES	Ellen Smith	JR	
4	JN	John Norris	JR	
5	MW	Mary West	SR	
6				
7				
8				
9	Rate_Jr			
10	65			
11				
12	Rate_Sr			
13	95			
14				

BOOK1.XLS

6. Name the range A2:C5 **ConsultantData**.

7. Name cell A10 **Rate_Jr** and name cell A13 **Rate_Sr**. (These cells define the billing rate for junior and senior consultants).

8. Activate the Invoice sheet. Remove gridlines using Tools ➤ Options ➤ View.

9. Enter the constants, set approximate column widths, and apply cell borders as pictured below:

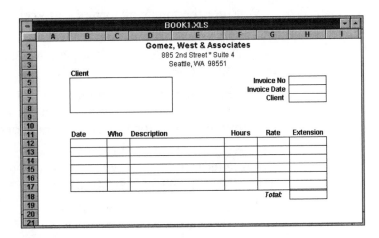

10. Name cell H7 **ClientCode**

11. Apply the following built-in number formats to the Invoice sheet:

Cell(s)	Format
B12:B17	Date—m/d/yy
F12:F17	Number—0.00
G12:G17	Number—0
H6	Date—m/d/yy
H12:H18	Number—#,##0.00

12. Enter the following formulas on the Invoice sheet:

a. Enter the following formula into cell B5—it looks up the client name based on client number entered in cell ClientCode:

=IF(ISTEXT(ClientCode),VLOOKUP(ClientCode,ClientData,2,FALSE),"")

b. Enter the following formula into cell B6—it looks up address line 1:

=IF(ISTEXT(ClientCode),VLOOKUP(ClientCode,ClientData,3,FALSE),"")

c. Enter the following formula into cell B7—it looks up address line 2:

=IF(ISTEXT(ClientCode),VLOOKUP(ClientCode,ClientData,4,FALSE),"")

d. Enter the following formula into cell B8—it looks up address line 3:

=IF(ISTEXT(ClientCode),VLOOKUP(ClientCode,ClientData,5,FALSE),"")

e. Enter the following formula into cell H4—it suggests a unique invoice number based on current date if an invoice number has not been entered and workbook is unsaved:

=IF(AND(ISBLANK(H5),CELL("filename")=""),"Suggested invoice:"&RIGHT(YEAR(NOW()),1)&TEXT(MONTH(NOW()),"00")&RIGHT(TEXT(NOW()*100.00,"#####"),3),"")

f. Enter the following formula into cell I6—it displays a prompt if there is not a valid date in H6, or if the date in H6 is more than 30 days ago, or if the date in H6 is later than the current date:

=IF(OR(ISERROR(YEAR(H6)),H6<TODAY()-30,H6>TODAY()),"Enter valid date","")

> **g.** Enter the following formula into cell I7—it displays an error message if the value in B5 is #N/A:

=IF(ISNA(B5),"Invalid Client!","")

> **h.** Enter the following formula into cell G12 (and copy it to G13:G17)—it looks up the consultant rate:

=IF(ISTEXT(C12),IF(VLOOKUP(C12,Consult-antData,3,FALSE)="SR",Rate_Sr,Rate_Jr),0)

> **i.** Enter this formula into cell H12 (copy to H13:H17)—it calculates the extension:

=F12*G12

> **j.** Enter the following formula into cell I12 (and copy it to I13:I17)—it displays an error message if the value in G12 is #N/A:

=IF(ISNA(G12),"Invalid Consultant Code!","")

> **k.** Enter this formula into cell H18—it totals the extensions:

=SUM(H12:H17)

13. Choose the Tools ➤ Options ➤ View command and uncheck the *Zero Values* setting (to suppress the display of zero values).

14. Choose the File ➤ Save command—enter file name Invoice. Use the File Save as Type drop-down to specify Template.

15. Close the template, then reopen it and test it.

▶ *Bulletproofing the Template*

Depending on how a template is used, varying levels of security measures may be required. For example, you'll probably want to prevent typos in the client code, and you will always want to prevent the user from accidentally overwriting formulas. Validation of entries may be important, to make sure the invoice contains correct information. Here are some additional features that could be added to the Invoice template to make it more bulletproof:

- Add an on-sheet list box control for entering client code (see Chapter 19).

- Unlock cells where data entry is allowed, then protect the sheet (see Chapter 11).

- Add validation to warn if entry in date or hours columns is invalid.

- The list of clients and consultants is part of the template, and thus is saved with each copy of the template. (Often, it is desirable to store such data in separate workbooks, or in an external database—see Chapter 18.)

▶▶ *Building Smart Templates*

The remainder of this chapter is dedicated to the development of templates that can be easily reused in worksheet models. The broader sense of the word *template* is now being used in that the techniques covered below are not specific to *official* templates. Essentially, the topic now becomes *how to construct modular building blocks*.

To illustrate modularity, a simple template will be constructed whose purpose is the analysis of data stored in a worksheet database. Step-by-step, features will be added that make the template applicable to a broader range of analysis situations. The business scenario is as follows:

- A computer company has two divisions: Commercial and OEM.

- Each division has three departments: Hardware, Software, and Services.

- The company sells into several regions worldwide—forecasts are tracked by division, department, and region.

- Accuracy of projections is vitally important: low forecasts result in too little inventory and lost sales; high forecasts result in overproduction.

- The purpose of the model is to compare the forecasts for any two regions.

Using Templates

Ch.
10

The template will start off simple in Exercise One, and become successively more modular in Exercises Two through Four. To fully understand the process, you will need to understand names (Chapter 8), and the VLOOKUP function (Chapter 9).

▶ Exercise One—Compare Regions within One Department

A forecast will be prepared for one department, Hardware, within the OEM division. The model will reside in one workbook containing two worksheets, which will contain:

- Hardware forecast data by region
- Formulas allowing any two regions to be compared side-by-side (think of this comparison sheet as a template)

▶ ▶ **N O T E**

The construction of this model is explained in tutorial format. It is not essential that you follow the tutorial precisely in order to understand it.

1. Create a new workbook with two worksheets; name the first sheet Hardware and name the second sheet Compare.

2. Enter the forecast database onto sheet Hardware:

BOOK1.XLS								
Region	Q1.Forecast	Q1.Actual	Q2.Forecast	Q2.Actual	Q3.Forecast	Q3.Actual	Q4.Forecast	Q4.Actual
USA	550	129	367	190	769	885	13	635
Canada	341	946	974	436	911	553	169	102
Mexico	832	538	229	320	994	303	441	365
Latin America	727	655	359	529	173	689	391	975
Western Europe	646	307	455	891	117	471	820	141
Eastern Europe	917	119	758	699	61	438	340	409
Far East	690	456	540	371	579	290	728	730

▶ ▶ **T I P**

Here is a shortcut for quickly entering random integers: select cells C3:J9, enter the formula =INT(RAND( )*1000), and press Ctrl+Enter. Replace the formulas with values using Edit ➤ Copy followed by Edit ➤ Paste Special, then choose Values.

3. Name cells B3:J9 Hardware.

▶ ▶ **T I P**

A meaningful naming strategy is a critical component in worksheet development.

4. Build the comparison sheet, which is intended to compare any two rows of the forecast data. Enter the following constants and formatting onto sheet Compare:

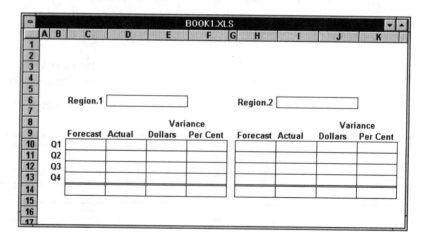

5. Name cell D6 Region.1—the first region being compared will be entered into this cell.

6. Name cell I6 Region.2—the second region being compared will be entered into this cell.

7. Enter the following formulas:

Cell(s)	Formula
C10	=VLOOKUP(Region.1,Hardware,2,FALSE)
C11	=VLOOKUP(Region.1,Hardware,4,FALSE)
C12	=VLOOKUP(Region.1,Hardware,6,FALSE)
C13	=VLOOKUP(Region.1,Hardware,8,FALSE)
D10	=VLOOKUP(Region.1,Hardware,3,FALSE)
D11	=VLOOKUP(Region.1,Hardware,5,FALSE)
D12	=VLOOKUP(Region.1,Hardware,7,FALSE)
D13	=VLOOKUP(Region.1,Hardware,9,FALSE)
E10	=D10-C10
E11	=D11-C11
E12	=D12-C12
E13	=D13-C13
F10	=E10/D10
F11	=E11/D11
F12	=E12/D12
F13	=E13/D13
C14	=SUM(C10:C13)
D14	=SUM(D10:D13)
E14	=SUM(E10:E13)
F14	=E14/D14

8. Copy the Region.1 formulas to Region.2 section:

- Copy cells C10:F14, and paste at cell H10.
- Select cells H10:I13—replace every occurrence of Region.1 with Region.2.

9. Enter valid regions into cells D6 and I6; if the model was constructed correctly, data for the two regions will display on the Compare sheet.

10. Save the workbook as **OEM.XLS**.

▶ *Exercise Two—Multiple Departments within the Workbook*

So far, the compare template is not very modular. The comparison formulas are hard-wired to the *hardware* forecast database. (The only flexibility is the ability to choose which regions are being compared.) In Exercise Two, *software* and *services* databases will be added to the workbook, and the comparison template will be changed to work with any of the three databases.

1. Create two new department sheets:

- Insert two new worksheets—name one Software and one Services.
- Enter forecast data on the two new sheets (copy range B2:J9 from the Hardware sheet, then change the data).
- On the Software sheet, name B3:J9 Software.
- On the Services sheet, name B3:J9 Services.

2. Add Department to Compare sheet:

- Enter **Department** into cell H4.
- Name cell I4 Department—this cell will determine which forecast database the Compare sheet will refer to.

3. Define the name Forecast to refer to:

=IF(Department="Hardware",Hardware,IF(Department="Software",Software,Services))

 ▶ ▶NOTE

This named formula refers to the one of the three forecast databases based on the contents of cell Department.

4. On Compare sheet, use the Edit ➤ Replace command to change every occurrence of Hardware to Forecast.

To use the template, enter a valid department into I4 and valid regions into D6 and I6.

▶ *Exercise Three—Allow Analysis of More than One Division*

The *compare* template has now achieved a level of modularity—it is able to analyze data in one of three departments *within the OEM division*. In Exercise Three, the compare template will be placed in a stand-alone workbook so that it can work with the forecast for the OEM *and* Commercial divisions which reside in two different workbooks. The benefits to this architecture are:

- Since the divisional forecasts will reside in different workbooks, each division can work on its respective forecast concurrently.

- Since the comparison template will reside in its own workbook, any changes to the design of the template need only be made in place.

- The template can be easily used for new divisions in the future.

In addition, the template logic will be expanded to allow comparisons across departments (so that, for example, OEM/Hardware/Europe can be compared with OEM/Software/Europe).

▶ ▶ N O T E

In this data model, with only two divisions, the *compare* template could easily live inside both divisional workbooks. But picture a situation where there are dozens of divisions—a single compare template saves a huge amount of time in development and maintenance.

1. Create a new workbook—move the Compare sheet from OEM.XLS to the new workbook (see Chapter 2—and save the new workbook as a template named COMPARE.XLT.)

▶ ▶**T I P**

> A shortcut for this task is to simply drag the Compare sheet and drop it outside of OEM.XLS, but not onto a different workbook. A new workbook is created automatically. Save OEM.XLS after dragging the Compare sheet out.

2. Create a workbook for the commercial division (save OEM.XLS as COM.XLS—change some numbers so that you will notice differences on the compare template).

3. Open OEM.XLS—all three workbooks (OEM.XLS, COM.XLS, and COMPARE.XLT) should now be open.

4. On COMPARE.XLT, enter the constants listed below:

Cell	Entry
C4	Dept.1
H4	Dept.2

5. Name the following cells:

Cell	Name
D4	Dept.1
I4	Dept.2

6. On COMPARE.XLT, activate Compare sheet and define the following names:

Name	Refers To
Hardware	=OEM.XLS!Hardware
Software	=OEM.XLS!Software
Services	=OEM.XLS!Services
Forecast.1	=IF(Dept.1="Hardware",Hardware,IF(Dept.1="Software",Software,Services))
Forecast.2	=IF(Dept.2="Hardware",Hardware,IF(Dept.2="Software",Software,Services))

7. On COMPARE.XLT, select cells C10:D13 and replace every occurrence of *Forecast* with *Forecast.1*

8. On COMPARE.XLT, select cells H10:I13 and replace every occurrence of *Forecast* with *Forecast.2*

Using the Template

Here is how to use the Compare template at the end of Exercise Three:

- Use the Edit ➤ Links command to point the template to the desired workbook (OEM.XLS or COM.XLS)—choose the Change Source button, then select the workbook from the displayed list.

- Enter valid departments into cells D4 and I4.

- Enter valid regions into cells D6 and I6.

- Workbooks containing source data do not have to be open— VLOOKUP works with closed workbooks.

▶ *Exercise Four—Allow Comparisons across Divisions*

So far, the template is able to make comparisons *within* one division. One more twist will be added that allows the template to make comparisons *across* divisions (for example, OEM/Software/Europe versus Commercial/Software/Europe).

1. All three workbooks (OEM.XLS, COM.XLS, and COMPARE.XLT) should be open.

2. Enter the following constants onto COMPARE.XLT:

Cell	Entry
C2	Div.1
H2	Div.2

3. Name cell D2 as **Div.1**—name cell I2 as **Div.2**.

4. Insert a new worksheet into COMPARE.XLT and name it Divisions.

5. Add the following to the Divisions sheet, then name cells B3:C4 DivisionList. (The purpose of this table is to maintain a cross-reference between "friendly" descriptions of the divisions and the corresponding workbook names.)

	A	B	C	D	E	F	G
1							
2		DivisionList					
3		Commercial	COM.XLS				
4		OEM	OEM.XLS				
5							
6							
7							
8							
9							

BOOK2.XLS

6. On COMPARE.XLT, activate the Compare sheet and define the following names:

Name	Refers To
Forecast.1	=INDIRECT(VLOOKUP(Div.1, DivisionList,2,TRUE)&"!"&Dept.1)
Forecast.2	=INDIRECT(VLOOKUP(Div.2, DivisionList,2,TRUE)&"!"&Dept.2)

Using the Template

Here is how to use the Compare template at the end of Exercise Four:

- Enter either OEM or Commercial into cells D2 and I2.

- Enter valid departments into cells D4 and I4.

- Enter valid regions into cells D6 and I6.

- Workbooks containing source data must be open. (The INDIRECT function cannot be used to access closed workbooks. The Compare template will display #REF! errors if opened before the precedent worksheets.)

► ► **CHAPTER 11**

Auditing
and Protecting
Your Work

►► *F*AST *T*RACK

▶ ▶ ***T*wo** of the biggest problems endemic to worksheet applications are security and maintainability. The most clever models are rendered useless if users are able to easily break them. Similarly, complex models that are difficult to support or modify will eventually collapse under their own weight. This chapter will provide you with the relatively simple security and auditing skills:

- *Prevent users from accidentally breaking worksheets by changing formulas and data that are not intended to be changed.*

- *Prevent users from accessing sensitive data and formulas.*

- *Allow workbooks to be effectively shared in a multi-user environment.*

- *Avoid the "spaghetti code" syndrome by documenting your work.*

- *Avoid getting lost when there are several levels of cell dependencies by learning to trace logic flow.*

- *Categorize files with file information settings.*

- *Search for files based on simple or advanced search criteria.*

▶ ▶ *File-Level Security*

There are several levels of protection that can be applied to a workbook. The topmost level of protection is set on the file level. When a workbook is first saved, and any time you choose the File ➤ Save As command, the Save As dialog box is displayed.

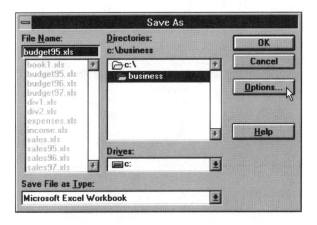

Click the Options button to display the Save Options dialog box (Figure 11.1)—this is where file-level security options are set.

FIGURE 11.1 ▶

Save Options

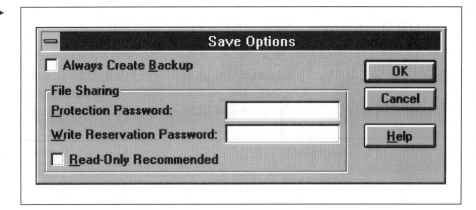

▶ *Requiring a Password to Open a Workbook*

The *protection password* entered in the Save Options dialog box (see Figure 11.1) requires that a password be entered in order to open or access the workbook. In general, this password is used on workbooks requiring the highest possible level of security.

- The password can be up to 15 characters, can include special characters, and is case-sensitive.

- You will be prompted for the password when you try to open the workbook.

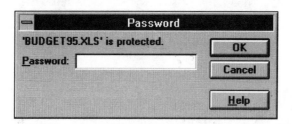

- You will be prompted for the password if the formula is entered into a different workbook that refers to cell(s) on the password-protected workbook (and the protected workbook is closed).

- If you forget the password, there is virtually nothing you can do to recover the workbook—and you will not get assistance from Microsoft technical support.

 ► ►**N O T E**

Macros are able to specify a password when opening a password-protected workbook in order to avoid the password prompt. While this requires that the password be embedded in a module (or macro sheet), the module itself can be protected.

▶ *Requiring a Password to Save a Workbook*

The *write-reservation password* entered in the Save Options dialog box (see Figure 11.1) requires that a password be entered in order to *save* the workbook. This allows users to open, view, and manipulate the workbook, but not save it without knowing the password. As with the protection password, the write-reservation password can be up to 15 characters long and is case-sensitive.

► ►W A R N I N G

Scrutiny of the write-reservation password reveals a critical shortcoming you should be aware of: application-managed file-level security is only as good as the underlying file system. You can open a file with a write-reservation password, change it, save it to a different name, and close it. Then copy the new file to the old file using File Manager or at the DOS prompt. Only security provided by the operating system can thwart this procedure.

► *Removing Protection and Write-Reservation Passwords*

Follow this procedure to remove a protection password or write-reservation password:

1. Open the workbook.

2. Choose the File ➤ Save As command, then click the Options button.

3. Clear the password(s)—asterisks will appear when there is a password.

4. Click OK to close the Save Options dialog box, then click OK to save the file.

5. Answer Yes when the following dialog box is displayed:

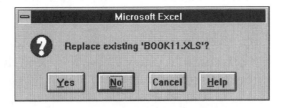

► *Read-Only Recommended*

The Read-Only Recommended setting in the Save Options dialog box (see Figure 11.1) causes Excel to display the dialog box on the next page when the file is opened.

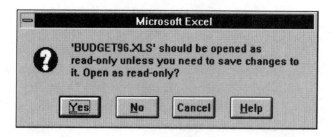

Click Yes to open the file read-only—. The text [Read Only] displays next to the file name on the title bar. If you Click No, the file is opened with full write privileges. The Read-Only Recommended setting is a handy solution for two scenarios:

- A workbook is used by more than one person; users should generally open it read-only in case somebody else needs to change it.

- Users are prevented from accidentally changing a workbook that is not supposed to be changed on a day-to-day basis, yet periodically requires maintenance.

▶ *Always Create Backup*

When checked, the Always Create Backup setting in the Save Options dialog box (see Figure 11.1) causes Excel to create a backup of the file every time it is saved. The backup file is saved with a .BAK extension in the same directory as the original file. Open the backup file if:

- The original file becomes corrupted.

- You make mistakes, and do not realize it until *after* you have saved the file.

Since files with a .BAK extension are not displayed in the File ➤ Open dialog box by default, you will have to type in the file name or else change the filter. (See Chapter 2.)

▶ ▶**W A R N I N G**

Automatic backups are saved with a .BAK extension. If you have files named FINANCE.XLS and FINANCE.XLT in the same directory, and both files are set to create backups, both backups will be saved as FINANCE.BAK and thus step on one another.

▶ *Any File Can Be Opened Read-Only*

Even when a write-reservation password is not defined, and Read-Only Recommended is not set, you can still open files read-only. Check the Read-Only setting in the lower right corner of the File ➤ Open dialog box. [Read-Only] will display next to the file name on the title bar.

▶ ▶ *Protection inside the Workbook*

The remainder of the security options serve to restrict what a user can do *after* the workbook has been opened. Essentially, there are three levels of security:

- Workbook level
- Worksheet level
- Object level (cells and graphical objects)

▶ *Workbook Protection*

Choose the Tools ➤ Protection ➤ Protect Workbook command to display the Protect Workbook dialog box:

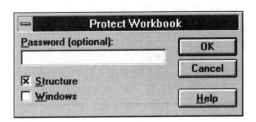

Protecting Your Work

▶ ▶
Ch.
11

Password	Optional password up to 255 characters; it can include special characters and is case-sensitive.
Structure	If checked, prevents changes to worksheet structure; you are prevented from deleting, inserting, renaming, copying, moving, hiding, or unhiding sheets.
Windows	If checked, prevents changes to workbook's window; the window control button becomes hidden and most windows functions (move, size, restore, minimize, maximize, new, close, split, and freeze panes) are disabled.

Since a protected structure prevents users from inserting new sheets, there are several unexpected side effects that you should be aware of. When a structure is protected you are unable to:

- Add a new chart sheet with ChartWizard

- Record a macro onto a new module or macro sheet

- Use the scenario manager to create a new report

- Display source data for a cell in a pivot table

To unprotect a workbook, choose the Tools ➤ Protection ➤ Unprotect Workbook command. You will be prompted for the password if one was specified when the workbook was protected.

▶ *Worksheet Protection*

Use worksheet protection to prevent users from changing the contents of a sheet. Choose the Tools ➤ Protection ➤ Protect Sheet command to display the Protect Sheet dialog box:

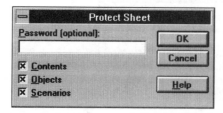

Password	Optional password up to 255 characters; it can include special characters and is case-sensitive.
Contents	Protects worksheet cells and chart items.
Objects	Protects graphic objects on worksheets (including charts).
Scenarios	Prevents changes to scenario definitions.

To unprotect a worksheet, choose the Tools ➤ Protection ➤ Unprotect Sheet command.

You will be prompted for the password if one was specified when the worksheet was protected.

Another way to discourage users from changing cells is by hiding all or part of the sheet:

Hiding an Entire Sheet Choose the Format ➤ Sheet ➤ Hide command to hide a worksheet.. To unhide a worksheet, choose the Format ➤ Sheet ➤ Unhide command. Remember, you can't hide or unhide worksheets if the *workbook* structure is protected. So, to achieve the highest level of security, hide sheets first, then protect the workbook structure. (You will have to unprotect the workbook before you can unhide the sheets.)

Hiding Rows Select the rows you want to hide, then choose the Format ➤ Row ➤ Hide command.

Hiding Columns Select the columns you want to hide, then choose the Format ➤ Column ➤ Hide command.

You can make it difficult for a user to unhide hidden rows and columns by protecting the worksheet, using the Tools ➤ Protection ➤ Protect Sheet command.

▶ **T I P**

> **How do you unhide hidden rows or columns when you are unable to select them? To unhide a hidden row or column, select a contiguous range of cells that includes the hidden row or column, then choose the Format ➤ Row ➤ Unhide command, or the Format ➤ Column ➤ Unhide command. Alternately, use the name box to select a hidden cell, then unhide the row or column.**

▶ Cell Protection

Choose the Format ➤ Cells command, then select the Protection tab.

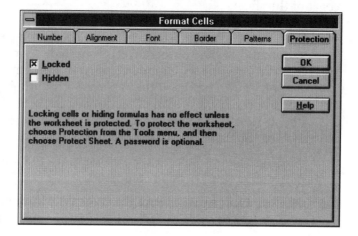

Locked	Cells can't be changed after sheet is protected.
Hidden	Hides formulas after sheet is protected.

Three simple facts can save you considerable confusion and frustration when working with cell protection:

- Inexplicably, Excel places the settings on the *format* dialog box—it is easy to forget this fact.

- Cell protection does not take effect unless the worksheet is protected with Contents checked (think of sheet protection as a master breaker switch, and cell protection as a single outlet on the breaker).

- By default, each cell is individually set with Locked checked—you must individually unlock each cell that users will be allowed to change before you protect the worksheet.

►►TIP

You can navigate between unlocked cells on a protected worksheet using the Tab key.

► *Object Protection*

If objects placed on a worksheet are not protected, users are able to move, resize, or even delete them. To protect an object:

1. Select the object.

2. Choose the Format ➤ Object command, then select the Protection tab.

3. Lock the object and/or object text.

Object locking works like cell protection; by default, objects are set with Locked on (checked), and only need to be unlocked if you want specific objects unprotected on an otherwise protected sheet.

Keep these facts in mind when protecting objects:

- All objects have a protection setting called *Locked*; when checked, the object cannot be deleted, resized, moved, or formatted. (If the worksheet is protected, that is. Remember, there's a two-tier structure.)

- Text boxes, buttons, and several controls have an additional setting called Lock Text; when checked, the text cannot be changed.

- Object protection does not take effect unless the worksheet is protected with Objects checked (think of sheet protection as a master breaker switch, and object protection as a single outlet on the breaker).

- By default, *all* objects are locked.

See Chapter 12 to learn about working with graphical objects on worksheets.

▶▶ *Documenting Your Work*

When you create worksheets and workbooks that work together to automate a function, as you did in Chapter 10, you have developed a "spreadsheet application". A spreadsheet application can be simple, like the Invoice template in Chapter 10, or it can be huge and extremely complex. In any case, documentation of the formulas and code running the application is important, both for verification of the application's results and for future modifications.

Spreadsheet applications have a notorious reputation for "spaghetti code" (formulas and macro codes which are disorganized and difficult to follow) and the blame falls directly on the shoulders of the people who build them. When spreadsheets were used solely for personal productivity, at least others weren't bearing the brunt of developers' bad habits. But spreadsheet programs have become popular tools used to create organizational solutions. Thorough documentation (e.g., cell notes that explain why a particular formula was used, where supporting information came from, etc.) is vitally important—particularly in complex models.

 ▶ ▶ **T I P**

> **Though it may be a practice that defies human nature, you are a lot better off if you document as you work. The formulas and logic are fresh in your mind, and a tedious task is not left for the end.**

There are three primary items used for documenting a worksheet model:

- Cell notes
- Text boxes and arrows
- Meaningful naming conventions (see Chapter 8)

LISTING ALL THE NAMES IN A WORKSHEET

If you use names extensively, it doesn't take long before a workbook can contain hundreds of names. Whether you are documenting your work or troubleshooting a problem, having a complete list of the names in a worksheet is very helpful. To create a list of all the names in a worksheet:

1. Select a cell in an empty area of the worksheet, so that the pasted list will not overwrite other data. The list will be pasted into two columns, beginning with the active cell.

2. Choose Insert ➤ Name ➤ Paste.

3. Click the Paste List button on the Paste Name dialog.

The pasted list will contain all the global names in the workbook, and local names only for the active worksheet. To compile a list including all the local names in the workbook, you must repeat this process for each worksheet in the book that contains local names. (See Chapter 8, "The Power of Names," to learn more about global and local names.)

▶▶ *Cell Notes*

 Cell notes are an outstanding facility for documenting formulas, assumptions, and results. Select a cell, then choose the Insert ➤ Note command to display the Cell Note dialog box:

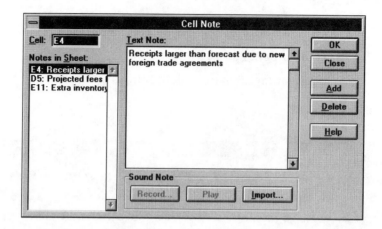

The dialog controls include:

Cell	Indicates which cell note is being edited.
Text Note	There is no limit to the length of a note other than available memory; words automatically wrap; press Enter to start a new line. To copy the displayed note to another cell, type a new reference in the Cell edit box and click the Enter button.
Notes in Sheet	Lists all the worksheet's cells that have notes, and the first few characters of each note; click to edit the note.
Sound Note	Facility for annotating a cell with sound; requires special hardware and software.

  **N O T E**

Before you start trying to liven up your worksheet with sound, remember that 30 seconds of speech can consume a couple of megabytes of disk storage!

Add	Adds the note, and leaves the dialog box displayed to edit other notes.
Delete	Deletes current note. You are given a warning "Note will be permanently deleted." This means that this action can not be reversed using the Edit ➤ Undo command.
·OK	Adds the note and closes the dialog box.

▶ *Viewing Notes*

Cells with notes are indicated with a small red dot in the upper right corner of the cell. (Note indicators can be turned on and off using the Note Indicator setting on the Tools ➤ Options ➤ View dialog box.) Select a cell with a note, then use one of the following procedures:

- Click the Note tool on the Auditing toolbar.
- Choose the Insert ➤ Note command.
- If in-cell editing is turned off, double-click the cell.

 ▶ ▶**T I P**

The Edit ➤ Find command can be used to search cell notes for a given text string. The Notes option can be found in the Look In dropdown of the Find dialog box.

▶ *Printing Notes*

When a worksheet is printed using the normal procedures, cell notes are not included in the printout. Follow this procedure to print cell notes:

1. Choose the File ➤ Page Setup command, then select the Sheet tab.

2. Check the Row and Column Headings setting to print the cell references before each note.

3. Check the Notes setting, then print.

▶ Clear Notes for Memory Efficiency

Sometimes cell notes are intended for the user of a worksheet to learn more about certain formulas or assumptions. Other times, notes are used by the developer and are *not* intended for users. In the latter case, you may want to clear the notes (for memory efficiency) before deploying the workbook:

1. Save a copy of the workbook *with* notes for future reference.
2. Select all cells on the sheet (use the Select All button, located at the top left intersection of the row and column headings).
3. Choose the Edit ➤ Clear ➤ Notes command.

▶ ADDING SOUND NOTES

In addition to text notes, you can add sound notes to cells. If your computer is equipped for sound, the sound will play when the Insert ➤ Note command is selected for an annotated cell. Cells with sound notes are identified with an asterisk in the Notes in Sheet list in the Cell Note dialog. You can add imported sound notes, or record your own.

To add an imported sound note to a cell, choose the Insert ➤ Note command and click the Import button. Browse for the sound file in the Import Sound dialog, and when you find a sound note file you want to use, click Import. Click the Add button to add more sound (or text) cell notes, or click OK to close the dialog.

You can record your own sound notes if your computer is set up to record. To record a sound note, select the cell you want to annotate with a sound note. Choose Insert ➤ Note and click the Record button. In the Record dialog, click the Record button to begin recording. Click the Stop button when you finish recording. You can click the Pause button to pause while recording, and click the Pause button again to resume recording. Click the Play button to play back the new recording. Keep in mind that although sound is fun, even short sound notes use up a significant amount of disk space.

▶▶ *Documenting with Text Boxes*

Sometimes it is desirable for notes to boldly stand out. Text boxes, combined with other on-sheet graphical objects, can add important information to a report, with style.

		BUDGET95.XLS					
A	B	C	D	E	F	G	H

1995 Budget

			Forecast	Actual		Receipts larger than forecast due to new foreign trade agreements
Receipts	Sales	130,000	170,000		
	Fees	8,000	7,500		
		138,000	177,500		
Expenses	Lease	50,000	50,000		
	Utilities	3,000	3,500		
	Payroll	45,000	45,000		
	Inventory	20,000	25,000		
	Equipment	10,000	8,726		
	Supplies	1,200	798		
		129,200	133,024		
Net Income		8,800	44,476		

See Chapter 12 to learn more about text boxes and other graphical objects.

▶▶ *Auditing Worksheets*

One of the most tedious tasks is troubleshooting complex worksheets. Excel 5 has added some powerful new features designed to simplify the process.

Protecting
Your Work

▶ ▶

Ch.
11

► *Dependent and Precedent Cells*

Assume that cell B1 has the formula =A1.

- B1 is the *dependent* cell; it depends on A1.
- A1 is the *precedent* cell; it precedes B1.

On complex worksheets, there can be many levels of dependency, which makes it difficult to trace the flow of dependencies. The auditing commands provide a graphical representation of cell relationships (see Figure 11.2).

FIGURE 11.2 ►

Tracer arrows

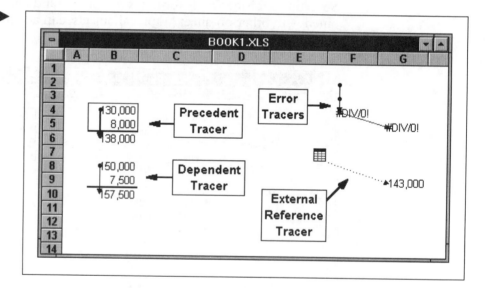

Tracing Precedents	Select a dependent cell, then choose the Tools ➤ Auditing ➤ Trace Precedents command; arrows are displayed pointing from precedent to dependent cells.
Tracing Dependents	Select a source cell, then choose Tools ➤ Auditing ➤ Trace Dependents; arrows are displayed pointing from precedent to dependent cells.

Tracing Errors

Select a cell containing an error value, then choose the Tools ➤ Auditing ➤ Trace Error command. Arrows are drawn from the error value in the active cell to the cells that might have caused the error.

Removing Arrows

Choose the Tools ➤ Auditing ➤ Remove All Arrows command; all arrows on the worksheet are removed.

There are three types of tracer arrows:

- **Formula** tracers are solid blue arrows (solid black on black-and-white monitors).

- **Error** tracers are solid red arrows (short black dashes on black-and-white monitors) from precedent formulas, solid blue arrows from precedent values.

- **External reference** tracers are dashed black lines with a worksheet icon (long black dashes with an icon on black-and-white monitors).

  TIP

> You can quickly locate cells containing links to other worksheets, workbooks, and applications by searching for an exclamation point (!). Choose Edit ➤ Find, and type ! in the Find What edit. Select Look In Formulas, and clear the Find Entire Cells Only checkbox.

Protecting Your Work

▶ ▶

Ch. **11**

TROUBLESHOOTING A LINK

When you move or copy a worksheet from one workbook to another, you may create unintended links in the new workbook. You may not notice the links until you open the new workbook and see the alert message "This document contains links. Re-establish links?" Sometimes links can be difficult to trace and eliminate.

▶

Here are some steps you can follow to find the cause of a link:

1. Choose Edit ➤ Links. The Links dialog lists all workbooks that the active workbook is linked to, and lets you change the links.

2. Names can point to ranges on other workbooks, which in turn create a link that is hard to find. Use the Insert ➤ Name ➤ Paste command, then click Paste List. It is easy to see external references in the list.

3. Display the formulas on each worksheet by pressing Ctrl+` (grave accent), then scan the formulas for external references. Press Ctrl+` again to display values on the worksheet.

4. If a chart in your workbook is created from data in another workbook, a link is created. These links are hard to isolate because you must examine each chart individually. Select the chart, and click the ChartWizard tool. The step 1 dialog will be displayed—check for external references in the *Range* edit. If the chart plots data from more than one worksheet, activate the chart and check the data source for each series (double-click the series, then select the Name and Values tab to see the data source).

5. Did you use the Data ➤ Get External Data command to perform a query, and check the Keep Query Definition setting? If yes, a link is automatically created, in a hidden name, to the MSQUERY.XLA add-in. If the link is caused by a query, select a cell within the data range. Choose Data ➤ Get External Data, then clear the Keep Query Definition checkbox to remove the query from the worksheet. (The data will remain on the worksheet.)

There are several ways to eliminate links once you've found them:

1. If the links are caused by references in formulas, you can replace the formulas with values. Select the cells containing linked formulas, choose Edit ➤ Copy, then choose Edit ➤ Paste Special and check Values.

2. If the links are in formulas and you want to keep the formulas, replace the external references with references in the current workbook. Use the Edit ➤ Replace command to speed up the process of replacing references.

3. If the links are in names, either redefine or delete the names.

4. If the link is in a chart, re-define the data source(s) for the chart.

▶ Selecting Special Cells

Choose the Edit ➤ Go To command, then click the Special button to display the Go To Special dialog box pictured below.

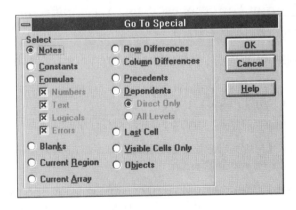

Make selections using the radio and checkbox controls as described:

Notes   All cells containing notes

Constants   All cells containing constant values

Formulas   All cells containing formulas; you can then narrow the selection by choosing only certain types of data returned by the formulas. You can:

- Select formulas that return numbers.
- Select formulas that return text.
- Select formulas that return logical values (TRUE and FALSE).
- Select formulas that return error values.

Blanks   All blank cells

Current Region   A rectangular range of data (the active cell must be within the data before choosing the command)

Current Array   The entire array that the active cell resides in (if it is part of an array)

Row Differences   Cells in the same row as the active cell, whose contents are different from the active cell

Column Differences   Same as row differences, but in columns

Precedents   Cells referred to by the formula in the active cell

Dependents   Cells whose formulas refer to the active cell

- **Direct Only** selects only cells with direct references.
- **All Levels** selects cells with both direct and indirect references (the entire network of related cells).

Last Cell   The last cell in the worksheet (or macro sheet) containing data or formatting

Visible Cells Only   Only visible cells on the worksheet (so changes will not affect hidden rows or columns)

Objects   All graphical objects (including chart objects)

Once the desired cells are selected, use the Tab key to cycle through them. If a range of cells is selected prior to choosing the Edit ➤ Go To command, only cells within the selected range will be searched.

Here are some shortcut keys for selecting special cells.

Keystroke	Selects
Ctrl +[	Direct precedents
Ctrl+Shift+{	All precedents
Ctrl+]	Direct dependents
Ctrl+Shift+}	All dependents
Ctrl+Shift+*	Current region
Ctrl+/	Entire array
Ctrl+End	Last cell in worksheet

 ▶ ▶**T I P**

> **Use the Edit ➤ Find command, covered in Chapter 3, to search for specific values or formulas. You can search cell values, formulas, or cell notes.**

▶ *Learn Everything about a Cell at Once*

The Info Window displays (almost) everything there is to know about the active cell:

1. Choose the Tools ➤ Options command, select the View tab, then check the Info Window setting to display the Info Window.

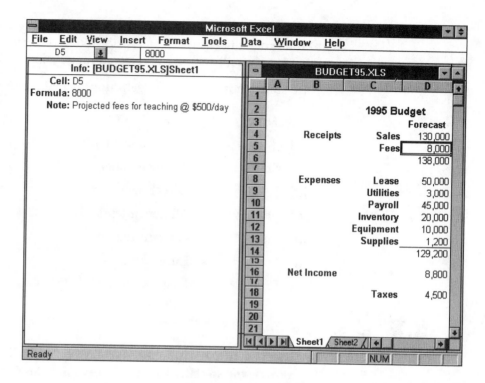

2. Use the Info menu (which only displays when the Info Window is active) to specify what information to include in the Info Window.

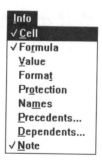

PRINTING FORMULAS

You might want to document the formulas in your worksheet by printing them. There are two ways to create a printout of the formulas in your worksheet: print the worksheet with formulas displayed instead of values, or use the Info Window.

To print the worksheet with formulas displayed, switch the worksheet to formula display mode by pressing Ctrl+` (grave accent). Long formulas will be truncated, but you can resize each column to display entire formulas by double-clicking the right border of the column header. Print the worksheet, or a selected part of the worksheet, using the File ➤ Print command. The advantage of this method is that formulas are displayed in position on the worksheet; the disadvantage is that the printout can be very long if there are lots of long formulas.

To print a listing of formulas using the Info Window, select the cells whose formulas you want to print (hold down Ctrl to select non-contiguous cells). Display the Info Window by clicking the Show Info Window tool on the Auditing toolbar (or choose Tools ➤ Options, the View tab, and check the Info Window checkbox). From the Info Window menu bar, choose Info ➤ Formula. (If the Formula command is checked, formulas are already selected for display—choosing the command will hide the Formula information.) With the Info Window still displayed, choose File ➤ Print. The advantage of this method is that a concise listing of cell information is printed; the disadvantage is that the row/column perspective of the worksheet is lost.

►► *Searching for Files*

Searching for files and categorizing files using *summary information* are important skills to help you organize your work.

► *Searching Based on the File Name*

Suppose you have saved budget data for each year in workbooks beginning with "BUDGET," such as BUDGET94.XLS and BUDGET95.XLS. You now want to view the files, but don't remember what directory they were saved in. This procedure will locate the files for you:

1. Choose the File ➤ Find File command (or click the Find File tool on the WorkGroup toolbar).

► ►**N O T E**

The very first time the File ➤ Find File command is chosen after Excel is installed, the Search dialog box will be displayed. After that, the File ➤ Find File command will display the Find File dialog box, which will list the files found in the last search.

2. Click the Search button to display the Search dialog box (see Figure 11.3).

3. Enter these search parameters in the Search dialog box:

- In File Name, enter the file name, with optional wildcards—for example, enter **budget*.xls** to search for every file beginning with "BUDGET" and ending with ".XLS" (see Table 11.1 for a list of supported wildcard characters).

- In Location, select a directory—use the drop-down list to specify the drive, then type a directory if desired.

- To search all subdirectories of the *Location*, check Include Subdirectories.

4. Click OK—The Find File dialog box is displayed again, with the results of the search displayed in the Listed Files window (see Figure 11.4).

To display a preview of the file, select Preview from the View drop-down list. This lets you quickly inspect the file before taking the time to actually open it. (See Figure 11.5.)

FIGURE 11.3 ▶

The Search dialog box

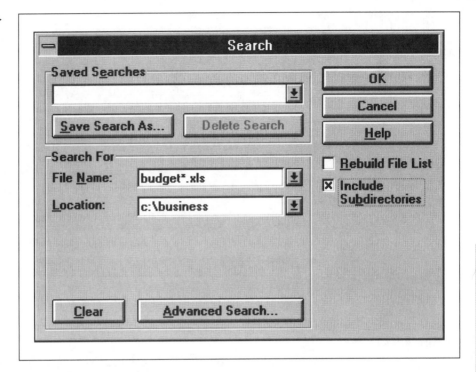

TABLE 11.1: *Wildcard Characters for Searches*

Character	Meaning
? (question mark)	Match single character
* (asterisk)	Match any number of characters
" " (double quotes)	Enclosed character is not wildcard (use to search for ?, *, &, etc.)
, (comma)	Indicates OR (search for information matching at least one item in list)
& (ampersand)	Indicates AND (search for information matching all items in list)
(space)	Same as &—Indicates AND (search for information matching all items in list)
~ (tilde)	Indicates NOT (exclude matching information from search)

FIGURE 11.4 ▶

The files are listed on the left, and summary information for the selected file is displayed on the right.

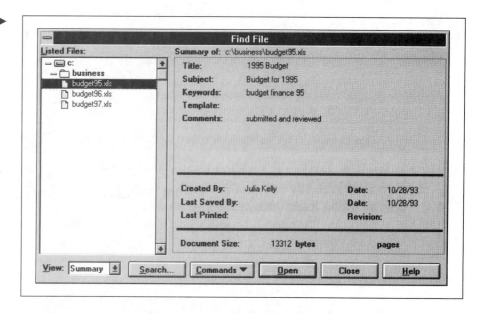

FIGURE 11.5 ▶

The upper-left corner of the top sheet is displayed in the preview.

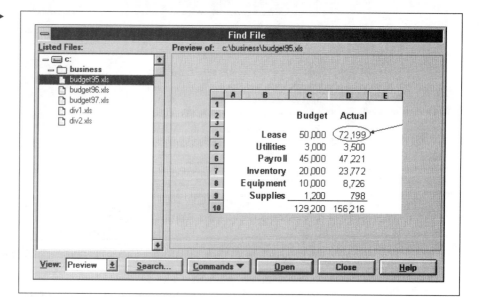

Click the Search button to conduct a new search. Click the Open button to open the file. When you click the Commands button, a drop-down menu is displayed.

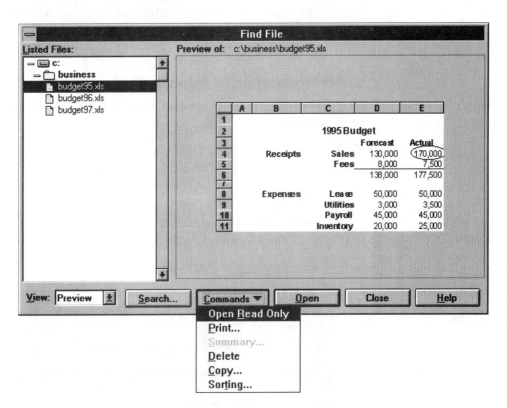

Open Read Only opens selected workbook(s) read-only.

Print displays dialog box to select printing options for selected workbook.

Summary (Inexplicably, this command is never available.)

Delete deletes selected workbook.

Copy displays Copy dialog box, to copy files to another directory/drive or create new directory.

Sorting displays Options dialog box for choosing how listed files are sorted.

▶ Performing an Advanced Search

There are several ways to search for files based on criteria other than the file name. For instance, your budget files may not always begin with "BUDGET." Before you can understand advanced searches, you need to understand how to enter summary information for a file.

Entering Summary Information

Summary information can be entered for each workbook that lets you enter a title, subject, author, keywords, and comments.

This information can help you locate workbooks, and is particularly useful in a workgroup environment. To enter summary information:

1. Open the workbook.
2. Choose the File ➤ Summary Info command.
3. Enter a title, subject, author name, any keywords which might be useful in a future search, and comments.

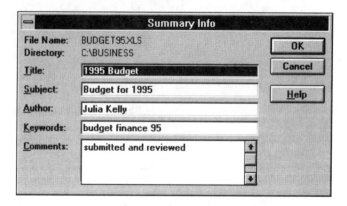

▶ ▶ **T I P**

To display the Summary Info dialog box every time a new worksheet is saved (or when the Save-As command is used), choose the Tools ➤ Options command, select the General tab, and check the Prompt for Summary Info setting. This setting is checked by default.

Keyword Search

The following exercise will search for files where the word "BUDGET" was entered as a keyword in summary information.

1. Choose the File ➤ Find File command. The results of the last search are displayed.

2. Click the Search button.

3. Click the Clear button (to clear all previous search parameters).

4. Enter ***.xls** in File Name (specifying all Excel workbooks).

5. Enter a Location (including a path to narrow the search).

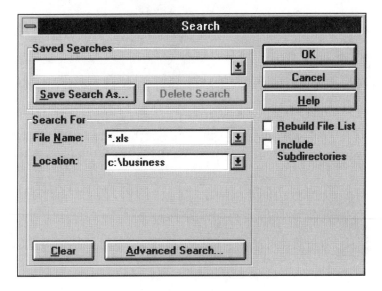

6. Click the Advanced Search button.

7. Select the Summary tab.

   • Enter **budget** in Keywords.
   • Select Create New List from the Options drop-down.

8. Click OK to close the Advanced Search dialog box, then click OK in the Search dialog box to begin the search.

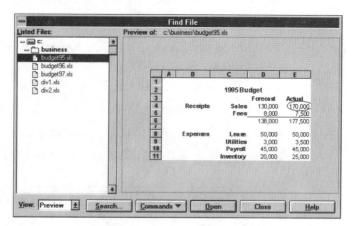

Saving the Search

Suppose this is a search that you want to perform regularly. Once a set of search criteria has been specified, it can be named and saved for future use. You can then perform the same search again at a later date without having to reenter the search parameters.

Follow these steps to name and save a search:

1. Specify the search criteria.

2. In the Search dialog box, click Save Search As (see Figure 11.3)

3. Type a name for the search in the Search Name edit box, and click OK.

To use a saved search, select it from the Saved Searches drop-down and click OK.

Table 11.1 explains the wildcard characters you can use in searches.

PART FOUR

▶ ▶ *In Part Four* you'll be introduced to graphic objects and charts. You will learn to format and manipulate worksheet objects, and to chart worksheet data. The new charting environment in Excel 5 is more powerful than in previous versions, and has many new features you will want to check out.

Working with Graphic Objects

▶▶ *F*AST *T*RACK

▶ ***To group objects*** **400**

Hold down Shift to select multiple objects, then click the Group tool.

▶ ***To draw perfect (symmetrical) shapes*** **401**

To draw a square, circle, 90-degree arc, or lines and arrows with perfect vertical, horizontal, or 45-degree alignment, hold down Shift while drawing the object.

▶ ***To link a textbox to a worksheet cell*** **404**

Select the textbox, click the formula bar, and enter a formula such as **=B3**.

▶ ***To create a picture of a cell*** **405**

Select the cells you want to take a picture of, click on the Camera tool, then click on the worksheet where you want to paste the picture.

► ► ***T**raditionally*, spreadsheet programs are used for number crunching. But Excel is a powerful graphics package in its own right and allows graphic objects to be placed on worksheets, which lets you:

- Put your company logo on a worksheet
- Use objects such as text boxes, arrows, and circles to emphasize information (with style!)
- Enhance worksheets by using pictures of cells

This chapter covers:

- *The different types of objects that can be created*
- *How objects are moved, sized, and formatted*
- *How to use the camera tool to create pictures*
- *How to protect objects*

See Chapter 25 to learn how to import and export graphics to and from other applications.

► ► *How to Draw Graphic Objects*

Suppose you have a worksheet with information that needs explanation or emphasis.

	A	B	C	D	E	F	G	H	I
BUDGET95.XLS

	Budget	Actual
Lease	50,000	⟨72,199⟩
Utilities	3,000	3,500
Payroll	45,000	47,221
Inventory	20,000	23,772
Equipment	10,000	8,726
Supplies	1,200	798
	129,200	156,216

Reflects one time startup costs. Next period will be under budget.

A text box, circle, and arrow are used to explain a figure on the work-sheet. These objects were drawn on the sheet using tools found on the drawing toolbar.

Objects such as circles, arrows, text boxes, and buttons are placed on worksheets by drawing them:

1. Display the Drawing toolbar by choosing the View ➤ Toolbars command, or clicking the Drawing tool on the Standard toolbar.

2. Click the tool for the object you want to draw. The mouse pointer becomes a crosshair.

3. Click on the worksheet, and drag the mouse.

4. Release the mouse button.

Table 12.1 explains the tools on the Drawing toolbar:

▶ **TABLE 12.1:** *Drawing Tools*

Tool	Function
╲	Line
↘	Arrow
ᔛ	Freehand Line

▶ **TABLE 12.1:** *Drawing Tools (continued)*

Tool	Function
	Filled Rectangle
	Unfilled Rectangle
	Filled Ellipse
	Unfilled Ellipse
	Filled Arc
	Unfilled Arc
	Filled Freeform Polygon
	Unfilled Freeform Polygon
	Text Box
	Create Button
	Drawing Selection (selects objects and controls)
	Bring To Front
	Send To Back
	Group
	Ungroup

▶ **TABLE 12.1:** *Drawing Tools (continued)*

Tool	Function
⬜	Reshape (displays vertices on freehand lines and freeform polygons)
⬜	Drop Shadow
⬜	Pattern (drop-down, tear-off palette of patterns)

Drawing Several of the Same Object

Suppose you want to draw several arrows. You can click the arrow tool and draw, then repeat the procedure for each arrow. But there is a quicker way:

1. Double-click a drawing tool (the drawing tool will remain in effect until you're done)

2. Draw the object—the tool remains in effect—draw another object.

3. Single-click the tool when you are done drawing.

▶▶ *How to Select Objects*

To format, move, resize, copy, or delete an object, it must first be selected. The procedure differs slightly depending on whether the object is *filled*:

Filled Objects A filled object is colored—it obscures the underlying cells, as pictured in Figure 12.1. (Some of the tools on the Drawing toolbar create filled objects that are colored white—this can be hard to distinguish from an unfilled object if worksheet gridlines are turned off.) You can click anywhere on a filled object to select it. You will learn how to fill objects in the formatting section later in this chapter.

Working with Graphic Objects

▶ ▶
Ch.
12

FIGURE 12.1 ▶

You can see gridlines behind the unfilled rectangle. Click the border in order to select it.

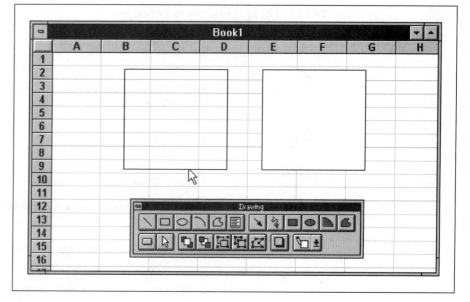

Unfilled Objects An unfilled object is an outline with no fill—you can see the cells behind the object. To select an unfilled object, you must click on the object's border.

To select an object, click on it. The name of the selected object displays in the Name box on the left of the formula bar.

A selected object has small markers on the border—these are called *handles*.

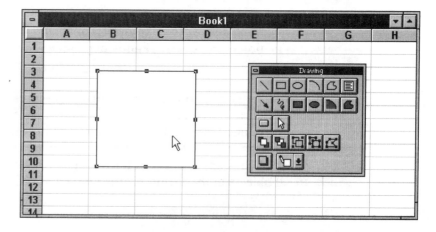

►▶**T I P**

> It is impossible to select a cell behind a filled object by clicking on the cell, because you will select the object instead. To select a cell behind a filled object, you can use the Name box or the Edit ➤ Go To command, or use the arrow keys to navigate to the cell behind a filled object.

▶▶ *Using the Object Shortcut Menu*

When you click an object with the right mouse button, the object is selected and a shortcut menu is displayed, as in Figure 12.2.

FIGURE 12.2 ▶

Click an object with the right mouse button to display the object shortcut menu.

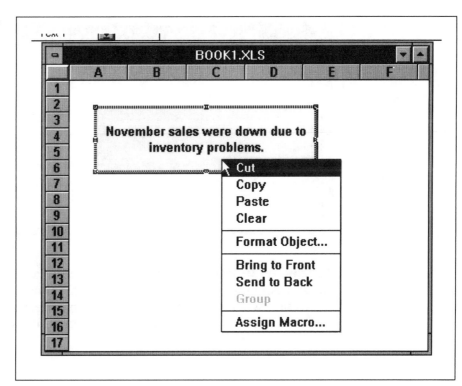

Working with
Graphic Objects

Ch.
12

The shortcut menu can save you several keystrokes when working with objects.

▶▶ *Manipulating Objects*

In this section you will learn how to move, resize, copy, and delete graphic objects.

▶ *Moving and Resizing Objects*

The mouse must be used to move and resize objects.

Moving an Object To move an object, select it with the mouse, then drag it across the worksheet. An outline of the object is displayed until you release the mouse button.

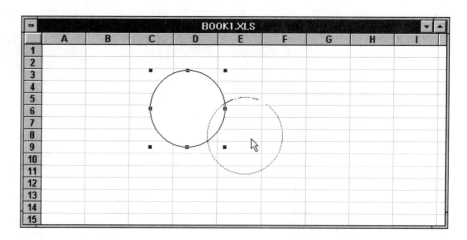

Resizing an Object To resize an object, select it, then drag one of its handles. An outline of the new size is displayed until the mouse button is released. When you click and hold on a handle, the cursor changes to a double-faced arrow, showing the direction(s) that you may resize.

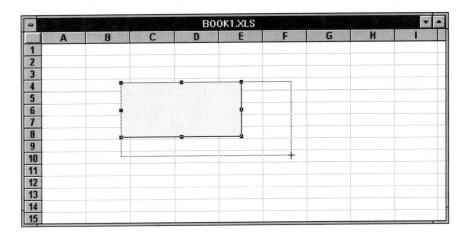

Suppose you want to resize a rectangle, but retain its precise proportions. This is nearly impossible to do freehand. In Excel, however, all you have to do is hold down the Shift key while dragging one of the corner handles.

Aligning Objects to the Worksheet Grid

A common problem is the task of perfectly aligning several objects, or making sure objects are the exact same size. When you try this freehand, no matter how careful you are, it is nearly impossible to align or size perfectly. When you look at a worksheet with imperfectly aligned objects, you may not be consciously aware of the imperfections, but the brain detects them anyway. You'll have a feeling that something just doesn't look right.

If you hold down the Alt key while moving or resizing an object, the object is snapped to the worksheet grid—even if gridlines are not displayed.

▶ Copying Objects

There are two ways to copy objects: by dragging and dropping, and with menu commands.

Using Drag and Drop The most efficient way to copy an object to a nearby location is to drag it and drop it. Here's how:

1. Hold down the Ctrl key.
2. Select the object, then drag and drop it—a copy of the object is created.

Using Menu Commands To copy (or cut) an object using menu commands:

1. Select the object.
2. Choose the Edit ➤ Copy or Edit ➤ Cut command.
3. Select a cell where you want to paste.
4. Choose the Edit ➤ Paste command.

Alternately, use the Cut, Copy, and Paste commands on the object shortcut menu.

► *Deleting Objects*

To delete an object:

1. Select the object.
2. Press the Delete key (or choose the Edit ➤ Clear command).

Alternately, use the Clear command on the object shortcut menu.

►► *Formatting Objects*

There are several different format settings that can be applied to objects. In addition, different objects have different types of format settings. For instance, only arrows have a formattable arrowhead. And only text boxes and buttons have formattable text.

In spite of the fact that some objects have unique formattable properties, all objects are formatted by displaying the Format Object dialog box pictured in Figure 12.3. There are three ways to display this dialog box:

- Double-click the object.
- Choose the Format Object command from the object shortcut menu.
- Select the object, then choose the Format ➤ Object command.

FIGURE 12.3 ▶

The contents of the Format Object dialog box vary depending on the type of object.

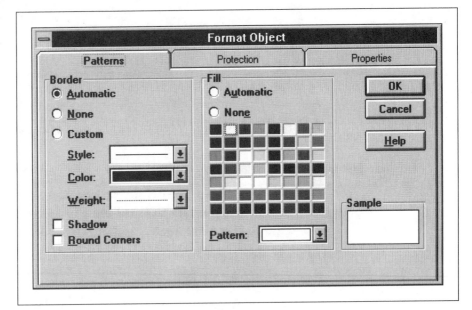

The following exercise will show how to format a text box using some visually effective formatting techniques:

1. Display the Drawing toolbar and use the Text Box tool to draw a text box.
2. Enter some text into the text box (press Esc when you are done). The object will still be selected.

Working with Graphic Objects

Ch. 12

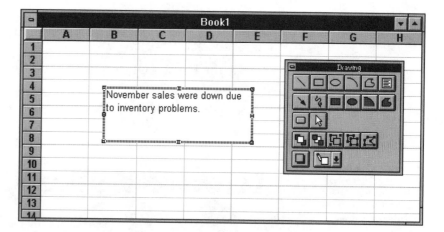

3. Select the Format ➤ Object command, then select the Patterns tab.

4. Check the Shadow border setting, and select a yellow fill color.

 ► ►**T I P**

To tone down the bright yellow, use a pattern. Drop down the pattern list and choose white. Drop down the pattern list again, and choose a hatch pattern.

5. Select the Font tab, and choose bold style.

6. Select the Alignment tab, and center horizontally and vertically.

7. Click OK.

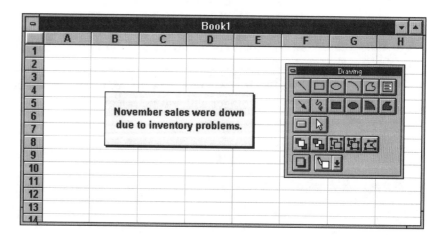

Use the Format Painter Tool to Quickly Format Several Objects

The same formatting can be applied to several objects using the Format Painter tool (on the Standard toolbar). In the preceding exercise, seven steps were required to format the text box. Suppose you want to format several text boxes the same way—the Format Painter will let you do it quickly.

1. Select an object which is already formatted the way you want.

2. Double-click the Format Painter tool.

3. Click on each object you want to format.

4. Click on the Format Painter to turn it off (or press Esc).

CREATE YOUR OWN COLOR PALETTE

Excel's color palette offers 56 built-in colors to choose from, but you are not limited to those colors. You can change any color in the palette to a custom color which you create using the Color Picker. It is especially useful to change the Chart Fills and Chart Lines colors (rows 3 and 4 in any color palette) because these are the default colors Excel uses when you create a chart. You can customize the colors in a specific order from left to right, and Excel will use the custom colors in the order in which you created them. For example, if you customize the Chart Fills colors as a succession of greens, then create a column chart, the chart series will be colored a succession of greens. Changing any of Excel's built-in colors is fairly simple.

1. Open the workbook in which you want to use custom colors.

2. Choose Tools ➤ Options, then select the Color tab.

3. Select the color you want to change, then click Modify.

Working with
Graphic Objects

Ch.
12

4. Create a new color using the Color Picker (this is the only tricky part—getting the color you want takes a bit of experimentation).

5. Click OK to close the Color Picker, then click OK to close the Options dialog.

Your custom color palette will be saved with the workbook in which you created it. If you want to copy the custom palette into another workbook:

1. Open both workbooks (the workbook containing the custom color palette and the workbook you want to copy the palette into).

2. Activate the workbook you want to copy the palette into.

3. Choose Tools ➤ Options, then select the Color tab.

4. In the Copy Colors From: edit box, select the name of the workbook containing the custom color palette.

▶▶ *Understanding Object Properties*

The Format Object dialog box has a tab called Properties (see Figure 12.4). This tab is identical for all types of objects.

FIGURE 12.4 ▶

The Properties tab controls object size and position relative to the underlying cells, and whether the object prints out.

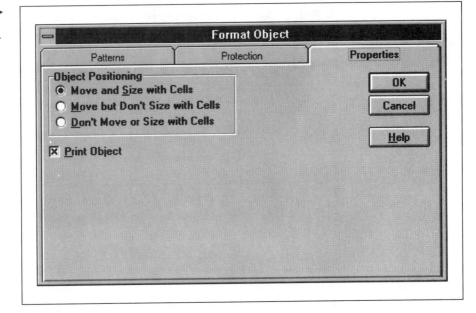

Controlling Object Size and Placement Relative to Underlying Cells

Suppose you draw a text box, enter some text, then manually size the text box:

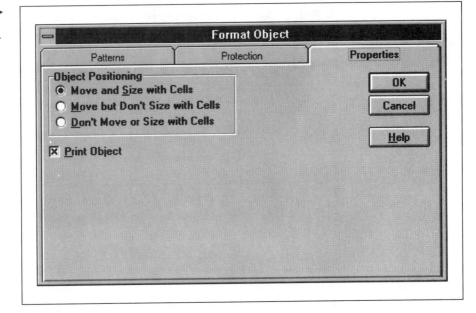

Working with
Graphic Objects

▶ *Ch.*

12

If you change the row height or column width of the underlying cells, the text box resizes accordingly:

The Object Positioning options (see Figure 12.4) control this behavior:

Move and Size with Cells An object will move if rows/columns are inserted or deleted. The object size will change as the row height or column width of underlying cells changes.

Move But Don't Size with Cells An object will move with the underlying cells, but will not resize.

Don't Move or Size with Cells An object will not move with the underlying cells, and will not resize.

Do You Want the Object to Print?

By default, all objects (except buttons) are included on the printout when the worksheet is printed. But some objects may be intended to display on the screen and not print. For example, a text box may instruct the user on how to enter data; this text box would be inappropriate on the printout. The *Print Object* setting (see Figure 12.4) determines whether an object will print or not.

CUTTING, COPYING, AND SORTING OBJECTS WITH CELLS

You have seen how the size and position of an object relative to the underlying cells are controlled by the Format ➤ Object ➤ Properties dialog tab. Objects can also be copied, cut, sorted, and deleted with their underlying cells. This behavior is controlled by an option on the Tools ➤ Options ➤ Edit dialog tab. When the Cut, Copy, and Sort Objects with Cells option is selected, objects on a worksheet are virtually attached to the underlying cells. If you move or copy the cells beneath an object, the object is also moved or copied. If you delete a cell using the Edit ➤ Delete command, objects attached to the cell will also be deleted. If an object fits entirely within a single cell, the object will sort with the cell.

▶▶ *Working with More than One Object at a Time*

More than one object can be selected at the same time, which lets you manipulate all of the selected objects at once. Suppose you want to move several objects, and retain their relative positions. You can select all of the objects and move them together, instead of moving them one by one.

Selecting Multiple Objects Using the Shift Key Hold down Shift while selecting objects with the mouse. This technique is probably the quickest if you need to select just two or three objects.

 Using the Drawing Selection Tool Click on the Drawing Selection tool (located on the Drawing toolbar), then draw a rectangle around the objects that you want to select. (When finished using the Drawing Selection tool, click it again to turn it off.) This tool is most useful when the objects you want to select are positioned close together.

► *Grouping and Ungrouping Objects*

You have learned how to select more than one object in order to manipulate more than one object at once. But you may want to semi-permanently *group* objects together. When you group objects, a new object is created.

1. Draw a text box and an arrow.

2. Select the text box and arrow, then choose the Format ➤ Placement ➤ Group command (or click the Group Objects tool on the Drawing toolbar).

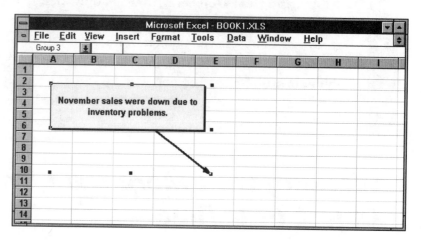

Notice that the two objects are now a single object, with a new name— Group 3. (Since Excel names objects using a sequential numeric suffix, the name of the new object depends on the number of objects that have already been created on the worksheet.)

You can also choose to ungroup objects that have been previously grouped:

1. Select the group object.

2. Choose the Format ➤ Placement ➤ Ungroup command, or click the Ungroup Objects tool.

▶▶ *Types of Objects*

So far in this chapter, you have read about objects in general. This section will describe the unique properties of each type of object.

▶ *Rectangles, Ellipses, and Arcs*

It is difficult, if not impossible, to draw perfect squares and circles freehand. If you hold down the Shift key, you can draw squares and circles, rather than rectangles and ovals. Pressing Shift while drawing an arc will create a 90° arc.

▶ ▶**T I P**

If you hold down the Shift key while clicking on an unfilled tool, it will draw a filled object. Likewise, if you hold down the Shift key while clicking on a filled tool, it will draw an unfilled object. See Table 7.3 for a list of other "reversible" tools.

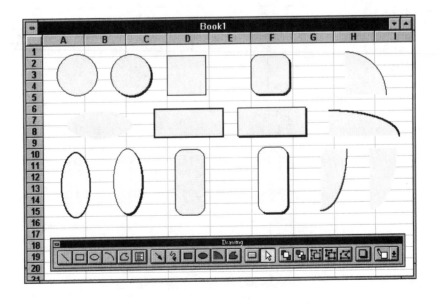

▶ *Lines and Arrows*

An arrow is simply a line formatted with an arrowhead (see examples in Figure 12.5). The Format Objects dialog box lets you specify the arrowhead type, if any:

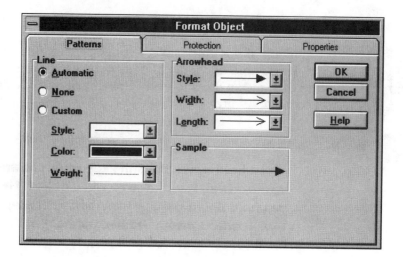

FIGURE 12.5 ▶

Various lines and arrowheads combined to make arrows

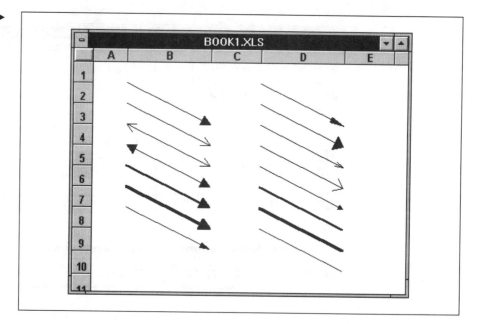

Lines can be drawn at perfect vertical, horizontal, and 45-degree angles by holding down Shift while drawing.

▶ *Text Boxes*

A text box is a rectangle in which you can enter and format text. It is very useful for adding comments and explanations to worksheets and charts, especially when combined with arrows and circles to point to specific information.

After you draw a text box, the text-insertion point will blink within the box, ready for you to type text. Text boxes automatically wrap text (press Enter to insert a hard break).

There are several format settings specific to text boxes:

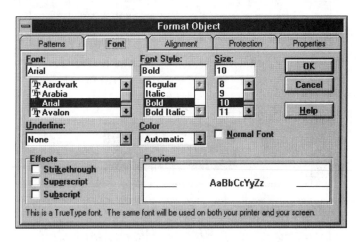

- The Alignment and Font tabs are used to format the text.
- The Automatic Size setting on the Alignment tab causes the text box to size automatically based on the text.
- The Lock Text setting on the Protection tab prevents users from changing text. (The worksheet must also be protected for this setting to take effect—see Chapter 11 to learn about sheet protection.)

You can also format the text in a text box using tools on the Formatting toolbar.

▶ ▶**T I P**

How can you place text inside an oval? Place a text box on top of the oval, then format the text box with no fill and no border. Group the two objects into a single object if you want to move or copy them (select both objects, then use the Format ➤ Placement ➤ Group command).

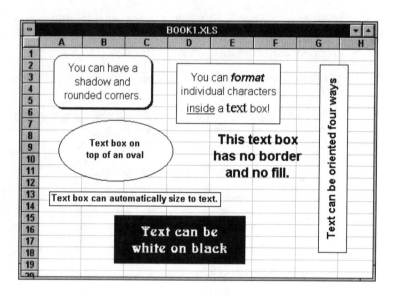

Linking a Text Box to Worksheet Cells

Suppose you want the contents of a text box to be variable. You can link a text box to a worksheet cell by entering a formula instead of a constant. Try this exercise:

1. On a new worksheet, enter the following formula into cell B2:

   =IF(ISNUMBER(B3),"You may now save the workbook.","Please enter a number into B3.")

2. Draw a text box.

3. Click in the formula bar and type **=B2**, then press Enter (see Figure 12.6).

WARNING

A common mistake is entering the formula into the text box rather than into the formula bar.

4. Enter a number in B3 and watch the text box change.

FIGURE 12.6

When a linked text box is selected, the cell reference displays in the formula bar, where the cell reference can be changed.

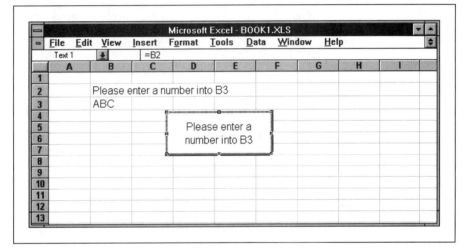

▶ *Linked Pictures*

A linked picture is a picture of one or more worksheet cells that remains linked to the source cell(s). Put to creative use, linked pictures can greatly enhance reports and presentations.

The camera tool is the easiest way to create a linked picture. It is not located on any of the built-in toolbars, so you will have to create a custom toolbar, or add the camera tool to an existing toolbar, in order to use the camera tool.

To create a linked picture using the camera tool:

1. Select source cell(s).

2. Click the camera tool.

Working with Graphic Objects

▶ ▶

Ch.

12

3. Click on a worksheet—a picture of the source cells is created (see Figure 12.7).

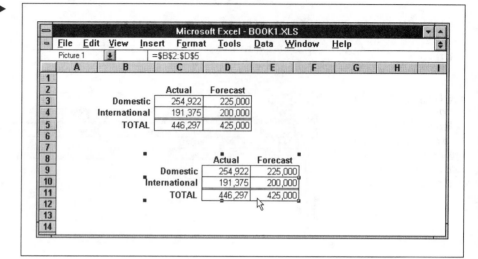

To create a linked picture using menu commands:

1. Select the source cell(s).

2. Choose the Edit ➤ Copy command.

3. Select the place on the worksheet where you want to paste, then hold down the Shift key, and choose the Edit ➤ Paste Picture Link command.

Here are some important properties of linked pictures:

- Any change to the source cells causes a linked picture to update.

- When a picture is first created, the picture object has its own border, independent of any borders or gridlines in the source cell(s)—use the Format ➤ Object command to remove the object border.

- The reference for the source cells displays on the formula bar when a linked picture is selected (see Figure 12.7).

- You can edit (or clear) the reference on the formula bar. If cleared, the link between the picture and the source cell(s) is broken and the picture becomes static.

Consider the worksheet in Figure 12.8.

FIGURE 12.8 ▶

Some people prefer charts and others prefer tabular data. A linked picture placed on a chart sheet satisfies all.

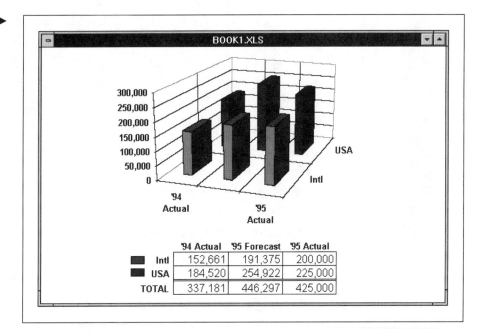

	'94 Actual	'95 Forecast	'95 Actual
Intl	152,661	191,375	200,000
USA	184,520	254,922	225,000
TOTAL	337,181	446,297	425,000

Application developers can derive two key benefits from linked pictures:

- Pictures can be placed on custom dialog boxes.
- When a linked picture is created, it refers to an absolute cell reference; however, a picture can refer to a named formula (see Chapter 8 to learn about named formulas). This lets user input dynamically change the picture source.

Working with Graphic Objects

▶ ▶
Ch.
12

▶ LINKING A PICTURE TO A NAMED FORMULA

Just as a picture can be linked to a named range, a picture can be linked to a named formula—a name that points to a variable range of cells. For example, suppose you have two named ranges, *Sales* and *Profits*. Create a cell named Choice, then create a formula named PictureChoice which points to *Sales* or *Profits* based on the value in cell Choice: =IF(Choice=1,Sales,Profits) (see Chapter 8 if you need help naming a formula). Take a picture of one of the named ranges (it doesn't matter which), then select the picture and change the formula bar to read =PictureChoice.

Enter a value in cell Choice to see the linked picture work. A value of 1 will display a picture of range Sales, while any other value will display a picture of range Profits. Option buttons are a good user interface for entering a value in cell Choice. See Chapter 19 to learn about option buttons and other worksheet controls.

▶ *Freehand Lines and Freeform Polygons*

 To draw a freehand line, click and drag the mouse to draw the line. The mouse pointer becomes a pencil while drawing the line. When you release the mouse button, the line is completed.

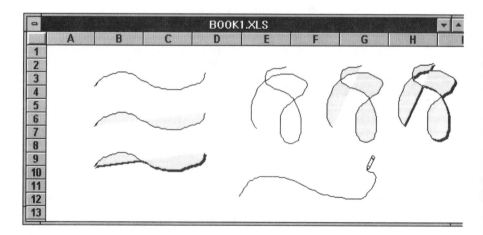

Freeform polygons can combine straight lines and freehand lines. To draw straight lines, click at the endpoint of the line. You can make a polygon side vertical, horizontal, or a 45-degree angle by holding down Shift while clicking.

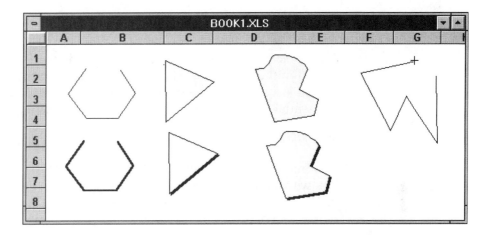

To alter the shape of a freehand line after it is drawn, select the line and click the Reshape tool. Each vertex of the line will have a handle, and you can drag each handle with the crosshair to reshape the line. To turn the Reshape tool off, click the tool again, or click outside the object.

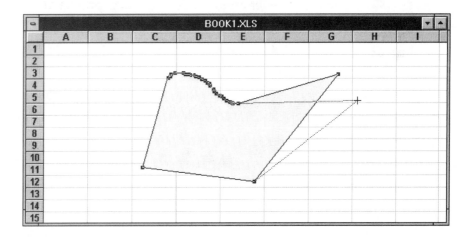

Working with Graphic Objects

Ch.
12

▶▶ *Special Information*

The following information may be of particular interest to macro writers and application developers.

Renaming Objects

Each object is named automatically when drawn—the name is displayed in the Name box when the object is selected. Excel names the objects using a prefix consisting of the object type, and a suffix that is a sequential number. For instance, when you draw a text box on a new workbook it is named *Text 1*. Then you draw a rectangle—it is named *Rectangle 2*. If you write macros, this can cause you trouble.

To rename an object, simply select it, overwrite the name in the Name box with something more meaningful, and press Enter. As pointed out in Chapter 8, object names have different rules then cell names—object names can have spaces, and they *cannot* have periods.

Protecting Objects

Like cells, objects are protected (locked) by default. To unlock an object, select the object, then choose Format ➤ Object. Select the Protection tab, then clear the Locked checkbox. The Protection settings do not take effect unless the worksheet is protected. See Chapter 11 to learn about worksheet protection.

▶ ▶ **CHAPTER** **13**

Charting
Basics

———

FAST TRACK

▶ ***To format a chart***   **440**

> Activate the chart by double-clicking on it, then double-click the element you want to format.

▶ ***To draw inside a chart***   **444**

> Activate the chart, then use the Drawing tools to draw objects (the objects you draw "live" in the chart, not on the worksheet).

▶ ***To paste a picture into a chart***   **444**

> Copy the picture using the Edit ➤ Copy command, then activate the chart and choose Edit ➤ Paste.

▶ ***To change the number format***   **447**

> Activate the chart, then right-click the axis and choose the Format Axis command. Select the Number tab and enter a format code.

▶ ***To add a title to a chart***   **448**

> Activate the chart, then choose Insert ➤ Titles. Select the type of title you want (chart or axis) and click OK, then enter your title text into the new text box.

▶ ***To change a chart border***   **449**

> Select the chart, then choose the Format ➤ Object command. Select the Patterns tab, then choose border options.

►► **C**hartsare an effective way to present information. They allow a lot of information to be absorbed quickly, whereas a traditional columnar report might require considerable study and analysis. Excel includes a powerful built-in charting facility that makes it very easy to create a variety of charts.

This chapter covers:

- *How to create charts with the ChartWizard, including how to select the type of chart you want to create*
- *The difference between embedded charts and chart sheets*
- *Adding data to an existing chart*
- *Formatting charts for maximum impact*
- *An exercise that will show you how to create and format a chart*

►► *Charts Are Easy*

Before you explore the many charting options covered later in this chapter, here is an exercise that will demonstrate how easy it is to create a chart:

1. Enter the following on a new worksheet:

	A	B	C	D	E	F
1						
2		Region	Actual	Forecast		
3		North	456	346		
4		South	562	854		
5		East	726	892		
6		West	851	238		
7						
8						
9						

BOOK1.XLS

2. Select cells B2:D6.

3. Click the ChartWizard tool (on the Standard toolbar).

4. Drag the mouse pointer across the worksheet to draw the chart frame (Figure 13.1).

5. When you release the mouse button, the ChartWizard (Step 1 of 5) dialog box will be displayed. Click the Finish button.

6. A chart using the default chart format is drawn on the worksheet (see Figure 13.2).

By default, charts are *linked* to the worksheet cells. To see this in action, change the source data in the worksheet—the chart will automatically redraw accordingly.

When a chart is active, the menus change. The Data menu goes away, and chart-specific commands appear on the View, Insert, and Format menus. Also, the Chart toolbar is displayed. Table 13.1 describes the tools on the Chart toolbar.

FIGURE 13.1 ▶

As you draw the chart, the chart outline is displayed.

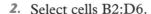

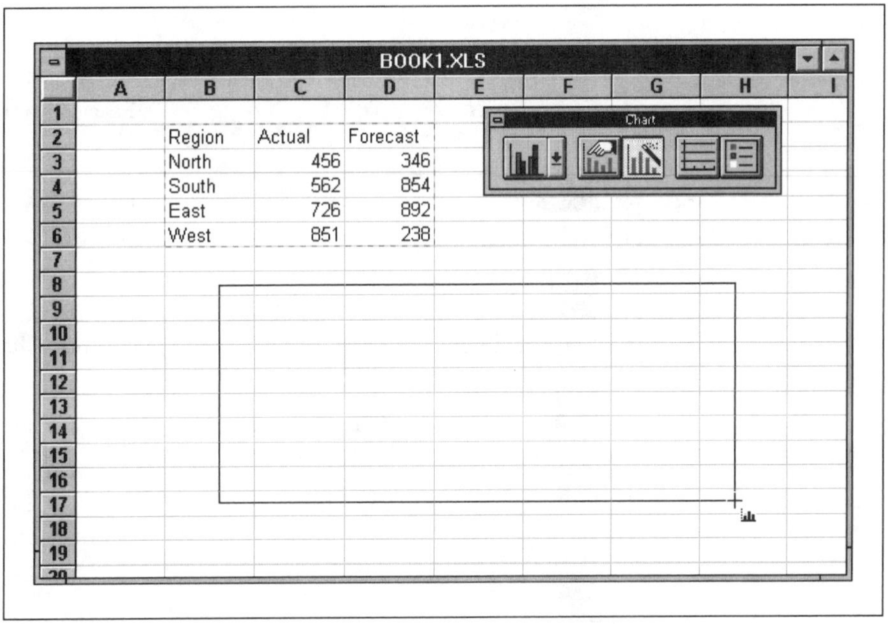

	A	B	C	D	E	F	G	H	I
1									
2		Region	Actual	Forecast					
3		North	456	346					
4		South	562	854					
5		East	726	892					
6		West	851	238					

BOOK1.XLS

Chart

FIGURE 13.2 ►

Default chart created with the ChartWizard.

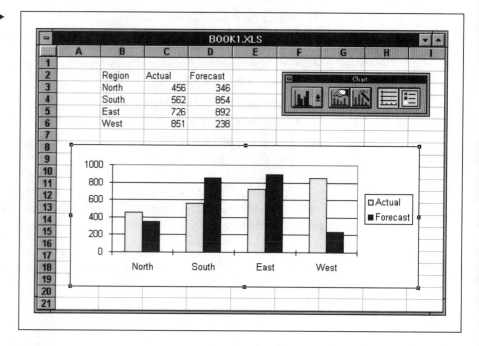

► **TABLE 13.1:** *Tools on the Chart Toolbar*

Tool Face	Tool	Function
	Chart Type	Drops down tear-off palette of chart types
	Default Chart	Creates default embedded chart without ChartWizard
	ChartWizard	Starts ChartWizard
	Horizontal Gridlines	Toggles display of horizontal gridlines on/off
	Legend	Toggles display of legend on/off

Charting Basics

Ch.
13

▶▶ *Embedded Charts vs. Chart Sheets*

The chart created in the previous exercise is an *embedded* chart. Charts can also reside on *chart sheets*.

▶ *About Embedded Charts*

An embedded chart is a graphic object that lies on a worksheet. It can be moved, resized, and deleted just as you would other graphical objects, such as text boxes. Click the chart to select it, then move the chart by dragging with the mouse, or resize the chart by dragging one of the handles. (See Chapter 12 to learn about graphical objects.) The primary advantage of embedded charts is that they can be viewed (and printed) side-by-side with worksheet data. You can place more than one embedded chart on a worksheet.

An embedded chart must be activated before you can format it, or make changes to it. Double-click an embedded chart to activate it. A heavy border is displayed around an active chart, as shown in Figure 13.3.

FIGURE 13.3 ▶

Embedded charts are activated by double-clicking the chart. A heavy border is displayed.

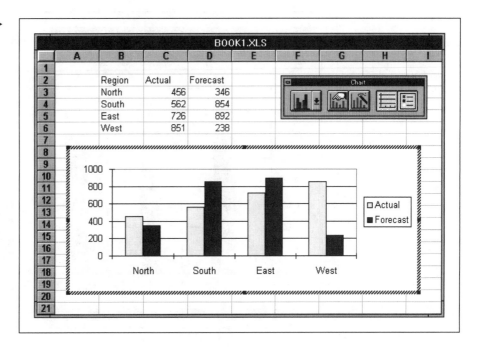

▶ ▶ N O T E

An embedded chart is *selected* by single-clicking it with the mouse, the same as with all graphic objects. When selected, it can be moved, resized, or deleted. Do not confuse *selecting* with *activating*—you must double-click an embedded chart to *activate* it.

▶ *About Chart Sheets*

Chart sheets are like worksheets, except there are no cells. A chart sheet is a separate page in a workbook—it contains one chart (see Figure 13.4). To create a chart sheet:

1. Select the data you want to chart.

2. Choose Insert ▶ Chart ▶ As New Sheet. The ChartWizard is started. (Alternatively, press F11 to create a new chart sheet, and circumvent the ChartWizard.

FIGURE 13.4 ▶

Column chart on a chart sheet

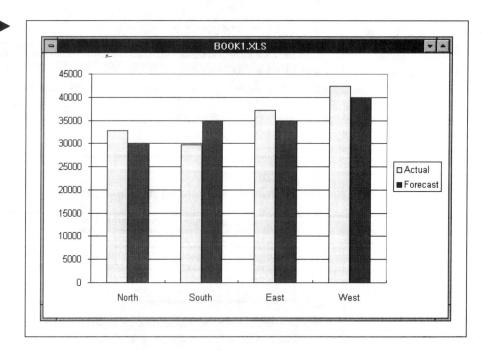

Chart sheets can be renamed, moved, copied, and deleted just as you would a worksheet. (See Chapter 2 to learn how to manage sheets.)

The primary advantages of chart sheets is they can be made to be full size without manual sizing, and when printed do not include any worksheet data. Also, there is a command that is available only for chart sheets: the View ➤ Sized with Window command controls whether the size of the chart is dependent on the size of the window. By default, this command is unchecked. If checked, the chart is automatically sized to fit the window. (This setting has no effect on how the chart will appear when printed.)

N O T E

In previous versions of Excel, it was impossible to place graphical objects on chart sheets. The restriction has been removed.

▶▶ *Understanding Data Series and Data Points*

When working with charts, it will help if you understand the difference between a *data series* and *data points*. These concepts are basic to understanding how your data is being represented in the chart, and to creating a chart that will display your data properly.

▶ *What Is a Data Point?*

A data point is an individual value that originated in a single worksheet cell. Data points are represented by columns, bars, dots, slices, or other shapes called *data markers*. In Figure 13.3, North-Actual is one data point; South-Forecast is another data point.

▶ *What Is a Data Series?*

A data series is a group of related data points which represents a single row or column of data. Each series is distinguished by a unique color or pattern. In Figure 13.3, Forecast is one data series and Actual is the other data series—each series consisting of four data points.

▶▶ *Chart Types*

Suppose you are ready to chart data for a presentation. The first question you need to answer is: what kind of chart? Excel offers so many chart types that this may not be an easy question to answer. Figure 13.6 shows the 15 built-in chart types available, and within each chart type there are several subtypes (as you can see in Figure 13.7, which shows column chart subtypes). In addition to the many built-in chart types and subtypes available, you can create hybrid types. For example, you can combine area, line, and column series in the same chart (as illustrated in Figure 14.6).

Each chart type is best suited for illustrating particular types of data. Here are some descriptions of the different chart types to help you choose. See Figure 13.6 for an illustration of each chart type.

Column and Bar

You are probably familiar with column and bar charts. They are useful for comparing values at different points in time (for example, quarterly earnings), or making comparisons between items (like total sales for each product line). You can create column and bar charts which display negative values below the X-axis (in a column chart) or left of the Y-axis (in a bar chart). You can stack series columns or bars to illustrate each data point's relationship to the whole more clearly. You can display more data in the chart by overlapping the data points in clusters. There are built-in column and bar subtypes for each of these display options, which you can choose from the ChartWizard step 3 dialog, or you can switch between options using the Format ▶ Group dialog.

Line

What if you want to show, for example, daily improvement in air quality after installation of a smokestack filter? A line chart is the optimum choice. Line charts are great for displaying continuity, trends, and changes over even intervals of time. (For uneven time intervals, a scatter chart is preferable.) With a line chart you can choose the classic zig-zag style, in which points are connected with straight lines, or you can choose a smoothed-out line which emphasizes continuity. You can choose not to connect the data points at all (the chart will resemble a scatter chart). You can also choose between linear and logarithmic scaling. Other variations of the line chart include a subtype for high-low charts (useful for plotting data like high, low, and average daily temperatures).

Suppose you want to chart the performance of stocks or securities? There are two line chart sub-types to be aware of: high-low-close (which charts the high price, low price, and closing price for the day) and open-high-low-close (which charts the opening price, as well as the high, low, and closing prices). If you want to create a high-low-close or an open-high-low-close chart, your data must be arranged on the worksheet in a specific order. The name of the chart subtype is a good way to remember - the open series first, followed by the high series, followed by low, followed by close.

Area

An area chart is just a line chart with the space below the line filled in. An area chart can have a lot more visual impact than a line chart, though. Suppose you want to chart the reduction in forested land in North America over the last 100 years? An area chart would show the reduction in acreage more dramatically than a line chart. You can also use an area chart to advantage by creating a hybrid line-area chart. Suppose you have created a line chart which has four or five series, and the lines are hard to read because they are crowding each other. Or perhaps you want to emphasize a single series apart from the others. You can select a single line and change its chart type to area, which will change the readability and visual impact of the chart considerably.

Pie

What is unique about a pie chart is that it can only plot one data series. Although you can plot a single data series in any chart type, a pie chart is especially good at showing the relationships of each data point to each other and to the whole. Also, you can emphasize a single point in the series by separating its wedge from the rest of the pie.

Suppose you want to portray this year's expenditures on various office supplies? A pie chart is a great chart for comparing how much of the supplies budget was spent on pens, paper clips, notepads, etc. You can label each wedge with total dollars spent on that item, or with percentage of the supplies budget spent on that item. You can emphasize that too much was spent on pens, for example, by separating the 'pens' wedge from the rest of the chart. When you create a pie chart, keep in mind that too many data points can make the chart illegible.

Doughnut

A doughnut chart is like a pie chart, but you can plot more than one series using a doughnut. Like the pie chart, you can label the data points by value or by percentage of the total series, and you can explode the doughnut into separate wedges or separate a single wedge. Doughnut charts are most useful in an environment where the audience is used to seeing and interpreting them. They are widely used in the Far East, and far less frequently in North America.

Radar

Suppose you own a landscaping business. You want to chart the seasonal job load for the last five years to determine when you need to hire more employees and when it's safe to schedule vacations. You can use a radar chart to portray seasonal fluctuations, and help you make a decision more quickly than when analyzing tabular data.

In a radar chart, the points in a data series are plotted in a circle around a central point. The central point of the chart represents the Y-axis. Each data point has its own spoke, or X-axis, and the value of the data point is displayed by its position on the spoke. Using the landscaping scenario, you would record the number of jobs each month for the last five years, and each year's data would be a data series in the chart. Like the doughnut chart, the radar chart is widely used in the Far East.

Scatter

Suppose you want to show the relationship between the adult heights of women and their mothers. A scatter chart is a good way to display the relationship. Each data point in a scatter chart is a coordinate composed of an X-value (a specific woman's height) and a Y-value (her mother's height). If there is a relationship between mother and daughter heights, the coordinate points in the chart will form a straight line or clusters. If there is not a relationship, the coordinate points will be scattered at random in the chart. Scatter charts show the correlation between two data series, and are widely used to present scientific data. They are particularly good for value changes over uneven intervals.

Combination

Suppose you want to chart the Dow Jones average and the total volume traded every day for a month? You can chart two data series with vastly different value scales on the same chart by using a combination chart. Combination charts are a hybrid of chart types, for example, column and area, or line and column. Commonly, combination charts have a secondary axis to display a data series on a different value scale. You can create a combination chart by selecting the Combination chart type from the ChartWizard step 2 dialog. But what if you have already created a chart, and you don't want to recreate it ? You can change a chart into a combination chart easily. Chapter 14 describes how to change an individual chart series type, and how to add a secondary axis to an existing chart.

3-D

Suppose you are putting together a presentation for the stockholder's meeting, and you want to impress and dazzle the stockholders with a terrific graphical display of the company's finances? 3-D charts are a good choice for visual appeal. Most of Excel's chart types have a three-dimensional format. (Radar, scatter, and combination charts do *not* have 3-D counterparts.) When you create a 3-D chart, remember to spin or tilt the chart until you have the best possible viewing angle (see Chapter 14 to learn about 3-D charts). Also, if you find that one data series is obscuring another (common in 3-D column charts), it's easy to put the data series in a different order so that all the data markers can be seen.

Surface

Surface charts look like topographical maps. They are unfamiliar to many users, but are extremely useful once you understand how to use and interpret them. In a surface chart, color is used to show value ranges rather than to identify series markers. You can use a surface chart to plot data from a continuum (such as temperatures, altitudes, or retail sales prices), rather than discrete data points (such as sales reps or product names). Chapter 14 explains surface charts with a real-world application.

▶▶ *Using the ChartWizard*

 In the previous exercise, the ChartWizard was used to create an embedded chart. But the exercise asked you to immediately click the Finish button, which skipped over most of the ChartWizard options. In this section, the five major ChartWizard steps will be thoroughly explained.

▶ *Starting the ChartWizard*

To begin creating a chart, select the data to be charted (including labels for columns and rows), then do one of the following:

- Click the ChartWizard tool if you want to create an embedded chart, then use the mouse to draw the chart object on the worksheet.

- Choose Insert ➤ Chart ➤ On This Sheet (same as the ChartWizard tool).

- Choose Insert ➤ Chart ➤ As New Sheet to create a new chart sheet.

The ChartWizard is displayed (see Figure 13.5). Each step of the ChartWizard includes Cancel, Back, Next, and Finish buttons:

- Click Cancel to stop the ChartWizard—no chart will be created.

- Click Back to go back to the previous step.

- Click Next to proceed to the next step.

- Click Finish when you are done specifying chart properties—the chart will be created immediately.

Step 1 of 5—Confirm the Data Range

Step 1 confirms that the selected range contains the data you want included in the chart (see Figure 13.5). If the range displayed is not correct, change it by typing a new reference or by selecting a different range. The chart data does not have to come from the active worksheet; you can specify a different worksheet, or even a different workbook:

If Data Is on a Different Worksheet Display the ChartWizard Step 1 dialog box. Select the worksheet, then select the range of cells containing the data. Click the Next button.

FIGURE 13.5 ▶

Step 1 of the ChartWizard displays the range that the chart will be based on, and lets you override it.

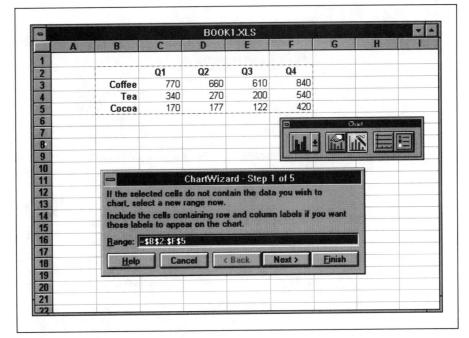

If Data Is in a Different Workbook Be sure the workbook containing the data (Book1, for example) is open, and the workbook where the chart will be drawn (Book2) is active. Display the ChartWizard Step 1 dialog box. Select Book1 from the Window menu, then select the worksheet and the range of cells containing the data. Click the Next button.

Include row and column headings if you want them to appear as labels in the chart. When the range is correct, click Next.

 ▶ ▶ **N O T E**

You can change the properties of the default chart. This procedure is described in Chapter 14.

Step 2 of 5—Choose the Type of Chart

Step 2 lets you choose the type of chart. In Figure 13.6, a column chart has been selected. Then click Next.

FIGURE 13.6 ►

Choose the type of
chart you want to
create.

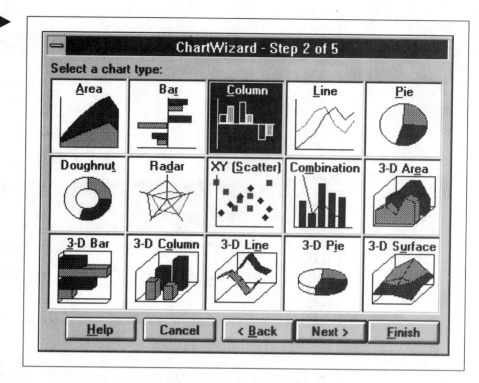

Step 3 of 5—Select a Type Format

Each type of chart has several different formats from which to choose.
Step 3, pictured in Figure 13.7, lets you choose the chart format. Click
Next to move to step four.

Step 4 of 5—Orient the Chart

Step 4, pictured in Figure 13.8, displays a preview of the chart, and lets
you specify how the data on the chart is oriented:

Data Series in: Rows This means that each data series is plotted from a row of data.

Data Series in: Columns If this option is selected, each data
series will be plotted from a column of data.

FIGURE 13.7 ▶

Choose the chart format.

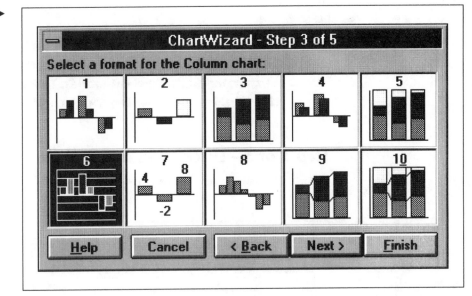

FIGURE 13.8 ▶

The ChartWizard guesses how the data should be oriented, but you can override these settings.

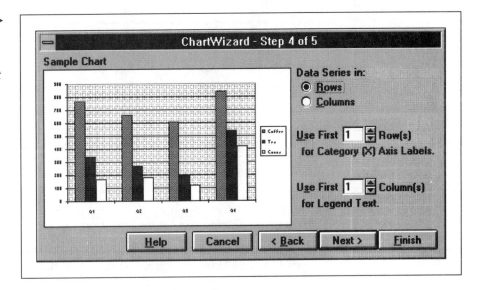

Use First *X* Row(s)   This setting lets you specify how many top rows contain X-axis labels.

Use First *X* Column(s)   This setting lets you specify how many left-hand columns contain the legend entries.

> ▶ ▶**N O T E**
>
> **Multiple rows and columns can be selected for X-axis labels and legend text because Excel is capable of charting multi-level categories. To learn more about charting multi-level categories, see Chapter 14.**

Step 5 of 5—Enter Titles and Legend

Step 5 lets you specify legend, chart title, and axis titles. (See Figure 13.9)

FIGURE 13.9 ▶

Choose chart and axis titles and a legend display.

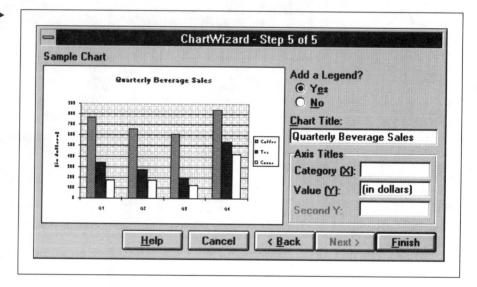

- If you don't want a legend, choose *No*—you can always add one later by clicking the Legend tool on the Chart toolbar.
- Type chart and/or axis titles if you want them—if left blank, titles can be added later with the Insert ▶ Titles command.

Click Finish to create the chart, as in Figure 13.10.

FIGURE 13.10 ►

Completed column chart created with ChartWizard

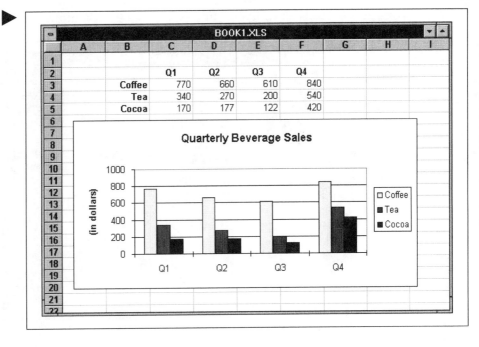

► *Changing a Chart Using the ChartWizard*

The ChartWizard can be used to change an existing chart. However, when changing a chart, only two of the original five steps are available.

1. If the chart is an embedded chart, select it (click it with the mouse); if it is a chart sheet, activate the sheet.

2. Click the ChartWizard tool.

   Step 1   Same as Step 1 when creating a new chart

   Step 2   Same as Step 4 when creating a new chart

► ► *Changing a Chart to a Different Type*

There are many built-in chart types to choose from (see Figure 13.6). Each type of chart has several basic formats, sometimes referred to by

Excel as subtypes. For example, a 2-D column chart has three subtypes.

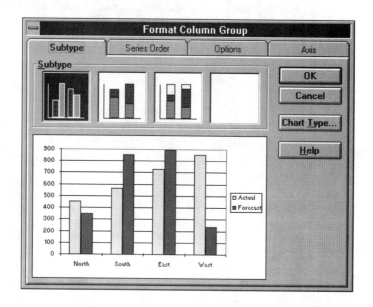

The previous exercise explained how to change a chart using the ChartWizard. There are several other ways to change a chart from one type to another, or change the subtype.

Changing the Chart Type Using the Main Menu Activate the chart (double-click it if it is an embedded chart), then choose Format ➤ Chart Type and select a new chart type.

 Changing the Chart Type Using the Chart Type Tool The Chart Type tool (on the Chart toolbar) contains a drop-down palette of chart types. These tools are faster to use than the Format ➤ Chart Type command, but do not offer the variety of subtypes that the command offers. To use the tools, select the chart (no need to activate it), then select a chart type from the palette.

 ▶ ▶ **T I P**

> The Chart Type tool has a tear-off palette. See Chapter 1 to learn how to use tear-off palettes.

Changing the SubType Using AutoFormat To use an AutoFormat, activate the chart, then choose Format ➤ AutoFormat. Select a type from the Galleries list, then choose a format from the Formats options. Click on OK to close the dialog box. If you don't like the result, choose Edit ➤ Undo to undo the AutoFormat, or choose a different AutoFormat.

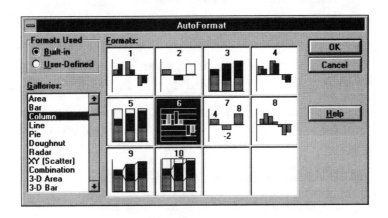

 ▶ ▶ **T I P**

> **You can create your own user-defined chart Auto-Formats. See Chapter 14 to learn how.**

▶ ▶ *Adding, Deleting, and Changing Chart Data*

Once created, a chart does not need to be recreated in order to add data, delete data, or reorganize the data.

▶ *Adding Data to a Chart*

There are several ways to add new data to an existing chart:

- Use Drag and Drop (embedded charts only)
- Use the Edit ➤ Copy and Edit ➤ Paste commands
- Use the Insert ➤ New Data command

Drag and Drop New Data onto an Embedded Chart

You can add a new data series, or new data points, using drag-and-drop.

Drag and Drop New Data Series To add a new series with drag-and-drop, select the new row or column of data on the worksheet and drag and drop it onto the chart.

Drag and Drop New Data Points To add new points to an existing series, select the points and drag and drop them onto the chart.

After you drag and drop, if Excel is unable to determine whether you are adding a series or data points, a dialog box is displayed which lets you specify the type of data being added.

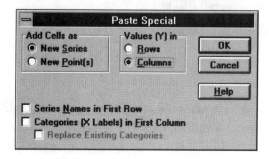

Suppose you have a worksheet which tracks sales by region, and charts the data. At the end of each month, data is added to the sheet, and needs to be added to the chart.

To add the new data to the chart in Figure 13.11:

1. Select F2:F4.
2. Drag and drop the cells onto the chart. (Drag the cells as if you were moving them, and drop them anywhere on the chart).

Adding Data Using Copy and Paste

New data can be added by copying from the worksheet, and pasting onto the chart. This works for embedded charts and chart sheets.

1. Select the data you are adding to the chart.
2. Choose Edit ➤ Copy.

FIGURE 13.11

The new data points are added at the end of each data series—it doesn't matter where on the chart you drop the cells.

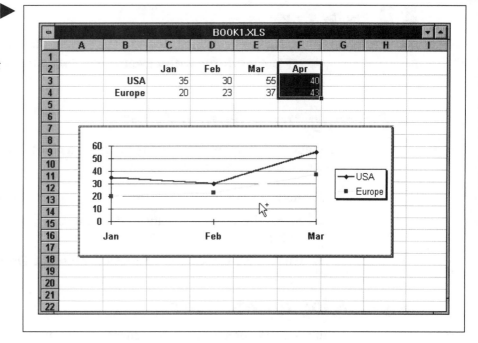

3. Select the chart:

   • If it is embedded, select it with the mouse.

   • If it is a chart sheet, activate the sheet by clicking the sheet tab.

4. Choose Edit ➤ Paste.

Adding Data Using Insert ➤ New Data

The Insert ➤ New Data command is available only when a chart is active. This technique works for both embedded charts and chart sheets.

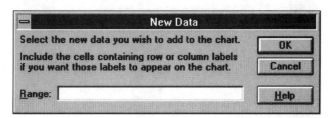

Enter a cell reference, or use the mouse to point-and-click the range, then click OK.

TIP

A chart can include data that comes from more than one worksheet, and even from more than one workbook.

▶ Deleting Data from a Chart

A data series can be deleted directly from a chart, and there is no impact on the underlying worksheet data.

1. Activate the chart.

2. Select the series you want to delete by clicking a data marker within the series.

3. Choose Edit ➤ Clear ➤ Series (or press the Delete key).

▶ Changing a Data Series

Suppose that after you create a chart, you want to change the source for one of the data series. In Figure 13.12, the budget and Y-T-D

FIGURE 13.12 ▶

The budget data series points to C3:C4. It needs to be changed to F3:F4.

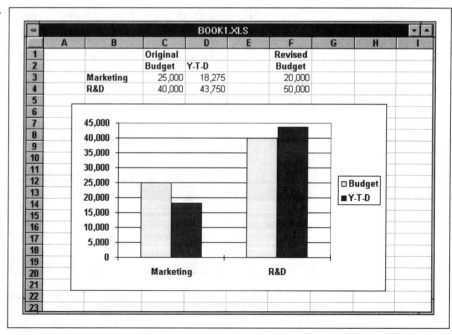

columns (C and D) are charted. Revised budget figures have been entered into column F, and the budget data series needs to point to the revised budget instead of the original budget.

1. Activate the chart.

2. Select the budget data series by single-clicking any data point in the series—in Figure 13.13 the budget data series is selected.

FIGURE 13.13

The S1 on the left part of the formula bar indicates that data series one is selected.

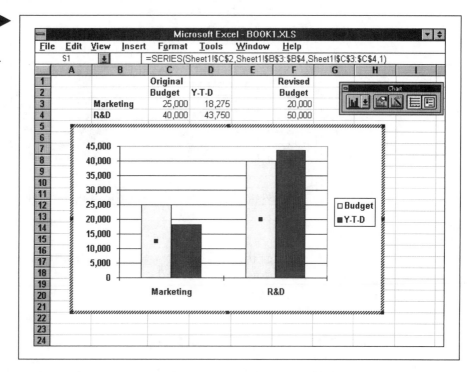

▶▶**T I P**

> **The first time you click a data point, the entire data series is selected. If you click the data point a second time, just the single point is selected.**

3. Choose Format ➤ Selected Data Series, then select the Name and Values tab (Figure 13.14).

FIGURE 13.14 ▶

The Name and Values tab in the Format Data Series dialog box

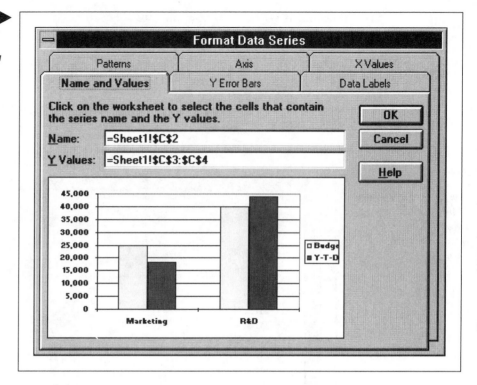

4. Change the Y Values to: **=Sheet1!$F$3:$F$4** (you can type this in, or you can point-and-click on the worksheet to fill it in).

5. Click OK.

▶ *Changing Data Orientation*

Suppose you want to change the orientation of the chart in Figure 13.11 so that the months are data series (on the legend) and the regions are categories (on the horizontal axis). The ChartWizard makes it easy to change the data orientation:

1. Activate the chart and click the ChartWizard tool.

2. Click Next on the Step 1 of 2 dialog box.

3. In the Step 2 of 2 dialog box, use the Data Series In options to specify columns instead of rows.

▶ *Charting Noncontiguous Ranges*

On Figure 13.15, suppose you want to chart only the TOTAL rows:

1. Select cells C2:F2.

2. Hold down Ctrl, then select cells C5:F5 and C9:F9.

3. Create the chart with ChartWizard.

Figure 13.15 illustrates charted noncontiguous data ranges.

FIGURE 13.15 ▶

Only the two TOTAL rows and labels are included in the chart

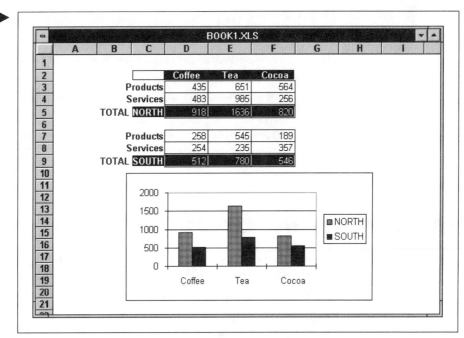

▶ ▶ *Deleting Charts*

Here is how to delete embedded charts and chart sheets:

▶ *Embedded Charts*

Deleting an embedded chart from the worksheet is the same as deleting any other object: Select the chart object and press Delete.

(Or right-click the chart and choose the Clear command from the shortcut menu.)

▶ *Chart Sheets*

Deleting a chart sheet is just like deleting any other sheet in a workbook: Activate the sheet, and choose Edit ➤ Delete Sheet. (Or right-click the sheet tab and choose the Delete command from the shortcut menu.)

 ▶ ▶ T I P

If you want to print a worksheet that contains an embedded chart, but don't want to include the chart in the printout, you need not delete the chart. Instead, select the chart and choose the Format ➤ Object command, select the Properties tab, and uncheck the Print Object setting. (See Chapter 12 to learn more about object properties.)

▶▶ *Formatting Chart Elements*

Formatting chart elements is not difficult. The topic seems complex only because there are so many different elements of a chart, each with unique formatting properties, as identified in Figure 13.16.

There are certain procedures that apply to formatting chart elements, regardless of which chart element you are formatting:

- The chart must be active in order to format any element in it. Activate embedded charts by double-clicking the chart; activate chart sheets by clicking the sheet tab.

- Double-click the chart element you want to format to display the Format dialog box (or right-click the element, and select the Format command from the shortcut menu). The name of the selected

FIGURE 13.16

Chart elements

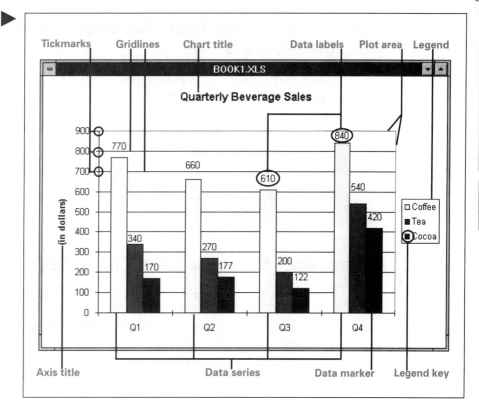

element is displayed in the Name box on the left part of the formula bar.

● Select the formatting options you want, then click OK.

Sometimes it is hard to select the right chart element. The element you want to select may not be visible, or another element may overlap it. A sure way to select an elusive chart element is to select any element, then use the left or right arrow keys to cycle through all of the elements.

▶ ▶ **T I P**

To delete a chart element, select the element and press Delete (or choose Clear from the shortcut menu).

▶ Using Formatting Tools for Quick Chart Element Formatting

Most of the tools on the Formatting toolbar can be used to format chart elements. As an example, follow these steps to format axis text to bold:

1. Display the Formatting toolbar (use the View ➤ Toolbars command).

2. Activate the chart.

3. Select an axis.

4. Click the Bold tool.

▶ Formatting an Embedded Chart Object

You just read about formatting the elements inside a chart. Embedded charts are just like other graphic objects, and the *chart object* itself can be formatted (as opposed to the elements inside the chart). In fact, the formatting options are identical to a rectangle. (See Chapter 12.) Formatting the *chart object* has nothing to do with formatting the chart elements that live inside the chart.

▶ ▶ **T I P**

Think of an embedded chart object as a boring box full of interesting stuff. Formatting the chart object makes the box a little bit more interesting, but has no bearing on the interesting stuff inside the box.

To format an embedded chart, select it and choose Format ➤ Object. (Remember, *selecting* is just one click, whereas *activating* requires a double-click.)

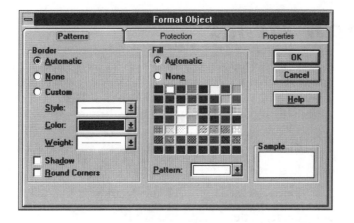

Figure 13.17 shows several embedded charts with different formatting.

FIGURE 13.17

The only difference between these embedded charts is the formatting of the chart object.

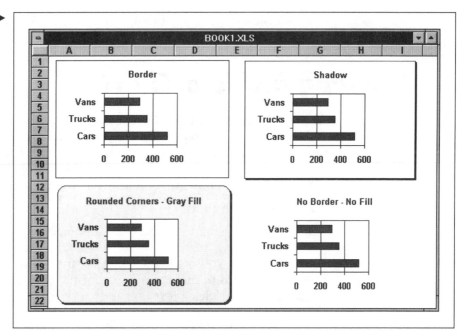

 ▶ ▶**TIP**

Embedded charts with no fill and no border are most effective on a worksheet with no gridlines.

►► *Shortcut Menus*

Many of the elements within a chart have shortcut menus providing context-sensitive commands. To use a shortcut menu, right-click on the chart element and choose a command. Here is a list of the elements within an active chart that can be right-clicked to display a shortcut menu:

Chart	Plot Area	Axis
Legend	Legend Entry	Legend Key
Data Series	Data Marker	Gridlines
Chart Title	Axis Title	Data Label
Trendline	Error Bars	Droplines
Series Lines	High-Low lines	Up-Down bars
Walls (3-D)	Floor (3-D)	Corner (3-D)

►► *Drawing inside a Chart*

In Chapter 12 you learned how to draw objects on a worksheet. Similarly, you can draw objects *inside* a chart. The procedure is the same as when you draw on a worksheet, except the chart must be active:

1. Display the Drawing toolbar.

2. Activate the chart.

3. Click a drawing tool, and draw an object on the chart.

The objects that you draw in a chart live inside the chart. The chart must be activated to move, resize, or format the objects. The chart in Figure 13.18 includes a text box and an arrow.

You can also copy pictures and objects into a chart. For example, if you have a company logo as a bitmap file, you can use the Insert ➤ Object or Insert ➤ Picture command to insert it in the worksheet, then copy the logo and paste it into an activated chart.

FIGURE 13.18 ▶

A text box and an arrow are drawn on the chart.

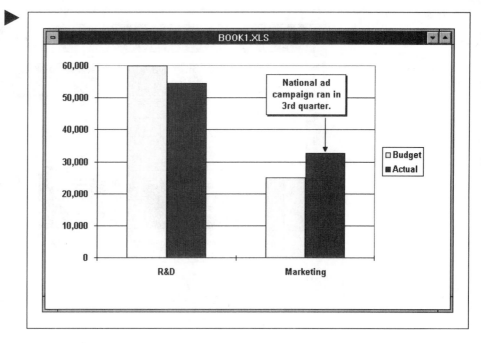

▶▶ *Charting Exercise*

In this exercise you will apply many of the skills learned in this chapter to create and format a chart.

1. Enter Data and Create a Chart

Enter the data in Figure 13.19 on a new worksheet, and use the ChartWizard to create a chart using default formatting (click Finish in the ChartWizard Step 1 dialog box).

2. Change the Colors of the Data Series

a. Right-click on one of the markers (notice that the whole series is selected, and a shortcut menu is displayed).

b. Choose the Format ➤ Data Series command, then select the Patterns tab.

c. Select a different color from the color palette, and click OK.

d. Repeat the process to change the color of the other series.

FIGURE 13.19 ▶

Since the default chart is customizable, your chart may not look identical to this one.

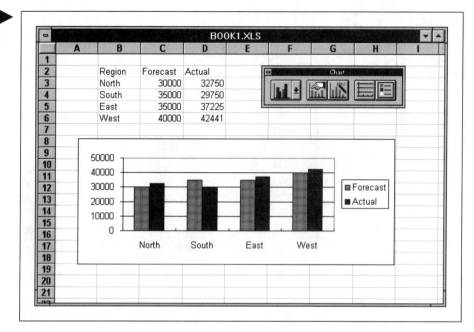

TIP

The Color tool on the Formatting toolbar can be used to color chart elements (use the tear-off Color palette to color chart elements quickly).

3. Change the Forecast Series Chart Type from Column to Area

a. Right-click on one of the Forecast series markers.

b. Choose the Chart Type command, then select Area and click OK.

4. Remove the Plot Area Color

a. Right-click on the plot area.

b. Choose Format Plot Area.

c. Select Area—None, then click OK.

5. Change the Chart Area Color to Dark Gray

a. Right-click near the perimeter of the chart to select the Chart area and display the shortcut menu.

b. Choose the Format Chart Area command, then select the Patterns tab.

c. Select a dark gray area color, then click OK.

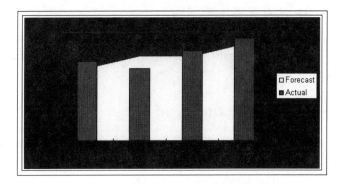

6. Change Axis Text to Bold and White

a. Right-click one axis and choose the Format Axis command.

b. Select the Font tab.

c. Select settings for bold and white, and click OK.

d. Select the other axis and choose Edit ➤ Repeat Format Axis.

7. Format Numbers on the Y-Axis to Display in Thousands

a. Right-click the Y-axis and choose the Format Axis command.

b. Select the Number tab, and type **#,###,** in the Code edit box (be sure to type both commas). See Chapter 5 to learn more about custom number formats.

c. Leave the Format Axis dialog box displayed for the next procedure.

8. Change Scale on the Y-Axis to Reduce Gridline Clutter

a. Select the Scale tab.

b. Type **10000** in the Major Unit edit box.

c. Click OK to close the Format Axis dialog box.

▶ ▶**N O T E**

> **Depending on how large you draw the chart, the default major unit may already be 10,000.**

9. Format the Legend

a. Right-click the legend and choose the Format Legend command.

b. Select the Patterns tab, and select a light gray area color and the border Shadow setting.

c. Select the Font tab and choose bold. Click OK to close the dialog box.

10. Add and Format a Chart Title

a. Choose Insert ➤ Titles, and check the Chart Title setting, then click OK

b. Double-click the title text to select it, then type **Sales**. Press Esc to deselect the title text.

c. Right-click the new title and choose the Format Chart Title command.

d. Format the title color, border, and text to match the legend. Then click OK.

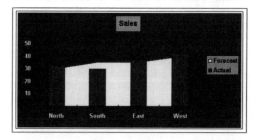

11. *Reshape the Legend and Plot Area to Reduce Empty Space*

a. Move the chart title over to the left side of the plot area, and move the legend to the top of the chart.

b. Reshape the legend (drag handles) to be wide and shallow, with the legend entries side-by-side.

c. Select the plot area. Drag the right-side handle to the right side of the chart, to fill in the empty space.

12. *Apply a Shadowed Border to the Chart*

a. Click a worksheet cell to deactivate the chart.

b. Right-click the chart and choose the Format Object command.

c. Select the Patterns tab. Select a fill color for the chart object which is the same as you chose for the chart area.

d. Select a medium-weight border, and check the Shadow, and Round Corners settings. Then click OK.

Now, turn off the gridlines on the worksheet, and the chart should look something like this:

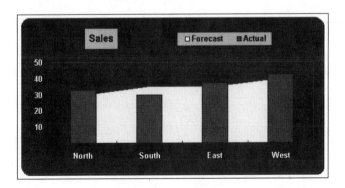

COPYING CHART FORMATS

Suppose you are looking at a workbook which contains a carefully formatted chart. Perhaps you spent a lot of time formatting it, or maybe someone else created it and you want to "borrow" the formatting to use on one of your charts. You can easily copy and paste the formatting of one chart onto another chart. To copy and paste formatting, activate the chart you want to copy. Select the Chart area—the Name box should read "Chart", then choose Edit ➤ Copy. Activate the chart where you want to paste the formatting, and choose Edit ➤ Paste Special. In the Paste Special dialog box, select the Formats option. If you want the format to be readily available in the future, you may want to create a custom AutoFormat, which is covered in Chapter 14.

Constructing Complex Charts Using Advanced Techniques

FAST TRACK

►► **C**hapter 13 covered the basics of working with charts. Once you have mastered the basics, this chapter will provide you with the advanced skills needed to create and format charts that are not of the everyday variety:

- *Creating custom AutoFormats, and changing the default chart*
- *Creating combination charts*
- *Forecasting with trendlines*
- *Creating picture charts*
- *The most important advanced skill: charting data dynamically*
- *Advanced tips and tricks*

►► Custom AutoFormats Can Save Time and Create Consistency

If you often create charts with similar formatting, you can save a lot of time by creating one or more custom AutoFormats. In addition to time savings, AutoFormats can help you create a consistent, professional look for reports and presentations.

Suppose you frequently chart two types of data using the same chart type, with the same colors, fonts, and other formatting—for example:

- Comparing budgeted expense versus actual expense
- Comparing sales to sales forecasts

One custom AutoFormat can be used for both of these charts. Here are the basic steps for creating a custom AutoFormat:

1. Create a chart (embedded chart or chart sheet)—apply all formatting such as fonts, gridlines, color, legend, etc.

2. Activate the chart, and choose Format ➤ AutoFormat.

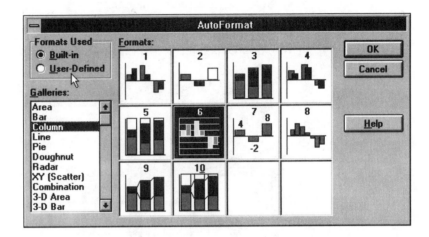

3. Select User-Defined option, then click the Customize button. The User-Defined AutoFormats dialog box will be displayed.

4. Click the Add button.

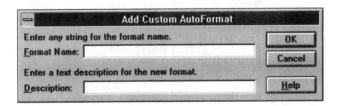

5. Type a name for the custom AutoFormat (and a brief identifying description, if desired) then click OK. The name is restricted to 31 characters in length, and the description is restricted to 32 characters.

6. Close the User-Defined AutoFormats dialog box.

▶ Applying a Custom AutoFormat

Once you have created a custom AutoFormat, follow these steps to apply it:

1. Create a new chart using default formats.

2. Select and activate the chart.

3. Choose the Format ➤ AutoFormat command.

4. Click User-Defined.

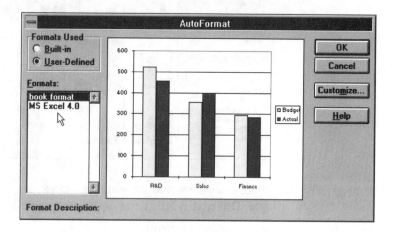

5. Select the custom AutoFormat from the Formats list—the Auto-Format is previewed in the dialog box—click OK.

The chart in Figure 14.1 was built and formatted, and then a custom AutoFormat was defined using the newly-created chart as the basis.

This AutoFormat can be applied to charts which are not necessarily identical to the original chart, as shown in Figures 14.2 and 14.3.

FIGURE 14.1 ▶

The title and legend have shadows, and are positioned to allow a large plot area. The fonts are bold. The colors are customized.

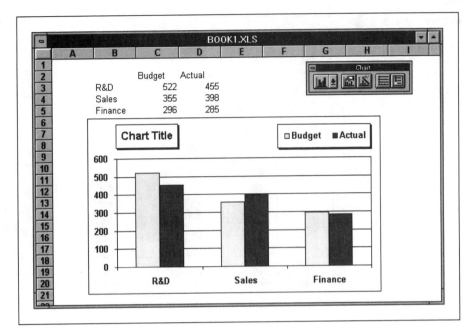

FIGURE 14.2 ▶

The AutoFormat is applicable even when there are more (or fewer) data series.

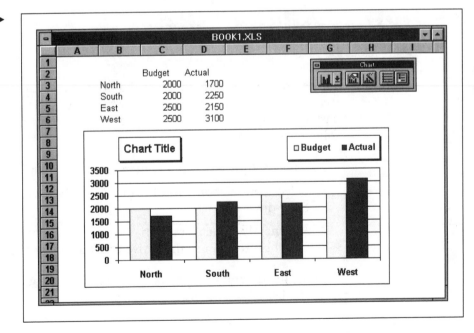

FIGURE 14.3 ▶

The AutoFormat is now applied to Forecast/Sales instead of Budget/Actual.

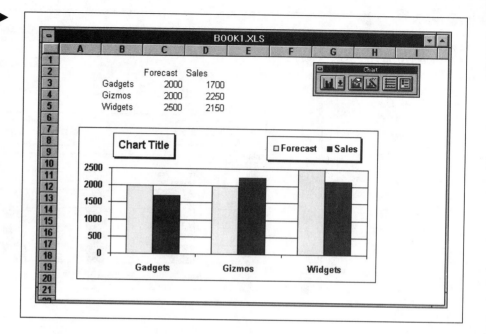

▶▶ *How to Change the Default Chart*

In the previous section, you learned how to create custom AutoFormats. Once you have created one or more custom AutoFormats, it is easy to configure Excel to use one of them as your default chart. Just follow these steps:

1. Choose Tools ➤ Options, then select the Chart tab (Figure 14.4).

2. Select your custom AutoFormat from the Default Chart Format drop-down list.

3. Alternately, if a chart is active, you can click the Use the Current Chart button to use the active chart as the default chart.

To reset the default chart back to the original default, select (Built-in) from the list of default chart formats.

FIGURE 14.4 ▶

The settings inside the Active Chart group, and the Use Current Chart button, are only available when a chart is active.

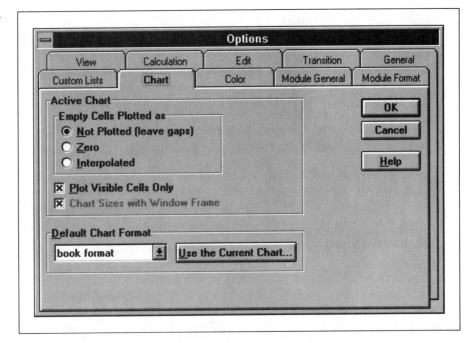

▶ *Other Chart Options*

The Active Chart settings, pictured in Figure 14.4, are also important to understand:

Setting	Function
Not Plotted	A gap is left in the chart when a plotted cell is blank.
Zero	Blank cells are treated as zero value.
Interpolated	Fills in lines by interpolating a value.
Plot Visible Cells Only	Only visible cells are plotted—hidden cells are ignored (particularly useful in conjunction with outlining).
Chart Sizes with Window	This setting pertains to chart sheets—when checked, the chart automatically sizes according to size of the window (same as the View ▶ Sized with Window command).

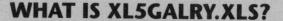

> ### WHAT IS XL5GALRY.XLS?
>
> When you create a custom chart autoformat, the formatting information is stored in a hidden file called XL5GALRY.XLS, located in Excel's XLSTART directory. XL5GALRY.XLS exists *only* to store custom chart autoformats. The first time you choose the Tools ➤ Options command during an Excel session, you may notice that XL5GALRY.XLS is opened before the dialog box appears (observe the status bar). If you delete XL5GALRY.XLS, you will lose all previously created custom chart autoformats. Excel will automatically create a new XL5GALRY.XLS the next time you create a custom chart autoformat or save a chart as the default chart format.

▶▶ Creating Combination Charts

Suppose you have charted actual and projected sales for a period. A combination chart may emphasize the relationship between the two data series better than a single chart type, as illustrated in Figure 14.5.

Follow these steps to create a combination chart:

1. Activate the chart and select the data series you want to change.
2. Choose Format ➤ Chart Type and select a type from the Chart Type dialog box.

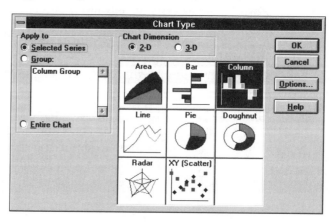

FIGURE 14.5 ▶

The combination chart (on the right)—which you may find easier to quickly absorb—combines a column chart and line chart.

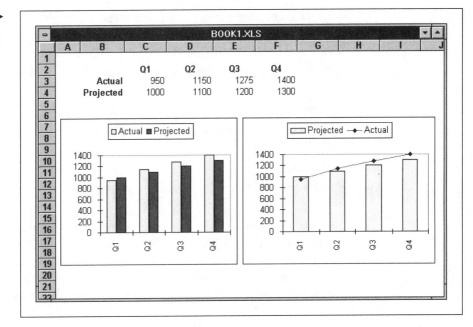

Unlike previous versions, Excel 5 is not limited to two chart types in a combo chart—as you can see in Figure 14.6.

FIGURE 14.6 ▶

Combination charts are particularly effective when printed on a black-and-white printer, where it can be difficult to distinguish gray scales.

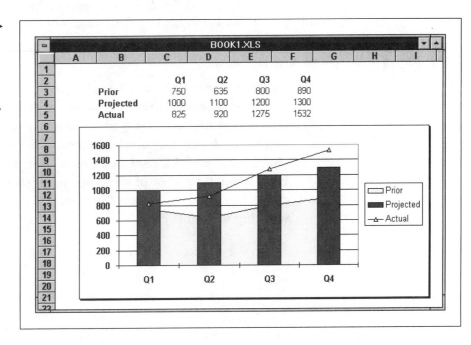

Constructing Complex Charts

Ch.
14

More facts about combination charts:

- 3-D charts cannot be combined.
- You can create any combination of area, column, line and scatter charts.
- You can include bar, pie, doughnut, or radar types in a combo chart, but only one series can be formatted using these types.

▶▶ *Working with 3-D Charts*

3-D charts are a mixed blessing. They are visually appealing, and sometimes allow complex data to be presented in a way that is easier to absorb than a 2-D chart. On the other hand, they present certain problems. For instance, a data series in a 3-D column chart might obscure another data series. But used judiciously, 3-D charts can enhance your reports and presentations.

▶ *Visual Appeal*

Some 3-D chart types and formats are essentially the same as their 2-D counterparts. The benefit is visual appeal, as illustrated in Figure 14.7.

 ▶ ▶ **W A R N I N G**

There is a problem with 3-D pie charts, which is often overlooked, and Figure 14.7 shows a good example of it. Most people don't pay attention to the fact that the angles of the corresponding portions in the two pie charts (2-D and 3-D) are not equal. Sure, it's because Excel is putting a bit of perspective on the second pie chart, but it is misleading. Be aware of this fact when working with 3-D pies!

FIGURE 14.7 ▶

Sometimes the difference between a 2-D and 3-D chart is purely aesthetic.

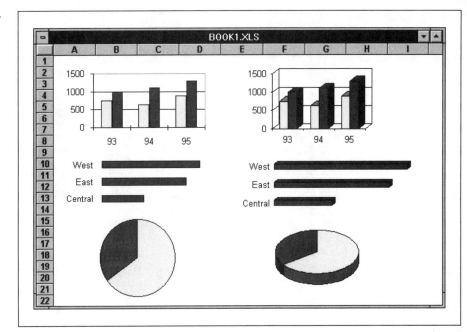

▶ *Practical Application*

The benefits of 3-D charts are not limited to aesthetics. The 3-D column chart in Figure 14.8 provides a result that would be difficult to achieve using 2-D.

▶ *Viewing a 3-D Chart from Different Angles*

For some 3-D chart formats, such as the column chart in Figure 14.8, it is possible for a data series to obscure another data series. When a 3-D chart is active, you can choose Format ➤ 3-D View to change the view angle.

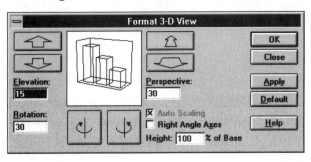

FIGURE 14.8 ►

Terminology for 3-D column charts

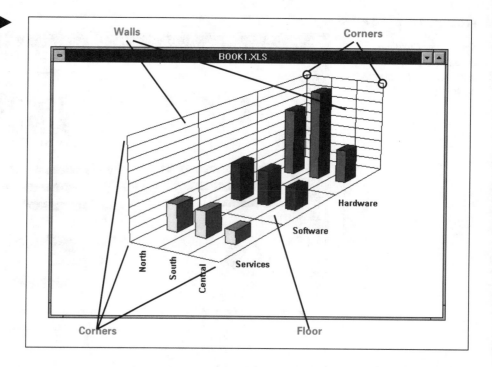

As you click the elevation, perspective, and spin buttons, the preview box gives you a general idea of how you are viewing the chart.

- Click OK to accept the view.
- Click Close to cancel the view changes.
- Click Apply to apply the view settings to the chart, but leave the dialog box displayed for more changes.
- Click Default to go back to the default 3-D view.

Another way to change 3-D view is by direct manipulation of the chart using the mouse. Follow these steps:

1. Activate the chart.
2. Select the corners by clicking any corner.
2. Click a corner again and hold down the mouse button. The mouse becomes a crosshair.
4. Drag the corner (hold down Ctrl while dragging the corner if you want to display outlines of the data markers while changing the

view, as pictured in Figure 14.9). Release the mouse button to re-display the full chart.

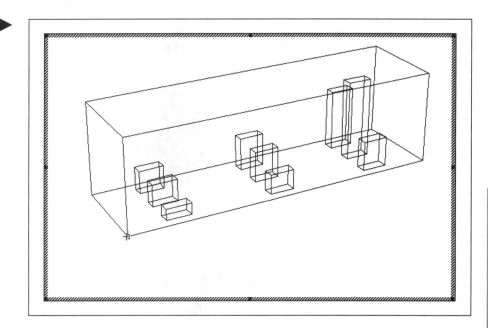

▶ *An Exercise in Creating and Formatting a 3-D Chart*

In this exercise, you will create and format a 3-D column chart.

1. Enter Data and Create a Chart

a. Enter the following on a new worksheet:

	A	B	C	D	E	F	
1							
2		Region	Hardware	Software	Services		
3		North	654	352	245		
4		South	871	325	235		
5		Central	322	212	121		
6							
7							
8							
9							

BOOK1.XLS

b. Choose Insert ➤ Chart ➤ As New Sheet to create a chart sheet—choose these options in the ChartWizard:

- Select the 3-D column chart in Step 2.
- Select format #6 in Step 3.
- Select no legend in Step 5.

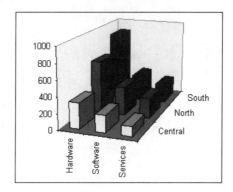

2. Change the Floor Color

a. Double-click the floor (or right-click the floor and choose Format Floor from the shortcut menu).

b. Choose a light gray area color from the Format Floor dialog box.

 ▶ ▶**T I P**

You can change the color of any chart element using the Color tool palette from the Formatting toolbar, and text color can be changed using the Font Color tool palette.

3. Change the Size and Spacing of Columns

a. Choose the Format ➤ 3-D Column Group command, then select the Options tab.

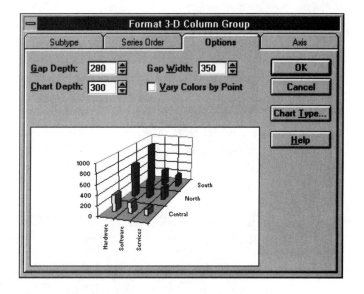

b. Change the Gap Depth setting to **280**.

c. Change the Chart Depth setting to **300**.

d. Change the Gap Width setting to **350**.

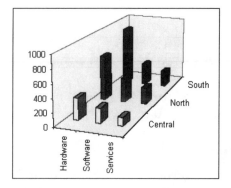

▶▶ *Special Formatting*

This section will explain how to add special lines, such as droplines and up-down bars, and how to separate pie wedges.

► Adding Lines and Bars

You can add droplines, series lines, high-low lines, and up-down bars to some charts. They are all added the same way:

1. Select the chart area, plot area, or series.

2. Choose the Format Group command (this will display as Format ► Line Group in a line chart, Format ► Area Group in an area chart, etc.)

3. Select the Options tab.

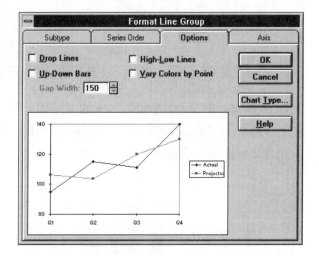

4. Check the setting for Drop Lines, Series Lines, High-Low Lines, or Up-Down Bars.

Droplines

Droplines are vertical lines which emphasize the location of the data point on the X-axis. They are applicable to area and line charts only.

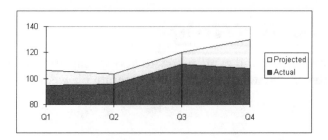

Series Lines

Series lines connect the series in stacked bar and column charts. They highlight the amount of value change between data points.

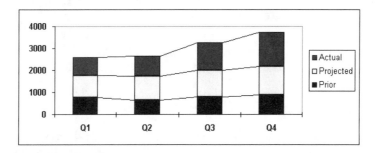

High-Low Lines

High-low lines emphasize the difference between the high and low data points within each category. They can be applied to line charts only, and are particularly useful on stock market charts.

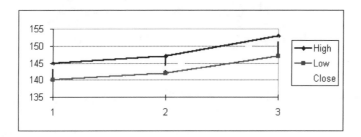

Up-Down Bars

Up-down bars highlight the performance of one data series relative to another data series. Suppose you have charted forecast vs. actual sales over several periods. In periods where actual exceeds forecast, the up-down bars display the variance in one color. When actual is less than forecast, the up-down bars display the variance in another color. Up-down bars can only be placed on line charts with at least two series.

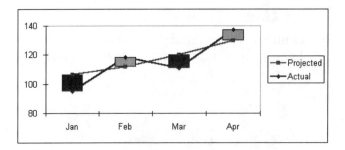

► *Separating Pie Slices*

Slices of pie charts can be separated from the rest of the pie for emphasis. A single slice can be separated, or all of the slices can be separated.

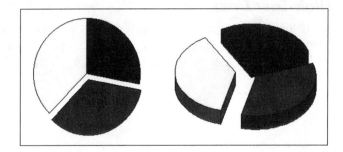

- To separate all of the slices, select the series (single-click any slice) and drag it away from the center of the pie.

- To separate only one slice, select the slice (single-click the slice, then single-click it again) and drag it away from the center of the pie.

- To join separated slices, drag the slice(s) back to the center of the pie.

►► *Changing Worksheet Values by Manipulating the Chart*

Some charts let you change underlying worksheet data by manipulating the chart with the mouse. This is a useful technique when doing what-if analysis. Only 2-D bar, 2-D column, and 2-D line charts allow direct manipulation of data markers. Try the following exercise:

1. Enter the following on a worksheet, then create a 2-D column chart:

	A	B	C	D	E
1					
2		Region	Actual	Forecast	
3		North	456	346	
4		South	562	854	
5		East	726	892	
6		West	851	238	
7					
8					

BOOK1.XLS

2. Select the North Actual marker by single-clicking it twice (not a double-click).

3. Drag the handle on top of the marker up or down (Figure 14.10), and notice that the value in cell C3 changes.

FIGURE 14.10 ▶

While dragging the marker, the mouse pointer becomes an up-down arrow. The underlying cell changes as soon as you release the mouse button.

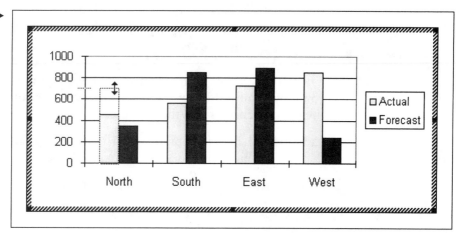

What If the Chart Is Based on a Cell Containing a Formula?

If you directly manipulate a data marker that points to a cell containing a formula, something different happens. Excel will not change the formula. Rather, it changes one of the cells that the formula depends on. The Goal Seek dialog box is displayed, allowing you to specify which cell should be changed.

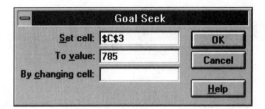

You are required to enter a cell reference that the charted cell depends on. (See Chapter 23 to learn more about Goal Seek.)

▶▶ *Changing the Way Data Is Plotted*

Once you have created a chart, there are several ways to change how the data is plotted.

▶ *Reversing the Plot Order*

There are two common reasons for reversing the plot order for an axis: you may want to look at the data differently, or you may have created the chart incorrectly in the first place.

In Figure 14.11, the data in B3:C7 is sorted by sales in descending order. Yet the bar chart goes from small to large.

Follow these steps to reverse the plot order:

1. Activate the chart.

2. Select the axis to reverse, and choose Format ▶ Axis—select the Scale tab.

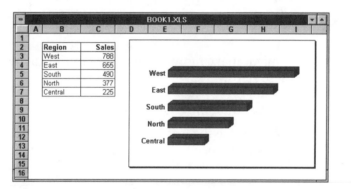

3. Check the Categories in Reverse Order setting, then click OK.

FIGURE 14.11 ▶

*An instance of the
data sheet and bar
chart being oriented in
reverse order*

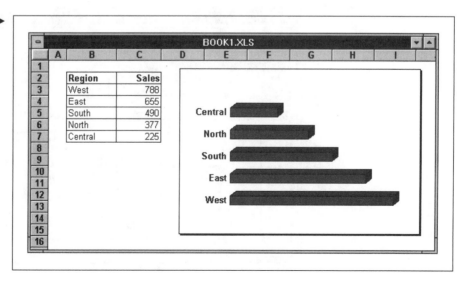

▶ *Changing the Series Order*

Suppose you have created a column chart with a data series for Y-T-D sales, and a data series for prior year sales.

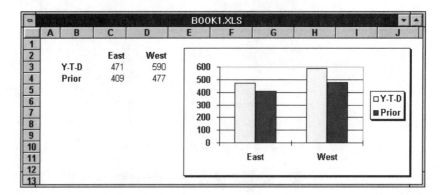

It might make more sense to place Prior to the left of Y-T-D. Follow these steps:

1. Activate the chart.

2. Choose the last command on the Format menu (the command will change based on the type of chart, e.g., Format ▶ Pie Group or Format ▶ Column Group)—select the Series Order tab.

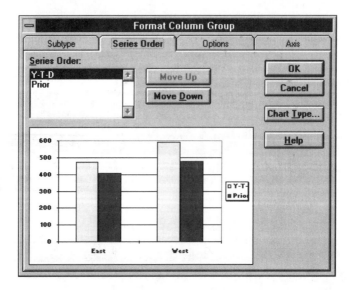

3. Select a series in the Series Order box, then click Move Up or Move Down to rearrange the order of the series, then click OK.

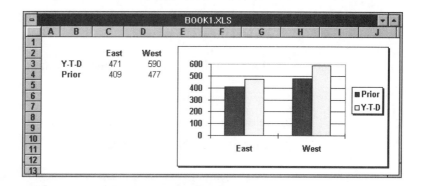

▶ *Using a Secondary Axis to Display Two Value Scales*

Suppose you want to chart two series with different value scales on the same chart. For example, one chart needs to show average home sales price and number of homes sold. The average sales price will be over $100,000, whereas the number of homes sold for a given period will be less than 100. Figure 14.12 shows an example of this.

FIGURE 14.12 ▶

A secondary axis typically requires a combination chart in order to create a meaningful result.

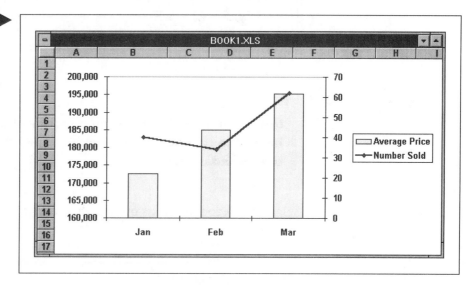

Constructing Complex Charts

▶ ▶
Ch.
14

To create a new chart with a secondary axis using the ChartWizard:

1. Select a combination chart in ChartWizard Step 2.
2. Select a format in ChartWizard Step 3 which includes a secondary axis.

To add a secondary axis to an existing chart:

1. Activate the chart.
2. Select the data series that is being placed on a secondary axis.
3. Choose Format ➤ Selected Data Series, then select the Axis tab.

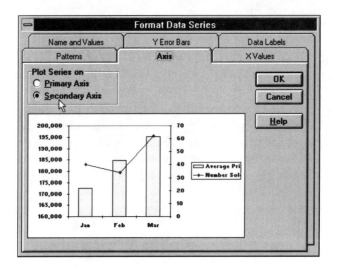

 ▶ ▶**T I P**

Unless you already have a combination chart, it is helpful to change the series chart type before creating the secondary axis.

4. Select the Secondary Axis option, then click OK.

▶ *Charting Multi-Level Categories*

You can get more useful information onto a single chart with Excel 5's new multi-level category capability. Suppose you want to chart data on sales of the same three products (shoes), to two different categories of buyers (men and women), in two different regions (east and west).

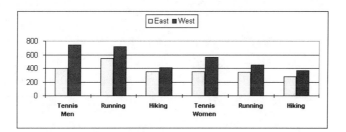

If all of the category labels (columns B and C) are included in the charted range, Excel creates multi-level category labels by default.

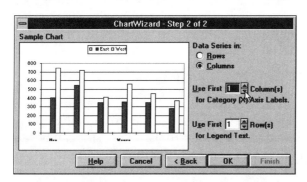

If you want to use only the first column (column B) as category labels, select the chart and click ChartWizard. On the Step 2 dialog box, change the Category (X) Axis Labels setting to Use First **1** Column.

▶

CHARTING DATA FROM MULTIPLE WORKSHEETS

Suppose you keep monthly financial data on separate monthly worksheets, yet all the data must be shown in a single chart? You could copy the data from each of the monthly worksheets onto another worksheet, but this is a lot of unnecessary work. Instead, you can create a chart directly from multiple worksheets.

Begin by charting the first month's data. (It doesn't matter where you create the chart—it can be embedded on one of the worksheets, or it can be a separate chart sheet.) Activate the chart, then choose Insert ➤ New Data to insert data from the second worksheet. To add the new data, you can type the reference or activate the next worksheet and drag over the reference. Excel may display a Paste Special dialog box if it's not certain whether the new data is new points or a new series (just as when dragging and dropping to add data to a chart). Repeat the Insert ➤ New Data command for each worksheet range you want to add to the chart. Keep in mind that the separate worksheet ranges should be identical—they should all have the same category labels, in the same order (although you don't have to add the labels with each set of data).

▶▶ *Special Types of Charts*

In this section, you will learn about picture charts, trend lines, error bars, and surface charts.

▶ *Creating Picture Charts*

You can replace the normal data markers used in various 2-D charts with pictures that are imported from a graphics program, or drawn with Excel's built-in drawing tools. The result can be very appealing when used in reports and presentations (see Figure 14.13).

FIGURE 14.13

*This picture was
pasted into the chart
from the Microsoft
PowerPoint clip-art
library.*

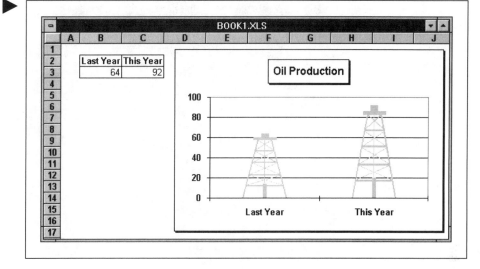

The procedure for using pictures in charts is simple. Follow these steps
to use a picture in an existing chart:

1. Copy a picture to the Clipboard:

   * Copy a graphic from another application.
   * Create a picture using Excel's drawing tools, then select it
     and choose Edit ➤ Copy.

2. Activate the chart.

3. Select the data series (or individual data point) that you want to
   replace with a picture.

4. Choose Edit ➤ Paste.

Formatting Picture Markers

There are formatting styles for picture markers. Select the marker, and
choose Format ➤ Selected Data Series (or if a single point, Format ➤
Selected Data Point). Then click the Patterns tab.

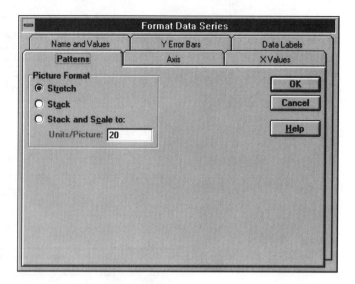

The picture in Figure 14.13 is stretched. The Stack option causes the picture to be stacked to the appropriate height:

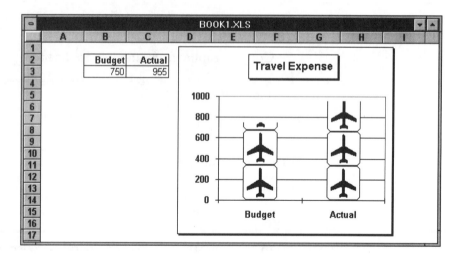

The Stack and Scale option lets you specify the size of the picture, in the same unit of measure as the chart axis.

More Facts about Picture Markers

- More than one picture can be used in a chart (for example, a chart showing statistics for USA, Mexico, and Canada could use the flag of each nation).

- To remove picture formats from a series, select the series and choose Edit ➤ Clear ➤ Formats—don't accidentally delete the entire data series by using the Edit Clear command on the shortcut menu.

- Charts with pictures can be saved as custom AutoFormats.

► *Using Trendlines*

In previous versions of Excel, if you wanted to plot a trend, the trend had to be calculated on the worksheet. Now, a chart is able to examine a set of data, and plot a trendline based on that data—without adding formulas to the worksheet to calculate the trend. Here are some potential applications:

- Forecast sales for the next six months based on the previous 18 months.

- A chemical analysis based on a standard curve can be validated with a linear regression.

- Chart the half-life of a radioactive compound into the future.

- Smooth out the daily fluctuations in stock prices to see performance trends more clearly.

Trendlines can extrapolate data backwards as well as forwards, and can be based on five different regression equations or on a moving average. Using a moving average, each average is calculated from the specified number of preceding data points.

Trendlines can be added to area, column, line, bar, and scatter charts, and are formatted and deleted just like other chart elements. They cannot be added to 3-D charts. Multiple trendlines can be added to the same data series.

Adding a Trendline to a Data Series

Here are the steps to add a trendline to a data series:

1. Activate the chart.

2. Select the series you want to add the trendline to, then choose Insert ▶ Trendline.

3. Select the Type tab, and choose the type of trend you want to chart.

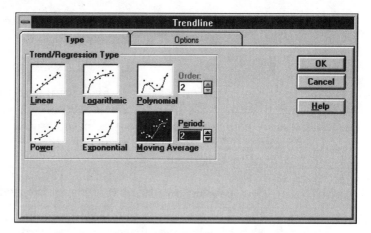

- For polynomial regression, specify the highest power for the
  independent variable in the Order edit box (must be an integer between 2 and 6).

- For a moving average, specify the number of periods the moving average is based on in the Period edit box.

4. Use the Options tab to name the trendline, and set the other options described in Table 14.1.

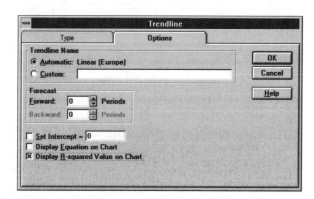

Table 14.1 explains the options available for applying trendlines.

▶ **TABLE 14.1:** *Trendline Options*

Setting	Function
Trendline Name	Displays in legend
Forecast	Selects number of periods forward and backward for trend forecast
Display Equation on Chart	Displays regression equation (can be formatted, moved)
Display R-squared Value on Chart	Displays R-squared value (can be formatted, moved)
Set Intercept	Changes Y-intercept value

▶ *Using Error Bars*

Error bars are used to display a degree of uncertainty (a plus/minus factor) surrounding a given data series, as shown in Figure 14.14. Error bars can be added to these 2-D chart types: line, column, area, bar,

FIGURE 14.14 ▶

This shows the predicted rate of return for three portfolios, and uses error bars to plot one standard deviation.

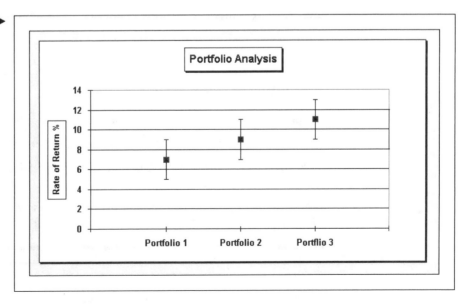

Constructing Complex Charts

▶ ▶

Ch.
14

and scatter charts. They cannot be used on 3-D charts. In scatter charts, error bars can be added to both axes. If the series values change, the error bars will be automatically adjusted.

Here are the steps to add an error bar to a data series:

1. Activate the chart and select the data series that you want to add error bars to.

2. Choose Insert ➤ Error Bars.

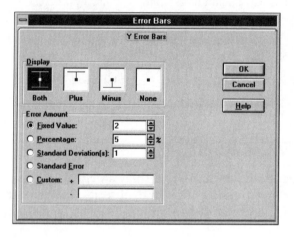

Table 14.2 explains the options available for applying error bars.

► **TABLE 14.2:** *Error Bars Options*

Setting	Function
Display	Error bar can display above and/or below the data point.
Fixed Value	Constant value used to plot the error bar.
Percent	Error bar is based on percentage calculated from each data point.
Standard Deviation	Enter the number of standard deviations from the data points.

▶ **TABLE 14.2:** *Error Bars Options (continued)*

Setting	Function
Standard Error	The standard error of the plotted values is displayed as the error amount.
Custom	Custom deviation values can be entered in a range of worksheet cells; then enter the work-sheet range in the Custom box. The worksheet range must contain the same number of values as there are data points in the series. You can enter positive deviation values, negative deviation values, or both.

▶ *Using Surface Charts*

A surface chart is a graph that shows one variable as a function of two other variables. Surface charts are often used for scientific data, but are also applicable for certain business requirements.

For a surface chart to make sense, the two variables need to represent continuous data. For instance, although an axis may represent temperatures in 10-degree increments, temperature is a continuous measurement—there are temperatures that lie between the 10-degree increments. But *product code* would be an illogical variable—it is not a continuous measurement.

Case Study

The following case study will use a surface chart to help a company establish a retail price for a new product, and establish a marketing budget.

- The company is in the business of making electronic toys—a new product is being introduced, with a retail price between $20 and $40.

- A marketing budget must be established between $500,000 and $2,500,000.

- Historical sales and profit data have been gathered for similar products where price and marketing expenditures were within the above parameters (see Figure 14.15).

Constructing Complex Charts

Ch. 14

FIGURE 14.15 ▶

Historical profitability based on similar products.

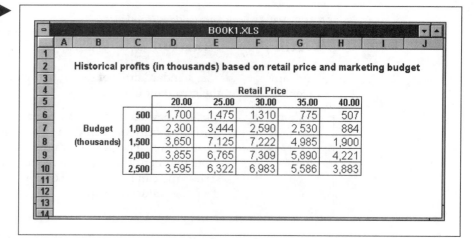

The historical profits (in thousands) based on retail price and marketing budget

			Retail Price				
			20.00	25.00	30.00	35.00	40.00
		500	1,700	1,475	1,310	775	507
	Budget	1,000	2,300	3,444	2,590	2,530	884
	(thousands)	1,500	3,650	7,125	7,222	4,985	1,900
		2,000	3,855	6,765	7,309	5,890	4,221
		2,500	3,595	6,322	6,983	5,586	3,883

● The historical data will be analyzed to determine a retail price and marketing budget most likely to yield maximum profitability (since marketing expenditures reduce profit, a point of diminishing returns must be determined).

One horizontal axis of the chart will represent list price. The second horizontal axis will represent marketing budget. The two axes define a horizontal plane equivalent to a flat map. To create a surface chart based on the data in Figure 14.15:

1. Select cells C5:H10.

2. Use the ChartWizard. Specify 3-D Surface at Step 2, then click Finish. The result is shown in Figure 14.16.

The contour reveals that a product priced in the $25 to $30 range, with a marketing budget of $1.5 to $2 million, is apt to produce the greatest profitability. As might be expected, a forty-dollar product with a marketing budget under one million is apt to fare poorly.

 ▶ ▶ **TIP**

A printed report of a 3-D surface chart might actually include two or three different charts based on the same data. Each chart could be set up from a different angle so that all areas of the contour can be viewed.

FIGURE 14.16 ▶

Elevation and perspective have been adjusted in order to clearly view the most profitable area of the surface. Spinning the chart to change perspective will alter the location of the axes.

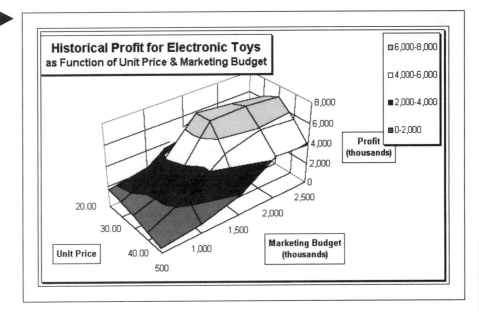

▶▶ *Protecting a Chart*

Protecting a chart prevents users from deleting, resizing, or otherwise manipulating the chart. Here are the procedures (and implications) for protecting charts:

▶ *Protecting Embedded Charts*

Protecting an embedded chart is exactly the same as protecting any graphic object (see Chapter 12). Select the chart object, choose Format ➤ Object, select the Protection tab, and check the Locked setting. The lock does not take effect until the worksheet containing the chart is protected.

▶ *Protecting Chart Sheets*

Protecting a chart sheet is exactly the same as protecting a worksheet (see Chapter 11). Activate the sheet, and choose Tools ➤ Protection ➤ Protect Sheet.

Constructing
Complex Charts

▶

Ch.

14

▶▶ *Printing Charts*

When you print a worksheet with an embedded chart, as you might expect, the printout includes the chart and surrounding worksheet. There may be circumstances where you want to print the worksheet without the chart, or visa versa. To print a worksheet without an embedded chart, select the chart by clicking it once (without activating it, which requires a double-click). Then choose Format ➤ Object, select the Properties tab, and clear the Print Object checkbox. To print an embedded chart without the surrounding worksheet, double-click the chart to activate it, then choose File ➤ Print.

Whether a chart is embedded or a separate sheet, you can change the printed size and layout of the chart. For example, suppose you want to print a chart on a separate page, but only 1/2 size, on the top half of the page. Select the chart sheet (or activate an embedded chart), then choose File ➤ Print Preview. Click the Margins button so that margin lines are displayed. Drag the margin lines to resize/reposition the chart. You can change the orientation of the printed chart to landscape or to portrait by clicking the Setup button and choosing landscape or portrait on the Page dialog tab.

If you choose File ➤ Page Setup when a chart is active, the Page Setup dialog box includes a Chart tab. The Chart tab has settings that control how the chart is resized. If you select Use Full Page, the chart can be resized both horizontally and vertically, but may lose its height-to-width ratio. If you select Scale to Fit Page, the chart will maintain its height-to-width ratio while you resize it. If you choose Custom, the chart can be cropped; for instance, you can crop out the legend without permanently removing the legend from the chart.

▶▶ *Charting Data Dynamically*

In a spreadsheet environment, there are often many sets of data with similar structure. For example, you may store budgeting data on a division, department, or cost-center level. The data may be stored in one workbook or many workbooks. But there is always a *budget* column and an *actual* column.

One of the most common design problems is that if you create too many charts, it's hard to be consistent.. Different charts are created for the division budget, department budget, cost-center budget, etc. This causes a problem in terms of maintenance and consistency. When your organization decides that all budget charts need to be modified to show original and revised budgets, you have a maintenance problem on your hands if there are dozens of similar charts floating around.

By applying a variety of Excel skills, you can learn what is arguably the most important charting skill: how to use a single chart on multiple data sets. In other words, dynamically bring data to your chart, as we've done in Figure 14.17, instead of "marrying" a given chart to a particular set of data. This can be accomplished in several ways:

- Use charts to point to cells containing formulas—user input drives the formulas, causing different data sets to be charted (typically, this will entail the use of functions like INDEX, VLOOKUP, OFFSET, MATCH, SUMIF, covered in Chapter 9, and the so-called D-functions, covered in Chapter 16).

- Use file links (controlled with the Edit ➤ Links command) to link a workbook to different workbooks (see Chapter 4).

FIGURE 14.17 ▶

A well-designed charting model can dynamically chart different sets of data.

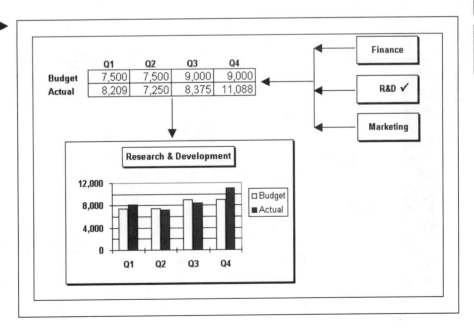

- Use dynamic names, covered in Chapter 8, to point to different data sets based on user input.

- Create charts based on Pivot Tables (see Chapter 17).

- Use workbook templates and chart templates to create reusable models (see Chapter 10).

▶ **DYNAMIC CHARTING WITH NAMED FORMULA**

Charts typically display the values contained in a specific ranges of cells. However, an individual series can dynamically point to different ranges, according to user input. For example, a single chart might display the data for one of several markets, depending on which market the user selects in a listbox. The way to accomplish this is to use a named formula in a series name and value.

1. Create a named formula which points dynamically to different ranges according to user input. (See the Named Formulas section in Chapter 8 for an example).

2. Create a chart from any one of the ranges.

3. Activate the chart, then right-click the series you want to make dynamic.

4. Choose Format Data Series.

5. Select the Name and Values tab.

6. In the Y Values edit box, type the name of the named formula, then click OK.

7. Use a listbox (see Chapter 19) to allow the user to choose which range is charted—selecting a choice from the listbox causes the worksheet to recalculate and the chart to update.

►► *Tools Not Found on the Built-in Toolbars*

There are a number of charting tools that are not on the Chart toolbar. In order to use these tools, you have to add them to a built-in toolbar, or create a custom toolbar. (See Chapter 26.)

Most of the tools described in Table 14.3 are AutoFormat shortcuts. These tools, like the Chart Type tools, let you draw a specific type of chart.

► **TABLE 14.3:** *Special Charting Tools*

Toolface	Tool	Function
	Vertical Gridlines	Adds/deletes vertical gridlines
	Line/Column Chart AutoFormat	Combination line/column chart
	Stacked Column Chart AutoFormat	Stacked column chart
	3-D Perspective Column Chart AutoFormat	3-D perspective column chart
	Pie Chart AutoFormat	Pie chart, percentage labels
	3-D Pie Chart AutoFormat	3-D pie chart, percentage labels
	Doughnut Chart AutoFormat	Doughnut chart, category labels
	Volume/Hi-Lo-Close Chart AutoFormat	Combination chart for stock prices

Constructing Complex Charts

►▼

Ch.
14

▶ ▶**N O T E**

Chapter 26, "Advanced Tips and Techniques," includes a section on charting.

PART FIVE

►► **In Part Five** you will learn how to manipulate data in Excel. You will learn about several new features for filtering, subtotaling, and sorting data on a worksheet, and how to use criteria ranges for advanced filtering procedures. Most importantly, you will learn to use Excel's new pivot tables to summarize and analyze data. Finally, you will learn how to use Microsoft Query to retrieve data from external sources, and how to use Query and pivot tables together to retrieve and summarize large amounts of external data.

► ► CHAPTER **15**

Working with Internal Databases or Lists

▶▶ FAST TRACK

As far as Excel is concerned, there are two distinct types of databases. *External databases*, such as dBASE, Paradox, FoxPro, SQL Server, and Oracle, and *internal databases*—databases that reside in worksheets (also called *lists* in Excel). You will learn how to work with external databases in Chapters 17 and 18. This chapter will show you how to work with internal databases. You will learn:

- *The pros and cons of internal databases*

- *Why internal database skills are vital—even if you don't permanently store databases in Excel*

- *How to build an internal database*

- *How to sort data*

- *How to filter a database (i.e., to view a subset of the data based on user-specified criteria)*

▶▶ *Database Skills Are Important for All Users*

 Many users have been put off by Excel's database features simply because the term *database* implies something complex and hard to learn. This perception was reinforced by the fact that database management in previous versions of Excel actually *was* hard to learn. In Excel 5, database features have been greatly simplified, and provide very powerful functionality for managing and analyzing data.

NOTE

The extraordinary level of confusion about databases in general, and Excel databases in particular, prompted Microsoft to practically abandon the term *database* altogether. The Excel manuals and on-line help instead refer extensively to *list management*.

There is another category of users who have avoided internal databases—people who use a "real" database management system (DBMS). An internal Excel database lacks certain features possessed by the simplest DBMS. Knowing this, DBMS aficionados skip over Excel's database features. Just because a range of cells is treated as a database doesn't mean that the worksheet is necessarily the permanent home for the data. Excel is an extraordinary tool for analyzing data stored in a DBMS, and the internal database features play an important role in this process. Here are a few reasons to become familiar with how Excel manages its internal databases:

- Much of Excel's database functionality is easy to learn.

- Most of the database functionality is *important* to learn, even if the problems you are solving are not, on the surface, database management problems.

- Even if your data is stored in an external DBMS, Excel database features can help you dissect, analyze, and report.

- Most tables of data on worksheets can be treated as databases.

▶▶ *Limitations of Spreadsheet Databases*

Excel provides outstanding facilities for entering, editing, analyzing, and manipulating data. But there are limitations inherent to all

Internal Databases

▶
Ch.
15

spreadsheet programs that you should be aware of before choosing Excel as the place to store your data:

- A worksheet is limited to 16,384 rows and 256 columns.

- Only one user can have write access to an internal database at a time.

- Enforcing data integrity (for example, by disallowing text in numeric columns) requires custom macros and dialog boxes.

- The entire database must be in memory (unless you are accessing an external database—see Chapter 18).

- Data stored on worksheets tends to consume more disk space than data stored in external databases (a worksheet stores formulas, formatting, graphics, etc.; a DBMS stores raw data).

Remember, even if your data is stored in an external DBMS, Excel is an outstanding tool for analyzing, manipulating, and reporting on external data.

▶▶ *For Users of Earlier Versions of Excel*

Excel's database features have been drastically improved. Many of the old commands are missing from the menu system, which may give you the *misconception* that there has been a loss of functionality. Here are some key differences and similarities between Excel 4 and Excel 5:

- Named ranges Database, Criteria, and Extract are no longer required, which is why the SET DATABASE, SET EXTRACT, and SET CRITERIA commands are no longer on the menu.

- Instead of relying on a named range Database, Excel automatically detects when the active cell is located within a range of data.

- There is a simplified interface for defining simple criteria and performing extracts (covered in this chapter).

- For complex problems, you can still define criteria and perform extracts the old way; see Chapter 16 to learn the Excel 5 nuances.

- Pivot Tables, covered in Chapter 17, are a dramatic improvement over Excel 4's crosstab facility.

►► *Setting Up a Database*

Setting up a database is quite simple. First, it will help if you understand these three terms:

Field   A column within a database

Record   A row within a database

Field Name   The top row of a database usually contains *field names*; a field name consists of unique text describing the field (there is no need to actually name the cells)

In the example shown in Figure 15.1,

- There are 7 fields (columns) in the database.

- There are 10 records (or rows) in the database; B3:H3 is the first record.

- Cells B2:H2 contain field names.

FIGURE 15.1 ►

An internal database consists of fields, field names, and records (or rows).

	A	B	C	D	E	F	G	H
1								
2		Client No	Name	Category	Region	MTD Sales	YTD Sales	Last Year
3		101	Argus Industries	Manufacturing	North	9,569	13,775	14,723
4		102	LEX Software	Services	South	3,527	10,534	12,887
5		103	National Bank	Financial	South	1,472	8,123	10,022
6		104	Kinsman & Nelson	Services	East	3,717	12,374	9,221
7		105	Northwest Investments	Financial	North	3,315	18,656	11,044
8		106	Nica Corporation	Manufacturing	West	6,542	58,229	52,559
9		107	MDC Enterprises	Manufacturing	East	8,167	23,613	25,733
10		108	Wilson & Roth CPA	Services	West	4,026	11,786	9,225
11		109	JK Associates	Financial	South	12,391	71,805	23,490
12		110	T.K. James Inc.	Services	North	3,146	19,104	11,373
13								
14								
15								
16								

BOOK1.XLS

Internal
Databases

► ►
Ch.
15

Field names are not required to use some database features, such as sorting. But to use all database features, you must enter field names. Unlike Excel 4, there are no particular rules for field names; they can contain spaces and special characters.

Setting up a database is extraordinarily simple: enter field names and data onto a worksheet. You have probably performed this task countless times.

N O T E

You may want to create the database pictured in Figure 15.1 so you can follow along; this database is referred to throughout this chapter.

T I P

For rapid data entry into a range of cells, select the range, then use the Tab key to navigate the range. (Use Shift+Tab to move backwards.)

▶▶ *Sorting a Database*

Data is more useful when it is organized, or sorted, so users can find the information they want quickly. For instance, a teacher might want to sort an attendance list by putting students' names in alphabetical order; alternatively, the attendance list might be more useful sorted by number of absences--putting the students with the most at the top of the list. A database or list can be sorted by any field in the database (e.g., name or number of absences), in ascending or descending order, and by custom sort orders (see Chapter 16, "Getting More Power From Databases," to learn about custom sort orders).

Here is the procedure for sorting a database:

1. Select any one cell within the database range.

2. Choose the Data ➤ Sort command.

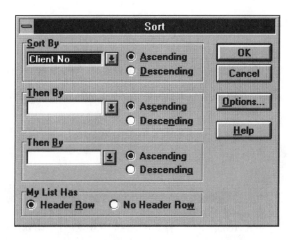

3. The Sort By drop-down displays all fields in the database—choose the field you want to sort by.

4. Use the option buttons to specify ascending (a,b,c; 1,2,3) or descending (z,y,x; 10,9,8) order.

5. The two Then By inputs are optional; they allow two more sort fields to be specified (up to three total).

6. Excel tries to determine if the database has a header row (field names), and sets the Header Row or No Header Row setting accordingly. Override this setting if required.

7. Click OK to sort.

► ►**W A R N I N G**

If the database has a header row, but you specify no header row, the headings (field names) will be sorted into the database as if the header row was a data record. Excel will make a guess concerning header/no header correctly 99% of the time, so users tend not to pay attention to this setting until the first time they lose the header row into the data. If you sort incorrectly, the sort can be undone using Edit ► Undo Sort.

Assume you want to sort the database pictured in Figure 15.1 by Category, and by YTD Sales within category from highest to lowest sales:

1. Select a cell inside the database, then choose Data ➤ Sort.
2. Select the Category field from the Sort By list; choose ascending order.
3. Select YTD Sales as the second sort field, and choose descending order.

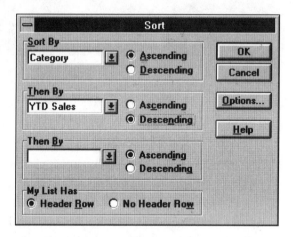

4. Click OK to sort the data as follows:

	Client No	Name	Category	Region	MTD Sales	YTD Sales	Last Year
3	109	JK Associates	Financial	South	12,391	71,805	23,490
4	105	Northwest Investments	Financial	North	3,315	18,656	11,044
5	103	National Bank	Financial	South	1,472	8,123	10,022
6	106	Nica Corporation	Manufacturing	West	6,542	58,229	52,559
7	107	MDC Enterprises	Manufacturing	East	8,167	23,613	25,733
8	101	Argus Industries	Manufacturing	North	9,569	13,775	14,723
9	110	T.K. James Inc.	Services	North	3,146	19,104	11,373
10	104	Kinsman & Nelson	Services	East	3,717	12,374	9,221
11	108	Wilson & Roth CPA	Services	West	4,026	11,786	9,225
12	102	LEX Software	Services	South	3,527	10,534	12,887

See Chapter 16 to learn how to sort by more than three fields.

▶ *More Facts about Sorting*

- Sorts are performed according to underlying cell value, not the formatted appearance of the cell.

- Sorts are case-insensitive by default; you can specify case-sensitive sorting by clicking the Options button on the Sort dialog box, and checking the case-sensitive checkbox.

- Logical value FALSE comes before TRUE in an ascending sort.

- All error values are considered the same.

- Blanks sort last for both ascending *and* descending sorts.

- Avoid text and numbers in the same field—it is generally a bad practice, and it makes the sort order unpredictable.

▶▶ *Filtering a Database Using AutoFilter*

Sometimes you will want to view only database records that meet certain criteria. This is accomplished by *filtering* the database. For example, suppose you have a mailing list of names and addresses for clients all over the country, and you want to send letters to only clients with Georgia addresses. You can filter the data so that only the records with Georgia addresses are visible, and then copy the filtered data to another worksheet, a report, or a word processing program for mailing. There are two types of filters:

- *AutoFilters*, covered in this chapter
- *Advanced filters*, covered in Chapter 16

Internal
Databases

▶ ▶
Ch.
15

Follow these steps to filter your database:

1. Select any cell in the database, then choose the Data ➤ Filter ➤ AutoFilter command. Drop-down controls are placed on top of the field names.

	A	B	C	D	E	F	G	H
			BOOK1.XLS					
1								
2		Client N⬇	Name ⬇	Category ⬇	Regio⬇	MTD Sal⬇	YTD Sal⬇	Last Ye⬇
3		109	JK Associates	Financial	South	12,391	71,805	23,490
4		105	Northwest Investments	Financial	North	3,315	18,656	11,044
5		103	National Bank	Financial	South	1,472	8,123	10,022
6		106	Nica Corporation	Manufacturing	West	6,542	58,229	52,559
7		107	MDC Enterprises	Manufacturing	East	8,167	23,613	25,733
8		101	Argus Industries	Manufacturing	North	9,569	13,775	14,723
9		110	T.K. James Inc.	Services	North	3,146	19,104	11,373
10		104	Kinsman & Nelson	Services	East	3,717	12,374	9,221
11		108	Wilson & Roth CPA	Services	West	4,026	11,786	9,225
12		102	LEX Software	Services	South	3,527	10,534	12,887
13								

2. Click a drop-down control to apply a filter to the field. The contents of a drop-down list are dictated by the contents of the field. For example, the Category drop-down will contain each unique data item found in the field, plus four other choices:

- Select one of the categories, such as Financial, to display only those records where the category is equal to Financial; when the filter is applied, the drop-down control changes color as an indicator that the filter is in effect (the row numbers also change color).

- Select (All) to turn off a filter for a given field (remember, you are turning off the filter for the one field only—filters for other fields are left in place).

- Select (Blanks) to display only those rows where the field is blank.

- Select (NonBlanks) to display only those rows where the field is not blank.

- Select (Custom...) to set a custom AutoFilter (covered below).

You can filter more than one field at a time. In this example, if you add a filter for Region equals South in addition to Category equals Financial, you will be viewing all records where Category equals Financial AND Region equals South (a total of two records—clients 109 and 103).

▶

USE A FILTERED LIST TO FIND TYPOS

Picture a worksheet that is used to store payments to suppliers. Each time you make a payment the supplier name is typed in, along with other data, and the list contains hundreds of rows. You want to consolidate the data to see how much you have paid to each supplier, but the consolidation requires that supplier names be typed identically each time they are entered. For example, ABC Corporation must always be entered as ABC Corporation, never as ABC Corp (because ABC Corp would show up in the consolidation as a separate supplier). How can you check a very long list for typographical errors without tediously looking through the entire list, item by item? You can add each supplier name to a custom dictionary, then spell check the worksheet. But every time you add a new supplier, you have to add the new name to your custom dictionary.

There is a quicker way: apply an AutoFilter to the list. When you click on the autofilter arrow for the supplier names column, the dropdown list displays all the unique names in the column, and any misspelled names will be immediately evident. For example, if ABC Corporation has been entered as ABC Corp, both names will show up on the dropdown list. You can select ABC Corp to filter those entries from the list, then quickly change all the ABC Corp entries to ABC Corporation.

▶ ▶

Ch.

15

▶ *Setting Custom AutoFilters*

The simple filters covered in the previous exercise are based on what a field is *equal* to (i.e., category *equals* Financial, region *equals* South).

Custom AutoFilters allow relationships other than *equal* to be specified. If you choose (Custom...) from the drop-down list, the Custom Auto-Filter dialog box is displayed.

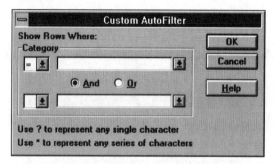

- The narrow drop-down lets you specify the relational operator (see Table 15.1).

- The wide drop-down lets you specify the field value; you can select an item from the list or type in a value (wildcard characters can be included).

- The bottom two drop-downs are used to specify an optional second comparison criterion.

▶ **TABLE 15.1:** *Custom AutoFilter Operators*

Operator	Meaning
=	Equal to
>	Greater than
<	Less than
>=	Greater than or equal to
<=	Less than or equal to
<>	Not equal

- Use the And Or options if you want to apply two comparison criteria:

  - Select And to display rows that meet both criteria.
  - Select Or to display rows that meet either criteria.

Using the database in Figure 15.1, assume that you want to analyze the north and east regions. Within those regions, you want to display only the larger clients—those with YTD sales greater than 15,000.

1. Choose Data ➤ Filter ➤ AutoFilter.

2. Click the Region drop-down.

3. Select Custom.

4. From the drop-downs, select **= north**, *or,* **= east** (as pictured below), then click OK.

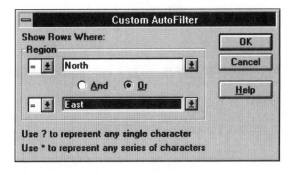

5. Click the YTD Sales drop-down.

6. Select Custom.

7. In the upper drop-downs, select **>** and enter **15000** (as pictured below).

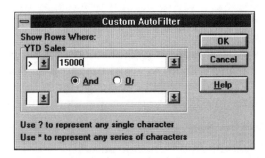

When the filtering exercise is complete, the worksheet will look like this:

		BOOK1.XLS					
Client N	**Name**	**Category**	**Regio**	**MTD Sal**	**YTD Sal**	**Last Ye**
105	Northwest Investments	Financial	North	3,315	18,656	11,044
107	MDC Enterprises	Manufacturing	East	8,167	23,613	25,733
110	T.K. James Inc.	Services	North	3,146	19,104	11,373

▶ Removing All Filters at Once

If one or more filters are set, use the Data ➤ Filter ➤ AutoFilter command to remove the filter(s). The command is unchecked, the drop-down controls are removed from the worksheet, and all records are displayed.

▶ Totaling Fields of a Filtered Database

Suppose that you want to see column totals for a filtered database. There are three things you need to know about totaling filtered data:

• Use the SUBTOTAL function (covered in Chapter 9); unlike SUM, it ignores rows that are hidden as a result of filtering.

• The AutoSum button, used on a cell beneath a database field, will place a SUBTOTAL function in the cell instead of SUM—but only if the database is filtered.

• If you calculate totals by placing SUM formulas on the row directly beneath the database, the Totals row will be treated as a database record—avoid this practice by using the SUBTOTAL function instead (see Chapter 9 to learn about SUBTOTAL).

For a short example of totaling fields of a filtered database, perform the following steps, using the worksheet pictured in Figure 15.1:

1. Filter the database to show region North only.

2. Select cells F13:H13.

3. Click the AutoSum button.

The results are shown in Figure 15.2.

FIGURE 15.2

*Filtered database with
column totals*

	A	B	C	D	E	F	G	H
			BOOK1.XLS					
1								
2		Client N	Name	Category	Regio	MTD Sal	YTD Sal	Last Ye
4		105	Northwest Investments	Financial	North	3,315	18,656	11,044
8		101	Argus Industries	Manufacturing	North	9,569	13,775	14,723
9		110	T.K. James Inc.	Services	North	3,146	19,104	11,373
13						16,030	51,535	37140
14								
15								
16								
17								
18								
19								
20								

TIP

For clarity and aesthetics, you may be tempted to place the word TOTALS in cell C13 or E13. However, this causes Excel to treat row 13 as a database record, and thus hide it when filters are applied. Skip a row, and place the totals on row 14 instead—it will not be treated as a database record. Or, enter the word TOTALS *after* you have subtotaled the filtered database—then Excel will not treat then entry as a record.

▶ Implications of Working with a Filtered Database

As you apply AutoFilters to a database, Excel is simply hiding the rows that do not match the filter criteria. However, rows that are hidden as a result of filtering are not the same as rows that are hidden using the Format ➤ Row ➤ Hide command. By and large, this is a very good thing. You should be aware of the following points concerning cells hidden as a result of a filter:

- They are unaffected by AutoFills.
- They are unaffected by formatting commands.

- They are not included in newly created charts (though this is can be overridden on a per-chart basis by clearing the Plot Visible Cells Only setting in the Tools ➤ Options ➤ Chart dialog box).

- They are unaffected by the Clear command.

- They are not copied with the Copy command.

- They are not deleted by the Delete Row command.

- They are unaffected by sorting.

- They are included in SUM functions—and are not included in SUBTOTAL functions.

- They are not printed.

▶▶ *Using the Built-in Data Form*

Typically, databases are entered and maintained by typing directly onto a worksheet. However, you could use a built-in *data form* instead. This form

- Displays one record at a time;

- Can be used to add new records, and edit existing records;

- Lets you view records matching specified criteria.

To display a data form, select a cell inside your database, then choose Data ➤ Form. The field names from the database are used as titles inside the form:

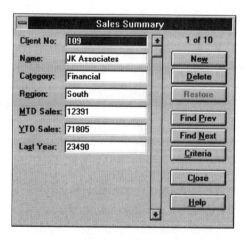

▶ *Adding New Records*

Follow these steps to add a new record to a database using a data form:

1. Click the New button to clear the form for a new record—New Record is displayed in the upper right corner of the dialog box.
2. Fill in the field values (you can use the Tab key to move between fields).
3. Click the New button to add record (new records are placed at the bottom of database).

▶ *Editing Records*

Here is how to edit database records using a data form:

1. Use the scroll bar to select the desired record—the record number is displayed in the upper right corner of the dialog box.
2. Edit the field values.
3. Click the New button to update the database.

▶ *Deleting Records*

To delete database records with a data form:

1. Use the scroll bar to select the desired record. The record number is displayed in the upper right corner of the dialog box.
2. Click the Delete button.

▶ *Displaying Records Matching Search Criteria*

The data form can be used to search for records that match criteria that you specify. Here is the procedure:

1. Click the Criteria button—the form will clear and Criteria is displayed in the upper right corner of the dialog box.
2. Enter criteria in the edit box next to the field you want to filter:

   • Enter the value to search for, such as *West.*

- Or, precede the value with relational operator (see Table 15.1), such as <>*West*.
- Enter criteria for any number of fields.

3. Click the Find Prev or Find Next button.

Using the database pictured in Figure 15.1, the following criteria would display every record where region is equal to north, month-to-date sales is other than zero, and year-to-date sales is greater than 10,000:

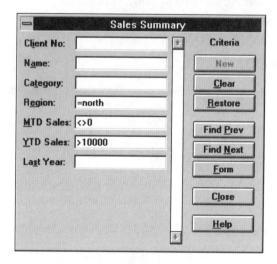

To clear the criteria, click the Criteria button, then manually clear the criteria from specific edit boxes (or click the Clear button to clear all criteria), and click the Form button.

▶ More Facts about Data Forms

- Values from calculated fields (cells with formulas) are displayed in the form, but cannot be edited.
- Hidden columns are not displayed.
- As new records are added, the data form will not overwrite data located underneath the database—it will disallow new records from being added.

CHAPTER 16

Getting More Power from Databases

FAST TRACK

▶ ***To use D functions*** *544*

D functions perform calculations on a specified column within a specified database, and use a criteria range to determine which records to include in the calculation. All D functions have the same syntax. For example, the DSUM syntax is *DSUM(DatabaseRange,Field,CriteriaRange)*

▶ ***To insert subtotals into a database*** *547*

Select a cell within the database range, and choose Data ➤ Subtotals.

▶ ***To create friendly-looking databases*** *550*

First, enter legal field names on the header row of the database. Then, enter field descriptions on the row(s) above the header row. Finally, hide the first row of the database (the header row).

▶▶ *he* previous chapter covered the basics of internal databases. This chapter will teach you more advanced techniques for working with internal databases:

- *Special database sorting techniques*
- *Defining criteria ranges*
- *Using advanced filters*
- *Using the so-called "D functions"—the family of database functions beginning with the letter D*
- *Placing embedded totals in a database*

▶▶ Special Sorting Problems

Chapter 15 explains how to address common sorts using up to 3 fields to sort rows in ascending or descending order. This section covers several other sorting requirements.

▶ Sorting by More than Three Fields

Consider the following database:

 **▶ ▶ N O T E**

The database in Figure 16.1 is essentially the same database used in Chapter 15, but with the Last Call field inserted. You may want to create this database on your system, as it will be referred to throughout this chapter.

FIGURE 16.1

Sample Database

A	B	C	D	E	F	G	H	I
1								
2	Client No	Name	Category	Region	Last Call	MTD Sales	YTD Sales	Last Year
3	107	MDC Enterprises	Mfg	East	1/30/94	8,167	23,613	25,733
4	104	Kinsman & Nelson	Services	East	2/7/95	3,717	12,374	9,221
5	110	T.K. James Inc.	Services	North	8/11/94	3,146	19,104	11,373
6	105	Pacific Investments	Financial	North	12/1/93	3,315	18,656	11,044
7	101	Argus Industries	Mfg	North	1/10/95	9,569	13,775	14,723
8	109	JK Associates	Financial	South	3/1/94	12,391	71,805	23,490
9	102	LEX Software	Services	South	4/23/94	3,527	10,534	12,887
10	103	National Bank	Financial	South	6/1/94	1,472	8,123	10,022
11	106	Nica Corporation	Mfg	West	2/25/94	6,542	58,229	52,559
12	108	Wilson & Roth	Services	West	11/1/93	4,026	11,786	9,225
13								
14								

BOOK1.XLS

Suppose that you want to sort the database using four fields: Region, Last Call, Category, and Name. Here are two ways to work around the three-field limit of the Data ➤ Sort command. Method One is the most commonly used method and the easiest to learn, but it requires at least two passes of the Data ➤ Sort command. Method Two requires only one sorting pass, but there is a bit of initial setup involved—this method is more suitable for a database which is re-sorted often, so that after the calculated sort field (explained below) is added to the database, only one sorting pass is needed.

Method One

Sort the data twice, starting with the least significant fields:

1. Choose Data ➤ Sort.
2. Select Last Call, Category, and Name.
3. Click OK to sort.
4. Choose Data ➤ Sort.
5. Select Region as the first field.
6. Select (none) as the second and third fields.
7. Click OK to sort.

► ►**T I P**

> **Dates and times, when sorted in ascending order, sort from oldest to newest. Sort order is based on the *underlying cell value*, not the formatted appearance.**

Method Two

Create a *calculated sort field* (a field that combines other fields):

1. Add a new field in column J using the field name Region—Last Call.

2. Place the following formula in cell J3, then fill it down through cell J12:

   =LEFT(E3&"   ",5)&F3

There are five spaces within the quotations. The LEFT function is padding the region field to five characters (assuming a maximum region length of five characters). Padding is only required when a field within a calculated sort field is not the last one, and is variable in length.

3. Choose Data ➤ Sort.

4. Select Region—Last Call as the first sort field.

5. Select Category and Name as the second and third sort fields.

6. Click OK to sort.

Note that with calculated sort fields, you lose the ability to specify ascending or descending order for the individual fields within the calculated field. What if you want to combine Region=ascending with YTD Sales=descending in column K? Use a formula in K3 such as:

   =LEFT(E3&"   ",5)&TEXT(1000000-H3,"0000000")

► Sorting Columns Instead of Rows

The columns in the following database are sorted alphabetically by region name. Assume that you want to sort the columns according to total sales in descending order:

	A	B	C	D	E	F	G
					BOOK1.XLS		
1							
2			East	North	South	West	
3		Q1	374	426	568	512	
4		Q2	750	236	682	875	
5		Q3	410	475	797	775	
6		Q4	409	225	450	922	
7		Total	1,943	1,362	2,497	3,084	
8							
9							
10							

1. Select cells C2:F7 (so as not to sort the row labels with the data).

2. Choose Data ➤ Sort.

3. Click the Options button to display the Sort Options dialog box.

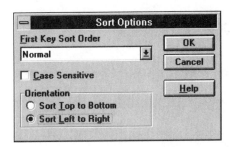

4. Select the Sort Left to Right option.

5. Click OK.

6. Sort by Row 7 (row number on worksheet, not row number within database).

7. Select the Descending option.

8. Click OK to sort the database as follows:

	A	B	C	D	E	F	G
					BOOK1.XLS		
1							
2			West	South	East	North	
3		Q1	512	568	374	426	
4		Q2	875	682	750	236	
5		Q3	775	797	410	475	
6		Q4	922	450	409	225	
7		Total	3,084	2,497	1,943	1,362	
8							
9							

▶ ▶ **T I P**

The Sort Options dialog box lets you specify case-sensitive sorts. An ascending case-sensitive sort will go *AaBbCc* etc.

▶ Using Custom Sort Orders

There are times when you may want to sort data using a sort order that is neither ascending nor descending. For example, your organization may sort regions on printed reports in roughly the order they appear on a map, rather than alphabetically. Or you may want to sort a list of office vendors with the most frequently used vendor on top.

On the following worksheet, the months are listed in date sequence.

	A	B	C	D
1				
2			Service	
3		Month	Calls	
4		January	51	
5		February	78	
6		March	49	
7		April	37	
8		May	34	
9		June	75	
10		July	69	
11		August	45	
12		September	65	
13		October	58	
14		November	63	
15		December	72	
16				

BOOK1.XLS

Suppose that your company has a fiscal year that begins October 1 and ends September 30. You can cut and paste to get the data in the right sequence, or you can use a custom list to determine the sort order.

Creating Custom Lists

Follow these steps to create a custom list for an October-through-September fiscal-year sort:

1. Enter the data on a worksheet in the desired sequence

(hint: you can type in October and November, then use the fill handle to fill down the remaining months).

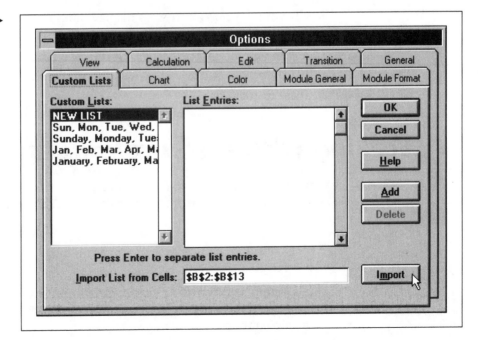

	A	B	C	D
1				
2		October		
3		November		
4		December		
5		January		
6		February		
7		March		
8		April		
9		May		
10		June		
11		July		
12		August		
13		September		
14				

BOOK1.XLS

2. Select B2:B13.

3. Choose Tools ➤ Options, then select the Custom Lists tab (Figure 16.2).

FIGURE 16.2

The Tools ➤ Options, Custom Lists tab

Options

View	Calculation	Edit	Transition	General
Custom Lists	Chart	Color	Module General	Module Format

Custom Lists:
NEW LIST
Sun, Mon, Tue, Wed,
Sunday, Monday, Tue:
Jan, Feb, Mar, Apr, M:
January, February, Ma

List Entries:

Press Enter to separate list entries.

Import List from Cells: $B$2:$B$13

OK
Cancel
Help
Add
Delete
Import

4. Click the Import button.

5. Click OK.

You only to have to create a custom list once. Since the list is not stored in a workbook, it is available globally.

▶ ▶**T I P**

Custom lists are also used by Excel's AutoFill feature. See Chapters 7 and 26 to learn more about performing AutoFills.

Using a Custom List to Drive a Sort

Once you have created a custom list, it is easy to use it to sort data. Follow these steps to sort a list using the October-September sort order defined in the previous exercise:

1. Select a cell inside the database or list, then choose Data ▶ Sort.

2. Select Month as the Sort By setting.

3. Click the Options button to display the Sort Options dialog box.

4. Use the First Key Sort Order drop-down, and select the item reading October, November, December, etc.

5. Click OK to close the Sort Options dialog box, then click OK again to sort.

▶▶ *Working with Criteria Ranges*

An important construct in advanced database manipulation is the *criteria range*—a range of cells that defines a database filter. Criteria ranges are used in two ways:

● They are used by advanced database filters—to display only those records that meet the criteria.

● They are used by *D functions*, a special category of function that uses a criteria range to determine which database records to use in calculations.

Using a criteria range requires two steps:

1. Define the criteria range.

2. Use the criteria range when performing an advanced filter, or in a D function—the criteria range by itself does nothing.

 ► ►**N O T E**

> **Learning about criteria ranges requires some patience. There is a lot of ground to cover before you will see how to put them to use. In this chapter we will present the basics of criteria ranges, proceed to the topic of computed criteria, and then move on to advanced filters and D functions. Initially, you might want to read just the basics of criteria ranges and then skip ahead to see how they are used in advanced filters before you finish the presentation of criteria ranges.**

► *Parts of a Criteria Range*

A criteria range consists of two parts:

- A header row, containing field names that must identically match the database field names
- One or more criteria rows

The following criteria range is used to filter the database in Figure 16.1:

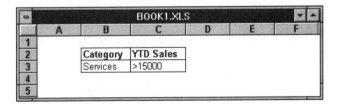

The criteria range in cells B2:C3 means: All records where the Category is equal to Services *and* YTD Sales are greater than 15,000. If this criteria range were used to filter the database shown in Figure 16.1, only row 5 would display.

▶ ▶**TIP**

If you are familiar with Structured Query Language (SQL), then you may recognize that a criteria range is the equivalent of a simple *where* clause.

▶ *Parts of the Criteria*

The criteria specification is identical to criteria entered in a data form. There is an optional relational operator, followed by a value. Table 16.1 defines the relational operators that can be used.

▶ **TABLE 16.1:** *Relational Operators*

Operator	Meaning
=	Equal to
>	Greater than
<	Less than
>=	Greater than or equal to
<=	Less than or equal to
<>	Not equal

Table 16.2 contains examples of criteria, as they would be entered into the criteria range.

▶ **TABLE 16.2:** *Criteria Examples*

Criteria	Meaning
=East	Equal to East
>B	Greater than B
<Jones	Less than Jones
>=West	Greater than or equal to West
<=West	Less than or equal to West
<>West	Not equal to West
Smith	Starts with Smith (Smith, Smithe, Smithsonian)

▶ **TABLE 16.2:** *Criteria Examples (continued)*

Criteria	Meaning
*Smith	Ends with Smith (Jane Smith, John Smith, Smith)
<>*Smith	Every value that does not end with Smith
car	Every value containing "car" (Carson, scare, car)
?ON	Finds Ron and Jon, but not Stone
=10	Equal to 10
>100	Greater than 100
<100	Less than 100
>=25	Greater than or equal to 25
<=25	Less than or equal to 25
<>0	Not equal to zero
100	Equal to 100

N O T E

The criteria examples in Table 16.2 that begin with an equal sign are not formulas; they are text constants beginning with an equal sign. However, when the first character entered into a cell is an equal sign, Excel assumes the entry is a formula. Precede the equal sign with an apostrophe to indicate a text entry.

▶ *Multiple Criteria*

Multiple criteria can be specified in two forms:

AND Records that match all criteria (where Region equals west *and* YTD Sales are greater than 15,000). Place the criteria on one row.

OR Records that match one of several criteria (where Region equals west *or* Sales are greater than 15,000). Place the criteria on different rows.

The examples shown in Figure 16.3 apply to the database pictured in Figure 16.1:

FIGURE 16.3 ▶

Examples of multiple criteria used with the database shown earlier in the chapter (in Figure 16.1)

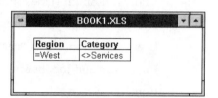

Where Region equals West and Category does not equal Services

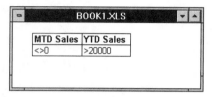

Where MTD Sales does not equal zero and YTD Sales is greater than 20000

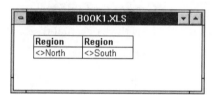

Where Region does not equal North and Region does not equal South

Where Region ends with TH and Category starts with FIN and Last Call is prior to 1/1/94

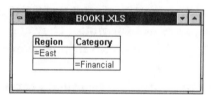

Where Region equals East or Category equals Financial

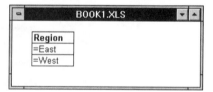

Where Region equals East or Region equals West

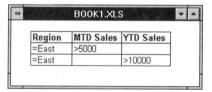

Where Region equals East and MTD Sales > 5000 OR where Region equals East and YTD Sales > 10000

▶ ▶**N O T E**

> **If you have never used a criteria range before, the topic may seem abstract at this point. This is a good time to jump ahead to advanced filters, where you will learn how to apply criteria ranges. Come back to computed criteria once you have a more solid understanding of the uses of criteria ranges.**

▶ *Computed Criteria*

Criteria specifications can be complex, especially if they include multiple criteria and relational operators. Picture a worksheet model with a database, a complex criteria range, and various D functions (covered later in this chapter) that use the criteria range to perform calculations on the database. By changing the data in the criteria range, you can ask different questions of the database. This provides a lot of power, but also presents two problems:

- When you change the criteria you run the risk of "breaking" the model with a typographical error.

- The model may be intended for use by people in your organization who neither understand criteria ranges nor wish to understand them.

Computed criteria can be used to solve these problems. They allow user input to be incorporated into a criteria range without the user of the model knowing about criteria ranges, or even being aware that a criteria range exists.

There are several important things to know about computed criteria:

- The term *computed criteria* tends to confuse people because of the unusual use of the word *computed*. Formulas can be entered into a criteria range, and these formulas *calculate* results, just like any formula. A computed criterion is just a criteria range that has formulas in it.

- Computed criteria are very powerful, and *vitally* important for serious worksheet development.

- The topic is widely misunderstood because there are two ways to express computed criteria: Method One is a logical extension of what you have learned so far; Method Two is somewhat idiosyncratic:

  - Method One is more powerful and easier to learn than Method Two, though Method Two does have one unique capability which makes it worth learning.
  - Inexplicably, the Excel manuals (and most third-party publications) explain only Method Two.
  - The lengthy coverage of Method Two here is not intended to place emphasis—it just requires more explanation.

- The two methods are *not* mutually exclusive.

▶ *Computed Criteria—Method One*

Very simply, you are *not limited to constant text values* in a criteria range. You can also use formulas which calculate the criteria. Using the database in Figure 16.1, suppose you want to ask the question, "How many clients had YTD Sales exceeding X (a user-specified threshold)?" The next exercise shows how to build a criteria range that incorporates variables:

1. Create the following worksheet:

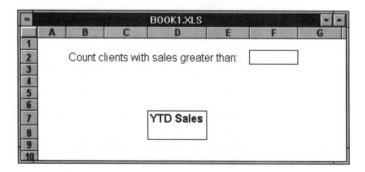

2. Enter this formula into D8: =">"&F2

3. Enter a number into F2; the formula in D8 causes the criteria to change. (Performing the count requires the use of a D function, covered later in this chapter.)

Perhaps you also want the ability to count the number of clients with MTD (month-to-date) Sales exceeding a user-specified threshold. Any cell within a criteria range can include a formula instead of a constant. Add the following to your model:

B4   Enter **M** (for MTD), or **Y** (for YTD):

D7   **=IF(F4="M","MTD Sales","YTD Sales")**

FIGURE 16.4 ▶

The user input in cells F2 and F4 is driving the criteria range D7:D8

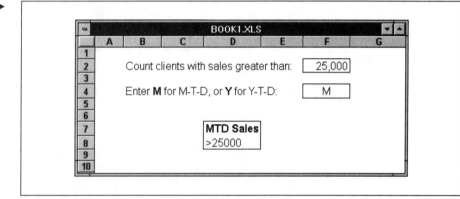

▶ *Computed Criteria—Method Two*

The second way of expressing computed criteria is the method that is taught in the Excel manual, and in most third-party publications. Though some find this method more complicated to use, it nonetheless provides an important capability that cannot be achieved with Method One: the ability to compare a field to one or more fields in the same record.

 ▶ ▶ N O T E

> **Remember, Methods One and Two are not mutually exclusive. Both techniques can be employed in the same criteria range.**

The database in Figure 16.5 is used to measure the efficiency of regional customer service departments for a fictional utility company.

FIGURE 16.5 ▶

The Calls 94 and Calls 95 fields contain the number of incoming calls for 1994 and 1995 respectively. Fields OK 94 and OK 95 contain the number of those calls resolved to the customer's satisfaction.

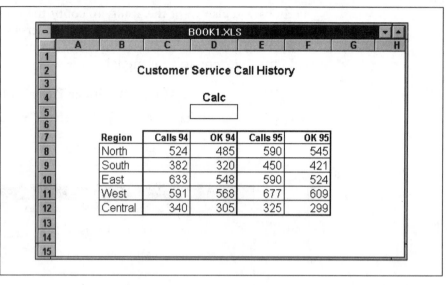

Region	Calls 94	OK 94	Calls 95	OK 95
North	524	485	590	545
South	382	320	450	421
East	633	548	590	524
West	591	568	677	609
Central	340	305	325	299

Customer Service Call History

Calc

Suppose that you want to create a criteria range that will be used to display only those regions where the number of calls received in 1995 exceeded the number of calls in 1994. Using the database and criteria range in Figure 16.5, entering the following formula in cell D5:

    =E8>C8

would cause an advanced filter (covered later in this chapter) to display only rows 8, 9, and 11—the rows where 1995 calls exceeded 1994 calls. The rules for constructing this type of relative comparison are:

- The formula must return logical values TRUE or FALSE.

- The field name used in the criteria range (i.e., cell D4 in Figure 16.5) must *not* match a field name in the database—in fact, it can be left blank.

- The cell references in the formula are relative, and point to the first record of the database (you can use absolute references, but not to compare fields within each record).

- Like Method One, the criteria range can contain more than one column.

Here are some more examples of Method Two criteria using the database in Figure 16.1. Each formula goes into cell D5:

Example 1:

Filter	Display every record where the total calls for 1994 and 1995 are greater than 1000.
Formula	=C8+E8>1000
Display	Rows 8, 10, and 11

Example 2:

Filter	Display every record where the percentage of successful call resolutions in 1995 is worse than 1994.
Formula	=(F8/E8)<(D8/C8)
Display	Rows 8 and 11

Example 3:

Filter	Display every record where the percentage of successful resolutions in 1995 is worse than 90%.
Formula	=(F8/E8)<.9
Display	Rows 10 and 11

Example 4:

Filter	Display every record where the percentage of successful resolutions in 1994 is better than the percentage contained in cell F5.
Formula	=(D8/C8)>$F$5 (Note the absolute reference $F$5; it is not contained in the database—an absolute comparison is being performed.)
Display	Depends on cell F5—if F5 contains 90%, rows 8 and 11 are displayed

▶▶ *Using Advanced Filters*

AutoFilters, covered in Chapter 15, allow simple data filters to be defined with ease, and provide an outstanding interface for specifying filter criteria. Custom AutoFilters provide a little more flexibility, but even they are limited. *Advanced filters* are able to:

- Use an unlimited number of criteria per field (using criteria ranges, covered earlier in this chapter)

- Use variables as part of the criteria (using computed criteria, covered earlier in this chapter)

 ▶ ▶ N O T E

To remove a filter and display all the data, choose the Data ➤ Filter ➤ Show All command.

▶ *Filtering "in Place"*

When you filter in-place, all records that do not meet a criteria specification are hidden, and all other records are displayed (in the same way that AutoFilters do). Here are the steps required to perform an advanced filter in-place:

1. Create a criteria range.

2. Select a cell within the database range.

3. Choose Data ➤ Filter ➤ Advanced Filter (Figure 16.6).

4. Select the Filter the List in-place option.

5. Enter the Criteria Range (you can type a cell reference, or point-and-click on the worksheet).

6. Click OK to filter.

7. To filter again with new criteria:

   - Enter new value into criteria range (on worksheet).

   - Then choose Data ➤ Filter ➤ Advanced Filter and click OK (the Advanced Filter dialog box remembers the settings from the last Advanced Filter).

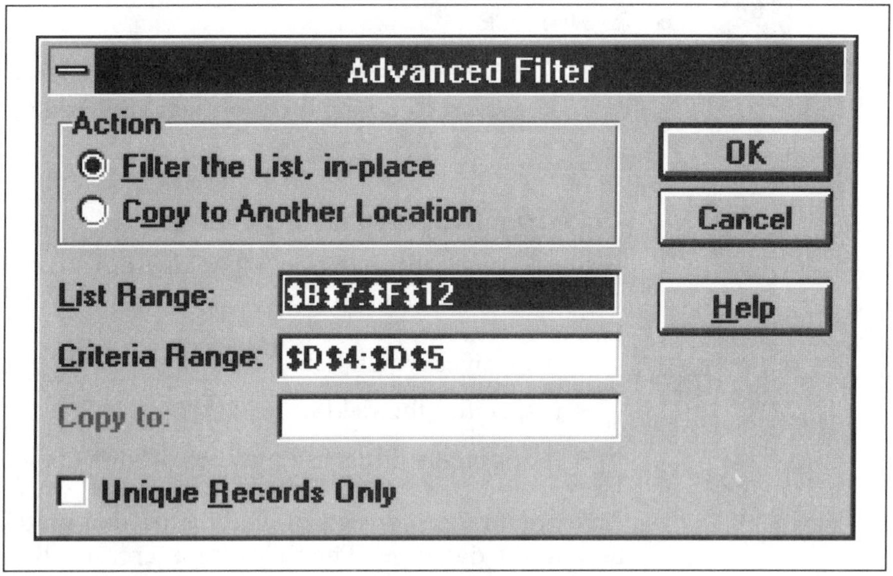

FIGURE 16.6 ▶

*Advanced AutoFilter
dialog box*

▶ *Copying Records to a New Location*

So far, every filter in this chapter (and the previous chapter) has filtered data in-place. As an alternative, filtered rows can be copied to a new location. Use the same steps as in the previous exercise, but with the following options:

- Choose the Copy to Another Location setting (see Figure 16.6)—this will make the Copy To setting available.

- Enter a Copy To range (type in a cell reference, or point-and-click on the worksheet).

Every record meeting the criteria specification is copied to the specified location.

Often, when you copy records to a new location, it is desirable to copy them to a different worksheet or a different workbook. There is a trick to this—you must activate the destination workbook/worksheet before choosing the Data ➤ Filter ➤ Advanced Filter command.

▶ ▶**N O T E**

In previous versions of Excel, the process of copying a record to a new location was referred to as a *data extract*.

Copying Only Specified Fields

If you do not want to extract all fields from a database, an *extract range* must be defined. An extract range serves three purposes:

- It specifies which fields to copy.
- It specifies the field order.
- It optionally limits the number of rows copied.

An extract range consists of field names that match the field names used in the database. The following exercise will copy records from the database in Figure 16.1:

1. Build a criteria range:

Cell	Entry
B14	**Region**
B15	**North**

2. Build an extract range:

Cell	Entry
C17	**Name**
D17	**YTD Sales**

3. Select a cell inside the database range, then choose Data ➤ Filter ➤ Advanced Filter. Excel will automatically detect the list (database) range $B$2:$I$12 (see Figures 16.7 and 16.8).

4. Select the Copy to Another Location option.

5. Enter a Criteria Range of **B14:B15**. (If you point-and-click the cells on the worksheet, the sheet name is automatically included as part of the range.)

6. Enter a Copy To range of **C17:D17**. (If you point-and-click the cells on the worksheet, the sheet name is automatically included as part of the range.)

7. Click OK.

FIGURE 16.7

This advanced filter will copy only the Name and YTD Sales fields.

	A	B	C	D	E	F	G	H	I
			BOOK1.XLS						
1									
2		Client No	Name	Category	Region	Last Call	MTD Sales	YTD Sales	Last Year
3		107	MDC Enterprises	Mfg	East	1/30/94	8,167	23,613	25,733
4		104	Kinsman & Nelson	Services	East	2/7/95	3,717	12,374	9,221
5		110	T.K. James Inc.	Services	North	8/11/94	3,146	19,104	11,373
6		105	Pacific Investments	Financial	North	12/1/93	3,315	18,656	11,044
7		101	Argus Industries	Mfg	North	1/10/95	9,569	13,775	14,723
8		109	JK Associates	Financial	South	3/1/94	12,391	71,805	23,490
9		102	LEX Software	Services	South	4/23/94	3,527	10,534	12,887
10		103	National Bank	Financial	South	6/1/94	1,472	8,123	10,022
11		106	Nica Corporation	Mfg	West	2/25/94	6,542	58,229	52,559
12		108	Wilson & Roth	Services	West	11/1/93	4,026	11,786	9,225
13									
14		Region							
15		North							
16									
17			Name	YTD Sales					
18									
19									

FIGURE 16.8

The criteria range caused only those records in region North to be copied. The extract range caused only the fields Name and YTD Sales to be copied.

	A	B	C	D	E	F	G	H	I
			BOOK1.XLS						
1									
2		Client No	Name	Category	Region	Last Call	MTD Sales	YTD Sales	Last Year
3		107	MDC Enterprises	Mfg	East	1/30/94	8,167	23,613	25,733
4		104	Kinsman & Nelson	Services	East	2/7/95	3,717	12,374	9,221
5		110	T.K. James Inc.	Services	North	8/11/94	3,146	19,104	11,373
6		105	Pacific Investments	Financial	North	12/1/93	3,315	18,656	11,044
7		101	Argus Industries	Mfg	North	1/10/95	9,569	13,775	14,723
8		109	JK Associates	Financial	South	3/1/94	12,391	71,805	23,490
9		102	LEX Software	Services	South	4/23/94	3,527	10,534	12,887
10		103	National Bank	Financial	South	6/1/94	1,472	8,123	10,022
11		106	Nica Corporation	Mfg	West	2/25/94	6,542	58,229	52,559
12		108	Wilson & Roth	Services	West	11/1/93	4,026	11,786	9,225
13									
14		Region							
15		North							
16									
17			Name	YTD Sales					
18			T.K. James Inc.	19,104					
19			Pacific Investments	18,656					
20			Argus Industries	13,775					
21									

TIP

> After setting an advanced filter, and copying to another location, the header row (field names) of the copied data is named Extract, and the criteria range is named Criteria.

▶▶ *Using the D Functions*

The database functions, or D functions, are different from most other functions because:

- They perform calculations on a specified column within a specified database (or any range of cells with a header row containing unique field names—see Chapter 15 to learn how to set up a database).

- They use a criteria range to determine which records to include in the calculation (criteria ranges are explained earlier in this chapter).

The D functions are all structured identically. Once you understand DSUM, you will be ready to use all of the D functions.

NOTE

> For most D functions, there is a non-database equivalent. For example, there is a DSUM function and a SUM function.

DSUM Syntax

The DSUM syntax is:

DSUM(DatabaseRange,Field,CriteriaRange)

Database-Range	A range of cells containing database—must include header row with unique field names (covered in Chapter 15)
Field	A field within DatabaseRange used in calculation
Criteria-Range	A range of cells containing criteria specification (covered earlier in this chapter)

In Figure 16.9, DSUM is used to calculate MTD Sales for all clients in region North.

FIGURE 16.9

As you can see from the DSUM arguments, the database is at B2:I12, the field being summed is MTD Sales, and the criteria range is at B14:B15.

BOOK1.XLS

	A	B	C	D	E	F	G	H	I
2		Client No	Name	Category	Region	Last Call	MTD Sales	YTD Sales	Last Year
3		101	Argus Industries	Mfg	North	1/10/95	9,569	13,775	14,723
4		102	LEX Software	Services	South	4/23/94	3,527	10,534	12,887
5		103	National Bank	Financial	South	6/1/94	1,472	8,123	10,022
6		104	Kinsman & Nelson	Services	East	2/7/95	3,717	12,374	9,221
7		105	Pacific Investments	Financial	North	12/1/93	3,315	18,656	11,044
8		106	Nica Corporation	Mfg	West	2/25/94	6,542	58,229	52,559
9		107	MDC Enterprises	Mfg	East	1/30/94	8,167	23,613	25,733
10		108	Wilson & Roth	Services	West	11/1/93	4,026	11,786	9,225
11		109	JK Associates	Financial	South	3/1/94	12,391	71,805	23,490
12		110	T.K. James Inc.	Services	North	8/11/94	3,146	19,104	11,373
13									
14		Region							
15		North		16030					
16									
17									
18									
19									

Contains formula:
=DSUM(B2:I12,"MTD Sales",B14:B15)

Here are some variations on the DSUM formula in Figure 16.9. All four of these examples are based on the criteria range B14:B15, which specifies region *North*.

An example summing *YTD Sales*:

```
=DSUM(B2:I12,"YTD Sales",B14:B15)
```

An example summing Last Year (assuming that the database range is named SalesData, and the criteria range is named SalesCriteria):

```
=DSUM(SalesData,"Last Year",SalesCriteria)
```

Now, assume that the text "Last Year" has been entered into C14. This formula demonstrates that the second argument, *field*, can be a variable:

```
=DSUM(B2:I12,C14,B14:B15)
```

Any worksheet function that requires range arguments can use embedded functions to calculate the range. The D functions are no exception. In the next example, the OFFSET function points to cells B14:B15 (see Chapter 9 to learn about OFFSET). While the next formula does not require the use of the OFFSET function, it still demonstrates a powerful capability: Since the arguments for OFFSET can be variables, user input can be used to dynamically point to different criteria ranges:

=DSUM(B2:I12,"MTD Sales",OFFSET(B13,1,0,2,1))

Table 16.3 contains all of the D functions. They all use the same arguments as DSUM, but perform different types of calculations.

► **TABLE 16.3:** *D Functions*

Function	Description
DAVERAGE	Calculates an average
DCOUNT	Counts cells containing numbers
DCOUNTA	Counts nonblank cells
DGET	Gets a single field from a single record
DMAX	Calculates a maximum value
DMIN	Calculates a minimum value
DPRODUCT	Multiplies values
DSTDEV	Estimates standard deviation based on a sample
DSTDEVP	Calculates standard deviation based on the entire population
DSUM	Sums values
DVAR	Estimates variance based on a sample
DVARP	Calculates variance based on the entire population

 ►

There are two functions in addition to the D functions that use criteria ranges: SUMIF and COUNTIF. Both are covered in Chapter 9.

►► *Inserting Embedded Subtotals in a Database*

The ability to embed subtotals into a range of data, in a semi-automated fashion, is an important new Excel 5 capability. This feature (and Pivot Tables, the subject of the next chapter) has significantly enhanced Excel's overall capability as a reporting tool.

Using the database pictured in Figure 16.1, assume you want to add subtotals and a grand total for the MTD Sales, YTD Sales, and Last Year fields by region. Here's how you could do it:

1. Sort the database by Region.
2. Select a cell within the database range.
3. Choose Data ➤ Subtotals to display the dialog box in Figure 16.10.
4. Choose Region from the At Each Change In list (subtotals will be inserted each time the region changes).

FIGURE 16.10 ▶

The Data ➤ Subtotals dialog box

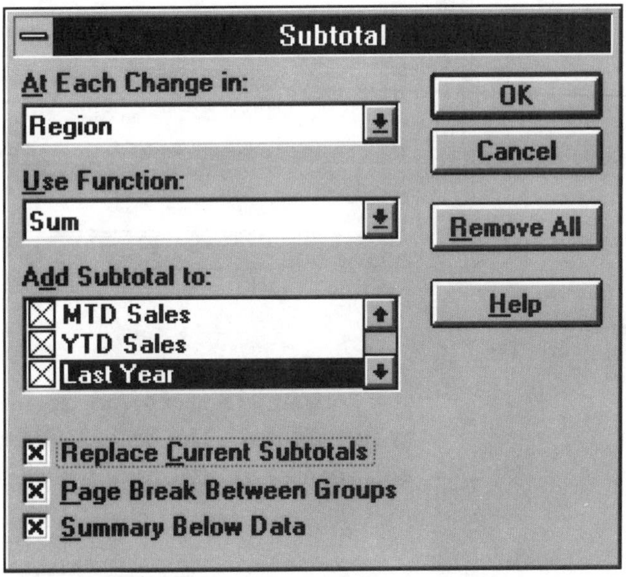

5. Select the SUM function from the Use Function list (see SUB-TOTAL in Chapter 9 for explanation of each function).

6. The Add Subtotal To list is used to specify which fields to sub-total—check MTD Sales, YTD Sales, and Last Year.

7. Check the Page Break Between Groups setting to insert a page break after each subtotal.

8. If Summary Below Data is checked, the subtotal row is placed beneath the data; otherwise it is placed on top.

9. Click OK to insert subtotals (pictured in Figure 16.11).

FIGURE 16.11 ▶

Database with sub-totals

	Client No	Name	Category	Region	Last Call	MTD Sales	YTD Sales
	107	MDC Enterprises	Mfg	East	1/30/94	8,167	23,613
	104	Kinsman & Nelson	Services	East	2/7/95	3,717	12,374
				East Total		11,884	35,987
	110	T.K. James Inc.	Services	North	8/11/94	3,146	19,104
	105	Pacific Investments	Financial	North	12/1/93	3,315	18,656
	101	Argus Industries	Mfg	North	1/10/95	9,569	13,775
				North Total		16,030	51,535
	109	JK Associates	Financial	South	3/1/94	12,391	71,805
	102	LEX Software	Services	South	4/23/94	3,527	10,534
	103	National Bank	Financial	South	6/1/94	1,472	8,123
				South Total		17,390	90,462
	106	Nica Corporation	Mfg	West	2/25/94	6,542	58,229
	108	Wilson & Roth	Services	West	11/1/93	4,026	11,786
				West Total		10,568	70,015
				Grand Total		55,872	247,999

BOOK1.XLS

▶ **TIP**

Use Format ➤ AutoFormat to format a range that contains subtotals. The built-in formats detect the subtotals, and format accordingly for optimum readability.

More Power
from Databases

Ch.
16

▶ *Inserting Subtotals Adds Outlining to the Sheet*

Notice the outline symbols in Figure 16.11.

Outlining is an automatic by-product when subtotals are inserted using Data ➤ Subtotals.

- To expand/collapse the outline, click the outline symbols.
- To hide/unhide outline symbols, use the Tools ➤ Options command, select the View tab, then use the Outline Symbols checkbox.

Outlining is covered in depth in Chapter 22.

▶ ## USING MULTIPLE SUBTOTAL FORMULAS

Take a look at Figure 16.11. In this worksheet, subtotals were added which sum sales by region. Suppose you want to show average sales by region, in addition to total sales by region? Adding a second subtotal function is easy. You've learned how to add a first set of subtotals, which in Figure 16.11 used the SUM function to sum both sales fields by region. To average both sales fields by region, repeat the procedure, but:

- Select AVERAGE from the Use Function dropdown list

- Clear the Replace Current Subtotals checkbox

Now each region will have two subtotal rows, one for Total and one for Average.

▶ Removing Embedded Subtotals

There are two ways to remove embedded subtotals that were inserted using Data ➤ Subtotals:

- To remove all embedded subtotals, choose the Data ➤ Subtotals command, and click Remove All.

- To add different subtotals to the same range, and remove the old subtotals at the same time, check the Replace Current Subtotals setting (see Figure 16.10).

▶▶ Creating Friendly-Looking Databases

Since field names must be unique, you often wind up with field names which, from a user perspective, are not very friendly. Figure 16.12 contains two databases, each with a different type of problem.

The 1994 database duplicates the field names Budget and Actual, which causes problems for many database operations. In addition, the Q1–Q4 descriptive labels above the database confuse Excel—when you

FIGURE 16.12 ▶

The 1994 database does not have unique field names. The field names in the 1995 database are not user-friendly.

BOOK1.XLS								

1994 Budget vs Actual

	Q1		Q2		Q3		Q4	
Division	Budget	Actual	Budget	Actual	Budget	Actual	Budget	Actual
R&D	7,000	7,225	7,000	6,808	8,000	7,855	8,000	8,120
Finance	3,500	3,445	3,500	3,515	3,500	3,382	4,000	4,020
Marketing	3,000	2,830	3,500	3,667	3,500	4,210	4,000	3,831

1995 Budget vs Actual

Division	Q1.Bud	Q1.Act	Q2.Bud	Q2.Act	Q3.Bud	Q3.Act	Q4.Bud	Q4.Act
R&D	8,000	7,925	8,500	8,780	8,500	8,345	8,500	8,224
Finance	4,000	3,775	4,000	4,201	4,000	3,879	4,500	4,320
Marketing	4,000	3,711	4,250	4,225	4,250	4,210	4,500	4,669

sort this database, Excel will attempt to include rows 2 and 3 in the data area.

The 1995 database uses unique field names—it is perfectly legal. But the field names are aesthetically displeasing, and potentially confusing to others.

There is a way to design your databases to combine the friendliness of the 1994 database with the correctness of the 1995 database. Consider Figures 16.13 and 16.14.

FIGURE 16.13 ▶

The database is at B5:J8. Rows 3 and 4 are for clarity only.

Division	Q1 Budget	Q1 Actual	Q2 Budget	Q2 Actual	Q3 Budget	Q3 Actual	Q4 Budget	Q4 Actual
Division	Q1.Bud	Q1.Act	Q2.Bud	Q2.Act	Q3.Bud	Q3.Act	Q4.Bud	Q4.Act
R&D	8,000	7,925	8,500	8,780	8,500	8,345	8,500	8,224
Finance	4,000	3,775	4,000	4,201	4,000	3,879	4,500	4,320
Marketing	4,000	3,711	4,250	4,225	4,250	4,210	4,500	4,669

FIGURE 16.14 ▶

The first row of the database, containing legal field names, is hidden.

Division	Q1 Budget	Q1 Actual	Q2 Budget	Q2 Actual	Q3 Budget	Q3 Actual	Q4 Budget	Q4 Actual
R&D	8,000	7,925	8,500	8,780	8,500	8,345	8,500	8,224
Finance	4,000	3,775	4,000	4,201	4,000	3,879	4,500	4,320
Marketing	4,000	3,711	4,250	4,225	4,250	4,210	4,500	4,669

Here is how you can create this database:

- Enter legal field names on the header row of the database.
- Enter field descriptions on the row(s) above the header row.
- Hide the first row of the database (the header row).

► ► CHAPTER **17**

Using Pivot Tables to Analyze Data

► ► *F*AST *T*RACK

▶ ***To control how a data field is calculated***   ***574***

First, select a cell inside the data area of the pivot table. Then, choose Data ➤ PivotTable Field. Finally, choose the type of calculation in the Summarize By list box.

▶ ***To perform a custom calculation***   ***575***

Start by selecting a cell inside the data area of the pivot table. Next, choose Data ➤ PivotTable Field, then click Options. Finally, choose from the Show Data As list.

▶ ***To base a pivot table on an external database***   ***584***

Select External Data Source at Step One of the PivotTable Wizard.

One of the biggest challenges in the real world is the need to derive important information from large quantities of raw data. *Pivot tables* provide a way to easily summarize and analyze data using special direct manipulation techniques. They are called pivot tables because you can change their layout by twisting and rearranging, or *pivoting*, the row and column headings quickly and easily. Pivot tables are arguably the most important new feature in Excel 5, and are well worth the time to learn and master. This chapter covers:

- *How to create a pivot table from a worksheet database*
- *How to change the layout of a pivot table*
- *Creating pivot tables from external databases*
- *Creating pivot tables from multiple consolidation ranges*

Using an Example Database for the Exercises

Through much of this chapter, a database will be used that is located in a sample workbook that comes with Excel. The workbook is named PRODUCTS.XLS, and can be found in the EXCELCBT directory, inside your Excel directory. The database is stored on the worksheet named Products (Figure 17.1).

If you want to follow the exercises in the chapter, you may want to copy this data to a new workbook so as not to accidentally change PRODUCTS.XLS, which is used in Excel's online Examples and Demos.

The database contains sales history for a fictitious company that sells produce and dairy products to supermarkets. Sales are tracked by product category, period (year and month), salesperson, and region.

FIGURE 17.1 ▶

Database of sales history

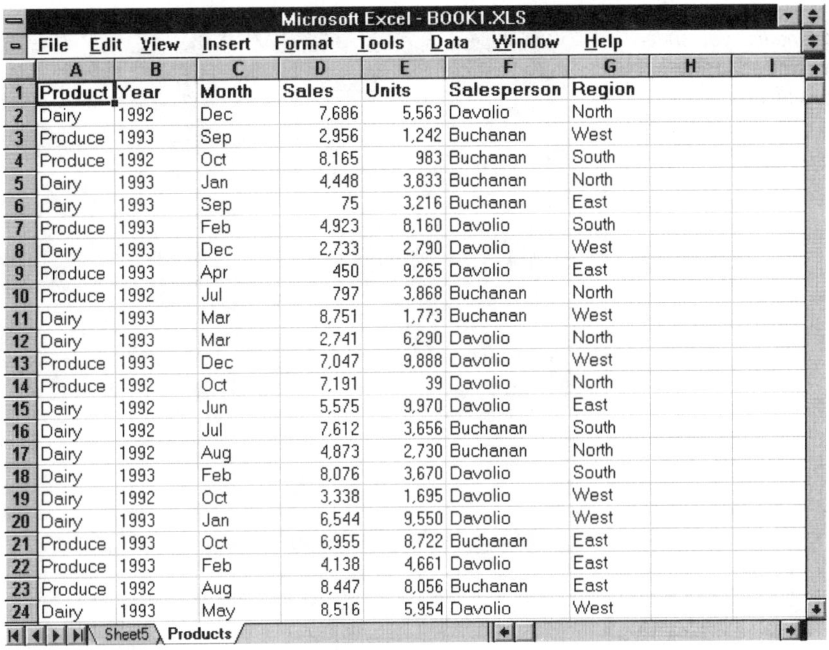

	A	B	C	D	E	F	G	H	I
1	Product	Year	Month	Sales	Units	Salesperson	Region		
2	Dairy	1992	Dec	7,686	5,563	Davolio	North		
3	Produce	1993	Sep	2,956	1,242	Buchanan	West		
4	Produce	1992	Oct	8,165	983	Buchanan	South		
5	Dairy	1993	Jan	4,448	3,833	Buchanan	North		
6	Dairy	1993	Sep	75	3,216	Buchanan	East		
7	Produce	1993	Feb	4,923	8,160	Davolio	South		
8	Dairy	1993	Dec	2,733	2,790	Davolio	West		
9	Produce	1993	Apr	450	9,265	Davolio	East		
10	Produce	1992	Jul	797	3,868	Buchanan	North		
11	Dairy	1993	Mar	8,751	1,773	Buchanan	West		
12	Dairy	1993	Mar	2,741	6,290	Davolio	North		
13	Produce	1993	Dec	7,047	9,888	Davolio	West		
14	Produce	1992	Oct	7,191	39	Davolio	North		
15	Dairy	1992	Jun	5,575	9,970	Davolio	East		
16	Dairy	1992	Jul	7,612	3,656	Buchanan	South		
17	Dairy	1992	Aug	4,873	2,730	Buchanan	North		
18	Dairy	1993	Feb	8,076	3,670	Davolio	South		
19	Dairy	1992	Oct	3,338	1,695	Davolio	West		
20	Dairy	1993	Jan	6,544	9,550	Davolio	West		
21	Produce	1993	Oct	6,955	8,722	Buchanan	East		
22	Produce	1993	Feb	4,138	4,661	Davolio	East		
23	Produce	1992	Aug	8,447	8,056	Buchanan	East		
24	Dairy	1993	May	8,516	5,954	Davolio	West		

▶▶ *Creating a Simple Pivot Table from an Internal Database*

There is a PivotTable Wizard that makes the job of creating pivot tables simple. The following exercise will walk you through the steps required to create a simple pivot table using the Products database pictured in Figure 17.1.

1. Starting the PivotTable Wizard

Follow these steps to start the PivotTable Wizard:

a. Open the products workbook.

b. Select a cell anywhere inside the database.

c. Choose the Data ➤ Pivot Table command—Step One of the Pivot-Table Wizard, pictured in Figure 17.2, is displayed.

FIGURE 17.2 ▶

*Step One lets you spec-
ify where the source
data is located.*

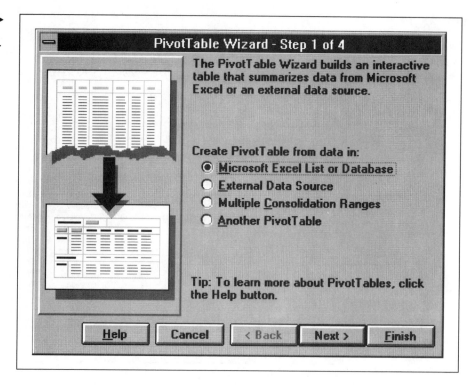

d. Since the source data is stored in an internal database, select the
Microsoft Excel List or Database option.

e. Click Next to proceed to Step Two.

2. Confirming the Database Range

Step Two of the PivotTable Wizard lets you confirm the database range.

If the active cell is inside a database when you choose the Data ➤ Pivot
Table command, the Wizard automatically detects the boundaries of

the database. You can enter a different range, or you can use the mouse to point, click, and drag a range of cells.

- If the source data is on a different worksheet, click the sheet tab, then select the database range.

- If the source data is in a different (open) workbook, use the window menu to activate the workbook, then select the database range.

- If the source data is stored in a workbook that is not open, click the Browse button to choose the workbook.

Click Next to proceed to Step Three.

3. Laying Out the Pivot Table

Step Three (Figure 17.3) is the heart of the pivot table.

The data fields are represented by a set of buttons at the right of the dialog box. You can select whichever buttons you want as row and column heads—and whichever one you want as the data inside the pivot table. The layout is created by dragging and dropping the field buttons

Pivot Tables

Ch. **17**

FIGURE 17.3 ▶

The database fields are displayed as buttons on the right part of the dialog box. The pivot table in the dialog box is a preview of the actual table that will be placed on a worksheet.

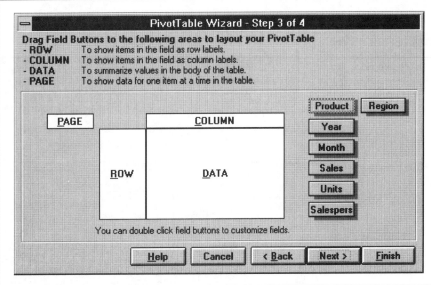

onto the pivot table. There are four places where you can drop a field button:

Row	field(s) used as row titles
Column	Field(s) used as column titles
Page	Field(s) used to show data for one item at a time
Data	The actual data that will be inside the pivot table (typically numeric fields)—at least one field must be placed in the data area

Using the Products database, suppose you want to see the how each salesperson has performed within each region—by product. Follow these steps, referring to Figure 17.4.

1. Drag the Salesperson field into the Row area.

2. Drag the Region field into the Column area.

3. Drag the Product field into the Page area.

4. Drag the Sales field into the Data area—the label changes to *Sum of Sales* as shown in Figure 17.4.

FIGURE 17.4 ►

Drag and drop field buttons onto the pivot table.

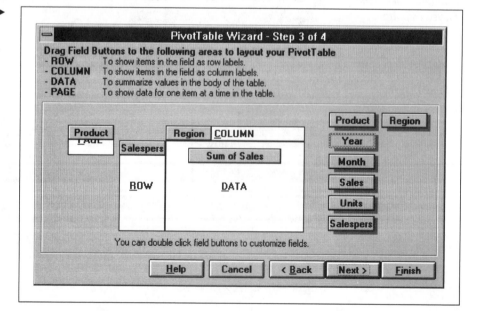

This example positions one data field at each of the four places that a field can be positioned: row field, column field, page field, and data field. However, you are not limited to one field per location—you can place more than one field at each of the four areas.

▶ ▶ **T I P**

If you place the wrong field onto the pivot table, it can be removed by dragging it anywhere outside of the table.

Click Next to proceed to the last step.

4. Finishing the Pivot Table

Step Four (Figure 17.5) lets you specify where the pivot table will be placed, and several other options.

    a. Specify where the pivot table goes using the Pivot Table Starting Cell:

        • If you do not specify a starting cell, the pivot table will be placed on a new worksheet that is inserted into the active workbook.

Pivot Tables

▶ ▶
Ch.
17

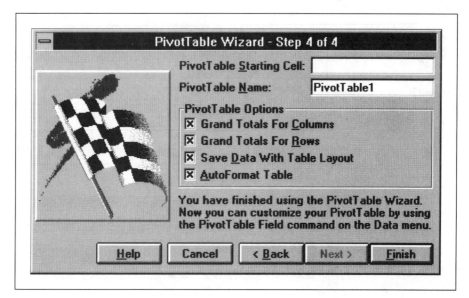

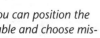

- You can place the pivot table anywhere in the active workbook—click on any sheet tab, and select a cell.
- To place the pivot table on a workbook other than the active workbook, use the Window menu to activate the book, click a tab, and select a cell.

b. The pivot table is named automatically—you can override the name if desired.

c. Set the pivot table options:

- Check Grand Totals for Columns to place totals at the bottom of each column.
- Check Grand Totals for Row to place totals at the end of each row.
- By checking Save Data with Table Layout, the data behind the pivot table is saved in a hidden cache—this allows the pivot table to be changed without the source data being open (the implications of this setting are discussed later in this chapter).
- Check AutoFormat Table to format the pivot table—the columns are sized and borders added to the table.

d. Click Finish—Figure 17.6 shows a finished pivot table.

FIGURE 17.6 ▶

You can change the table layout by dragging the field buttons on the worksheet, without using the PivotTable Wizard.

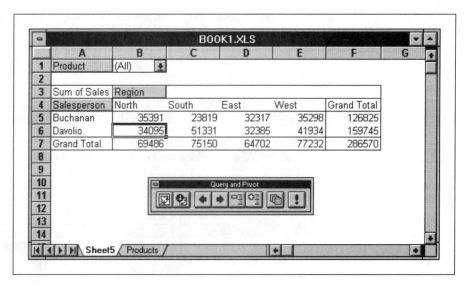

The pivot table in Figure 17.6 shows how each salesperson performed within each region. The layout, specified in Step Three of the Pivot-Table Wizard (see Figure 17.3), determines the level of summarization. In the example just described, a database containing over fifty records (rows) was summarized into an informative, concise format.

You cannot edit the cells inside a pivot table. However, in the next section, you will learn how to change the layout of a pivot table using special simple, direct manipulation techniques. First, notice that two changes to the workspace have occurred:

- If no starting cell was specified at Step 4 of the PivotTable Wizard (see Figure 17.5), the pivot table is placed on a new worksheet inserted next to the sheet containing the source data.

- The Query and Pivot toolbar is displayed (it is displayed anytime you activate a worksheet containing a pivot table, not just when the table is first created).

T I P

> **There is no limit, other than available memory, to the number of pivot tables that can be defined in the same workbook—or even on the same worksheet.**

▶▶ *Changing the Layout of a Pivot Table*

Once a pivot table has been created, there are two ways to change the layout: interacting directly with the table on the worksheet, or using the PivotTable Wizard.

▶ *Change a Pivot Table Interactively*

One of the best aspects of pivot tables is that you can manipulate them directly on the worksheet, without having to restart the PivotTable Wizard. Most users are of the opinion that this method for changing a pivot table layout is the most intuitive—once you become familiar with pivot tables, the interaction becomes second nature.

Using the Page Field to Filter the Data

The pivot table in Figure 17.6 has a page field—Product. This drop-down control lets you filter the data displayed in the pivot table. By default, when a pivot table is first created, the page will be set to (All), a combination of dairy and produce products. Suppose you only want to view information pertaining to dairy products. Click the drop-down arrow, and select Dairy from the list. The data in the table changes accordingly.

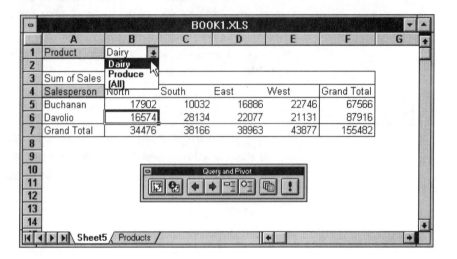

Now, suppose you want to print two separate reports, one for dairy and one for produce. First, use the page button to switch back to (All). Then follow these steps:

1. Select a cell anywhere inside the pivot table.

2. Click the Show Pages tool on the Query and Pivot Toolbar. Depending on your layout, there can be more than one page field. The Show Pages dialog box is displayed, letting you select which field will determine the page breaks.

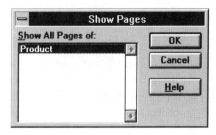

3. Select Product from the list, and click OK. Figure 17.7 shows the result.

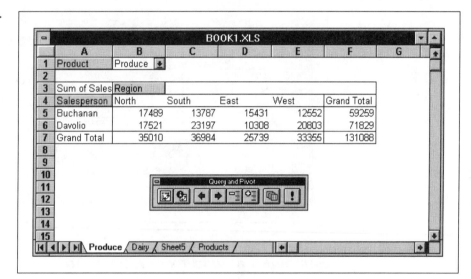

Notice in Figure 17.7 that two new worksheets have been inserted into the workbook—one for Produce and one for Dairy.

Changing the Layout by Moving Field Buttons

As you saw in Figure 17.6, the field buttons are placed on the pivot table. This allows you to change your view of the data by dragging the buttons on the sheet, without having to redisplay the PivotTable Wizard.

For instance, using the pivot table in 17.6, suppose you want to see sales by product for each sales rep—just click the Product button, and drag it just beneath the Salesperson button. The pivot table will recalculate, as pictured in Figure 17.8.

The best way to learn about pivot tables is through experimenting. Try positioning each button as a row category, column category, and page break—the pivot table will reveal different information about the underlying data with each layout.

FIGURE 17.8 ▶

Sales by region by product by salesperson.

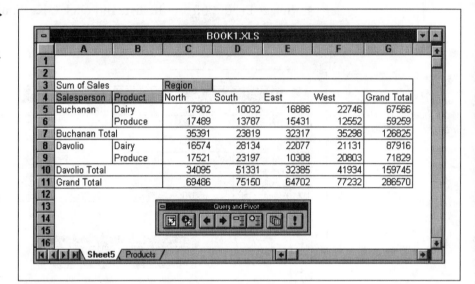

Removing a Field from a Pivot Table

To remove a field from a pivot table, simply drag the field button outside the pivot table range. When a large × displays, as shown in Figure 17.9, release the mouse button.

Remember, removing a field from a pivot table does not affect the underlying data, nor does it affect the hidden cache.

Drilling Down into the Detailed Data

When viewing summary data in a pivot table, you may observe a number that requires explanation. You can double-click any value within the data area, including subtotals and totals, to view the detailed data behind the number. For instance, using the pivot table in Figure 17.6, suppose you want to see what factors contributed to Davolio's high

FIGURE 17.9

Drag a field button outside of the pivot table to remove it from the table.

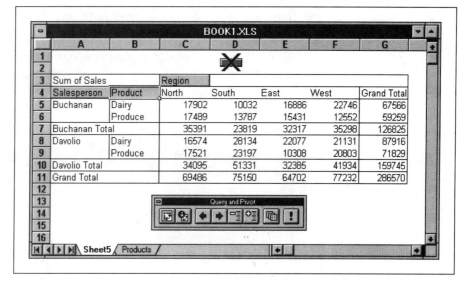

sales in region South: Simply double-click cell C6. A new worksheet is inserted into the workbook, and every record (row) from the source database where salesperson is equal to Davolio, and region is equal to South, is displayed (see Figure 17.10).

FIGURE 17.10

Double-click a cell in the data area of a pivot table to view the detail behind the number.

	A	B	C	D	E	F	G	H
1	Product	Year	Month	Sales	Units	Salesperson	Region	
2	Dairy	1993	Feb	8076	3670	Davolio	South	
3	Dairy	1992	Jul	9082	8966	Davolio	South	
4	Dairy	1992	Sep	3947	9132	Davolio	South	
5	Dairy	1993	Jul	7029	6853	Davolio	South	
6	Produce	1993	Feb	4923	8160	Davolio	South	
7	Produce	1993	Oct	7347	5881	Davolio	South	
8	Produce	1992	May	9566	7406	Davolio	South	
9	Produce	1992	Jun	1361	1824	Davolio	South	

BOOK1.XLS — Sheet1 / Sheet5 / Products

Pivot Tables

Ch.

17

Collapsing and Expanding a Pivot Table

Sometimes, within a pivot table, you may want to view more or less detail. When there are more than one row or column categories, the level of detail can be easily expanded and collapsed. Consider the pivot table in Figure 17.11.

FIGURE 17.11 ▶

Double-click the salesperson row categories, A5 or A10, to collapse and expand the pivot table.

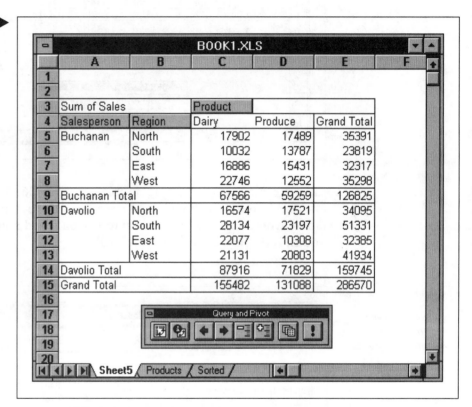

The pivot table in Figure 17.11 is still small, but suppose there are dozens of regions instead of only four—the data for a single salesperson may not fit in the window. Double-click the salesperson row categories, cells A5 and/or A10, to collapse the pivot table. Figure 17.12 shows the pivot table after cell A5 has been double-clicked.

By double-clicking A5 again, the Buchanan rows are unhidden.

The database includes sales history from 1992 and 1993. Suppose, using the pivot table in Figure 17.11, you want to see the breakdown of

FIGURE 17.12

The Buchanan rows have been collapsed, leaving only the Buchanan total row.

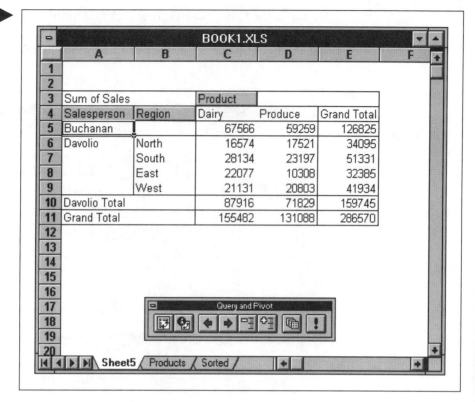

1992/1993 sales for Dairy and/or Produce. Double-click the Dairy column heading (cell C4). Since Excel is not sure how you want to expand the pivot table, the Show Detail dialog box is displayed.

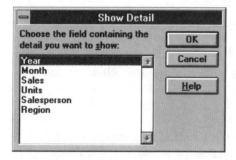

Select Year from the list, then click OK. A breakdown of 1992/1993 is added to the pivot table for Dairy and Produce, even though it is only displayed for Dairy (see Figure 17.13). Double-click the Produce column heading (cell F3) to show the 1992/1993 breakdown. Also, notice that the field button Year has been added to the table.

FIGURE 17.13 ▶

Double-click the Dairy column heading, cell C4, to expand and collapse the pivot.

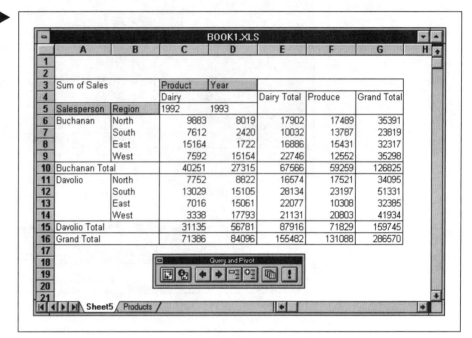

▶ *Changing a Pivot Table Using the PivotTable Wizard*

Another way to change a pivot table is with the PivotTable Wizard. Follow these steps:

1. Select a cell inside the pivot table.

 ▶ ▶**N O T E**

If the active cell is not inside the pivot table when you choose the Data ▶ Pivot Table command, Excel assumes that you want to create a new pivot table. There can be more than one pivot table on a worksheet.

2. Start the PivotTable Wizard using the Data ➤ Pivot Table command, or click the corresponding tool (pictured to the left) on the Query and Pivot toolbar.

3. The wizard is displayed starting at Step Three (see Figure 17.3). The procedure for changing the layout is the same as when the pivot table was first created.

▶ *Use Names to Simplify Synchronization*

When the source for a pivot table is an Excel database, or multiple consolidation ranges, you will likely specify a cell reference as the source data (e.g., $A$1:$E$99). Later, if you add records to the source database (or delete records), the pivot table definition needs to be changed using these steps:

1. Select a cell inside the pivot table, then choose Data ➤ PivotTable.

2. Step Three of the wizard is displayed. Click Back to display Step Two.

3. Change the range, then click Finish.

However, there is a much better way to synchronize the pivot table with the source data using names:

1. Name the source data range, e.g., **MyData**.

2. When you create the pivot table, at Step Two of the wizard, refer to the source data by name.

When rows are deleted from the source data range, the named range contracts automatically. If you insert one or more rows into the source range, the name expands automatically. (If you add a row beneath the named range, you will have to redefine the name.) In all cases, the

Pivot Tables

▶ ▶
Ch.
17

pivot table refreshes correctly after choosing Data ➤ Refresh Data. (See Chapter 8 to learn about names.)

▶▶ *Controlling How Data Fields Calculate*

When a data field inside a pivot table is numeric, then, by default, the numbers in the data area of sum fields come from the source database. (If the data field is text, a count is performed by default.) However, there are many other types of calculations that can be performed.

Using the Wizard Double-click the value field button on Step Three of the PivotTable Wizard, then choose the type of calculation in the Summarize By list box. (The different types of calculations are described in Table 17.1.)

On the Worksheet Select a cell inside the data area of the pivot table, then choose Data ➤ PivotTable Field. Choose the type of calculation in the Summarize By list box. (The different types of calculations are described in Table 17.1.)

▶ **TABLE 17.1:** *Calculations That Can Be Performed in a PivotTable Value Field*

Use...	To Calculate...
Sum	Sum (total) of the values
Count	Number of records (rows)
Average	Average value in underlying data
Max	Maximum value in underlying data
Min	Minimum value in underlying data
Product	Product of the underlying data
Count Nums	Number of records (rows) containing numbers
StdDev	Estimated standard deviation of population where the underlying data represents the sample

▶ **TABLE 17.1:** *Calculations That Can Be Performed in a PivotTable Value Field (continued)*

Use...	To Calculate...
StdDevp	Standard deviation of population where the underlying data represents the entire population
Var	Variance of population where underlying data represents the sample
Varp	Variance of population where underlying data represents entire population

▶ *Performing Custom Calculations*

In a pivot table, you can perform certain custom calculations where a value is compared in one of several ways to another value. For example, using Figure 17.6, suppose you want to see each sales rep's percentage rather than dollars of total sales. Follow these steps:

1. Select a value cell inside the data area of the pivot table, then choose Data ▶ PivotTable Fields.

2. From the PivotTable Fields dialog box, click Options to expand the dialog box.

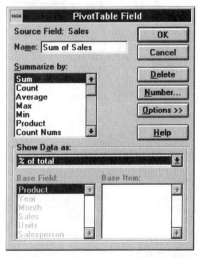

3. From the Show Data As list, choose % of Total, then click OK.

The results are demonstrated in Figure 17.14.

You can also define custom calculations from Step Three of the Pivot-Table Wizard. Double-click the value field button, then repeat steps 2 and 3 of the previous exercise.

FIGURE 17.14 ▶

Every value cell is repre-sented as a percentage of the grand total—cell F7.

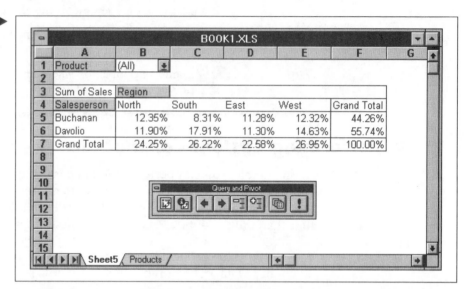

USING BLOCK TOTALS IN PIVOT TABLES

Consider the pivot table shown in Figure 17.11. It includes each salesperson's total sales, because outer fields are subtotaled auto-matically. But suppose you also want to display the subtotal of sales for each region, regardless of who made the sales. To display subtotals for both inner (Region) and outer (Salesperson) row fields, you'll need to create block totals. Double-click the inner field button (the Region button) to display the PivotTable Field dialog box (you can also right-click an inner-field cell and choose PivotTable Field). Under Subtotals, select Custom, then select the type of subtotal you want (Sum, Average, etc.). At the bottom of the pivot table, a "block" of region totals will be added (they'll read North Sum, South Sum, etc).

▶▶ *Customizing a Pivot Table*

Pivot tables are flexible, and you can change field labels, set number formats, and control how data is grouped.

▶ *Changing Field Button Labels*

The text that is used on the field buttons is determined by the field names in your database. These names may not be very friendly, so you may want to change them—without changing the source database.

Using the Wizard Double-click the field button on Step Three of the PivotTable Wizard. Change the Name in the PivotTable field dialog box.

On the Worksheet Click the field button—the button text displays on the formula bar. Use the formula bar to edit the text, just as you would edit the contents of a cell. (Or, double-click the field button, and change the Name in the PivotTable Field dialog box.)

 ▶ ▶ T I P

> **When you create a pivot table from multiple consolidation ranges (covered later in this chapter), generic button labels are automatically created (e.g., Column and Row). It is likely you will want to change these button labels.**

▶ RENAMING A PIVOT TABLE DATA FIELD NAME

Suppose you create the pivot table shown in Figure 17.18, but you don't want the data field name (in cell A2) to read Sum of Amount. You want it to read Amount, but when you try to enter the text Amount, Excel displays an alert which says "Pivot table field name already exists" and will not accept your entry. Try this trick: Place a trailing space after the word Amount. This prevents the name from conflicting with the field names in the pivot table.

▶ *Formatting Numbers in the Data Area*

You can apply number formats to the cells in a pivot table just as you would format any cell. But, if you change the layout, the formatting does not automatically adjust. Instead, use one of the following procedures.

Using the Wizard Double-click the field button on Step Three of the PivotTable Wizard, then click the Number button. Select a format from the Format Cell dialog box, pictured in Figure 17.15.

On the Worksheet Select a cell inside the data area of the pivot table, then choose Data ▶ PivotTable Field. Click the Number button to display the Format cell dialog box, pictured in Figure 17.15.

FIGURE 17.15 ▶

The numeric formats available for pivot table data are the same as when you format a cell using the Format ▶ Cell command.

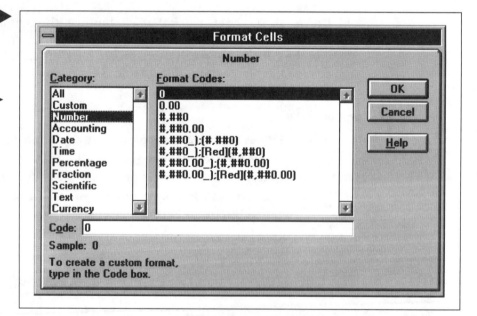

▶ *Grouping and Ungrouping Data*

There are times when the source database is structured in a way that does not fit the way you want to group the data in the pivot table. A good example of this problem can be seen with dates. Consider Figure 17.16.

FIGURE 17.16

Invoice Database to be used as source for pivot table.

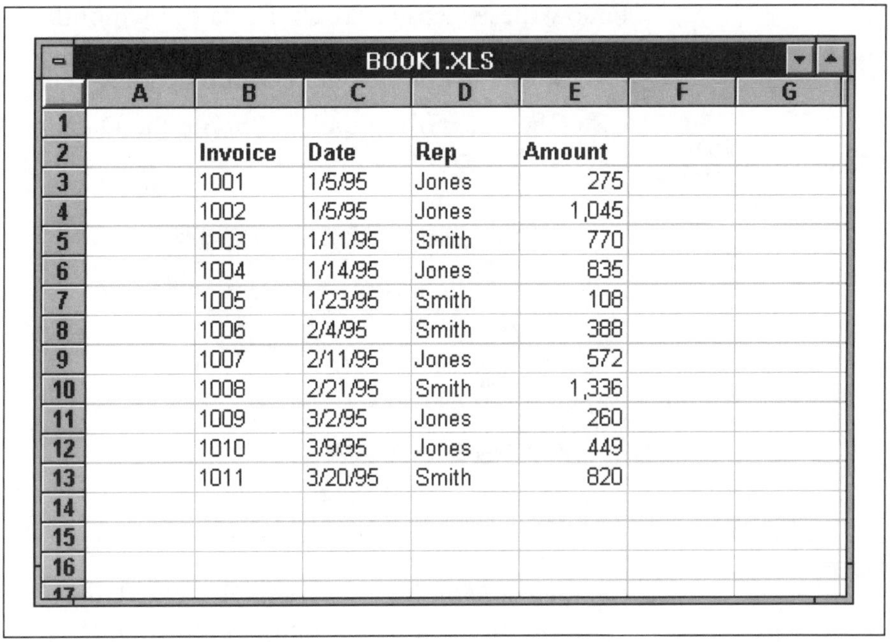

	A	B	C	D	E	F	G
1							
2		**Invoice**	**Date**	**Rep**	**Amount**		
3		1001	1/5/95	Jones	275		
4		1002	1/5/95	Jones	1,045		
5		1003	1/11/95	Smith	770		
6		1004	1/14/95	Jones	835		
7		1005	1/23/95	Smith	108		
8		1006	2/4/95	Smith	388		
9		1007	2/11/95	Jones	572		
10		1008	2/21/95	Smith	1,336		
11		1009	3/2/95	Jones	260		
12		1010	3/9/95	Jones	449		
13		1011	3/20/95	Smith	820		
14							
15							
16							

Suppose you want to design a pivot table that shows the sales reps, Smith and Jones, on separate rows, and their total sales for each month in columns. The pivot table in Figure 17.17 uses *Rep* as a row category, *Date* as a column category, and *Amount* as a data value. As you can see, each discrete date in the source database occupies a separate column.

FIGURE 17.17

The date columns are too detailed—the goal is to see totals for each month.

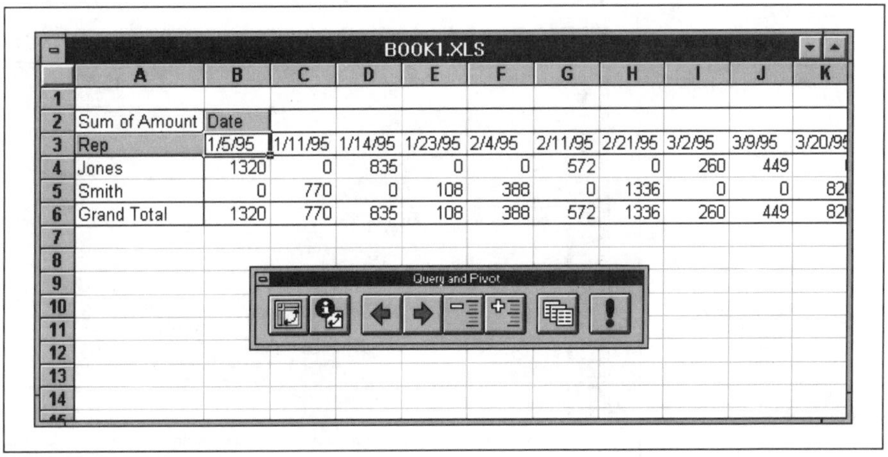

	A	B	C	D	E	F	G	H	I	J	K
1											
2	Sum of Amount	Date									
3	Rep	1/5/95	1/11/95	1/14/95	1/23/95	2/4/95	2/11/95	2/21/95	3/2/95	3/9/95	3/20/9
4	Jones	1320	0	835	0	0	572	0	260	449	
5	Smith	0	770	0	108	388	0	1336	0	0	82
6	Grand Total	1320	770	835	108	388	572	1336	260	449	82

Follow these steps to group the dates by month:

1. Select any of the date-column heading cells.

2. Click the Group tool, or choose the Data ➤ Group and Outline ➤ Group command.

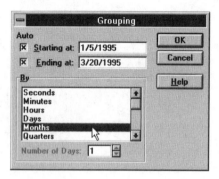

3. Select Months, then click OK. The date columns are rolled up into months, as pictured in Figure 17.18.

Follow these steps to ungroup the columns:

1. Select any of the date (month) column heading cells.

2. Click the Ungroup tool. Or, choose the Data ➤ Group and Outline ➤ Ungroup command.

FIGURE 17.18 ▶

You can group dates by any number of days (such as weeks), months, quarters, or years.

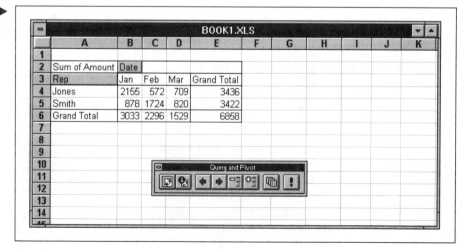

▶

GROUPING PIVOT TABLE ROW FIELDS AND COLUMN FIELDS

Suppose that you have a database that contains three years' worth of sales data by date. If you use the dates as a row field or column field in a pivot table, Excel recognizes dates and makes it easy for you to group them into several kinds of date groups. For example, you can group the dates into months, the months into quarters, and the quarters into years. The user can then show or hide the monthly, quarterly, or yearly figures by double-clicking the fields. To create multiple-level group dates, right-click a date cell in the pivot table, then choose Group And Outline ➤ Group. The By list is a multi-select list. This means you can choose Months, Quarters, and Years, then click OK.

Now let's assume that you have data of a different kind—perhaps sales figures by city, and the cities are a row field in the pivot table, and you want to group the cities in the pivot table by state. If you select a city cell and attempt to group, Excel will display the alert "Cannot group that selection." In this case you have to create the group definition explicitly: Select all the cities to be grouped into one state. (Hold down Control to select non-contiguous cells.) Then choose Data ➤ Group And Outline ➤ Group. The selected cities will be grouped together as Group 1. Finish grouping the cities, then change the group names to state names.

▶ Sorting a Pivot Table

You can sort the data inside a pivot table, using the Data ➤ Sort command, and the logical organization of the data within the table will be left intact. Consider the pivot table in Figure 17.11. Suppose that within the data for salesperson Buchanan, you want to list the regions in order of how well Buchanan performed—in descending order (from best to worst). Follow these steps:

1. Select any cell in the Grand Total column that corresponds to Buchanan (E5:E8).

2. Choose Data ➤ Sort.

3. Choose the Descending option, then click OK. Figure 17.19 shows the sorted pivot table.

FIGURE 17.19 ▶

Buchanan's regions are sorted in descending order based on the Grand Total column.

	A	B	C	D	E	F
			BOOK1.XLS			
1						
2						
3	Sum of Sales		Product			
4	Salesperson	Region	Dairy	Produce	Grand Total	
5	Buchanan	North	17902	17489	35391	
6		West	22746	12552	35298	
7		East	16886	15431	32317	
8		South	10032	13787	23819	
9	Buchanan Total		67566	59259	126825	
10	Davolio	North	16574	17521	34095	
11		West	21131	20803	41934	
12		East	22077	10308	32385	
13		South	28134	23197	51331	
14	Davolio Total		87916	71829	159745	
15	Grand Total		155482	131088	286570	
16						
17				Query and Pivot		
18						
19						
20						

Figure 17.19 also illustrates a problem you should be aware of when you sort a pivot table. Notice that Davolio's regions were placed in the exact same order as Buchanan's—even though Davolio's sort is illogical. There is no way to override this behavior. (See Chapters 15 and 16 to learn more about sorting.)

▶▶ *Creating a Pivot Table from an External Database*

So far in this chapter, you have learned how to create a pivot table based on a database that resided on a worksheet. You can also create pivot tables based on an external database, such as Access, dBASE, Paradox, Oracle, or SQL Server.

 ▶ ▶**N O T E**

> **The databases you can access depend on the ODBC drivers installed on your system, and the appropriate network connections to the database. See Chapter 18 to learn more about accessing external databases.**

▶ *What Is Microsoft Query?*

Creating a pivot table from an external database requires that you use Microsoft Query. Microsoft Query is a separate program that comes with Excel that serves two purposes:

- It is a stand-alone program that can be used to query databases— a separate manual for Microsoft Query is included in the Excel retail package.

- It is used by Excel to retrieve data from external databases. In this capacity, it acts as an intermediary between Excel and the external database.

When you originally installed Excel, installing Microsoft Query was optional. If it is not installed on your system, you will be unable to create pivot tables from external databases. You must run the Excel setup program to add Microsoft Query, and associated files, to your system.

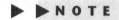

N O T E

Microsoft Query is included with Microsoft products other than Excel. Even if you chose not to install it when you installed Excel, it may be on your system anyway. It is usually located under the MSAPPS directory, which is inside your Microsoft Windows directory.

▶ *Performing the Database Query*

Step One of the PivotTable Wizard (see Figure 17.2) has an option called External Data Source. When you choose this option, then click Next, Step Two of the PivotTable Wizard is displayed. But this is different than the Step Two when creating a pivot table from a worksheet database.

If the text in the dialog box states "No data retrieved," click the Get Data button—Microsoft Query is started, and you will now define a query.

Defining the Query

You are now working inside Microsoft Query. In this discussion, only the basic steps are provided. However, Chapter 18 includes a more detailed discussion on how to define a query—refer to the heading entitled "Using Microsoft Query to Define a Query" within Chapter 18.

1. Select a data source.

2. Add one or more tables where the data is stored.

3. Add the fields to the query.

4. Optionally, add a criterion.

5. From the Microsoft Query menu, choose the File ➤ Return Data to Microsoft Excel command.

 ➤ 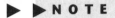**N O T E**

> **You do not have to save the query definition in Microsoft Query. When the data is returned to Excel, the SQL statement generated by Microsoft Query is stored in the Excel workbook, though it is hidden.**

▶ Back to Excel

Step Two of the PivotTable Wizard is again displayed. If you successfully defined a query in Microsoft Query, the text in the dialog box will read "Data Retrieved."

Until it says data retrieved, you will be unable to proceed. Click the Next button.

Step Three of the PivotTable Wizard is displayed. Use it the same as when defining a pivot table from an Excel database (covered previously in the chapter). Click Next when you are done designing the pivot table layout.

Step Four of the Pivot Table Wizard is displayed. As with Step Three, it works just the same as when you created a pivot table from an Excel database. Click Finish to complete the pivot table.

▶ Working with a Pivot Table Created from External Data

Once the pivot table is placed on a worksheet, working with it is very similar to working with pivot tables created from an Excel database.

You can:

- Drag the field buttons to change your view of the data.

- Double-click data cells inside the pivot table to display detailed source records.

- Double-click row or column headings to expand and contract the pivot table.

- Select a cell inside the table, and choose Data ➤ Pivot Table to change the table.

▶ *Refreshing the Pivot Table*

The detailed data that came from Microsoft Query is stored in the workbook in a special hidden cache, rather than as a link to a source. So, if the pivot table is created from a large database, all of the source data is stored hidden in the workbook and can make the workbook file quite large (more on the hidden cache later in this chapter, in "Save Data with Table Layout" and "Creating a Pivot Table From Another Pivot Table"). When you change the layout of the pivot table, the cache is driving the table, not the source database.

Suppose that you save the workbook containing the pivot table, then re-open it days or weeks later. What if the source database is a transaction file that changes daily? Your pivot table will not be in sync with the source database. Choose the Data ➤ Refresh Data command to refresh the pivot table from the source database. Behind the scenes, Excel will re-query the database, refresh the hidden cache, and then refresh the pivot table.

 ▶ ▶ **T I P**

When you refresh a pivot table created from an external database, Excel uses an XLL (a special Excel DLL) to re-query the database—not Microsoft Query. This makes the query go faster, and uses less of your system's memory.

▶ *Changing the Source Data*

There are several circumstances when you may want to change the database query behind a pivot table. You may want to...

- Add new fields
- Add or change the query criteria
- Completely redefine the query

Follow these steps to change the query that is driving a pivot table:

1. Select a cell inside the pivot table.
2. Choose Data ➤ Pivot Table—Step Three of the PivotTable Wizard is displayed.
3. Click the Back button to display Step Two.
4. Click the Get Data button—Microsoft Query is started with the original query loaded.
5. Change the query, or choose File ➤ New and create a new query.
6. Choose File ➤ Return Data to Microsoft Excel.

Step Three of the PivotTable Wizard is displayed—follow the normal procedures to complete the table layout.

▶ ▶ *Creating a Pivot Table from Multiple Consolidation Ranges*

Suppose your organization, a distributor of electronic goods, has several regional offices, and each office submits a sales forecast by product. It is your job to create a report that consolidates these forecasts. Consider the workbooks in Figure 17.20.

With the four workbooks open, follow these steps to consolidate the information onto a new workbook:

1. Choose File ➤ New to create a new workbook.

FIGURE 17.20 ▶

Four regional sales forecasts that need to be consolidated.

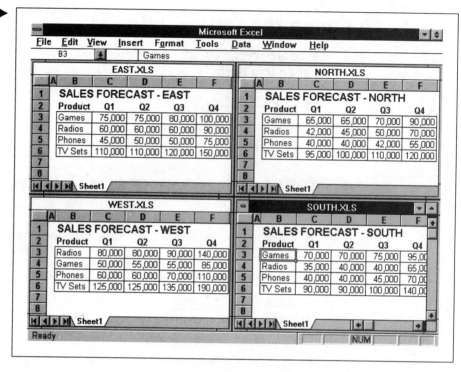

2. Choose Data ➤ Pivot Table—Step One of the PivotTable Wizard is displayed.

3. Select Multiple Consolidation Ranges, then click Next. Step 2a of the PivotTable Wizard, pictured in Figure 17.21, is displayed.

4. Select the option Create a Single Page for Me, then click Next to proceed to Step 2b of the PivotTable Wizard (pictured in Figure 17.22).

▶▶**N O T E**

When you select the option Create a Single Page for Me, the wizard creates a separate page for each consolidated range. The option I will Create the Page Fields lets you override the default pagination.

5. Enter the range by pointing and clicking on the workbooks—click on WEST.XLS, and select cells B2:F6, then click Add.

FIGURE 17.21 ▶

Step 2a is a special step that applies only when consolidating multiple consolidation ranges.

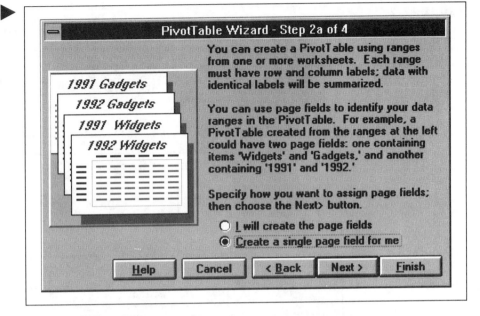

FIGURE 17.22 ▶

Step 2b lets you specify the ranges to be consolidated.

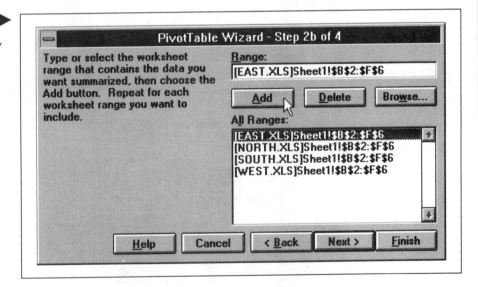

6. Repeat step 5 above for EAST.XLS, NORTH.XLS, and SOUTH.XLS, then click Next to proceed to Step Three of the PivotTable Wizard (Figure 17.23).

FIGURE 17.23 ►

Double-click the field buttons to customize them. For aesthetic reasons only, you may want to change the name Page1 to Region, Row to Product, and Column to Quarter.

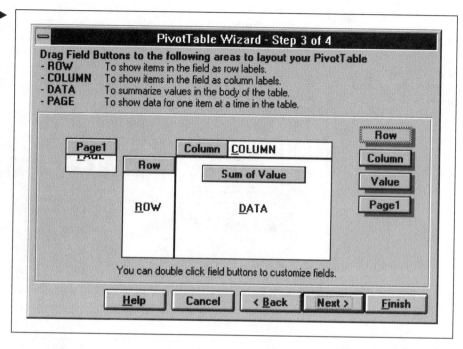

7. The field button in the data area must read Sum of Value. If it doesn't (the PivotTable Wizard is somewhat unpredictable as to what type of calculation will be used as the default), double-click the button, and select Sum from the Summarize By list.

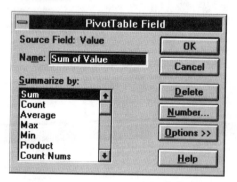

8. Click Next to proceed to Step Four. Check all four options, then click Finish to create the pivot table pictured in Figure 17.24.

FIGURE 17.24

The four regions are consolidated. The drop-down lets you select any of the four regions, or all of them (All is chosen by default).

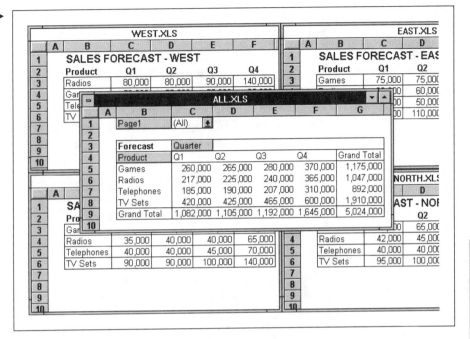

There is one key fact to keep in mind when creating a pivot table from multiple consolidation ranges: The consolidation is based on the column labels (field names), and the row labels (the values in the first column of each range). Matching labels are consolidated, though the position of the label within the range is not a factor.

▶▶ *Creating a Pivot Table from Another Pivot Table*

So far, you have learned how to create pivot tables based on three different data sources: an Excel database, an external database, and multiple consolidation ranges. A pivot table can also be based on another pivot table.

There are two reasons why you might want to base a pivot table on another pivot table. The most important reason is memory usage. You learned earlier that a pivot table is driven by a hidden cache of data stored in the workbook. When you create a pivot table based on another pivot table, the two tables share the same hidden cache. The other reason you might want to base a pivot table on another pivot table is efficiency—when you refresh either pivot table, both are refreshed.

If you choose Data ➤ PivotTable when there is already a pivot table defined in the active workbook (and if the active cell is not inside the existing pivot table), Step One of the PivotTable Wizard makes the Another PivotTable option available (see Figure 17.2). After clicking Next, Step Two lets you pick which existing pivot table you want to use.

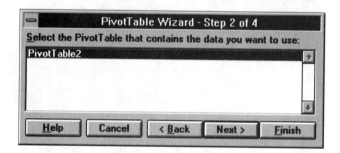

Choose a pivot table from the list, then click Next to proceed to Step Three of the PivotTable Wizard.

 ▶ ▶ **T I P**

When you create a new pivot table, Step Four of the PivotTable wizard lets you override the default name assigned by the wizard. Meaningful names can come in handy if you create more than one pivot table in a workbook, then create a new pivot table based on an existing table. With meaningful names, you can distinguish the tables from one another.

As you have learned, when a pivot table uses another pivot table as its source, then both tables are driven by the same hidden cache. If you uncheck the Save Data with Pivot Table option in Step Four (see Figure 17.5) for either table, both tables are impacted.

▶▶ *Save Data with Table Layout?*

Step Four of the Pivot Table Wizard, pictured in Figure 17.5, has a setting called Save Data With Table Layout. When checked, the source data is saved, inside the workbook, in a special hidden cache. It is useful to understand the implications of this setting.

- When checked, the pivot table can be changed without having to access the source data. This can save you the trouble of opening up workbooks, or the time it takes to query an external database.

- When unchecked, you need to make sure the hidden cache is not out of sync with the source data. (The Data ➤ Refresh Data command refreshes the cache, and, accordingly, the pivot table itself.)

In general, you will get better performance by saving the data with the table layout. But you pay a memory usage penalty, and must be mindful of data synchronization.

▶▶ *Charting a Pivot Table*

You can create charts using the data in a pivot table. The procedure is no different than charting any other worksheet data. (See Chapter 13 to learn the basics of charting.) In Figure 17.25, the source data for the chart is B5:D8.

Figure 17.26 is the same worksheet as Figure 17.25. However, the pivot table layout has been changed. The **Year** field has been repositioned as a page field. The **Region** field has been repositioned as a column heading. The chart has automatically redrawn accordingly.

FIGURE 17.25 ▶

When a different region is selected from the page drop-down, the chart redraws accordingly. The chart title is linked to cell C2.

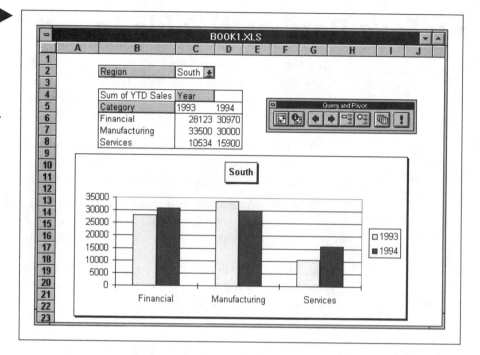

FIGURE 17.26 ▶

The chart redraws after the pivot table layout is changed.

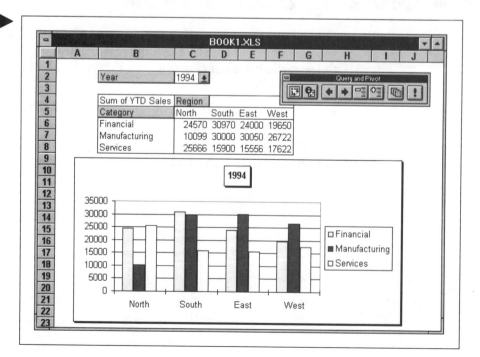

TWO IMPORTANT POINTS ABOUT CHARTING FROM A PIVOT TABLE

You have already seen how pivot tables are a terrific tool for presenting data. They are also a great data-staging tool for charts. You can create a chart directly from a pivot table. Then, when you pivot the pivot table, the chart "pivots", too. Whatever is displayed in the pivot table (data, labels, more detail, less detail, etc.) is displayed in the chart. When you create a chart from a pivot table, there are two important details you should keep in mind.

- Create the pivot table without totals. To do this, uncheck the Grand Totals options in Step 4. Although you can chart a pivot table which includes totals, the chart will be illegible because of the scale of the total data.

- Chart the entire pivot table, or the chart will not re-draw properly when the pivot table is pivoted. The easiest way to select the entire pivot table is to click a cell in the pivot table, then click the Select Current Region tool (or press Ctrl+Shift+*). Then click the ChartWizard tool and draw your chart.

►► *The Pivot Table Shortcut Menu*

If you click anywhere in a pivot table using the right mouse button, a shortcut menu is displayed.

This is the same shortcut menu that is displayed when you right-click a normal cell, but with six commands added that are specific to pivot tables.

 Refresh Data Same as Data ➤ Refresh Data. Updates the pivot table from the source data.

 Show Pages Places each page of a multi-page pivot table onto a separate worksheet.

Group and Outline Displays a submenu that lets you hide detail, unhide detail, group data, and ungroup data.

 Add Field This command lets you add column fields, row fields, or data fields to the pivot table—depending on which type of cell is selected when the command is chosen.

PivotTable Displays the PivotTable Wizard.

 PivotTable Field Lets you customize a field. Same as the Data ➤ PivotTable Field command.

▶▶ *More Facts about Pivot Tables*

Here are some more facts about pivot tables that are important to know.

Excel 4 Users

Pivot tables are a replacement for *crosstabs*, which were introduced in Excel 4. The menu commands that were used in Excel 4 to create crosstabs have been replaced with the pivot table commands. Follow these steps to convert an Excel 4 crosstab to a pivot table:

1. Open the Excel 4 worksheet.
2. Select a cell inside the crosstab range, and choose Data ➤ Pivot Table.
3. Step Three of the PivotTable Wizard is displayed.
4. Click Finish.

Once you save the file, the crosstab is permanently converted to an Excel 5 pivot table. You will no longer be able to open the file under Excel 4.

When the Source Database Is Filtered

If you create a pivot table from an Excel database that has been filtered (using Data ➤ Filter), the filtering is ignored. Therefore, you may want to remove the filter before creating the pivot table.

When the Source Database Includes Embedded Subtotals

If you create a pivot table from an Excel database that has embedded subtotals (for either rows or columns), the subtotal rows are treated as separate records in the database. Accordingly, you *must* remove embedded subtotals to get meaningful results in the pivot table. (If the embedded subtotals were inserted using Data ➤ Subtotals, then choose Data ➤ Subtotals and click Remove All.)

Freezing a Pivot Table

Suppose that you include a pivot table in a report, and want to keep an exact copy. Since you may inadvertently refresh the pivot table at a later date, follow these steps to make a frozen copy:

1. Select the entire table.
2. Choose Edit ➤ Copy.
3. Select a cell where you want to place the copy, then choose Edit ➤ Paste Special.
4. Select the Values option, then click OK.

The copy of the pivot table is not an actual pivot table. It cannot be pivoted, or changed with the PivotTable Wizard.

Two Calculation on One Data Field

Suppose that you want to calculate the sum of a data field, and calculate the average of the same field. The same field can be placed into the data area more than once.

USING D FUNCTIONS WITH A PIVOT TABLE

You can use D functions (like DSUM, DAVERAGE, DCOUNT, etc. —see Chapter 16) to tap into a pivot table's hidden cache of data. Calculations can be performed on any field in the hidden data cache, even if that field is not displayed in the pivot table. Set up the D function using *field* and *criteria* arguments which correspond to fields in the pivot table's database. To insert the *database* argument, click on any cell in the pivot table. The D function will use the pivot table's hidden data cache in place of a database range.

Here is an example using the pivot table in Figure 17.6. You will use the DSUM function to sum units sold by a specific salesperson. Enter Salesperson in cell H3, and the criteria Davolio in cell H4. (Cells H3:H4 will be the criteria range for the D function.) Units is a field name in the underlying database, even though it is not displayed in the pivot table. Enter a DSUM function in cell H7. To enter the *database* argument, click on a cell in the pivot table. To enter the *field* argument, type "Units". For the criteria argument, enter the range H3:H4. The formula will return the number of units sold by Davolio. Because the D function is using the underlying data as the *database* argument, pivoting or filtering the pivot table will not change the value returned by the D function.

Accessing External Databases

F**AST** T**RACK**

▶ *To add fields to a query* **612**

Double-click the field name in the table, or drag and drop fields from the table to the data pane. To add all fields in the table, double-click the asterisk at the top of the table.

▶ *To add criteria to a query* **614**

Choose the Criteria ➤ Add Criteria command, or click the Show/Hide Criteria tool.

▶ *To refresh a query* **619**

When you first create the query, check the Keep Query Definition option. Then, to refresh the query, select a cell inside the data and choose Data ➤ Refresh Data.

▶ *To change a query definition* **620**

First select any cell inside the data, then choose Data ➤ Get External Data. Finally, click Edit Query—change the query in Microsoft Query.

▶ *To format a column of data retrieved by a query* **620**

Format the entire column—the next time the query is performed, more rows may be retrieved.

▶ *To perform queries without Microsoft Query* **621**

First, load the ODBC add-in (XLODBC.XLA). Then, use the SQL.REQUEST worksheet function.

► ► *I*n Chapters 16 and 17 you learned how to manage and manipulate databases residing on a worksheet. But in a corporate environment, source data is typically stored in an external database, such as dBASE, Paradox, SQL Server, Oracle, or DB2. Accessing such data is one of the biggest obstacles faced by corporate users, and a lot of time is spent manually entering data into worksheet models when, ideally, data would be imported into worksheets electronically.

There is a separate program that comes with Excel called *Microsoft Query*, which makes the process of querying external databases relatively simple. Microsoft Query uses a technology called *Open Database Connectivity* (ODBC) to access data. This chapter will explain:

- *The various ways you can get external data into your worksheets*
- *How to perform queries using Microsoft Query*
- *How to place query results onto a worksheet*
- *Performing queries with the SQL.REQUEST function*

 ► ►**N O T E**

The Excel retail package includes an entire manual on Microsoft Query. This chapter is intended to provide a condensed primer to get you up and running quickly.

When you originally installed Excel, you were provided the option of installing Microsoft Query. (It will have been installed in the MSAPPS\MSQUERY directory which is located in the Microsoft Windows directory.) If Microsoft Query is not installed, you may want to use the Excel setup program to install it before reading this chapter.

▶▶NOTE

Microsoft Query is also included with Microsoft applications other than Excel. Even if you did not install it when you installed Excel, it might already be on your system.

▶▶ *There Are Several Ways to Get External Data into Excel*

There are a number of ways to get external data into your worksheets. This chapter will show you how to issue queries to an external database using Microsoft Query (and using the SQL.REQUEST function), which in turn uses a Microsoft technology called ODBC, which stands for Open Database Connectivity. ODBC provides access to many types of databases. However, you may want to access a database for which there is no ODBC driver. Or, your organization may not have the required networking infrastructure in place to support a direct "conversation" between Excel and a certain database. You should be aware of the alternatives:

Opening dBASE Files

You can use the File ➤ Open command to open a dBASE file (or compatible files created with xBASE programs such as Fox and Clipper). You can even edit and save the data. However, the size of the file may not exceed Excel's limit of 16,384 rows and 256 columns. See Chapter 25 for more information on the types of files than can be opened directly.

Importing Text Files

If your mainframe application is capable of outputting text files, you can import them into Excel with the File ➤ Open command. (The various options are explained in Chapter 25.)

External Databases

▶▶
Ch.
18

Exporting Excel Worksheets from Your Database Application

Some database applications, such as Microsoft Access, have the ability to save data in Excel format. Then, there is nothing special to be done on the Excel end—you just open the file that was output from the database application.

Pivot Tables

Pivot tables, covered in Chapter 17, provide a powerful, intuitive interface for accessing and viewing external (and internal) databases. (Pivot tables require the use of Microsoft Query, and thus ODBC.)

▶▶ Definition of Terms

It is relatively simple to perform database queries, and to place the results of a query onto a worksheet. But with two different applications involved, Microsoft Excel and Microsoft Query, there are a number of ways to perform queries. To fully understand the options, it will help if you understand the various pieces of the puzzle. Here are some of the terms that will be referred to in this chapter.

Structured Query Language There is an industry-standard language used to communicate with databases which is called *Structured Query Language,* or *SQL* (generally pronounced "sequel"). When you perform queries from Excel or from Microsoft Query, whether you know it or not, the query is translated into SQL.

Microsoft Query This program is a stand-alone application that is included with Excel. It provides an interface that lets you create SQL statements without having to know (or even see) SQL. You can use MS Query to perform queries, then paste the results onto an Excel worksheet. (You can even paste a query *definition* onto an Excel worksheet, in which case the query can be fired directly from Excel, even though MS Query is doing the real work behind the scenes.)

ODBC Manager ODBC stands for Open Database Connectivity, a Microsoft technology that allows different applications, such as Excel and MS Query, to communicate with a variety of database types. Whenever you perform a query from Excel (or MS Query), a SQL statement is sent to the ODBC manager—ODBC acts as an intermediary between the application and the database. This means that the same query syntax can be used to query a database server, such as SQL Server and Oracle, and "flat" files such as dBASE and Paradox.

ODBC Driver The ODBC Manager does not actually "talk" directly to a database. Rather, it communicates through *drivers*. Included in the Excel package are drivers for Access, dBASE, FoxPro, Paradox, SQL Server, Oracle, Excel worksheets, and text files. Additional drivers can be purchased from database vendors, or from third-party companies that publish ODBC drivers. (To learn how to install ODBC drivers, refer to Appendix B of the Microsoft Query manual.)

Data Sources When performing a query, it is not enough to know what type of database you are accessing. A *Data Source*, defined in the ODBC manager, tells the ODBC manager the type of data, where to find the database, and in some cases, how to connect to the data. For example, you may have several different dBASE databases on your computer, each of which is considered a discrete data source.

ODBC Add-In This Excel add-in, named XLODBC.XLA, allows Excel to talk to the ODBC manager directly, circumventing MS Query. The SQL.REQUEST worksheet function, covered later in this chapter, is a service provided by the ODBC add-in. In addition, the ODBC add-in provides an API for application developers.

Microsoft Query Add-In This Excel add-in, named XLQUERY.XLA, serves to integrate Excel with Microsoft Query. It adds two commands to Excel's Data menu, and one command to MS Query's File menu. These commands make it easier to work with the two programs. (See Chapter 24 for more information on add-ins.)

 ▶▶**N O T E**

> When installing Excel, if you did not choose to install the data-access components, the ODBS add-in and the Microsoft Query add-in will not be in your system. They are required if you want to apply the skills discussed in this chapter. You can use the Excel setup program to install them.

External Databases

▶▶
Ch.
18

The NorthWind Traders Database A sample database is included with MS Query for a fictitious company called Northwind Traders. The data is in dBASE format, and is defined as data source NWind. Exercises in this chapter will query this database.

▶▶ Retrieving Data from an External Database

The query add-in helps to integrate Excel with Microsoft Query, and simplify the process of retrieving data from an external database. In this section, you will learn how to use Microsoft Query and add-ins to:

- load the query add-in
- define a query
- place the query results, and query definition, on a worksheet
- refresh the query at a later date without having to redefine it in MS Query

▶ Loading the Query Add-In

The query add-in, XLQUERY.XLA, is an Excel add-in that appends two commands to Excel's Data menu:

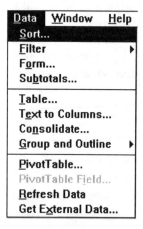

If the commands Refresh Data and Get External Data are not on your Data menu, then the query add-in is not loaded. Use the File ➤ Open command to open XLQUERY.XLA—it is located in the LIBRARY\MSQUERY directory, located in the directory where you installed Excel.

➤ ➤ **T I P**

> **The add-in manager, displayed with the Tools ➤ Add-Ins command, can be used to configure Excel so that the query add-in loads automatically every time you start Excel. (See Chapter 24 to learn more about add-ins.)**

➤ *Starting Microsoft Query*

Once the query add-in is loaded, choose the Data ➤ Get External Data command to start Microsoft Query.

Since Microsoft Query is a separate application, you can run it by double-clicking its icon from Program Manager, but the Data ➤ Get External Data command does two special things: It adds a command to the Microsoft Query menu that returns you to Excel after the query is defined, and it leaves Excel in a state where it is ready to complete the process once you return from Microsoft Query. Thus, the Data ➤ Get External Data command makes things a lot easier.

➤ *Using Microsoft Query to Define a Query*

After choosing the Data ➤ Get External Data command, you will be working inside Microsoft Query. This chapter will walk you through the basic steps involved in defining a query. Remember, a separate manual on Microsoft Query comes in the Excel package.

Selecting a Data Source

Once inside Microsoft Query, the first step is to select a data source—see Figure 18.1.

The precise meaning of data source differs somewhat depending on the type of database you are accessing. Table 18.1 describes several commonly used database types, and the corresponding meaning of data source.

FIGURE 18.1 ▶

Microsoft Query—select a data source.

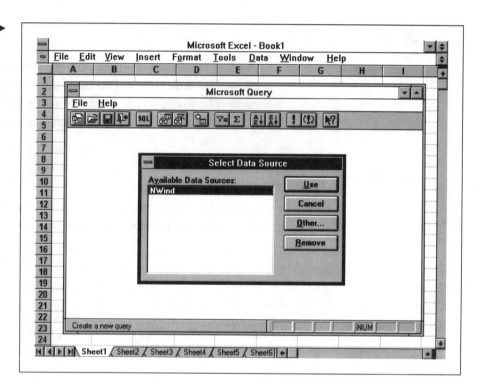

▶ **TABLE 18.1:** *Meaning of Data Source in Various Types of Databases*

Type of Database	Meaning of *Data Source*
dBASE, FoxPro, and Paradox	A group of related files stored in a discrete directory
Text	A text file containing records and fields
SQL Server and Oracle	A database defined on a server—the data source specifies the server, the network containing the server, and other information required to make the connection to the database

Select the NWind data source (the sample Northwind database included with MS Query), then click the Use button. Refer to the Microsoft Query manual to learn how to define new data sources.

▶ *Choosing the Tables*

Next, you must specify which tables (files) you wish to retrieve data from. The Add Tables dialog box lists all of the dBASE files in the Northwind database:

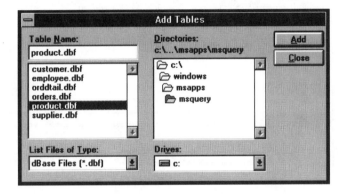

▶▶**N O T E**

If the .DBF files are not displayed in the Table Name list, use the dialog box to navigate your way to the Microsoft Windows directory, then to the MSAPPS\MSQUERY directory that is contained within your Windows directory—this is where the NWind data should be stored on your system.

Select product.dbf from the list of tables, then click Add (see Figure 18.2). A query can retrieve data from more than one table. We are going to start with a simple query, so click the Close button to close the Add Tables dialog box.

External Databases

▶ ▶

Ch.

18

FIGURE 18.2 ▶

The product table has been added to the query definition.

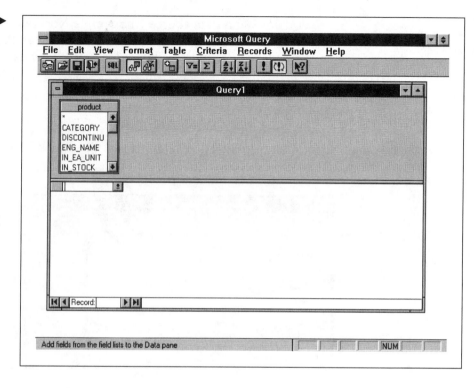

▶ *Choosing the Fields*

Next, you must specify which fields you want to include in the query. There are several ways to add fields to the query:

● Double-click the field names.

● Select one or more fields (use the Ctrl or Shift keys to select more than one field), then drag and drop them onto the bottom part of the window.

● Use the ✱ (asterisk) to add all fields to the query.

Use one of these techniques to add the fields PRODUCT_ID, PROD_NAME, CATEGORY, IN_STOCK, and UNIT_PRICE to the query (see Figure 18.3).

FIGURE 18.3 ▶

*The query results are
displayed in the query
window.*

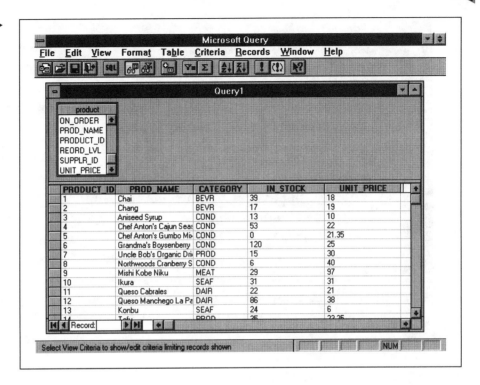

 ▶ ▶ T I P

> **Each time you add a field to the query, the query is re-
> issued. You can use the Records ➤ Automatic Query
> command to control this behavior.**

▶

UNDERSTANDING TABLE JOINS

A *join* combines records from two tables in a database. The join re-
lates, or connects, the data in the two tables, provided the tables
have at least one field in common. For example, in the NWind database which is provided with MS Query, the *customer* table and
orders table are joined because they share the *CUSTMR_ID* field.
The join makes it possible to look up order shipping dates for
specific customers, even though no single table contains both

External
Databases

▶ ▶

Ch.
18

▶ customer names and shipping dates. Here's another example: in the Nwind database you can look up the customers for whom a specific employee has filled orders, even though the *customer* and *employee* tables are not joined, because both tables are joined to the *orders* table.

MS Query recognizes joins automatically in databases that support primary keys (a *primary key* is a field or fields whose values uniquely identify each record in the table). An automatic join is recognized if one table has a primary key field, and the other table has a field with the same name and data type. You can create joins explicitly by joining fields that share similar data and the same data type. To create a join, display both tables. Click on the field to be joined in one table, then drag and drop the field icon onto the equivalent field in the other table.

▶ Adding Criteria

If you want to retrieve a subset of the records, you must add a criterion. Follow these steps to select only those products in the beverage category:

1. Choose the Criteria ➤ Add Criteria command, which displays the Add Criteria dialog box.

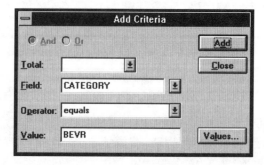

2. Use the Field drop-down list to select *CATEGORY*.

3. Use the Operator drop-down list to choose *equals*.

4. Click the Values button.

5. Select Bevr from the list (beverages).

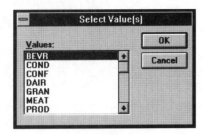

6. Click OK to close the Select Value dialog box.

7. Click the Add button—a criteria grid is added to the query window.

NOTE

The criteria grid is almost identical to an advanced criterion defined on a worksheet. See Chapter 16 to learn how to apply advanced criteria to worksheet databases.

8. Click the Close button to close the Add Criteria dialog box.

The query window will now display only those products in the beverage category (see Figure 18.4).

TIP

To see the SQL statement that MS Query is generating behind the scenes, choose the View ➤ SQL command, or click the SQL button on MS Query's toolbar.

External Databases

Ch.
18

FIGURE 18.4 ▶

Behind the scenes, the criterion causes a where clause to be added to the SQL statement.

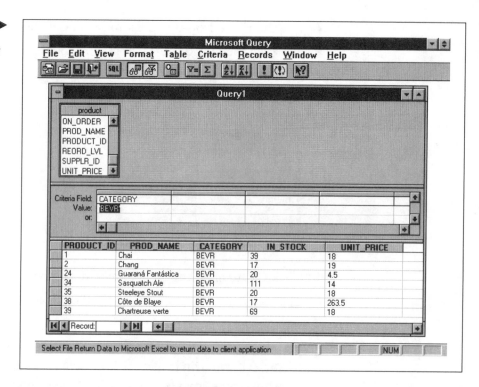

UNDERSTANDING QUERY CRITERIA

The ability to use criteria to filter only the information that you want is what makes queries so useful. There are a number of different ways to add criteria to a query.

● You can choose Criteria ➤ Add Criteria, then select a Field, Operator, and Value from lists in the Add Criteria dialog. If you click in a field (column) in the data pane before choosing Criteria ➤ Add Criteria, the Add Criteria dialog will default to the selected field. You can choose from a complete list of operators in the Operator drop-down list. You can type in a Value, or select a value by clicking the Values button and selecting from the list.

- Choose View ➤ Criteria, then use the criteria pane which is displayed. Click in a *Criteria Field* cell in the criteria pane, then click the drop-down arrow which is displayed and select a field from the drop-down list. Type a value into the *Value* cell, or double-click the *Value* cell and select/type an operator and value in the Edit Criteria dialog.

- Select a single item (for example, a company name) from a data field, then click the Criteria Equals tool to display all records where the field is equivalent.

- Choose View ➤ SQL, then type the criteria (*where* clause) into the SQL statement yourself.

If you choose Criteria ➤ Add Criteria, the Add Criteria dialog is displayed. At the top of the dialog are option buttons labeled *And* and *Or*. These options allow you to combine criteria for very specific data filtering. Initially the *And* and *Or* options are dimmed, but after you create one criteria, these options become available. If you choose *And*, then add a second criteria, the query will select records which meet both the first and the second criteria. For instance, if you want to display all the records where you had orders of more than $500 from companies in New York, create criteria where orders are greater than 500 *And* state is equal to New York. If you choose *Or*, then add a second criteria, the query will select records which meet either of the criteria. For example, if you want to display records of all your suppliers in Canada and in France, create criteria where supplier country is equal to Canada *Or* supplier country is equal to France.

External
Databases

Ch.
18

▶ *Placing the Data onto an Excel Worksheet*

Now that there is data in the query window, choose the File ▶ Return Data to Microsoft Excel command (from the MS Query menu). Excel takes over, and displays the Get External Data dialog box (Figure 18.5):

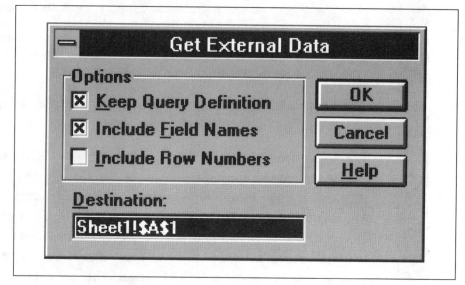

Remember, the Return Data to Microsoft Excel command only appears on the File menu if MS Query was started from Excel.

Keep Query Definition causes the query definition to be stored on the active worksheet (the data source, and the SQL statement generated by MS Query), which in turn allows the query to be processed in the future without having to reconstruct it in MS Query.

Include Field Names causes the field names to be pasted onto the worksheet, in addition to the data.

Include Row Numbers adds sequential row numbers to the records (once they are pasted onto the worksheet).

Check Keep Query Definition and Include Field Names, then click OK. The data will be pasted onto the worksheet (Figure 18.6), and the query definition is stored as a hidden name.

FIGURE 18.6

The data is pasted onto the active worksheet.

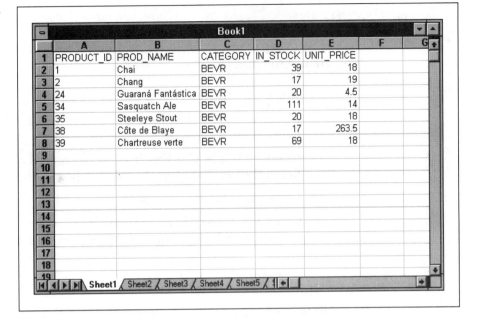

	A	B	C	D	E	F	G
1	PRODUCT_ID	PROD_NAME	CATEGORY	IN_STOCK	UNIT_PRICE		
2	1	Chai	BEVR	39	18		
3	2	Chang	BEVR	17	19		
4	24	Guaraná Fantástica	BEVR	20	4.5		
5	34	Sasquatch Ale	BEVR	111	14		
6	35	Steeleye Stout	BEVR	20	18		
7	38	Côte de Blaye	BEVR	17	263.5		
8	39	Chartreuse verte	BEVR	69	18		

Book1 — Sheet1 / Sheet2 / Sheet3 / Sheet4 / Sheet5

▶ *Refreshing a Query*

Once query results are placed on a worksheet, you may want to refresh the query at a later date. Otherwise, if the source data changes, the worksheet will not be synchronized with the source data. This is the reason for checking the Keep Query Definition option (see Figure 18.5)—it allows the query to be refreshed without having to redefine the query. If Keep Query Definition was checked, you can use this procedure to refresh the query:

1. Make sure the query add-in (XLQUERY.XLA) is loaded.

2. Select any cell within the range of data retrieved from the previous query.

3. Choose the Data ➤ Refresh Data command—the database is requeried and the results are placed on the worksheet. (Or click the Refresh Data tool which is found on the Query and Pivot toolbar.)

External
Databases

▶ ▶
Ch.
18

▶ *Changing a Query*

If you keep a query definition, as described above, follow these steps to change the query:

1. Make sure the query add-in (XLQUERY.XLA) is loaded.

2. Select any cell within the range of data retrieved from the previous query.

3. Choose Data ➤ Get External Data—since a query was already defined, the Get External Data dialog box is displayed.

4. Click Edit Query—MS Query is started.

5. Change the query in MS Query, and choose File ➤ Return Data to Microsoft Excel (from the MS Query menu).

▶ *Working with Query Results*

Often, retrieving data onto a worksheet is just the first part of the job. You may want to format the data, or use Excel to further analyze the data. Here are some ideas:

How to Quickly Format the Data Select a cell within the data, and choose Format ➤ AutoFormat to apply a built-in table format.

How to Apply a Number Format Look at the UNIT_PRICE column in Figure 18.6. The numbers are not properly formatted as dollar and cents. You could format the range E2:E8. But, when you refresh the query at a later date, more rows may be retrieved—the additional rows will not be formatted. Instead, apply the number format to the entire column (as long as there is no other numeric data in the same column elsewhere on the worksheet using a different format).

Manipulating the Data on the Worksheet The Data ➤ Filter command can be used to filter the data on the worksheet. The Data ➤ Sort command can be used to sort the data. (See Chapters 15 and 16 for more information.)

Build a Pivot Table Use the Data ➤ Pivot Table command to build a pivot table based on the retrieved data.

►► *Using the SQL.REQUEST Worksheet Function*

The SQL.REQUEST function provides a different way of retrieving data from an external database. It uses the ODBC add-in (XLODBC.XLA), which allows Excel to communicate directly with the ODBC Manager, circumventing MS Query. There are pros and cons to this approach:

PROS:

- User input can be dynamically incorporated into the SQL statement.
- It will take less time to perform a query.

CONS:

- The SQL.REQUEST function must be entered as an array formula that anticipates the maximum number of rows that may be retrieved—plus, array formulas are limited in size.
- The data source must be known, and the SQL statement must be entered manually (though it can be pasted from MS Query).
- Column widths are not automatically adjusted.

► *Loading the ODBC Add-In*

Before you can use the SQL.REQUEST function, the ODBC add-in must be loaded. (If you enter a formula with SQL.REQUEST and get a #NAME! error, the add-in is not loaded.) Use the File ➤ Open command to open XLODBC.XLA, stored in the LIBRARY\MSQUERY directory, under the Excel directory. (See Chapter 24 to learn how to load add-ins automatically.)

► *Function Syntax*

The SQL.REQUEST function accepts the following arguments:

Connection_String   text string specifying the *data source name* (used by the ODBC manager), and other information required to make connection to the database

(user ID, password, server, database)   Samples based on database type:

dBASE	DSN=NWind
Text	DSN=My Text Data
Oracle	DSN=My Oracle Data; DBQ=MYSERVER; UID=Jane; PWD=Password
SQL Server	DSN=My SQL Server; UID=Jane; PWD=123; Database=Pubs

Output_Ref   cell reference (or name) where the completed connection string is to be placed—if omitted, no connection string returned

Driver_Prompt   specifies if the ODBC manager dialog box (or boxes) displayed, and which options are available to the user

1	Always display dialog box.
2	Only display dialog box if Connection_String does not provide enough information to make connection.
3	Only display dialog box if Connection_String does not provide enough information to make connection—options that are not required are disabled.
4	If connection cannot be made, no dialog box is displayed and an error is returned (defaults to 2 if omitted).

SQL_Statement   SQL text, such as: SELECT Product, Qty FROM Products WHERE Qty<>0

Field_Names   logical (TRUE or FALSE) specifies whether to return field names with query—if omitted defaults to FALSE

Array-Entering the Formula

One of the biggest disadvantages of SQL.REQUEST is that you must *array-enter* the formula into a range of cells that anticipates the maximum number of rows and columns that will be retrieved. If the retrieved data does not fill the range, the remainder of the range is filled with blanks.

Follow these steps to retrieve 2 fields, and up to 20 rows (plus field names), from the *product* master file in the Northwind sample data. Only those products where quantity in stock is less than 5 will be retrieved.

1. Make sure XLODBC.XLA is loaded.

2. Select B2:C22.

3. Enter the following formula (but do not press Enter)—use the precise upper/lower case specified.

   =SQL.REQUEST("DSN=NWind",,2,"SELECT PROD_NAME, IN_STOCK FROM product.dbf WHERE IN_STOCK<5",TRUE)

4. To array-enter the formula, hold down Ctrl+Shift keys, then press Enter—Figure 18.7 shows the result.

FIGURE 18.7 ▶

Five products have stock less than 5—the last argument TRUE causes field names to be placed on the sheet.

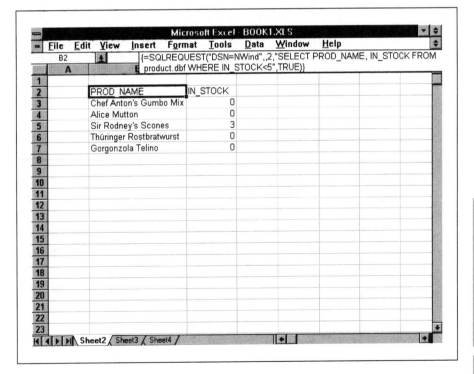

External Databases

Ch. **18**

► ►**N O T E**

> When you array-enter a formula, brackets are placed around the formula. You cannot type the brackets— you must "Ctrl+Shift+Enter" the formula. (See Chapter 26 to learn more about array formulas.)

► *Incorporating Variables into the SQL Statement*

An important benefit of the SQL.REQUEST function is the ability to dynamically incorporate variables into the SQL statement. In the previous example, the SQL statement is hard-coded into the formula. The only way to change the query is by changing the array formula, which is awkward.

The *where* clause of the SQL statement specifies a threshold (5) that determines which products will be retrieved. Suppose that you want to be able to enter this threshold easily—without changing the array formula. The following steps allow you to use a cell, E2, to enter the threshold.

1. Enter the number 10 into cell E2.

2. Select cells B2:C22.

► ►**T I P**

> You cannot edit a portion of an array—the entire array must be selected before revising the formula. A shortcut for selecting an array is to select a cell within the array, then choose the Edit ➤ Go To command, click Special, then choose the Current Array option (or select a cell and press Ctrl+/).

3. Edit the formula to read as follows—remember, don't press Enter.

=SQL.REQUEST("DSN=NWind",,2,"SELECT PROD_NAME, IN_STOCK FROM product.dbf WHERE IN_STOCK<"&E2,TRUE)

4. Press Ctrl+Shift+Enter to array-enter the formula—Figure 18.8 shows the result.

5. Enter the number 20 into cell E2 and watch the data change.

6. Remember these important facts:

   - The dimensions of the array formula limit the number of rows and columns that will be retrieved—in the previous example, no matter how large a number you enter into cell E2, the data will stop at C22. (Don't hesitate to create large arrays to avoid this problem.)

   - If the value in cell E2 results in an invalid SQL statement, the whole array will display the error #N/A.

FIGURE 18.8 ▶

Cell E2 determines the threshold for quantity in stock.

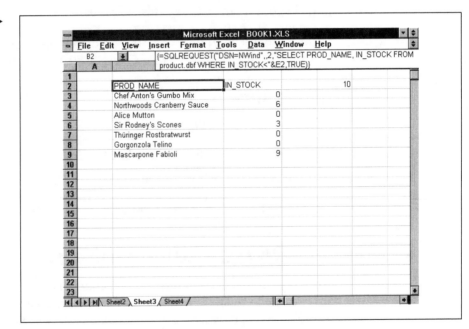

When a SQL Statement Requires Embedded Quotation Marks

A SQL statement *where* clause that performs a numeric comparison might read:

    WHERE IN_STOCK < 100

External Databases

Ch.
18

But when comparing a text value, the text must be quoted using single quote marks (apostrophe). The *where* clause might read:

WHERE CATEGORY = 'BEVR'

If the *where* clause contains variables, as with the previous exercise, and a formula is constructing the SQL statement, the formula must place the single quotes around the text string. Such formulas are difficult to read and edit, due to the proliferation of double quotes and single quotes. Notice how difficult it is to discern the single and double quotes at the end of the following formula:

="SELECT * FROM product.dbf WHERE CATEGORY = '"&B2&"'"

A trick that simplifies the job of entering and editing such formulas is to define a named constant that is equal to a single quote, then use the name in your formulas. Try this exercise:

1. Use Insert ▶ Name ▶ Define to create the name **Q**—it refers to a single quotation mark (see Chapter 8 to learn more about named constants).

2. Enter **BEVR** into cell B2.

3. Enter the following formula into a cell:

   ="SELECT * FROM product.dbf WHERE CATEGORY = "&Q&B2&Q

4. This formula will result in:

   SELECT * FROM product.dbf WHERE CATEGORY = 'BEVR'

▶ Working with Long SQL Statements

Text strings in Excel are limited to 255 characters. This is a severe restriction because SQL statements can be quite long. To overcome this limit, the SQL statement can be placed in a range of cells. The following example combines a long SQL statement with some creative use of variables.

On a blank worksheet, define the name **Q** to refer to a single quote (see previous example). Then enter the following:

In cell B2   **Enter Category:**

In cell C2   **BEVR**

In cell B4   **select PROD_NAME,CATEGORY,IN_STOCK, REORD_LVL,SUPPLR_ID from product.dbf** (and enter a trailing space after product.dbf)

In cell B5   **where IN_STOCK < (REORD_LVL + 100)** (and enter a trailing space)

In cell B6   **=IF(ISBLANK(C2),"","and CATEGORY = "&Q&C2&Q&")**

In cell B7   **order by CATEGORY,PROD_NAME**

In cell B9:F50   **=SQL.REQUEST ("DSN=NWind",,2,B4:B7,TRUE)** (array-enter the formula)

Depending on how your system is configured, you may have to specify the full path to the product file in cell B4. For example:

…from C:\WINDOWS\MSAPPS\MSQUERY\product.dbf product

All products in the beverage category are retrieved. Change cell C2 to COND, and all products in the condiment category are retrieved (Figure 18.9). Clear cell C2, and all products are retrieved.

FIGURE 18.9 ▶

The SQL statement referred to by the SQL.REQUEST function can reside in a range of cells, overcoming the 255-character limit for a cell.

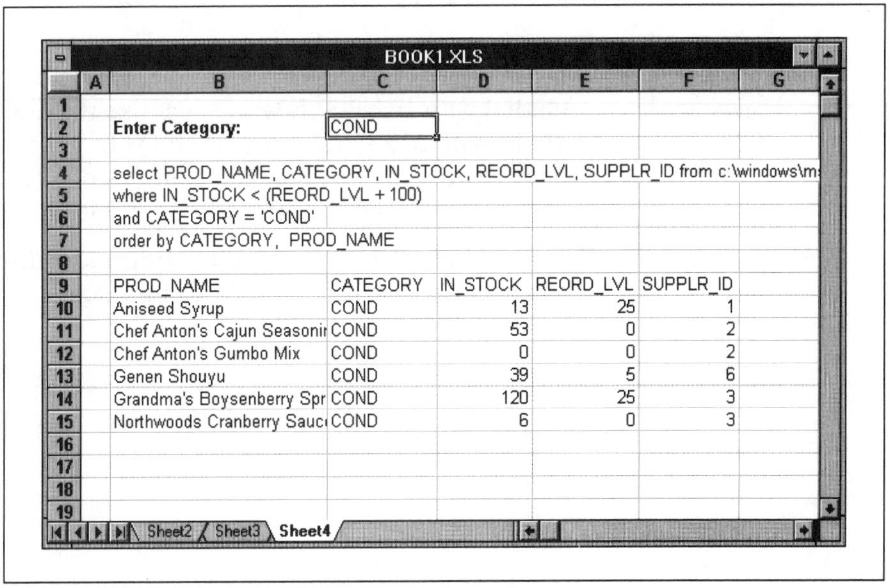

External Databases

Ch. **18**

This demonstrates the following points.

- The formula in B6 appends the where clause only if a value is entered in C2.

- When the SQL statement is sent to the ODBC manager, the values in B4:B7 are concatenated into one long string—without the trailing spaces, the query would fail.

►► *For Users of Earlier Versions of Excel*

Earlier versions of Excel used a utility called Q+E to perform queries. Microsoft Query takes the place of Q+E, and most users will find it to be a considerable improvement. If you have written macros to perform queries using Q+E, there are two important facts to be aware of.

- The DDE interface to MS Query is compatible with Q+E. In your macro code, all you have to do is change the name of the executable from QE.EXE to MSQUERY.EXE.

- Previously, the interface between Excel and Q+E was simplified by an add-in named QE.XLA. An add-in of the same name is included with Excel 5. It works just like the old QE.XLA, except it works with MS Query instead of Q+E. This means that if you have written macros that call routines on QE.XLA, the macros should work properly under Excel 5 without modification.

- If for some reason you want to continue to use Q+E, Excel 5 is still capable of sending DDE commands to Q+E.

PART SIX

▶ ▶ **I**n Part Six you'll learn how to create and use Excel's new worksheet controls and custom dialog boxes to customize worksheet interfaces without programming. You will also learn to automate everyday tasks using the Macro Recorder, and then you will put all these techniques together as you develop a real-life application.

CHAPTER 19

Using Worksheet Controls and Custom Dialog Boxes

►► *F*AST *T*RACK

▶ ***To create a custom dialog box***   *658*

Choose Insert ➤ Macro ➤ Dialog; or, right-click a sheet
tab and choose Insert, then select Dialog from the Insert
dialog box.

▶ ***To rename a control***   *661*

Select the control and change the name in the Name box.

▶ ***To change the tab order of the controls on a custom
dialog box***   *663*

Choose Tools ➤ Tab Order, or right-click the dialog frame
and choose the Tab Order command. Select a control and
use the Move buttons to change its position in the list.

▶ ***Dialog box properties can be controlled
programmatically***   *668*

You can hide and unhide objects; you can disable and enable objects; you can change the text associated with the
control; and you can change the dialog box caption.

▶ ▶ **U***sers* are drawn to spreadsheet products in large part because of the openness of the spreadsheet environment. However, this same openness is one of the biggest obstacles when trying to deploy bulletproof solutions. Validating user input, and performing certain actions based on user input, are among the most common development tasks. This chapter covers the two primary techniques used to control user input:

- *Enhancing the user interface by placing controls, such as list boxes and checkboxes, directly on worksheets*

- *Creating custom dialog boxes when bulletproof programmatic control is required*

▶ ▶ *Understanding Custom Controls*

A *control* is a special type of object that is placed on a worksheet or dialog sheet (a dialog sheet is a special worksheet which is used to build a custom dialog box). Controls are used to facilitate user input. For example, one type of control is a list box—it allows you to make selections from a list rather than typing in a response. Controls are placed on worksheets and dialog sheets by drawing them, just as you would draw a graphic object such as a rectangle. (See Chapter 12 to learn about graphic objects.)

The most important thing to understand about controls is that there is much similarity between controls on worksheets and controls on dialog sheets:

- All of the controls that can be used on a worksheet can also be used on a dialog sheet.

- Most controls are *active*—when clicked, something happens.

- Some controls are *passive*; they are not interacted with—for instance, you do not interact with a group box.

- Controls have many traits in common with other graphical objects, such as text boxes and drawing objects (see Chapter 12)—they can be formatted, locked, sent to back, brought to front, or hidden.

On the other hand, dialog sheets support several controls that cannot be used on worksheets.

▶ ▶**N O T E**

> **To insert a dialog sheet into a workbook, choose Insert ➤ Macro ➤ Dialog. Or, Control+click a sheet tab, choose the Insert command, then select Dialog from the Insert dialog box.**

▶ *The Forms Toolbar*

The tools that are used to draw controls are found on the Forms toolbar.

The Forms toolbar is displayed automatically when a dialog sheet is active. (Dialog sheets are explained later in this chapter.) When a worksheet is active, use the View ➤ Toolbars command to display the Forms toolbar.

Table 19.1 lists all of the drawing tools on the Forms toolbar. The table specifies which controls can be placed on worksheets, and also specifies which controls are passive (in other words, they are not clicked or otherwise interacted with).

►► **TABLE 19.1:** *Drawing Tools on the Forms Toolbar*

Tool	Description	Usable On Worksheets?	Passive?
Aa	Label (text)	Yes	Yes
abl	Edit control	No	No
XYZ	Group Box	Yes	Yes
▢	Button	Yes	No
☒	Check Box	Yes	No
◉	Option Button	Yes	No
List Box icon	List Box	Yes	No
Drop-down list box icon	Drop-down list box	Yes	No
List box linked icon	List box linked to edit control	No	No
Combination drop-down icon	Combination drop-down/edit control	No	No
Scroll bar icon	Scroll bar control	Yes	No
⬍	Spinner control	Yes	No

Several controls (checkbox, option button, list box, drop-down list box, scroll bar, spinner) can be linked to a worksheet cell. These controls...

- Can be linked to only one cell (though a cell can have multiple controls linked to it)

- Are typically linked to a cell in the same workbook, but can also be linked to a cell in a different one (in which case the workbook must be open for the control to work)

- Have a tab called Control which allows the cell link to be defined (but only when the control has been selected, and when the Format ➤ Object command has been chosen)

▶▶ *Controls on Worksheets*

Effective user interfaces can be created with controls on worksheets. You can make it easier for users to interact with your model, and also avoid data entry errors.

- Controls can be linked to cells—certain data entry is simplified, and data integrity enforced.

- Adding controls to a worksheet is easy—knowledge of macros is not required.

- When combined with advanced naming techniques (see Chapter 8) and the macro recorder (see Chapter 20), advanced functionality can be added to a worksheet model with relative ease.

▶ *To Place a Control on a Worksheet*

Follow these steps to draw a control on a worksheet:

1. Display the Forms toolbar using View ➤ Toolbars.

2. Click a tool on the Forms toolbar (one of the tools designated in Table 19.1 as usable on worksheets)—the mouse pointer becomes a crosshair.

3. Draw the object on the worksheet using the mouse (as you would draw any graphic object).

▶ ▶**N O T E**

> **Excel will not let you to draw a control on a worksheet if the particular control is not allowed there—Excel just beeps when you click one of these tools.**

▶ *Formatting Controls*

The term *format*, when applied to controls, encompasses all of the control's properties, not just the visual format. This discussion will explain how to access the formatting dialog box for controls.

Unlike "normal" graphic objects, active controls perform an action when clicked. Follow these steps to format them.

1. Select the object by holding down the Ctrl key while clicking the object.

2. Choose the Format ▶ Object command.

▶ ▶**T I P**

> **Any graphic object can have a macro assigned to it. When the object is clicked, the macro runs. To select such objects on a worksheet, hold down the Ctrl key, then click the object.**

Another way to format a control is to right-click it, then choose the Format Object command from the shortcut menu pictured below.

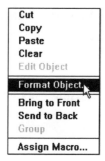

▶ *Setting Control Properties*

Active controls have *control properties*. This is where cell linkage is defined, as well as other behavioral settings. (Later in this chapter, each type of control will be discussed.) Regardless of the type of control, here are two ways to access the control properties:

- Follow the procedures for formatting the control (described above), then select the Control tab.

Format Object		
Protection	Properties	Control

Current Value: 0

Minimum Value: 0

Maximum Value: 100

Incremental Change: 1

Page Change: 10

Cell Link:

☒ 3D Shading

OK

Cancel

Help

- Select the control, and click the Control Properties tool (located on the Forms toolbar).

▶ UNDERSTANDING OBJECT PROTECTION

All worksheet objects, including drawing objects, charts, and on-sheet controls, can be protected so that users can't delete, resize, or move them. Individual objects are protected by *locking* them. By default, all newly created objects are locked. However, the lock does not take effect until the worksheet is protected. (This is much the same as with cell protection.) To lock or unlock an object, select the object, choose Format ➤ Object, select the Properties tab, then check the Locked checkbox. To better understand the two tier protection scheme, consider a table lamp plugged into an electrical outlet where the outlet is controlled by a wall switch. If the wall

▶

switch is turned off, you are unable to turn on the lamp using the lamp's own switch. But once you turn on the wall switch, the lamp's switch takes effect. Using this metaphor, the object lock is like the lamp switch, and worksheet protection is like the wall switch.

Objects that can contain text (such as text boxes, buttons, option buttons, and checkboxes) have an additional property that locks the *text*. For example, you can create a text box which is locked but the text is unlocked. Once the worksheet is protected, you will be able to change the text, but not move, resize, or delete the text box. Conversely, you can lock the text in an unlocked text box—the user will be able to move or resize the text box, but not alter the text.

▶ Moving and Resizing Controls

Controls are simply graphic objects, though they possess special properties. They are moved and resized using the same procedures for moving and resizing other types of objects.

▶ Worksheet Controls

The controls discussed in this section can all be used on worksheets (and on dialog sheets).

Labels

Labels are used for text, and they are passive. They are of little value on worksheets because they are less flexible than text boxes. Unlike a text box, a label cannot be formatted, nor can a formula be used. (The text format on labels is automatically the same as the text on built-in dialog boxes.)

Checkboxes

Checkboxes are used to toggle between logical values TRUE and FALSE (for inputs that require a yes/no answer). To create a checkbox linked to a cell:

1. Draw a checkbox on a worksheet.

2. With the checkbox object still selected, choose the Format ➤ Object command, then select the Control tab.

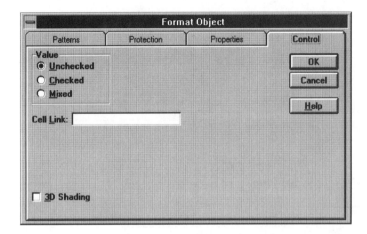

3. Enter a cell reference or cell name into Cell Link (this is a range edit—you can point and click on the worksheet to specify the cell).

▶ ▶ **N O T E**

The current value setting is not particularly useful for controls on worksheets; it is used to set default values for controls on dialog sheets. This is true of all the controls which allow an initial value to be set.

4. Click OK, then test the checkbox. It will enter TRUE or FALSE into the linked cell (see Figure 19.1).

It is common for the linked cell to be located out of view. There is no particular reason for the user to see the TRUE/FALSE value, even if the cell is referenced by other cells in the model.

FIGURE 19.1 ▶

The checkbox is linked to cell B6. When checked, B6 is set to TRUE. When unchecked, B6 is set to FALSE.

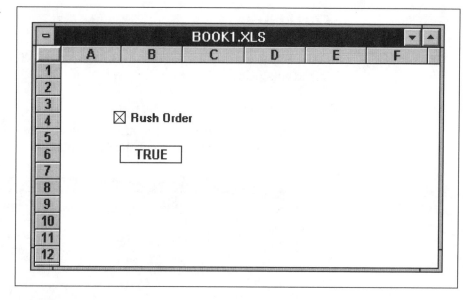

Scroll bars

Scroll bars are used to control an integer value in a cell (Figure 19.2).

FIGURE 19.2 ▶

Scroll bars control the integer value in a cell.

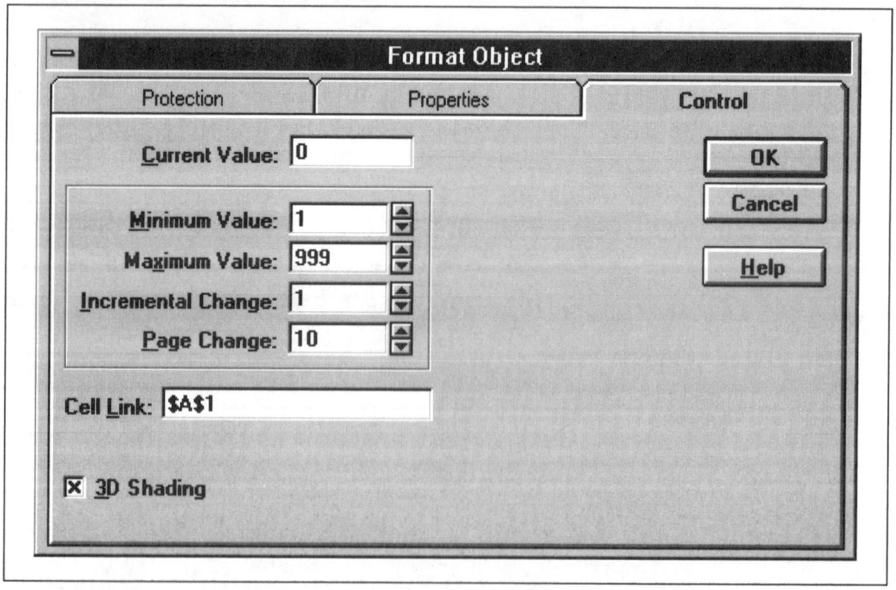

- Minimum and Maximum values constrain the cell value—these values can be no less than zero and no greater than 30,000 (meaning that the cell must contain a number from 0 to 30,000).

- Incremental Change is controlled by clicking the up or down arrows.

- Page Change is controlled by clicking the scroll bar itself, or by dragging the scroll box—the box between the up and down arrows.

- Enter the cell reference (or cell name) in Cell Link.

The scroll bar settings in Figure 19.2 would add or subtract one from cell A1 when the arrows are clicked, and add or subtract 10 when the bar is clicked. The cell will not go below 1 or above 999.

Scroll bars can be oriented vertically or horizontally (Figure 19.3).

FIGURE 19.3 ▶

Scroll bars can be oriented vertically or horizontally.

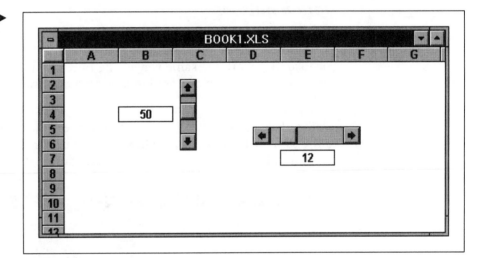

Spinners

Spinners are identical to scroll bars, except there is no Page Change setting available, and they can only be oriented vertically.

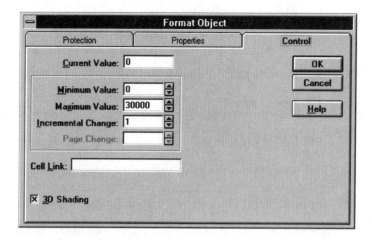

Option Buttons

Option buttons are used to select one option from a list of two or more exclusive choices. Option buttons are sometimes called radio buttons because they work the same way as the buttons on a car radio—since you can only listen to one station at a time, the choices are mutually exclusive.

The worksheet in Figure 19.4 includes three option buttons, all linked to the same cell. However, the linkage only needs to be set for one of the option buttons—the other buttons are automatically linked.

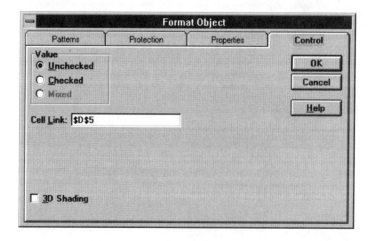

FIGURE 19.4 ▶

All of the option buttons are linked to cell D5. When the first button is chosen, D5 is set to 1. When the second button is chosen, D5 is set to 2, etc.

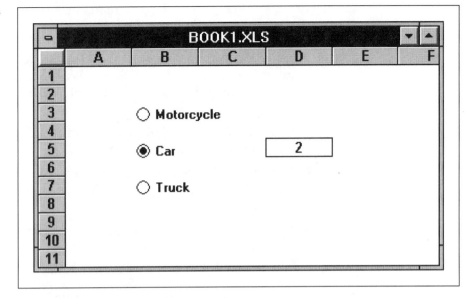

 Option buttons can be placed inside of a Group Box. The group box groups the buttons not only visually, but logically as well (see Figure 19.5).

FIGURE 19.5 ▶

The option buttons in the Media group box are linked to B7. The option buttons in the Category group box are linked to D7.

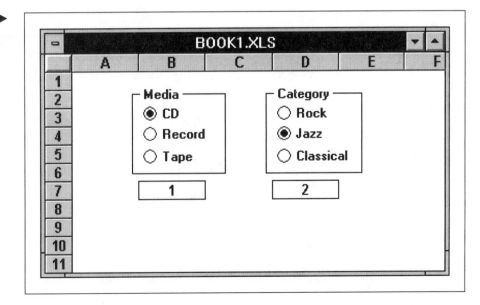

Here are some important facts to remember about the behavior of option buttons and group boxes:

- All option buttons on a worksheet that are *not* inside a group box are part of the same logical group. When you link any of them to a cell, all of the others are automatically linked to the same cell.

- All options buttons within a group box are part of the same logical group. When you link any of them to a cell, all of the others are automatically linked to the same cell.

- There can be more than one group box on a sheet containing option buttons. And, on the same sheet, there can be option buttons that are not inside a group box.

- If you resize a group box so that an option button that was previously not inside the box is then inside, the new member automatically becomes part of the logical group. Conversely, if you resize a group box so that one of the option buttons is no longer in the box, the "orphaned" option button ceases to be a member of the logical group.

- Other controls, such as checkboxes and list boxes, can be placed inside a group box (see Figure 19.6). The sole purpose is aesthetics—there is no logical side effect.

FIGURE 19.6 ▶

Controls other than option buttons can be placed in a group box, with no effect on the behavior of the controls. Group boxes only affect the behavior of option buttons.

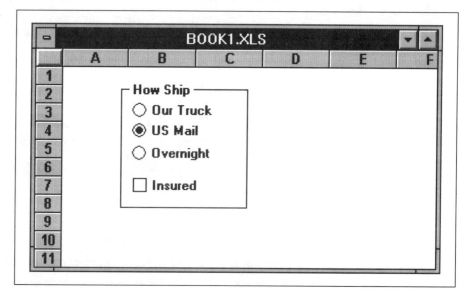

List Boxes

List boxes let the user select an item from a list, and place a result in a linked cell. They require two separate cell linkages:

- An input range—the range of cells that contains the list of choices
- A cell link—when an item is selected in the list box, this cell contains the position within the list of the selected item

Here are the control properties for the list box in Figure 19.7:

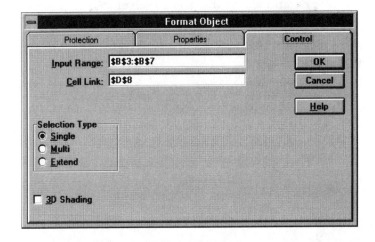

FIGURE 19.7 ▶

The input range for the list box is B3:B7. The cell link is D8. Since the second item in the list is selected, D8 contains the number 2.

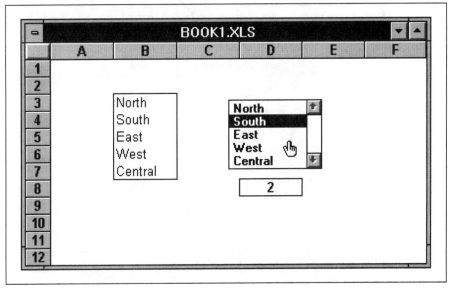

You can use names in place of cell addresses for the list box cell linkages. For example, in Figure 19.7, you could name B3:B7 **Regions**, then enter **Regions** as the input range.

The Selection Type setting allows you to control the way users select items:

- Single allows one selection at a time.
- Multi allows the user to select and de-select multiple items in the list by clicking them.
- Extend allows the user to select a contiguous range of items by holding down the Shift key (like in the File ➤ Open dialog box).

▶ ▶ **T I P**

> For *all* controls that are linked to cells, a cell name can be entered for the link. When the control and the linked cell are in the same workbook, the benefit is clarity. But if the control and linked cell are on separate workbooks, the benefit is integrity, and in this type of case, it is very important to refer to cells by name.

Drop-Down List Boxes

Drop-down list boxes are identical to standard list boxes, except you can specify how high the list box is, measured in lines, when dropped down.

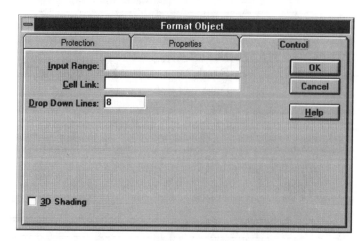

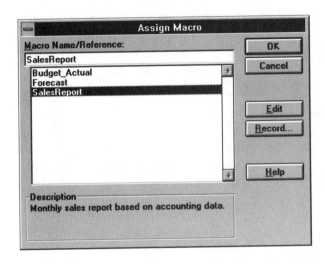

Buttons

Buttons are not linked to cells—their sole purpose is to run a macro. When you draw a button, a dialog box displays allowing you to assign a macro.

At this stage, there are three ways to assign a macro:

- Select an existing macro from the list.
- Click New to write a new macro—a shell for a new macro will be placed on a VBA module, and displayed so that you can write the actual macro.
- Click Record to record a macro—the Record New Macro dialog box is displayed.

Chapter 20 provides more information on how to assign macros to buttons, and how to record macros.

  T I P

> **Any graphic object can be assigned to a macro, not just "official" buttons. Just select the object and choose Tools ➤ Assign Macro. As with official buttons, when the object is clicked the macro is run.**

In terms of formatting, buttons are similar to text boxes (see Chapter 12). You can format the font, and set the text alignment. Figure 19.8 shows some buttons with different formatting.

FIGURE 19.8 ▶

Examples of buttons with different formatting

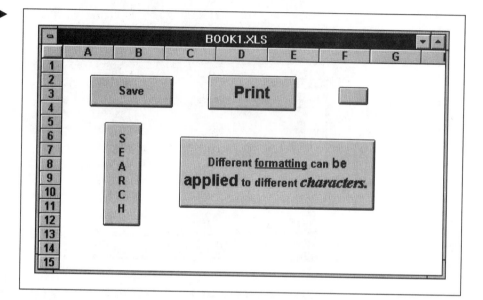

By default, buttons do not print (whereas by default, all other controls do). This can be changed using the Print Object setting, on the Properties tab of the Format Object dialog box.

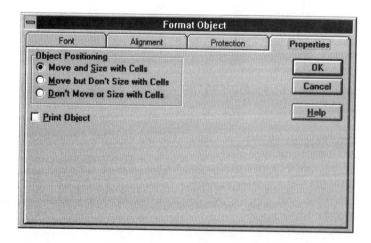

CONTROLS WON'T WORK IF LINKED CELLS ARE LOCKED AND PROTECTED

Here's a frustrating scenario: you're developing an application that allows users to display data for a given month by clicking a spinner control. The spinner allows the user to enter a number from 1 to 12 into a cell named Month. When the application is complete, you protect the worksheet so that users will not be able to delete objects, or edit certain locked cells. But now, when you click the spinner, you get an error message. Remember, all cells are locked by default. So after the worksheet was protected, the spinner was trying to place data into the cell Month, which is locked.

You can get around this problem without sacrificing the security afforded by cell and worksheet protection. The linked cell (Month) does not have to be on the same worksheet as the control—it can be placed on a separate, hidden worksheet. But how does the user know which month is selected? A locked cell on the visible sheet can refer to the unlocked cell on the hidden sheet using the formula =*Month*. In fact, using a hidden worksheet for all of the behind-the-scenes machinery in your model is a very good way to build applications.

▶ Design Techniques

Here are some tips to help you design effective user interfaces using controls:

- Use option buttons when there are only a few choices, and the choices are relatively static. Otherwise, a list box is probably a better bet. Adding more choices to a list box only involves expanding the input range, as opposed to redesigning the sheet to accommodate more option buttons. Figures 19.9 and 19.10 show some examples using option buttons and list boxes.

FIGURE 19.9 ▶

List boxes require less maintenance than option buttons when the contents of the list changes, since they are data driven. And when the list is long, list boxes are more aesthetic.

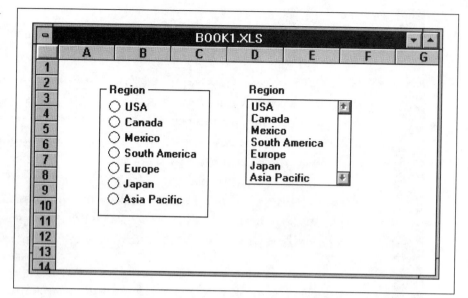

FIGURE 19.10 ▶

Option buttons are very effective when there are few choices, and the choices are relatively static. List boxes with only two or three choices are not aesthetically appealing.

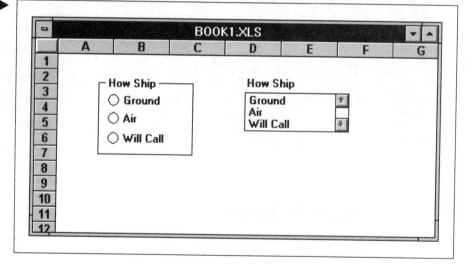

- Technically, one checkbox can serve the same purpose as a group of two option buttons. But sometimes two option buttons provide more clarity, as shown in Figure 19.11.

- Group boxes are not limited to grouping option buttons—all related controls can be grouped together, as pictured in Figure 19.12. In fact, a group box might contain no option buttons.

FIGURE 19.11 ▶

*The one checkbox can
perform the same logi-
cal function as the two
option buttons. But in
this example, the op-
tion buttons provide
more clarity because
the meaning of each
choice is spelled out.*

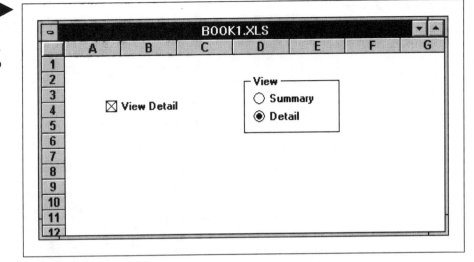

FIGURE 19.12 ▶

*You can place controls
other than option but-
tons in a group box.
The Ordered By input
is not a control—it is a
cell with a border.*

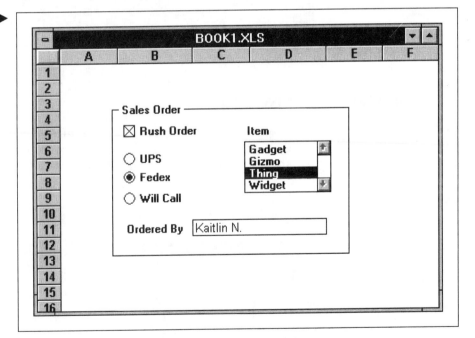

- A worksheet can be made to look similar to a "real" custom dialog
  box. Color the cells grey and remove gridlines from the sheet, as
  pictured in Figure 19.13.

FIGURE 19.13 ▶

A worksheet formatted to look like a dialog box. The controls are formatted with 3-D shading.

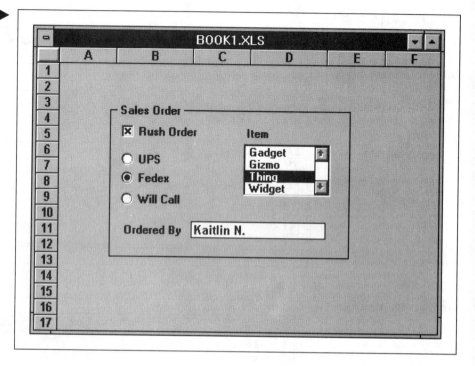

▶ Dynamic List Boxes

Here is an advanced technique that combines named formulas (covered in Chapter 8) with list boxes. This exercise uses named formulas to dynamically change the contents of a list box—without having to write custom macros.

1. On a new worksheet, enter these values in range B2:D15:

2. Name the ranges indicated on the worksheet.

3. Define the name **CourseList** referring to:

=INDIRECT("List."&DeptChoice)

4. Add grouped option buttons to the worksheet:

   • Draw a group box.
   • Draw four option buttons inside the group box, and link one of them to cell DeptChoice (the rest will be linked automatically).

5. Add a list box to the worksheet:

   • Input range: **CourseList**
   • Cell link: **CourseChoice**

 ▶ ▶**TIP**

 **The formula =OFFSET(CourseList,CourseChoice-1,1,1,1)
will return the code for the course selected in the list box.**

Another common problem is a list with a variable number of rows. For example, a list may be built by querying an external database, and the number of rows may vary from time to time. The standard approach to this problem is to programmatically (or manually!) define a named range after performing the query. Alternately, the list box can use a name that dynamically calculates the number of rows in the list. Consider the following worksheet:

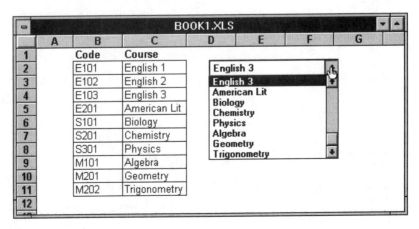

- The name CourseList is defined as:

=OFFSET($C$2,1,0,COUNTA(OFFSET($C$2,1,0,999,1)),1)

(This formula assumes a maximum of 999 rows.)

- The Input range for list box is CourseList.

- If new rows of data are added to bottom of list, the drop-down list box automatically includes the new rows.

►► *Custom Dialog Boxes*

So far, this chapter has covered how to place controls directly on worksheets. Custom dialog boxes provide greater programmatic control of events, and are a key component in application development.

 ► ►**NOTE**

Everything that has been discussed in this chapter pertaining to controls on worksheets also pertains to custom dialog boxes. This section explains only the unique aspects of custom dialog boxes.

- Custom dialog boxes are modal, whereas worksheets are not. A modal dialog box is one which retains the focus until the dialog box is dismissed.

- Worksheet controls do not support accelerator (shortcut) keys or tab order, as do custom dialog box controls.

- Custom dialog boxes must be displayed programmatically.

- All controls that can be placed on worksheets can be placed on custom dialog boxes; custom dialog boxes support several additional controls.

► *Creating a New Dialog Box*

To create a new dialog box, insert a dialog sheet into your workbook: Choose the Insert ➤ Macro ➤ Dialog command. When you insert a new dialog sheet, you will notice that two things happen (see Figure 19.14):

- The Forms toolbar displays automatically.
- A dialog frame containing two buttons (OK and Cancel) is placed on the new dialog sheet.

FIGURE 19.14 ▶

A new dialog sheet in-cludes three objects: a dialog frame, an OK button, and a Cancel button.

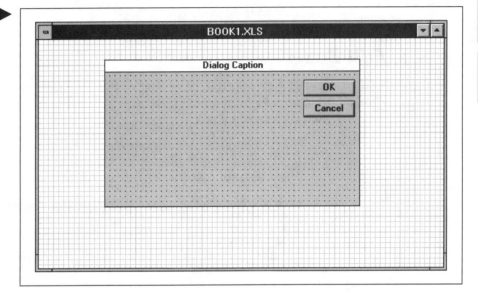

▶ *The Dialog Frame*

The dialog frame (see Figure 19.14) is a separate object. It can be moved, resized, and the caption can be changed. To select the dialog frame, click anywhere on its title or outer border.

▶ *Moving and Sizing Controls*

The procedures for moving and resizing controls on dialog boxes differ somewhat from controls on worksheets. When gridlines are displayed, controls automatically snap to the gridlines when the control is drawn, moved, or resized. This behavior can be overridden in two ways:

- Turn off gridlines using the Toggle Grid tool (located on the Forms toolbar).

▶ ▶**TIP**

The Toggle Grid tool can also be used to toggle gridlines on a worksheet.

- Hold down the Alt key while moving/sizing to temporarily override snap to grid.

▶ *Edit Boxes*

An *edit box* is used to enter text or numeric data, and can also be used to enter a cell reference. Here are the steps to draw an edit box, and then set its properties:

1. Click the Edit Box tool, and draw the object inside the dialog frame.

2. With the edit box still selected, click the Control Properties tool.

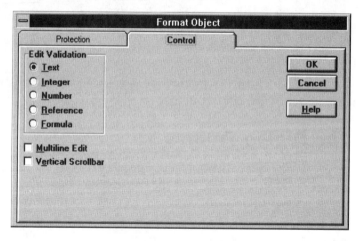

Text	Up to 255 characters can be entered
Integer	Limits input to values from –32,765 to 32,767
Number	Any valid number
Reference	Requires valid cell reference—allows input by pointing and clicking on worksheet

Formula	Any valid formula
Multiline Edit	Causes input to wrap within the control
Vertical Scroll bar	Places vertical scroll bars beside the control when the dialog box is run

▶ *Combination List*

 A combination list-edit (or combo list-edit) box is actually two separate controls that work together—a list box and an edit box. The edit box is automatically linked to the list box. When an item is chosen from the list box, the text is automatically placed in the edit box. You can also type directly into the edit box (the entry does not have to match an item in the list).

 Drop-down combo list-edits are identical to combo list-edits, except the list is a drop-down.

▶ *Placing Graphic Objects on Dialog Boxes*

You are not limited to the controls found on the Forms toolbar when placing objects on a dialog box. Any graphic object can be placed on a dialog box, including pictures, charts, text boxes, and any of the drawing objects. There are specific benefits to using these objects:

Text Boxes	Unlike labels, text boxes can be formatted, and can contain a formula.
Pictures	Pictures linked to cells are a convenient way of displaying formatted, tabular data on a dialog box.
Charts	Just like charts embedded on worksheets, chart objects on dialog boxes remain linked to source cells.

▶ *Use Meaningful Names for Controls*

When you draw objects on a worksheet, they are automatically named by Excel using the object type, followed by a sequential number.

Controls drawn on dialog sheets are automatically named the same way. For example, a new dialog sheet contains three objects:

- Dialog Frame 1
- Button 2 (OK button)
- Button 3 (Cancel button)

If you add an edit box, it will be named **Edit Box 4**. Add a label after that, and it will be named **Label 5**, and so on. You can rename the controls using meaningful names that will make your macros more readable. To rename a control:

1. Select the control.
2. Overwrite the name in the Name Box.

For example, in Figure 19.15, Edit Box 4 has been renamed **Company Edit** (the name of the control can be seen in the Name box, and is different from the caption on the dialog).

FIGURE 19.15 ▶

Rename a control by selecting it and overwriting its name in the Name Box.

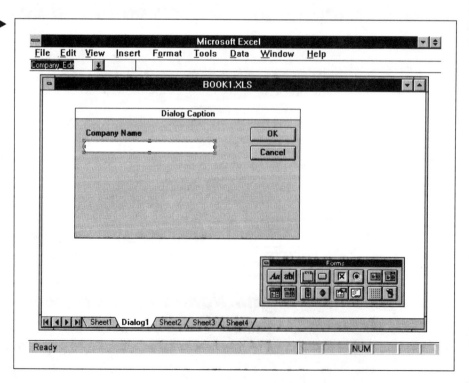

▶ ▶ **W A R N I N G**

If macros refer to a control named, say, *List Box 7*, then you rename the list box to ListRegions, the macros must be edited accordingly.

▶ *Setting the Tab Order*

When a dialog box is displayed, the tab key moves the focus from control to control. By default, the tab order of a custom dialog box is determined by the order in which the controls were created. To change the tab order, choose the Tools ➤ Tab Order command (or click the dialog frame with the right mouse button and select Tab Order from the shortcut menu).

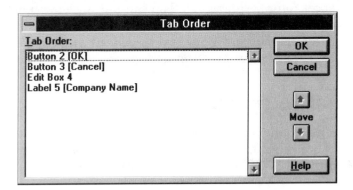

Select an item in the list, and click the up/down arrows to move it up or down.

▶ *Assigning Accelerator Keys*

Accelerator keys are shortcuts that let you move to a specific control in a dialog box. They are used in conjunction with the Alt key. For example, in the Go To dialog box (displayed by pressing F5), you press Alt+R to move to the Reference box. You can define accelerator keys in your custom dialog boxes. To assign an accelerator key, select the control, and click the Control Properties tool. Then select the Control tab.

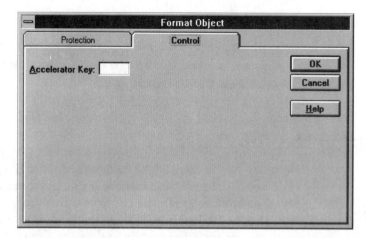

Buttons, checkboxes, option buttons, labels, and group boxes can have accelerator keys assigned. You can use any letter, number, or special character; however, user-interface conventions dictate that you use a letter that appears in the text associated with the control. Accelerator keys are displayed with an underscore.

▶ Controlling Events

Custom dialog boxes are able to run macros when three types of events occur: when the dialog box is displayed (*on-show*), when a control is clicked (*on-click*), or when a control is changed (*on-change*).

On-Show

You can assign a macro to run automatically when the dialog box is initially displayed. On-show macros are often used to set default values for dialog box controls. To create an on-show macro, select the dialog frame, then use one of the following two procedures:

- If the macro does not exist, click the Edit Code tool; a new macro (procedure) will be placed on a VBA module (see Figure 19.16). Place your VBA code between the Sub and End Sub. (If there is no module in the workbook, a new module is inserted.)

- If the macro already exists, choose the Tools ▶ Assign Macro command; a list of macros will be displayed from which to choose.

FIGURE 19.16 ▶

A new macro (proce-dure) is created. Place the code between the Sub and End Sub.

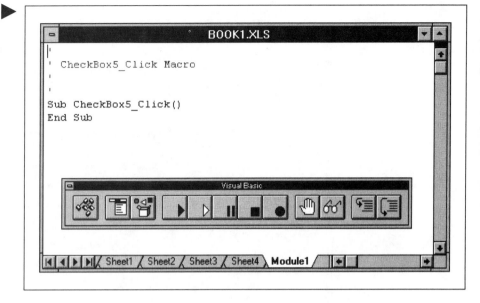

 ▶ ▶**N O T E**

> **When you create a new macro (procedure) using the Edit Code tool, Excel automatically names the macro. The name of the object is included as part of the macro name. There is no special meaning to these names, and they can be overridden with a name of your choosing.**

 ▶ ▶**T I P**

> **If a macro is already assigned to a control, the Edit Code tool will display the macro.**

On-Click

An *on-click* macro is run when it is clicked by the user. You can assign an on-click macro to the following controls:

- Button
- Checkbox

- Option button
- Any graphic object

Buttons have some special properties that determine their on-click behavior. Draw a button on a dialog frame, select it, then click the Control Properties tool, then select the Control tab.

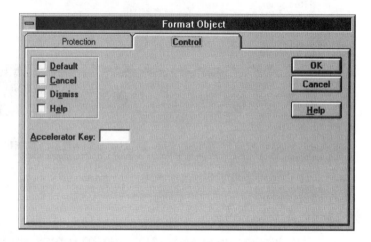

Default	Sets button as the default—when checked, pressing Enter on the keyboard is the equivalent of clicking the button
Cancel	Determines if the button is triggered when the dialog box is canceled
Dismiss	Determines if the button will close the dialog box when clicked
Help	Determines if the button is triggered when F1 is pressed while the dialog box is displayed

On-click macros are created, assigned, and edited the same way as on-show macros.

On-Change

An on-change macro is run when user input occurs. You can assign an on-change macro to the following controls:

- Edit box
- List box
- Combo edit-list

In the case of edit boxes, the macro is run each time a character is typed, deleted, or changed. On-change macros are created the same way as on-show macros.

▶ Testing the Dialog Box

 Choose the Tools ➤ Run Dialog command, or click the Run Dialog tool, to test the dialog box. All event macros are run (as events dictate) when the dialog box is tested in this manner.

▶ Running the Dialog Box for Real

A dialog box is displayed from a VBA macro (procedure) using the Show method. The following code sample assumes that a dialog box resides on a dialog sheet named EnterStats, and the VBA module resides in the same workbook as the dialog sheet:

```
Sub ProcessStats()
    DialogSheets("EnterStats").Show
End Sub
```

Typically, a macro will take different action if an OK button dismisses the dialog box rather than a Cancel button. The following code sample tests for this condition:

```
Sub ProcessStats()
    If  DialogSheets("EnterStats").Show Then
     MsgBox "You clicked the OK button"
    End If
End Sub
```

If an on-click macro were assigned to the OK button on the EnterStats dialog box, events would occur in the following sequence when OK is clicked:

1. On-click macro runs (not shown above)
2. Dialog box closes
3. In-line code is processed (message box displayed)

► When Not to Link Controls to Cells

Controls that are linked to cells edit the cell immediately. This causes two often undesirable side-effects:

● Cells are edited regardless of whether OK or Cancel is pressed.

● Each change to a cell can trigger a worksheet recalculation.

Thus, controls on dialog boxes are often *not* linked to cells, which requires cell updates to be handled programmatically.

► Controlling Dialog Box Properties Programmatically

The controls on a dialog sheet can be manipulated programmatically from VBA. They can be disabled or enabled, have their text changed—virtually any of the properties can be set from VBA code. The code samples below manipulate properties of the dialog box pictured in Figure 19.17. The dialog box resides on a dialog sheet named *StudentInfo*.

Disabling a Control

The following code disables the Skills edit box. This code might be part of an on-click macro assigned to the checkbox:

```
Sub DisableCheckBox()
    DialogSheets("StudentInfo").CheckBoxes(1).Enabled = False
End Sub
```

FIGURE 19.17

*Student information
dialog box*

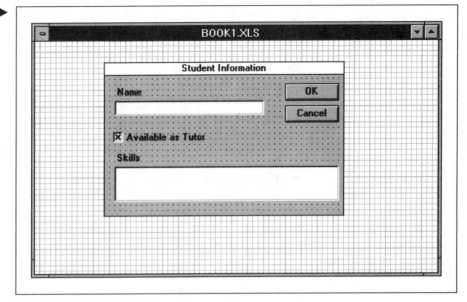

CheckBoxes(1) refers to the first checkbox in the dialog box. Here is
another way to disable the checkbox, this time referring to it by name
(Check Box 10):

```
Sub DisableCheckBox()
    DialogSheets("StudentInfo").CheckBoxes("Check Box 10").En-
abled = False
End Sub
```

TIP

**Macros are easier to read if you rename controls with
meaningful names. For example, VBA code that refers
to a control as "Tutor CheckBox" makes more sense
than "Check Box 10".**

Conditionally Disable/Enable a Control

Using the dialog box in Figure 19.17, if a student is not available to tutor, the dialog box needs to prohibit entry into the Skills edit box (the
second edit box). In addition, the label Skills (the second label) will
also be enabled/disabled in order to provide the user with a visual cue

as to the status of the edit box. The following macro, which is run when the checkbox is clicked, disables the edit box and the label when the checkbox is unchecked, and vice-versa when checked:

```
Sub HandleEditBox()
    Dim Check As Integer
    Check = DialogSheets("StudentInfo").CheckBoxes(1).Value
    If Check = 1 Then
     DialogSheets("StudentInfo").Labels(2).Enabled = True
     DialogSheets("StudentInfo").EditBoxes(2).Enabled = True
    Else
     DialogSheets("StudentInfo").Labels(2).Enabled = False
     DialogSheets("StudentInfo").EditBoxes(2).Enabled = False
    End If
End Sub
```

The use of a With statement makes the same macro somewhat less verbose:

```
Sub HandleEditBox()
    With DialogSheets("StudentInfo")
    Dim Check As Integer
    Check = .CheckBoxes(1).Value
    If Check = 1 Then
       .Labels(2).Enabled = True
       .EditBoxes(2).Enabled = True
    Else
       .Labels(2).Enabled = False
       .EditBoxes(2).Enabled = False
    End If
    End With
End Sub
```

Setting Dialog Box Properties

The dialog frame is an object whose properties can be set programmatically. The following macro changes the caption of the StudentInfo dialog box:

```
Sub SetCaption()
 DialogSheets("StudentInfo").Dialog boxFrame.Caption = "Hello!"
End Sub
```

This macro sets the focus to Edit Box 12:

```
Sub SetFocus()
    DialogSheets("StudentInfo").Focus = "Edit Box 12"
End Sub
```

▶ *Creating a Functional Dialog*

The following exercise walks you through the creation of a full-featured, functional dialog box that...

- Sets default values using an on-show macro
- Accepts user inputs, and disables controls based on certain conditions
- Validates user input when OK is clicked
- Places user inputs onto a worksheet

The dialog box will be used to enter information for job applicants. Input to the supervisor edit box can occur only if the applicant was previously employed at the company, and a name must be entered.

This exercise uses the worksheet and dialog box pictured in Figures 19.18 and 19.19.

1. Create a new workbook with a worksheet named **Apply**; insert a dialog sheet and name it **DataEntry**.

2. Build the Apply worksheet, as pictured in Figure 19.18. Name the cells as indicated.

3. Draw the controls pictured in Figure 19.19 (on dialog sheet DataEntry).

4. The controls that will be referred to from macro code will be renamed for clarity; rename them as follows:

Control	Name
Name edit box	**Edit_Name**
Department list box	**List_Dept**
Checkbox	**Check_Prev**
Supervisor label	**Label_Super**
Supervisor edit box	**Edit_Super**

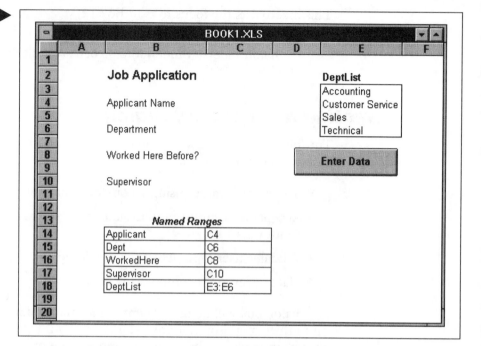

5. Assign an input range for the list box of Apply!DeptList (the named range on worksheet Apply).

6. An on-show macro will set default values so that the dialog box does not retain values from the last time it was used. Since most applicants apply for technical positions, the department will default to *technical*; edit boxes will be set to *null*, the checkbox unchecked, and the supervisor edit box disabled:

   - Select the dialog frame, then click the Edit Code tool.
   - Enter the following macro:

```
Sub DialogFrame1_Show()
    With DialogSheets("DataEntry")
    Dim Check As Integer
      .EditBoxes("Edit_Name").Text = ""
      .ListBoxes("List_Dept").Value = 4
      .CheckBoxes("Check_Prev").Value = False
      .Labels("Label_Super").Enabled = False
      .EditBoxes("Edit_Super").Enabled = False
      .EditBoxes("Edit_Super").Text = ""
      .Focus = "Edit_Name"
    End With
End Sub
```

7. When the checkbox is checked, the supervisor edit must be enabled; when it is unchecked the supervisor must be cleared and disabled:

   - Select the checkbox, then click the Edit Code tool.
   - Enter the following macro:

```
Sub Check_Prev_Click()
    Dim Checked As Integer
    With DialogSheets("DataEntry")
    Checked = .CheckBoxes("Check_Prev").Value
    If Checked = 1 Then
        .EditBoxes("Edit_Super").Enabled = True
        .Labels("Label_Super").Enabled = True
    Else
        .EditBoxes("Edit_Super").Enabled = False
        .Labels("Label_Super").Enabled = False
        .EditBoxes("Edit_Super").Text = ""
```

```
        End If
      End With
   End Sub
```

8. Change the OK button so that it does *not* dismiss the dialog box (verification that a name was entered must occur, and an on-click event will decide whether to dismiss the dialog box).

9. Define an on-click macro for the OK button:

   - Select the OK button then click the Edit Code tool.
   - Enter the following macro:

```
Sub Button2_Click()
Set Dial = DialogSheets("DataEntry")
   If Dial.EditBoxes("Edit_Name").Text = "" Then
    MsgBox "You must enter a name."
    Dial.Focus = "Edit_Name"
   Else

  Set Sheet = Worksheets("Apply")

  Sheet.Range("Applicant").Value =
   Dial.EditBoxes("Edit_Name").Text

  Sheet.Range("Dept").Value =
   Sheet.Range("DeptList")(Dial.ListBoxes("List_Dept").Value)

  Dim Worked As String

  If Dial.CheckBoxes("Check_Prev").Value = 1 Then Worked =
   "Yes" Else Worked = "No"

  Sheet.Range("WorkedHere").Value = Worked

  Sheet.Range("Supervisor").Value =
   Dial.EditBoxes("Edit_Super").Text

  Dial.Hide
  End If

  End Sub
```

10. Test the dialog box using the Run Dialog box tool

11. Write the macro to initially show the dialog box:

   - Activate the module.
   - Enter the following macro:

```
Sub EnterApplicantData()
    DialogSheets("DataEntry").Show
End Sub
```

12. Draw a button to display the dialog box:

   - Draw a button on worksheet Apply.
   - Assign the macro EnterApplicantData.

Your dialog box should be ready to go. Click the new button on worksheet Apply to try it.

▶ ▶ ▶ **CHAPTER** **20**

Macro
Basics

▶▶ *F*AST *T*RACK

▶ **To assign a macro to a new button**　　**697**

First, draw the button. Then, select a macro from the list in the Assign Macro dialog box.

▶ **To assign a macro to any graphic object**　　**697**

First, select the object. Then, choose Tools ➤ Assign Macro. Finally, select a macro from the list in the Assign Macro dialog box.

▶ **To assign a macro to a tool**　　**698**

Display the toolbar containing the tool, then choose View ➤ Toolbars. Click the Customize button, then click the tool (on the toolbar) to which you want to assign the macro. Finally, choose Tools ➤ Assign Macro.

▶ **To create a custom menu system**　　**700**

Activate a module and choose Tools ➤ Menu Editor.

▶ **To run a macro automatically when a workbook is first opened**　　**700**

Name the macro **Auto_Open**.

►► ***T****here* are two types of people who create macros: everyday users (nonprogrammers), who can use the *macro recorder* to automate simple tasks; and application developers, who create complete custom applications. This chapter provides some useful information for both ends of the spectrum, but with an emphasis on skills for the nonprogrammer:

- *Programming Excel overview*
- *Recording macros*
- *Running macros*
- *User-defined functions (function macros)*

►► *Programming Excel Overview*

Excel is the first application to support VBA—Microsoft's *Visual Basic, Applications Edition*—a language based on the popular Visual Basic programming language. Microsoft intends VBA to be the common macro language used in all of its programmable applications, making it strategically important for application developers. Eventually, VBA will be the programming language for Microsoft Access, Microsoft Word, and other Microsoft products. VBA code (and knowledge) is easily transferable between Microsoft applications.

- The old macro language, *XLM*, is still supported and has been extended to support features that are new in Excel 5. You can run your old macros, and continue to write XLM macros if so desired.

- Future versions of Excel will continue to support XLM, but will not extend the functionality of XLM. Microsoft has made it very clear that VBA is where the future lies. Accordingly, the focus of this chapter is VBA.

- VBA macros can call XLM macros, and vice-versa. This allows users with an investment in XLM code to gradually transition to VBA.

- Excel is able to run Lotus 1-2-3 macros, without the need to translate them. See Chapter 25 for more information on Lotus compatibility.

- For serious programmers, VBA provides scoped variables and debugging facilities—features that were sorely lacking in XLM.

- Excel macros are compatible across Windows and Macintosh platforms. If your organization uses Windows and Mac, you can create applications that run on both.

▶ ▶**NOTE**

This chapter does not attempt to teach the details of how to program in VBA. That is an exhaustive topic that requires a lot of coverage to do it justice. Instead, it will provide a general orientation for you to build upon. Refer to the *Visual Basic User's Guide* for more information.

All macros reside in workbooks: VBA macros reside on *modules*, and XLM macros reside on *XLM sheets*. There is no limit, other than available memory, to the number of modules and/or XLM sheets in a workbook.

▶**NOTE**

The Excel documentation uses the terms *macro* and *procedure* interchangeably, as does this book.

Macro Basics

▶ ▶

Ch.

20

▶ ▶ *The Macro Recorder*

The *macro recorder* is a tool that translates your actions into macro code, without the need to understand the underlying macro syntax. It works like a tape recorder: When you turn the recorder on, it "records" everything you do. Later, you can play back (run) the macro, and the actions that you previously recorded are repeated. The macro recorder provides two primary benefits:

- Simple, repetitive tasks can be automated without the need to know VBA.

- The recorder is an excellent tool for learning VBA.

When used in conjunction with general Excel know-how, surprisingly complex tasks can be reliably automated. But using the recorder *effectively* requires that you understand its limitations, and carefully plan a course of action before you start recording. Here are some typical tasks that could be automated with recorded macros:

- Format a range of cells as bold font, with borders.

- Open a workbook, print it, then close it.

- Open a text file that was output by a mainframe application, sort the data, insert subtotals and grand totals, then print the report.

- Open several workbooks, consolidate information onto a new workbook, then save the new workbook.

- Perform a query, then chart the results.

As you can see from these examples, creating reports is a task that is ideally suited for automation by recording macros.

▶ *How to Start Recording a Macro*

Here are the steps to begin recording a new macro.

1. Plan exactly what you want to accomplish, and how to go about it. In fact, you should run through the precise keystrokes that you plan on recording before actually recording them.

2. Turn on the recorder using the Tools ➤ Record Macro ➤ Record New Macro command.

Record New Macro	
Macro Name: Macro1	OK
	Cancel
Description: Macro recorded 11/26/94 by Bill Rothwell	Options >>
	Help

 ► ►**N O T E**

If there are no visible workbooks at the time you plan to start recording, then the Tools menu does not display. In this case, start recording with the File ➤ Record New Macro command.

3. Enter a meaningful name for your macro. The name can be up to 255 characters long, and consist of letters, numbers, and underscores. There can be no spaces or other punctuation marks—including hyphens. (If you need to separate words use underscores.) The name must begin with a letter.

Valid Names	Invalid Names	Reason
MyMacro	My Macro	Contains a space
Sales_Report	Sales.Report	Contains a period
Summary95	95Summary	Starts with a number
Get_YTD_Info	Y-T-D	Contains illegal characters

4. By default, the Description will include your name and the date—this text is placed above the actual macro in the VBA module, as comments. You can add additional comments to explain the purpose of the macro.

At this point, you can click OK to begin recording. Otherwise, there are additional settings that you can access by clicking the Options button.

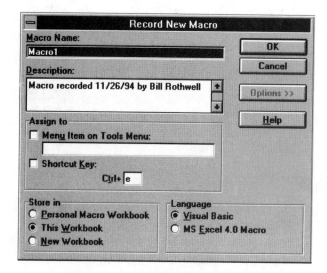

Menu Item on Tools Menu Check this option if you want to add the macro to Excel's built-in *Tools* menu. The text you enter in the box beneath the checkbox is used as the command text on the Tools menu.

Shortcut Key Check this option if you want to assign a shortcut key for the macro you are about to record. Then, enter a key that is to be used in conjunction with the Ctrl key to run the macro. If you check Shortcut Key, and enter **x** as the Ctrl+ key, then after the macro is recorded, pressing Ctrl+x will run the macro.

Store In These options specify where the soon-to-be-recorded macro will be placed.

Personal Macro Workbook This workbook, named PERSONAL.XLS, is automatically opened, and hidden, each time you start Excel. This is a good place to store macros that you want available at all times. (It is discussed later in this chapter.)

This Workbook Places the macro in the active workbook. If there is no active workbook, this option is not available.

New Workbook A new workbook will be created, and the macro will be recorded in it.

Language Specifies which language the macro will be recorded in. Visual Basic is the default choice—choose MS Excel 4.0 Macro if you want to record a macro in the old XLM language.

▶ Recording Your Actions

As soon as you click OK on the Record New Macro dialog box, every action you take is recorded (including mistakes!). The word "Recording" is displayed on the status bar, and a Stop tool is displayed (see Figure 20.1).

FIGURE 20.1 ▶

Click the Stop tool to stop recording. The tool also serves as a visual reminder that you are recording a macro.

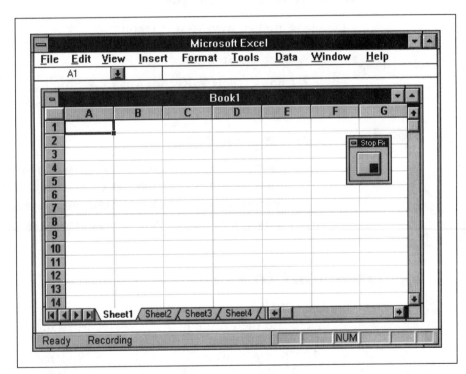

At this point, you simply perform the actions that you want to record. For example, you might open a workbook, create a chart, and then print the workbook.

▶ ▶ N O T E

The recorder tries not to record wasted actions. Suppose you select cell A2, then realize you made a mistake, and then immediately select B2. The selecting of cell A2 will not be recorded. Or, suppose you display the wrong dialog box. If you click Cancel, the action will not be recorded.

▶ *Stopping the Recorder*

There are two ways to stop recording:

- Click the Stop tool.
- Choose Tools ➤ Record Macro ➤ Stop Recording. (Or, if there is no active workbook, choose File ➤ Stop Recording.)

▶ ▶ W A R N I N G

Don't forget to stop recording when you've finished your macro. Many users forget to do this and unwittingly record a huge, useless macro. As the macro becomes larger and larger, your computer will start to slow down.

▶ *From Start to Finish*

The following exercise will walk you through the steps of recording a macro and then running the newly recorded macro:

1. Choose Tools ➤ Record Macro ➤ Record New Macro to display the Record New Macro dialog box. Enter a name for your macro.

2. Click Options, and assign **m** as the Ctrl key. Then choose to store the macro in a new workbook (so as not to pollute your personal workbook with this learning exercise). Click OK to start recording.

3. Perform the following actions:

   - Choose File ➤ New.

- Enter some data onto the new workbook.
- Apply some formatting.

4. Stop the recorder by choosing Tools ➤ Record Macro ➤ Stop Recording.

Before running the macro, close the workbook where you entered and formatted data (no need to save it). Then, press Ctrl+m to run the macro. Just like the first time, a new workbook is created, data is entered, and formatting is applied.

▶ ▶ **T I P**

It is wise to save your work, including the workbook containing the newly recorded macro, before running the macro. Until a macro is tested, consider it capable of unpredictable consequences.

Viewing the Macro

In the previous exercise, you recorded a macro into a new workbook. This means there is a new, unsaved workbook, named Book2 or Book3 (or Book whatever) in memory. Use the Window menu to locate the workbook—it will have a sheet in it named Module1. Click the Module1 tab to view the macro. Figure 20.2 shows a newly recorded macro named Enter_Then_Format.

Even if you don't understand macro syntax, you can usually distinguish some of your actions in the macro code. Observe the following:

- The description entered in the Record New Macro dialog box is placed on the module, above the macro. (Any line that starts with an apostrophe is a comment line, and has no effect on the macro.)

- As you might deduce, the statement **Range("B2").Select** selects cell B2.

- When you enter the cursor into a cell, an **ActiveCell.FormulaR1C1** command is recorded.

- Look at the command that enters a SUM formula—even though the workspace is set to A1 reference style, an R1C1 reference is recorded.

FIGURE 20.2 ▶

Macros (procedures) re-side in a special kind of sheet called modules.

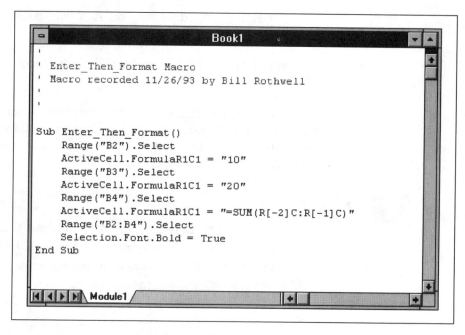

```
                              Book1

' Enter_Then_Format Macro
' Macro recorded 11/26/93 by Bill Rothwell
'
'

Sub Enter_Then_Format()
    Range("B2").Select
    ActiveCell.FormulaR1C1 = "10"
    Range("B3").Select
    ActiveCell.FormulaR1C1 = "20"
    Range("B4").Select
    ActiveCell.FormulaR1C1 = "=SUM(R[-2]C:R[-1]C)"
    Range("B2:B4").Select
    Selection.Font.Bold = True
End Sub

◄◄ ► ►► Module1
```

  ▶ ▶ T I P

Macros created with the recorder are not very efficient. Where the recorder creates two lines of code, one line will often do the job. For example, a handwritten macro can place a formula into a cell without selecting the cell first. Once you understand macro syntax, you can edit your recorded macros to make them more efficient.

▶ *What Can Go Wrong?*

The initial feeling of empowerment provided by the macro recorder can quickly vanish as you try to solve real-world problems. Here are four common ways you might get into trouble:

Ambiguous Intent Many actions you record can be interpreted in several ways. For example, assume cell B2 is the active cell, the macro recorder is on, and you select cell B3. Do you really mean B3? Or do you mean the top row of a database? Or did you mean to move down one row?

Things Happen Picture an automobile with a trip recorder. You want to automate the task of getting to work each day, so you get in the car, turn on the recorder, drive to work, then turn off the recorder. But everything goes wrong when the macro is played back the next morning. The problem stems from the fact that things are different when you play back the macro: a bike is in the driveway, the traffic light is red, and there is a traffic jam. Similarly, obstacles may arise unexpectedly when you play back your recorded macros.

Over-Recording Many recorded macros start out with a blank slate—unnecessarily. By using templates (covered in Chapter 10) you can simplify macro recording. Templates can be pre-formatted, and they can contain pre-defined names, styles, and formulas that make the job easier.

Inherent Limitations The macro recorder is pretty good at automating everyday tasks. But if you want to create serious applications, you will need to learn how to write macros yourself.

▶ *Recording in Relative or Absolute Reference Mode*

By default, the macro recorder records absolute cell references. Sometimes, you will want to record relative references. Use the Tools ➤ Record Macro ➤ Use Relative References command to switch to relative recording. (This command is a toggle—use the same command to switch back to absolute recording.) The following example illustrates the usefulness of this option.

Suppose you want to record a macro that adds the active cell and the number above the active cell. The macro will place a formula in the cell beneath the active cell (see Figure 20.3).

Create the worksheet in Figure 20.3, then record a macro the wrong way:

1. Select B3.

2. Start the recorder. (Make sure you are recording absolute references—the Tools ➤ Record Macro ➤ Use Relative References command should *not* have a checkmark.)

FIGURE 20.3 ▶

The macro needs to act relative to the active cell at the time the macro is run. If B3 is active, the formula should be placed in B4. If D3 is active, the formula should be placed in D4.

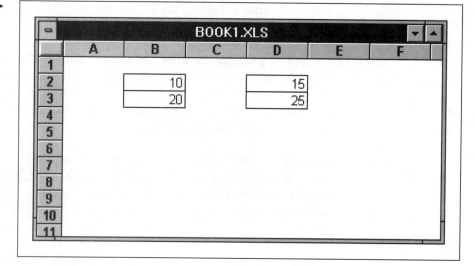

3. Select B4. Enter the formula **=B2+B3**.

4. Stop recording.

To see how it worked, clear B4. Then select D3 and run your new macro. Since you were in Absolute mode when the macro was recorded, the formula is placed in B4, not in D4. Regardless of which cell is active, the macro will always place the formula in B4.

Now, record the same macro again. This time switch to relative reference mode before you do step 3. After you are done recording, test the new macro:

- Clear B4 and D4.

- Select B3 and run the macro.

- Select D3 and run the macro.

Since you recorded the macro in relative mode, the macro enters formulas relative to the active cell.

> **TIP**
>
> **You can switch back and forth between absolute reference mode and relative reference mode at any time while recording a macro.**

- When you record in absolute reference mode, Excel records the absolute reference of every cell you select.

- When you record in relative reference mode, and you select one or more cells, Excel records the selection relative to the previously selected cell.

▶ *Recording Macros That Work As Intended*

As you use the macro recorder, you will discover that it often misinterprets your intent. Sometimes the only way to make it right is by manually editing the recorded macro. But there are some specific techniques you can use to cause the recorder to correctly interpret your actions.

Selecting Variable Size Ranges

Suppose that every month you are responsible for creating a report based on data that is output from a mainframe. (See Chapter 25 to learn more about importing data.) The mainframe outputs a text file in CSV format (comma separated values). The data needs to be copied into another workbook, which contains related information. Figure 20.4 shows the text file, opened in Excel.

The plan of action for recording the macro is:

1. Start recording.
2. Open the workbook where the source data needs to be copied (REPORT.XLS).
3. Open the text file—by default, A1 is the active cell.
4. Select the data, and copy it to the Clipboard.
5. Activate REPORT.XLS and select destination cell.
6. Paste.

Macro Basics

▶ ▶

Ch.

20

FIGURE 20.4 ▶

Sales data output as text file from mainframe. The number of rows varies from month to month.

	A	B	C	D	E	F
			DATA.CSV			
1	Product	Forecast	Actual			
2	Decals	1000	1178			
3	Handlebars	10000	10602			
4	Horns	2750	2619			
5	Packs	3500	3450			
6	Seats	8000	9900			
7	Wheels	20000	23250			
8						
9						
10						
11						
12						
13						

7. Print.

8. Stop recording.

There is one small, yet typical, problem that you must deal with: The number of rows in the text file is variable. It does no good to record the selection of A1:C7 as an absolute reference, because next month, the data may reside in A1:C10. Therefore, the task of selecting the data to be copied (step 4) presents a problem.

The solution is to use a command that selects the *current region*, rather then using the mouse to select A1:C7. At step 4, choose Edit ▶ Go To, then click Special, to display the Go To Special dialog box.

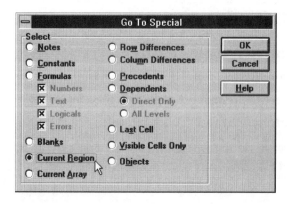

Choose Current Region, then click OK. Easier yet, click the Select Current Region tool. A1:C7 is selected, but the recorded macro is different than if you had selected A1:C7 with the mouse.

The following is the command that is recorded when you select an absolute range:

```
Range("A1:C7").Select
```

The following is the command that is recorded when you select Current Region:

```
Selection.CurrentRegion.Select
```

Formatting a Column of Numbers

Figure 20.5 is a slight variation of Figure 20.4. There is a column for units (an integer value), and dollars (currency).

The recorded macro must apply a currency format to the Dollars column. You can't select the current region, as in the previous problem, because you would mistakenly format the Units column. The solution is simple: Select the entire column C before applying the currency format. It doesn't matter that a number format will be applied to C1—the format has no effect on text.

Macro Basics

FIGURE 20.5 ▶

The recorded macro must apply a currency format to the values in the dollars column. The number of rows varies from month to month.

Ch.
20

	A	B	C	D	E
			DATA.CSV		
1	Product	Units	Dollars		
2	Decals	320	1178.55		
3	Handlebars	299	10602.2		
4	Horns	266	2619.75		
5	Packs	309	3450.03		
6	Seats	245	9900.8		
7	Wheels	504	23250.32		
8					
9					
10					
11					
12					
13					

Charting a Variable Number of Rows

Suppose that you want to record a macro that charts the data in Figure 20.4. Remember, the number of rows varies from month to month. Don't use the ChartWizard to create the chart—no matter how you go about it, recording the ChartWizard results in a macro that charts an absolute range. Here is a procedure that works:

1. Start recording.

2. Open the file.

3. Select the current region (using the Current Region tool, or the commands presented in previous group of steps).

4. Create the chart using one of these techniques:

   - Press F11 to create a chart sheet.
   - Use the default chart tool (not the Chart Wizard) to draw an embedded chart.

5. Stop recording.

Summing a Column with a Variable Number of Rows

Using the data in Figure 20.5, suppose that your recorded macro must add a total to the bottom of column C. This presents two problems:

- How do you select the cell at the bottom of column C? (Remember, the number of rows is variable.)

- How do you write the formula? Regardless of the reference mode, the AutoSum tool will record the wrong formula.

Follow these steps to record a macro that will work regardless of the number of rows:

1. Start recording.

2. Open the file.

3. Select C1.

4. Hold down the End key, then press the down arrow key (selects the last number in the column).

5. Switch to relative reference mode.

6. Press the down arrow (moving the active cell to C8).

7. Enter the formula **=SUM(OFFSET($C$1,1,0,ROW()-2))**.

8. Stop recording.

In English, the formula reads: Sum the range of cells beginning one cell beneath C1, and include the number of rows equal to the row number containing the formula, minus two (accounting for the header row). The OFFSET and ROW functions are among the most useful worksheet functions—they are both covered in Chapter 9.

BE AWARE OF THE ACTIVE CELL WHEN YOU START RECORDING

Suppose you want to record a macro to enter a formula into cell A5 which sums cells A1:A4. You enter your numbers into cells A1:A4, then select cell A5. You turn on the macro recorder, enter your sum formula, and stop recording. To test the macro you clear cell A5 and run the macro, and it works fine. Later you run the macro again—but this time cell D6 is the active cell. The macro enters the formula =SUM(D2:D5) into cell D6—not at all what you intended.

The problem is that your macro does not have a defined starting position. You have recorded a macro which sums the four cells above the active cell, wherever the active cell happens to be. Fixing the problem is simple—for the first step of the macro, you must record the selection of the cell where you want to enter the formula (in this example, cell A5). So, start the macro recorder, click on the cell where you want the macro to begin, then record the rest of the macro. If the starting cell is already selected when you begin recording, click on it anyway. You can also begin a macro by going to a named cell or range with Edit ➤ Go To or with the Name box, and the macro will record the selection by name.

Macro Basics

Ch.
20

►► *Running Macros*

There are several ways to run a macro. Earlier in this chapter, you learned how to assign a shortcut key to a recorded macro. In this section, you will learn how to run a macro...

- Using the Excel menu
- From a button
- From a tool
- From a custom menu
- When a workbook is opened or closed
- When a worksheet is activated or deactivated

► *Running a Macro Using Menu Commands*

Choose the Tools ➤ Macro command to display the Macro dialog box.

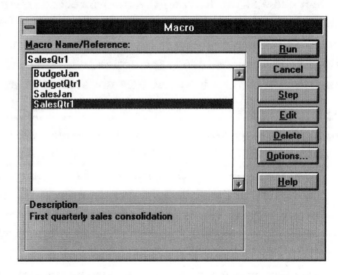

Macros that are contained on all currently open workbooks are displayed in the list. To run a macro, select it from the list and click Run.

The Macro dialog box provides several additional capabilities:

Step	Click this button to run the macro step-by-step. Stepping through a macro is useful for debugging purposes.
Edit	The module containing the macro is activated, and the macro is displayed for editing purposes.
Delete	Deletes the selected macro. (You can also delete macros by activating the module and clearing the macro.)
Options	Lets you add a command to Excel's Tools menu that runs the macro, and change the description of the macro.

▶ *Assigning a Macro to a Button*

You can assign a macro to a button (or any graphic object). When the button is clicked, the macro runs. Follow these steps to create a new button, and assign a macro to it:

1. Display the Forms toolbar.

2. Click the Button tool, then draw the button on the worksheet. (Drawing a button is just like drawing other objects—see Chapter 12 to learn about graphic objects and drawing tools.)

3. The Assign Macro dialog box is displayed.

Macro Basics

▶ ▶
Ch.
20

4. Select a macro from the list, and click OK.

If you want to record a new macro to assign to the button, click the Record button. Click Edit to display the module containing the macro.

Follow these steps to change the macro assignment of an existing button:

1. Hold down the Ctrl key, and click the button.
2. Choose Tools ➤ Assign Macro.

Follow these steps to assign a macro to any graphic object:

1. Select the object.
2. Choose Tools ➤ Assign Macro

Here are two important implications of assigning macros to buttons:

● If the macro is in a different workbook than the button, a link is established to the workbook containing the macro. (The workbook will display in the Edit ➤ Links dialog box.) If the workbook containing the macro is closed, and you click the button, the workbook containing the macro is opened automatically, and the macro runs.

● If you delete a button that is assigned to a macro, the macro is not deleted.

▶ *Assigning a Macro to a Tool*

When a macro is assigned to a button on a worksheet, it is only available when the worksheet containing the button is active. Macros assigned to button tools (on toolbars) are available whenever the toolbar is displayed.

Typically, you will assign macros to custom tools. But in fact, you can assign macros to any of Excel's built-in tools, which overrides the tool's built-in functionality. Follow these steps to assign a macro to any tool that already exists on a toolbar. (See Chapter 26 to learn how to customize toolbars.)

1. Display the toolbar containing the tool using the View ➤ Toolbars command.

2. Choose View ➤ Toolbars, then click Customize. (You will not actually use the Customize dialog box, but it must be displayed in order to customize tools or toolbars.)

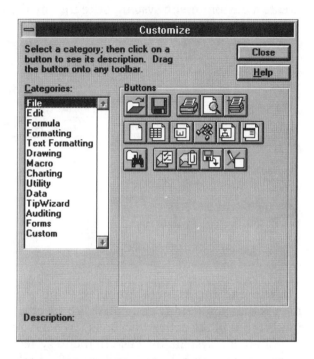

3. Click the tool that you want to assign a macro to. (Be sure to click the tool on the actual toolbar, not a tool inside the Customize dialog box.)

4. Choose Tools ➤ Assign Macro.

5. Select a macro from the list, and click OK.

6. Close the Customize dialog box.

Here are some general guidelines to decide whether to assign a macro to a button on a worksheet, or to a tool on a toolbar:

- Use buttons on worksheets when the macro is specific to the worksheet.

- Use tools (on toolbars) when the macro must be available globally.

▶ Creating a Custom Menu System

With a module active, choose the Tools ▶ Menu Editor command to create a custom menu system, or to modify the built-in menus.

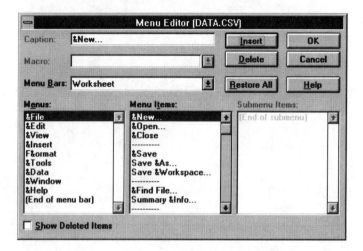

There is one important fact to understand about the menu editor: The menus that you modify and create are specific to the active workbook (and stored in the active workbook). When you open a workbook with a custom menu system, the custom menu system takes over. When you close the workbook, Excel's built-in menus take over and revert to their default state.

▶ Running Macros Automatically when a Workbook Is Opened or Closed

You can create special macros (procedures) that run automatically when a workbook is opened or closed. This is accomplished by placing macros in the workbook that are named using special reserved names:

Auto_Open   If there is a macro named Auto_Open in a workbook, it runs automatically when the workbook is opened.

Auto_Close   If there is a macro named Auto_Close in a workbook, it runs automatically *before* the workbook is closed.

Suppose that you want to suppress an Auto_Open or Auto_Close macro from running. How do you do it? Just hold down the Shift key while you open or close the workbook.

▶▶NOTE

> **Auto_Open and Auto_Close macros do *not* run when a workbook is opened or closed programmatically, though your macro can explicitly run them if desired.**

▶ Running Macros Automatically when a Worksheet Is Activated or Deactivated

Macros can be automatically triggered when a worksheet is activated or deactivated. These macros will run when you activate or deactivate a worksheet by using any of these methods:

- Click worksheet tabs
- Press Ctrl+Page Up or Ctrl+Page Down
- Change the active workbook

These activate and deactivate macros are defined using special names that are placed on the worksheet. To cause a macro named Create-Report to run when a sheet named *MySheet* is activated:

1. Activate the worksheet *MySheet*.
2. Choose Insert ➤ Name ➤ Define.
3. Enter the name: **MySheet!Auto_Activate**
4. Enter **refers to: =CreateReport**

▶TIP

> **If the macro is located in a different workbook, the book name must be included, using the syntax =BOOK1.XLS!ModuleName.MacroName.**

You can use the same steps to create a deactivate macro, except the name is defined as **MySheet!Auto_Deactivate**.

▶ *More Events That Can Run Macros*

Here are the other events in Excel that can cause a macro to run. (See the Visual Basic User's Guide to learn how to implement these event-handling facilities.)

OnTime Method Causes a macro to run at a specified time.

OnWindow Property Runs a macro when a specified window is activated.

OnKey Method Runs a macro when a specified key is pressed.

OnCalculate Property Runs a macro when a worksheet recalculation occurs.

OnEntry Property Runs a macro when an entry occurs into a worksheet cell.

OnData Property Runs a macro when data is received from another application via dynamic data exchange (DDE).

OnRepeat Method Runs a macro when user chooses Edit ➤ Repeat (or clicks Repeat tool).

OnUndo Method Runs a macro when user chooses Edit ➤ Undo (or clicks Undo tool).

▶▶ *User-Defined Functions*

Excel includes hundreds of built-in functions, such as SUM, PRODUCT, and INDEX. You can write your own functions using VBA, and use them on a worksheet in much the same way that you refer to built-in functions like SUM.

N O T E

Previous versions of Excel have referred to user-defined functions as *function macros*.

All user-defined functions have two common characteristics:

- They accept one or more arguments.
- They return a result.

Don't let the terminology confuse you—this is no different than a built-in function. For instance, SUM takes an argument (a range of cells), and returns a result (the sum of the range). The only difference is that you get to define the arguments and the calculation that produces the result.

Consider the worksheet pictured in Figure 20.6. On this example invoice, Column E requires a formula that multiplies column C by column D, then adds a 7% sales tax.

FIGURE 20.6 ▶

A user-defined function can be used to calculate the extension, plus sales tax.

	A	B	C	D	E	F
1						
2				Unit	Extension	
3		Item	Qty	Price	(Plus Tax)	
4		Gadgets	5	20.00		
5		Gizmos	10	6.00		
6		Things	3	100.00		
7		Widgets	7	8.50		
8						
9						
10						
11						
12						
13						
14						

BOOK1.XLS

Macro Basics

Ch.
20

> ✎ ▶ ▶**N O T E**
>
> **This problem does not require a user-defined function—
> it can be solved with a relatively simple worksheet
> formula. Therein lies the paradox of user-defined
> functions: the ones that are easy to write are usually
> not needed!**

The following exercise will walk you through all of the steps to create, and apply, a user-defined function.

1. In a new workbook, enter the data in Figure 20.6.

2. Insert a VBA module by choosing the Insert ➤ Macro ➤ Module command. A new module is inserted (see Figure 20.7).

3. Enter the following three lines in the module:

As you can see, there are three parts of a user-defined function:

- The first line defines the name of the function, and the arguments it will receive. The above function is named *Extension*, and it receives two arguments: *Qty* and *Price*. Arguments are separated by commas.

- The last line of the function is a terminator. All functions must end with End Function.

- In the middle, the actual calculation occurs. In this simple example, the calculation only requires one line of code. But there is virtually no limit to the length of the function. Notice the use of the three variables: the function name and the two arguments. The variable name *Extension* calculates the final result.

FIGURE 20.7 ▶

A new VBA module is inserted in the workbook, and the Visual Basic toolbar is automatically displayed.

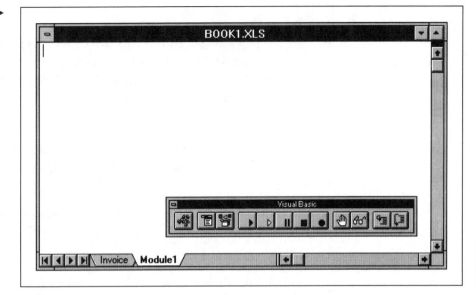

Next, the function is entered on the worksheet in the same way you enter a built-in function:

1. Activate the Invoice worksheet.

2. Enter the formula **=Extension(C4,D4)** into E4. (Notice the sequence of the two arguments corresponds to the first line of the function on the module.)

3. Copy E4 to E5:E7.

▶▶ *The Personal Macro Workbook*

When you read about recording macros, earlier in this chapter, you learned how to record macros into a *personal macro workbook* named PERSONAL.XLS. When you first install Excel, the personal macro workbook does not exist. PERSONAL.XLS is created the first time you record a macro into it. It is stored in the XLSTART directory (located in the directory where you installed Excel).

▶ ▶ **T I P**

All workbooks in the XLSTART directory are automatically opened each time you start Excel. You can also place templates in XLSTART, which is covered in Chapter 10.

PERSONAL.XLS is a good place to store macros that are used on an everyday basis. Here are some important things you should know about it:

- It is automatically opened each time you start Excel, and it is hidden.
- You can manually edit PERSONAL.XLS. Use the Window ➤ Unhide command to view it.
- Since it is opened every time you start Excel, you may want to avoid placing large macros on it that are not used regularly.

Turn to Chapter 21 to see how to create a custom application from start to finish.

Custom Application— Start to Finish

▶▶ F_{AST} T_{RACK}

▶▶ **T**his chapter will walk you through all the steps to create a powerful custom application—a *decision support system* (DSS) used to analyze the performance of a fictitious company that sells bicycle parts. Skills that you have learned throughout the book will be utilized, and several new techniques will be introduced along the way. The application will include:

- *Powerful worksheet functions like INDEX, OFFSET, and COUNTA*
- *Pivot tables*
- *Recorded macros (you do not need to understand macros to create this application, though you should be familiar with the macro recorder)*
- *Controls (list boxes and option buttons)*
- *Criteria ranges and the DSUM function*
- *Advanced naming techniques*

▶ The Business Requirement

The management of *Western BikeStuff* needs to track actual sales performance against their forecast.

- The company carries four product lines: helmets, handlebars, seats, and racks. More may be added in the future, so the application must be insensitive to the number of product lines.

- Products are sold in two markets: USA and Europe. Even if new markets are added in the future, management will combine all foreign markets into one for analysis purposes.

- Sales and forecast data is tracked per market, per product, per month.

- As is typical of decision support systems, the program is read-only. It analyzes existing data.

- The program must start off by displaying a high-level summary, and then allow the users to "drill down" to a greater level of detail.

▶▶ *Getting Started*

Create a directory to house the application. It doesn't matter where the directory is located. Then create a new workbook, and save it in the application directory—name it DSS.XLS.

To start with, DSS.XLS will contain six worksheets. (More will be created later.) Name the worksheets: **Home, Trend, Breakdown, Data, Settings**, and **Products** (see Figure 21.1).

▶ ▶**N O T E**

The instructions in this chapter do not instruct you to save your work. Needless to say, however, you should save the workbook periodically.

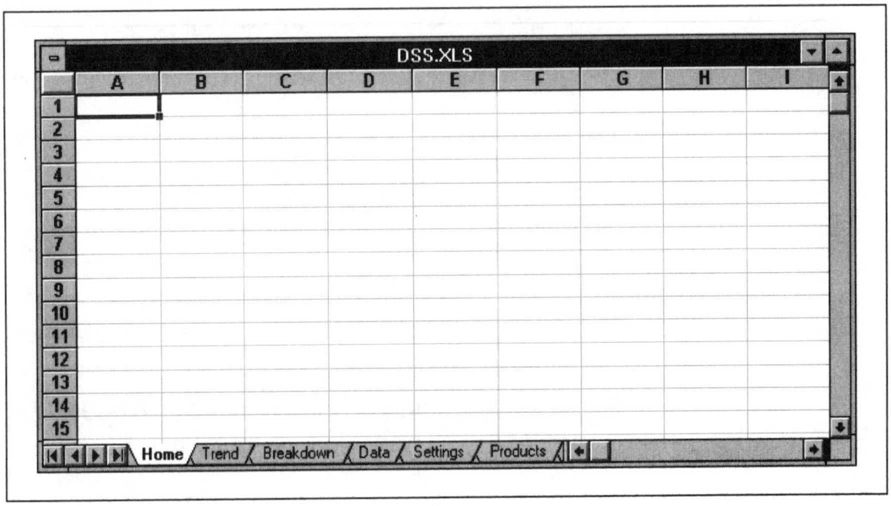

FIGURE 21.1 ▶

To rename a work-sheet, choose Format ▶ Sheet ▶ Rename (or click the tab with the right mouse button, and choose Rename from the shortcut menu).

Custom Application

▶ ▶
Ch.
21

▶▶ *Building the Database*

The database driving the application is 96 rows by 6 columns. Fortunately, there are some shortcuts that will make it easy to enter this data:

1. On worksheet Data, enter the following information:

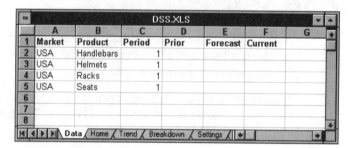

2. Copy range A2:C5, and paste at the bottom of the data (A6). Then change the number in C6:C9 to a **2** (for period 2).

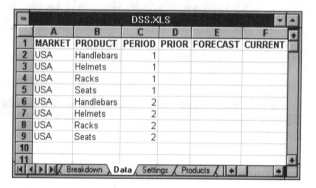

3. Repeat step 2 ten more times, for periods 3 through 12. (When this step is complete, the data will extend to row 49.)

4. Copy range A2:C49, and paste starting at A50. Then change A50:A96 to **Europe**.

5. Select D2:F96 and enter: **=INT(RAND()*10000)** Enter the formula into the selected range by pressing Ctrl+Enter.

NOTE

The formula places random numbers into the range, which will probably create some illogical data. You can edit the data later if desired.

6. With D2:F96 still selected, choose Edit ➤ Copy, then Edit ➤ Paste Special. Choose *Values*. (This replaces the formulas with the underlying values, so that the random numbers don't constantly recalculate.)

➤ Name the Range Using a Named Formula That Counts the Rows

The database range will be named to facilitate some of the formulas that will be used later on. At the end of this exercise, the data will be saved as a dBASE file, and a query will be performed to retrieve the data onto the worksheet. In the real world, you won't know how many rows are contained in the database. Accordingly, the database range will be named using a formula that dynamically calculates the number of rows.

With worksheet Data active, choose Insert ➤ Name ➤ Define. Create a name **Database** that refers to:

=OFFSET(Data!$A$1,0,0,COUNTA(OFFSET(Data!$A$1,0,0,9999)),6)

TIP

The name Database will automatically expand or contract based on the number of values in column A. Since a named formula is not a "real" named range, it will not display in the name box. However, press F5 and type Database—the range will be selected. (Named formulas are covered in Chapter 8.)

▶ *Name the Product List*

There are several places in the application where the user will select from a list of products. In two cases, pivot tables will do the work for you. But there is one instance where the list must reside in a range of cells. Activate the Products sheet, and enter the information shown below:

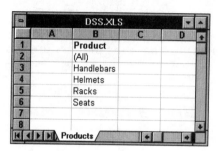

Remember, the application is supposed to be insensitive to the number of products. (Later, you will learn how to create this list by performing a query.) So the named range must use the same technique as was used for the Database range. In addition, two different names will be created—one that includes *(All)* and one that does not (in case there is a need to display both lists).

Activate worksheet Products, then follow these steps:

1. Define the name **Products.Plus.All** referring to:

=OFFSET($B$1,1,0,COUNTA(OFFSET($B$1,1,0,999,1))

This name counts the number of products, allowing for a maximum of 999.

2. Define the name **Product.List** referring to:

=OFFSET(Products.Plus.All,1,0,ROWS(Products.Plus.All)-1)

This name uses Products.Plus.All, less the first row.

To test the names, press F5 to display the Go To dialog box, then type the name into the reference box.

▶▶ *Setting Up the Globals*

Most applications include various settings and calculations that are used by worksheets throughout the application. You can save a lot of time by defining such settings one time only—on a worksheet whose sole purpose is to store *global* settings. The BikeStuff DSS application, as designed, has only one such setting. Still, it is worthwhile to set up the globals worksheet as a learning exercise.

In this application, the sheet named *Settings* is being used to store globals. Activate Settings, and follow these steps:

1. Name cell C2 **Current.Year**.
2. Enter the formula **=YEAR(NOW())** into C2 to calculate the current year.

▶▶ *Building the Home Worksheet*

The worksheet named Home will be the first sheet displayed when the application is started. (The finished sheet is displayed in Figure 21.2.) It provides a very high-level summary, from which the user can "drill down" into a greater level of detail.

▶ *Place the Supporting Data on a Separate Worksheet*

In order to create the chart, several calculations have to be performed first. The user doesn't have to see these interim calculations, so they will be placed on a separate sheet that will eventually be hidden from view. Insert a new worksheet, and name it **Home_Hide**. This name will serve as a reminder that the sheet contains calculations supporting the Home sheet, and that it needs to be hidden later.

FIGURE 21.2 ▶

Completed Home worksheet

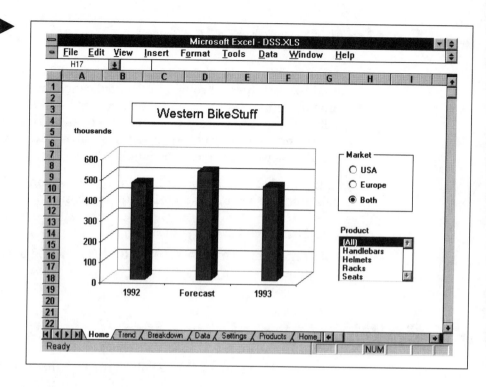

Activate Home_Hide and follow these steps:

1. Name C2 **Market.Choice** and name cell C3 **Product.Choice**. (The controls on Home will be linked to these cells.) The quickest way to name these cells is by placing labels in B2 and B3 (see Figure 21.3), then use Insert ▶ Name ▶ Create see Chapter 8 to review creating names.)

2. Build the criteria range by entering the following onto Home_Hide:

Cell	Entry
B7	**Market**
C7	**Product**
B8	**=CHOOSE(Market.Choice,"USA", "Europe","")**
C8	**=IF(Product.Choice=1,"",INDEX (Product.List,Product.Choice-1))**

FIGURE 21.3 ▶

Completed Home_Hide worksheet

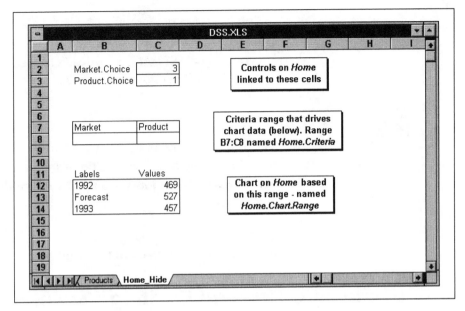

▶ ▶ **T I P**

> **This is a criteria range that uses formulas which, based on user input, calculate the second row of the criteria range—this type of criteria range is sometimes called a *computed criteria*. See Chapter 16 to learn about computed criteria.**

3. Name B7:C8 **Home.Criteria**

4. Build the range of data that the final chart is based on—add the following to Home_Hide:

Cell	Entry
B12	=Current.Year-1
C12	=DSUM(Database,"Prior",Home.Criteria)/1000
B13	Forecast
C13	=DSUM(Database,"Forecast", Home.Criteria)/1000

Custom Application

▶ ▶

Ch.
21

Cell	Entry
B14	=Current.Year
C14	=DSUM(Database,"Current", Home.Criteria)/1000

▶ ▶ **T I P**

The DSUM formulas divide by 1000 because the chart is based on thousands—this is done for aesthetic purposes. See Chapter 16 to learn about DSUM, and other D functions.

5. Name B12:C14 **Home.Chart.Range**

▶ *Adding a Title and Creating the Chart*

Now that the supporting data is ready, the chart on the Home sheet can be built. Activate Home, and follow these steps:

1. Draw a text box, and enter the company name. The text box pictured in Figure 21.2 has a border and a shadow.

▶ ▶ **T I P**

A text box gives you control of text position—when text is placed in cells, you have to fight the worksheet grid when designing the sheet. See Chapter 12 to learn about text boxes, and other graphic objects.

2. Click the ChartWizard tool, and draw the chart border on the worksheet. (Chapter 13 covers the ChartWizard.)

3. At Step 1, specify range as **=Home.Chart.Range**.

4. At Step 2, choose 3-D column chart.

5. At Step 3, choose format #4.

6. At Step 4, set Data Series In to Columns, and Use First Column(s) to 1.

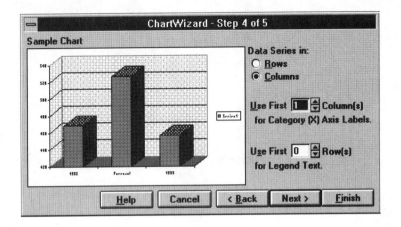

7. At Step 5, set Add a Legend to No.

At this point your chart won't have data in it. Next, you'll create worksheet controls which will point the chart toward the data you choose. Figure 21.2 shows the finished chart. Some extra formatting has been performed, so it will not look identical to the chart that you create.

▶ *Adding Controls*

Worksheet controls will let the user specify what data to chart. (See Chapter 19 to learn about controls.) With the Home sheet active, follow these steps:

1. Display the Forms toolbar (View ➤ Toolbars).

2. Draw a group box, and place three option buttons inside it. Change the text on the group box and option buttons as shown in Figure 21.2.

3. Right-click the first option button, choose Format Object, and link it to cell Market.Choice.

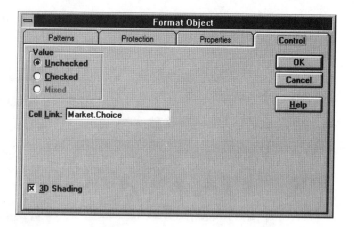

▶ ▶ T I P

The other two option buttons inside the group box are automatically linked to cell Market.Choice.

4. Draw a list box. With the list box still selected, choose Format ➤ Object. Specify an input range **Products.Plus.All**. Specify cell link **Product.Choice**.

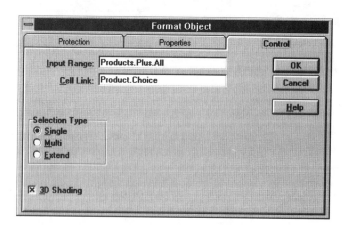

Test the controls. As you click different options, the chart should change. If not, verify the settings for the controls, and verify the entries on Home_Hide.

TIP

To see the model work, be sure all controls have been created and linked, *and* that selections have been made in the controls.

▶▶ *Comparing the Current Year to the Prior Year*

The Home sheet displays a high-level summary. Now, you will build the Trend worksheet, which compares current-year sales to prior-year sales using a line chart. (The finished Trend sheet is pictured in Figure 21.6.) A pivot table will be used to organize the data for charting. (See Chapter 17 to learn about pivot tables.)

▶ *Creating the Pivot Table*

Activate Trend, then follow these steps:

1. Choose Data ➤ Pivot Table to start the PivotTable Wizard.

2. At Step 1 of the Wizard, choose Microsoft Excel List or Database.

3. At Step 2, enter **Database** for the range. (Since the name Database is already defined in the workbook, Step 2 should default to Database.)

4. At Step 3, drag the field buttons to the locations shown in Figure 21.4.

5. The text labels Sum of Prior and Sum of Current are not very friendly. Still at Step 3, double-click these field buttons, and change the names (text) to **Last Year** and **This Year** respectively.

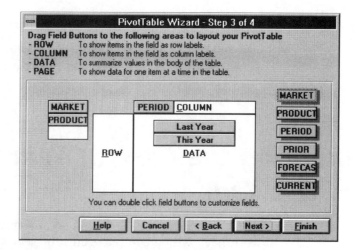

6. At Step 4, change the starting cell to **=$B$2** (to leave some space above the table, for aesthetic purposes). Only the setting Save Data With Table Layout should be checked. See Figure 21.5. Click Finish.

▶ Creating the Chart

The pivot table has organized the data exactly the way the soon-to-be-created line chart requires. But there are still a couple of problems:

● If the user moves the Data or Period buttons (see Figure 21.5), the pivot table layout changes, in which case the chart changes as well.

FIGURE 21.4 ▶

A pivot table can have multiple page fields, and multiple data fields.

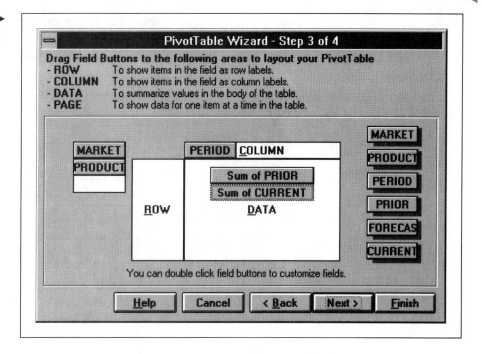

FIGURE 21.5 ▶

The finished pivot table. Don't worry about the appearance—the chart is going to obscure most of the pivot table.

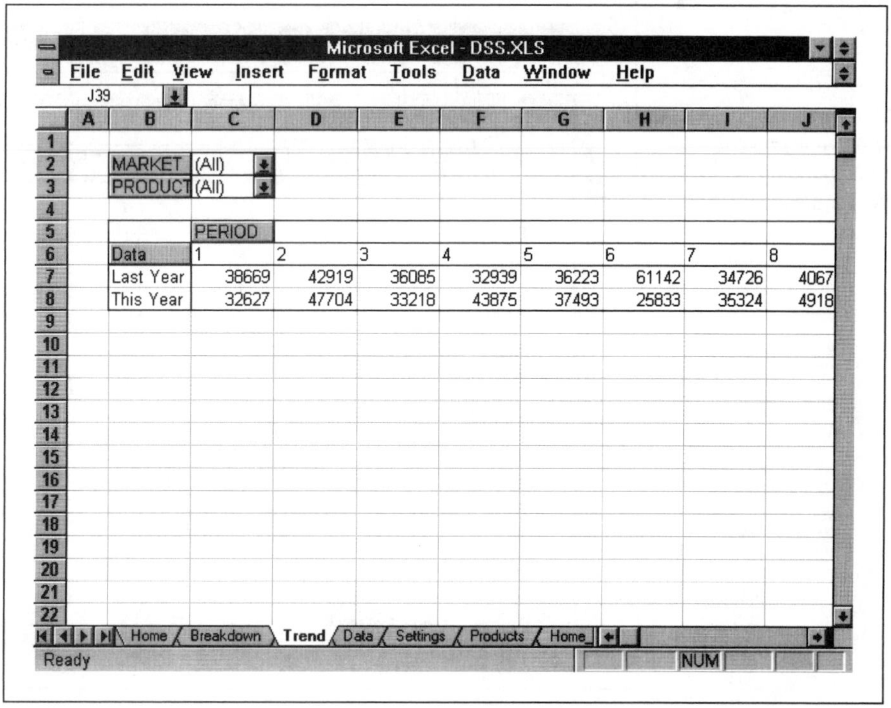

Custom
Application

Ch.
21

Sometimes this is desirable. But in this case, the application dictates that chart layout not change. To discourage the user from changing the pivot table layout, the chart will be placed on top of the pivot table.

- The chart won't be large enough to cover all 13 columns of the pivot table.

Follow these steps to create the chart:

1. Set the width of columns D through N to **1**. The pivot table will then be small enough to be covered by the chart.

2. Use the ChartWizard to draw a line chart.

   - Select the cell range **B6:N8.**
   - Click on the ChartWizard, then draw a chart which covers the data area of the pivot table.
   - Leave the Market and Product page buttons showing, so the user can change the data being charted (See Figure 21.6).

FIGURE 21.6 ▶

Completed Trend sheet. The user is discouraged (though not completely prevented) from changing the pivot table layout.

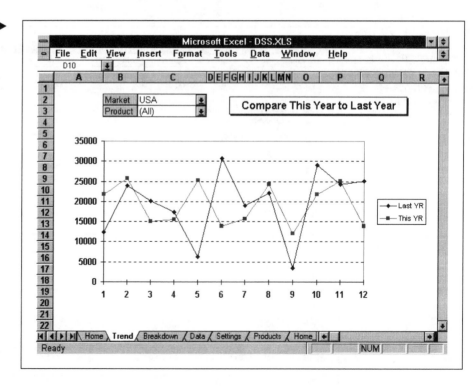

Change the market and product using the two drop-down lists, and watch the chart change.

▶▶ *Creating the Product Breakdown*

The Breakdown worksheet will use a pie chart to show how the products have performed within each market, or for both markets combined. (The finished worksheet is shown in Figure 21.9) As with the Trend sheet, a pivot table will organize the data for the chart.

▶ *Creating the Pivot Table*

Activate Breakdown, and follow these steps:

1. Choose Data ➤ PivotTable.

2. At Step 1 of the Wizard, choose Microsoft Excel List or Database.

3. At Step 2, enter **Database** for the range. (Since the name Database is already defined in the workbook, Step 2 should default to Database.)

4. At Step 3, drag the field buttons to the locations shown in Figure 21.7.

5. At Step 4, change the starting cell to **=$B$2** (to leave some space above the table, for aesthetic purposes). Only the setting Save Data With Table Layout should be checked. Figure 21.8 shows the finished pivot table.

▶ *What if Products Are Added?*

Since the application must be insensitive to the number of products, the chart will be based on names that dynamically expand and contract, rather than on the absolute reference $B$6:$C$9. With Breakdown active, define the following two names:

1. Define the name **Pie.Labels** referring to:

   =OFFSET($B$5,1,0,COUNTA(OFFSET($B$5,1,0,999,1)))

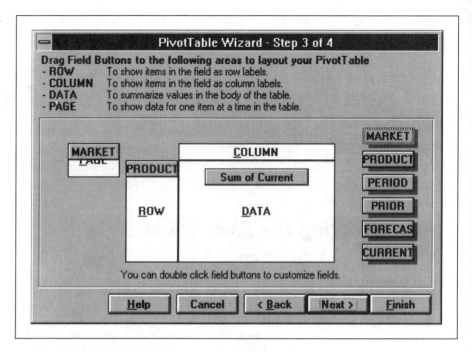

FIGURE 21.8 ►

This pivot table will be used to create a pie chart.

2. Define the name **Pie.Data** referring to:

=OFFSET($C$5,1,0,COUNTA(OFFSET($C$5,1,0,999,1)))

Test the names: Press F5 and enter the names—Pie.Labels should select B6:B9, and Pie.Data should select C6:C9.

▶ *Creating the Pie Chart*

With Breakdown still active, follow these steps to create the pie chart:

1. Select B6:C9, then draw the chart using the ChartWizard tool— do not override the range at Step 1 of the wizard.

2. At Step 2 of the wizard, choose 3-D Pie.

3. At Step 3, choose format #7.

4. At Step 4, choose Data Series in Columns, and Use First 1 Column.

5. At Step 5 of the wizard, enter a chart title. (The text doesn't matter, because it will be replaced with a formula later.)

6. Size the chart to cover the data region of the pivot table, but leave the market drop-down showing. (The finished chart shown in Figure 21.9 has been formatted, and won't look identical to the one you created.)

Now, the chart needs to be modified to use the two named formulas:

7. Double-click the chart object to activate it. Then, single-click any pie wedge. The entire data series (S1) will be selected.

8. Carefully change the formula (in the formula bar) to read:

=SERIES(,Breakdown!Pie.Labels,Breakdown!Pie.Data,1)

9. Change the chart title to refer to the drop-down selection at cell $C$2: Single-click the title, and enter the following formula on the formula bar:

=Breakdown!$C$2

Deselect the chart, and test it: place some text in B10, and a number in C10—the pie should automatically add a fifth wedge. Use the market drop-down to change the pivot table—the chart title should change accordingly. (Remember to clear B10:C10 when done testing.)

Custom Application

▶ ▶
Ch.
21

FIGURE 21.9 ▶

The finished Break-down sheet

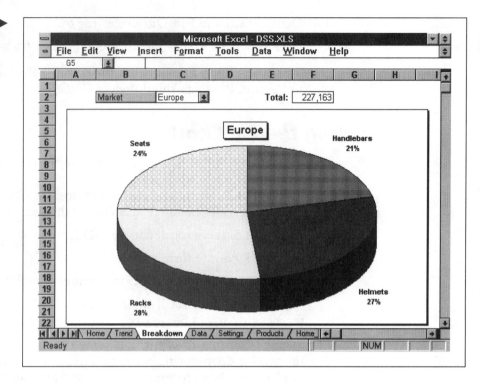

How Big Is the Pie?

The pie chart (see Figure 21.9) shows the percentage of each product's contribution to the whole pie. But how big is the pie? Add the following to the Breakdown sheet to let the user know how big the pie is:

Cell	Entry
E2	**Total:**
F2	**=SUM(Pie.Data)**

 ▶ ▶ **N O T E**

> **One of the original assumptions was insensitivity to the number of products. However, pie charts have an inherent limitation: When there are too many wedges, the pie loses its impact.**

▶▶ *Moving the Data to an External Database*

The data that resides on the Data worksheet will now be moved to an external database—a dBASE file. The application will be set up to query the database each time it is started, so that it is always working with current data. Before you can proceed with this step, there are two requirements:

- Microsoft Query must be installed on your system. (Chapter 18 explains how to determine if this is the case.)

- The Excel query add-in, which provides the interface between Excel and Microsoft Query, must be installed on your system. (The file XLQUERY.XLA must be on your system, loaded under your Excel directory in LIBRARY\MSQUERY, though not necessarily configured to load automatically with Tools ➤ Add-Ins.)

These components can be installed using the Excel setup program.

 ▶ ▶**N O T E**

> **If your system is not set up properly, or if you do not want to store the data in an external database, skip ahead to the section "Recording the Startup Macro."**

▶ *Saving the Data in dBASE Format*

Follow these steps to save the database as a dBASE file. (See Chapter 25 for more information on this topic.)

1. Activate the worksheet named Data.

2. Arrange the workspace so that you can see the Excel desktop, as pictured in Figure 21.10.

3. Hold down the Ctrl key, then drag the Data worksheet tab onto the Excel desktop—a new workbook is created with a copy of the Data sheet.

FIGURE 21.10 ▶

If the workbook is maximized, click the Document Restore button or choose Window ➤ Arrange in order to see the Excel desktop.

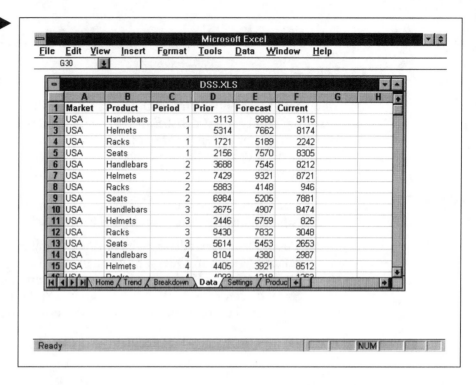

4. Choose File ➤ Save As. Select dBASE IV file type, and name the file **BIKES.DBF**.

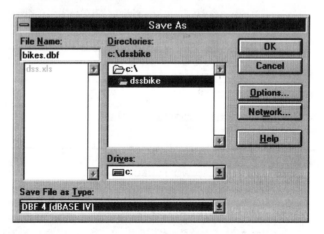

5. Close the file. (Answer *No* when asked again if you want to save the file.)

► Defining the Query

In this section, the query will be defined that retrieves the data from the dBASE file and places it onto the Data worksheet. (See Chapter 18 to learn more about this topic.)

Starting Microsoft Query

Follow these steps to start Microsoft Query:

1. Make sure the query add-in is loaded. (If it is loaded, there will be a command called Get External Data on the Data menu.) If not loaded, open the file MSQUERY.XLA located under your Excel directory, under LIBRARY\MSQUERY.

2. Select cell A1 on the Data worksheet.

3. Choose Data ➤ Get External Data—Microsoft Query is started.

Defining an ODBC Data Source

Follow these steps to define an ODBC data source for BIKES.DBF:

1. At the Select Data Source dialog box, click Other.

2. At the ODBC Data Sources dialog box, click New.

3. At the Add Data Source dialog box, select dBASE Files, and click OK.

4. At the ODBC dBASE Setup dialog box, enter data source named BikeStuff, and any description you want.

5. Click Select Directory. The directory should be set to the application directory, and BIKES.DBF should display in the list of files. (If not, use this dialog box in the same way you use a File ➤ Open dialog box to navigate to the application directory.) Click OK.

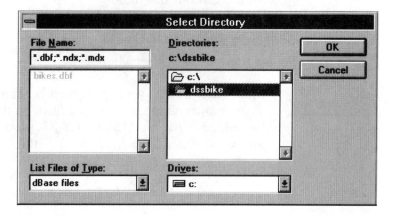

6. The ODBC dBASE Setup dialog box will display the name of the application directory. Click OK.

7. At the ODBC Data Sources dialog box, select BikeStuff from the list, then click OK.

8. At the Select Data Source dialog box, select BikeStuff, and click Use.

▸▸ **T I P**

There is one good piece of news about this tedious procedure: it only needs to be performed once for a given data source. Any application that uses ODBC can then utilize the same ODBC data source.

Completing the Query Definition

Follow these steps to complete the query definition in Microsoft Query, and then place the results onto the Data worksheet:

1. At the Add Tables dialog box, select BIKES.DBF, and click Add. Then click Close.

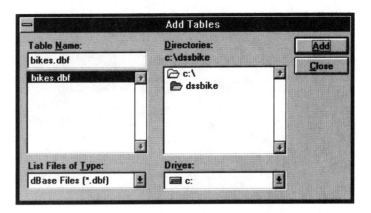

2. In the Bikes table, at the top of the query window (see Figure 21.11), double-click the asterisk to add all of the fields to the query.

3. Choose File ➤ Return Data to Microsoft Excel. Control is transferred back to Excel.

4. At the Get External Data dialog box, check Keep Query Definition and Include Field Names. Then click OK.

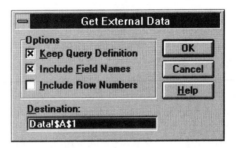

 ▶ ▶ **N O T E**

Since the sales data was already on the Data sheet, you may wonder why all this work, and with no visible change as a result: The query definition is now stored on the worksheet, hidden, and the data can be painlessly refreshed.

FIGURE 21.11 ▶

Double-click the asterisk as a shortcut to add all of the fields to the query.

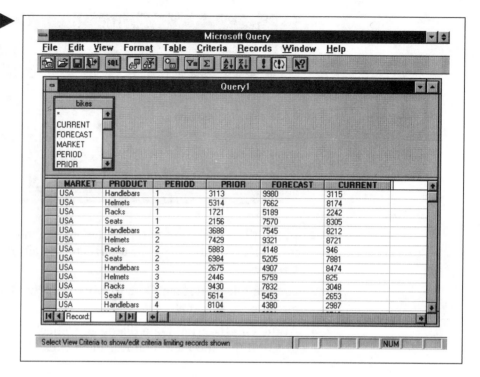

To test the query, clear several cells inside the database on the Data worksheet. Then choose Data ➤ Refresh Data. The data will be retrieved from the dBASE file, and the cells that you cleared should contain data.

Querying the List of Products

The list on the Products worksheet needs to be refreshed each time the application is run. In the real world, it is likely that there would be a product master file. Without a master file, the list can still be derived from BIKES.DBF. The inclusion of *(All)* at the top of the list introduces a wrinkle.

Activate the Products worksheet, and follow these steps to define the query:

1. Select cell B3, then choose Data ➤ Get External Data.

2. At the Select Data Source dialog box, pick BikeStuff, then click Use.

3. At the Add Tables dialog box, pick BIKES.DBF, then click Add. Then click Close.

4. In the Bikes table, at the top of the query window (see Figure 21.11), double-click the Product field to add it to the query.

5. Choose View ➤ Query Properties, and check Unique Values Only, then click OK.

6. Choose Records ➤ Sort. Pick Ascending, then click Add.

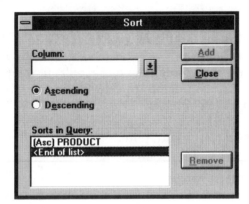

 ▶ ▶ **N O T E**

Even though the products may be sorted correctly, there is no guarantee that they will remain sorted as the database changes.

7. Choose File ➤ Return Data To Microsoft Excel. Control is transferred back to Excel.

8. At the Get External Data dialog box, check only the Keep Query Definition setting, then click OK.

Custom
Application

▶ ▶
Ch.
21

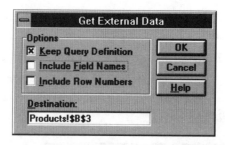

 ▶ ▶**W A R N I N G**

> **It is critical that you do not check Include Field Names. Otherwise, the word "Product" will be included in the product list.**

▶▶ *Recording the Startup Macro*

Next, you will record a macro that will automatically be run every time the application is started (by opening the workbook). The macro will perform two major tasks:

- Pivot tables do not refresh automatically. The macro must make sure these tables contain current data.

- In the real-world scenario, the source database (BIKES.DBF) is constantly changing. The macro needs to refresh the database on worksheet Data by querying BIKES.DBF.

 ▶ ▶**N O T E**

> **Querying the dBASE file requires the use of the query add-in, MSQUERY.XLA. Excel can be configured to automatically open the add-in using Tools ➤ Add-Ins (covered in Chapter 24). However, if the application is being deployed to other desktops in your organization, you may not want to make the assumption that these desktops are properly configured. (This topic is discussed later in this chapter.)**

▶ *Starting the Recorder*

Recording a complex macro requires advance planning. All of your actions—including mistakes—are recorded. (See Chapter 20 to learn about recording macros.) Create a plan, and perform each step carefully. Before you begin recording:

- Make sure the query add-in is loaded (unless you chose not to save the data in a dBASE file).

- Activate the Home worksheet.

Follow these steps to start the recording process:

1. Choose Tools ➤ Record Macro ➤ Record New Macro.

2. Enter the macro name **Auto_Open,** then click Options. The macro must be stored in This Workbook.

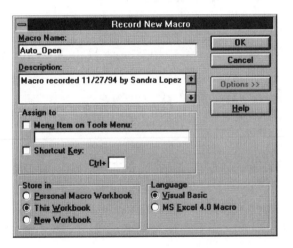

3. Click OK—you are now recording.

4. Make sure the Tools ➤ Record Macro ➤ Use Relative References command is *not* checked.

Custom Application

▶ ▶

Ch.
21

► ►**TIP**

> **The name Auto_Open is a special keyword. When the workbook is opened, the Auto_Open macro is automatically run.**

► *Refreshing the Data*

Follow these steps to refresh the database. (Skip this section if you chose not to store the data in a dBASE file.)

1. Click the Data worksheet tab.
2. Select cell A1, then choose Data ➤ Refresh Data.

That takes care of the database stored on worksheet Data. But now, the product list must be refreshed:

3. Click the Products worksheet tab.
4. Select cell B3, then choose Data ➤ Refresh Data.

► *Refreshing the Pivot Tables*

Follow these steps to refresh the two pivot tables:

1. Click the Trend worksheet tab.
2. Select cell C2, then choose Data ➤ Refresh Data.
3. Click the Breakdown worksheet tab.
4. Select cell C2, then choose Data ➤ Refresh Data.

► *Finishing Up*

There's only one more step to record: Click the Home worksheet tab. Then choose Tools ➤ Record Macro ➤ Stop Recording. The new macro resides on a VBA module that was inserted into the workbook by the macro recorder. It is shown in Figure 21.12.

You can test the macro by choosing the Tools ➤ Macro command, picking Auto_Open from the list, and clicking Run.

FIGURE 21.12 ▶

Even if you are unfamiliar with VBA syntax, you can still recognize the recorded actions.

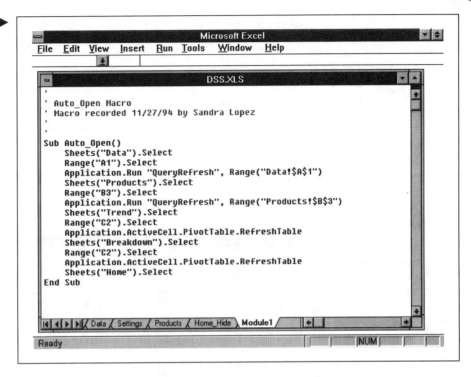

```
Microsoft Excel
File   Edit   View   Insert   Run   Tools   Window   Help

                    DSS.XLS
'
' Auto_Open Macro
' Macro recorded 11/27/94 by Sandra Lopez
'
'
Sub Auto_Open()
    Sheets("Data").Select
    Range("A1").Select
    Application.Run "QueryRefresh", Range("Data!$A$1")
    Sheets("Products").Select
    Range("B3").Select
    Application.Run "QueryRefresh", Range("Products!$B$3")
    Sheets("Trend").Select
    Range("C2").Select
    Application.ActiveCell.PivotTable.RefreshTable
    Sheets("Breakdown").Select
    Range("C2").Select
    Application.ActiveCell.PivotTable.RefreshTable
    Sheets("Home").Select
End Sub

Data / Settings / Products / Home_Hide \ Module1 /
Ready                                           NUM
```

▶▶ *Putting on the Finishing Touches*

There are a few more steps required to complete the application.

1. Hide the worksheets that are not supposed to be seen by the users of the application (Home_Hide, Data, Settings, Products, and Module 1). Select each sheet, and choose Format ➤ Sheet ➤ Hide.

▶ ▶ **T I P**

> **By grouping the sheets, they can be hidden with one command. (See Chapter 2.)**

2. Remove gridlines and remove row and column headings (on all the visible sheets) by using Tools ➤ Options, then selecting the View tab (see Figure 21.13).

Custom
Application

▶▶
Ch.
21

You can also remove the horizontal and vertical scrollbars, since the information on each sheet fits in the window.

▶ ▶ **N O T E**

The scrollbar settings are not specific to a given worksheet. They apply to the entire workbook.

3. Activate Home, and save the workbook.

FIGURE 21.13 ▶

Choose Tools ➤ Options, and select the View tab, to remove gridlines, row and column headings, and scrollbars.

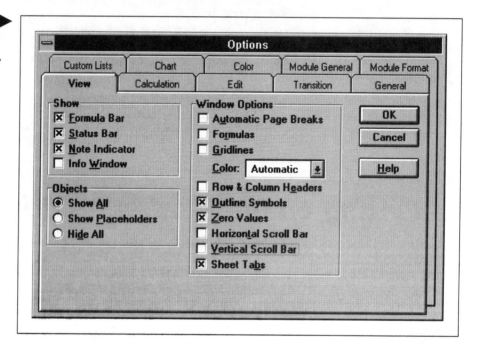

▶▶ *Comments and Caveats*

Here are some comments about the application, some ideas on how to improve it, and some thoughts about application development in general.

▶ *Suppressing Screen Updates While Macros Run*

When you open the workbook, the Auto_Open macro runs automatically. You can watch the various sheets being activated, and charts being repainted. This slows down the macro, and some people consider it unaesthetic.

Insert the following VBA command at the beginning of the Auto_Open macro to suppress the screen display while the macro is running. (Once the macro stops, the screen updates as usual.)

```
Application.ScreenUpdating = False
```

There is a trade-off involved. When the screen update is suppressed...

- The macro runs faster.
- The user is looking at an hourglass, instead of being entertained by watching the macro work.

In other words, you have to weigh the difference between *actual* elapsed time, and *perceived* elapsed time.

▶ *Prototyping vs. Real-World Development*

If you examine the effort that went into the development of this simple application, you will see that many of the tasks were dictated by the requirement that the application be insensitive to the number of products in the database. Therein lies one of the biggest differences between prototyping and developing truly data-driven applications.

It may be relatively easy to grind out prototype quality applications. But such applications require constant maintenance. Changes to the underlying data require that the application be modified. A well designed, data-driven application takes more time to develop up front, but is worth the effort in the long run.

▶ *Loading the Query Add-In*

The application assumes that Excel is configured to load the query add-in (MSQUERY.XLA) automatically. When an application is being deployed to many desktops, be careful before you make such assumptions.

You could add a step to the recorded macro to open MSQUERY.XLA. But even this introduces two problems:

- Computers configured to open MSQUERY.XLA automatically will display an alert when the macro tries to open the file, since it will already be open.

- MSQUERY.XLA is located underneath the Excel directory. However, the Excel directory may be different from machine to machine. The macro would fail on a computer where Excel was installed in a directory different than on your computer.

The real solution is to write a brief macro that opens the add-in only if it is not already loaded. The macro can also determine where Excel is installed, and thus locate the query add-in regardless of where Excel is installed on each system.

▶ Using Microsoft Query

The application uses Microsoft Query to retrieve data from the dBASE file. As a result, there are two issues to consider:

- Microsoft Query is left in memory after you run the application, which could be confusing to users. To solve this problem, you can modify the macro to shut down Microsoft Query.

- There is a faster way to perform queries. There is an add-in included with Excel that provides an API to the ODBC manager, circumventing Microsoft Query. The add-in is named XLODBC.XLA. (This add-in also provides the SQL.REQUEST worksheet function, covered in Chapter 18.)

▶ Hiding the Formula Bar

This application does not require that the formula bar be displayed, because there is no data entry taking place. You could hide it when you record the Auto_Open macro, but this introduces a problem: this is a global setting, and Excel "remembers" it from session to session. If the Auto_Open macro hides the formula bar, it will remain hidden until it is manually unhidden (using View ➤ Formula Bar)—even in future Excel sessions. This is not a big problem when you are the only user, but it can be a support problem if the application is being deployed to many desktops.

The solution is to record an Auto_Close macro, which restores the formula bar.

➤ *Bulletproofing the Application*

The more people who use an application, the more important it is for the application to be *bulletproof*. In other words, no matter what the user does, they cannot cause an error, harm the data, or change the program.

 ➤ ➤ **N O T E**

Bulletproofing is a matter of degree. It is kind of like the temperature absolute zero—you can get very close, but it is ultimately unachievable. You need to weigh the development cost of each bulletproofing measure against the benefits realized (reduced support cost, and overall user satisfaction).

Here are some things you can do to bulletproof the application:

Create a Custom Menu System An application is not even remotely bulletproof if the built-in menus are displayed. There are too many commands that will break the application.

Trapping Keyboard Shortcuts Even with a custom menu system, the user can still use keyboard shortcuts to perform all kinds of disruptive tasks. You can write a macro to trap every insidious keystroke.

Protecting the Worksheets Minimally, the worksheets should be protected so that users cannot delete the objects (embedded charts and controls). You can also protect cells, but this has many side-effects that you should be aware of. For instance, you can't manipulate a pivot table on a worksheet where the cells are protected, nor can macros write data to cells that are protected. Also, certain worksheet controls (i.e. listboxes, checkboxes, and option buttons) won't work if the cells they

Custom Application

➤ ▶
Ch.
21

are linked to are locked and protected. (See Chapter 11 to learn more about protection.)

Protecting the Workbook If you protect the workbook structure, users will not be able to unhide hidden worksheets, or delete worksheets. (See Chapter 11 to read more about this topic.)

Save the File as Read-Only With the data stored in an external database, there is no reason for users to be able to change the workbook. Use File ➤ Save As, then click Options, to save the workbook as a read-only file (using the write-reservation password).

PART SEVEN

▶ ▶ **I**n *Part Seven* you will learn to use consolidation, outlining, and what-if analysis tools (like Goal Seek and Solver) to find business solutions. You will also learn about Excel's add-ins and other add-ins you can use with Excel to solve specific business problems. Part Seven explains the concepts behind OLE, and how you can use Excel in conjunction with other programs (like Microsoft Word 6). Finally, you will get lots of advanced tips and techniques to help you become more productive.

► ► **CHAPTER 22**

Consolidating and Outlining

FAST **T**RACK

▶ **To create an automatic outline** **773**

    Choose Data ➤ Group And Outline ➤ Auto Outline.

▶ **To expand and collapse an outline** **774**

    Click the level tools in the upper left corner of the work-sheet to hide or show entire levels of detail, or click the show or hide details symbols in the top and left margins of the worksheet to expand or collapse groups.

▶ **To hide outline symbols** **775**

    Click the Show Outline Symbols tool, or choose Tools ➤ Options, select the View tab, and uncheck the Outline Symbols setting.

▶ **To remove outlining** **780**

    Choose Data ➤ Group And Outline ➤ Clear Outline.

▶▶ **C** *onsolidating* information from multiple sources is a task often performed using spreadsheet software. This chapter is going to show how to use Excel's consolidation features to create a multi-level budgeting model. You will learn how to:

- *Use the Data ➤ Consolidate command*
- *Link the consolidation to source data*
- *Outline consolidated data*
- *Solve a real-world business problem using consolidation*

This chapter will also cover outlining. Several commands in Excel, such as Consolidate, create worksheet outlines as an automatic by-product. You can also create your own outlines. You will learn how to:

- *Create automatic outlines*
- *Use outline symbols to expand and collapse outlines*
- *Create "manual" outlines*

▶▶ Consolidating Data

In a sense, many of the formulas placed on a worksheet serve to consolidate data, using a broad definition for this term. But this section covers a specific command: Data ➤ Consolidate.

Data consolidations are used to roll-up and summarize data from more than one source. For example, suppose that you have workbooks storing population statistics for each county within a state, with one workbook for each county. You need to take the information from the county workbooks and create a state-wide report that summarizes all of the counties. You can painstakingly open each workbook, copy the information to a new workbook, and then write formulas to summarize the information.

Better yet, you can use Excel's built-in consolidation capabilities to simplify this process. Using the Data ➤ Consolidate command, you can:

- Consolidate information stored on different worksheets within the same workbook

- Consolidate information stored on different workbooks (without the need to open the workbooks)

- Consolidate multiple ranges on the same worksheet

- Consolidate data on the basis of row and column labels, regardless of position on the worksheet

- Use different calculations when you consolidate, such as sum, count, and average

- Link the consolidation to the source data

 ▶ ▶**N O T E**

> **Pivot tables, covered in Chapter 17, provide a powerful, flexible way to analyze data. They can consolidate data from multiple sources, summarize detailed data, and create multi-level outlines. If you need to perform consolidations, pivot tables are a *must learn* topic.**

▶ *The Business Problem*

In this section, you will learn how to perform a two-level consolidation for a fictitious company, Electronic Gizmos Corp. (EGC), that distributes electronic products nationwide.

- EGC has four distribution centers, which are designated as A through D.

- Two distribution centers, A and B, are in the eastern region. Centers C and D are in the western region. There is a regional manager for each of the two regions.

- Every year, during the 4th quarter, the distribution centers prepare a proposed budget for the following year and submit it to the regional manager for approval.

- The regional managers submit consolidated budgets for their respective regions to the VP of Finance for approval.

▶ *Using a Template for Conformity*

To simplify the consolidation process, a template will be used that forces the distribution centers to enter data in the same format. The budget template is shown in Figure 22.1.

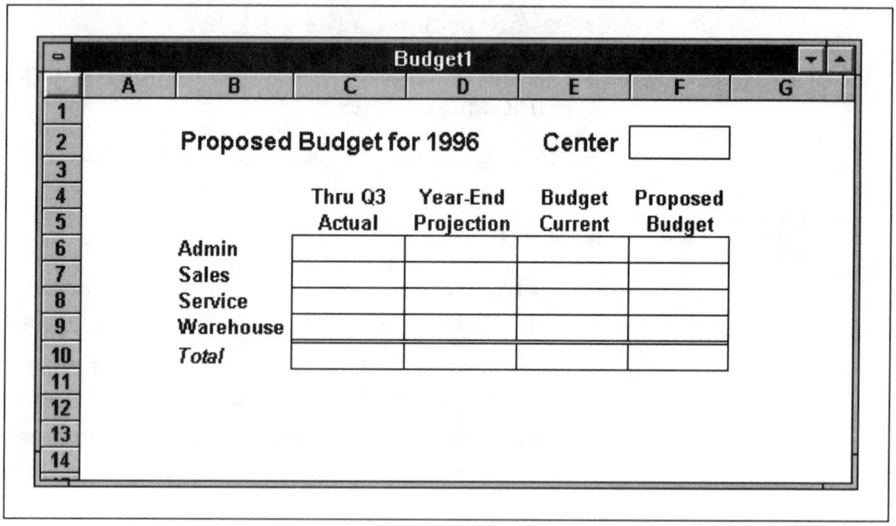

FIGURE 22.1 ▶

Budgets are submitted for four departments. Notice that the row labels (B6:B10) and column labels (C5:F5) are unique.

Follow these steps to create the template pictured in Figure 22.1:

1. Create a new workbook—delete every worksheet except Sheet1.

2. Enter the row and column labels shown in Figure 22.1.

3. Hide the gridlines (using Tools ➤ Options, View tab).

4. Apply borders as shown in Figure 22.1. (See Chapter 5 to learn about cell formatting.)

▶ ▶**T I P**

> Place the double border on the top of row 10 rather
> than the bottom of row 9. Later, when you copy D6 to
> D7:D9, the double border won't get overwritten.

5. Enter the following formulas:

D6	**=C6*1.33**
C10	**=SUM(C6:C9)**

▶ ▶**N O T E**

> The distribution centers submit budget proposals for
> the upcoming year during the 4th quarter—before 4th
> quarter data is available. The formula in D6 is intended
> to predict 4th quarter expenses on the basis of the
> previous three quarters.

6. Copy the formula in D6 to D7:D9.

▶ ▶**T I P**

> Use the fill handle to AutoFill D6 down through D9.
> (AutoFill is discussed in Chapter 7.)

7. Copy the formula in C10 to D10:F10.
8. Name the range B5:F10 **Budget_Area**.

▶ ▶**T I P**

> To suppress the display of zero values, choose Tools ▶
> Options, click the View tab, and uncheck Zero Values.

9. Choose File ➤ Save. Enter the file name **BUDGET**. Using the Save File as Type drop-down, choose Template.

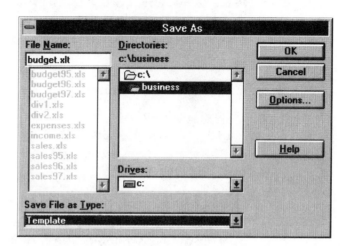

 ► ►**T I P**

> **If you want to prevent users from overwriting formulas, all cells where data entry is allowed should be unlocked, and all other cells should be locked. (All cells are locked by default). The cell lock takes effect when the worksheet cells are protected using Tools ➤ Protection ➤ Protect Worksheet. (See Chapter 11 to learn about protecting worksheets.)**

The template is complete. When you close it and re-open it, a copy of the template is loaded into memory, instead of the original. (See Chapter 10 to learn about templates.)

 ► ►**T I P**

> **To open an original template rather than a copy, hold down the Shift key while you open the template.**

▶ Using a File Naming Convention

For reasons you will discover later, a file naming convention is vitally important when performing workbook consolidations. EGC has chosen the following conventions:

- Distribution center workbook names begin with the name of the parent region, followed by an underscore, followed by the one character distribution center ID. For example, center C, which is in the western region, will create a budget workbook named WEST_C.XLS. Center A, in the eastern region, will create a workbook named EAST_A.XLS, and so on.

- The regional managers create workbooks beginning with REG, followed by an underscore, followed by the region. These two workbooks will be named REG_EAST.XLS and REG_WEST.XLS.

- The corporate summary workbook will be named CORP.XLS, though the name of this workbook is not as critical as are the names of the lower level workbooks.

▶ Consolidating by Position or Category

Before creating a consolidation, there is an important issue to consider: The Data ➤ Consolidate command lets you consolidate on the basis of position or on the basis of row/column categories.

Consolidating by Position

Consolidation based on position requires that the data be structured identically, relative within each data source:

- Each cell being consolidated must reside in the same relative position within the source range, as is the case with the EGC model.

- The row and column heading in the source range(s) are ignored, even if they are included as part of the consolidation range.

- Data ➤ Consolidate lets you consolidate multiple ranges from the same worksheet. Therefore, the *relative* position of cells within each range is critical—not the absolute position on the worksheet. (See Figure 22.2)

FIGURE 22.2 ▶

F7:G8 is a consolidation of the two source ranges, C4:D5 and C11:D12.

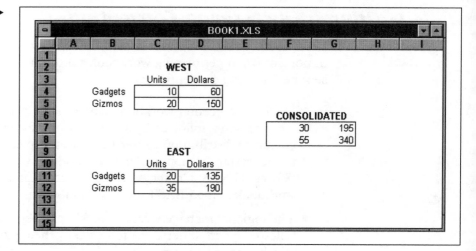

- Since the row and column headings are not part of the source data (and are not copied to the consolidation even if included), the source data and the consolidation are often based on a template.

Generally, consolidating by position is a risky proposition. A minor change to source data can cause erroneous results.

Consolidating by Category

When you consolidate on the basis of category, the row and/or column labels are used to determine how to perform the consolidation. Accordingly, the source data ranges do not have to be structured identically.

- The source ranges can contain a varying number of rows or columns and must include the row and/or column labels.

- The sequence of the row and/or column labels doesn't matter.

To perform a consolidation by category, check the Top Row and/or Left Column checkboxes in the Data ➤ Consolidate dialog box. Figure 22.3 shows a consolidation by category, with the source ranges and the consolidation located on the same worksheet.

Consolidating by category provides greater data integrity and more flexibility than consolidating by position.

FIGURE 22.3 ▶

F7:H10 is a consolidation of the two source ranges, B3:D6 and B12:D14. Consolidation by category allows the source ranges to differ.

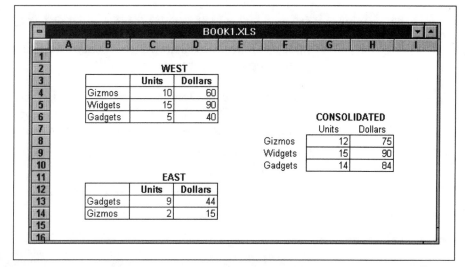

▶ *To Link or Not to Link*

The second major choice you are presented with when consolidating is whether to link the consolidation to the source data ranges.

When to Link A consolidation that is linked to source data recalculates automatically, when links are refreshed. Linking is a good idea if the source data is subject to change, and the consolidation needs to stay in sync with the source data. For instance, using the EGC model, suppose that the budgeting process is iterative. A distribution center submits a proposal. The manager reviews the numbers and sends it back for revision. The center makes changes, the manager reviews again, and so on. In this scenario, the workbooks will remain in sync without manual effort.

When Not to Link You should not link if the consolidation is a one-time process—the consolidation will be a "frozen" report, with no formulas pointing back to the source data. Otherwise, you run the risk of the consolidation inadvertently changing because of a change in the source.

▶ *Step One—The Distribution Center Budget*

Suppose you are the controller for distribution center C. Follow these steps to prepare your budget proposal:

1. Choose File ➤ Open to open the template created in the previous exercise—BUDGET.XLT. (Notice that a copy of the template, named Budget1, is loaded into memory—not the original.)

2. Enter **C** into F2. Enter numbers into C6:C9, E6:E9, and F6:F9. (See Figure 22.4)

3. Choose File ➤ Save, and name the file **WEST_C.XLS**.

FIGURE 22.4 ▶

The completed budget proposal for distribution center C.

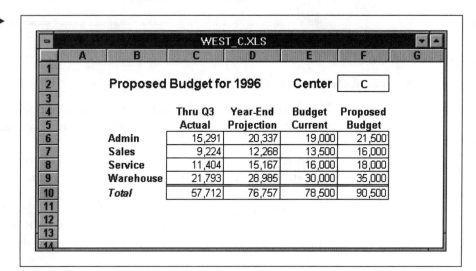

		Thru Q3 Actual	Year-End Projection	Budget Current	Proposed Budget
Admin		15,291	20,337	19,000	21,500
Sales		9,224	12,268	13,500	16,000
Service		11,404	15,167	16,000	18,000
Warehouse		21,793	28,985	30,000	35,000
Total		57,712	76,757	78,500	90,500

Proposed Budget for 1996 — Center: C

In the next step, the western region manager will consolidate centers C and D. You can repeat the previous steps for center D, or take a short-cut: Save WEST_C.XLS as **WEST_D.XLS**, then change a few numbers so that the workbooks can be distinguished later, then save again.

▶ *Step Two—The Regional Consolidation*

Suppose you are the western regional manager for EGC. It is your job to consolidate the proposed budgets submitted by the distribution centers within your region. The structure of the template will allow a consolidation by position. However, the personnel at center D are known to break the rules from time to time, so the safest bet is a consolidation by category. Follow these steps:

1. Close WEST_C.XLS and WEST_D.XLS.

▶ ▶ **T I P**

> **The source workbooks do not have to be open in order to perform a consolidation. This is an important feature, especially when there are dozens of source workbooks instead of only two.**

2. Create a new workbook.

▶ ▶ **N O T E**

> **When performing a consolidation by category, the row and column headings are part of the source data ranges. As such, the template provides marginal value, as the consolidation process will copy row and column headings for you.**

3. Select B2 (the upper left corner of the consolidation range) and choose Data ➤ Consolidate. The Consolidate dialog box is shown in Figure 22.5.

4. Enter **WEST_?.XLS!Budget_Area** in the Reference box, then click Add.

FIGURE 22.5 ►

The Data ➤ Consolidate dialog box.

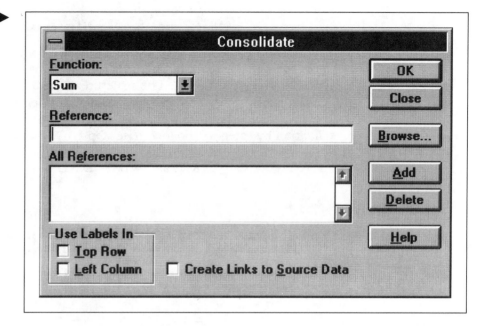

5. Check Top Row and Left Column, which causes the consolidation to be based on category, rather than position. Check Create Links to Source Data.

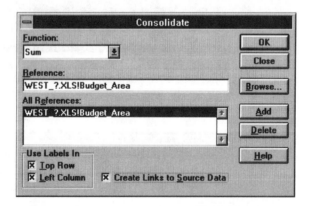

6. Click OK to perform the consolidation. The result is shown in Figure 22.6.

7. Name the range B5:F10 **Budget_Area** (this will be used for the corporate consolidation).

FIGURE 22.6

When you create links to the source data, the sheet is automatically outlined.

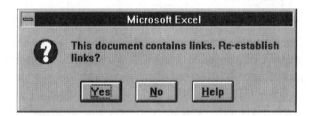

	A	B	C	D	E	F	G	H
				REG_WEST.XLS				
1								
2				Actual	Projection	Current	Budget	
5		Admin		27,516	36,596	36,000	41,500	
8		Sales		19,368	25,759	26,500	31,000	
11		Service		22,067	29,349	31,000	34,000	
14		Warehouse		39,633	52,712	55,000	62,000	
17		Total		108,584	144,417	148,500	168,500	
18								
19								
20								
21								
22								
23								

Consolidating and Outlining

Ch. **22**

▶ *Refreshing a Linked Consolidation*

A linked consolidation behaves just like any workbook that is linked to one or more source workbooks. When the file is opened, the following dialog box is displayed.

Microsoft Excel

? This document contains links. Re-establish links?

[Yes]   [No]   [Help]

Click OK to recalculate the links. New values are retrieved from the source workbooks, even if they are closed.

▶ ▶ **T I P**

If you want dependent workbooks to update links without a prompt, choose Tools ▶ Options, click the Edit tab, and uncheck Ask to Update Automatic Links. This is a global setting that pertains to all workbooks.

▶ *Using Wildcards and Named Ranges*

Two vitally important techniques were used in the previous exercise, the benefits of which can not be over-estimated if you intend to perform, and rely upon, consolidations.

Using Wildcards in the File Name

You can include asterisks and question marks in the file name as wildcard characters. The use of wildcards adheres to software conventions: The asterisk is used as a place marker for any number of characters, and the question mark is used as a place marker for any one character. The EGC file naming convention, discussed earlier in this chapter, is intended to support this wildcard-based consolidation methodology.

The file name WEST_?.XLS will consolidate from all files in the current directory with a prefix of WEST_, any character in the sixth position, and a suffix of .XLS (i.e., WEST_C.XLS, WEST_D.XLS, WEST_Z.XLS). The benefit may not be obvious with the EGC model, consisting of two source workbooks, but consider the following:

- Consolidations can be performed on a large number of workbooks, without the tedious effort of specifying each source range.

- If a new workbook is added to the directory and the name of the workbook matches the wildcard specification, it will be included automatically the next time the consolidation workbook recalculates.

Referring to the Source Data by Name

The second vital technique used in the previous exercise was the reference to a named range, Budget_Area. (Earlier in the chapter, when the template was created, the name was defined.) By using a name:

- When creating links to source data, the name helps ensure the integrity of the external reference. (Refer to Chapter 8 to learn more about names.)

- New categories can be inserted into one or more source data ranges. The name expands automatically, and the next time the consolidation recalculates, everything stays in sync.

▶ *Automatic Outlining*

The worksheet shown in Figure 22.7 contains outline symbols, which are an automatic by-product when you create links to source data. When you click the outline symbols in the left margin, the outline expands. (Outlining is covered in depth later in this chapter.)

FIGURE 22.7 ▶

On the detail rows, Column C contains the workbook prefix indicating which row comes from which source.

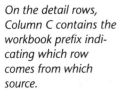

	A	B	C	D	E	F	G	H
1								
2				Actual	Projection	Current	Budget	
3			West_C	15,291	20,337	19,000	21,500	
4			West_D	12,225	16,259	17,000	20,000	
5		Admin		27,516	36,596	36,000	41,500	
8		Sales		19,368	25,759	26,500	31,000	
11		Service		22,067	29,349	31,000	34,000	
14		Warehouse		39,633	52,712	55,000	62,000	
17		Total		108,584	144,417	148,500	168,500	
18								
19								
20								
21								

REG_WEST.XLS

The numbers on the detail rows contain formulas that refer to the source workbooks.

▶ *Entering Source References*

In the previous exercise, the source reference was entered manually. But there are several other ways to enter this information.

- If the source workbook is open, you can point and click the source range.

- Click the Browse button (see Figure 22.5) to select a closed workbook, then type the sheet name and source range following the workbook name.

- Use a single 3-D reference to consolidate source areas that are identically positioned on different sheets in the same workbook. (See Chapters 4 and 8 to learn more about 3-D references.)

Consolidating and Outlining

Ch.
22

▶ Using Category Labels in the Consolidation Range

In the previous exercise, one cell (B2) was selected when the Data ➤ Consolidate command was chosen. However, if you select more than one cell when you choose Data ➤ Consolidate, and the range contains category labels, the labels control what data is consolidated. The following exercise demonstrates the technique:

1. On a new workbook, build the worksheet shown in Figure 22.8.

FIGURE 22.8 ▶

A consolidation will be created of the East and West data.

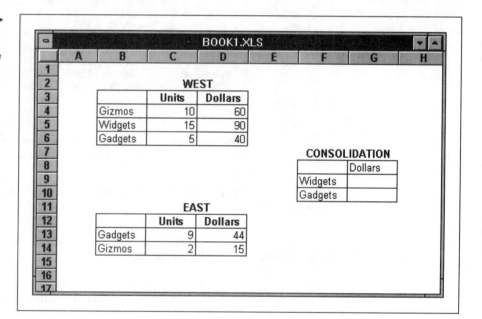

2. Select F8:G10 and choose Data ➤ Consolidate.

3. With the Consolidate dialog box displayed, select B3:D6 (which enters the range into the Reference in the consolidate dialog box), then click Add.

4. Add the second source range: Select B12:D14 and click Add.

5. Check both Top Row and Left Column.

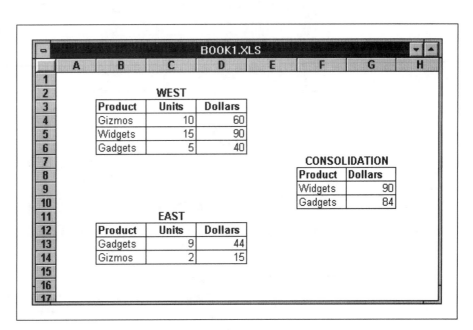

▶ ▶NOTE

**When the consolidation is on the same sheet as the
source data, you cannot create a link to the source.**

Click OK to perform the consolidation. Figure 22.9 shows the result.

FIGURE 22.9 ▶

Product Gizmos *and
column* Units *were
excluded from the
consolidation.*

Since category labels were included in the selected range when Data ➤ Consolidate was chosen, the labels controlled which data was consolidated.

Using Wildcards in the Categories

There is an interesting and powerful variation to the technique described above. If the categories in the consolidation range include wildcards, all categories matching the wildcard are summarized. Consider the worksheet in Figure 22.10.

FIGURE 22.10 ▸

Category labels inside the consolidation range can include wildcard characters.

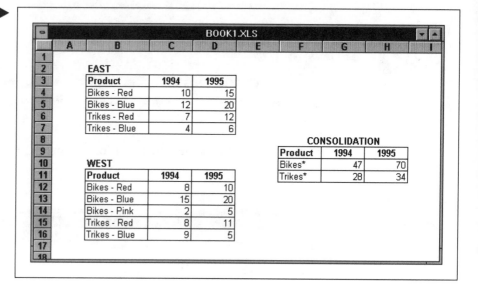

When the consolidation in Figure 22.10 was created, F9:H11 was selected. The asterisk caused all bikes, and all trikes, to be summarized.

▸ Consolidation Functions

While consolidation is most often performed to sum data, you can also perform consolidations that use other functions:

Count	Counts cells containing a value—text or number (equivalent to COUNTA function)
Average	Calculates average

Max	Finds the maximum value
Min	Finds the minimum value
Product	Calculates the product
Count Nums	Counts numbers (equivalent to COUNT function)
StDev	Calculates the standard deviation of a sample
StDevP	Calculates the standard deviation of the population
Var	Calculates the variance of a sample
VarP	Calculates the variance of the population

▶ *Multi-Level Consolidations*

There are some important things to understand about multi-level consolidations. Let's re-visit the EGC model.

At Step two, the western region consolidation was completed, and saved as REG_WEST.XLS. Suppose that the eastern region consolidation was also performed and saved as REG_EAST.XLS. (Remember, both of these consolidations are linked to the distribution center source data.)

Consolidating the two regions into a corporate total involves the same basic procedure as when the regional consolidations were created. (The only difference is the file name.) Here are the implications of EGC's two-level linked model:

- The regional budgets are linked to the distribution center budgets. When the regional budgets are opened, the links are (optionally) recalculated.

- The corporate budgets are linked to the regional budgets. When the corporate budget is opened, the links are (optionally) recalculated.

- Link recalculation only goes down one level. Suppose a change is made to a distribution center (bottom level) budget. Then, the corporate (top level) workbook is opened. The change at the bottom level will not flow to the top level. The workbooks must be recalculated in reverse order of the hierarchy.

▶ *More Facts about Consolidation*

- Only one consolidation can be defined on a (destination) worksheet (you can perform many consolidations on the same worksheet, but only the most recent consolidation will remain defined in the Data ➤ Consolidate dialog box as a reusable model).

- Consolidation dialog settings are persistent—the same consolidation model can be used repeatedly without setting it up from scratch each time.

- Destination cells are formatted using the number formats in the first source selected for consolidation.

- An unlinked consolidation can be reversed by choosing Edit ➤ Undo immediately following the consolidation.

- A linked consolidation cannot be reversed with Edit ➤ Undo. (It can be reversed by closing the workbook without saving the consolidation.)

- If the source and destination areas are on the same worksheet, you cannot create a linked consolidation.

▶▶ *Worksheet Outlining*

An outlined worksheet lets you easily and quickly view various levels of detail—for rows and/or columns. Figure 22.11 shows a worksheet with outlining.

There are several operations in Excel that create outlines for you automatically:

- Data ➤ Subtotals (see Chapter 16)

- Data ➤ Consolidate, when the Link To Source option is chosen (covered earlier in this chapter)

- A summary report created with Solver (see Chapter 23)

This section will explain how to create your own outlines, and how to use outlining symbols—regardless of how the outline was created.

FIGURE 22.11 ▶

The outline symbols in the left and top margins let you expand and collapse the outline.

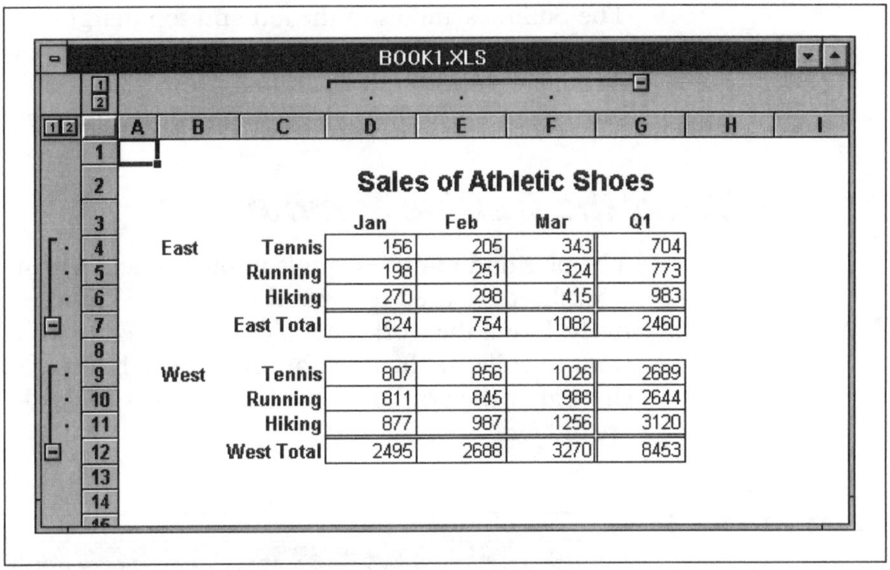

▶ *Creating Automatic Outlines*

The easiest way to create an outline is with the Data ➤ Group And Outline ➤ Auto Outline command. Excel looks for formulas on the active sheet, and on the basis of the formulas, determines where the summary and detail rows/columns are located. Consider the outlined worksheet in Figure 22.12.

FIGURE 22.12 ▶

Automatic outlining was applied to this worksheet.

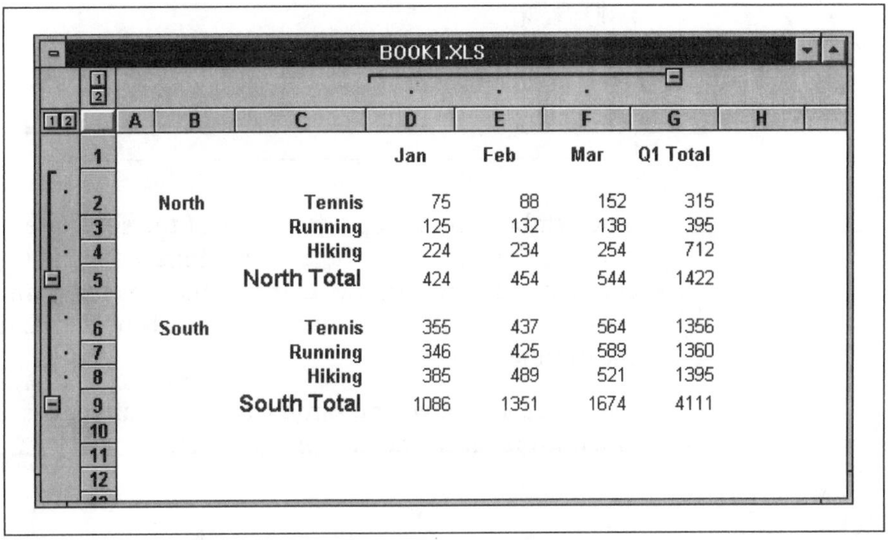

The outline symbols in the left and top margins indicate where the summary rows and columns are located. Since row 7 sums rows 4 through 6, it becomes a summary row in the outline. Since column G sums columns D through F, it becomes a summary column.

▶ Using the Outline Symbols

The plus and minus symbols in the top and left margins of an outlined worksheet are used to expand or collapse sections of the outline selectively. Using the worksheet pictured in Figure 22.12, suppose that you want to collapse the data for region North. Figure 22.13 shows the sheet after the symbol to the left of row is clicked—rows 4 through 6 are hidden.

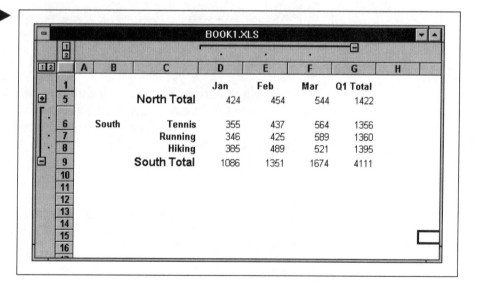

The symbols in the top left corner of the sheet are used to expand and collapse the entire outline at once. Figure 22.13 shows two buttons for changing the row outline, and two buttons for changing the column outline. The number of buttons depends upon the number of levels in the outline.

Figure 22.14 shows the same worksheet, after pressing both of the level one buttons in the corner of the sheet.

FIGURE 22.14

Use the symbols in the upper left corner to expand and collapse the entire outline at once.

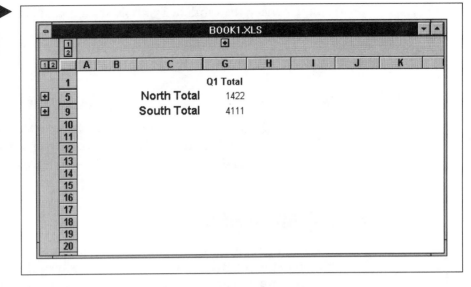

Using Menu Commands to Expand and Collapse Outlines

Menu commands can be used in lieu of the outline symbols to expand or collapse an outline. Follow these steps to collapse a section of an outline using menu commands:

1. Select a summary cell for the group you want to collapse.

2. Choose Data ➤ Group And Outline ➤ Hide Detail.

To expand an outline group (display details) using menu commands:

1. Select a summary cell for the group you want to expand.

2. Choose Data ➤ Group And Outline ➤ Show Detail.

Hiding the Outline Symbols

Suppose you are distributing an outlined worksheet to co-workers, and you do not want the outline symbols displayed. Follow these steps to hide the symbols:

1. Choose Tools ➤ Options, and select the View tab.

2. Uncheck the Outline Symbols setting, and click OK.

 You can also use the Show Outline Symbols tool to toggle outline symbols, or from the keyboard, press Ctrl+8.

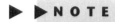

▶ ▶**N O T E**

> **Hiding the outline symbols does not remove the underlying outline from the worksheet. The outline is still in place, and can still be manipulated with menu commands.**

▶ *Creating Manual Outlines*

Automatic outlining is convenient because it does all the work for you. But sometimes you may want more control over the outline, in which case you must define the outline manually. Here are several scenarios in which manual outlining might be used:

- If there are no formulas on the worksheet (for example, data downloaded from a mainframe)
- To outline just a portion of the worksheet
- If the data is not organized for automatic outlining (for instance, one section has summary data above detail data, and another section has summary data below detail data)

Consider the worksheet in Figure 22.15:

Suppose you want the ability to collapse just the East section (see Figure 22.16).

1. Select the rows you want to outline (rows 2:9).

 2. Choose Data ➤ Group And Outline ➤ Group (or click on the Group tool).

▶ *Formatting Worksheet Outlines*

You can manually format an outline, as you would any range of cells. But there are two more effective techniques: styles and table AutoFormats.

FIGURE 22.15

You can outline just the East section of the worksheet by creating a manual outline.

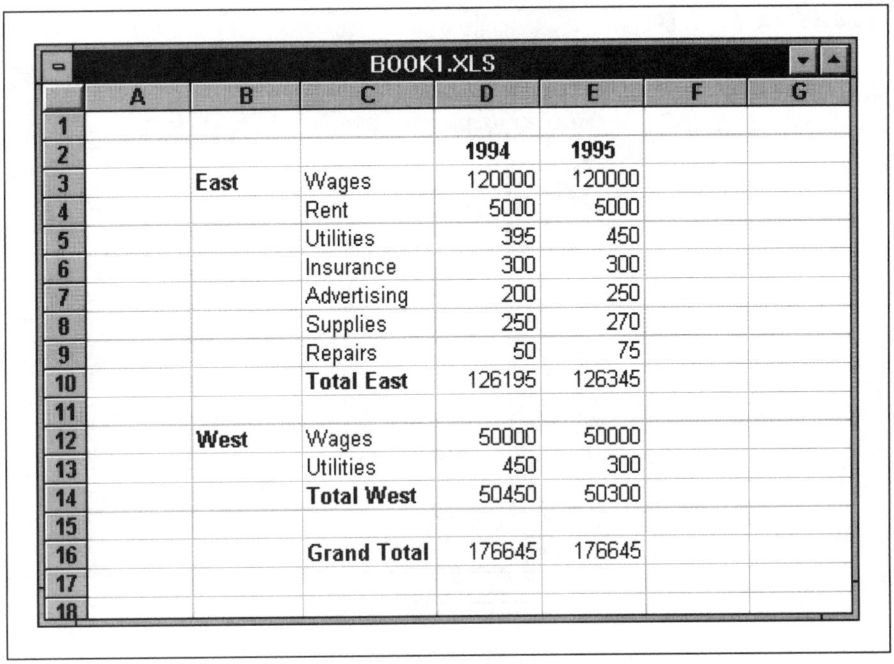

BOOK1.XLS

	A	B	C	D	E	F	G
1							
2				**1994**	**1995**		
3		**East**	Wages	120000	120000		
4			Rent	5000	5000		
5			Utilities	395	450		
6			Insurance	300	300		
7			Advertising	200	250		
8			Supplies	250	270		
9			Repairs	50	75		
10			**Total East**	126195	126345		
11							
12		**West**	Wages	50000	50000		
13			Utilities	450	300		
14			**Total West**	50450	50300		
15							
16			**Grand Total**	176645	176645		
17							
18							

FIGURE 22.16

The manual outline created for Region East has been collapsed.

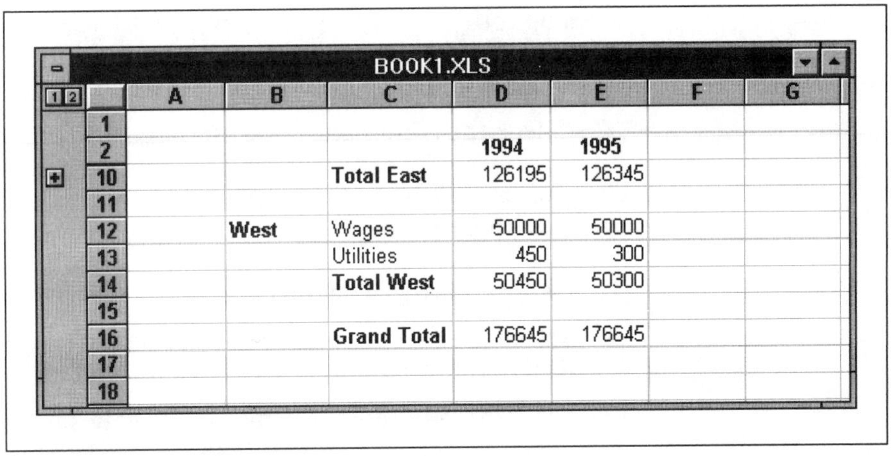

BOOK1.XLS

	A	B	C	D	E	F	G
1							
2				**1994**	**1995**		
10			**Total East**	126195	126345		
11							
12		**West**	Wages	50000	50000		
13			Utilities	450	300		
14			**Total West**	50450	50300		
15							
16			**Grand Total**	176645	176645		
17							
18							

Applying Styles to Outlines

You can apply built-in styles to different levels of an outline, as shown in Figure 22.17. As with cell styles, if you change a style definition, every outline level using the given style will be automatically reformatted.

FIGURE 22.17 ►

Outline with styles defined for each of three levels.

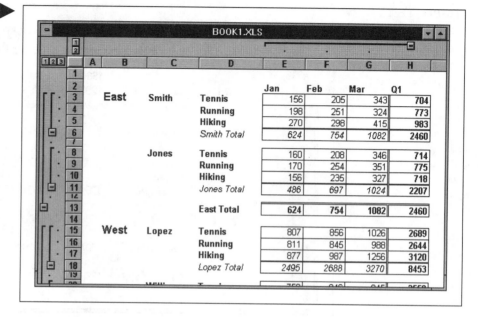

To apply automatic styles to an outline, the Automatic Styles option must be selected before creating the outline. To select the Automatic Styles option:

1. Choose Data ➤ Group and Outline ➤ Settings.

2. Check the Automatic Styles setting.

Then, when an automatic outline is created, the outline styles are automatically applied. To change the definition of a style:

1. Choose Format ➤ Style.

2. Select the style from the Style Name list (the styles are named RowLevel_1, ColumnLevel_1, and so on).

3. Click the Modify button and make your changes, then click OK to close the Format Cells dialog box. Click OK again to close the Style dialog box. (See Chapter 5 to learn more about styles.)

The new style definition is automatically applied.

Applying Table AutoFormats to Outlines

You can apply AutoFormats to a worksheet before or after outlining the data. The AutoFormat feature is "smart"—it detects summary and detail levels using the formulas. Follow these steps to apply an AutoFormat:

1. Select a cell within the data range.

2. Choose Format ➤ AutoFormat.

3. Select an AutoFormat from the list of Table Formats.

 ▶ ▶**N O T E**

If only one cell is selected when the Format ➤ AutoFormat command is chosen, the format will be applied to all contiguous data. If the range you want to AutoFormat contains blank rows or columns, you must select the entire range before choosing the command.

 ▶ ▶**T I P**

By default, charts created from outlined data automatically change when the outline is expanded or collapsed.

▶ CREATING CHARTS FROM OUTLINES

Suppose you have a large table of sales data, and you have outlined it so that the data can be easily viewed on a summary or detail level. Now, you want to chart the sales data. By default, charting is based on visible data only, so that as the outline is collapsed and expanded, the chart changes accordingly. However, an expanded outline can result in a chart with so many data series that the chart becomes unreadable. So another option is to create a chart that is based on the summary level, even if the outline is expanded to a detail level. To create a chart that will not expand, begin by collapsing the outline to a summary level. Select the entire table, then select only the visible cells in the table by choosing Edit ➤ Go To, clicking the Special button, and selecting Visible Cells Only. Now, when you create the chart, it will not expand when the outline is expanded.

Consider the opposite scenario: Suppose you want the chart to always show detail, even when the outline is collapsed. Select all of the data in the expanded outline and create the chart. With the chart active, choose Tools ➤ Options, and select the Chart tab. Clear the Plot Visible Cells Only checkbox.

▶ *Removing an Outline*

You can remove outlining from an entire worksheet, or from selected rows or columns.

To remove outlining from the entire worksheet:

1. Select any cell on the worksheet.
2. Choose Data ➤ Group And Outline ➤ Clear Outline.

To remove outlining from a group of rows or columns:

1. Select the rows or columns you want to remove outlining from.

2. Choose Data ➤ Group And Outline ➤ Ungroup (or click on the Ungroup tool)

23

What-If
Analysis

►►FAST TRACK

▶ ***Use Scenario Manager***   ***800***

    to create and save different sets of input values with their
    results.

▶ ***To create a scenario***   ***802***

    First, choose Tools ➤ Scenarios. Then, click the Add but-
    ton to add new scenarios with different input values.

▶ ***To create scenario summary reports***   ***804***

    Click the Summary button on the Scenario Manager dia-
    log box, and select the Scenario Summary option.

▶ ***To merge scenarios***   ***805***

    First, open all workbooks to be merged, and activate the
    worksheet to which the scenarios will be merged. Then,
    choose Tools ➤ Scenarios, and click the Merge button. Fi-
    nally, on the Merge Scenarios dialog box, select the work-
    books and worksheets to be merged.

►► **G**enerally, a worksheet with simple SUM functions is performing *what-if* analysis. When you change a cell, you can see what happens as a result. This means that almost everything you do with worksheets can be characterized as what-if analysis, using a broad definition of the term. This chapter, however, explains three specific tools to help with complex what-if analysis:

- *Goal Seek, which determines the input required to produce a desired result.*
- *Solver, which finds the optimum solution to complex problems involving multiple variables and constraints.*
- *Scenario Manager, which allows you to create and save sets of input values that produce different results.*

 ►►**NOTE**

The Excel manual and various third-party publications include *data tables* when discussing what-if analysis. There is virtually nothing that can be done in a data table that cannot be done using "normal" worksheet formulas—and you don't have to learn a new construct.

►► Solving Simple Problems Using Goal Seek

Essentially, *Goal Seek* solves formulas backwards. Use Goal Seek when you know the result you want, but need to determine how much to change a single input to get that result. For example, here are two typical problems that can be solved with Goal Seek:

- You want to take out a loan to buy a car, but the maximum payment your budget will allow is $300 per month. What is the most expensive car you afford?

- You are taking a course in Biology, and the final grade is based on the weighted average of six exams. You have taken five of the six exams, and want to know the minimum score you need on the sixth exam in order to get a B for the course.

To use Goal Seek, select a cell containing a formula, then choose the Tools ➤ Goal Seek command.

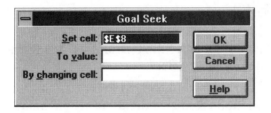

- *Set cell* must be a cell which contains a formula—it defaults to the active cell.

- *To value* must be a constant value (not a cell reference).

- *By changing cell* must be a cell containing a constant value, and must be directly or indirectly referenced by the cell specified in *Set cell*. The reference can be several levels away, and can be located in another worksheet or another workbook.

▶ *Goal Seek—Case One*

Suppose you want to buy a new car. Here's what you know:

- You can get a bank loan at 9%.

- The loan requires a 20% down payment.

- The maximum monthly payment you can afford is $300.

What's the most expensive car you can afford? Follow this exercise, using the PMT function and Goal Seek, to find out:

1. Enter the following on a new worksheet:

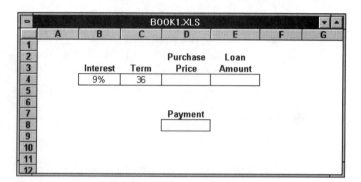

2. In cell E4, enter the formula **=D4*0.8** (the loan amount is 80% of
   the purchase price).

3. Enter the formula **=PMT(B4/12,C4,-E4)** in cell D8 (the PMT
   function calculates the monthly payment).

4. With cell D8 selected, choose Tools ► Goal Seek. Fill in the dialog box as shown below.

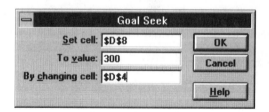

5. Click OK, and Goal Seek finds the answer. To keep the answer
   (and change the values in the worksheet), click OK on the Goal
   Seek Status dialog box. (See Figure 23.1)

► *Goal Seek—Case Two*

You are taking a course in Biology, and you want to know what grade
you have to get on the final exam in order to get a B for the course.

FIGURE 23.1 ▶

*Goal seek has deter-
mined the maximum
purchase price.*

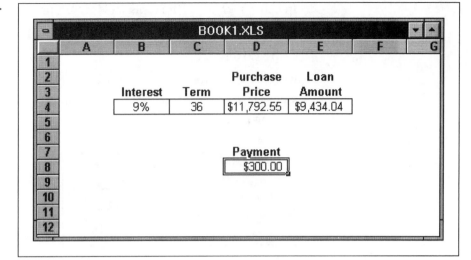

- There are six exams given during the course, and you have taken five of them—you scored 75, 80, 95, 76, and 62.

- The exams scores are weighted. Exams #1, #2, #4, and #5 are each worth 10% of the final grade, exam #3 is worth 20%, and exam #6 is worth 40%.

- The final score is calculated from the average of the six weighted exam scores.

Goal Seek will change an indirectly referenced value (the sixth exam score) to reach a final weighted average of 80% (which will give you a final grade of B).

1. Enter the following on a new worksheet:

What-If Analysis

▶ ▶
Ch.
23

2. In cell E4, enter the formula **=C4*D4**. Then copy it down to E5:E9.

3. In cell D10, enter the formula **=SUM(D4:D9)**.

4. Copy D10 to E10.

5. In cell F10, enter the formula **=E10/D10**.

6. Select F10, then choose Tools ➤ Goal Seek. Fill in the dialog box as shown below.

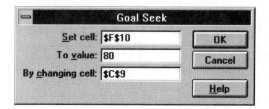

7. Click OK, then Goal Seek finds the answer (Figure 23.2). To keep the new values in the worksheet, click OK on the Goal Seek Status dialog box.

FIGURE 23.2 ▶

*Goal Seek has deter-
mined the score
required on the final
exam (C9) in order to
get a B for the course.*

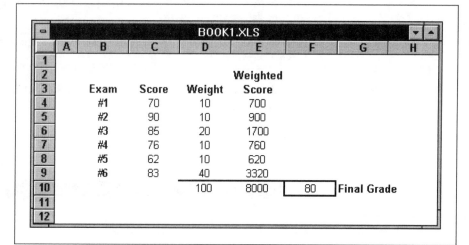

► ►**TIP**

> **If you create a chart based on cells containing form-**
> **ulas, and then change a charted value by dragging a**
> **data marker, the Goal Seek dialog box is displayed.**
> **(See Chapter 14.)**

► *If You Make a Mistake*

Here are some of the error messages you'll see if you enter invalid information in the Goal Seek dialog box.

- If the By Changing Cell contains a formula, you'll see:

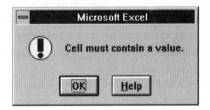

- If the cell entered in Set Cell contains a constant, you'll see:

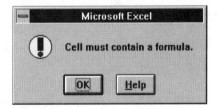

► ► *Solving Complex Problems with Solver*

Solver is used to find solutions to problems involving multiple variables
and constraints—problems that are more complex than Goal Seek can
handle. While Goal Seek finds a specific solution, Solver finds the best,
or optimal, solution.

Solver is a complex tool, but is worth the time to learn if you must find optimal solutions to complex problems. Solver can save money and resources in your business by finding better, more efficient ways to allocate resources. It can also save you the time spent finding solutions by trial-and-error. Solver can help you to solve problems such as:

- How to find the optimal allocation of parts inventory to minimize production costs.

- How to create the most efficient personnel schedule to minimize costs while meeting business needs and individual scheduling requests.

- How to optimize allocation of funds in an investment portfolio to minimize risk and maximize return.

There may be different optimal solutions to a problem, depending on the mathematical techniques Solver uses to solve the problem. The default Solver settings are appropriate for many problems, but experimentation with the different Solver Options settings (see Figure 23.3) may yield better results.

FIGURE 23.3 ▶

In the Solver Options dialog box, you can change the allowable time and number of iterations and experiment with different mathematical techniques.

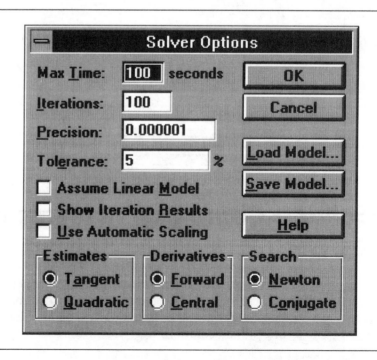

▶ *Types of Problems Solver Can Analyze*

Solver can analyze and solve three types of problems:

Linear Problems A problem in which the variables are related through linear functions of the type $y = k_1x$ plus k_2 —where x and y are the variables and k_1 and k_2 are constants. If you know that your problem is linear, check the Assume Linear Model setting on the Solver Options dialog box (Figure 23.3) to speed up the calculation. This is especially important if the data model is large.

Non-Linear Problems A problem in which the variables cannot all be related through linear functions. Examples would include polynomials, exponential functions, and sine waves.

Integer Problems A problem in which any of the variables is constrained to an integer value. Solver takes a longer time to solve integer problems.

▶ *Business Case*

Suppose you are the manager of a dairy farm, and one of your responsibilities is to determine a livestock feed mixture that meets certain protein requirements but is still cost-effective. Ingredient costs are continually changing, and as they change, you must recalculate the ingredient mix to minimize cost. Here's what you know:

- The feed mixture is composed of oats, corn, and barley.
- The final mix must have a protein content of between 9.2% and 9.5%.

Finding a solution to this kind of problem can be a lengthy trial-and-error process if you use conventional methods. Instead, Solver can find a solution for you.

First, you must understand three definitions:

- *Target cell* is the specific objective of the problem—the cell whose value Solver will set to be a minimum, maximum, or a specific value. In this problem, the target cell is the cost (which is to be minimized) of the final mix.

What-If Analysis

▶

Ch.

23

- *Changing cells* are cells whose values Solver will manipulate to meet the target cell objective. In this problem, the changing cells are the proportions of each ingredient in the final mix.

- *Constraints* are the limits set on the values in any of these cells—there can be constraints on changing cells, the target cell, or any cells involved in the calculations. In this problem, the constraints are:

  - The final protein concentration must be between 9.2% and 9.5%.

  - The amount of each ingredient must be at least 0 lbs. (This constraint prevents Solver from using a negative value.)

  - The total of the ingredients must equal 100%.

1. Make sure the Solver add-in is loaded, then enter the following on a new worksheet:

	A	B	C	D	E	F	G	H	I
					lbs feed in	cost per	lbs protein/		
3		feed	% protein	price/lb	100 lbs mix	100 lbs mix	100 lbs mix		
4		oats	9.50%	0.23					
5		corn	8.50%	0.08					
6		barley	9.00%	0.14					
7								% protein	

2. Enter these formulas:

Cell	Formula
E7	=SUM(E4:E6)
F4	=E4*D4
G4	=E4*C4

3. Copy the formulas:

   - Copy the formula in E7 to F7 and G7.
   - Copy the formula in F4 to F5 and F6.
   - Copy the formula in G4 to G5 and G6.

4. Choose Tools ➤ Solver.

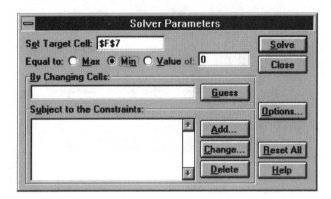

5. Enter cell F7 as the target cell, and set the *Equal To* setting to *Min*.
6. Click on the By Changing Cells edit box, then select cells E4:E6 (the changing cells).
7. Click the Add button to display the Add Constraint dialog box:

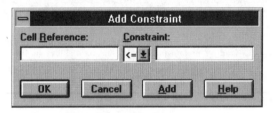

8. Add the following constraints. Click the Add button between each entry.

Cell	Operator	Constraint
E7	=	100
G7	>=	9.2
G7	<=	9.5
E4:E6	>=	0

9. Click OK after you add the last constraint. (Verify the constraints in the Solver Parameters dialog box, and use the Add, Change, and Delete buttons to make corrections as needed—see Figure 23.4.)
10. Click the Solve button to start Solver. Figure 23.5 shows the results.

What-If Analysis

Ch.
23

FIGURE 23.4 ▶

The Solver Parameters dialog box is set up to find the lowest-cost mixture of feeds within the constraints allowed.

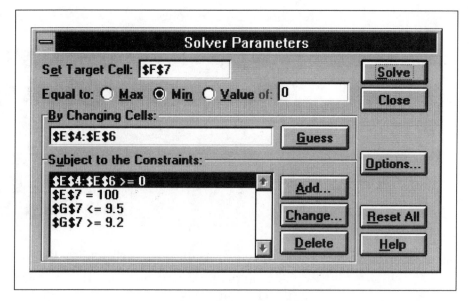

FIGURE 23.5 ▶

Solver has found the lowest-cost mixture which meets the protein requirements.

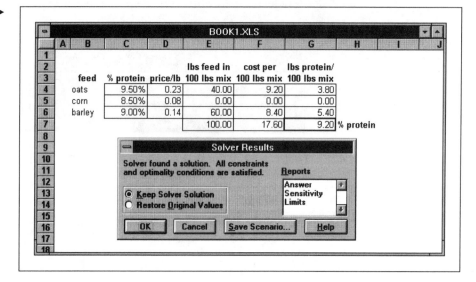

11. Select the Keep Solver Solution option and click the OK button to keep the new values in the worksheet. At this point, you can also save the solution as a named scenario by clicking the Save Scenario button and entering a name for the scenario in the Save Scenario dialog box. (Scenarios are covered later in this chapter.)

Solver works by trying different values in the changing cells and observing the results. By default, Solver is allowed 100 seconds and 100 tries, or *iterations*, to solve the problem. Complex problems (or slower computers) may require more time or iterations to reach a solution. If Solver runs out of time before reaching a solution, a dialog box will be displayed informing you that the maximum time limit was reached.

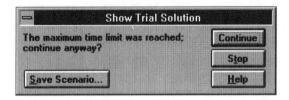

Click the Continue button if you want to disregard the limit and continue the process.

To change the time or number of iterations allowed, click the Options button on the Solver Parameters dialog box (Figure 23.4) to display the Solver Options dialog box (Figure 23.3). Enter a new time and/or number of iterations, and click OK.

 ▶ ▶ **T I P**

Although you can start Solver with the changing cells blank, Solver works faster if you enter some rough estimates into the changing cells.

The Solver settings are saved with the worksheet. When the price of corn changes and the feed mix must be recalculated, all you need to do is open the workbook, change the price on the worksheet, choose Tools ▶ Solver, and click the Solve button.

▶ Solver Reports

The Solver Results dialog box provides three reports to choose from. To produce any of these reports, select the report(s) from the list (hold down Ctrl while clicking to select more than one) and click OK.

The Answer Report The Answer report (Figure 23.6) displays the starting and final values of the target and changing cells, and an analysis of the constraint cells. (Whether the constraint could be met, and how much difference, or *slack*, there is between the constraints and the final values). If a constraint is *binding*, the final value of the cell is limited by the constraint. (Notice that where a constraint is binding, the final value of the cell equals the constraint).

The Sensitivity Report The Sensitivity report (see Figure 23.7) tells you how much of a difference changes in the changing cells (or constraints) would make in the target cell.

▶ ▶ N O T E

> **A different version of the Sensitivity report is created if the Assume Linear Model setting was checked in the Solver Options dialog box.**

FIGURE 23.6 ▶

The Answer report displays an analysis of the constraints used to solve the problem.

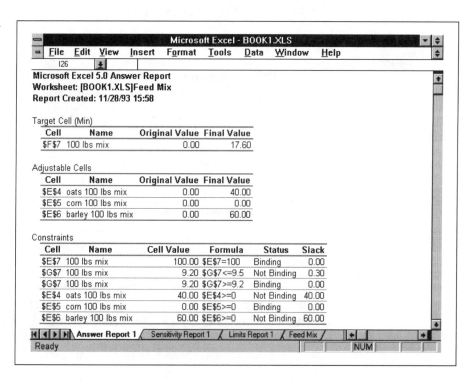

FIGURE 23.7 ▶

The Sensitivity report tells you how sensitive the target value is to changes in constraints or changing values.

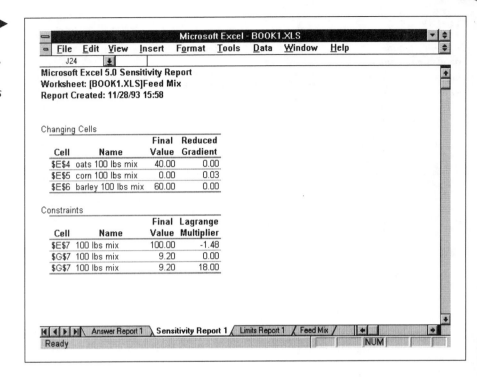

What-If Analysis

▶ ▶

Ch. **23**

The Limits Report The Limits report (see Figure 23.8) lists the values of the target and changing cells, and their upper and lower limits (as specified by the constraints). Essentially, this report shows the margin of variation for each changing cell.

▶ *More Facts about Solver*

- Up to 200 changing cells can be specified in a single problem.

- Solver settings (parameters and options) are persistent, and are saved on the worksheet. To save different settings on the same worksheet, save the settings as a *model*. To save a model, click the Save Model button in the Solver options dialog box.

- If you want to watch the values on the worksheet change as Solver tries different values, check the *show iteration results* setting on the Solver Options dialog box. Each major change in values will be displayed on the worksheet, and a dialog box will ask if you want to continue the process after each change.

FIGURE 23.8 ▶

The Limits report shows the margin for variation in the changing cells.

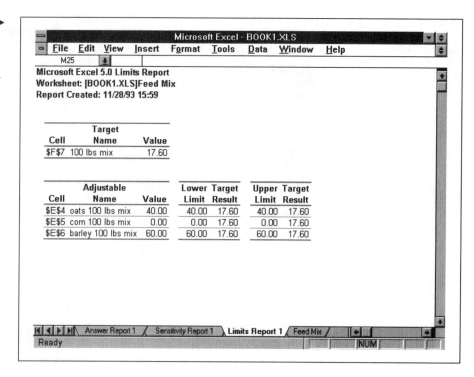

● Excel provides several sample Solver problems in the EXCEL\EXAMPLES\SOLVER file.

▸▸ *Using Scenario Manager*

Scenario manager lets you create and save different sets of input values, with their results, as *scenarios*. A scenario is a group of input values (called changing cells) saved with a name. Each scenario represents a set of what-if assumptions that you can apply to a workbook model to see the effects on other parts of the model.

Use the scenario manager to:

● Create multiple scenarios with multiple sets of changing cells.

● View the results of each scenario on your worksheet.

● Create a summary report of all input values and results.

▶ *Business Case*

Suppose you have been looking for a new home, and have narrowed your choices down to two: one for $200,000, the other for $300,000. The following information will apply to either home:

- The interest rate is 7%, and a 20% down payment is required.
- The term of the loan can be either 15 years or 30 years.

There are four different scenarios: Either the $300,000 house or the $200,000 house, with either the 15-year or 30-year loan. Scenario manager can help organize, manage, and summarize these scenarios.

Begin by creating a scenario for the $300,000 home, with a 15-year loan.

1. Enter the following on a new worksheet:

2. Name cells B3:E4 and B7:B8 using the Insert ▶ Name ▶ Create command.

3. Enter the following formulas:

Cell	Formula
E4	=**Price*.8** (the loan amount is 80% of the purchase price)
B8	=**PMT(Rate/12,Term*12,-Amount)**

4. Choose Tools ➤ Scenarios.

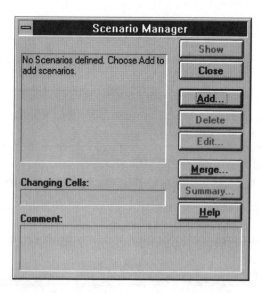

5. Click the Add button on the Scenario Manager dialog box.

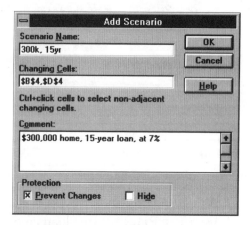

6. Type **300k, 15yr** as a scenario name.

7. Double-click the Changing Cells Edit box (to highlight it), then:

   • Click cell B4.
   • Hold down Ctrl and click cell D4.
   • Click OK.

The Scenario Values dialog box will be displayed, with the names of the changing cells and their values.

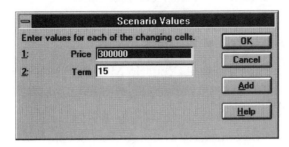

8. Since the values for the first scenario are already entered, click Add to set up the next scenario.

9. Type **300k, 30yr** to create (and name) the second scenario, and click OK.

10. In the Scenario Values dialog box, change the *Term* value to **30**.

11. Repeat steps 8, 9, and 10 to set up two more scenarios:

    • Create the scenario **200k, 15yr** with values of **$200,000** and **15**.
    • Create the scenario **200k, 30yr** with values of **$200,000** and **30**.

12. Click OK after creating the fourth scenario. The Scenario Manager dialog box now contains your list of four scenarios.

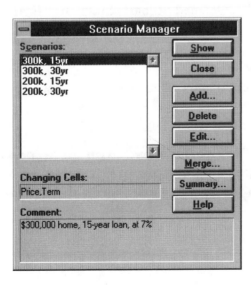

What-If Analysis

▶▶
Ch.
23

To see any single scenario displayed on the worksheet, select the name of the scenario and click the Show button. The worksheet values will change according to the selected scenario.

▶ Scenario Summary Reports

One of the best parts of Scenario Manager lies in its ability to summarize all of the scenarios in a summary report. Follow these steps to create a summary report:

1. Click the Summary button on the Scenario Manager dialog box. The Scenario Summary dialog box will be displayed.

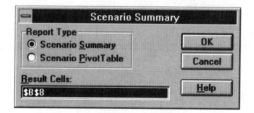

2. Select the Scenario Summary option, and be sure the Result Cell is $B$8 (the cell displaying the payment).

3. Click OK.

A new sheet, named Scenario Summary (Figure 23.9), will be added to the workbook.

Notice the outline symbols along the top and left side of the summary report. You can use these to hide or show levels of detail in the summary—see Chapter 22 to learn more about outlines.

 ▶ ▶**N O T E**

> **The PivotTable option on the Scenario Summary dialog box creates a pivot table based on the scenario. See Chapter 17 to learn more about pivot tables.**

FIGURE 23.9 ▶

The Scenario Summary is an outlined report of all the scenarios you created.

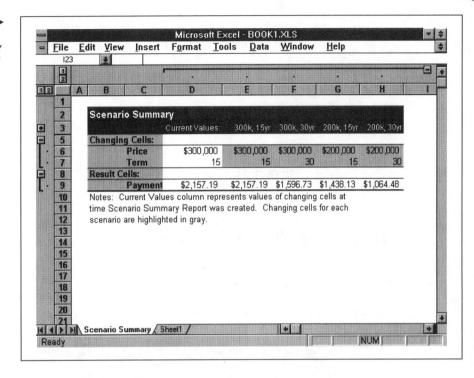

▶ *Merging Scenarios*

Suppose that you have created a number of budget scenarios based on revenue forecasts, and someone else in your department has created other budget scenarios based on different assumptions. The scenarios, defined in two separate workbooks, can be merged into a single model.

Follow these steps to merge scenarios:

1. Open the workbooks that contain the scenarios you want to merge. (For example, HIS_BOOK and MY_BOOK.) Make sure the worksheet which will contain the merged scenarios is active (in this case, MY_BOOK!Sheet1).

2. Choose Tools ➤ Scenarios, and click the Merge button on the Scenarios dialog box. The Merge Scenarios dialog box will be displayed, with a list of all open workbooks and a list of the worksheets in each workbook.

What-If Analysis

Ch.
23

3. Select the workbook (HIS_BOOK) and worksheet (Sheet1) you want to merge from, then click OK.

▶ Deleting Scenarios

To delete a scenario:

1. Choose Tools ➤ Scenarios.
2. Select the scenario to be deleted.
3. Click the Delete button.

▶ Using the Scenarios Tool

The Scenarios tool on the Workgroup toolbar offers an easy way to add, edit, or display scenarios.

Until scenarios are created, the tool is an empty listbox.

To add scenarios using the Scenarios tool:

1. Enter the values you want to use into the changing cells on the worksheet.
2. Select all the changing cells to be included in the scenario (hold down Ctrl while clicking to select non-adjacent cells).
3. Type a scenario name in the Scenarios tool, and press Enter.

To display a scenario using the Scenarios tool, select the scenario you want from the drop-down list.

To edit scenarios using the Scenarios tool:

1. Display the scenario to be edited.
2. Edit the values in the changing cells.

3. Select or type the scenario name in the scenarios tool, and press Enter.

A dialog box will be displayed asking if you want to redefine the scenario based on current cell values—click Yes.

▶ Protecting Scenarios

Scenarios can be protected by the Prevent Changes setting on the Add Scenario and Edit Scenario dialog boxes. By default, this setting is checked, and takes effect when the worksheet is protected.

The Tools ➤ Protection ➤ Protect Sheet dialog box also has a Scenarios setting which prevents changes to the definition of a scenario when the sheet is protected. See Chapter 11, Protecting and Auditing Your Work, to learn more about worksheet protection.

▶ More Facts about Scenario Manager

- Up to 32 changing cells can be defined per scenario.

- Scenario Manager can be used to save scenarios created with Solver (click the Save Scenario button in the Solver Results dialog box).

- When a scenario is created or edited, the user name and date are recorded by Scenario Manager. This information is displayed in the Scenario Manager dialog box and in the first outline level of the Summary report.

What-If Analysis

Ch.
23

CHAPTER **24**

Using Excel Add-Ins

FAST TRACK

▶ **To define reports**   **820**

First, load the Report Manager add-in. Then, choose File
➤ Print Report, and click Add. Finally, add sheets (sections) to the report, each containing an optional view and
scenario.

▶ **To print a report**   **821**

Choose File ➤ Print Report, then select a report and
click Print.

▶ **To use special scientific, engineering, and financial
functions**   **823**

Load the Analysis ToolPak add-in. Functions become available, just like built-in functions.

▶ **To save a workbook as an add-in**   **824**

First, open the workbook and activate a module or macro
sheet. Then, choose Tools ➤ Make Add-In.

▶ **Add-ins can't be modified**   **824**

Therefore, save a copy of your original workbook.

▶▶ **A**s the name implies, add-ins are not part of the Excel core program—they are separate components which, if designed properly, seamlessly extend the power of Excel. There are a number of add-ins that come with Excel, and you may have already used one or more of them without realizing what they were.

This chapter covers:

- *How to configure Excel to load add-ins automatically.*
- *How to use add-ins that come with Excel: AutoSave, View Manager, Report Manager, and the Analysis ToolPak.*
- *How to create your own add-ins.*

Several add-ins are discussed in other chapters. The MS Query and the ODBC add-ins are covered in Chapter 18; the Solver is covered in Chapter 23.

 ▶ ▶ **N O T E**

> **Scenario Manager was an add-in under Excel 4, but is now built into the core Excel program (see Chapter 23). The Excel 4 Scenario Manager add-in is still included with Excel 5 for backwards compatibility.**

►► *Installing and Configuring Add-Ins*

This section explains how to configure Excel so that the add-ins you want available all times will open automatically when you start the program.

► *Installation Issues*

When you first install Excel, there are a number of optional components that you can choose to install, many of which are add-ins. Something happens when you install add-ins that is very important to understand: in some cases, the Excel setup program not only copies the add-in to your hard disk, but also configures Excel to load the add-in automatically. (Or in some cases, a small part of the add-in is loaded automatically which, when evoked, opens the entire add-in.) If the add-ins are not used on an everyday basis, this introduces two problems:

- It takes longer to start Excel when lots of add-ins are automatically loaded.
- Add-ins consume memory.

In the following discussion, you will learn how to configure Excel to automatically load add-ins. Don't be surprised if, when you first use the add-in configuration utility, you find that a handful of add-ins are being automatically opened every time you start Excel—including some obscure ones that you may never use.

 ► ►**N O T E**

> **The Excel setup program can be used to install components that were not installed when you first set up Excel on your system.**

► *Configuring Excel to Load Add-Ins Automatically*

Choose the Tools ➤ Add-Ins command to display the add-in dialog box, which is used to set which add-ins load automatically.

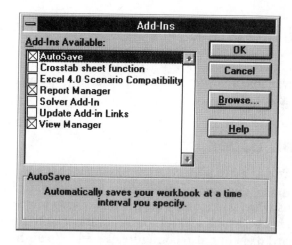

Using the checkboxes (in the list box), check the add-ins you want Excel to load automatically. Uncheck the ones you will never (or seldom) use.

 ► ►**N O T E**

> **When you un-check an add-in, it is *not* removed from your disk. You can always re-check and add-in later.**

You can purchase third-party add-in products, or create your own. Click Browse to search for add-ins other than the ones that come with Excel.

 ► ►**T I P**

> **To use an add-in that is not set up to load automatically, use Tools ➤ Add-Ins. When done, use Tools ➤ Add-Ins to unload it.**

► *How Add-Ins Behave*

Different add-ins behave differently. Some, such as the Analysis Tool-Pak, are practically invisible. The ToolPak adds special worksheet functions; it does not add any commands to the Excel menu system. Other add-ins, such as View Manager and Report Manager, add one or more commands to the Excel menu system.

An add-in can be a custom application that takes over the Excel workspace, and displays a custom menu system (though none of the add-ins that come with Excel behave this way). Later in this chapter, you will learn how to save a workbook as an add-in.

▶▶ *Save Your Files Automatically Using AutoSave*

The AutoSave add-in automatically saves your work at specified time intervals. Choose Tools ➤ AutoSave to display the AutoSave dialog box.

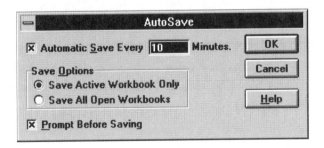

- Check the checkbox to activate AutoSave, or clear it to de-activate the feature.
- Enter the number of minutes between AutoSave.
- Specify whether you want just the active workbook saved, or all open workbooks.
- Check Prompt Before Saving if want the chance to confirm/cancel the save.

► ►WARNING

Saving files automatically, without the option to confirm, can be a risky proposition. Just imagine that the save occurs right after you make a serious mistake, and just before you are about to choose the Edit ➤ Undo command.

►► *Using View Manager*

The View Manager add-in is a tool that lets you define different *views* on a worksheet, and display them with ease. A view definition consists of:

- A view name.
- A range of cells.
- Display settings such as gridlines, scroll bars, and row and column headings.
- Print settings (optional).
- Hidden row and column settings (optional).

► ►NOTE

The View Manager add-in must be loaded in order to use View Manager. This topic is discussed earlier in this chapter.

Choose the View ➤ View Manager command to display the view manager dialog box.

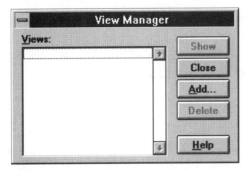

Adding a View

To add a new view, click the Add button on the View Manager dialog box. The Add View dialog box is displayed.

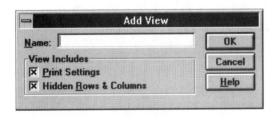

Name Behind the scenes, a hidden name is created containing the view settings. Thus, the rules for the view name are the same as those for a cell name: it has to start with a letter; no spaces allowed; it can contain only letters, numbers, periods, and underscores; it can't exceed 255 characters.

Print Settings If checked, the current print settings are stored as part of the view definition.

Hidden Rows & Columns If checked, the view tracks which rows/columns are hidden. When you add a new view, the current status of the workspace (e.g., gridlines, scroll bars) is stored as part of the view definition.

Showing and Deleting Views

Showing a View Choose View ➤ View Manager, select a view from the list, then click Show.

Using Excel
Add-Ins

▸▸

Ch.
24

Deleting a View Choose View ➤ View Manager, select a view from the list, then click Delete.

Real-World Application

View Manager is a carry-over from Excel 4 and some of its functionality has been obviated by the Excel 5 workbook model. Since individual worksheets within a workbook can be formatted differently (i.e. with gridlines, row & column headings, etc.), the fact that View Manager stores such settings is only marginally useful. (View Manager does, however, allow multiple views per worksheet.)

View Manager is especially useful when it is used on an outlined worksheet. Different views can be defined for different outline levels. Try this brief exercise to get a better feel for how View Manager works.

1. On a new worksheet, select B2:D5 and choose View ➤ View Manager. Click Add.

2. Enter a name, check both settings, then click OK.

 ▶ ▶ **T I P**

> **View settings are stored as a hidden name on the active worksheet.**

3. Choose Tools ➤ Options, click the View tab, and uncheck the Gridlines and Row & Column Headers settings.

4. Hide column B.

5. Select D4:D9 and choose View ➤ View Manager. Click Add.

6. Enter a name, check both settings, then click OK.

Now, show the two views to see how they work:

7. Choose View ➤ View Manager, choose the view defined at Step 2, and click Show.

8. Choose View ➤ View Manager, choose the view defined at Step 6, and click Show.

As you show each view, the workspace is changed according to the settings at the time the view was defined.

NOTE

> **You probably don't want to use View Manager as an aid for simple worksheet navigation. It is a large add-in, and probably not worth the load-time or memory penalties.**

▶▶ *Using Report Manager*

The Report Manager add-in lets you define one or more custom *reports* which are stored in the active workbook. A report consists of one or more sections which will be printed as separate pages in the report. In each section you specify:

- The name of the worksheet.
- Optionally, one scenario on that worksheet (see Chapter 23 to learn about Scenario Manager).
- Optionally, one view that has been defined on the worksheet (see preceding section on Views in this chapter).

Here are some typical problems that can be solved with Report Manager:

- A workbook contains numerous worksheets. When you print the workbook, you want to print only three of the sheets, in a specified sequence.
- A worksheet contains three scenarios created with Scenario Manager: Optimistic, Pessimistic, and Realistic. When you print the sheet, you want to print each scenario.
- A worksheet contains two noncontiguous ranges that you want to print on the same report, using the same page number sequence. (Each range is setup as a view using View Manager.)

For every task that you perform with Report Manager (creating reports, printing reports, etc.), the first step is to activate the desired workbook, then choose the File ➤ Print Report command.

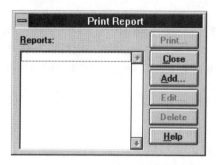

▶ Creating a Report

To create a new report, click the Add button on the Print Report dialog box. The Add Report dialog box is displayed.

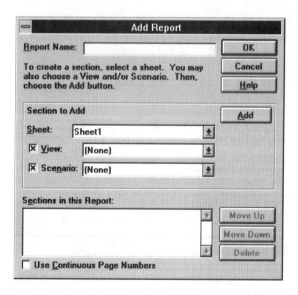

Report Name Enter a report name consisting of letters, numbers, and spaces. Special characters are not permitted.

Sheet Add sheets to the report by selecting a sheet name from the drop-down list. Then click the Add button. You can add the same sheet to the report more than once.

View You can include a view (defined by View Manager) as part of the definition for each section of the report. Only the view range will print on the page (including all of the view settings). Choose the view from the drop-down list.

Scenario A scenario (created by Scenario Manager) can be included as part of the section definition. Choose the scenario from the drop-down list.

Move Up and Move Down The sections of the reports as they display in the list box determine their print order. Use the Move Up and Move Down buttons to change the order of the sections within the list.

Delete Click Delete to remove the selected section from the report.

Use Continuous Page Numbers When checked, the entire report uses the same page number sequence.

 ▶ ▶ **T I P**

You can create more than one report per workbook.

▶ *Editing, Printing, and Deleting Reports*

For each of these procedures, start by choosing File ➤ Print Report. Select a report from the list of reports. Then,

- To edit a report, click Edit. The Edit Report dialog box works the same way as the Add Report dialog box.

- To print a report, click Print.

- To delete a report, click Delete.

Using Excel Add-Ins

▶ ▶

Ch.
24

USING SLIDE SHOW

Suppose you have an on-screen presentation to prepare, and you don't have a separate presentation program (like Microsoft Power-Point). You can create on-screen presentations of worksheets and charts using Excel's Slide Show. Slide Show is an add-in that allows you to create an on-screen presentation of your data. With Slide Show, you can incorporate charts, graphics, and worksheet data into your screen or overhead presentation. The charts and data in your slides can be linked or unlinked, as you choose. To use Slide Show, it must have been installed in Excel, and then the add-in must be loaded. To load it, choose Tools ➤ Add-ins and check the Slideshow Template checkbox. Then, when you choose File ➤ New, the File New dialog will be displayed and you can select Slide. (For the template to show up in the File ➤ New dialog box, you must quit Excel and start again after loading the add-in.)

To create slides, you copy the data, charts, etc. you want to show, then paste it into a slide workbook using the Paste Slide button on the Slides template. Slides will be linked to the source workbooks, so any changes you make to source data will be automatically updated in the slides.

During your presentation you can change slides manually or time them, and you can create a number of transition effects. You can set these features in the Edit Slide dialog which is displayed when you click the Edit Slide button. To run the Slide Show, click the Start Show button on the template. Press the space bar to change slides (if the show is not set to timed slides). To stop the show at any point, press Escape—from the Slide Show Options dialog, you can choose Stop, Continue, or Go To any slide number you choose.

▶▶ *Analysis ToolPak*

The Analysis ToolPak is different than the other add-ins discussed so far in this chapter in that it does not add commands to the Excel menu. Instead, it adds a wide variety of special worksheet functions. When the add-in is loaded, the functions are available for use just like built-in functions, such as SUM. (See how to load add-ins earlier in this chapter.)

The functions included in the ToolPak are in the following categories:

- Engineering functions
- Functions for statistical analysis
- Financial functions

Appendix B lists all of the functions included in the Analysis ToolPak.

▶▶ *Creating Add-Ins*

As you have learned so far in this chapter, add-ins come in a variety of sizes and flavors. If you want to, though, you can also create your own. You might, for example, want to create an add-in to do any of the following:

- Add new worksheet functions, like the Analysis ToolPak.
- Add a special feature, like View Manager and Report Manager.
- Be an entire custom application, like a portfolio analysis system, or an executive information system.

Needless to say, the real work involved in creating an add-in is the process of writing the program itself. Add-ins can be written using Visual Basic, Applications Edition (VBA), and/or the old Excel macro language (XLM).

Using Excel
Add-Ins

▶▶
Ch.
24

Your programs will reside in a workbook, on VBA modules, or on XLM macro sheets. (Refer to Chapter 20 to get acquainted with some of the issues involved.) Follow these procedures to transform your workbook into an add-in:

1. Activate the workbook.
2. Activate any VBA module or XLM macro sheet.
3. Choose Tools ➤ Make Add-In.

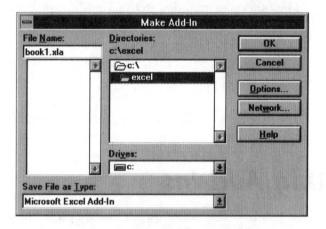

4. Use the Make Add-in dialog box just as you use the File ➤ Save dialog box: enter a file name, and choose a directory. Notice the file type is set to Microsoft Excel Add-In. Click OK.

A copy of your workbook is created as an add-in, and the original workbook is left intact. It is very important that you retain the original workbook, because the add-in cannot be modified.

For more information on creating add-ins, refer to the *Visual Basic User's Guide* that comes with Excel.

▶▶ *Commercial Add-Ins*

There are a number of Excel add-ins that can be purchased from various software vendors. Here are some of the more notable ones.

BrainCel

A forecasting tool based on neural network technology—a non–rules-based method for analyzing data. BrainCel is available from:

> Promised Land Technologies, Inc.
> (203) 562-7335

Crystal Ball

A forecasting and risk analysis tool that creates Monte Carlo simulations. Crystal Ball is available from:

> Decisioneering
> (800) 289-2550

Evolver

A genetic algorithm problem-solver used to provide optimal results for problems with unlimited variables. Evolver is available from:

> Axcelis, Inc.
> (206) 632-0885

Microsoft Open EIS Pak

An Excel-based application generator that helps you develop executive information systems (EIS) and decision support systems (DSS), without having to know how to program. This product is available from:

> Microsoft Corporation
> (800) 426-9400

@RISK

Provides advanced analysis capabilities used for forecasting and financial modeling. @RISK is available from:

> Palisade Corporation
> (607) 277-8000

Worksheet Wizard

An add-in that helps users create common worksheet models such as income statements and balance sheets. Worksheet Wizard is available from:

Graphitti Software Corporation
(209) 299-7849

CHAPTER 25

Working with Other Programs and Data

FAST TRACK

▶ ***To insert an object into Excel using Excel menu commands*** **842**

First, choose Insert ➤ Object. Then, select the Create New tab to create a new object, or select the Create from File tab to insert an object from an existing file.

▶ ***To import a text file*** **846**

Open the file using File ➤ Open, then specify import options using the Text Import Wizard.

▶ ***To import dBASE, Lotus 1-2-3, and QuattroPro files*** **853**

Use the File ➤ Open command.

▶ ***To export an Excel file to different format*** **853**

Choose File ➤ Save As. Select the file type from Save File As Type list.

▶ ***To get help if you are a Lotus 1-2-3 user*** **854**

Choose Help ➤ Lotus 1-2-3; or choose Tools ➤ Options, click the Transition tab, and select the Lotus 1-2-3 Help option.

▶▶ **N**o software program is an island. The ability to work with other programs—and the data created by them—is an important feature in any modern software package. Excel is an outstanding citizen in this regard. This chapter covers:

- *Transferring data to and from other applications using the Clipboard*
- *Sharing data with other programs using Object Linking and Embedding (OLE)*
- *Importing text files*
- *Importing data from other applications, such as dBASE and Lotus 1-2-3*
- *Exporting data*
- *Switching from Lotus 1-2-3 to Excel*

For a review of how to query external databases from Excel, refer to Chapter 18.

▶▶ Exchanging Data with Other Applications Using the Clipboard

Excel has several powerful facilities for importing and exporting data, such as object linking and embedding. But for everyday manual tasks, the Clipboard is a convenient way to move information in and out of Excel. Most Windows programs are capable of using the Clipboard, and it can be used to copy text and graphics.

▶ Copying Text into Excel

Here is an exercise that demonstrates how to copy text from Notepad into Excel:

1. Start Notepad, and enter some text.
2. Select the text with the mouse, and Choose Edit ➤ Copy. (This places the text on the Clipboard.)
3. Activate Excel, and choose Edit ➤ Paste. (This pastes the text from the Clipboard.)

The text is placed into one or more cells. It's that simple. Every other use of the Clipboard is simply a variation on the above exercise.

▶ Copying Graphics into Excel

The procedure for copying graphics into Excel is very similar. Use a program such as Paintbrush, then use the Edit ➤ Copy command to copy a graphic to the Clipboard. Activate Excel, and choose Edit ➤ Paste. The graphic is placed on the worksheet as a graphic object, as shown in Figure 25.1.

Graphics copied into Excel can be moved, resized, and deleted just like any other graphic object. (See Chapter 12 for a review of working with graphic objects.)

▶ Copying Data out of Excel

Copying data (text or graphics) out of Excel involves the same procedure used to copy into Excel, but in the opposite direction. Follow this exercise to copy some information from Excel into Write (the word processor that comes with Microsoft Windows).

1. Select a range of cells, and choose Edit ➤ Copy.
2. Activate Write, and choose Edit ➤ Paste.

Figure 25.2 shows a Write file where two different paste operations have occurred.

FIGURE 25.1 ▶

This Canadian flag was copied from the Microsoft PowerPoint clipart library. The object is selected, and its name is displayed in the name box, just like any graphic object in Excel.

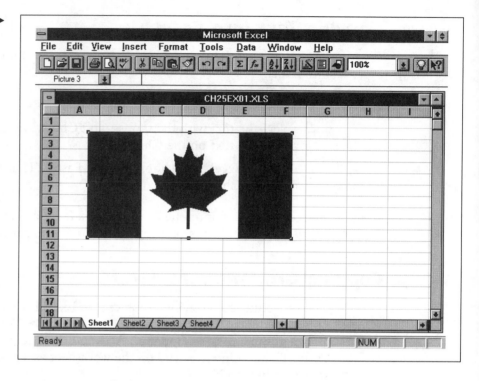

FIGURE 25.2 ▶

The same data from Excel was pasted two times, using different paste methods available in Write.

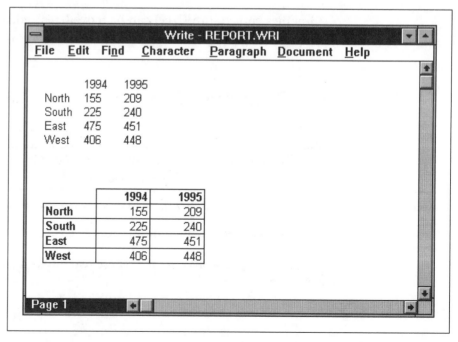

The first table of numbers in Figure 25.2 is text. The second table is a graphic (bitmap). Write can import the data in different formats, using its Edit ➤ Paste Special command. This illustrates an important point: the type of data that pastes into the other program is dependent on that program's capabilities. For example, Notepad is not capable of importing graphics. If you wanted to paste the data pictured in Figure 25.2 into Notepad, the only option would be to paste text.

▶▶ *Using Object Linking and Embedding*

Object Linking and Embedding (OLE) is a technology that allows different applications to share data with one another. The term OLE is derived from the fact that a piece of data, called an *object*, which is created in one application can be *embedded* in another. And the embedded object can be *linked* to the source document.

▶ ▶NOTE

OLE is not limited to Microsoft products. Many non-Microsoft applications support OLE, including most major word processing and graphics applications.

Unfortunately, there's a lot of jargon necessary to explain OLE. Nevertheless, OLE is really quite simple. In this section, you will walk through a simple exercise to see how OLE works.

▶ ▶NOTE

Many applications, including Excel, support version two of the OLE specification. Since OLE 2 is here today, and since it is the future direction for most major Windows applications, the discussion of OLE in this chapter will focus on OLE 2.

To illustrate how OLE works, the following examples will use Excel 5 and Microsoft Word for Windows 6.

▶ Copying an Excel Object into Word

Suppose you are writing a business plan in Word, and that you have built a worksheet (Figure 25.3) in Excel that contains supporting data. The following exercise shows you how to copy part of the worksheet to the Word document:

1. In Excel, select the cells you want to copy. Then choose Edit ➤ Copy.

2. Activate Word. Place the cursor at the place where you want to paste the object.

3. In Word, choose Edit ➤ Paste Special. The dialog box in Figure 25.4 is displayed.

FIGURE 25.3 ▶

Supporting data for a business plan

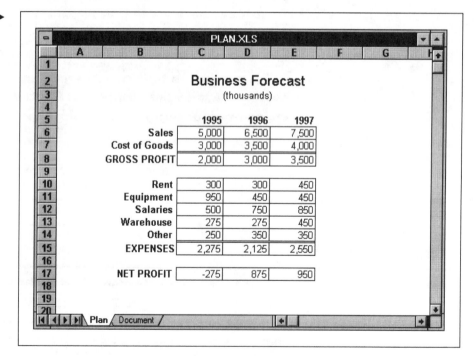

	PLAN.XLS						
	A	B	C	D	E	F	G	H

Business Forecast
(thousands)

	1995	1996	1997
Sales	5,000	6,500	7,500
Cost of Goods	3,000	3,500	4,000
GROSS PROFIT	2,000	3,000	3,500
Rent	300	300	450
Equipment	950	450	450
Salaries	500	750	850
Warehouse	275	275	450
Other	250	350	350
EXPENSES	2,275	2,125	2,550
NET PROFIT	-275	875	950

Plan / Document /

FIGURE 25.4 ▶

The Paste Special dialog box. As you can see from the first item in the list, Word senses that the soon-to-be pasted object is coming from Excel.

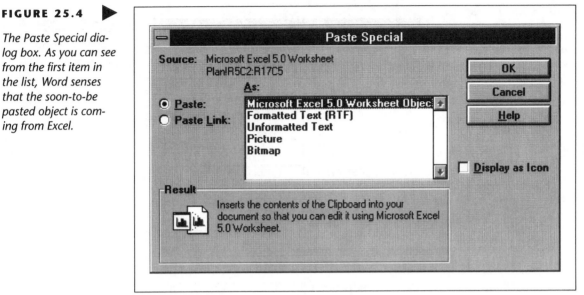

4. Select Microsoft Excel 5.0 Worksheet Object, and select how you want to paste:

- *Paste* places an embedded object into Word. The Excel object then "lives" inside the Word document, with no link to the original Excel document. (You will still be able to edit the Excel object using Excel, as you will soon see.)

- *Paste Link* links the object to the original Excel document. Changes to the original Excel document will cause the linked object to update.

5. Click OK. The Word document is shown in Figure 25.5.

Using Drag and Drop

Instead of using menu commands, you can drag and drop information from Excel to Word. Arrange your workspace so that you can see both applications at once. Activate Excel, and follow these steps:

1. Select the cell(s) you want to copy.

FIGURE 25.5 ►

The Excel information is pasted into the Word document as an Excel object.

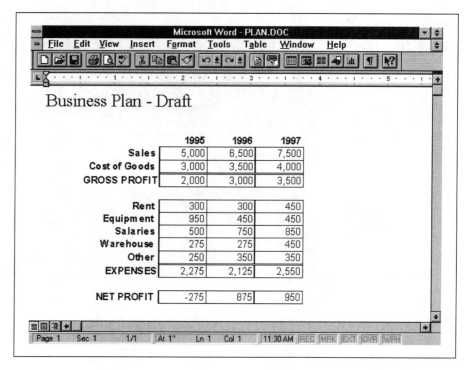

Microsoft Word - PLAN.DOC

File Edit View Insert Format Tools Table Window Help

Business Plan - Draft

	1995	1996	1997
Sales	5,000	6,500	7,500
Cost of Goods	3,000	3,500	4,000
GROSS PROFIT	2,000	3,000	3,500
Rent	300	300	450
Equipment	950	450	450
Salaries	500	750	850
Warehouse	275	275	450
Other	250	350	350
EXPENSES	2,275	2,125	2,550
NET PROFIT	-275	875	950

Page 1   Sec 1   1/1   At 1"   Ln 1   Col 1   11:30 AM REC MRK EXT OVR WPH

2. Click on the outermost border of the selected range, and while holding down the mouse button, drag the cells using one of these methods:

- Drag the cells onto the Word document to *cut and paste*.
- Hold down the Ctrl key while dragging to *copy and paste*.

 ►►**TIP**

You are not limited to cells when copying Excel objects to other applications. You can also copy Excel charts and other graphic objects. Just drag and drop the chart onto a Word document, for instance, to embed the chart in Word.

▶ *Understanding How Embedded Objects Work*

Consider the dialog box in Figure 25.4. Suppose that you choose the Paste option. This means:

- The Excel object is *embedded* in the Word document. It is physically stored there.

- There is no link to the original Excel worksheet. A change to the original Excel worksheet has no effect on the embedded object.

- If you double-click the embedded object (in the Word document), Excel is activated and takes control—even though you do not leave the Word document (See Figure 25.6). At this point, you are using Excel, but within the context of the Word document. This is called *in-place editing*.

- If you edit the embedded Excel object, there is no effect on the original Excel worksheet, since there is no link.

- When you click outside the embedded object (within the Word document), Word assumes control again.

FIGURE 25.6 ▶

The Excel object on the Word document has been double-clicked. The Excel menu takes over, and the object becomes an editable Excel worksheet.

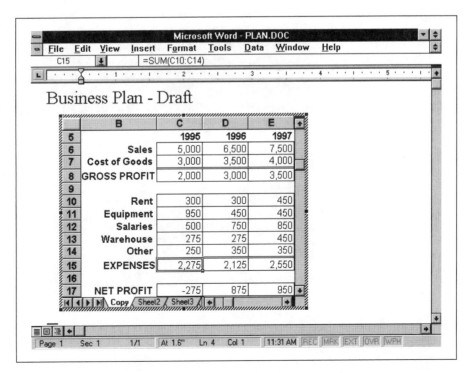

Other Programs and Data

▶▶ Ch. **25**

▶ *Understanding How Linked Objects Work*

Suppose, on the other hand, that you choose the *Paste Link* option from the dialog box pictured in Figure 25.4. This means:

- The Excel object is *linked* to the original worksheet. The object is simply a copy of the worksheet cells.

- When the worksheet changes, the linked object changes.

- If you double-click the linked object (in the Word document), the original worksheet is loaded into Excel (unlike the in-place editing that occurs for embedded objects).

▶ *Placing a Word Object into Excel*

Placing OLE objects into Excel involves identical concepts and procedures similar to the previous exercises—but in reverse. Since Word and Excel are both Microsoft products, even the dialog boxes are similar. Figure 25.7 shows Excel's Edit ▶ Paste Special dialog box.

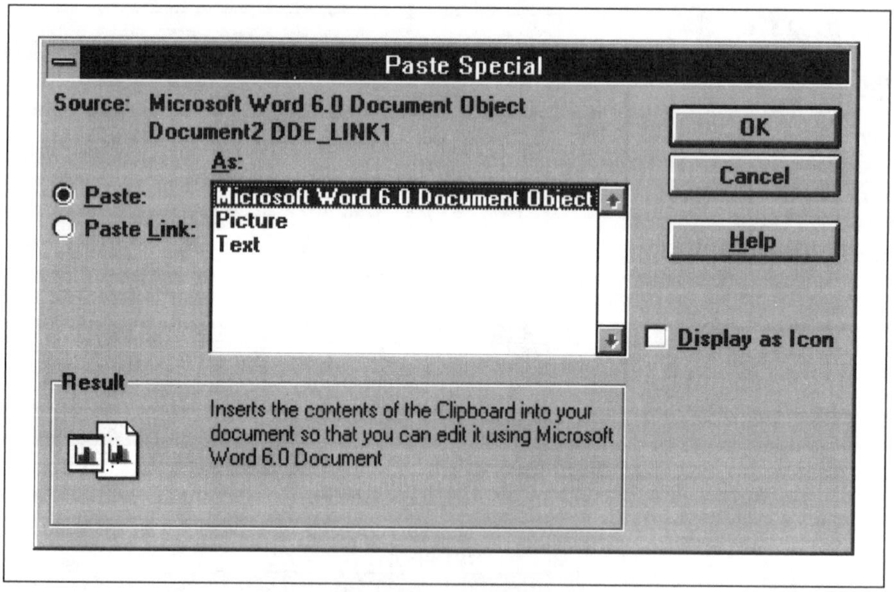

FIGURE 25.7 ▶

Excel's Edit ▶ Paste Special dialog box is similar to the Word dialog box.

> ▶ **N O T E**
>
> **Excel's Edit ➤ Paste Special dialog box is different, depending on the contents of the Clipboard at the time the command is chosen. If the Clipboard contains data from another application (non-Excel data), it looks like Figure 25.7. If, however, the Clipboard contains Excel data, the dialog box provides different options.**

Figure 25.8 shows an Excel worksheet with an embedded Word object. Notice that when the object is selected, the formula bar shows where the object came from.

FIGURE 25.8

A Word object embedded in Excel

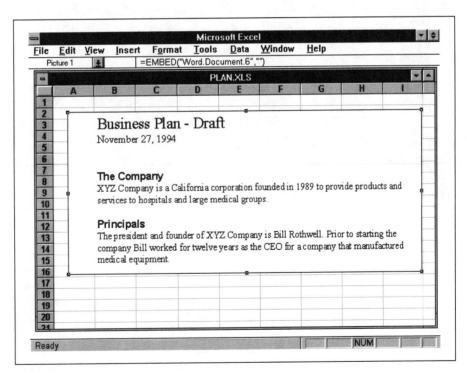

▶
LINK A WORD OBJECT INTO EXCEL WITH AN ICON

Suppose you have information in a Word document which is supplemental to your Excel report, and you don't want the information displayed unless the user specifically asks to see it. If the report is going to be used primarily electronically, you can display the Word object as an icon on the worksheet. When the user double-clicks the icon, the Word document is opened.

Both embedded and linked objects can be displayed as icons. To display an embedded or linked object as an icon, check the Display as Icon setting on the Paste Special dialog.

▶ *Embedding an Object in Excel Using the Excel Menu*

You have seen how to copy objects from one application to another when both applications are running. You can also insert OLE objects into Excel by starting out with a command on the Excel menu. Choose Insert ▶ Object to display the dialog box pictured in Figure 25.9.

Inserting a New Object The Create New tab (see Figure 25.9) lists the different types of OLE objects that you are able to create. Choose an object from the list, then click OK. The program that is responsible for the given object is started—when you quit the program, the object

FIGURE 25.9 ▶

The Object dialog box lets you create a new object or import one from an existing file.

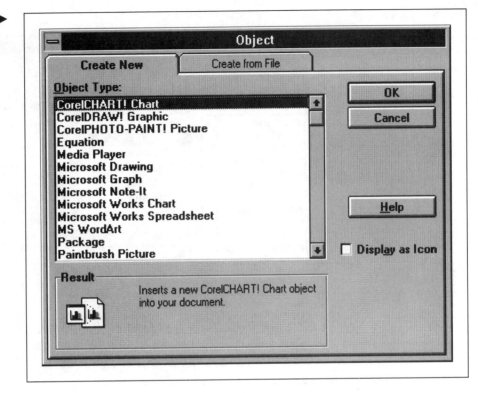

is placed on the worksheet. (The precise behavior depends on the individual program.)

Inserting an Object from an Existing File The Create from File tab (see Figure 25.10) lets you insert an existing file into the active worksheet. Select a file from the list of files. Check Link to File to link the object to the file. Check Display as Icon to place an icon on the worksheet representing the object.

Working with OLE Applets

There are several OLE mini-apps, sometimes referred to as *applets*, that are included with various Microsoft products. Some examples of these applets are *Microsoft Graph*, *Microsoft Note-It*, and *Microsoft ClipArt Gallery*. These applications cannot be run stand-alone—their sole purpose is to provide OLE services.

FIGURE 25.10 ►

Select the file you
want to place on the
worksheet.

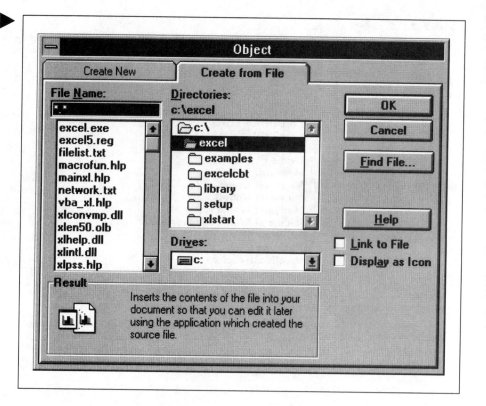

> ### N O T E
>
> **The applets are stored in the MSAPPS directory, under
> the directory where Windows is installed.**

If any of these applications are installed on your system, they will display in the Object dialog box (Figure 25.9). Try inserting a Note-It object, or an object from the ClipArt Gallery.

► *Working with OLE Objects in Excel*

OLE objects on Excel worksheets are very similar to "normal" graphic
objects.

To Set an OLE Object as Non-Printing By default, an OLE object will
print when the worksheet is printed. If you don't want it to print, select

the object, choose Format ➤ Object, click the Properties tab, and un-check the Print Object Setting.

To Move, Resize, and Format Use the same procedures as for other graphic objects, described in Chapter 12.

To Create a Static Picture of an OLE Object Select the object, choose Edit ➤ Copy, select a cell, choose Edit ➤ Paste Special. Choose Picture.

To Convert the Object Type When you click on an OLE object with the right mouse button, a special command is displayed on the shortcut menu. The command text varies, based on the type of object selected, as do the commands on the sub-menu. Choose the Convert command to change the object type—use this command when you do not have the application on your system that is responsible for the object.

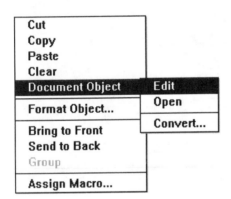

▶▶ *Importing Text Files*

Since most applications are able to export data in text format, import-ing text files is usually fairly easy. Unfortunately, however, there are sev-eral different text file formats—something which has confounded users of earlier Excel versions. To avoid confusion, Excel 5 employs a Text Im-port Wizard to simplify the job of importing text files.

▶ ▶ N O T E

This discussion is based on text files that contain data oriented as records, with each record containing fields of data, as opposed to random text. Random textual data can easily be copied into Excel using the Clipboard, from a text program such as Notepad.

The first step to import a text file is to choose the File ▶ Open command. Select Text Files from the list of file types, then open the desired file.

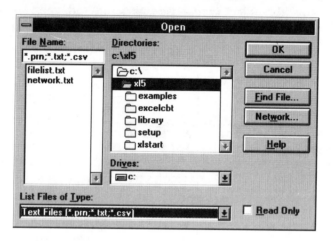

What happens next depends on the format of the text file.

▶ Text Files with Delimiters

Delimiters are special characters that separate fields, allowing Excel to place each field into a new column on the worksheet. When a text file is delimited, importing it into Excel is easy. There are several delimiters that are frequently used. Perhaps the most common one is *comma delimited*, referred to as CSV (for comma separate values). Figure 25.11 shows a CSV file which has been opened using Notepad.

If you import a certain text file on a regular basis, and have any control of the file format, use CSV format. When you open a CSV file, the data

FIGURE 25.11 ▶

This comma delimited text file contains 4 rows (records) and 5 columns (fields).

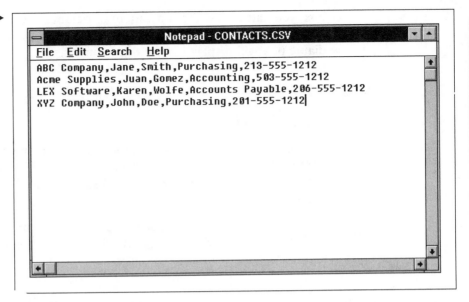

is automatically placed into rows and columns. Figure 25.12 shows the same text file opened in Excel.

When other types of delimiters are used (tabs, for instance), the Text Import Wizard verifies the delimiter before placing the data onto the worksheet. After you check Delimited in the Text Import Wizard Step 1 dialog

FIGURE 25.12 ▶

When a CSV file is opened in Excel, the data is automatically placed in rows and columns without manual intervention.

	A	B	C	D	E	F
1	ABC Company	Jane	Smith	Purchasing	213-555-1212	
2	Acme Supplies	Juan	Gomez	Accounting	503-555-1212	
3	LEX Software	Karen	Wolfe	Accounts Payable	206-555-1212	
4	XYZ Company	John	Doe	Purchasing	201-555-1212	
5						
6						
7						
8						
9						
10						
11						
12						
13						
14						

CONTACTS.CSV

Sheet1

box, you can choose from a variety of delimiters in the Step 2 dialog box. When the correct delimiter is selected, the preview in the Step 2 dialog box will display the data in columns.

▶ Using the Text Import Wizard for Fixed-Width Files

If your text file does not use delimiters, then the fields will be fixed-width. This, too, is a very common format, and has historically caused users the most trouble. Figure 25.13 shows a text file with fixed-field widths, opened in Notepad.

The Text Import Wizard makes it relatively easy to import fixed-width text files. Here are the steps required to import the text file pictured in Figure 25.13:

FIGURE 25.13 ▶

The fields of a fixed-width text file are typically padded with spaces. The fourth field of the third row, containing Accounts Payable, is the maximum width for the fourth field, and thus has no trailing spaces.

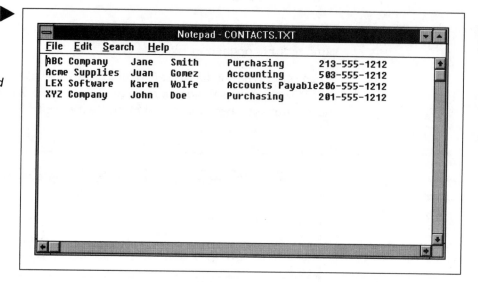

1. Open the File

Choose File ➤ Open, and open the file as usual. Step One of the Text Import Wizard is shown in Figure 25.14.

Original Data Type The Wizard detects that the file is fixed-width, though you can override this option if the Wizard is wrong.

FIGURE 25.14 ▶

*Step One lets you con-
firm the text file format.*

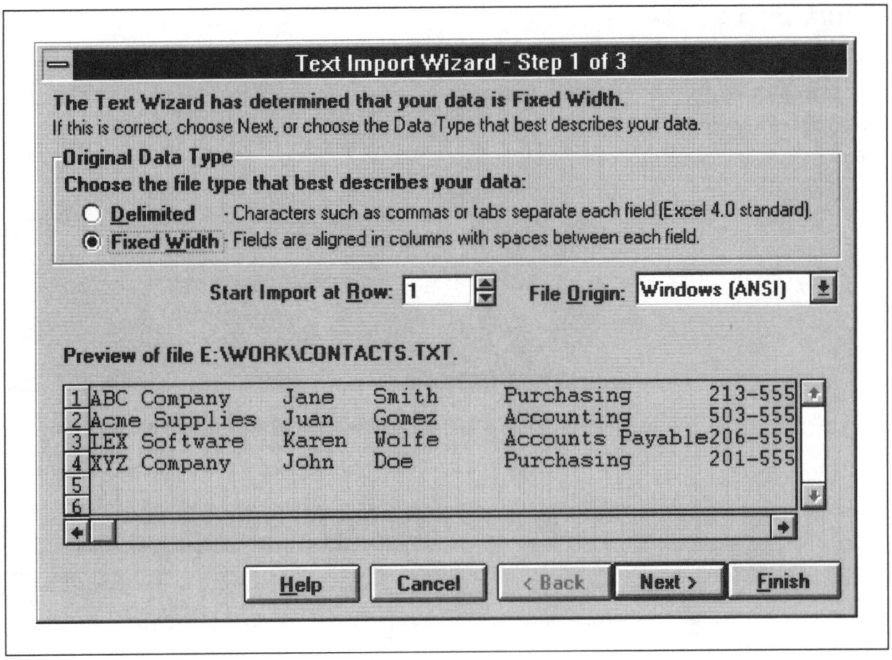

Start Import at Row This lets you specify the starting row number.
This setting is useful if the file contains a header row, and you don't
want to import it.

File Origin There are slight differences between files originated on different platforms, i.e., the character that indicates a new row. The Wizard will usually determine this setting correctly, but you can select
from the drop-down list to override the choice.

Preview Area This scrollable part of the dialog box lets you examine
the file.

Click Next to move to Step Two of the Wizard.

2. Specify the Column Breaks

Step Two of the Wizard (Figure 25.15) lets you specify where the column breaks are located. The Wizard tries to determine the column
breaks for you and usually does a pretty good job. But as you can see in
Figure 25.15, the third row of the file has confused the Wizard—it has
not detected the column break at position 48.

FIGURE 25.15 ►

Step Two provides thorough instruction on how to set the column breaks.

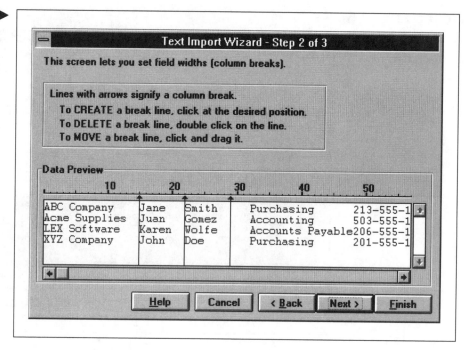

To correct the column breaks shown in Figure 25.15, drag the line at position 29 to position 32. Click position 48 to add a new column break. If you make a mistake, double-click a column line to remove it. Click Next to proceed to Step Three of the Wizard.

3. Format the Columns

Step Three of the Wizard (Figure 25.16) lets you format columns, or exclude them from being imported entirely.

To format a column, click on it with the mouse. Then choose the appropriate column format option.

General If a column is formatted as General format, Excel will automatically determine the data type.

Text Select this option when a column contains numeric values that should be text, e.g., zip codes or social security numbers.

Date Select the date option (and the associated drop-down list) to format a column as dates.

FIGURE 25.16

Step Three is used to format the columns.

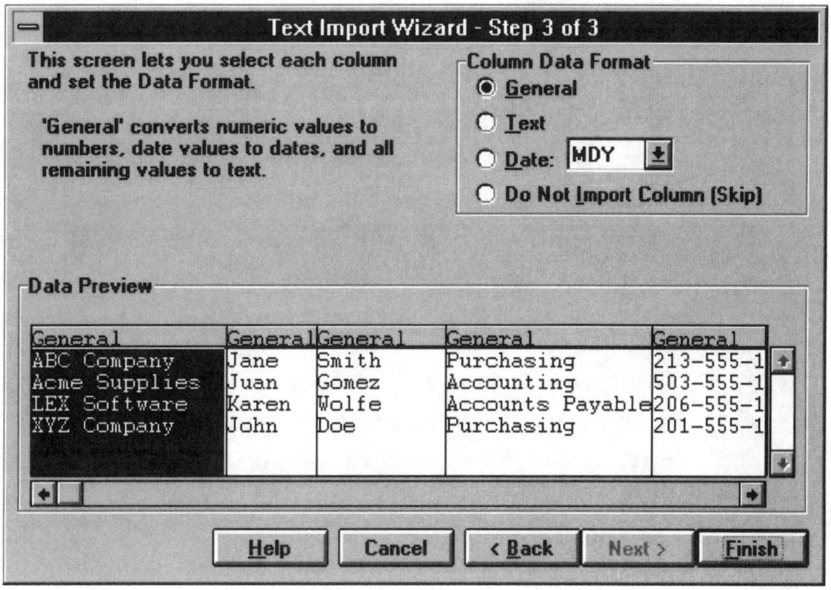

Text Import Wizard - Step 3 of 3

This screen lets you select each column and set the Data Format.

'General' converts numeric values to numbers, date values to dates, and all remaining values to text.

Column Data Format

- ◉ General
- ○ Text
- ○ Date: MDY ▼
- ○ Do Not Import Column (Skip)

Data Preview

General	General	General	General	General
ABC Company	Jane	Smith	Purchasing	213-555-1
Acme Supplies	Juan	Gomez	Accounting	503-555-1
LEX Software	Karen	Wolfe	Accounts Payable	206-555-1
XYZ Company	John	Doe	Purchasing	201-555-1

Help   Cancel   < Back   Next >   Finish

Ch. **25**

Other Programs and Data

Do Not Import Column   Select this option to exclude the column entirely.

When you click Finish, the text file is imported onto the active worksheet into rows and columns.

TIP

> **Suppose that you create reports each month based on a fixed-width text file that is output by a mainframe application. You can automate this task by recording a macro. (See Chapter 20 for a review.)**

CORRECTING DATA PARSING PROBLEMS

Suppose you routinely download tab-delimited data from a mainframe, and it is always imported into Excel with columns parsed appropriately. One day you open a text file which is comma-delimited, and because the file has a .txt extension, Excel automatically displays the Text Import Wizard to guide you in selecting the correct delimiter for the text file. You select the comma delimiter and open the text file, and the data parses correctly into columns.

Next, you download the data from the mainframe as usual, but the data appears on the worksheet all in a single column. It might even have garbage characters mixed in with it. What happened?

The problem is that Excel tried to import the tab-delimited mainframe data using a comma delimiter, because you set the delimiter to comma when you imported the text file. Delimiter settings are persistent, and Excel will keep using the comma delimiter until you change it. If you happen to be importing data which is tab-delimited (or use any delimiter other than comma), the data will be imported entirely into one column. You can fix any data parsing problem using the Text Import Wizard. To parse the imported data into columns correctly, select a single data cell in the column of data, then press Ctrl+Shift+* to select the entire data region. Then choose Data ➤ Text to Columns. The Text Import Wizard dialog will be displayed. In step 2 of the dialog, specify the correct delimiter. Look at the Data Preview window to be sure you've selected the correct delimiter—when you've got the right delimiter, the preview data will be in columns.

▶▶ *Importing Other File Formats*

Excel is capable of importing several popular file formats using the File ➤ Open command. Here are the supported formats:

- Text (covered earlier in this chapter)
- Lotus 1-2-3 (covered below)
- QuattroPro
- Microsoft Works
- dBASE III and dBASE IV
- SYLK
- Data Interchange (DIF)
- Multiplan

▶▶ *Exporting Data*

Excel workbooks can be saved in a variety of file formats, which are listed below. Choose the File ➤ Save As command, and choose the file format from the Save File as Type list.

Workbooks can be saved as:

- Template (see Chapter 10)
- Text file (space, tab, or comma delimited)
- Excel 2.1, 3.0, 4.0 worksheet
- Excel 4.0 workbook
- Lotus 1-2-3
- QuattroPro
- dBASE II, III, IV
- Data Interchange Format (DIF)
- SYLK

►► *Switching from Lotus 1-2-3*

Excel has many features to help out Lotus 1-2-3 users.

Opening 1-2-3 Files Lotus 1-2-3 spreadsheets can be opened using the File ➤ Open command, and saved using the File ➤ Save command (though Excel-specific information cannot be saved). You can build Excel models that use 1-2-3 sheets and even refer to names defined on them.

Running Macros You can run 1-2-3 macros under Excel, without having to translate them.

Getting Help The Help ➤ Lotus 1-2-3 command provides detailed help for Lotus users.

Special Transition Settings Choose Tools ➤ Options, then click the Transition tab. Select the Lotus 1-2-3 Help option. The slash key (/) will then help you write formulas using 1-2-3 syntax. Click the Help button on the Transition tab to learn more about Lotus help.

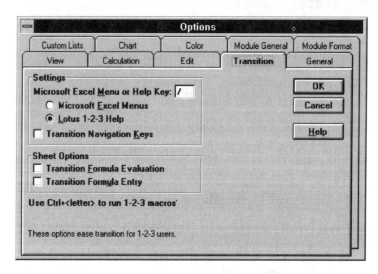

▶ ▶ **CHAPTER** **26**

Advanced
Tips & Techniques

FAST **T**RACK

▶ ***To enter an array formula***   *870*

Select one or more contiguous cells, then type the formula and press Ctrl+Shift+Enter.

▶ ***To change an array formula***   *871*

You cannot change an individual cell within an array—you must select the entire array (press Ctrl+/), edit the formula, and then press Ctrl+Shift+Enter.

▶ ***To copy/paste while a dialog box is displayed***   *876*

Press Ctrl+C to copy, and Ctrl+V to paste.

▶ ***To perform unit-of-measure conversions***   *877*

Use the CONVERT function in the Analysis ToolPak add-in.

*T**his** chapter covers three major topics:

- *Using custom AutoFills*
- *Customizing toolbars*
- *Using array formulas*

At the end of this chapter, you will also find a variety of tips and techniques that will enhance your overall productivity.

▶▶ *Using Custom AutoFills*

The AutoFill feature, covered in Chapter 7, lets you quickly fill a range of cells with months, dates, numbers, and certain text values. This section explains how to define custom lists that are recognized by AutoFill. For example, suppose your company operates in four regions (North, South, East, and West), and you are constantly typing the regions onto worksheets. A custom AutoFill will save you a lot of data-entry time.

▶ *Defining Custom Lists*

Follow these steps to define a custom list:

1. Enter the list into a (contiguous) range of cells, in a row or column.

2. Select the range of cells containing the list.

3. Choose Tools ➤ Options, then select the Custom Lists tab (see Figure 26.1).

4. Click the Import button—the list will be displayed in the Custom List box.

FIGURE 26.1

Custom lists can be autofilled.

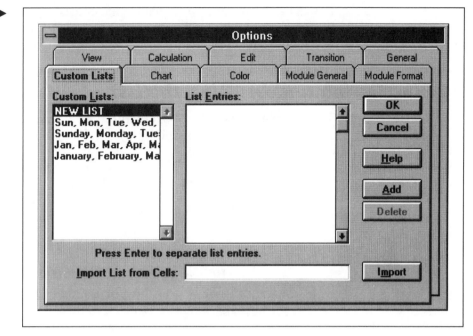

5. Click OK.

▶ **T I P**

> **You do not have to enter the list into cells first. The list can be typed into List Entries (pictured in Figure 26.1), though cells are *generally* easier to work with.**

Once you define a custom list, it is available globally. It is not stored in a specific workbook.

▶ *Performing a Custom AutoFill*

Performing an AutoFill on a custom list is no different than on a built-in list:

1. Enter any one of the values from the list into a cell.

2. Grab the fill handle with the mouse, and drag it (in any direction).

For example, suppose you create a list consisting of regions North, South, East, and West. You can enter any of the four regions into a cell, and then perform the AutoFill.

▶ *Editing and Deleting the List*

The Custom Lists dialog box, pictured in Figure 26.1, can be used to edit or delete a custom list. Display the dialog box, select a list in the Custom Lists box, then:

- To delete the list, click the Delete button.
- To edit the list, edit the contents of the List Entries box.

▶ ▶ **T I P**

You can also use custom lists to sort data in other than ascending or descending order. See Chapter 16 to learn how.

▶▶ *Customizing Toolbars*

Toolbars provide the quickest way of performing everyday tasks. In this section, you will learn how to:

- Create new toolbars
- Modify built-in toolbars
- Create your own toolfaces

▶ ▶ **N O T E**

See Chapter 7 to learn how to display toolbars, hide them, and position them on the screen.

There are approximately twelve different toolbars, and if they were all displayed they would consume too much screen real estate. However, you can customize one or more toolbars to contain the tools you use most often, and you can build your own toolbars.

▶ Adding Tools to a Toolbar

There are many tools that are not located on *any* toolbar, many of which are very useful. The following exercise shows how to add the Camera tool (covered in Chapter 12) to the Standard toolbar.

1. Click any toolbar using the right mouse button to display the toolbar shortcut menu.

```
√ Standard
   Formatting
   Chart
   Drawing
   Forms
   Visual Basic
   Auditing
   WorkGroup
   Microsoft

   Toolbars...
   Customize...
```

2. Select Customize from the shortcut menu to display the Customize dialog box, shown in Figure 26.2.

- The tools are organized by category. Click a category to display a different group of tools.

- There are tools in many of the categories that are not assigned to any toolbar.

- When you click a tool, a brief description appears on the bottom of the dialog box.

3. Click the Utility category.

4. Click and drag the Camera tool, and drop it onto the Standard toolbar.

5. Click Close.

Advanced Tips & Techniques

Ch.
26

FIGURE 26.2 ►

Add tools to any tool-bar by dragging them from the Customize dialog box and dropping them onto the toolbar.

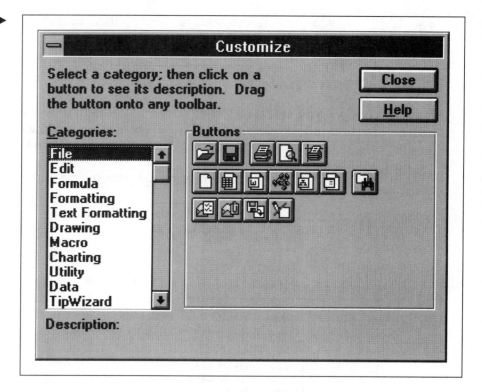

While the Customize dialog box is displayed, you can drag tools to and from various places to customize toolbars:

To Create a New Toolbar Drag a tool from the Customize dialog box, and drop it onto a worksheet or onto the Excel workspace.

To Remove a Tool from a Toolbar Drag the tool off the toolbar and onto a worksheet, or onto the Excel workspace.

To Move a Tool from One Toolbar to Another Drag the tool off of one toolbar, and drop it onto the other.

To Reorganize Tools on a Toolbar Drag the tool to a new position on the toolbar.

To Delete a Custom Toolbar Drag each tool onto a worksheet or onto the Excel workspace. When the last tool is removed, the toolbar is automatically deleted.

▶ *Naming Your Custom Toolbars*

When you create new toolbars using drag and drop, they are automatically named Toolbar1, Toolbar2, and so on. These names cannot be changed. To create a new toolbar you can name, follow these steps:

1. Choose View ➤ Toolbars.

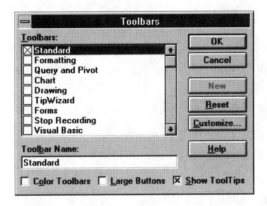

2. Type a name into the Toolbar Name text box, then click New. A new, blank toolbar is created and the Customize dialog box (see Figure 26.2) is displayed.

3. Drag tools onto the toolbar.

▶ *Deleting a Custom Toolbar*

Custom toolbars can be deleted by choosing View ➤ Toolbars. Select the name of the custom toolbar you want to delete, and click the Delete button. (Built-in toolbars cannot be deleted.)

▶ ▶ **T I P**

At some time you may want to restore a built-in toolbar to its default state. Choose View ➤ Toolbars, select the toolbar from the list, and click Reset.

Advanced Tips & Techniques

▶ ▶

Ch.
26

▶ CUSTOMIZE TOOLS BY EDITING TOOLFACES

You can customize tools by changing toolface images. This is most useful when you want to create a new tool to run a macro, but you can change the face of any tool. First, display a toolbar containing the tool you want to edit. If you want a new tool to run a macro, you can choose from several empty tools (including one with a blank face) in the Custom category of the Customize dialog. Then, display the Customize dialog. (You won't actually use the Customize dialog, but it must be displayed in order to customize tools or toolbars.) On the toolbar, right-click the tool you want to edit, then choose Edit Button Image from the shortcut menu. The Button Editor dialog will be displayed, and you can change the toolface by re-coloring pixels in the image.

To use the Button Editor, click on a color in the Colors palette, then click or drag through the pixels you want to color. If you want to start with a blank face, click the Clear button. When you have created the image you want, you can move the entire image up, down, or sideways in the frame by clicking the Move arrows. Glance at the Preview to see the image actual-size (this is important because an intricate image can be hard to see once it's reduced to toolface size).

If you change your mind after editing a toolface, you can reset the default toolface by choosing Reset Button Image from the toolface shortcut menu. You can also copy an image created in another graphics application and paste it onto a toolface (use the Paste Button Image command on the toolface shortcut menu), but keep in mind that it's difficult to scale down a larger image to toolface size (16 by 15 pixels) without losing the clarity of the image.

▶ *Useful Tools Not on Any Built-in Toolbar*

The tools in the next four tables (Tables 26.1 through 26.4) are not available on built-in toolbars. You must add these tools to a built-in toolbar, or to a custom one, to make them available.

▶ **TABLE 26.1:** *Editing Tools*

Tool Face	Tool Name	Function
	Set Print Area	Set selected cells as print area
	Select Current Region	Select region containing the active cell
	Insert Worksheet	Create new worksheet page
	Insert Chart Sheet	Create new chart page
	Paste Values	Paste only values
	Paste Formats	Paste only formats
	Clear Contents	Clear only formulas or values
	Clear Formats	Clear only formats
	Delete	Delete selected cells
	Insert	Insert cells
	Delete Row	Delete selected row
	Insert Row	Insert blank row
	Delete Column	Delete selected column

► **TABLE 26.1:** *Editing Tools (continued)*

Tool Face	Tool Name	Function
	Insert Column	Insert blank column
	Fill Right	Copy values, formulas, and formats right or left
	Fill Down	Copy values, formulas, and formats down or up

► **TABLE 26.2:** *Formatting Tools*

Tool Face	Tool Name	Function
Normal	Style	Apply/define cell style
	Increase Font Size	Increase font size of selected text
	Decrease Font Size	Decrease font size of selected text
	Justify Align	Justify text
	Cycle Font Color	Change text color
	Vertical Text	Align letters vertically
	Rotate Text Up	Rotate text sideways, reading bottom to top
	Rotate Text Down	Rotate text sideways, reading top to bottom

▶ **TABLE 26.2:** *Formatting Tools (continued)*

Tool Face	Tool Name	Function
	Double Underline	Double-underline selected text
	AutoFormat	Apply last table format set
	Dark Shading	Apply dark shading
	Light Shading	Apply light shading

▶ **TABLE 26.3:** *Miscellaneous But Important Tools*

Tool Face	Tool Name	Function
	Camera	Paste picture of linked selection
	Freeze Panes	Freeze/unfreeze split in active window
	Lock Cell	Lock/unlock selected cells and objects
	Zoom In	Increase magnification
	Zoom Out	Decrease magnification
	Calculate Now	Calculate formulas
	Show Outline Symbols	Show/hide outline symbols
	Select Visible Cells	Select only visible cells within selection

Advanced Tips & Techniques

Ch. **26**

▶ **TABLE 26.4**: *Drawing Tools*

Tool Face	Tool Name	Function
◁	Polygon	Draw polygons
◀	Filled Polygon	Draw filled polygons

▶▶ *Using Array Formulas*

Array formulas are special formulas that operate on data arrays (matrices). They have been favored by Excel power users for years and are used to perform matrix arithmetic calculations. In the following discussion, you will learn how to enter array formulas and see a couple of examples where they might be applied.

An array formula is entered into a contiguous, rectangular range of cells, even if the range consists of just one cell. The following exercise uses a primitive example intended to show the mechanics of entering array formulas:

1. Select cells B2:C3.

2. Enter: **=1**

3. Complete the formula by holding down Ctrl+Shift while pressing Enter.

The single array formula is entered into all four cells. On the formula bar, there are braces around the formula: {*=1*}. This formula is said to have been *array-entered.* The braces are a result of having array-entered the formula. If you were to actually type the braces, you would enter a text constant, not an array formula.

Array formulas impose several restrictions:

● You cannot change an individual cell within an array formula. You must select the entire array, then change the formula.

▶ ▶**T I P**

> To select an entire array, select any cell within the array,
> choose Edit ➤ Go To, click Special, choose the Current Array
> option, and click OK. The keyboard shortcut is Ctrl+/.

- You cannot insert or delete cells within an array formula.
- When you edit the formula, you must terminate the entry, using Ctrl+Shift+Enter, just as when the formula was first entered.
- An array formula is limited to approximately 1600 cells.

▶ ▶**N O T E**

> Arrays can be expressed as constants. See Chapter 8 to
> learn about named constants.

▶ *Putting Array Formulas to Work*

Here are a few examples that illustrate the use of array formulas.

Avoiding Interim Calculations

Consider the following worksheet:

	A	B	C	D	E	F	G
1							
2		Qty	Dollars				
3		2	10.00				
4		3	15.00				
5		4	20.00				
6		5	25.00				
7							
8			TOTAL				
9							
10							
11							
12							

BOOK1.XLS

Suppose you want to know the total of Qty * Dollars. The traditional way to solve this problem is to add formulas to D3:D6 that multiply

Advanced Tips &
Techniques

▶ ▶
Ch.
26

column B by column C, then add a formula that sums column D. The following array formula, entered into a single cell (C9), can perform the same calculation in one step:

{=SUM(B3:B6*C3:C6)}

Remember, the formula must be terminated with Ctrl+Shift+Enter—do not type the braces.

Performing Matrix Calculations

In the next example, an array formula entered into a range of cells performs a calculation on another range. On the following worksheet, suppose that in F5:G8 you want to display the word "High," where the population growth exceeds 3%:

	A	B	C	D	E	F	G	H
				BOOK1.XLS				
1								
2			**Population Growth**					
3								
4			**1994**	**1995**		**1994**	**1995**	
5		Seattle	2.7%	3.8%				
6		Portland	3.2%	2.0%				
7		San Francisco	1.5%	3.1%				
8		Los Angeles	-1.4%	0.8%				
9								
10								

This exercise performs the calculation with one array formula:

1. Select F5:G8.

2. Type the following:

=IF(C5:D8>0.03,"High","")

3. Press Ctrl+Shift+Enter.

The one formula calculates which cells in C5:D8 are greater than 3%.

Using Array Functions

There are a number of worksheet functions that can be used to perform array calculations. The following exercise uses the MMULT function to perform matrix (array) multiplication.

On the following worksheet, suppose you want to multiply the two bordered ranges:

The dimensions of the resulting matrix (array) must be four rows by three columns in this case, reflecting the four rows of the left-hand multiplier and the three columns of the right-hand multiplier. The number of columns in the left multiplier must equal the number of rows in the right multiplier, which is fulfilled in this example:

1. Select C9:E12.

2. Type the following:

   =MMULT(B2:C5,E2:G3)

3. Press Ctrl+Shift+Enter.

The array formula calculates as follows:

	A	B	C	D	E	F	G
1							
2		2	-3		-2	3	-3
3		-1	0		5	1	2
4		1	3				
5		4	2				
6							
7							
8			Result Set				
9		-19	3	-12			
10		2	-3	3			
11		13	6	3			
12		2	14	-8			
13							
14							

BOOK1.XLS

▶ ▶NOTE

> Historically, a special syntax for array formulas has been used to conditionally sum a range of cells and to perform other types of summarization. By and large, these uses for array formulas have been obviated by pivot tables (which summarize), and the worksheet functions SUMIF and COUNTIF (covered in Chapter 8), which perform conditional calculations.

Table 26.5 lists other worksheet functions that are applicable when performing array operations.

▶ **TABLE 26.5:** *Functions Used in Array Operations*

Function	Comments
COLUMN	Returns array when argument is a range
COLUMNS	Argument must be array or range
GROWTH	Argument can be array or range—can return an array
HLOOKUP	Argument must be array or range
INDEX	Argument must be array or range—can return array
LINEST	Always returns array
LOGEST	Always returns array
LOOKUP	Argument must be array or range
MATCH	Argument must be array or range
MDETERM	Argument must be array
MINVERSE	Always returns array
MMULT	Always returns array
ROW	Returns array when argument is a range
ROWS	Argument must be array or range
SUMPRODUCT	Argument can be array, range, or values
TRANSPOSE	Always returns array
TREND	Argument must be array or range—can return an array
VLOOKUP	Argument must be array or range

Advanced Tips &
Techniques

Ch.
26

▶▶ *Tips and Techniques*

In this section are various tips and techniques to enhance your productivity. The tips are in random order, so you can jump around to find topics of interest.

▶ *Using the Clipboard to Transfer Data in and out of Dialog Boxes*

The Clipboard can be used to copy information into (or out of) dialog boxes. Here are two examples that illustrate the technique.

Copying Information Out of a Dialog Box

Assume that you are preparing hardcopy documentation for a workbook, and there are cell notes that you want to move to a word processing document:

1. Select the cell containing the note, and choose Insert ➤ Note.

2. Select the text in the Text Note box, using the mouse.

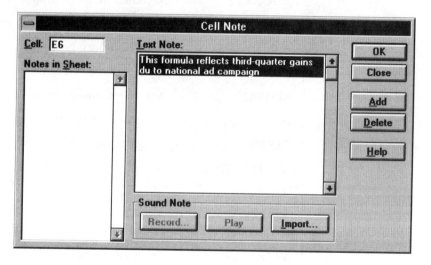

3. Press Ctrl+C to copy the selected text to the Clipboard, then close the dialog box.

4. Activate your word processor, then choose Edit ➤ Paste (or press Ctrl+V).

Pasting Information Into a Dialog Box

The following exercise will transfer data into a dialog box. Assume that you want to replace every occurrence of the name *Bach* with the name

Shostokovich. You don't want to risk misspelling Shostokovich, so you will paste it into the dialog box from a word processing document:

1. Activate the word processing document—select the word(s) you want to copy, and choose Edit ➤ Copy (or press Ctrl+C) to copy to the Clipboard.

2. Activate Excel.

3. Choose the Edit ➤ Replace command—type Smith into Find What, then tab down and enter the following in Replace with:

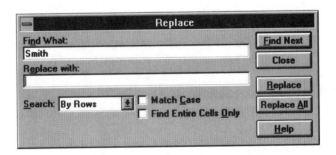

4. Press Ctrl+V to paste text into the dialog box from the Clipboard.

Remember, this technique is not specific to Excel. It can be employed in other Windows programs.

▶ Checking Spelling in a Chart

Checking spelling in the chart is as important as in any other part of a report. To check chart spelling:

1. Activate the chart window.

2. Choose Tools ➤ Spelling (or click the Check Spelling tool).

▶ Converting Units of Measure

To perform all kinds of unit-of-measure conversions, use the CONVERT function, found in the Analysis ToolPak. (See Chapter 24 to learn how to load the ToolPak and other add-ins.) For example, CONVERT can be used to convert from miles to kilometers, or grams to ounces.

The syntax for CONVERT is

CONVERT(number,from_unit,to_unit)

number is the quantity, measured in *from_unit*, to be converted

from_unit is a code representing the original unit of measure (case-sensitive)

to_unit is a code representing the new unit of measure (case-sensitive)

Here is an example that converts 12 teaspoons to cups (returning .25):

=CONVERT(12,"tsp","cup")

The codes for the various units of measure that can be converted are shown below.

Weight and Mass

Gram	"g"
Slug	"sg"
Pound	"lbm"
U (atomic mass unit)	"u"
Ounce	"ozm"

Distance

Meter	"m"
Statute mile	"mi"
Nautical mile	"Nmi"
Inch	"in"
Foot	"ft"
Yard	"yd"
Angstrom	"ang"
Pica ($^1/_{72}$ in.)	"Pica"

Time

Year	"yr"
Day	"day"
Hour	"hr"
Minute	"mn"
Second	"sec"

Pressure

Pascal	"Pa"
Atmosphere	"atm"
mm of Mercury	"mmHg"

Force

Newton	"N"
Dyne	"dyn"
Pound force	"lbf"

Energy

Joule	"J"
Erg	"e"
Thermodynamic calorie	"c"
IT calorie	"cal"
Electron volt	"eV"
Horsepower-hour	"HPh"
Watt-hour	"Wh"
Foot-pound	"flb"
BTU	"BTU"

Power

Horsepower	"HP"
Watt	"W"

Magnetism

Tesla	"T"
Gauss	"ga"

Temperature

Degree Celsius	"C"
Degree Fahrenheit	"F"
Degree Kelvin	"K"

Liquid Measure

Teaspoon	"tsp"
Tablespoon	"tbs"
Fluid ounce	"oz"
Cup	"cup"
Pint	"pt"
Quart	"qt"
Gallon	"gal"
Liter	"l"

Special Prefixes

There are several prefixes that can be used as part of the From_unit or To_unit arguments that act as multipliers. For example, the prefix *k* means kilo (multiplying by 1000). As with the *from* and *to* arguments, the prefix multiplier is case-sensitive.

Here is a formula that converts 1000 yards into meters:

```
=CONVERT(1000,"yd","m")
```

Now, using the *k* prefix, the following formula converts 1000 yards to kilometers:

=CONVERT(1000,"yd","km")

Here is a list of the prefixes you can use:

Prefix	Multiplier	Abbreviation
exa	1000000000000000000 (1E+18)	"E"
peta	1000000000000000 (1E+15)	"P"
tera	1000000000000 (1E+12)	"T"
giga	1000000000 (1E+09)	"G"
mega	1000000 (1E+06)	"M"
kilo	1000	"k"
hecto	100	"h"
dekao	10	"e"
deci	.1	"d"
centi	.01	"c"
milli	.001	"m"
micro	.000001 (1E-06)	"u"
nano	.000000001(1E-09)	"n"
pico	.000000000001 (1E-12)	"p"
femto	.000000000000001 (1E-15)	"f "
atto	.000000000000000001 (1E-18)	"a"

▶ *Transposing Rows and Columns*

Suppose you have data oriented in rows, and you want to reorient it in columns. Consider the example on the following page.

Advanced Tips & Techniques

Ch.
26

BOOK1.XLS					
A	B	C	D	E	F
1					
2	Q1	Q2	Q3	Q4	
3	374	750	410	409	
4					
5					
6					
7					
8					
9					
10					
11					

Follow these steps to transpose the data:

1. Select cells B2:E3.

2. Choose Edit ➤ Copy.

3. Select cell B5.

4. Choose Edit ➤ Paste Special.

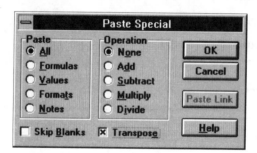

5. Check the Transpose setting, and click OK. The data is transposed from rows into columns.

BOOK1.XLS					
A	B	C	D	E	F
1					
2	Q1	Q2	Q3	Q4	
3	374	750	410	409	
4					
5	Q1	374			
6	Q2	750			
7	Q3	410			
8	Q4	409			
9					
10					
11					

▶ *3-D Fills*

In Chapter 7 you learned how to fill data on a worksheet horizontally or vertically. Use Edit ➤ Fill ➤ Across Worksheets to fill (copy) information across multiple sheets. Create a new workbook, and try this exercise:

1. On Sheet1, enter some information into B2:C3.

2. Select B2:C3.

3. With the Ctrl key held down, select the worksheets you want to fill—in this case, Sheet2 and Sheet4.

4. Choose Edit ➤ Fill ➤ Across Worksheets—the following dialog box is displayed:

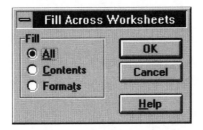

5. Select the information you want to fill—in this case All—and click OK.

The information in Sheet1!B2:C3 is copied to the same range on Sheet2 and Sheet4.

  T I P

To ungroup sheets, Shift+click the tab of the active worksheet.

Advanced Tips & Techniques

▶ ▶

Ch.
26

APPENDICES

Cross Reference of Changed Menu Commands

▶ **TABLE A.1:** *Cross Reference of Changed Menu Commands*

Excel 4 Command	Excel 5 Command	Remarks
File ➤ Links	Edit ➤ Links	
File ➤ Save Workbook	File ➤ Save	All files are workbooks in Excel 5
File ➤ Delete	File ➤ Find File	Click Commands button, choose delete
Edit ➤ Paste Link	Edit ➤ Paste Special	Click Paste Link button
Edit ➤ Insert	Insert ➤ Cells, Rows, Columns	
Edit ➤ Insert Object	Insert ➤ Object	
Edit ➤ Fill Right	Edit ➤ Fill ➤ Right	
Edit ➤ Fill Down	Edit ➤ Fill ➤ Down	
Formula ➤ Paste Name	Insert ➤ Name ➤ Paste	
Formula ➤ Paste Function	Insert ➤ Function	
Formula ➤ Define Name	Insert ➤ Name ➤ Define	
Formula ➤ Create Names	Insert ➤ Name ➤ Create	
Formula ➤ Apply Names	Insert ➤ Name ➤ Apply	
Formula ➤ Note	Insert ➤ Note	
Formula ➤ Go To	Edit ➤ Go To	
Formula ➤ Find	Edit ➤ Find	
Formula ➤ Replace	Edit ➤ Replace	

▶ **TABLE A.1:** *Cross Reference of Changed Menu Commands (continued)*

Excel 4 Command	Excel 5 Command	Remarks
Formula ➤ Select Special	Edit ➤ Go To	Click Special button
Formula ➤ Show Active Cell	(none)	Ctrl+backspace
Formula ➤ Outline	Data ➤ Group and Outline	
Formula ➤ Goal Seek	Tools ➤ Goal Seek	
Format ➤ Number	Format ➤ Cells	Select Number tab
Format ➤ Alignment	Format ➤ Cells	Select Alignment tab
Format ➤ Font	Format ➤ Cells	Select Font tab
Format ➤ Border	Format ➤ Cells	Select Border tab
Format ➤ Patterns	Format ➤ Cells	Select Patterns tab
Format ➤ Cell Protection	Format ➤ Cells	Select Protection tab
Format ➤ Row Height	Format ➤ Row ➤ Height	
Format ➤ Column Width	Format ➤ Column ➤ Width	
Format ➤ Justify	Format ➤ Cells	Select Alignment tab
Format ➤ Bring to Front	Format ➤ Placement ➤ Bring to Front	
Format ➤ Send to Back	Format ➤ Placement ➤ Send to Back	
Format ➤ Group	Format ➤ Placement ➤ Group	
Format ➤ Object Properties	Format ➤ Object	Select Properties tab
Data ➤ Find	Data ➤ Filter	

Changed Menu Commands

Ap.
A

► **TABLE A.1:** *Cross Reference of Changed Menu Commands (continued)*

Excel 4 Command	Excel 5 Command	Remarks
Data ➤ Extract	Data ➤ Filter ➤ Advanced Filter	
Data ➤ Delete	(none)	
Data ➤ Set Database	(none)	Not required—use Insert ➤ Name ➤ Define if desired
Data ➤ Set Criteria	(none)	Not required—use Insert ➤ Name ➤ Define if desired
Data ➤ Set Extract	(none)	Not required—use Insert ➤ Name ➤ Define if desired
Data ➤ Series	Edit ➤ Fill Series	Not required—use Autofill if desired
Data ➤ Parse	Data ➤ Text to Columns	
Options ➤ Set Print Area	File ➤ Page Setup	Select Sheet tab
Options ➤ Set Print Titles	File ➤ Page Setup	Select Sheet tab
Options ➤ Set Page Break	Insert ➤ Page Break	
Options ➤ Display	Tools ➤ Options	Select View tab
Options ➤ Toolbars	View ➤ Toolbars	
Options ➤ Color Palette	Tools ➤ Options	Select Color tab
Options ➤ Protect Document	Tools ➤ Protection	

▶ **TABLE A.1:** *Cross Reference of Changed Menu Commands (continued)*

Excel 4 Command	Excel 5 Command	Remarks
Options ➤ Calculation	Tools ➤ Options	Select Calculation tab
Options ➤ Workspace	Tools ➤ Options	Select View tab
Options ➤ Add-Ins	Tools ➤ Add-Ins	
Options ➤ Spelling	Tools ➤ Spelling	
Options ➤ Group Edit	(none)	Ctrl+click sheet tabs to select multiple sheets
Macro ➤ Run	Tools ➤ Macro	
Macro ➤ Record	Tools ➤ Record Macro	
Macro ➤ Start Recorder	Tools ➤ Record Macro	
Macro ➤ Set Recorder	Tools ➤ Record Macro	
Macro ➤ Relative Record	Tools ➤ Record Macro ➤ Use Relative References	
Macro ➤ Assign to Object	Tools ➤ Assign Macro	
Window ➤ Zoom	View ➤ Zoom	
Help ➤ Introducing Microsoft Excel	Help ➤ Quick Preview	
Help ➤ Learning Microsoft Excel	Help ➤ Examples and Demos	

APPENDIX **B**

Alphabetical List of
Worksheet Functions

►► *T*his appendix has complete descriptions of the Excel functions, including both the built-in worksheet functions and the functions that are contained in the Analysis Toolpak add-in. Table B.1 shows all these functions (broken down by category), a brief description of each, and the page number on which detailed information can be found. For more information about using functions, see Chapter 4.

► **TABLE B.1:** *Excel Functions by Category*

Function	Description	Page
Database and List Management Functions		
DAVERAGE	Returns the average of selected database entries	933
DCOUNT	Counts the cells containing numbers from a specified database using a criteria range	935
DCOUNTA	Counts nonblank cells from a specified database using a criteria range	935
DGET	Extracts from a database a single record that matches the specified criteria	937
DMAX	Returns the maximum value from selected database entries using a criteria range	938
DMIN	Returns the minimum value from selected database entries using a criteria range	938

▶ **TABLE B.1:** *Excel Functions by Category (continued)*

Function	Description	Page
DPRODUCT	Multiplies the values in a particular field of records using a criteria range	939
DSTDEV	Estimates the standard deviation based on a sample of selected database entries	939
DSTDEVP	Calculates the standard deviation based on the entire population of selected database entries	940
DSUM	Adds the numbers in the field column of records using a criteria range	940
DVAR	Estimates variance based on a sample from selected database entries	940
DVARP	Calculates variance based on the entire population of selected database entries	941
SQLREQUEST	Connects with an external data source and runs a query from a worksheet, then returns the result as an array without the need for macro programming	1069
SUBTOTAL	Returns a subtotal in a list or database	1000
Date and Time Functions		
DATE	Returns the serial number of a particular date	932
DATEVALUE	Converts a date in text form to a serial number	933
DAY	Converts a serial number to a day of the month	933

▶ **TABLE B.1:** *Excel Functions by Category (continued)*

Function	Description	Page
DAYS360	Calculates the number of days between two dates based on a 360-day year	933
EDATE	Returns the serial number of the date that is the indicated number of months before or after the start date	1036
EOMONTH	Returns the serial number of the last day of the month before or after a specified number of months	1037
HOUR	Converts a serial number to an hour	952
MINUTE	Converts a serial number to a minute	969
MONTH	Converts a serial number to a month	971
NETWORKDAYS	Returns the number of whole workdays between two dates	1051
NOW	Returns the serial number of the current date and time	975
SECOND	Converts a serial number to a second	994
TIME	Returns the serial number of a particular time	1006
TIMEVALUE	Converts a time in text form to a serial number	1007
TODAY	Returns the serial number of today's date	1008
WEEKDAY	Converts a serial number to a day of the week	1016
WORKDAY	Returns the serial number of the date before or after a specified number of workdays	1064
YEAR	Converts a serial number to a year	1017
YEARFRAC	Returns the year fraction representing the number of whole days between start_date and end_date	1066

▶ **TABLE B.1:** *Excel Functions by Category (continued)*

Function	Description	Page
Engineering Functions		
BESSELI	Returns the modified Bessel function $In(x)$	1021
BESSELJ	Returns the Bessel function $Jn(x)$	1021
BESSELK	Returns the modified Bessel function $Kn(x)$	1022
BESSELY	Returns the Bessel function $Yn(x)$	1022
BIN2DEC	Converts a binary number to decimal	1023
BIN2HEX	Converts a binary number to hexadecimal	1023
BIN2OCT	Converts a binary number to octal	1024
COMPLEX	Converts real and imaginary coefficients into a complex number	1025
CONVERT	Converts a number from one measurement system to another	1025
DEC2BIN	Converts a decimal number to binary	1032
DEC2HEX	Converts a decimal number to hexadecimal	1032
DEC2OCT	Converts a decimal number to octal	1033
DELTA	Tests whether two values are equal	1033
ERF	Returns the error function	1037
ERFC	Returns the complementary error function	1038
GESTEP	Tests whether a number is greater than a threshold value	1040
HEX2BIN	Converts a hexadecimal number to binary	1040
HEX2DEC	Converts a hexadecimal number to decimal	1041

▶ **TABLE B.1:** *Excel Functions by Category (continued)*

Function	Description	Page
HEX2OCT	Converts a hexadecimal number to octal	1041
IMABS	Returns the absolute value (modulus) of a complex number	1041
IMAGINARY	Returns the imaginary coefficient of a complex number	1042
IMARGUMENT	Returns the argument theta, an angle expressed in radians	1042
IMCONJUGATE	Returns the complex conjugate of a complex number	1043
IMCOS	Returns the cosine of a complex number	1043
IMDIV	Returns the quotient of two complex numbers	1043
IMEXP	Returns the exponential of a complex number	1044
IMLN	Returns the natural logarithm of a complex number	1044
IMLOG2	Returns the base-2 logarithm of a complex number	1045
IMLOG10	Returns the base-10 logarithm of a complex number	1044
IMPOWER	Returns a complex number raised to an integer power	1045
IMPRODUCT	Returns the product of two complex numbers	1045
IMREAL	Returns the real coefficient of a complex number	1046
IMSIN	Returns the sine of a complex number	1046
IMSQRT	Returns the square root of a complex number	1047

▶ **TABLE B.1:** *Excel Functions by Category (continued)*

Function	Description	Page
IMSUB	Returns the difference of two complex numbers	1047
IMSUM	Returns the sum of complex numbers	1047
OCT2BIN	Converts an octal number to binary	1052
OCT2DEC	Converts an octal number to decimal	1052
OCT2HEX	Converts an octal number to hexadecimal	1053
SQRTPI	Returns the square root of (*number* ★ pi)	1062
Financial Functions		
ACCRINT	Returns the accrued interest for a security that pays periodic interest	1018
ACCRINTM	Returns the accrued interest for a security that pays interest at maturity	1019
AMORDEGRC	Returns the depreciation for each accounting period	1020
AMORLINC	Returns the depreciation for each accounting period	1020
COUPDAYBS	Returns the number of days from the beginning of the coupon period to the settlement date	1026
COUPDAYS	Returns the number of days in the coupon period that contains the settlement date	1026
COUPDAYSNC	Returns the number of days from the settlement date to the next coupon date	1027
COUPNCD	Returns the next coupon date after the settlement date	1028

▶ **TABLE B.1:** *Excel Functions by Category (continued)*

Function	Description	Page
COUPNUM	Returns the number of coupons payable between the settlement and maturity dates	1029
COUPPCD	Returns the previous coupon date before the settlement date	1029
CUMIPMT	Returns the cumulative interest paid between two periods	1030
CUMPRINC	Returns the cumulative principal paid on a loan between two periods	1031
DB	Returns the depreciation of an asset for a specified period using the fixed-declining balance method	934
DDB	Returns the depreciation of an asset for a specified period using the double-declining balance method or some other method you specify	936
DISC	Returns the discount rate for a security	1034
DOLLARDE	Converts a dollar price expressed as a fraction into a dollar price expressed as a decimal number	1034
DOLLARFR	Converts a dollar price expressed as a decimal number into a dollar price expressed as a fraction	1035
DURATION	Returns the annual duration of a security with periodic interest payments	1035
EFFECT	Returns the effective annual interest rate	1037
FV	Returns the future value of an investment	948
FVSCHEDULE	Returns the future value of an initial principal amount after applying a series of compound interest rates	1039

▶ **TABLE B.1:** *Excel Functions by Category (continued)*

Function	Description	Page
INTRATE	Returns the interest rate for a fully invested security	1048
IPMT	Returns the interest payment for an investment for a given period	956
IRR	Returns the internal rate of return for a series of cash flows	956
MDURATION	Returns the Macauley modified duration for a security with an assumed par value of $100	1049
MIRR	Returns the internal rate of return where positive and negative cash flows are financed at different rates	969
NOMINAL	Returns the annual nominal interest rate	1051
NPER	Returns the number of periods for an investment	975
NPV	Returns the net present value of an investment based on a series of periodic cash flows and a discount rate	976
ODDFPRICE	Returns the price per $100 face value of a security with an odd first period	1053
ODDFYIELD	Returns the yield of a security with an odd first period	1054
ODDLPRICE	Returns the price per $100 face value of a security with an odd last period	1055
ODDLYIELD	Returns the yield of a security with an odd last period	1056
PMT	Returns the periodic payment for an annuity	980

▶ **TABLE B.1:** *Excel Functions by Category (continued)*

Function	Description	Page
PPMT	Returns the payment on the principal for an investment for a given period	982
PRICE	Returns the price per $100 face value of a security that pays periodic interest	1059
PRICEDISC	Returns the price per $100 face value of a discounted security	1057
PRICEMAT	Returns the price per $100 face value of a security that pays interest at maturity	1058
PV	Returns the present value of an investment	985
RATE	Returns the interest rate per period of an annuity	988
RECEIVED	Returns the amount received at maturity for a fully invested security	1060
SLN	Returns the straight-line depreciation of an asset for one period	996
SYD	Returns the sum-of-years' digits depreciation of an asset for a specified period	1003
TBILLEQ	Returns the bond-equivalent yield for a Treasury bill	1062
TBILLPRICE	Returns the price per $100 face value for a Treasury bill	1063
TBILLYIELD	Returns the yield for a Treasury bill	1063
VDB	Returns the depreciation of an asset for a specified or partial period using a declining balance method	1015

▶ **TABLE B.1:** *Excel Functions by Category (continued)*

Function	Description	Page
XIRR	Returns the internal rate of return for a schedule of cash flows that is not necessarily periodic	1064
XNPV	Returns the net present value for a schedule of cash flows that is not necessarily periodic	1065
YIELD	Returns the yield on a security that pays periodic interest	1067
YIELDDISC	Returns the annual yield for a discounted security	1068
YIELDMAT	Returns the annual yield of a security that pays interest at maturity	1068
Information Functions		
CELL	Returns information about the location, formatting, or contents of a cell	923
COUNTBLANK	Counts the number of blank cells within a range	931
INFO	Returns information about the current operating environment	954
ISBLANK	Returns TRUE if the value is blank	957
ISERR	Returns TRUE if the value is any error value except #N/A	958
ISERROR	Returns TRUE if the value is any error value	958
ISEVEN	Returns TRUE if the number is even	1048
ISLOGICAL	Returns TRUE if the value is a logical value	958
ISNA	Returns TRUE if the value is the #N/A error value	958
ISNONTEXT	Returns TRUE if the value is not text	959

► **TABLE B.1:** *Excel Functions by Category (continued)*

Function	Description	Page
ISNUMBER	Returns TRUE if the value is a number	959
ISODD	Returns TRUE if the number is odd	1049
ISREF	Returns TRUE if the value is a reference	959
ISTEXT	Returns TRUE if the value is text	959
N	Returns a value converted to a number	972
NA	Returns the error value #N/A	972
TYPE	Returns a number indicating the data type of a value	1011
Logical Functions		
AND	Returns TRUE if all its arguments are TRUE	917
FALSE	Returns the logical value FALSE	943
IF	Specifies a logical test to perform	953
NOT	Reverses the logic of its argument	974
OR	Returns TRUE if any argument is TRUE	978
TRUE	Returns the logical value TRUE	1010
Lookup and Reference Functions		
ADDRESS	Creates a cell address as text, given specified row and column numbers	916
AREAS	Returns the number of areas in a reference	917
CHOOSE	Chooses a value from a list of values	925
COLUMN	Returns the column number of a reference	927

▶ **TABLE B.1:** *Excel Functions by Category (continued)*

Function	Description	Page
COLUMNS	Returns the number of columns in a reference	927
HLOOKUP	Looks in the top row of an array and returns the value of the indicated cell	951
INDEX	Uses an index to choose a value from a reference or an array	954
INDIRECT	Returns a reference indicated by a text value	954
LOOKUP	Looks up values in a vector or an array	965
MATCH	Looks up values in a reference or an array	966
OFFSET	Returns a reference offset from a given reference	977
ROW	Returns the row number of a reference	992
ROWS	Returns the number of rows in a reference	993
TRANSPOSE	Returns the transpose of an array	1008
VLOOKUP	Looks in the first column of an array and moves across the row to return the value of a cell	1016

Math and Trigonometry Functions

ABS	Returns the absolute value of a number	915
ACOS	Returns the arccosine of a number	915
ACOSH	Returns the inverse hyperbolic cosine of a number	916
ASIN	Returns the arcsine of a number	918

▶ **TABLE B.1:** *Excel Functions by Category (continued)*

Function	Description	Page
ASINH	Returns the inverse hyperbolic sine of a number	918
ATAN	Returns the arctangent of a number	919
ATAN2	Returns the arctangent from x- and y- coordinates	919
ATANH	Returns the inverse hyperbolic tangent of a number	920
CEILING	Rounds a number to the nearest integer or to the nearest multiple of significance	922
COMBIN	Returns the number of combinations for a given number of objects	928
COS	Returns the cosine of a number	929
COSH	Returns the hyperbolic cosine of a number	930
COUNTIF	Counts the number of nonblank cells within a range that meet the given criteria	931
DEGREES	Converts radians to degrees	937
EVEN	Rounds a number up to the nearest even integer	941
EXP	Returns *e* raised to the power of a given number	942
FACT	Returns the factorial of a number	943
FACTDOUBLE	Returns the double factorial of a number	1038
FLOOR	Rounds a number down, toward zero	946
GCD	Returns the greatest common divisor	1039
INT	Rounds a number down to the nearest integer	955

TABLE B.1: *Excel Functions by Category (continued)*

Function	Description	Page
LCM	Returns the least common multiple	1049
LN	Returns the natural logarithm of a number	962
LOG	Returns the logarithm of a number to a specified base	962
LOG10	Returns the base-10 logarithm of a number	963
MDETERM	Returns the matrix determinant of an array	967
MINVERSE	Returns the matrix inverse of an array	969
MMULT	Returns the matrix product of two arrays	970
MOD	Returns the remainder from division	971
MROUND	Returns a number rounded to the desired multiple	1050
MULTINOMIAL	Returns the multinomial of a set of numbers	1051
ODD	Rounds a number up to the nearest odd integer	977
PI	Returns the value of pi	980
POWER	Returns the result of a number raised to a power	982
PRODUCT	Multiplies its arguments	984
QUOTIENT	Returns the integer portion of a division	1060
RADIANS	Converts degrees to radians	986
RAND	Returns a random number between 0 and 1	987
ROMAN	Converts an arabic numeral to roman, as text	990

▶ **TABLE B.1:** *Excel Functions by Category (continued)*

Function	Description	Page
ROUND	Rounds a number to a specified number of digits	991
ROUNDDOWN	Rounds a number down, toward zero	991
ROUNDUP	Rounds a number up, away from zero	992
SERIESSUM	Returns the sum of a power series based on the formula	1061
SIGN	Returns the sign of a number	994
SIN	Returns the sine of the given angle	995
SINH	Returns the hyperbolic sine of a number	995
SQRT	Returns a positive square root	997
SQRTPI	Returns the square root of (*number* * pi)	1062
SUM	Adds its arguments	1001
SUMIF	Adds the cells specified by a given criteria	1001
SUMPRODUCT	Returns the sum of the products of corresponding array components	1002
SUMSQ	Returns the sum of the squares of the arguments	1002
SUMX2MY2	Returns the sum of the difference of squares of corresponding values in two arrays	1002
SUMX2PY2	Returns the sum of the sum of squares of corresponding values in two arrays	1003
SUMXMY2	Returns the sum of squares of differences of corresponding values in two arrays	1003
TAN	Returns the tangent of a number	1005

TABLE B.1: *Excel Functions by Category (continued)*

Function	Description	Page
TANH	Returns the hyperbolic tangent of a number	1005
TRUNC	Truncates a number to an integer	1010

Statistical Functions

AVEDEV	Returns the average of the absolute deviations of data points from their mean	920
AVERAGE	Returns the average of its arguments	920
BETADIST	Returns the cumulative beta probability density function	921
BETAINV	Returns the inverse of the cumulative beta probability density function	922
BINOMDIST	Returns the individual term binomial distribution probability	1024
CHIDIST	Returns the one-tailed probability of the chi-squared distribution	924
CHIINV	Returns the inverse of the one-tailed probability of the chi-squared distribution	924
CHITEST	Returns the test for independence	925
CONFIDENCE	Returns the confidence interval for a population mean	929
CORREL	Returns the correlation coefficient between two data sets	929
COUNT	Counts how many numbers are in the list of arguments	930
COUNTA	Counts how many values are in the list of arguments	930
COVAR	Returns covariance, the average of the products of paired deviations	931

▶ **TABLE B.1:** *Excel Functions by Category (continued)*

Function	Description	Page
CRITBINOM	Returns the smallest value for which the cumulative binomial distribution is less than or equal to a criterion value	932
DEVSQ	Returns the sum of squares of deviations	937
EXPONDIST	Returns the exponential distribution	942
FDIST	Returns the F probability distribution	943
FINV	Returns the inverse of the F probability distribution	944
FISHER	Returns the Fisher transformation	945
FISHERINV	Returns the inverse of the Fisher transformation	945
FORECAST	Returns a value along a linear trend	946
FREQUENCY	Returns a frequency distribution as a vertical array	947
FTEST	Returns the result of an F-test	947
GAMMADIST	Returns the gamma distribution	949
GAMMAINV	Returns the inverse of the gamma cumulative distribution	949
GAMMALN	Returns the natural logarithm of the gamma function, $\sim;G(x)$	950
GEOMEAN	Returns the geometric mean	950
GROWTH	Returns values along an exponential trend	951
HARMEAN	Returns the harmonic mean	951
HYPGEOMDIST	Returns the hypergeometric distribution	953
INTERCEPT	Returns the intercept of the linear regression line	955

▶ **TABLE B.1:** *Excel Functions by Category (continued)*

Function	Description	Page
KURT	Returns the kurtosis of a data set	960
LARGE	Returns the k-th largest value in a data set	960
LINEST	Returns the parameters of a linear trend	961
LOGEST	Returns the parameters of an exponential trend	963
LOGINV	Returns the inverse of the lognormal distribution	964
LOGNORMDIST	Returns the cumulative lognormal distribution	964
MAX	Returns the maximum value in a list of arguments	966
MEDIAN	Returns the median of the given numbers	967
MIN	Returns the minimum value in a list of arguments	968
MODE	Returns the most common value in a data set	971
NEGBINOMDIST	Returns the negative binomial distribution	973
NORMDIST	Returns the normal cumulative distribution	973
NORMINV	Returns the inverse of the normal cumulative distribution	973
NORMSDIST	Returns the standard normal cumulative distribution	974
NORMSINV	Returns the inverse of the standard normal cumulative distribution	974
PEARSON	Returns the Pearson product moment correlation coefficient	978

► **TABLE B.1:** *Excel Functions by Category (continued)*

Function	Description	Page
PERCENTILE	Returns the k-th percentile of values in a range	978
PERCENTRANK	Returns the percentage rank of a value in a data set	979
PERMUT	Returns the number of permutations for a given number of objects	979
POISSON	Returns the Poisson distribution	981
PROB	Returns the probability that the values in a range are between two limits	983
QUARTILE	Returns the quartile of a data set	986
RANDBETWEEN	Returns a random number between the numbers you specify	1060
RANK	Returns the rank of a number in a list of numbers	987
RSQ	Returns the square of the Pearson product moment correlation coefficient	993
SKEW	Returns the skewness of a distribution	996
SLOPE	Returns the slope of the linear regression line	996
SMALL	Returns the k-th smallest value in a data set	997
STANDARDIZE	Returns a normalized value	998
STDEV	Estimates standard deviation based on a sample	998
STDEVP	Calculates standard deviation based on the entire population	999

TABLE B.1: *Excel Functions by Category (continued)*

Function	Description	Page
STEYX	Returns the standard error of the predicted y-value for each x in the regression	999
TDIST	Returns the Student's t-distribution	1006
TINV	Returns the inverse of the Student's t-distribution	1007
TREND	Returns values along a linear trend	1008
TRIMMEAN	Returns the mean of the interior of a data set	1010
TTEST	Returns the probability associated with a Student's t-Test	1011
VAR	Estimates variance based on a sample	1013
VARP	Calculates variance based on the entire population	1013
WEIBULL	Returns the Weibull distribution	1017
ZTEST	Returns the two-tailed P-value of a z-test	1017

Text Functions		
CHAR	Returns the character specified by the code number	923
CLEAN	Removes all nonprintable characters from text	926
CODE	Returns a numeric code for the first character in a text string	927
CONCATENATE	Joins several text items into one text item	928
DOLLAR	Converts a number to text, using currency format	938

► **TABLE B.1:** *Excel Functions by Category (continued)*

Function	Description	Page
EXACT	Checks to see if two text values are identical	941
FIND	Finds one text value within another (case-sensitive)	944
FIXED	Formats a number as text with a fixed number of decimals	945
LEFT	Returns the leftmost characters from a text value	961
LEN	Returns the number of characters in a text string	961
LOWER	Converts text to lowercase	966
MID	Returns a specific number of characters from a text string starting at the position you specify	968
PROPER	Capitalizes the first letter in each word of a text value	984
REPLACE	Replaces characters within text	989
REPT	Repeats text a given number of times	989
RIGHT	Returns the rightmost characters from a text value	990
SEARCH	Finds one text value within another (not case-sensitive)	993
SUBSTITUTE	Substitutes new text for old text in a text string	1000
T	Converts its arguments to text	1004
TEXT	Formats a number and converts it to text	1006
TRIM	Removes spaces from text	1009
UPPER	Converts text to uppercase	1012
VALUE	Converts a text argument to a number	1012

▶▶ *Built-In Worksheet Functions*

ABS

The ABS function returns the absolute value of a number.

Syntax

ABS(number)

Number   is the real number for which you want the absolute value.

Examples

ABS(43)

returns 43—43 is the absolute value of 43.

ABS(-105)

returns 105—105 is the absolute value of -105.

ACOS

Returns the arccosine of a number. The returned angle is given in radians in the range 0 to p.

Syntax

ACOS(number)

Number   is the cosine of the angle you want, and must be between -1 and 1. If you want to convert the result from radians to degrees, multiply the result by 180/PI().

Examples

ACOS(-0.5)

returns 2.094395 (2p/3 radians)

ACOS(-0.5)*180/PI()

returns 120 (degrees)

ACOSH

Returns the inverse hyperbolic cosine of a number (number must be greater than or equal to 1).

Syntax

ACOSH(number)

Number   is any real number equal to or greater than 1.

Examples

ACOSH(10)

returns 2.993223.

ADDRESS

Creates a cell address as text, given specified row and column numbers.

Syntax

ADDRESS(row_num,column_num,abs_num,a1,sheet_text)

Row_num   is the row number to use in the cell reference.

Column_num   is the column number to use in the cell reference.

Abs_num   specifies the type of reference to return. If abs_num is 1 or omitted, an absolute reference is returned; if abs_num is 2, an absolute row/relative column reference is returned; if abs_num is 3, a relative row/absolute column reference is returned; if abs_num is 4, a relative reference is returned.

A1   is a logical value that specifies the A1 or R1C1 reference style. If A1 is TRUE or omitted, ADDRESS returns an A1-style reference; if FALSE, ADDRESS returns an R1C1-style reference.

Sheet_text   is text specifying the name of the worksheet or macro sheet to be used as the external reference. If sheet_text is omitted, no sheet name is used.

Examples

ADDRESS(2,3)

returns "$C$2"

    ADDRESS(2,3,2,FALSE)

returns "R2C[3]"

AND

The AND function joins test conditions. Returns TRUE if all its logical arguments are TRUE; returns FALSE if one or more logical arguments is FALSE. Logical arguments are statements which return a value of true or false.

Syntax

    AND(logical1,logical2,...)

Logical1,logical2,... are conditions you want to test; conditions can be either TRUE or FALSE. Up to 30 arguments can be tested.

Examples

    AND(TRUE,TRUE)

returns TRUE.

    AND(TRUE,FALSE)

returns FALSE.

    AND(2+2=4,2+3=5)

returns TRUE.

AREAS

Returns the number of areas in a reference. An area is a single cell or a range of contiguous cells.

Syntax

    AREAS(reference)

Reference is a reference to a cell or range of cells and can refer to multiple areas. If you want to specify several references as a single argument, then you must include extra sets of parentheses so that Microsoft Excel will not interpret the comma as a field separator (see the second example).

Examples

AREAS(B2:D4)

returns 1

AREAS((B2:D4,E5,F6:I9))

returns 3

If the name Sales refers to the areas B1:D4, B2, and E1:E10, then:

AREAS(Sales)

returns 3

ASIN

Returns the arcsine of a number. To express the arcsine in degrees, multiply the result by 180/PI().

Syntax

ASIN(number)

Number   is the sine of the angle you want and must be from -1 to 1.

Examples

ASIN(-0.5)

returns -0.5236 (-p/6 radians)

ASIN(-0.5)*180/PI()

returns -30 (degrees)

ASINH

Returns the inverse hyperbolic sine of a number.

Syntax

ASINH(number)

Number   is any real number.

Examples

ASINH(-2.5)

returns -1.64723

ATAN

Returns the arctangent of a number. To express the arctangent in degrees, multiply the result by 180/PI().

Syntax

ATAN(number)

Number   is the tangent of the angle you want.

Examples

ATAN(1)

returns 0.785398 (p/4 radians)

ATAN(1)*180/PI()

returns 45 (degrees)

ATAN2

Returns the arctangent from x- and y- coordinates. To express the arctangent in degrees, multiply the result by 180/PI().

Syntax

ATAN2(x_num,y_num)

X_num   is the x-coordinate of the point.

Y_num   is the y-coordinate of the point.

Examples

ATAN2(1,1)

returns 0.785398 (p/4 radians)

ATAN2(-1,-1)

returns -2.35619 (-3p/4 radians)

ATAN2(-1,-1)*180/PI()

returns -135 (degrees)

ATANH

Returns the inverse hyperbolic tangent of a number.

Syntax

ATANH(number)

Number is any real number between 1 and -1.

Examples

ATANH(0.76159416)

returns 1 (approximately)

ATANH(-0.1)

returns -0.10034

AVEDEV

Returns the average of the absolute deviations of data points from their mean.

Syntax

AVEDEV(number1,number2,...)

Number1,number2,... are 1 to 30 arguments for which you want the average of the absolute deviations. You can also use a single array or a reference to an array instead of arguments separated by commas.

Example

AVEDEV(4,5,6,7,5,4,3)

returns 1.020408

AVERAGE

Returns the average of its arguments.

Syntax

AVERAGE(number1,number2,...)

Number1,number2,... are 1 to 30 numeric arguments for which you want the average.

 ▶ ▶ T I P

When averaging cells, bear in mind the difference between empty cells and cells containing the value zero, especially if you have cleared the Zero Values check box in the View tab of the Tools ➤ Options dialog box. Empty cells are not included in the average, but zero values are.

Examples

If A1:A5 is named Scores and contains

the numbers 10, 7, 9, 27, and 2, then:

AVERAGE(A1:A5)

returns 11

AVERAGE(Scores)

returns 11

BETADIST

Returns the cumulative beta probability density function.

Syntax

BETADIST(x,alpha,beta,A,B)

X is the value between A and B at which to evaluate the function.

Alpha is a parameter to the distribution.

Beta is a parameter to the distribution.

A is an optional lower bound to the interval of x.

B is an optional upper bound to the interval of x.

Example

BETADIST(2,8,10,1,3)

returns 0.685470581

BETAINV

Returns the inverse of the cumulative beta probability density function.

Syntax

BETAINV(probability,alpha,beta,A,B)

Probability   is a probability associated with the beta distribution.

Alpha   is a parameter to the distribution.

Beta   is a parameter to the distribution.

A   is an optional lower bound to the interval of x.

B   is an optional upper bound to the interval of x.

Example

BETAINV(0.685470581,8,10,1,3)

returns 2

CEILING

Rounds a number away from zero to the nearest integer or to the nearest multiple of significance.

For example, if you want to avoid using pennies in your prices and your product is priced at $5.47, use the formula =CEILING(5.47,0.05) to round prices up to the nearest nickel.

Syntax

CEILING(number,significance)

Number   is the value you want to round.

Significance   is the multiple to which you want to round.

Examples

CEILING(2.5,1)

returns 3

CEILING(-2.5,-2)

returns -4

CEILING(0.234,0.01)

returns 0.24

CELL

Returns information about the formatting, location, or contents of a cell. The CELL function is provided for compatibility with other spreadsheet programs.

Syntax

CELL(info_type,reference)

Info_type   is a text value that specifies what type of

cell information you want.

Reference   is the cell that you want information about.

See the On-line Help Worksheet Function Reference for a listing of info types.

Examples

CELL("row",A20)

returns 20

If A3 contains TOTAL, then:

CELL("contents",A3)

returns "TOTAL"

CHAR

Returns the character specified by the code number. You can use CHAR to translate code numbers you might get from files on other types of computers into characters.

Syntax

CHAR(number)

Number   is a number between 1 and 255 specifying which character you want. The character is from the character set used by your computer (e.g. Windows uses the ANSI character set).

Examples

CHAR(65)

returns "A"

CHAR(33)

returns "!"

CHIDIST

Returns the one-tailed probability of the chi-squared distribution.

Syntax

CHIDIST(x,degrees_freedom)

X   is the value at which you want to evaluate the distribution.

Degrees_freedom   is the number of degrees of freedom.

Example

CHIDIST(18.307,10)

returns 0.050001

CHIINV

Returns the inverse of the chi-squared distribution. CHIINV uses an iterative technique for calculating the function. Given a probability value, CHIINV iterates until the result is accurate to within $\pm 3 \times 10^{-7}$. If CHIINV does not converge after 100 iterations, the function returns the #N/A error value.

Syntax

CHIINV(probability,degrees_freedom)

Probability   is a probability associated with the chi-squared distribution.

Degrees_freedom   is the number of degrees of freedom.

Example

CHIINV(0.05,10)

returns 18.30703

CHITEST(actual_range,expected_range)

Returns the test for independence.

Syntax

CHITEST(actual_range,expected_range)

Actual_range   is the range of data that contains observations to test against expected values.

Expected_range   is the range of data that contains the ratio of the product of row totals and column totals to the grand total.

See the On-line Help worksheet function reference for information about the equation used to calculate CHITEST and an example.

CHOOSE

Uses the argument index_num to choose a value from the list of value arguments. You can use CHOOSE to select one of up to 29 values based on the index number. For example, if value1 through value7 are the days of the week, CHOOSE returns one of the days if index_num is a number between 1 and 7.

Syntax

CHOOSE(index_num,value1,value2,...)

Index_num   specifies which value argument is selected. Index_num must be a number between 1 and 29, or a formula or reference to a cell containing a number between 1 and 29.

- If index_num is 1, CHOOSE returns value1; if it is 2, CHOOSE returns value2; and so on.

- If index_num is less than 1 or greater than the number of the last value in the list, CHOOSE returns the #VALUE! error value.
- If index_num is a fraction, it is truncated to the lowest integer before being used.

Value1,value2,...   are up to 29 value arguments from which CHOOSE selects a value or an action to perform based on index_num. The arguments can be numbers, cell references, defined names, formulas, macro functions, or text.

Examples

CHOOSE(2,"1st","2nd","3rd","Finished")

returns "2nd"

SUM(A1:CHOOSE(3,A10,A20,A30))

is equivalent to SUM(A1:A30)

If A10 contains 4, then:

CHOOSE(A10,"Nails","Screws","Nuts","Bolts")

returns "Bolts"

CLEAN

Removes all nonprintable characters from text. You can use CLEAN on text imported from other applications which contains characters that may not print with your operating system. For example, you can use CLEAN to remove some low-level computer code that is frequently at the beginning and end of data files and cannot be printed.

Syntax

CLEAN(text)

Text   is any worksheet information from which you want to remove nonprintable characters.

Example

CHAR(7) returns a nonprintable character.

CLEAN(CHAR(7)&"text"&CHAR(7))

returns "text"

CODE

Returns a numeric code for the first character in a text string. The character is from the character set used by your computer (e.g. Windows uses the ANSI character set).

Syntax

CODE(text)

Text   is the text for which you want the code of the first

character.

Examples

CODE("A")

returns 65

CODE("Alphabet")

returns 65

COLUMNS

Returns the number of columns in a reference or array. (See Chapter 9 for in-depth coverage and examples of COLUMNS.)

Syntax

COLUMNS(array)

Array   is an array, array formula, or reference to a range of cells for which you want the number of columns.

COLUMN

Returns the column number of the reference. (See Chapter 9 for in-depth coverage and examples of COLUMN.)

Syntax

COLUMNeference)

Reference   is the cell or range of cells for which you want the column number.

COMBIN

Returns the number of combinations for a given number of objects.

Syntax

COMBIN(number,number_chosen)

Number   is the number of objects.

Number_chosen   is the number of objects in each combination.

Example

Suppose you want to know the odds of winning a lottery in which each entry is a combination of 6 numbers between 1 and 49.

COMBIN(49,6)

returns 13,983,816 possible combinations.

CONCATENATE

Joins several text items into one text item. The "&" operator can be used instead of CONCATENATE to join text items.

Syntax

CONCATENATE (text1,text2,...)

Text1,text2,...   are up to 30 text items to be joined into a single text item. The text items can be text strings, numbers, or single-cell references.

Examples

CONCATENATE("Total ","Value")

 returns "Total Value". This is equivalent to typing "Total"&" "&"Value".

Suppose in a stream survey worksheet, cell C2 contains "species", C5 contains " brook trout", and C8 contains the total 32.

CONCATENATE("Stream population for ",C5," ",C2," is ",C8,"/mile")

returns "Stream population for brook trout species is 32/mile"

CONFIDENCE

Returns a confidence interval for a population.

Syntax

CONFIDENCE(alpha,standard_dev,size)

Alpha   is the significance level used to compute the confidence level. The confidence level equals 100(1 - alpha)%, or in other words, an alpha of 0.05 indicates a 95% confidence level.

Standard_dev   is the population standard deviation for the data range, and is assumed to be known.

Size   is the sample size.

See the On-line Help worksheet function reference for information about the equation used to calculate CONFIDENCE and an example.

CORREL

Returns the correlation coefficient between two data sets.

Syntax

CORREL(array1,array2)

Array1   is a cell range of values.

Array2   is a second cell range of values.

Example

CORREL({3,2,4,5,6},{9,7,12,15,17})

returns 0.997054

COS

Returns the cosine of the given angle. If the angle is in degrees, multiply it by PI()/180 to convert it to radians.

Syntax

COS(number)

Number   is the angle (in radians) for which you want the cosine.

Examples

COS(1.047)

returns 0.500171

COS(60*PI()/180)

returns 0.5, the cosine of 60 degrees

COSH

Returns the hyperbolic cosine of a number.

Syntax

COSH(number)

Number is the number for which you want the hyperbolic cosine.

Examples

COSH(4)

returns 27.30823

COSH(EXP(1))

returns 7.610125, where EXP(1) is e, the base of the natural logarithm.

COUNT

Counts how many numbers are in the list of arguments.(See Chapter 9 for in-depth coverage and examples of COUNT.)

Syntax

COUNT(value1,value2,...)

Value1,value2,... are up to 30 arguments that can contain or refer to a variety of data types, but only numbers are counted.

COUNTA

Counts the number of nonblank values in the list of arguments. Use COUNTA to count the number of cells with data in a range or array.(See Chapter 9 for in-depth coverage and examples of COUNTA.)

Syntax

COUNTA(value1,value2,...)

Value1,value2,... are up to 30 arguments representing the values you want to count. In this case, a value is any type of information, including empty text ("") but not including empty cells. If an argument is an array or reference, empty cells within the array or reference are ignored.

COUNTBLANK

Counts the number of blank cells within a single range.(See Chapter 9 for in-depth coverage and examples of COUNTBLANK.)

Syntax

COUNTBLANKange)

Range is the range within which you want to count the blank cells.

COUNTIF

Counts the number of nonblank cells within a range that meet the given criteria.(See Chapter 9 for in-depth coverage and examples of COUNTIF.)

Syntax

COUNTIFange,criteria)

Range is the range of cells from which you want to

count cells.

Criteria is the expression that defines which cells will be counted.

COVAR

Returns covariance, the average of the products of paired deviations. Covariance helps to determine the relationship between two data sets (for example, whether greater income accompanies greater levels of education).

Syntax

COVAR(array1,array2)

Array1   is the first cell range of integers.

Array2   is the second cell range of integers.

Example

COVAR({3,2,4,5,6},{9,7,12,15,17})

returns 5.2

CRITBINOM

Returns smallest value for which cumulative binomial distribution is less than or equal to criterion value.

Syntax

CRITBINOM(trials,probability_s,alpha)

Trials   is the number of Bernoulli trials.

Probability_s   is the probability of a success on each trial.

Alpha   is the criterion value.

Example

CRITBINOM(6,0.5,0.75)

returns 4

DATE

Returns the serial number of a particular date.(See Chapter 9 for in-depth coverage and examples of DATE.)

Syntax

DATE(year,month,day)

Year   is a number from 1900 to 2078 in Microsoft Excel for Windows.

Month   is a number representing the month of the year.

Day   is a number representing the day of the month.

Worksheet Functions

Ap.
B

DATEVALUE

Converts a date in the form of text to a serial number.

Syntax

DATEVALUE(date_text)

Date_text is text that returns a date in a Microsoft Excel date format.

Example

DATEVALUE("8/22/55")

returns 20323 in the 1900 date system.

DAVERAGE

Returns the average of selected database entries.

Syntax

DAVERAGE(database,field,criteria)

Database is the range of cells that make up the database.

Field indicates which field is used in the function.

Criteria is the range of cells that contains the database criteria.

DAY

Converts a serial number to a day of the month.(See Chapter 9 for in-depth coverage and examples of DAY.)

Syntax

DAY(serial_number)

Serial_number is the date-time code used by Microsoft Excel for date and time calculations.

DAYS360

Calculates the number of days between two dates on the basis of a 360-day year.

Syntax

DAYS360(start_date,end_date,method)

Start_date,end_date   are the two dates between which you want to know the number of days (can be either text strings using numbers to represent the month, day, and year, or they can be serial numbers representing the dates).

Method   is a logical value that specifies whether the European or US method should be used in the calculation.

- **FALSE or omitted**   US (NASD). If the starting date is the 31st of a month, it becomes equal to the 30th of the same month. If the ending date is the 31st of a month and the starting date is less than the 30th of a month, the ending date becomes equal to the 1st of the next month, otherwise the ending date becomes equal to the 30th of the same month.
- **TRUE**   European method. Starting dates or ending dates which occur on the 31st of a month become equal to the 30th of the same month.

Example

DAYS360("1/30/93","2/1/93")

returns 1

  T I P

> **To determine the number of days between two dates in a normal year, you can use normal subtraction—for example, "12/31/93"-"1/1/93" equals 364.**

DB

Returns the depreciation of an asset for a specified period using the fixed-declining balance method.

Syntax

DB(cost,salvage,life,period,month)

Cost   is the initial cost of the asset.

Salvage   is the value at the end of the depreciation (sometimes called the salvage value of the asset).

Life   is the number of periods over which the asset is being depreciated (sometimes called the useful life of the asset).

Period   is the period for which you want to calculate the depreciation. Period must use the same units as life.

Month   is the number of months in the first year. If month is omitted, it is assumed to be 12.

Examples

Suppose a factory purchases a new machine. The machine costs $1,000,000 and has a lifetime of six years. The salvage value of the machine is $100,000. The following examples show depreciation over the life of the machine (the results are rounded to whole numbers).

> DB(1000000,100000,6,1,7)

returns $186,083

> DB(1000000,100000,6,2,7)

returns $259,639

DCOUNT

Counts the cells containing numbers from a specified database using a criteria range.

Syntax

DCOUNT(database,field,criteria)

Database   is the range of cells that make up the database.

Field   indicates which field is used in the function.

Criteria   is the range of cells that contains the database criteria.

DCOUNTA

Counts nonblank cells from a specified database using a criteria range.

Syntax

DCOUNTA(database,field,criteria)

Database   is the range of cells that make up the database.

Field   indicates which field is used in the function.

Criteria   is the range of cells that contains the database criteria.

DDB

Returns the depreciation of an asset for a specified period using double-declining balance method.

Syntax

DDB(cost,salvage,life,period,factor)

Cost   is the initial cost of the asset.

Salvage   is the value at the end of the depreciation (sometimes called the salvage value of the asset).

Life   is the number of periods over which the asset is being depreciated (sometimes called the useful life of the asset).

Period   is the period for which you want to calculate the depreciation. Period must use the same units as life.

Factor   is the rate at which the balance declines. If factor is omitted, it is assumed to be 2 (the double-declining balance method).

All five arguments must be positive numbers.

Examples

Suppose a factory purchases a new machine. The machine costs $2400 and has a lifetime of 10 years. The salvage value of the machine is $300. The following examples show depreciation over several periods. The results are rounded to two decimal places.

DDB(2400,300,3650,1)

returns $1.32, the first day's depreciation (Excel automatically assumes that factor is 2).

DDB(2400,300,120,1,2)

returns$40.00, the first month's depreciation.

DEGREES

Converts radians to degrees.

Syntax

DEGREES(angle)

Angle   is the angle in radians that you want to convert.

Example

DEGREES(PI())

returns180

DEVSQ

Returns the sum of squares of deviations.

Syntax

DEVSQ(number1,number2,...)

Number1,number2,...   are up to 30 arguments for which you want to calculate the sum of squared deviations. You can also use a single array or a reference to an array instead of arguments separated by commas.

- The arguments should be numbers, or names, arrays, or references that contain numbers.

- If an array or reference argument contains text, logical values, or empty cells, those values are ignored; however, cells with the value zero are included.

Example

DEVSQ(4,5,8,7,11,4,3)

returns 48

DGET

Extracts from a database a single record that matches the specified criteria.

Syntax

DGET(database,field,criteria)

Database   is the range of cells that make up the database.

Field   indicates which field is used in the function.

Criteria   is the range of cells that contains the database criteria.

DMAX

Returns the maximum value from selected database entries using a criteria range.

Syntax

DMAX(database,field,criteria)

Database   is the range of cells that make up the database.

Field   indicates which field is used in the function.

Criteria   is the range of cells that contains the database criteria.

DMIN

Returns the minimum value from selected database entries using a criteria range.

Syntax

DMIN(database,field,criteria)

Database   is the range of cells that make up the database.

Field   indicates which field is used in the function.

Criteria   is the range of cells that contains the database criteria.

DOLLAR

Converts a number to text, using currency format.

Syntax

DOLLAR(number,decimals)

Number   is a number, a reference to a cell containing a number, or a formula that evaluates to a number.

Decimals   is the number of digits to the right of the decimal point. If decimals is negative, number is rounded to the left of the decimal point. If you omit decimals, it is assumed to be 2.

> **N O T E**
>
> **The difference between formatting a cell with the Format ➤ Cell command and formatting a number directly with the DOLLAR function is that the result of the DOLLAR function is text, while a number in a formatted cell is still a number. You can use numbers formatted with DOLLAR in formulas, because numbers entered as text are converted to numbers when Excel calculates.**

Examples

DOLLAR(1234.567,2)

returns "$1234.57"

DOLLAR(1234.567,-2)

returns "$1200"

DPRODUCT

Multiplies the values in a particular field of records using a criteria range.

Syntax

DPRODUCT(database,field,criteria)

Database   is the range of cells that make up the database.

Field   indicates which field is used in the function.

Criteria   is the range of cells that contains the database criteria.

DSTDEV

Estimates the standard deviation on the basis of a sample of selected database entries.

Syntax

DSTDEV(database,field,criteria)

Database   is the range of cells that make up the database.

Field   indicates which field is used in the function.

Criteria   is the range of cells that contains the database criteria.

DSTDEVP

Calculates the standard deviation on the basis of the entire population of selected database entries.

Syntax

DSTDEVP(database,field,criteria)

Database   is the range of cells that make up the database.

Field   indicates which field is used in the function.

Criteria   is the range of cells that contains the database criteria.

DSUM

Adds the numbers in the field column of records in the database using a criteria range.

Syntax

DSUM(database,field,criteria)

Database   is the range of cells that make up the database.

Field   indicates which field is used in the function.

Criteria   is the range of cells that contains the database criteria.

DVAR

Estimates variance on the basis of a sample from selected database entries.

Syntax

DVAR(database,field,criteria)

Database   is the range of cells that make up the database.

Field indicates which field is used in the function.

Criteria is the range of cells that contains the database criteria.

DVARP

Calculates variance on the basis of the entire population of selected database entries.

Syntax

DVARP(database,field,criteria)

Database is the range of cells that make up the database.

Field indicates which field is used in the function.

Criteria is the range of cells that contains the database criteria.

EVEN

Rounds a number up to the nearest even integer.

Syntax

EVEN(number)

Number/p/is the value to round.

Examples

EVEN(1.5)

returns 2

EVEN(3)

returns 4

EXACT

Checks to see if two text values are identical (it is case sensitive). You can use EXACT to test text entries.

Syntax

EXACT(text1,text2)

Text1 is the first text string.

Text2 is the second text string.

Examples

EXACT("word","word")

returns TRUE

EXACT("Word","word")

returns FALSE

EXP

Returns e raised to the power of a given number.

Syntax

EXP(number)

Number is the exponent applied to the base e.

Examples

EXP(2)

returns e2, or 7.389056

EXP(LN(3))

returns 3

EXPONDIST

Returns the exponential distribution.

Syntax

EXPONDIST(x,lambda,cumulative)

X is the value of the function.

Lambda is the parameter value.

Cumulative is a logical value that indicates which form of the exponential function to provide.

Examples

EXPONDIST(0.2,10,TRUE)

returns 0.864665

EXPONDIST(0.2,10,FALSE)

returns 1.353353

FACT

Returns the factorial of a number.

Syntax

FACT(number)

Number   is the nonnegative number you want the factorial of. If number is not an integer, it is truncated.

Examples

FACT(1)

returns 1

FACT(1.9)

returns FACT(1) equals 1

FALSE

Returns the logical value FALSE.

Syntax

FALSE()

You can also type the word FALSE directly into the worksheet or formula, and Microsoft Excel interprets it as the logical value FALSE.

FDIST

Returns the F probability distribution.

Syntax

FDIST(x,degrees_freedom1,degrees_freedom2)

X   is the value at which to evaluate the function.

Degrees_freedom1   is the numerator degrees of freedom.

Degrees_freedom2   is the denominator degrees of freedom.

Example

FDIST(15.20675,6,4)

returns 0.01

FIND

Finds one text value within another (case-sensitive). (See Chapter 9 for in-depth coverage and examples of FIND.)

Syntax

FIND(find_text,within_text,start_num)

Find_text   is the text you want to find.

Within_text   is the text containing the text you want to find.

Start_num   specifies the character at which to start the search. The first character in within_text is character number 1. If you omit start_num, it is assumed to be 1.

FINV

Returns the inverse of the F probability distribution. FINV uses an iterative technique for calculating the function. Given a probability value, FINV iterates until the result is accurate to within $\pm 3 \times 10^{-7}$. If FINV does not converge after 100 iterations, the function returns the #N/A error value.

Syntax

FINV(probability,degrees_freedom1,degrees_freedom2)

Probability   is a probability associated with the F cumulative distribution.

Degrees_freedom1   is the numerator degrees of freedom.

Degrees_freedom2   is the denominator degrees of freedom.

Example

FINV(0.01,6,4)

returns 15.20675

FISHER

Returns the Fisher transformation.

Syntax

FISHER(x)

X   is a numeric value for which you want the transformation.

Example

FISHER(0.75)

returns 0.972955

FISHERINV

Returns the inverse of the Fisher transformation.

Syntax

FISHERINV(y)

Y   is the value for which you want to perform the inverse of the transformation.

Example

FISHERINV(0.972955)

returns 0.75

FIXED

Formats a number as text with a fixed number of decimals.

Syntax

FIXED(number,decimals,no_commas)

Number   is the number you want to round and convert to text.

Decimals   is the number of digits to the right of the decimal point.

No_commas   is a logical value that, if TRUE, prevents FIXED from including commas in the returned text. If no_commas is

FALSE or omitted, then the returned text includes commas as usual.

Examples

FIXED(1234.567,1)

returns "1234.6"

FIXED(1234.567,-1)

returns "1230"

FLOOR

Rounds a number down, toward zero.

Syntax

FLOOR(number,significance)

Number   is the numeric value you want to round.

Significance   is the multiple to which you want to round.

Examples

FLOOR(2.5,1)

returns 2

FLOOR(-2.5,-2)

returns -2

FORECAST

Returns a value along a linear trend.

Syntax

FORECAST(x,known_y's,known_x's)

X   is the data point for which you want to predict a value.

Known_y's   is the dependent array or range of data.

Known_x's   is the independent array or range of data.

Example

FORECAST(30,{6,7,9,15,21},{20,28,31,38,40})

returns 10.60725

FREQUENCY

Returns a frequency distribution as a vertical array.

Syntax

FREQUENCY(data_array,bins_array)

Data_array   is an array of or reference to a set of values for which you want to count frequencies. If data_array contains no values, FREQUENCY returns an array of zeros.

Bins_array   is an array of or reference to intervals into which you want to group the values in data_array. If bins_array contains no values, FREQUENCY returns the number of elements in data_array.

Example

Suppose a worksheet lists scores for a test. The scores are 79, 85, 78, 85, 83, 81, 95, 88, 97, and are entered into cells A1:A9. The data_array would contain a column of these test scores. The bins_array would be another column of intervals by which the test scores are grouped. In this example, bins_array would be C4:C6 and would contain the values 70, 79, 89. When entered as an array, you can use FREQUENCY to count the number of scores corresponding to the letter grade ranges 0-70, 71-79, 80-89, and 90-100 (this example assumes all test scores are integers). The following formula is entered as an array formula after selecting four vertical cells adjacent to your data.

FREQUENCY(A1:A9,C4:C6)

returns {0;2;5;2}

FTEST

Returns the result of an F-test.

Syntax

FTEST(array1,array2)

Array1   is the first array or range of data.

Array2   is the second array or range of data.

Example

FTEST({6,7,9,15,21},{20,28,31,38,40})

returns 0.648318

FV

Returns the future value of an investment.

Syntax

FVate,nper,pmt,pv,type)

Rate   is the interest rate per period.

Nper   is the total number of payment periods in an annuity.

Pmt   is the payment made each period; it cannot change over the life of the annuity. Typically, pmt contains principal and interest but no other fees or taxes. Payment arguments are entered as negative numbers.

Pv   is the present value, or the lump-sum amount that a series of future payments is worth right now. If pv is omitted, it is assumed to be 0.

Type   is the number 0 or 1 and indicates when payments are due. If type is 0, payments are due at the end of the period; if type is 1, payments are due at the beginning of the period. If type is omitted, it is assumed to be 0.

Examples

FV(0.5%,10,-200,-500,1)

returns $2581.40

FV(11%/12,35,-2000,,1)

returns $82,846.25

Suppose you want to save money for a special project occurring a year from now. You deposit $1000 into a savings account that earns 6 percent annual interest compounded monthly (monthly interest of 6%/12, or 0.5%). You plan to deposit $100 at the beginning of every month for the next 12 months. How much money will be in the account at the end of 12 months?

FV(0.5%,12,-100,-1000,1)

returns $2301.40

GAMMADIST

Returns the gamma distribution.

Syntax

GAMMADIST(x,alpha,beta,cumulative)

X   is the value at which you want to evaluate the distribution.

Alpha   is a parameter to the distribution.

Beta   is a parameter to the distribution. If beta=1, GAMMADIST returns the standard gamma distribution.

Cumulative   is a logical value that determines the form of the function. If cumulative is TRUE, GAMMADIST returns the cumulative distribution function; if FALSE, it returns the probability mass function.

Examples

GAMMADIST(10,9,2,FALSE)

returns 0.032639

GAMMADIST(10,9,2,TRUE)

returns 0.068094

GAMMAINV

Returns the inverse of the gamma cumulative distribution. GAMMAINV uses an iterative technique for calculating the function. Given a probability value, GAMMAINV iterates until the result is accurate to within ± 3x10^-7. If GAMMAINV does not converge after 100 iterations, the function returns the #N/A error value.

Syntax

GAMMAINV(probability,alpha,beta)

Probability   is the probability associated with the gamma distribution.

Alpha   is a parameter to the distribution.

Beta   is a parameter to the distribution. If beta=1, GAMMAINV returns the standard gamma distribution.

Example

GAMMAINV(0.068094,9,2)

returns 10

GAMMALN

Returns the natural logarithm of the gamma function, G(x).

Syntax

GAMMALN(x)

X   is the value for which you want to calculate GAMMALN.

Examples

GAMMALN(4)

returns 1.791759

EXP(GAMMALN(4))

returns 6 or (4-1)!

GEOMEAN

Returns the geometric mean.

Syntax

GEOMEAN(number1,number2,...)

Number1,number2,...   are up to 30 arguments for which you want to calculate the mean. You can also use a single array or a reference to an array instead of arguments separated by commas.

Example

GEOMEAN(4,5,8,7,11,4,3)

returns 5.476987

GROWTH

Returns values along an exponential trend. See the On-line Help worksheet function reference for more information and examples.

Syntax

GROWTH(known_y's,known_x's,new_x's,const)

Known_y's is the set of y-values you already know in the relationship $y=b*m^x$.

Known_x's is an optional set of x-values that you may already know in the relationship $y=b*m^x$.

New_x's are new x-values for which you want GROWTH to return corresponding y-values.

Const is a logical value specifying whether to force the constant b to equal 1.

HARMEAN

Returns the harmonic mean.

Syntax

HARMEAN(number1,number2,...)

Number1,number2,... are up to 30 arguments for which you want to calculate the mean. You can also use a single array or a reference to an array instead of arguments separated by commas.

Example

HARMEAN(4,5,8,7,11,4,3)

returns 5.028376

HLOOKUP

Looks in the top row of an array and returns the value of the indicated cell.

Syntax

HLOOKUP(lookup_value,table_array,row_index_num,range_lookup)

Lookup_value   is the value to be found in the first row of the table.

Table_array   is a table of information in which data is looked up. Use a reference to a range or a range name.

Row_index_num   is the row number in table_array from which the matching value should be returned. A row_index_num of 1 returns the first row value in table_array, a row_index_num of 2 returns the second row value in table_array, and so on.

Range_lookup   is a logical value that specifies whether you want HLOOKUP to find an exact match or an approximate match. If TRUE or omitted, an approximate match is returned (if an exact match is not found, the next largest value that is less than lookup_value is returned). If FALSE, HLOOKUP will find an exact match. If one is not found, the error value #N/A is returned.

Examples

Suppose you have an inventory worksheet of auto parts. Cells A1:A4 contain "Axles", 4, 5, 6. Cells B1:B4 contain "Bearings", 4, 7, 8. Cells C1:C4 contain "Bolts", 9, 10, 11.

HLOOKUP("Axles",A1:C4,2,TRUE)

returns 4

HLOOKUP("Bearings",A1:C4,3,FALSE)

returns 7

HOUR

Converts a serial number to an hour. (See Chapter 9 for in-depth coverage and examples of HOUR.)

Syntax

HOUR(serial_number)

Serial_number   is the date-time code used by Excel for date and time calculations. You can give serial_number as text, such as

"16:48:00" or "4:48:00 PM", instead of as a number (the text is automatically converted to a serial number).

HYPGEOMDIST

Returns the hypergeometric distribution.

Syntax

HYPGEOMDIST(sample_s,num_sample,population_s,num_population)

Sample_s   is the number of successes in the sample.

Num_sample   is the size of the sample.

Population_s   is the number of successes in the population.

Num_population   is the population size.

Example

A sampler of chocolates contains 20 pieces. Eight pieces are caramels, and the remaining 12 are nuts. If a person selects 4 pieces at random, the following function returns the probability that exactly 1 piece is a caramel.

HYPGEOMDIST(1,4,8,20)

returns 0.363261

IF

Specifies a logical test to perform.

Syntax

IF(logical_test,value_if_true,value_if_false)

Logical_test   is any value or expression that can be evaluated to TRUE or FALSE.

Value_if_true   is the value that is returned if logical_test is TRUE. If logical_test is TRUE and value_if_true is omitted, TRUE is returned.

Value_if_false   is the value that is returned if logical_test is FALSE. If logical_test is FALSE and value_if_false is omitted, FALSE is returned.

Up to seven IF functions can be nested as value_if_true and value_if_false arguments to construct more elaborate tests.

Examples

See Chapter 10, Using Templates, for several examples of IF functions.

INDEX

Uses an index to choose a value from a reference or array. (See Chapter 9 for in-depth coverage and examples of INDEX.)

Syntax 1

INDEX(array,row_num,column_num)

Syntax 2

INDEXeference,row_num,column_num,area_num)

Reference   is a reference to one or more cell ranges.

Row_num   is the row number within the range.

Column_num   is the column number within the range.

Area_num   is the specific area from a multi-area range reference.

INDIRECT

Returns a reference indicated by a text value. (See Chapter 9 for in-depth coverage and examples of INDIRECT.)

Syntax

INDIRECTef_text,a1)

Ref_text   is a reference to a cell that contains an A1- style reference, an R1C1-style reference, or a name defined as a reference.

A1   is a logical value that specifies what type of reference is contained in the cell ref_text.

INFO

Returns information about the current operating environment. See the On-line Help worksheet function reference for information about INFO, examples, and a list of type_text arguments.

Syntax

INFO(type_text)

Type_text   is text specifying what type of information you want returned.

INT

Rounds a number down to the nearest integer.

Syntax

INT(number)

Number   is the real number you want to round down to an integer.

Examples

INT(8.9)

returns 8

INT(-8.9)

returns -9

INTERCEPT

Returns the intercept of the linear regression line.

Syntax

INTERCEPT(known_y's,known_x's)

Known_y's   is an array of the dependent set of observations or data.

Known_x's   is the independent set of observations or data, expressed as an array.

Example

INTERCEPT({2,3,9,1,8},{6,5,11,7,5})

returns 0.0483871

IPMT

Returns the interest payment for an investment for a given period.

Syntax

IPMTate,per,nper,pv,fv,type)

Rate   is the interest rate per period.

Per   is the period for which you want to find the interest, and must be in the range 1 to nper.

Nper   is the total number of payment periods in an annuity.

Pv   is the present value, or the lump-sum amount that a series of future payments is worth right now.

Fv   is the future value, or a cash balance you want to attain after the last payment is made. If fv is omitted, it is assumed to be 0 (the future value of a loan, for example, is 0).

Type   is the number 0 or 1 and indicates when payments are due. Type 0 means payments are due at the end of the period; type 1 means payments are due at the beginning of the period. If type is omitted, it is assumed to be 0.

Examples

The following formula calculates the interest due in the first month of a three-year $8000 loan at 10 percent annual interest:

IPMT(0.1/12,1,36,–8000)

returns $66.67

The following formula calculates the interest due in the last year of a three-year $8000 loan at 10 percent annual interest, where payments are made yearly:

IPMT(0.1,3,3,–8000)

returns $292.45

IRR

Returns the internal rate of return for a series of cash flows. Excel uses an iterative technique for calculating IRR. Starting with guess, IRR cycles through the calculation until the result is accurate within 0.00001 percent. If IRR can't find a result that works after 20 tries, the #NUM! error value is returned.

Syntax

IRR(values,guess)

Values   is an array or a reference to cells that contain numbers for which you want to calculate the internal rate of return.

Guess   is a number that you guess is close to the result of IRR.

Examples

Suppose you want to start a restaurant business. You estimate it will cost $70,000 to start the business and expect to net the following income in the first five years: $12,000, $15,000, $18,000, $21,000, and $26,000. B1:B6 contain the following values: $-70,000, $12,000, $15,000, $18,000, $21,000 and $26,000, respectively.

To calculate the investment's internal rate of return after four years:

IRR(B1:B5)

returns -2.12%

To calculate the internal rate of return after five years:

IRR(B1:B6)

returns 8.66%

To calculate the internal rate of return after two years, you need to include a guess:

IRR(B1:B3,-10%)

returns -44.35%

ISBLANK

Returns TRUE if the value is blank.

Syntax

ISBLANK(value)

Value   is the value you want tested. Value can be a blank (empty cell), error, logical, text, number, or reference value, or name referring to any of these, that you want to test.

ISERR

Returns TRUE if the value is any error value except #N/A.

Syntax

ISERR(value)

Value   is the value you want tested. Value can be a blank (empty cell), error, logical, text, number, or reference value, or name referring to any of these, that you want to test.

ISERROR

Returns TRUE if the value is any error value.

Syntax

ISERROR(value)

Value   is the value you want tested. Value can be a blank (empty cell), error, logical, text, number, or reference value, or name referring to any of these, that you want to test.

ISLOGICAL

Returns TRUE if the value is a logical value.

Syntax

ISLOGICAL(value)

Value   is the value you want tested. Value can be a blank (empty cell), error, logical, text, number, or reference value, or name referring to any of these, that you want to test.

ISNA

Returns TRUE if the value is the #N/A error value.

Syntax

ISNA(value)

Value   is the value you want tested. Value can be a blank (empty cell), error, logical, text, number, or reference value, or name referring to any of these, that you want to test.

ISNONTEXT

Returns TRUE if the value is not text.

Syntax

ISNONTEXT(value)

Value   is the value you want tested. Value can be a blank (empty cell), error, logical, text, number, or reference value, or name referring to any of these, that you want to test.

ISNUMBER

Returns TRUE if the value is a number.

Syntax

ISNUMBER(value)

Value   is the value you want tested. Value can be a blank (empty cell), error, logical, text, number, or reference value, or name referring to any of these, that you want to test.

ISREF

Returns TRUE if the value is a reference.

Syntax

ISREF(value)

Value   is the value you want tested. Value can be a blank (empty cell), error, logical, text, number, or reference value, or name referring to any of these, that you want to test.

ISTEXT

Returns TRUE if the value is text.

Syntax

ISTEXT(value)

Value   is the value you want tested. Value can be a blank (empty cell), error, logical, text, number, or reference value, or name referring to any of these, that you want to test.

KURT

Returns the kurtosis of a data set.

Syntax

KURT(number1,number2,...)

Number1,number2,...   are 1 to 30 arguments for which you want to calculate kurtosis. You can also use a single array or a reference to an array instead of arguments separated by commas.

Example

KURT(3,4,5,2,3,4,5,6,4,7)

returns -0.1518

LARGE

Returns the k-th largest value in a data set.

Syntax

LARGE(array,k)

Array   is the array or range of data for which you want to determine the k-th largest value.

K   is the position (from the largest) in the array or cell range of data to return.

Examples

LARGE({3,4,5,2,3,4,5,6,4,7},3)

returns 5

LARGE({3,4,5,2,3,4,5,6,4,7},7)

returns 4

LEFT

Returns the leftmost characters from a text value. (See Chapter 9 for in-depth coverage and examples of LEFT.)

Syntax

LEFT(text,num_chars)

Text   is the text string containing the characters you want to extract.

Num_chars   specifies how many characters you want LEFT to return.

LEN

Returns the number of characters in a text string. (See Chapter 9 for in-depth coverage and examples of LEN.)

Syntax

LEN(text)

Text   is the text whose length you want to find. Spaces count as characters.

LINEST

Uses the "least squares" method to calculate a straight line that best fits your data and returns an array that describes the line. The equation for the line is $y=mx+b$. LINEST is often unnecessary in Excel 5 because of the new trendline capability in charts. See Chapter 14, "Constructing Complex Charts Using Advanced Techniques" to learn about trendlines. See the On-line Help worksheet function reference for detailed information about LINEST and examples.

Syntax

LINEST(known_y's,known_x's,const,stats)

Known_y's   is the set of y-values you already know in the relationship y=mx+b.

Known_x's   is an optional set of x-values that you may already know in the relationship y=mx+b.

Const   is a logical value specifying whether to force the constant b to equal 0.

Stats   is a logical value specifying whether to return additional regression statistics.

LN

Returns the natural logarithm of a number.

Syntax

LN(number)

Number   is the positive real number for which you want the natural logarithm.

Examples

LN(86)

returns 4.454347

LN(2.7182818)

returns 1

LOG

Returns the logarithm of a number to a specified base.

Syntax

LOG(number,base)

Number   is the positive real number for which you want the logarithm.

Base   is the base of the logarithm. If base is omitted, it is assumed to be 10.

Examples

LOG(10)

returns 1

LOG(8,2)

returns 3

LOG10

Returns the base-10 logarithm of a number.

Syntax

LOG10(number)

Number is the positive real number for which you want the base-10 logarithm.

Examples

LOG10(86)

returns 1.934498451

LOG10(10)

returns 1

LOG10(10^5)

returns 5

LOGEST

Returns the parameters of an exponential trend. See the On-line Help worksheet function reference for detailed information about LOGEST and examples. LOGEST is often unnecessary in Excel 5 because of the new trendline capability in charts. See Chapter 14, "Constructing Complex Charts Using Advanced Techniques" to learn about trendlines.

Syntax

LOGEST(known_y's,known_x's,const,stats)

Known_y's is the set of y-values you already know in the relationship $y=b*m^x$.

Known_x's is an optional set of x-values that you may already know in the relationship $y=b*m^x$.

Const is a logical value specifying whether to force the constant b to equal 1.

Stats is a logical value specifying whether to return additional regression statistics.

LOGINV

Returns the inverse of the lognormal distribution.

Syntax

LOGINV(probability,mean,standard_dev)

Probability   is a probability associated with the lognormal distribution.

Mean   is the mean of ln(x).

Standard_dev   is the standard deviation of ln(x).

Example

LOGINV(0.039084,3.5,1.2)

returns 4.000014

LOGNORMDIST

Returns the cumulative lognormal distribution.

Syntax

LOGNORMDIST(x,mean,standard_dev)

X   is the value at which to evaluate the function.

Mean   is the mean of ln(x).

Standard_dev   is the standard deviation of ln(x).

Example

LOGNORMDIST(4,3.5,1.2)

returns 0.039084

LOOKUP (vector form)

Looks up values in a vector (an array that contains only one row or one column). The vector form of LOOKUP looks in a vector for a value, moves to the corresponding position in a second vector, and returns this value. Use this form of the LOOKUP function when you want to be able to specify the range that contains the values you want to match.

See the On-line Help worksheet function reference for examples of LOOKUP.

Syntax

LOOKUP(lookup_value,lookup_vector,result_vector)

Lookup_value   is a value that LOOKUP searches for in the first vector. Lookup_value can be a number, text, a logical value, or a name or reference that refers to a value.

Lookup_vector   is a range that contains only one row or one column. The values in lookup_vector can be text, numbers, or logical values.

Result_vector   is a range that contains only one row or column. It should be the same size as lookup_vector.

LOOKUP (array form)

Looks up values in an array. The array form of LOOKUP looks in the first row or column of an array for the specified value, moves down or across to the last cell, and returns the value of the cell. Use this form of LOOKUP when the values you want to match are in the first row or column of the array. See the On-line Help worksheet function reference for examples of LOOKUP.

 ► ►**T I P**

> In general, it's best to use the HLOOKUP or VLOOKUP function instead of the array form of LOOKUP. This form of LOOKUP is provided for compatibility with other spreadsheet programs.

Syntax

LOOKUP(lookup_value,array)

Lookup_value   is a value that LOOKUP searches for in an array. Lookup_value can be a number, text, a logical value, or a name or reference that refers to a value.

Array   is a range of cells that contains text, numbers, or logical values that you want to compare with lookup_value.

LOWER

Converts text to lowercase.

Syntax

LOWER(text)

Text   is the text you want to convert to lowercase. LOWER does not change characters in text that are not letters.

Examples

LOWER("E. E. Cummings")

returns "e. e. cummings"

LOWER("Apt. 2B")

returns "apt. 2b"

MATCH

Looks up values in a reference or array. (See Chapter 9 for in-depth coverage and examples of MATCH.)

Syntax

MATCH(lookup_value,lookup_array,match_type)

Lookup_value   is the value you use to find the value you want in a table.

Lookup_array   is a contiguous range of cells containing possible lookup values. Lookup_array can be an array or an array reference.

Match_type   is the number -1, 0, or 1. Match_type specifies how Microsoft Excel matches lookup_value with values in lookup_array.

MAX

Returns the maximum value in a list of arguments.

Syntax

MAX(number1,number2,...)

Number1,number2,... are 1 to 30 numbers for which you want to find the maximum value.

Examples

If A1:A5 contains the numbers 10, 7, 9, 27, and 2, then:

MAX(A1:A5)

returns 27

MAX(A1:A5,30)

returns 30

MDETERM

Returns the matrix determinant of an array.

Syntax

MDETERM(array)

Array is a numeric array with an equal number of rows and columns.

Examples

MDETERM({1,3,8,5;1,3,6,1;1,1,1,0;7,3,10,2})

returns 88

MDETERM({3,6,1;1,1,0;3,10,2})

returns 1

MEDIAN

Returns the median of the given numbers.

Syntax

MEDIAN(number1,number2,...)

Number1,number2,... are up to 30 numbers for which you want the median.

Examples

MEDIAN(1,2,3,4,5)

returns 3

MEDIAN(1,2,3,4,5,6)

returns 3.5 (the average of 3 and 4)

MID

Returns a specific number of characters from a text string starting at the position you specify. (See Chapter 9 for in-depth coverage and examples of MID.)

Syntax

MID(text,start_num,num_chars)

Text   is the text string containing the characters you want to extract.

Start_num   is the position of the first character you want to extract in text. The first character in text has start_num 1, and so on.

Num_chars   specifies how many characters to return from text.

MIN

Returns the minimum value in a list of arguments.

Syntax

MIN(number1,number2,...)

Number1,number2,...   are up to 30 numbers for which you want to find the minimum value.

Examples

If A1:A5 contains the numbers 10, 7, 9, 27, and 2, then:

MIN(A1:A5)

returns

MIN(A1:A5,0)

returns 0

MINUTE

Converts a serial number to a minute. (See Chapter 9 for in-depth coverage and examples of MINUTE.)

Syntax

MINUTE(serial_number)

Serial_number   is the date-time code used by Microsoft Excel for date and time calculations.

MINVERSE

Returns the matrix inverse of an array.

Syntax

MINVERSE(array)

Array   is a numeric array with an equal number of rows and columns.

Examples

MINVERSE({4,-1;2,0})

returns {0,0.5;-1,2}

MINVERSE({1,2,1;3,4,-1;0,2,0})

returns {0.25,0.25,-0.75;0,0,0.5;0.75,-0.25,-0.25}

MIRR

Returns the internal rate of return where positive and negative cash flows are financed at different rates.

Syntax

MIRR(values,finance_rate,reinvest_rate)

Values   is an array or a reference to cells that contain numbers. These numbers represent a series of payments (negative values) and income (positive values) occurring at regular periods.

Finance_rate   is the interest rate you pay on the money used in the cash flows.

Reinvest_rate   is the interest rate you receive on the cash flows as you reinvest them.

Examples

Suppose you're a commercial fisherman just completing your fifth year of operation. Five years ago, you borrowed $120,000 at 10 percent annual interest to purchase a boat. Your catches have yielded $39,000, $30,000, $21,000, $37,000, and $46,000. During these years you reinvested your profits, earning 12% annually. In a worksheet, your loan amount is entered as -$120,000 in B1, and your five annual profits are entered in B2:B6. To calculate the investment's modified rate of return after five years:

MIRR(B1:B6,10%,12%)

returns 12.61%

To calculate the modified rate of return after three

years:

MIRR(B1:B4,10%,12%)

returns -4.80%

MMULT

Returns the matrix product of two arrays.

Syntax

MMULT(array1,array2)

Array1,array2   are the arrays you want to multiply.

Examples

MMULT({1,3;7,2},{2,0;0,2})

returns {2,6;14,4}

MMULT({3,0;2,0},{2,0;0,2})

returns {6,0;4,0}

MOD

Returns the remainder from division.

Syntax

MOD(number,divisor)

Number   is the number for which you want to find the remainder.

Divisor   is the number by which you want to divide number. If divisor is 0, MOD returns the #DIV/0! error value.

Examples

MOD(3,2)

returns 1

MOD(-3,2)

returns

MODE

Returns the most common value in a data set.

Syntax

MODE(number1,number2,...)

Number1,number2,...   are up to 30 arguments for which you want to calculate the mode. You can use a single array or a reference to an array instead of arguments separated by commas.

Example

MODE({5.6,4,4,3,2,4})

returns 4

MONTH

Converts a serial number to a month. (See Chapter 9 for in-depth coverage and examples of MONTH.)

Syntax

MONTH(serial_number)

Serial_number   is the date-time code used by Excel for date and time calculations.

N

Returns a value converted to a number. This function is provided for compatibility with other spreadsheet programs

Syntax

N(value)

Value   is the value you want converted. If value is a number, N returns the number; if value is a date (in an Excel date format), N returns the serial number of the date; if value is TRUE, N returns 1; if value is anything else, N returns 0.

Examples

If A1 contains "7", A2 contains "Even", and A3 contains "TRUE", then:

N(A1)

returns 7

N(A2)

returns 0, because A2 contains text

N(A3)

returns 1, because A3 contains TRUE

NA

Returns the error value #N/A. You can also type the value #N/A directly into a cell. The NA function is provided for compatibility with other spreadsheet programs.

Syntax

NA()

NEGBINOMDIST

Returns the negative binomial distribution.

Syntax

NEGBINOMDIST(number_f,number_s,probability_s)

Number_f   is the number of failures.

Number_s   is the threshold number of successes.

Probability_s   is the probability of a success.

Example

NEGBINOMDIST(10,5,0.25

returns 0.055049

NORMDIST

Returns the normal cumulative distribution.

Syntax

NORMDIST(x,mean,standard_dev,cumulative)

X   is the value for which you want the distribution.

Mean   is the arithmetic mean of the distribution.

Standard_dev   is the standard deviation of the distribution.

Cumulative   is a logical value that determines the form of the function.

Example

NORMDIST(42,40,1.5,TRUE)

returns 0.908789

NORMINV

Returns the inverse of the normal cumulative distribution.

Syntax

NORMINV(probability,mean,standard_dev)

Probability   is a probability corresponding to the normal distribution.

Mean   is the arithmetic mean of the distribution.

Standard_dev   is the standard deviation of the distribution.

Example

NORMINV(0.908789,40,1.5)

returns 42

NORMSDIST

Returns the standard normal cumulative distribution.

Syntax

NORMSDIST(z)

Z   is the value for which you want the distribution.

Example

NORMSDIST(1.333333)

returns 0.908789

NORMSINV

Returns the inverse of the standard normal cumulative distribution.

Syntax

NORMSINV(probability)

Probability   is a probability corresponding to the normal distribution.

Example

NORMSINV(0.908789)

returns 1.3333

NOT

Reverses the logic of its argument.

Syntax

NOT(logical)

Logical is a value or expression that can be evaluated to TRUE or FALSE. If logical is FALSE, NOT returns TRUE; if logical is TRUE, NOT returns FALSE.

Examples

NOT(FALSE)

returns TRUE

NOT(1+1=2)

returns FALSE

NOW

Returns the serial number of the current date and time. (See Chapter 9 for in-depth coverage and examples of NOW.)

Syntax

NOW()

NPER

Returns the number of periods for an investment.

Syntax

NPERate,pmt,pv,fv,type)

Rate is the interest rate per period.

Pmt is the payment made each period; it cannot change over the life of the annuity. Typically, pmt contains principal and interest but no other fees or taxes.

Pv is the present value, or the lump-sum amount that a series of future payments is worth right now.

Fv is the future value, or a cash balance you want to attain after the last payment is made. If fv is omitted, it is assumed to be 0 (the future value of a loan, for example, is 0).

Type   is the number 0 or 1 and indicates when payments are due. 0 or omitted means payments are due at the end of the period; 1 means payments are due at the beginning of the period.

Examples

NPER(12%/12,-100,-1000,10000,1)

returns 60

NPER(1%,-100,-1000,10000)

returns 60

NPV

Returns the net present value of an investment on the basis of a series of periodic cash flows and a discount rate.

 ▶ ▶**WARNING**

The NPV function is actually a present value function, but there are a couple of methods of using NPV as a true net present value function. The first method is: do not include the initial cash flow in the list of cash flows; instead, add the initial cash flow to the NPV function result. The second method is: include the initial cash flow in the list of cash flows, then multiply the NPV result by 1+I (I is the discount rate).

Syntax

NPVate,value1,value2,...)

Rate   is the rate of discount over the length of one period.

Value1,value2,...   are 1 to 29 arguments representing the payments and income.

Example

Suppose you're considering an investment in which you pay $10,000 one year from today and receive an annual income of $3000, $4200, and $6800 in the three years that follow. Assuming an annual discount rate of 10 percent, the net present value of this investment is:

NPV(10%,-10000,3000,4200,6800)

returns $1188.44

ODD

Rounds a number up to the nearest odd integer.

Syntax

ODD(number)

Number   is the value to round.

Examples

ODD(1.5)

returns 3

ODD(3)

returns 3

ODD(2)

returns 3

OFFSET

Returns a reference offset from a given reference. (See Chapter 9 for in-depth coverage and examples of OFFSET.)

Syntax

OFFSETeference,rows,cols,height,width)

Reference   is the reference from which you want to base the offset.

Rows   is the number of rows, up or down, that you want the upper-left cell to refer to.

Cols   is the number of columns, to the left or right, that you want the upper-left cell of the result to refer to.

Height   is the height, in number of rows, that you want the returned reference to be.

Width   is the width, in number of columns, that you want the returned reference to be.

OR

Returns TRUE if any argument is TRUE.

Syntax

OR(logical1,logical2,...)

Logical1,logical2,...   are 1 to 30 conditions you want to test that can be either TRUE or FALSE.

Examples

OR(1+1=1,2+2=5)

returns FALSE

If A1:A3 contains the values TRUE, FALSE, and TRUE, then:

OR(A1:A3)

returns TRUE

PEARSON

Returns the Pearson product moment correlation coefficient, which reflects the extent of a linear relationship between two data sets.

Syntax

PEARSON(array1,array2)

Array1   is a set of independent values.

Array2   is a set of dependent values.

Example

PEARSON({9,7,5,3,1},{10,6,1,5,3})

returns 0.699379

PERCENTILE

Returns the k-th percentile of values in a range. You can use PERCENTILE, for example, to examine candidates that score above the 90th percentile.

Syntax

PERCENTILE(array,k)

Array   is the array or range of data that defines relative standing.

K   is the percentile value in the range 0..1, inclusive.

Example

PERCENTILE({1,2,3,4},0.3)

returns 1.9

PERCENTRANK

Returns the percentage rank of a value in a data set. You can use PER-CENTRANK, for example, to evaluate the standing of a test score among a population of test scores.

Syntax

PERCENTRANK(array,x,significance)

Array   is the array or range of data with numeric values that defines relative standing.

X   is the value for which you want to know the rank.

Significance   is an optional value that identifies the number of significant digits for the returned percentage value. If omitted, PERCENTRANK uses three digits (0.xxx%).

Example

PERCENTRANK({1,2,3,4,5,6,7,8,9,10},4)

returns 0.333

PERMUT

Returns the number of permutations for a given number of objects. You can use PERMUT for lottery-style probability calculations.

Syntax

PERMUT(number,number_chosen)

Number   is an integer that describes the number of objects.

Number_chosen is an integer that describes the number of objects in each permutation.

Example

Suppose you want to calculate the odds of selecting a winning lottery number. Each lottery entry contains three numbers, each of which can be between 0 and 99, inclusive. The following function calculates the number of possible permutations.

    PERMUT(100,3)

returns 970,200

PI

Returns the value of pi (3.14159265358979), accurate to 15 digits.

Syntax

    PI()

Examples

    PI()/2

returns 1.57079...

    SIN(PI()/2)

returns 1

PMT

Returns the periodic payment for an annuity based on constant payments and a constant interest rate.

Be consistent about the units used for rate and nper. For example, if you make monthly payments on a four-year loan at 12 percent annual interest, use 12%/12 for rate and 4*12 for nper; to make annual payments on the same loan, use 12% for rate and 4 for nper.

Syntax

    PMTate,nper,pv,fv,type)

Rate is the interest rate per period.

Nper is the total number of payment periods in an annuity.

Pv   is the present value, the total amount that a series of future payments is worth now.

Fv   is the future value, or a cash balance you want to attain after the last payment is made. If fv is omitted, it is assumed to be 0 (the future value of a loan, for example, is 0).

Type   is the number 0 or 1 and indicates when payments are due. If type is 0 or omitted, payments are due at the end of the period; If type is 1, payments are due at the beginning of the period.

Examples

The following formula returns the monthly payment on a $10,000 loan at an annual rate of 8% that you must pay off in 10 months:

    PMT(8%/12,10,–10000)

returns $1037.03

For the same loan, if payments are due at the beginning of the period, the payment is:

    PMT(8%/12,10,10000,0,1)

returns –$1030.16

  T I P

To find the total amount paid over the duration of the annuity, multiply the returned PMT value by nper.

POISSON

Returns the Poisson distribution.

Syntax

    POISSON(x,mean,cumulative)

X   is the number of events.

Mean   is the expected numeric value.

Cumulative   is a logical value that determines the form of the probability distribution returned. If cumulative is TRUE, POISSON returns the cumulative Poisson probability that the number of random events occurring will be between zero and x inclusive; if FALSE, it returns the Poisson probability mass function that the number of events occurring will be exactly x.

Examples

POISSON(2,5,FALSE)

returns 0.084224

POISSON(2,5,TRUE)

returns 0.124652

POWER

Returns the result of a number raised to a power.

Syntax

POWER(number,power)

Number   is the base number. It can be any real number.

Power   is the exponent, to which the base number is raised.

Examples

POWER(5,2)

returns 25

POWER(98.6,3.2)

returns 2401077

POWER(4,5/4)

returns 5.656854

PPMT

Returns the payment on the principal for a given period for an investment based on periodic, constant payments and a constant interest rate.

Be consistent about the units used for rate and nper. For example, if you make monthly payments on a four-year loan at 12 percent annual interest, use 12%/12 for rate and 4*12 for nper; to make annual payments on the same loan, use 12% for rate and 4 for nper.

Syntax

PPMTate,per,nper,pv,fv,type)

Rate   is the interest rate per period.

Per   specifies the period and must be in the range 1 to nper.

Nper   is the total number of payment periods in an annuity.

Pv   is the present value, the total amount that a series of future payments is worth now.

Fv   is the future value, or a cash balance you want to attain after the last payment is made. If fv is omitted, it is assumed to be 0 (the future value of a loan, for example, is 0).

Type   is the number 0 or 1 and indicates when payments are due. If type is 0 or omitted, payments are due at the end of the period; If type is 1, payments are due at the beginning of the period.

Examples

The following formula returns the principal payment for the first month of a two-year $2000 loan at 10% annual interest:

PPMT(10%/12,1,24,–2000)

returns $75.62

The following function returns the principal payment for the last year of a 10-year $200,000 loan at 8% annual interest:

PPMT(8%,10,10,–200000)

returns $27,598.05

PROB

Returns the probability that values in a range are between two limits.

Syntax

PROB(x_range,prob_range,lower_limit,upper_limit)

X_range   is the range of numeric values of x with which there are associated probabilities.

Prob_range   is a set of probabilities associated with values in x_range.

Lower_limit   is the lower bound on the value for which you want a probability.

Upper_limit   is the optional upper bound on the value for which you want a probability.

Examples

PROB({0,1,2,3},{0.2,0.3,0.1,0.4},2)

returns 0.1

PROB({0,1,2,3},{0.2,0.3,0.1,0.4},1,3)

returns 0.8

PRODUCT

Multiplies its arguments.

Syntax

PRODUCT(number1,number2,...)

Number1,number2,...   are up to 30 numbers that you want to multiply.

Examples

If cells A2:C2 contain 5, 15, and 30:

PRODUCT(A2:C2)

returns 2250

PRODUCT(A2:C2,2)

returns 4500

PROPER

Capitalizes the first letter in each word of a text value.

Syntax

PROPER(text)

Text   is text enclosed in quotation marks, a formula that returns text, or a reference to a cell containing the text you want to partially capitalize.

Examples

> PROPER("this is a TITLE")

returns "This Is A Title"

> PROPER("2-cent's worth")

returns "2-Cent's Worth"

> PROPER("76BudGet")

returns "76Budget"

PV

Returns the present value of an investment (the total amount that a series of future payments is worth now). For example, when you borrow money, the loan amount is the present value to the lender.

- Be consistent about the units used for rate and nper. For example, if you make monthly payments on a four-year loan at 12 percent annual interest, use 12%/12 for rate and 4*12 for nper; to make annual payments on the same loan, use 12% for rate and 4 for nper.

- For all the arguments, the cash you pay out (e.g. deposits to savings) is represented by negative numbers; the cash you receive (e.g. dividend checks) is represented by positive numbers.

Syntax

> PVate,nper,pmt,fv,type)

Rate   is the interest rate per period.

Nper   is the total number of payment periods in an annuity.

Pmt   is the payment made each period and cannot change over the life of the annuity.

Fv   is the future value, or a cash balance you want to attain after the last payment is made. If fv is omitted, it is assumed to be 0. The future value of a loan is 0; however, if you want to save $50,000 to pay for a special project in 18 years, then $50,000 is the future value.

Type   is the number 0 or 1 and indicates when payments are due. If type is 0 or omitted, payments are due at the end of the period; if type is 1, payments are due at the beginning of the period.

Example

Suppose you're thinking of buying an insurance annuity that pays $500 at the end of every month for the next 20 years. The cost of the annuity is $60,000 and the money paid out will earn 8%. You want to determine whether this would be a good investment. Using the PV function you find that the present value of the annuity is:

PV(0.08/12,12*20,–500,,0)

returns $59,777.15

QUARTILE

Returns the quartile of a data set. You can use QUARTILE, for example, to find the top 25% of incomes in a population.

Syntax

QUARTILE(array,quart)

Array   is the array or cell range of numeric values for which you want the quartile value.

Quart   indicates which value to return. If quart equals 0, QUARTILE returns the minimum value; if quart equals 1, QUARTILE returns the first quartile (25th percentile); if quart equals 2, QUARTILE returns the median value (50th percentile); if quart equals 3, QUARTILE returns the third quartile (75th percentile); if quart equals 4, QUARTILE returns the maximum value.

Example

QUARTILE({1,2,4,7,8,9,10,12},1)

returns 3.5

RADIANS

Converts degrees to radians.

Syntax

RADIANS(angle)

Angle   is an angle in degrees that you want to convert.

Example

RADIANS(270)

returns 4.712389 (3p/2 radians)

RAND

Returns a random number between 0 and 1. The random number will recalculate every time the worksheet recalculates—to freeze the random values, copy the numbers, then choose Paste Special, Values.

Syntax

RAND( )

▶ ▶ **T I P**

To generate a random number between a and b, use the formula =RAND()*(b-a)+a.

Examples

To generate a random number greater than or equal to 0 but less than 100:

RAND()*100

returns a random number between 0 and 100.

INTAND()*100)

returns a random integer between 0 and 100.

RAND()*(49-2)+2

returns a random number between 2 and 49.

RANK

Returns the rank of a number in a list of numbers.

Syntax

RANK(number,ref,order)

Number   is the number whose rank you want to find.

Ref   is an array of, or a reference to, a list of numbers (non-numeric values in ref are ignored).

Order   is a number specifying how to rank number.

Examples

If A1:A5 contain the numbers 7, 3.5, 3.5, 1, and 2, respectively, then:

    RANK(A2,A1:A5,1)

returns 3

    RANK(A1,A1:A5,1)

returns 5

RATE

Returns the interest rate per period of an annuity.

Syntax

    RATE(nper,pmt,pv,fv,type,guess)

Nper   is the total number of payment periods in an annuity.

Pmt   is the payment made each period and cannot change over the life of the annuity.

Pv   is the present value (the total amount that a series of future payments is worth now).

Fv   is the future value, or a cash balance you want to attain after the last payment is made. If fv is omitted, it is assumed to be 0 (the future value of a loan, for example, is 0).

Type   is the number 0 or 1 and indicates when payments are due. If type is 0 or omitted, payments are due at the end of the period; If type is 1, payments are due at the beginning of the period.

Guess   is your guess for what the rate will be.

Example

To calculate the monthly rate of a four-year, $8000 loan with monthly payments of $200:

    RATE(48,-200,8000)

returns 0.77%

REPLACE

Replaces characters within text.

Syntax

REPLACE(old_text,start_num,num_chars,new_text)

Old_text is text in which you want to replace some characters.

Start_num is the position of the character in old_text that you want to replace with new_text.

Num_chars is the number of characters in old_text that you want to replace with new_text.

New_text is the text that will replace characters in old_text.

Examples

The following formula replaces the last two digits of 1990 with 91:

REPLACE("1990",3,2,"91")

returns "1991"

If cell A2 contains "123456", then:

REPLACE(A2,1,3,"@")

returns "@456"

REPT

Repeats text a given number of times.

Syntax

REPT(text,number_times)

Text is the text you want to repeat.

Number_times is a positive number specifying the number of times to repeat text. If number_times is 0, REPT returns "" (empty text). If number_times is not an integer, it is truncated. The result of the REPT function cannot be longer than 255 characters.

Examples

REPT("*-",3)

returns "*-*-*-"

If A3 contains "Sales", then:

REPT($A$3,2.9)

returns "SalesSales"

RIGHT

Returns the rightmost characters from a text value. (See Chapter 9 for in-depth coverage and examples of RIGHT.)

Syntax

RIGHT(text,num_chars)

Text is the text string containing the characters you want to extract.

Num_chars specifies how many characters you want to extract.

ROMAN

Converts an Arabic numeral to Roman, as text.

Syntax

ROMAN(number,form)

Number is the Arabic numeral you want converted.

Form is a number specifying the type of Roman numeral you want. The Roman numeral style ranges from Classic (form 0, TRUE, or omitted) to Simplified (form 4 or FALSE), becoming more concise as the value of form increases.

Examples

ROMAN(499,0)

returns "CDXCIX"

ROMAN(499,1)

returns "LDVLIV"

> ROMAN(499,2)

returns "XDIX"

ROUND

Rounds a number to a specified number of digits.

Syntax

> ROUND(number,num_digits)

Number   is the number you want to round.

Num_digits   specifies the number of digits to which you want to round the number. If num_digits is greater than 0, then number is rounded to the specified number of decimal places; if num_digits is 0, then number is rounded to the nearest integer; if num_digits is less than 0, then number is rounded to the left of the decimal point.

Examples

> ROUND(2.149,1)

returns 2.1

> ROUND(-1.475,2)

returns -1.48

> ROUND(21.5,-1)

returns 20

ROUNDDOWN

Rounds a number down, toward zero.

Syntax

> ROUNDDOWN(number,num_digits)

Number   is any real number that you want rounded down.

Num_digits   is the number of digits (to the right of the decimal point) to which you want to round the number.

Examples

ROUNDDOWN(3.2,0)

returns 3

ROUNDDOWN(76.9,0)

returns 76

ROUNDDOWN(3.14159,3)

returns 3.141

ROUNDUP

Rounds a number up, away from zero.

Syntax

ROUNDUP(number,num_digits)

Number   is any real number that you want rounded up.

Num_digits   is the number of digits (to the right of the decimal point) to which you want to round the number.

Examples

ROUNDUP(3.2,0)

returns 4

ROUNDUP(76.9,0)

returns 77

ROUNDUP(-3.14159,1)

returns -3.2

ROW

Returns the row number of a reference. (See Chapter 9 for in-depth coverage and examples of ROW.)

Syntax

ROWeference)

Reference   is the cell or range of cells for which you want the row number.

ROWS

Returns the number of rows in a reference. (See Chapter 9 for in-depth coverage and examples of ROWS.)

Syntax

ROWS(array)

Array   is an array, an array formula, or a reference to a range of cells for which you want the number of rows.

RSQ

Returns the square of the Pearson product moment correlation coefficient.

Syntax

RSQ(known_y's,known_x's

Known_y's   is an array or range of data points.

Known_x's   is an array or range of data points.

Example

RSQ({2,3,9,1,8,7,5},{6,5,11,7,5,4,4})

returns 0.05795

SEARCH

Finds one text value within another. (See Chapter 9 for in-depth coverage and examples of SEARCH.)

Syntax

SEARCH(find_text,within_text,start_num)

Find_text   is the text you want to find. You can use the wildcard characters, question mark (?) and asterisk (*), in find_text.

Within_text   is the text in which you want to search for find_text.

Start_num   is the character number in within_text, counting from the left, at which you want to start searching.

SECOND

Converts a serial number to a second.

Syntax

SECOND(serial_number)

Serial_number   is the date-time code used by Excel for date and time calculations.

Examples

SECOND("4:48:18 PM")

returns 18

SECOND(0.01)

returns 24

SECOND(4.02)

returns 48

SIGN

Determines the sign of a number. Returns 1 if number is positive, 0 if number is 0, and -1 if the number is negative.

Syntax

SIGN(number)

Number   is any real number.

Examples

SIGN(10)

returns 1

SIGN(4-4)

returns 0

SIGN(-0.00001)

returns -1

SIN

Returns the sine of the given angle.

Syntax

SIN(number)

Number   is the angle in radians for which you want the sine. If your argument is in degrees, multiply it by PI()/180 to convert it to radians.

Examples

SIN(PI())

returns 1.22E-16, which is approximately zero.

SIN(PI()/2)

returns 1

SIN(30*PI()/180)

returns 0.5, the sine of 30 degrees.

SINH

Returns the hyperbolic sine of a number.

Syntax

SINH(number)

Number   is any real number.

Examples

SINH(1)

returns 1.175201194

SINH(-1)

returns -1.175201194

SKEW

Returns the skewness of a distribution.

Syntax

SKEW(number1,number2,...)

Number1,number2...   are 1 to 30 arguments for which you want to calculate skewness.

Example

SKEW(3,4,5,2,3,4,5,6,4,7)

returns 0.359543

SLN

Returns the straight-line depreciation of an asset for one period.

Syntax

SLN(cost,salvage,life)

Cost   is the initial cost of the asset.

Salvage   is the value at the end of the depreciation (sometimes called the salvage value of the asset).

Life   is the number of periods over which the asset is being depreciated (sometimes called the useful life of the asset).

Example

Suppose you've bought a truck for $30,000 that has a useful life of 10 years and a salvage value of $7500. The depreciation allowance for each year is:

SLN(30000,7500,10)

returns $2250

SLOPE

Returns the slope of the linear regression line.

Syntax

SLOPE(known_y's,known_x's)

Known_y's is an array or cell range of numeric dependent data points.

Known_x's is the set of independent data points.

Example

SLOPE({2,3,9,1,8,7,5},{6,5,11,7,5,4,4})

returns 0.305556

SMALL

Returns the k-th smallest value in a data set.

Syntax

SMALL(array,k)

Array is an array or range of numerical data for which you want to determine the k-th smallest value.

K is the position (from the smallest) in the array or range of data to return.

Example

SMALL({3,4,5,2,3,4,5,6,4,7},4)

returns 4

SMALL({1,4,8,3,7,12,54,8,23},2)

returns 3

SQRT

Returns a positive square root.

Syntax

SQRT(number)

Number is the number for which you want the square root. If the number is negative, SQRT returns the #NUM! error value.

Examples

SQRT(16)

returns 4

SQRT(-16)

returns #NUM!

SQRT(ABS(-16))

returns 4

STANDARDIZE

Returns a normalized value.

Syntax

STANDARDIZE(x,mean,standard_dev)

X   is the value you want to normalize.

Mean   is the arithmetic mean of the distribution.

Standard_dev   is the standard deviation of the distribution.

Example

STANDARDIZE(42,40,1.5)

returns 1.333333

STDEV

Estimates standard deviation based on a sample.

Syntax

STDEV(number1,number2,...)

Number1,number2,...   are 1 to 30 number arguments corresponding to a sample of a population. You can also use a single array or a reference to an array instead of arguments separated by commas.

Example

Suppose 10 tools stamped from the same machine during a production run are collected as a random sample and measured for breaking strength. The sample values (1345, 1301, 1368, 1322, 1310, 1370, 1318, 1350, 1303, 1299) are stored in A2:E3, respectively. STDEV estimates the standard deviation of breaking strengths for all the tools.

STDEV(A2:E3)

returns 27.46

STDEVP

Calculates standard deviation on the basis of the entire population.

Syntax

STDEVP(number1,number2,...)

Number1,number2,...   are 1 to 30 number arguments corresponding to a population. You can also use a single array or a reference to an array instead of arguments separated by commas.

Example

Using the same data from the STDEV example and assuming that only 10 tools are produced during the production run, STDEVP measures the standard deviation of breaking strengths for all the tools.

STDEVP(A2:E3)

returns 26.05

STEYX

Returns the standard error of the predicted y-value for each x in the regression.

Syntax

STEYX(known_y's,known_x's)

Known_y's   is an array or range of dependent data points.

Known_x's   is an array or range of independent data points.

Example

STEYX({2,3,9,1,8,7,5},{6,5,11,7,5,4,4})

returns 3.305719

SUBSTITUTE

Substitutes new text for old text in a text string.

Syntax

SUBSTITUTE(text,old_text,new_text,instance_num)

Text   is the text or the reference to a cell containing text for which you want to substitute characters.

Old_text   is the text you want to replace.

New_text   is the text you want to replace old_text with.

Instance_num   specifies which occurrence of old_text you want to replace with new_text. If you specify instance_num, only that instance of old_text is replaced. Otherwise, every occurrence of old_text in text is changed to new_text.

Examples

SUBSTITUTE("Sales Data","Sales","Cost")

returns "Cost Data"

SUBSTITUTE("Quarter 1, 1991","1","2",1)

returns "Quarter 2, 1991"

SUBSTITUTE("Quarter 1 1991","1","2",3)

returns "Quarter 1, 1992"

SUBTOTAL

Returns a subtotal in a list or database. (See Chapter 9 for in-depth coverage and examples of SUBTOTAL.)

Syntax

SUBTOTAL(function_num,reference)

Function_num is the number 1 to 11 that specifies which function to use in calculating subtotals within a list.

Ref is range or reference for which you want the subtotal.

SUM

Adds its arguments.

Syntax

SUM(number1,number2,...)

Number1,number2,... are 1 to 30 arguments for which you want the sum.

Examples

SUM(3,2)

returns 5

If cells A2:C2 contain 5, 15, and 30:

SUM(A2:C2)

returns 50

SUMIF

Adds the cells specified by a given criteria. (See Chapter 9 for in-depth coverage and examples of SUMIF.)

Syntax

SUMIFange,criteria,sum_range)

Range is the range of cells you want evaluated.

Criteria is the criteria in the form of a number, expression, or text that defines which cells will be added. For example, Criteria can be expressed as 32, "32", ">32", "apples".

Sum_range are the actual cells to sum. The cells in sum_range are summed only if their corresponding cells in range match the criteria.

SUMPRODUCT

Returns the sum of the products of corresponding array components.

Syntax

SUMPRODUCT(array1,array2,array3,...)

Array1,array2,array3,... are 2 to 30 arrays whose components you want to multiply and then add.

See the On-line Help worksheet function reference for an example.

SUMSQ

Returns the sum of the squares of the arguments.

Syntax

SUMSQ(number1,number2,...)

Number1,number2,... are 1 to 30 arguments for which you want the sum of the squares.

Example

SUMSQ(3,4)

returns 25

SUMX2MY2

Returns the sum of the difference of squares of corresponding values in two arrays.

Syntax

SUMX2MY2(array_x,array_y)

Array_x is the first array or range of values.

Array_y is the second array or range of values.

Example

SUMX2MY2({2,3,9,1,8,7,5},{6,5,11,7,5,4,4})

returns -55

SUMX2PY2

Returns the sum of the sum of squares of corresponding values in two arrays.

Syntax

SUMX2PY2(array_x,array_y)

Array_x is the first array or range of values.

Array_y is the second array or range of values.

Example

SUMX2PY2({2,3,9,1,8,7,5},{6,5,11,7,5,4,4})

returns 521

SUMXMY2

Returns the sum of squares of differences of corresponding values in two arrays.

Syntax

SUMXMY2(array_x,array_y)

Array_x is the first array or range of values.

Array_y is the second array or range of values.

Example

SUMXMY2({2,3,9,1,8,7,5},{6,5,11,7,5,4,4})

returns 79

SYD

Returns the sum-of-years' digits depreciation of an asset for a specified period.

Syntax

SYD(cost,salvage,life,per)

Cost is the initial cost of the asset.

Salvage is the value at the end of the depreciation (sometimes called the salvage value of the asset).

Life is the number of periods over which the asset is being depreciated (sometimes called the useful life of the asset).

Per is the period and must use the same units as life.

Examples

If you've bought a truck for $30,000 that has a useful life of 10 years and a salvage value of $7500, the yearly depreciation allowance for the first year is:

    SYD(30000,7500,10,1)

returns $4090.91

The yearly depreciation allowance for the 10th year is:

    SYD(30000,7500,10,10)

returns $409.09

T

Returns the text referred to by value. You do not generally need to use the T function in a formula since Excel automatically converts values as necessary (this function is provided for compatibility with other spreadsheet programs).

Syntax

    T(value)

Value is the value you want to test. If value is or refers to text, T returns value. If value does not refer to text, T returns "" (empty text).

Examples

If B1 contains the text "Rainfall":

    T(B1)

returns "Rainfall"

If B2 contains the number 19:

>   T(B2)

returns """"

TAN

Returns the tangent of a number. If your argument is in degrees, multiply it by PI()/180 to convert it to radians.

Syntax

>   TAN(number)

>   **Number**   is the angle in radians for which you want the tangent.

Examples

>   TAN(0.785)

returns 0.99920

>   TAN(45*PI()/180)

returns 1

TANH

Returns the hyperbolic tangent of a number.

Syntax

>   TANH(number)

>   **Number**   is any real number.

Examples

>   TANH(-2)

returns -0.96403

>   TANH(0.5)

returns 0.462117

TDIST

Returns the Student's t-distribution.

Syntax

TDIST(x,degrees_freedom,tails)

X is the numeric value at which to evaluate the distribution.

Degrees_freedom is an integer indicating the number of degrees of freedom.

Tails specifies the number of distribution tails to return. If tails=1, TDIST returns the one-tailed distribution. If tails=2, TDIST returns the two-tailed distribution.

Example

TDIST(1.96,60,2)

returns 0.054645

TEXT

Formats a number and converts it to text.

Syntax

TEXT(value,format_text)

Value is a numeric value, a formula that evaluates to a numeric value, or a reference to a cell containing a numeric value.

Format_text is a number format in text form from the Number tab in the Cell Properties dialog box.

Examples

TEXT(2.715,"$0.00")

returns "$2.72"

TEXT("4/15/91","mmmm dd, yyyy")

returns "April 15, 1991"

TIME

Returns the serial number of a particular time.

Syntax

TIMEVALUE(time_text)

Time_text   is a text string that gives a time in any one of the Microsoft Excel time formats. Date information in time_text is ignored.

Examples

TIMEVALUE("2:24 AM")

returns 0.1

TIMEVALUE("22-Aug-55 6:35 AM")

returns 0.274305556

TIMEVALUE

Converts a time in the form of text to a serial number.

Syntax

TIMEVALUE(time_text)

Time_text   is a text string that gives a time in any one of the Microsoft Excel time formats. Date information in time_text is ignored.

Examples

TIMEVALUE("2:24 AM")

returns 0.1

TIMEVALUE("22-Aug-55 6:35 AM")

returns 0.274305556

TINV

Returns the inverse of the Student's t-distribution.

Syntax

TINV(probability,degrees_freedom)

Probability   is the probability associated with the two-tailed Student's t-distribution.

Degrees_freedom is the number of degrees of freedom to characterize the distribution.

Example

TINV(0.054645,60)

returns 1.96

TODAY

Returns the serial number of today's date. (See Chapter 9 for in-depth coverage and examples of TODAY.)

Syntax

TODAY()

TRANSPOSE

Returns the transpose of an array.

Syntax

TRANSPOSE(array)

Array is an array on a worksheet or macro sheet that you want to transpose. Array can also be a range of cells.

Example

Suppose A1:C1 contain 1, 2, 3, respectively. When the following formula is entered as an array into cells A3:A5:

TRANSPOSE($A$1:$C$1)

returns the same respective values, but in A3:A5.

TREND

Returns values along a linear trend.

Syntax

TREND(known_y's,known_x's,new_x's,const)

Known_y's is the set of y-values you already know in the relationship y=mx+b.

Known_x's   is an optional set of x-values that you may already know in the relationship y=mx+b.

New_x's   are new x-values for which you want TREND to return corresponding y-values.

Const   is a logical value specifying whether to force the constant b to equal 0. If const is TRUE or omitted, b is calculated normally. If const is FALSE, b is set equal to 0 and the m-values are adjusted so that y=mx.

Example

Suppose a business wants to purchase a tract of land in July, the start of the next fiscal year. The business collected cost information that covers the most recent 12 months for a typical tract in the desired area. known_y's contains the set of known values ($133,890, $135,000, $135,790, $137,300, $138,130, $139,100, $139,900, $141,120, $141,890, $143,230, $144,000, $145,290), and are stored in B2:B13, respectively.

When entered as a vertical array in the range C2:C6, the following formula returns the predicted prices for March, April, May, June, and July:

    TREND(B2:B13,,{13;14;15;16;17})

returns {146172;147190;148208;149226;150244}

TRIM

Removes spaces from text. Use TRIM to remove extra spaces when downloading fixed-width data from a mainframe.

Syntax

    TRIM(text)

Text   is the text from which you want spaces removed.

Example

    TRIM(" First   Quarter   Earnings ")

returns "First Quarter Earnings"

TRIMMEAN

Returns the mean of the interior of a data set. TRIMMEAN calculates the mean taken by excluding a percentage of data points from the top and bottom tails of a data set. Use this function when you want to exclude outlying data from your analysis.

Syntax

TRIMMEAN(array,percent)

Array   is the array or range of values to trim and average.

Percent   is the fractional number of data points to exclude from the calculation. For example, if percent=0.2, 4 points are trimmed from a data set of 20 points (20 x 0.2), 2 from the top and 2 from the bottom of the set.

Example

TRIMMEAN({4,5,6,7,2,3,4,5,1,2,3},0.2)

returns 3.777778

TRUE

Returns the logical value TRUE.

Syntax

TRUE()

TRUNC

Truncates a number to an integer.

Syntax

TRUNC(number,num_digits)

Number   is the number you want to truncate.

Num_digits   is a number specifying the precision of the truncation. The default value for num_digits is zero.

Examples

TRUNC(8.9)

returns 8

> TRUNC(-8.9)

returns -8

> TRUNC(PI())

returns 3

TTEST

Returns the probability associated with a Student's t-Test.

Syntax

> TTEST(array1,array2,tails,type)

Array1   is the first data set.

Array2   is the second data set.

Tails   specifies the number of distribution tails. If tails=1, TTEST uses the one-tailed distribution. If tails=2, TTEST uses the two-tailed distribution.

Type   is the kind of t-test to perform. If type equals 1, a paired test is performed; if type equals 2, a two-sample equal variance (homoscedastic) test is performed; if type equals 3, a two-sample unequal variance (heteroscedastic) test is performed.

Example

> TTEST({3,4,5,8,9,1,2,4,5},{6,19,3,2,14,4,5,17,1},2,1)

returns 0.196016

TYPE

Returns a number indicating the data type of a value.

Syntax

> TYPE(value)

Value   can be any Microsoft Excel value, such as a number, text, logical value, and so on. If value is a number, TYPE returns 1; if value is text, TYPE returns 2; if value is a logical value, TYPE returns 4; if value is a formula, TYPE returns 8; if value is an error value, TYPE returns 16; if value is an array, TYPE returns 64.

Examples

If A1 contains the text "Smith", then:

TYPE(A1)

returns 2

TYPE("MR. "&A1)

returns 2

UPPER

Converts text to uppercase.

Syntax

UPPER(text)

Text   is the text you want converted to uppercase (text can be a reference or text string).

Examples

UPPER("total")

returns"TOTAL"

If E5 contains "yield", then

UPPER(E5)

returns "YIELD"

VALUE

Converts a text argument to a number. This function is provided for compatibility with other spreadsheet programs.

Syntax

VALUE(text)

Text   is the text enclosed in quotation marks or a reference to a cell containing the text you want to convert. Text can be in any of the constant number, date, or time formats recognized by Excel. If text is not in one of these formats, VALUE returns the #VALUE! error value.

Examples

VALUE("$1,000")

returns 1,000

VALUE("16:48:00")-VALUE("12:00:00")

returns 0.2, the serial number equivalent to 4 hours and 48 minutes.

VAR

Estimates variance on the basis of a sample. If your data represents the entire population, you should compute the variance using VARP.

Syntax

VAR(number1,number2,...)

Number1,number2,...   are 1 to 30 number arguments corresponding to a sample of a population.

Example

Suppose 10 tools stamped from the same machine during a production run are collected as a random sample and measured for breaking strength. The sample values (1345, 1301, 1368, 1322, 1310, 1370, 1318, 1350, 1303, 1299) are stored in A2:E3, respectively. VAR estimates the variance for the breaking strength of the tools.

VAR(A2:E3)

returns 754.3

VARP

Calculates variance on the basis of the entire population. If your data represents a sample of the population, you should compute the variance using VAR.

Syntax

VARP(number1,number2,...)

Number1,number2,...   are 1 to 30 number arguments

corresponding to a population.

Example

Using the data from the VAR example and assuming that only 10 tools are produced during the production run, VARP measures the variance of breaking strengths for all the tools.

    VARP(A2:E3)

returns 678.8

VDB

Returns the depreciation of an asset for a specified or partial period using a declining balance method.

Syntax

    VDB(cost,salvage,life,start_period,end_period,factor,no_switch)

Cost   is the initial cost of the asset.

Salvage   is the value at the end of the depreciation (sometimes called the salvage value of the asset).

Life   is the number of periods over which the asset is being depreciated (sometimes called the useful life of the asset).

Start_period   is the starting period for which you want to calculate the depreciation. Start_period must use the same units as life.

End_period   is the ending period for which you want to calculate the depreciation. End_period must use the same units as life.

Factor   is the rate at which the balance declines. If factor is omitted, it is assumed to be 2 (the double-declining balance method). Change factor if you do not want to use the double-declining balance method.

No_switch   is a logical value specifying whether to switch to straight-line depreciation when depreciation is greater than the declining balance calculation.

Examples

Suppose a factory purchases a new machine. The machine costs $2400 and has a lifetime of 10 years. The salvage value of the machine is $300. The following examples show depreciation over several periods. The results are rounded to two decimal places.

VDB(2400,300,3650,0,1)

returns $1.32, the first day's depreciation. Excel automatically assumes that factor is 2.

VDB(2400,300,120,0,1)

returns $40.00, the first month's depreciation.

VDB(2400,300,10,0,1)

returns $480.00, the first year's depreciation.

VLOOKUP

Looks in the first column of an array and moves across the row to return the value of a cell. (See Chapter 9 for in-depth coverage and examples of VLOOKUP.)

Syntax

VLOOKUP(lookup_value,table_array,col_index_num,range_lookup)

Lookup_value   is the value to be found in the first column of the array.

Table_array   is the table of information in which data is looked up.

Col_index_num   is the column number in table_array from which the matching value should be returned.

Range_lookup   is a logical value that specifies whether you want VLOOKUP to find an exact match or an approximate match. If TRUE or omitted, an approximate match is returned (values must be sorted in ascending order).

WEEKDAY

Converts a serial number to a day of the week. (See Chapter 9 for in-depth coverage and examples of WEEKDAY.)

Syntax

WEEKDAY(serial_number,return_type)

Serial_number   is the date-time code used by Excel for date and time calculations.

Return_type   is a number that determines the type of return value.

WEIBULL

Returns the Weibull distribution.

Syntax

WEIBULL(x,alpha,beta,cumulative)

X is the value at which to evaluate the function.

Alpha is a parameter to the distribution.

Beta is a parameter to the distribution.

Cumulative determines the form of the function.

Examples

WEIBULL(105,20,100,TRUE)

returns 0.929581

WEIBULL(105,20,100,FALSE)

returns 0.035589

YEAR

Converts a serial number to a year. (See Chapter 9 for in-depth coverage and examples of YEAR.)

Syntax

YEAR(serial_number)

Serial_number is the date-time code used by Excel for date and time calculations.

ZTEST

Returns the two-tailed P-value of a z-test.

Syntax

ZTEST(array,x,sigma)

Array is the array or range of data against which to test x.

X is the value to test.

Sigma   is the population (known) standard deviation. If omitted, the sample standard deviation is used.

Example

ZTEST({3,6,7,8,6,5,4,2,1,9},4)

returns 0.090574

►► *Analysis Toolpak Functions*

The following functions are contained in the Analysis ToolPak add-in (see Chapter 24).

ACCRINT

Returns the accrued interest for a security that pays periodic interest.

Syntax

ACCRINT(issue,first_interest,settlement,rate,par,frequency,basis)

Issue   is the security's issue date, expressed as a serial date number.

First_interest   is the security's first interest date, expressed as a serial date number.

Settlement   is the security's settlement date, expressed as a serial date number.

Rate   is the security's annual coupon rate.

Par   is the security's par value. If you omit par, ACCRINT uses $1000.

Frequency   is the number of coupon payments per year. For annual payments, frequency=1; for semiannual, frequency=2; for quarterly, frequency=4.

Basis   is the type of day count basis to use. If basis is 0 or omitted, day count basis is US (NASD) 30/360; if basis is 1, day count basis is Actual/actual; if basis is 2, day count basis is Actual/360; if basis is 3, day count basis is Actual/365; if basis is 4, day count basis is European 30/360.

Example

A Treasury bond has the following terms: February 28, 1993 issue date; May 1, 1993 settlement date; August 31, 1993 first interest date; 10.0% coupon; $1000 par value; frequency is semiannual; 30/360 basis. The accrued interest (in the 1900 Date System) is:

ACCRINT(34028,34212,34090,0.1,1000,2,0)

returns 16.94444.

ACCRINTM

Returns accrued interest for a security that pays interest at maturity.

Syntax

ACCRINTM(issue,maturity,rate,par,basis)

Issue   is the security's issue date, expressed as a serial date number.

Settlement   is the security's maturity date, expressed as a serial date number.

Rate   is the security's annual coupon rate.

Par   is the security's par value. If you omit par, ACCRINTM uses $1000.

Basis   is the type of day count basis to use. If basis is 0 or omitted, day count basis is US (NASD) 30/360; if basis is 1, day count basis is Actual/actual; if basis is 2, day count basis is Actual/360; if basis is 3, day count basis is Actual/365; if basis is 4, day count basis is European 30/360.

Example

A note has the following terms:

April 1, 1993 issue date; June 15, 1993 maturity date; 10.0% coupon; $1000 par value; Actual/365 basis. The accrued interest (in the 1900 Date System) is:

ACCRINTM(34060,34135,0.1,1000,3)

returns 20.54795

Worksheet Functions

Ap.
B

AMORDEGRC

Returns the depreciation for each accounting period.

Syntax

AMORDEGRC(cost,date_purchased,first_period,salvage,period,rate,basis)

Cost is the cost of the asset.

Date_purchased is the date of the purchase of the asset.

First_period is the date of the end of the first period.

Salvage is the salvage value at the end of the life of the asset.

Period is the period.

Rate is the rate of depreciation.

Basis is the year_basis to be used. If basis is 0, date system is 360 days (NASD method); if basis is 1, date system is Actual; if basis is 3, date system is 365 days in a year; if basis is 4, date system is 360 days in a year (European method).

Example

Suppose a machine bought on August 19, 1993 costs $2400 and has a salvage value of $300, with a 15% depreciation rate. December 31, 1993 is the end of the first period.

AMORDEGRC(2400,34199,34334,300,1,0.15,1)

returns a first period depreciation of $775.

AMORLINC

Returns the depreciation for each accounting period.

Syntax

AMORLINC(cost,date_purchased,first_period,salvage, period,rate,basis)

Cost is the cost of the asset.

Date_purchased is the date of the purchase of the asset.

First_period is the date of the end of the first period.

Salvage is the salvage value at the end of the life of the asset.

Period is the period.

Rate is the rate of depreciation.

Basis is the year_basis to be used. If basis is 0, date system is 360 days (NASD method); if basis is 1, date system is Actual; if basis is 3, date system is 365 days in a year; if basis is 4, date system is 360 days in a year (European method).

Example

Suppose a machine bought on August 19, 1993 costs $2400 and has a salvage value of $300, with a 15% depreciation rate. December 31, 1993 is the end of the first period.

AMORLINC(2400,34199,34334,300,1,0.15,1)

returns a first period depreciation of $360.

BESSELI

Returns the modified Bessel function In(x). (See the On-line Help worksheet function reference for information about the equation used to calculate BESSELI.)

Syntax

BESSELI(x,n)

X is the value at which to evaluate the function.

N is the order of the Bessel function. If n is not an integer, it is truncated.

Example

BESSELI(1.5,1)

returns 0.981666

BESSELJ

Returns the Bessel function Jn(x). (See the On-line Help worksheet function reference for information about the equation used to calculate BESSELJ.)

Syntax

BESSELJ(x,n)

X is the value at which to evaluate the function.

N is the order of the Bessel function. If n is not an integer, it is truncated.

Example

BESSELJ(1.9,2)

returns 0.329926

BESSELK

Returns the modified Bessel function Kn(x). (See the On-line Help worksheet function reference for information about the equation used to calculate BESSELK.)

Syntax

BESSELK(x,n)

X is the value at which to evaluate the function.

N is the order of the Bessel function. If n is not an integer, it is truncated.

Example

BESSELK(1.5,1)

returns 0.277388

BESSELY

Returns the Bessel function Yn(x). (See the On-line Help worksheet function reference for information about the equation used to calculate BESSELY.)

Syntax

BESSELY(x,n)

X is the value at which to evaluate the function.

N is the order of the Bessel function. If n is not an integer, it is truncated.

Example

BESSELY(2.5,1)

returns 0.145918

BIN2DEC

Converts a binary number to decimal.

Syntax

BIN2DEC(number)

Number is the binary number you want to convert.

Examples

BIN2DEC(1100100)

returnsls 100

BIN2DEC(1111111111)

returns -1

BIN2HEX

Converts a binary number to hexadecimal.

Syntax

BIN2HEX(number,places)

Number is the binary number you want to convert.

Places is the number of characters to use. If places is omitted, BIN2HEX uses the minimum number of characters necessary.

Examples

BIN2HEX(11111011,4)

returns 00FB

BIN2HEX(1110)

returns E

BIN2OCT

Converts a binary number to octal.

Syntax

BIN2OCT(number,places)

Number is the binary number you want to convert.

Places is the number of characters to use. If places is omitted, BIN2OCT uses the minimum number of characters necessary.

Examples

BIN2OCT(1001,3)

returns 011

BIN2OCT(01100100)

returns 144

BINOMDIST

Returns the individual term binomial distribution probability.

Syntax

BINOMDIST(number_s,trials,probability_s,cumulative)

Number_s is the number of successes in trials.

Trials is the number of independent trials.

Probability_s is the probability of success on each trial.

Cumulative is a logical value that determines the form of the function. If cumulative is TRUE, then BINOMDIST returns the cumulative distribution function, which is the probability that there are at most number_s successes; if FALSE, it returns the probability mass function, which is the probability that there are number_s successes.

Example

The flip of a coin can only result in heads or tails. The probability of the first flip being heads is 0.5, and the probability of exactly 6 of 10 flips being heads is:

BINOMDIST(6,10,0.5,FALSE)

returns 0.205078

COMPLEX

Converts real and imaginary coefficients into a complex number.

Syntax

COMPLEXeal_num,i_num,suffix)

Real_num   is the real coefficient of the complex number.

i_num   is the imaginary coefficient of the complex number.

Suffix   is the suffix for the imaginary component of the complex number. If omitted, suffix is assumed to be "i".

Examples

COMPLEX(3,4)

returns 3 + 4I

COMPLEX(3,4,"j")

returns 3 + 4j

COMPLEX(0,1)

returns i

CONVERT

Converts a number from one measurement system to another. (See Chapter 26, Converting Units of Measure, for in-depth coverage and examples of CONVERT.)

Syntax

CONVERT(number,from_unit,to_unit)

Number   is the value in from_units to convert.

From_unit   is the units for number.

To_unit   is the units for the result.

COUPDAYBS

Returns the number of days from the beginning of the coupon period to the settlement date.

Syntax

COUPDAYBS(settlement,maturity,frequency,basis)

Settlement   is the security's settlement date, expressed as a serial date number.

Maturity   is the security's maturity date, expressed as a serial date number.

Frequency   is the number of coupon payments per year. For annual payments, frequency=1; for semiannual, frequency=2; for quarterly, frequency=4.

Basis   is the type of day count basis to use. If basis is 0 or omitted, day count basis is US (NASD) 30/360; if basis is 1, day count basis is Actual/actual; if basis is 2, day count basis is Actual/360; if basis is 3, day count basis is Actual/365; if basis is 4, day count basis is European 30/360.

Example

A bond has the following terms: January 25, 1993 settlement date; November 15, 1994 maturity date; Semiannual coupon; Actual/actual basis. The number of days from the beginning of the coupon period to the settlement date (in the 1900 Date System) is:

COUPDAYBS(33994,34653,2,1)

returns 71

COUPDAYS

Returns the number of days in the coupon period that contains the settlement date.

Syntax

COUPDAYS(settlement,maturity,frequency,basis)

Settlement   is the security's settlement date, expressed as a serial date number.

Maturity is the security's maturity date, expressed as a serial date number.

Frequency is the number of coupon payments per year. For annual payments, frequency=1; for semiannual, frequency=2; for quarterly, frequency=4.

Basis is the type of day count basis to use. If basis is 0 or omitted, day count basis is US (NASD) 30/360; if basis is 1, day count basis is actual/actual; if basis is 2, day count basis is actual/360; if basis is 3, day count basis is actual/365; if basis is 4, day count basis is European 30/360.

Example

A bond has the following terms: January 25, 1993 settlement date; November 15, 1994 maturity date; Semiannual coupon; Actual/actual basis. The number of days in the coupon period that contains the settlement date (in the 1900 Date System) is:

    COUPDAYS(33994,34653,2,1)

returns

COUPDAYSNC

Returns the number of days from the settlement date to the next coupon date.

Syntax

    COUPDAYSNC(settlement,maturity,frequency,basis)

Settlement is the security's settlement date, expressed as a serial date number.

Maturity is the security's maturity date, expressed as a serial date number.

Frequency is the number of coupon payments per year. For annual payments, frequency=1; for semiannual, frequency=2; for quarterly, frequency=4.

Basis is the type of day count basis to use. If basis is 0 or omitted, day count basis is US (NASD) 30/360; if basis is 1, day count basis is Actual/actual; if basis is 2, day count basis is Actual/360; if basis is 3, day count basis is Actual/365; if basis is 4, day count basis is European 30/360.

Example

A bond has the following terms: January 25, 1993 settlement date; November 15, 1994 maturity date; Semiannual coupon; Actual/actual basis. The number of days from the settlement date to the next coupon date (in the 1900 Date System) is:

COUPDAYSNC(33994,34653,2,1)

returns 110

COUPNCD

Returns the next coupon date after the settlement date.

Syntax

COUPNCD(settlement,maturity,frequency,basis)

Settlement is the security's settlement date, expressed as a serial date number.

Maturity is the security's maturity date, expressed as a serial date number.

Frequency is the number of coupon payments per year. For annual payments, frequency=1; for semiannual, frequency=2; for quarterly, frequency=4.

Basis is the type of day count basis to use. If basis is 0 or omitted, day count basis is US (NASD) 30/360; if basis is 1, day count basis is actual/actual; if basis is 2, day count basis is actual/360; if basis is 3, day count basis is actual/365; if basis is 4, day count basis is European 30/360.

Example

A bond has the following terms: January 25, 1993 settlement date; November 15, 1994 maturity date; Semiannual coupon; Actual/actual basis. The next coupon date after the settlement date (in the 1900 Date System) is:

COUPNCD(33994,34653,2,1)

returns 34104 or May 15, 1993

COUPNUM

Returns the number of coupons payable between the settlement date and maturity date.

Syntax

COUPNUM(settlement, maturity, frequency, basis)

Settlement is the security's settlement date, expressed as a serial date number.

Maturity is the security's maturity date, expressed as a serial date number.

Frequency is the number of coupon payments per year. For annual payments, frequency=1; for semiannual, frequency=2; for quarterly, frequency=4.

Basis is the type of day count basis to use. If basis is 0 or omitted, day count basis is US (NASD) 30/360; if basis is 1, day count basis is actual/actual; if basis is 2, day count basis is actual/360; if basis is 3, day count basis is actual/365; if basis is 4, day count basis is European 30/360.

Example

A bond has the following terms: January 25, 1993 settlement date; November 15, 1994 maturity date; Semiannual coupon; Actual/actual basis. The number of coupon payments (in the 1900 Date System) is:

COUPNUM(33994,34653,2,1)

returns 4

COUPPCD

Returns the previous coupon date before the settlement date.

Syntax

COUPPCD(settlement,maturity,frequency,basis)

Settlement is the security's settlement date, expressed as a serial date number.

Maturity is the security's maturity date, expressed as a serial date number.

Frequency is the number of coupon payments per year. For annual payments, frequency=1; for semiannual, frequency=2; for quarterly, frequency=4.

Basis is the type of day count basis to use. If basis is 0 or omitted, day count basis is US (NASD) 30/360; if basis is 1, day count basis is actual/actual; if basis is 2, day count basis is actual/360; if basis is 3, day count basis is actual/365; if basis is 4, day count basis is European 30/360.

Example

A bond has the following terms: January 25, 1993 settlement date; November 15, 1994 maturity date; semiannual coupon; actual/actual basis. The previous coupon date before the settlement date (in the 1900 Date System) is:

COUPPCD(33994,34653,2,1)

returns 33923 or November 15, 1992

CUMIPMT

Returns the cumulative interest paid between two periods.

Syntax

CUMIPMTate,nper,pv,start_period,end_period,type)

Rate is the interest rate.

Nper is the total number of payment periods.

Pv is the present value.

Start_period is the first period in the calculation. Payment periods are numbered beginning with 1.

End_period is the last period in the calculation.

Type is the timing of the payment. If type is 0, payments are due at the end of the period; if type is 1, payments are due at the beginning of the period.

Examples

A home mortgage loan has the following terms: Interest rate, 9.00% per annum ate=9.00%/12=0.0075); term, 30 years (nper=30*12=360); present value, $125,000. The total interest paid in the second year of payments (periods 13 through 24) is:

    CUMIPMT(0.0075,360,125000,13,24,0)

returns −11135.23

The interest paid in a single payment, in the first month, is:

    CUMIPMT(0.0075,360,125000,1,1,0)

returns 937.50

CUMPRINC

Returns the cumulative principal paid on a loan between two periods.

Syntax

    CUMPRINCate,nper,pv,start_period,end_period,type)

Rate   is the interest rate.

Nper   is the total number of payment periods.

Pv   is the present value.

Start_period   is the first period in the calculation. Payment periods are numbered beginning with 1.

End_period   is the last period in the calculation.

Type   is the timing of the payment. If type is 0, payments are due at the end of the period; if type is 1, payments are due at the beginning of the period.

Examples

A home mortgage loan has the following terms: Interest rate, 9.00% per annum ate= 9.00%/12=0.0075); term, 30 years (nper=30*12=360); present value, $125,000. The total principal paid in the second year of payments (periods 13 through 24) is:

    CUMPRINC(0.0075,360,−125000,13,24,0)

returns 934.1071

The principal paid in a single payment, in the first month, is:

CUMPRINC(0.0075,360,–125000,1,1,0)

returns 68.27827

DEC2BIN

Converts a decimal number to binary.

Syntax

DEC2BIN(number,places)

Number   is the decimal integer you want to convert.

Places   is the number of characters to use. If places is omitted, DEC2BIN uses the minimum number of characters necessary.

Examples

DEC2BIN(9,4)

returns 1001

DEC2BIN(-100)

returns 1110011100

DEC2HEX

Converts a decimal number to hexadecimal.

Syntax

DEC2HEX(number,places)

Number   is the decimal integer you want to convert.

Places   is the number of characters to use. If places is omitted, DEC2HEX uses the minimum number of characters necessary.

Examples

DEC2HEX(100,4)

returns 0064

DEC2HEX(-54)

returns FFFFFFFFCA

DEC2OCT

Converts a decimal number to octal.

Syntax

DEC2OCT(number,places)

Number is the decimal integer you want to convert.

Places is the number of characters to use. If places is omitted, DEC2OCT uses the minimum number of characters necessary.

Examples

DEC2OCT(58,3)

returns 072

DEC2OCT(-100)

returns 7777777634

DELTA

Tests whether two values are equal.

Syntax

DELTA(number1,number2)

Number1 is the first number.

Number2 is the second number. If omitted, number2 is assumed to be zero.

Examples

DELTA(5,4)

returns 0

DELTA(5,5)

returns 1

DELTA(0.5,0)

returns 0

DISC

Returns the discount rate for a security.

Syntax

DISC(settlement,maturity,pr,redemption,basis)

Settlement   is the security's settlement date, expressed as a serial date number.

Maturity   is the security's maturity date, expressed as a serial date number.

Pr   is the security's price per $100 face value.

Redemption   is the security's redemption value per $100 face value.

Basis   is the type of day count basis to use. If basis is 0 or omitted, day count basis is US (NASD) 30/360; if basis is 1, day count basis is actual/actual; if basis is 2, day count basis is actual/360; if basis is 3, day count basis is actual/365; if basis is 4, day count basis is European 30/360.

Example

A bond has the following terms: February 15, 1993 settlement date; June 10, 1993 maturity date; $97.975 price; $100 redemption value; actual/360 basis. The bond discount rate (in the 1900 Date System) is:

DISC(34015,34130,97.975,100,2)

returns 0.063391 or 6.3391%

DOLLARDE

Converts a dollar price expressed as a fraction into a dollar price expressed as a decimal number.

Syntax

DOLLARDE(fractional_dollar,fraction)

Fractional_dollar   is a number expressed as a fraction.

Fraction   is the integer to use in the denominator of the fraction.

Examples

DOLLARDE(1.02,16)

returns 1.125

DOLLARDE(1.1,8)

returns 1.125

DOLLARFR

Converts a dollar price expressed as a decimal number into a dollar price expressed as a fraction.

Syntax

DOLLARFR(decimal_dollar,fraction)

Decimal_dollar   is a decimal number.

Fraction   is the integer to use in the denominator of a fraction.

Examples

DOLLARFR(1.125,16)

returns 1.02

DOLLARFR(1.125,8)

returns 1.1

DURATION

Returns the annual duration of a security with periodic interest payments.

Syntax

DURATION(settlement,maturity,coupon,yld,frequency,basis)

Settlement   is the security's settlement date, expressed as a serial date number.

Maturity   is the security's maturity date, expressed as a serial date number.

Coupon   is the security's annual coupon rate.

Yld   is the security's annual yield.

Frequency   is the number of coupon payments per year. For annual payments, frequency=1; for semiannual, frequency=2; for quarterly, frequency=4.

Basis   is the type of day count basis to use. If basis is 0 or omitted, day count basis is US (NASD) 30/360; if basis is 1, day count basis is actual/actual; if basis is 2, day count basis is actual/360; if basis is 3, day count basis is actual/365; if basis is 4, day count basis is European 30/360.

Example

A bond has the following terms: January 1, 1986 settlement date; January 1, 1994 maturity date; 8% coupon; 9.0% yield; frequency is semiannual; actual/actual basis. The duration (in the 1900 Date System) is:

DURATION(31413,34335,0.08,0.09,2,1)

returns 5.993775

EDATE

Returns the serial number of the date that is the indicated number of months before or after the start date.

Syntax

EDATE(start_date,months)

Start_date   is a serial date number that represents the start date.

Months   is the number of months before or after start_date. A positive value for months yields a future date; a negative value yields a past date.

Examples

EDATE(DATEVALUE("01/15/91"),1)

returns 33284 or 02/15/91

EDATE(DATEVALUE("03/31/91"),-1)

returns 33297 or 02/28/91

EFFECT

Returns the effective annual interest rate.

Syntax

EFFECT(nominal_rate,npery)

Nominal_rate   is the nominal interest rate.

Npery   is the number of compounding periods per year.

Example

EFFECT(5.25%,4)

returns 0.053543 or 5.3543%

EOMONTH

Returns the serial number of the last day of the month before or after a specified number of months.

Syntax

EOMONTH(start_date,months)

Start_date   is a serial date number that represents the start date.

Months   is the number of months before or after start_date. A positive value for months yields a future date; a negative value yields a past date.

Examples

EOMONTH(DATEVALUE("01/01/93"),1)

returns 34028 or 2/28/93

EOMONTH(DATEVALUE("01/01/93"),-1)

returns 33969 or 12/31/92

ERF

Returns the error function integrated between lower_limit and upper_limit.

Syntax

ERF(lower_limit,upper_limit)

Lower_limit   is the lower bound for integrating ERF.

Upper_limit   is the upper bound for integrating ERF. If omitted, ERF integrates between zero and lower_limit.

Examples

ERF(0.74500)

returns 0.70793

ERF(1)

returns 0.84270

ERFC

Returns the complementary error function integrated

between x and.

Syntax

ERFC(x)

X   is the lower bound for integrating ERF.

Example

ERFC(1)

returns 0.1573

FACTDOUBLE

Returns the double factorial of a number.

Syntax

FACTDOUBLE(number)

Number   is the value for which to return the double factorial. If number is not an integer, it is truncated.

Examples

FACTDOUBLE(6)

returns 48

FACTDOUBLE(7)

returns 105

FVSCHEDULE

Returns the future value of an initial principal after applying a series of compound interest rates.

Syntax

FVSCHEDULE(principal,schedule)

Principal   is the present value.

Schedule   is an array of interest rates to apply.

Example

FVSCHEDULE(1,{0.09,0.11,0.1})

returns 1.33089

GCD

Returns the greatest common divisor.

Syntax

GCD(number1,number2,...)

Number1, number2,...   are up to 29 values. If any value is not an integer, it is truncated.

Examples

GCD(5,2)

returns 1

GCD(24,36)

returns 12

    GCD(7,1)

returns 1

GESTEP

Tests whether a number is greater than a threshold value.

Syntax

    GESTEP(number,step)

Number   is the value to test against step.

Step   is the threshold value. If you omit a value for step, GESTEP uses zero.

Examples

    GESTEP(5,4)

returns 1

    GESTEP(5,5)

returns 1

HEX2BIN

Converts a hexadecimal number to binary.

Syntax

    HEX2BIN(number,places)

Number   is the hexadecimal number you want to convert.

Places   is the number of characters to use. If places is omitted, HEX2BIN uses the minimum number of characters necessary.

Examples

    HEX2BIN("F",8)

returns 00001111

    HEX2BIN("B7")

returns 10110111

HEX2DEC

Converts a hexadecimal number to decimal.

Syntax

HEX2DEC(number)

Number   is the hexadecimal number you want to convert.

Examples

HEX2DEC("A5")

returns 165

HEX2DEC("FFFFFFFF5B")

returns -165

HEX2OCT

Converts a hexadecimal number to octal.

Syntax

HEX2OCT(number,places)

Number   is the hexadecimal number you want to convert.

Places   is the number of characters to use. If places is omitted, HEX2OCT uses the minimum number of characters necessary.

Examples

HEX2OCT("F",3)

returns 017

HEX2OCT("3B4E")

returns 35516

IMABS

Returns the absolute value (modulus) of a complex number.

Syntax

IMABS(inumber)

Inumber   is a complex number for which you want the absolute value.

Example
IMABS("5+12i")

returns 13

IMAGINARY
Returns the imaginary coefficient of a complex number.

Syntax
IMAGINARY(inumber)

Inumber   is a complex number for which you want the imaginary coefficient.

Examples

IMAGINARY("3+4i")

returns 4

IMAGINARY("0-j")

returns -1

IMARGUMENT
Returns the argument theta, an angle expressed in radians.

Syntax
IMARGUMENT(inumber)

Inumber   is a complex number for which you want the argument.

Example
IMARGUMENT("3+4i")

returns 0.927295

IMCONJUGATE

Returns the complex conjugate of a complex number.

Syntax

IMCONJUGATE(inumber)

Inumber   is a complex number for which you want the conjugate.

Example

IMCONJUGATE("3+4i")

returns 3 - 4i

IMCOS

Returns the cosine of a complex number.

Syntax

IMCOS(inumber)

Inumber   is a complex number for which you want the cosine.

Example

IMCOS("1+i")

returns 0.83373 - 0.988898i

IMDIV

Returns the quotient of two complex numbers.

Syntax

IMDIV(inumber1,inumber2)

Inumber1   is the complex numerator or dividend.

Inumber2   is the complex denominator or divisor.

Example

IMDIV("-238+240i","10+24i")

returns 5 + 12i

IMEXP

Returns the exponential of a complex number.

Syntax

IMEXP(inumber)

Inumber   is a complex number for which you want the exponential.

Example

IMEXP("1+i")

returns 1.468694 + 2.287355i

IMLN

Returns the natural logarithm of a complex number.

Syntax

IMLN(inumber)

Inumber   is a complex number for which you want the natural logarithm.

Example

IMLN("3+4i")

returns 1.609438 + 0.927295i

IMLOG10

Returns the base-10 logarithm of a complex number.

Syntax

IMLOG10(inumber)

Inumber   is a complex number for which you want the common logarithm.

Example

IMLOG10("3+4i")

returns 0.69897 + 0.402719i

IMLOG2

Returns the base-2 logarithm of a complex number.

Syntax

IMLOG2(inumber)

Inumber   is a complex number for which you want the base-2 logarithm.

Example

IMLOG2("3+4i")

returns 2.321928 + 1.337804i

IMPOWER

Returns a complex number raised to an integer power.

Syntax

IMPOWER(inumber,number)

Inumber   is a complex number you want to raise to a power.

Number   is the power to which you want to raise the complex number.

Example

IMPOWER("2+3i",3)

returns -46 + 9i

IMPRODUCT

Returns the product of two complex numbers.

Syntax

IMPRODUCT(inumber1,inumber2,...)

inumber1,inumber2,... are 1 to 29 complex numbers to multiply.

Examples

IMPRODUCT("3+4i","5-3i")

returns 27 + 11I

IMPRODUCT("1+2i",30)

returns 30 + 60i

IMREAL

Returns the real coefficient of a complex number.

Syntax

IMREAL(inumber)

Inumber is a complex number for which you want the real coefficient.

Example

IMREAL("6-9i")

returns 6

IMSIN

Returns the sine of a complex number.

Syntax

IMSIN(inumber)

Inumber is a complex number for which you want the sine.

Example

IMSIN("3+4i")

returns 3.853738 - 27.016813i

IMSQRT

Returns the square root of a complex number.

Syntax

IMSQRT(inumber)

Inumber   is a complex number for which you want the square root.

Example

IMSQRT("1+i")

returns 1.098684 + 0.45509i

IMSUB

Returns the difference of two complex numbers.

Syntax

IMSUB(inumber1,inumber2)

Inumber1   is the complex number from which to subtract inumber2.

Inumber   is the complex number to subtract from inumber1.

Example

IMSUB("13+4i","5+3i")

returns 8 + i

IMSUM

Returns the sum of complex numbers.

Syntax

IMSUM(inumber1,inumber2,...)

Inumber1,inumber2,...   are 1 to 29 complex numbers to add.

Example

IMSUM("3+4i","5-3i")

returns 8 + i

INTRATE

Returns the interest rate for a fully invested security.

Syntax

INTRATE(settlement,maturity,investment,redemption,basis)

Settlement is the security's settlement date, expressed as a serial date number.

Maturity is the security's maturity date, expressed as a serial date number.

Investment is the amount invested in the security.

Redemption is the amount to be received at maturity.

Basis is the type of day count basis to use. If basis is 0 or omitted, day count basis is US (NASD) 30/360; if basis is 1, day count basis is actual/actual; if basis is 2, day count basis is actual/360; if basis is 3, day count basis is actual/365; if basis is 4, day count basis is European 30/360.

Example

A bond has the following terms: February 15, 1993 settlement (issue) date; May 15, 1993 maturity date; 1,000,000 investment; 1,014,420 redemption value; Actual/360 basis. The bond discount rate (in the 1900 Date System) is:

INTRATE(34015, 34104,1000000,1014420,2)

returns 0.058328 or 5.8328%

ISEVEN

Returns TRUE if the number is even.

Syntax

ISEVEN(value)

Value   is the value you want tested.

ISODD

Returns TRUE if the number is odd.

Syntax

ISODD(value)

Value   is the value you want tested.

LCM

Returns the least common multiple.

Syntax

LCM(number1,number2,...)

Number1,number2,...   are 1 to 29 values for which you want the least common multiple. If value is not an integer, it is truncated.

Examples

LCM(5,2)

returns 10

LCM(24,36)

returns 72

MDURATION

Returns the Macauley modified duration for a security with an assumed par value of $100.

Syntax

MDURATION(settlement,maturity,coupon,yld,frequency,basis)

Settlement   is the security's settlement date, expressed as a serial date number.

Maturity is the security's maturity date, expressed as a serial date number.

Coupon is the security's annual coupon rate.

Yld is the security's annual yield.

Frequency is the number of coupon payments per year. For annual payments, frequency=1; for semiannual, frequency=2; for quarterly, frequency=4.

Basis is the type of day count basis to use. If basis is 0 or omitted, day count basis is US (NASD) 30/360; if basis is 1, day count basis is actual/actual; if basis is 2, day count basis is actual/360; if basis is 3, day count basis is actual/365; if basis is 4, day count basis is European 30/360.

Example

A bond has the following terms: January 1, 1986 settlement date; January 1, 1994 maturity date; 8.0% coupon; 9.0% yield; frequency is semiannual; actual/actual basis. The modified duration (in the 1900 Date System) is:

MDURATION(33239,36631,0.08,0.09,2,1)

returns 5.73567

MROUND

Returns a number rounded to the desired multiple.

Syntax

MROUND(number,multiple)

Number is the value to round.

Multiple is the multiple to which you want to round number.

Examples

MROUND(10,3)

returns 9

MROUND(-10,-3)

returns -9

MULTINOMIAL

Returns the multinomial of a set of numbers.

Syntax

MULTINOMIAL(number1,number2,...)

Number1,number2,... are 1 to 29 values for which you want the multinomial.

Example

MULTINOMIAL(2,3,4)

returns 1260

NETWORKDAYS

Returns the number of whole workdays between two dates.

Syntax

NETWORKDAYS(start_date,end_date,holidays)

Start_date is a serial date number that represents the start date.

End_date is a serial date number that represents the end date.

Holidays is an optional set of one or more serial date numbers to exclude from the working calendar, such as state and federal holidays and floating holidays.

Example

NETWORK-
DAYS(DATEVALUE("10/01/91"),DATEVALUE("12/01/91"),DATEVALUE
("11/28/91"))

returns 43

NOMINAL

Returns the annual nominal interest rate.

Syntax

NOMINAL(effect_rate,npery)

Effect_rate   is the effective interest rate.

Npery   is the number of compounding periods per year.

Example

NOMINAL(5.3543%,4)

returns

OCT2BIN

Converts an octal number to binary.

Syntax

OCT2BIN(number,places)

Number   is the octal number you want to convert.

Places   is the number of characters to use. If places is omitted, OCT2BIN uses the minimum number of characters necessary.

Examples

OCT2BIN(3,3)

returns 011

OCT2BIN(7777777000)

returns 1000000000

OCT2DEC

Converts an octal number to decimal.

Syntax

OCT2DEC(number)

Number   is the octal number you want to convert.

Examples

OCT2DEC(54)

returns 44

OCT2DEC(7777777533)

returns -165

OCT2HEX

Converts an octal number to hexadecimal.

Syntax

OCT2HEX(number,places)

Number   is the octal number you want to convert.

Places   is the number of characters to use. If places is omitted, OCT2HEX uses the minimum number of characters necessary.

Examples

OCT2HEX(100,4)

returns 0040

OCT2HEX(7777777533)

returns FFFFFFFF5B

ODDFPRICE

Returns the price per $100 face value of a security with an odd first period.

Syntax

ODDFPRICE(settlement,maturity,issue,first_coupon,rate,yld,redemption,frequency,basis)

Settlement   is the security's settlement date, expressed as a serial date number.

Maturity   is the security's maturity date, expressed as a serial date number.

Issue   is the security's issue date, expressed as a serial date number.

First_coupon   is the security's first coupon date, expressed as a serial date number.

Rate   is the security's interest rate.

Yld   is the security's annual yield.

Redemption is the security's redemption value per $100 face value.

Frequency is the number of coupon payments per year. For annual payments, frequency=1; for semiannual, frequency=2; for quarterly, frequency=4.

Basis is the type of day count basis to use. If basis is 0 or omitted, day count basis is US (NASD) 30/360; if basis is 1, day count basis is actual/actual; if basis is 2, day count basis is actual/360; if basis is 3, day count basis is actual/365; if basis is 4, day count basis is European 30/360.

Example

A treasury bond has the following terms: November 11, 1986 settlement date; March 1, 1999 maturity date; October 15, 1986 issue date; March 1, 1987 first coupon date; 7.85% coupon; 6.25% yield; $100 redemptive value; frequency is semiannual; actual/actual basis. The price per $100 face value of a security having an odd (short or long) first period (in the 1900 date system) is:

    ODDFPRICE(31727,36220,31700,31837,0.0785,0.0625,100,2,1)

returns 113.597717

ODDFYIELD

Returns the yield of a security with an odd first period.

Syntax

    ODDFYIELD(settlement,maturity,issue,first_coupon,rate, pr,redemp-
    tion,frequency,basis)

Settlement is the security's settlement date, expressed as a serial date number.

Maturity is the security's maturity date expressed as a serial date number.

Issue is the security's issue date, expressed as a serial date number.

First_coupon is the security's first coupon date, expressed as a serial date number.

Rate is the security's interest rate.

Pr is the security's price.

Redemption is the security's redemption value per $100 face value.

Frequency is the number of coupon payments per year. For annual payments, frequency=1; for semiannual, frequency=2; for quarterly, frequency=4.

Basis is the type of day count basis to use. If basis is 0 or omitted, day count basis is US (NASD) 30/360; if basis is 1, day count basis is actual/actual; if basis is 2, day count basis is actual/360; if basis is 3, day count basis is actual/365; if basis is 4, day count basis is European 30/360.

Example

A bond has the following terms: January 25, 1991 settlement date; January 1, 1996 maturity date; January 18, 1991 issue date; July 15, 1991 first coupon date; 5.75% coupon; $84.50 price; $100 redemptive value; Frequency is semiannual; 30/360 basis. The yield of a security that has an odd (short or long) first period is:

    ODDFYIELD(33263,35065,33256,33434,0.0575,084.50,100,2,0)

returns .09758 or 9.76%

ODDLPRICE

Returns the price per $100 face value of a security with an odd last period.

Syntax

    ODDLPRICE(settlement,maturity,last_interest,rate,yld,redemption,frequency,basis)

Settlement is the security's settlement date, expressed as a serial date number.

Maturity is the security's maturity date, expressed as a serial date number.

Last_interest is the security's last coupon date, expressed as a serial date number.

Rate is the security's interest rate.

Yld   is the security's annual yield.

Redemption   is the security's redemption value per $100 face value.

Frequency   is the number of coupon payments per year. For annual payments, frequency=1; for semiannual, frequency=2; for quarterly, frequency=4.

Basis   is the type of day count basis to use. If basis is 0 or omitted, day count basis is US (NASD) 30/360; if basis is 1, day count basis is actual/actual; if basis is 2, day count basis is actual/360; if basis is 3, day count basis is actual/365; if basis is 4, day count basis is European 30/360.

Example

A bond has the following terms: February, 7, 1987 settlement date; June 15, 1987 maturity date; October 15, 1986 last interest date; 3.75% coupon; 4.05% yield; $100 redemptive value; frequency is semiannual; 30/360 basis. The price per $100 of a security having an odd (short or long) last coupon period is:

ODDLPRICE(31815,31943,31700,0.0375,0.0405,100,2,0)

returns 99.87829

ODDLYIELD

Returns the yield of a security with an odd last period.

Syntax

ODDLYIELD(settlement,maturity,last_interest,rate,pr, redemption,frequency,basis)

Settlement   is the security's settlement date, expressed as a serial date number.

Maturity   is the security's maturity date, expressed as a serial date number.

Last_interest   is the security's last coupon date, expressed as a serial date number.

Rate   is the security's interest rate.

Pr   is the security's price.

Redemption   is the security's redemption value per $100 face value.

Frequency   is the number of coupon payments per year. For annual payments, frequency=1; for semiannual, frequency=2; for quarterly, frequency=4.

Basis   is the type of day count basis to use. If basis is 0 or omitted, day count basis is US (NASD) 30/360; if basis is 1, day count basis is actual/actual; if basis is 2, day count basis is actual/360; if basis is 3, day count basis is actual/365; if basis is 4, day count basis is European 30/360.

Example

A bond has the following terms: April 20, 1987 settlement date; June 15, 1987 maturity date; October 15, 1986 last interest date; 3.75% coupon; $99.875 price; $100 redemptive value; frequency is semiannual; 30/360 basis. The yield of a security that has an odd (short or long) first period is:

    ODDLYIELD(31887,31943,31770,0.0375,99.875,100,2,0)

returns 0.044873.

PRICEDISC

Returns the price per $100 face value of a discounted security.

Syntax

    PRICEDISC(settlement,maturity,discount,redemption,basis)

Settlement   is the security's settlement date, expressed as a serial date number.

Maturity   is the security's maturity date, expressed as a serial date number.

Discount   is the security's discount rate.

Redemption   is the security's redemption value per $100 face value.

Basis   is the type of day count basis to use. If basis is 0 or omitted, day count basis is US (NASD) 30/360; if basis is 1, day count

basis is actual/actual; if basis is 2, day count basis is actual/360;
if basis is 3, day count basis is actual/365; if basis is 4, day count
basis is European 30/360.

Example

A bond has the following terms: February 15, 1993 settlement date;
March 1, 1993 maturity date; 5.25% discount rate; $100 redemption
value; Actual/360 basis. The bond price (in the 1900 Date System) is:

PRICEDISC(34015,34029,0.0525,100,2)

returns 99.79583

PRICEMAT

Returns the price per $100 face value of a security that pays interest at
maturity.

Syntax

PRICEMAT(settlement,maturity,issue,rate,yld,basis)

Settlement is the security's settlement date, expressed as a serial date number.

Maturity is the security's maturity date, expressed as a serial
date number.

Issue is the security's issue date, expressed as a serial date number.

Rate is the security's interest rate at date of issue.

Yld is the security's annual yield.

Basis is the type of day count basis to use. If basis is 0 or omitted, day count basis is US (NASD) 30/360; if basis is 1, day count
basis is actual/actual; if basis is 2, day count basis is actual/360; if
basis is 3, day count basis is actual/365; if basis is 4, day count basis is European 30/360.

Example

A bond has the following terms: February 15, 1993 settlement date;
April 13, 1993 maturity date; November 11, 1992 issue date; 6.1%

semiannual coupon; 6.1% yield; 30/360 basis. The price (in the 1900 Date System) is:

PRICEMAT(34015,34072,33919,0.061,0.061,0)

returns 99.98449888

PRICE

Returns the price per $100 face value of a security that pays periodic interest.

Syntax

PRICE(settlement,maturity,rate,yld,redemption,frequency,basis)

Settlement   is the security's settlement date, expressed as a serial date number.

Maturity~Mis the security's maturity date, expressed as a serial date number.

Rate   is the security's annual coupon rate.

Yld   is the security's annual yield. Redemption is the security's redemption value per $100 face value.

Frequency   is the number of coupon payments per year. For annual payments, frequency=1; for semiannual, frequency=2; for quarterly, frequency=4.

Basis   is the type of day count basis to use. If basis is 0 or omitted, day count basis is US (NASD) 30/360; if basis is 1, day count basis is actual/actual; if basis is 2, day count basis is actual/360; if basis is 3, day count basis is actual/365; if basis is 4, day count basis is European 30/360.

Example

A bond has the following terms: February 15, 1991 settlement date; November 15, 1999 maturity date; 5.75% semiannual coupon; 6.50% yield; $100 redemption value; frequency in semiannual; 30/360 basis. The bond price (in the 1900 Date System) is:

PRICE(33284,36479,0.0575,0.065,100,2,0)

returns 95.04287

QUOTIENT

Returns the integer portion of a division.

Syntax

QUOTIENT(numerator,denominator)

Numerator   is the dividend.

Denominator   is the divisor.

Examples

QUOTIENT(5,2)

returns 2

QUOTIENT(4.5,3.1)

returns 1

RANDBETWEEN

Returns a random number between two specified numbers.

Syntax

RANDBETWEEN(bottom,top)

Bottom   is the smallest integer RANDBETWEEN will return.

Top   is the largest integer RANDBETWEEN will return.

 ▶ ▶ **T I P**

> **You can get the same result without loading the Analysis Toolpak by using the RAND function. To generate random numbers between a and b, where a is the bottom number and b is the top number, use the formula RAND()*(b-a)+a.**

RECEIVED

Returns the amount received at maturity for a fully invested security.

Syntax

RECEIVED(settlement,maturity,investment,discount,basis)

Settlement is the security's settlement date, expressed as a serial date number.

Maturity is the security's maturity date, expressed as a serial date number.

Investment is the amount invested in the security.

Discount is the security's discount rate.

Basis is the type of day count basis to use. If basis is 0 or omitted, day count basis is US (NASD) 30/360; if basis is 1, day count basis is actual/actual; if basis is 2, day count basis is actual/360; if basis is 3, day count basis is actual/365; if basis is 4, day count basis is European 30/360.

Example

A bond has the following terms: February 15, 1993 settlement (issue) date; May 15, 1993 maturity date; 1,000,000 investment; 5.75% discount rate; Actual/360 basis. The total amount to be received at maturity(in the 1900 Date System) is:

RECEIVED(34015,34104,1000000,0.0575,2)

returns 1,014,420.266

SERIESSUM

Returns the sum of a power series on the basis of the formula.

Syntax

SERIESSUM(x,n,m,coefficients)

X is the input value to the power series.

N is the initial power to which you want to raise x.

M is the step by which to increase n for each term in the series.

Coefficients is a set of coefficients by which each successive power of x is multiplied. The number of values in coefficients determines the number of terms in the power series. For example, if there are three values in coefficients, then there will be three terms in the power series.

See Excel's On-Line Help worksheet function reference for an example of SERIESSUM.

SQRTPI

Returns the square root of (number*PI).

Syntax

SQRTPI(number)

Number is the number by which pi is multiplied.

Examples

SQRTPI(1)

returns 1.772454

SQRTPI(2)

returns 2.506628

TBILLEQ

Returns the bond-equivalent yield for a Treasury bill.

Syntax

TBILLEQ(settlement,maturity,discount)

Settlement is the Treasury bill's settlement date, expressed as a serial date number.

Maturity is the Treasury bill's maturity date, expressed as a serial date number.

Discount is the Treasury bill's discount rate.

Example

A Treasury bill has the following terms: March 31, 1993 settlement date; June 1, 1993 maturity date; 9.14% discount rate. The bond equivalent yield for a treasury bill (in the 1900 Date System) is:

TBILLEQ(34059,34121,0.0914)

returns 0.094151 or 9.4151%

TBILLPRICE

Returns the price per $100 face value for a Treasury bill.

Syntax

TBILLPRICE(settlement,maturity,discount)

Settlement is the Treasury bill's settlement date, expressed as a serial date number.

Maturity is the Treasury bill's maturity date,

expressed as a serial date number.

Discount is the Treasury bill's discount rate.

Example

A Treasury bill has the following terms: March 31, 1993 settlement date; June 1, 1993 maturity date; 9% discount rate. The Treasury bill price (in the 1900 Date System) is:

TBILLPRICE(34059,34121,0.09)

returns 98.45

TBILLYIELD

Returns the yield for a Treasury bill.

Syntax

TBILLYIELD(settlement,maturity,pr)

Settlement is the Treasury bill's settlement date, expressed as a serial date number.

Maturity is the Treasury bill's maturity date, expressed as a se-rial date number.

Pr is the Treasury bill's price per $100 face value.

Example

A Treasury bill has the following terms: March 31, 1993 settlement date; June 1, 1993 maturity date; 98.45 price per $100 face value. The Treasury bill yield (in the 1900 Date System) is:

    TBILLYIELD(34059,34121,98.45)

returns 9.1417%

WORKDAY

Returns the serial number of the date before or after a specified number of workdays.

Syntax

    WEEKDAY(serial_number,return_type)

Serial_number   is the date-time code used by Excel for date and time calculations. You can give serial_number as text, such as "15-Apr-1993" or "4-15-93", instead of as a number. The text is automatically converted to a serial number.

Return_type   is a number that determines the type of return value. If Return-type is 1 or omitted, the number returned is 1 (Sunday) through 7 (Saturday) (behaves like previous versions of Microsoft Excel); if Return-type is 2, the number returned is 1 (Monday) through 7 (Sunday); if Return-type is 3, the number returned is 0(Monday) through 6 (Sunday).

Examples

    WEEKDAY("2/14/90")

returns 4 (Wednesday).

    WEEKDAY(29747.007)

returns 4 (Wednesday)in the 1900 date system.

XIRR

Returns the internal rate of return for a schedule of cash flows. Excel uses an iterative technique for calculating XIRR. Using a changing rate (starting with guess), XIRR cycles through the calculation until the result is accurate within 0.000001%. If XIRR can't find a result that works after 100 tries, the #NUM! error value is returned.

Syntax

XIRR(values,dates,guess)

Values   is a series of cash flows that correspond to a schedule of payments in dates. The first payment is optional, and corresponds to a cost or payment that occurs at the beginning of the investment. All succeeding payments are discounted based on a 365-day year.

Dates   is a schedule of payment dates that corresponds to the cash flow payments. The first payment date indicates the beginning of the schedule of payments. All other dates must be later than this date, but they may occur in any order.

Guess   is a number that you guess is close to the result of XIRR.

Example

Consider an investment that requires a $10,000 cash payment on January 1, 1992, and returns $2750 on March 1, 1992, $4250 on October 30, 1992, $3250 on February 15, 1993, and $2750 on April 1, 1993. The internal rate of return (in the 1900 Date System) is:

XIRR({10000,2750,4250,3250,2750},{33604,33664,33907,34015, 34060},0.1)

returns 0.373363 or 37.3363%

XNPV

Returns the net present value for a schedule of cash flows.

Syntax

XNPVate,values,dates)

Rate   is the discount rate to apply to the cash flows.

Values   is a series of cash flows that correspond to a schedule of payments in dates. The first payment is optional, and corresponds to a cost or payment that occurs at the beginning of the investment. All succeeding payments are discounted based on a 365-day year.

Dates   is a schedule of payment dates that corresponds to the cash flow payments. The first payment date indicates the beginning

Worksheet Functions

Ap. B

of the schedule of payments. All other dates must be later than this date, but they may occur in any order.

Example

Consider an investment that requires a $10,000 cash payment on January 1, 1992, and returns $2750 on March 1, 1992, $4250 on October 30, 1992, $3250 on February 15, 1993, and $2750 on April 1, 1993. Assume that the cash flows are discounted at 9%. The net present value is:

XNPV(0.09,{10000,2750,4250,3250,2750},{33604,33664,33907, 34015,34060})

returns 2086.647602

YEARFRAC

Returns the year fraction representing the number of whole days between start_date and end_date.

Syntax

YEARFRAC(start_date,end_date,basis)

Start_date   is a serial date number that represents the start date.

End_date   is a serial date number that represents the end date.

Basis   is the type of day count basis to use. If basis is 0 or omitted, day count basis is US (NASD) 30/360; if basis is 1, day count basis is actual/actual; if basis is 2, day count basis is actual/360; if basis is 3, day count basis is actual/365; If basis is 4, day count basis is European 30/360.

Examples

YEARFRAC(DATEVALUE("01/01/93"),DATEVALUE("06/30/93"),0)

returns 0.5

YEARFRAC(DATEVALUE("01/01/93"),DATEVALUE("07/01/93"),3)

returns 0.49863

YIELD

Returns the yield on a security that pays periodic interest. If there is more than one coupon period until redemption, YIELD is calculated through a hundred iterations. The resolution uses the Newton method based on the formula used for the function PRICE. The yield is changed until the estimated price given the yield is close to price.

Syntax

YIELD(settlement,maturity,rate,pr,redemption,frequency,basis)

Settlement   is the security's settlement date, expressed as a serial date number.

Maturity   is the security's maturity date, expressed as a serial date number.

Rate   is the security's annual coupon rate.

Pr   is the security's price per $100 face value.

Redemption   is the security's redemption value per $100 face value.

Frequency   is the number of coupon payments per year. For annual payments, frequency=1; for semiannual, frequency=2; for quarterly, frequency=4.

Basis   is the type of day count basis to use. If basis is 0 or omitted, day count basis is US (NASD) 30/360; if basis is 1, day count basis is actual/actual; if basis is 2, day count basis is actual/360; if basis is 3, day count basis is actual/365; if basis is 4, day count basis is European 30/360.

Example

A bond has the following terms: February 15, 1991 settlement date; November 15, 1999 maturity date; 5.75% coupon; 95.04287 price; $100 redemption value; frequency is semiannual; 30/360 basis. The bond yield (in the 1900 Date System) is:

YIELD(33284,36479,0.0575,95.04287,100,2,0)

returns 0.065 or 6.5%

YIELDDISC

Returns the annual yield for a discounted security. For example, a treasury bill.

Syntax

YIELDDISC(settlement,maturity,pr,redemption,basis)

Settlement   is the security's settlement date, expressed as a serial date number.

Maturity   is the security's maturity date, expressed as a serial date number.

Pr   is the security's price per $100 face value.

Redemption   is the security's redemption value per $100 face value.

Basis   is the type of day count basis to use. If basis is 0 or omitted, day count basis is US (NASD) 30/360; if basis is 1, day count basis is actual/actual; if basis is 2, day count basis is actual/360; if basis is 3, day count basis is actual/365; if basis is 4, day count basis is European 30/360.

Example

A bond has the following terms: February 15, 1993 settlement date; March 1, 1993 maturity date; 99.795 price; $100 redemption value; Actual/360 basis. The bond yield (in the 1900 Date System) is:

YIELDDISC(34015,34029,99.795,100,2)

returns 5.2823%

YIELDMAT

Returns the annual yield of a security that pays interest at maturity.

Syntax

YIELDMAT(settlement,maturity,issue,rate,pr,basis)

Settlement   is the security's settlement date, expressed as a serial date number.

Maturity   is the security's maturity date, expressed as a serial date number.

Issue   is the security's issue date, expressed as a serial date number.

Rate   is the security's interest rate at date of issue.

Pr   is the security's price per $100 face value.

Basis   is the type of day count basis to use. If basis is 0 or omitted, day count basis is US (NASD) 30/360; if basis is 1, day count basis is actual/actual; if basis is 2, day count basis is actual/360; if basis is 3, day count basis is actual/365; if basis is 4, day count basis is European 30/360.

Example

A bond has the following terms: March 15, 1993 settlement date; November 3, 1993 maturity date; November 8, 1992 issue date; 6.25% semiannual coupon; 100.0123 price; 30/360 basis. The yield (in the 1900 Date System) is:

YIELDMAT(34043,34276,33916,0.0625,100.0123,0)

returns 0.060954 or 6.0954%

▶▶ ODBC Function (database access)

The following function is contained in the ODBC add-in (see Chapter 18).

SQL.REQUEST

Connects with an external data source and runs a query from worksheet—returns query results as an array. Strings are limited to a length of 255 characters. If query_text exceeds that length, enter the query in a vertical range of cells and use the entire range as the query_text. The values of the cells are concatenated to form the complete SQL statement.

Syntax

SQL.REQUEST(connection_string,output_ref,driver_prompt, query_text,column_names_logical)

Connection_string supplies information, such as the data source name, user ID, and passwords, required by the driver being used to connect to a data source and must follow the driver's format. The following list provides three example connection strings for three drivers.

> **dBASE** DSN=NWind;PWD=test
>
> **SQL Server** DSN=MyServer;
> UID=dbayer;PWE=123;Database=Pubs
>
> **ORACLE** DNS=My Oracle Data
> Source;DBQ=MYSER VER;UID=JohnS;PWD=Sesame

N O T E

You must define the Data Source Name (DSN) used in connection_string before you try to connect to it.

Output_ref is a cell reference where you want the completed connection string placed. Use output_ref when you want SQL.REQUEST to return the completed connection string.

Driver_prompt specifies when the driver dialog box is displayed and which options are available. Use one of the numbers described in the following list. If driver_prompt is omitted, SQL.REQUEST uses 2 as the default.

1 Driver dialog box is always displayed.

2 Driver dialog box is displayed only if information provided by the connection string and the data source specification is not sufficient to complete the connection. All dialog box options are available.

3 Driver dialog box is displayed only if information provided by the connection string and the data source specification is not sufficient to complete the connection. Dialog box options are dimmed and unavailable if they are not required.

4 Dialog box is not displayed. If the connection is not successful, it returns an error.

Query_text is the SQL statement that you want to execute on the data source. See examples of query_text below.

Column_names_logical   indicates whether column names are returned as the first row of the results. Set this argument to TRUE if you want the column names to be returned as the first row of the results. Use FALSE if you do not want the column names returned (if column_names_logical is omitted, SQL.REQUEST does not return column names).

Examples

Suppose you want to make a query of a dBASE database named DBASE4. When you enter the following formula in a cell, an array of query results is returned, with the first row being the column names.

```
SQL.REQUEST("DSN=NWind;DBQ=c:\msquery;FIL=dBASE4",
c15,2,"Select Custmr_ID,Due_Date from Orders
WHEREorder_Amt>100",TRUE)
```

If this function completes all of its actions, it returns an array of query results or the number of rows affected by the query.

You can update a query by concatenating references into query_text. In the following example, every time $A$3 changes, SQL.REQUEST uses the new value to update the query.

"SELECT Name FROM Customers WHERE Balance > "'&$A$3'.

▶ ▶   APPENDIX **C**

Keyboard
Shortcuts

___

►► *This* appendix contains 15 tables, summarizing the usage of shortcut keys in Excel.

- Changes from Excel 4
- Entering and editing
- Command keys
- Function keys
- Moving and selecting in worksheets and workbooks
- Moving and selecting while in End mode
- Moving and selecting with Scroll Lock on
- Selecting special cells
- Formatting
- Outlining
- Print Preview mode
- Selecting chart items when chart is active
- Using AutoFilter
- Window commands
- Switching applications

For keyboards with only ten function keys:

- Use Alt+F1 for F11.
- Use Alt+F2 for F12.

Changes from Excel 4

F4	Repeat last action
F7	Check spelling
Ctrl+F	Find
Ctrl+H	Replace
Shift+F4	Find next
Ctrl+Shift+F4	Find previous
Ctrl+N	Open new workbook
Ctrl+O	Open
Ctrl+S	Save
Ctrl+P	Print
Ctrl+Tab	Next window
Ctrl+Shift+Tab	Previous window
Ctrl+PgDn	Move to next sheet in workbook
Ctrl+PgUp	Move to previous sheet in workbook
Ctrl+A	Select all

Entering and Editing

F2	Edit active cell
Esc	Cancel entry
Backspace	Delete character to left of insertion point, or delete selection
Shift+F2	Edit cell note
F3	Paste name into formula
Shift+F3	Display Function Wizard
Ctrl+A	After typing valid function name in formula, display step 2 of Function Wizard

Ctrl+Shift+A	After typing valid function name in formula, insert argument names for the function
Alt+=	Insert AutoSum formula
Ctrl+semicolon	Enter date in cell or formula bar
Ctrl+Shift+colon	Enter time in cell or formula bar
Ctrl+D	Fill down
Ctrl+R	Fill right
Ctrl+Del	Delete text to end of line
Alt+Enter	Insert carriage return
Ctrl+Alt+Tab	Insert tab
Arrow keys	Move one character up, down, left, or right
Ctrl+Shift+"	Copy value from cell above the active cell
Ctrl+' (apostrophe)	Copy formula from cell above the active cell
Ctrl+` (single left quotation mark)	Alternate between displaying values or formulas
Ctrl+Enter	Fill a selection of cells with current entry
Ctrl+Shift+Enter	Enter array formula
F4	Change cell reference type (absolute-relative-mixed)

Command Keys

Ctrl+N	New workbook
Ctrl+O (or Ctrl+F12)	Open
Ctrl+S (or Shift+F12)	Save
F12	Save As

Ctrl+P (or Ctrl+Shift+F12)	Print
Alt+F4	Close Excel
Ctrl+Z (or Alt+ Backspace)	Undo
F4	Repeat
Ctrl+X (or Shift+ Delete)	Cut
Ctrl+C (or Ctrl+ Insert)	Copy
Ctrl+V (or Shift+ Insert)	Paste
Ctrl+D	Fill down
Ctrl+R	Fill right
Del	Clear contents (in worksheet); clear selected item (in chart)
Ctrl+F	Display Find dialog box
Ctrl+H	Display Replace dialog box
Shift+F4	Find next
Ctrl+Shift+F4	Find previous
F5	Go To
Ctrl+minus sign	Display Delete dialog box
Ctrl+Shift+plus sign	Display Insert dialog box
Shift+F11	Insert new worksheet
F11	Insert new chart sheet
Ctrl+F11	Insert new Excel 4.0 macro sheet
Ctrl+F3	Display Define Name dialog box
F3	Display Paste Name dialog box (if names are defined)
Ctrl+Shift+F3	Display Create Names dialog box
Alt+' (apostrophe)	Display Style dialog box

Ctrl+1	Display Format Cells dialog box
Ctrl+9	Hide rows
Ctrl+Shift+(	Unhide rows
Ctrl+0 (zero)	Hide columns
Ctrl+Shift+)	Unhide columns
F7	Check spelling
Ctrl+F6	Next window
Ctrl+Shift+F6	Previous window
F6	Next pane
Shift+F6	Previous pane
F1	Help Contents screen
Shift+F1	Show Help Pointer
Ctrl+7	Show or hide Standard toolbar
F9 or Ctrl+=	Calculate all open workbooks
Shift+F9	Calculate active sheet

Function Keys

F1	Help Contents screen
Shift+F1	Display help pointer
F2	Activate formula bar
Shift+F2	Insert note
Ctrl+F2	Display Info window
F3	Display Paste Name dialog box (if names are defined)
Shift+F3	Display Function Wizard
Ctrl+F3	Display Define Name dialog box
Ctrl+Shift+F3	Display Create Names dialog box

F4	When editing a formula, change cell reference type (absolute-relative-mixed); when not editing a formula, repeat last action
Ctrl+F4	Close window
Alt+F4	Close Excel
F5	Go To
Ctrl+F5	Restore window size
F6	Next pane
Shift+F6	Previous pane
Ctrl+F6	Next window
Ctrl+Shift+F6	Previous window
F7	Check spelling
Ctrl+F7	Move command (document Control menu)
F8	Turn Extend mode on or off
Shift+F8	Turn Add mode on or off
Ctrl+F8	Size command (document Control menu)
F9	Calculate all sheets in all open workbooks
Shift+F9	Calculate active sheet
Ctrl+F9	Minimize workbook
F10	Activate menu bar
Shift+F10	Activate shortcut menu
Ctrl+F10	Maximize workbook
F11	Insert new chart sheet
Shift+F11	Insert new worksheet
Ctrl+F11	Insert new Excel 4.0 macro sheet
F12	Save As
Shift+F12	Save

Ctrl+F12	Open
Ctrl+Shift+F12	Print

Moving and Selecting in Worksheets and Workbooks

Enter	Move down through selected cells
Shift+Enter	Move up through selection
Tab	Move right through selection; move among unlocked cells in protected worksheet
Shift+Tab	Move left through selection
Ctrl+Backspace	Scroll to display active cell
Arrow key	Move by one cell in direction of arrow
Shift+any arrow key	Extend selection by one cell
Ctrl+↑ or Ctrl+↓	Move up or down to edge of current data region
Ctrl+← or Ctrl+→	Move left or right to edge of current data region
Ctrl+Shift+any arrow key	Extend selection to edge of current data region (in direction of arrow)
Home	Move to beginning of row
Shift+Home	Extend selection to beginning of row
Ctrl+Home	Move to beginning of worksheet
Ctrl+Shift+Home	Extend selection to beginning of worksheet
Ctrl+End	Move to last cell in worksheet (lower-right corner)
Ctrl+Shift+End	Extend selection to last cell in worksheet (lower-right corner)

Ctrl+spacebar	Select entire column
Shift+spacebar	Select entire row
Ctrl+A	Select entire worksheet
Shift+Backspace	Collapse selection to active cell
PgDn	Move down one screen
PgUp	Move up one screen
Alt+PgDn	Move right one screen
Alt+PgUp	Move left one screen
Ctrl+PgDn	Move to next sheet in workbook
Ctrl+PgUp	Move to previous sheet in workbook
Shift+PgDn	Extend selection down one screen
Shift+PgUp	Extend selection up one screen
Ctrl+Shift+*	Select current region
Ctrl+Shift+spacebar	When an object is selected, select all objects on sheet
Ctrl+6	Alternate between hiding objects, displaying objects, and displaying placeholders for objects

If Enter does not move to the next cell, choose Tools ➤ Options, then select the Edit tab and check the Move Selection After Entry setting.

If the selection is one column, pressing Enter or Tab moves the active cell down (Shift+Enter or Shift+Tab moves the active cell up). If the selection is one row, pressing Enter or Tab moves the active cell right (Shift+Enter or Shift+Tab moves the active cell left).

Moving and Selecting While in End Mode

End	Turn End mode on/off
End, arrow key	Move by one block of data within a row or column
End, Shift+arrow key	Extend selection to end of data block in direction of arrow

End, Home	Move to last cell in worksheet (lower-right corner)
End, Shift+Home	Extend selection to last cell in worksheet (lower-right corner)
End, Enter	Move to last cell in current row
End, Shift+Enter	Extend selection to last cell in current row

End, Enter and End, Shift+Enter are unavailable if you have selected the Transition Navigation Keys setting on the Transition tab in the Tools ▶ Options dialog box.

Moving and Selecting with Scroll Lock

Scroll Lock	Turn scroll lock on/off
↑ or ↓	Scroll screen up or down one row
← or →	Scroll screen left or right one column
Home	Move to upper-left cell in window
End	Move to lower-right cell in window
Shift+Home	Extend selection to upper-left cell in window
Shift+End	Extend selection to lower-right cell in window

Selecting Special Cells

Ctrl+Shift+?	Select all cells containing a note
Ctrl+Shift+*	Select rectangular range of cells around the active cell—range selected is an area enclosed by any combination of blank rows and blank columns
Ctrl+/	Select entire array, if any, to which active cell belongs
Ctrl+\	Select cells whose contents are different from the comparison cell in each row

Ctrl+Shift+¦	Select cells whose contents are different from the comparison cell in each column
Ctrl+[	Select only cells directly referred to by formulas in selection
Ctrl+Shift+{	Select all cells directly or indirectly referred to by formulas in selection
Ctrl+]	Select only cells with formulas that refer directly to active cell
Ctrl+Shift+}	Select all cells within formulas that directly or indirectly refer to active cell
Alt+semicolon	Select only visible cells in current selection

Formatting

Alt+' (apostrophe)	Display Style dialog box
Ctrl+Shift+~	General number format
Ctrl+Shift+$	Currency format with two decimal places (negative numbers appear in parentheses)
Ctrl+Shift+%	Percentage format with no decimal places
Ctrl+Shift+^	Exponential number format with two decimal places
Ctrl+Shift+#	Date format with day, month, and year
Ctrl+Shift+@	Time format with hour and minute (indicate a.m. or p.m.)
Ctrl+Shift+!	Two-decimal-place format with commas
Ctrl+Shift+&	Apply outline border
Ctrl+Shift+_ (underscore)	Remove all borders

Ctrl+B	Apply or remove bold (toggle)
Ctrl+I	Apply or remove italic (toggle)
Ctrl+U	Apply or remove underline (toggle)
Ctrl+5	Apply or remove strikethrough (toggle)
Ctrl+9	Hide rows
Ctrl+Shift+(	Unhide rows
Ctrl+0 (zero)	Hide columns
Ctrl+Shift+)	Unhide columns

Outlining

Alt+Shift+←	Ungroup a row or column
Alt+Shift+→	Group a row or column
Ctrl+8	Display or hide outline symbols
Ctrl+9	Hide selected rows
Ctrl+Shift+(	Unhide selected rows
Ctrl+0 (zero)	Hide selected columns
Ctrl+Shift+)	Unhide selected columns

Print Preview Mode

Arrow keys	Move around page when zoomed in
↑, ↓	Move by one page when zoomed out
PgUp, PgDn	Move by one page when zoomed out; move around page when zoomed in
Ctrl+↑ or Ctrl+←	Move to first page when zoomed out
Ctrl+↓ or Ctrl+→	Move to last page when zoomed out

Selecting Chart Items When Chart Is Active

↓	Select previous group of items
↑	Select next group of items
→	Select next item within group
←	Select previous item within group

Using AutoFilter

Alt+↓	Display drop-down list for selected column label
Alt+↑	Close drop-down list for selected column label
↑	Select previous item in list
↓	Select next item in list
Home	Select first item in list (All)
End	Select last item in list (NonBlanks)
Enter	Filter worksheet list using selected item

Window Commands

Ctrl+F4	Close window
Ctrl+F5	Restore window size
Ctrl+F6 or Ctrl+Tab	Next window
Ctrl+Shift+F6 or Ctrl+Shift+Tab	Previous window
Ctrl+F7	Move command (Control menu)
Ctrl+F8	Size command (Control menu)
Ctrl+F9	Minimize window
Ctrl+F10	Maximize window

Keyboard
Shortcuts

► ►
Ap.
C

Switching Applications

Alt+Esc	Next application
Alt+Shift+Esc	Previous application
Alt+Tab	Next Windows application
Alt+Shift+Tab	Previous Windows application
Ctrl+Esc	Display Task List dialog box

Glossary

Absolute Reference A cell reference which specifies the exact address of a cell. An absolute reference takes the form $A$1, $B$3, etc.

Activate (Chart) Select a chart for editing or formatting. To activate a chart sheet, click the sheet tab. To activate an embedded chart, double-click the chart.

Active Cell The selected cell. You can enter or edit data in the active cell.

Active Sheet The sheet that you are currently working on. When a sheet is active, the name on the sheet tab is bold.

Active Window The window that you are currently using or that is currently selected. Only one window can be active at a time, and keystrokes and commands affect the active window.

Add-In Add-ins are files that can be installed to add commands and functions to Excel.

Address The location of a cell on a sheet. The cell address consists of a row address and a column address, such as F12, in which F is the sixth column on the sheet and 12 is the twelfth row on the sheet.

Alternate Startup Directory A directory you can specify in addition to XLSTART which contains workbooks or other files you want to start automatically when you start Excel. Templates placed in this directory are added to the New dialog, which is displayed when you choose File ➤ New.

Argument Information you supply to a function for calculation. An argument can be a value, reference, name, formula, or another function.

Array Data used to build single formulas that produce multiple results or that operate on a group of arguments arranged in rows or columns.

Array Range A type of array that consists of a rectangular range of cells that share a common formula.

Array Constant A specially arranged group of constants that is used as an argument in a formula.

AutoFill AutoFill is a feature which allows you to create a series of incremental or fixed values on a worksheet by dragging the fill handle with the mouse.

AutoFormat (for Charts) A combination of chart type, chart subtype, and other formatting characteristics, such as patterns and font, that you can quickly apply to a chart to change its appearance. In addition to Excel's built-in autoformats, you can create your own custom (user-defined) autoformats.

Autotemplate A workbook that you save as a template in the XLSTART directory or alternate startup directory using specific file-names (i.e., BOOK.XLT, SHEET.XLT, CHART.XLT, DIALOG.XLT, MACRO.XLT). You can use autotemplates as the basis for all new workbooks and all new worksheets that you insert into your workbooks.

Axes Borders on the plot area which provide a frame of reference for measurement or comparison. On most charts, data values are plotted along the Y axis and categories are plotted along the X axis. On a typical column chart, the X axis is the horizontal axis and the Y axis is the vertical axis. Pie and doughnut charts have no axes, radar charts have a single central axis, and scatter charts have two value axes. Some 3-D charts have three axes (X, Y, and Z) for values, categories, and series.

Cell The intersection of a column and a row.

Cell Note A note that adds supplementary information or comments to the data in a specific cell.

Cell Reference The set of row and column coordinates which identify a cell location on a worksheet. Also referred to as the cell address.

Ap.
D

Chart A graphical representation of worksheet data. A chart can be embedded (created and saved on a worksheet) or can be a chart sheet (a separate sheet in a workbook). Charts are linked to the data they were created from, and are automatically updated when worksheet changes are made.

Chart Area The entire region surrounding the chart, just outside the plot area. When the chart area is selected, uniform font characteristics can be applied to all text in the chart.

Chart Object An un-activated embedded chart. A chart object behaves like other worksheet objects.

Chart Sheet A sheet in a workbook containing a chart. When a chart sheet is active, the chart on the chart sheet is automatically activated.

Chart Text Text in a chart is either linked to worksheet data or un-linked. Unlinked text (e.g., axis and chart titles, text boxes, and trend-line labels) can be added after creating a chart, then edited, formatted, and moved. Linked text (e.g., legend entries, tick-mark labels, and data labels) is based on text or values in the worksheet, and can be formatted and moved. Editing linked text can break the link.

Chart Toolbar Contains the Chart Type, Default Chart, ChartWizard, Horizontal Gridlines, and Legend tools. Clicking the Chart Type tool displays a palette of chart types from which you can choose to change the chart type of a selected data series or an entire chart.

Chart Type A chart type is a specific kind of chart. All Excel chart types are based on these chart types: area, bar, column, line, pie, dough-nut, radar, XY (scatter), 3-D area, 3-D bar, 3-D column, 3-D line, 3-D pie, 3-D doughnut, 3-D surface. Each chart type has at least one sub-type that is a variation of the original chart type.

Chart Type Group A group of data series that are formatted as one chart type and displayed on the same axis. For example, a chart show-ing columns overlaid by lines contains two chart groups, a column group and a line group.

ChartWizard ChartWizard is a series of dialog boxes that guides you through the steps required to create a new chart (or modify settings for an existing chart).

Check Box A control composed of a box that indicates with a check mark whether an option is set, regardless of the state of other options in the dialog box.

Circular References A formula that refers to its own cell, either directly or indirectly. Formulas containing circular references can be solved if iteration is turned on (Tools ➤ Options, Calculation tab).

Clipboard A temporary holding area for data that is cut or copied. The data remains on the Clipboard until you cut or copy other data or quit Excel. You can paste cut or copied data from the Clipboard to another location, worksheet, workbook, or application.

Column A vertical range of cells. Each column is identified by a unique letter or letter combination (e.g., A, Z, CF).

Combination Drop Down-Edit Box A control composed of an empty edit box and an arrow button, paired with a drop-down list that appears when the user clicks on the arrow.

Combination List-Edit Box A control composed of a single box with editable text and an arrow button, paired with a drop-down list that appears when the user clicks on the arrow.

Comparison Criteria A set of search conditions used to find data by querying by example. Comparison criteria can be a series of characters you want matched, such as "Northwind Traders", or an expression, such as ">300".

Comparison Operator A mathematical symbol used to compare two values (i.e., =, >, <, =>, =<, <>). See Table 16.1, Relational Operators, for meanings.

Computed Criteria Search criteria that is the result of a formula. Use computed criteria with the Data ➤ Filter ➤ Advanced Filter command to find a subset of data in a database or list.

Constant A cell value that does not start with an equal sign. For example, the date, the value 345, and text are all constants.

Constraints Limitations placed on a Solver problem. Constraints can be applied to changing cells, the target cell, or other cells directly or indirectly related to your problem. You can apply two constraints to each changing cell, and up to 200 other constraints per Solver problem.

Criteria Range A cell range containing a set of search conditions that you use with the Data ➤ Filter ➤ Advanced Filter command to filter data in a list. A criteria range consists of one row of criteria labels and at least one row that defines the search conditions.

Cursor The flashing vertical line that shows where text is entered (for example, in a cell during in-cell editing). Also referred to as the insertion point.

Custom Calculation A calculation that summarizes the values in selected cells in the data area of a PivotTable by using the values in other cells in the data area. For example, the custom calculation "% of Row" displays the value of each cell in the row as a percentage of the row total.

Custom Sort Order A non-alpha, non-numeric sort order, such as Low, Medium, High or Monday, Tuesday, Wednesday. You can use one of the built-in custom sort orders, or create your own using the Tools ➤ Options, Custom Lists dialog tab.

Data Form A dialog box that you can use to see, change, add, and delete records from a list or database, or to find specific records based on criteria you specify. You can display the data form for a list or database by choosing the Data ➤ Form command.

Data Label A label that provides additional information about a data marker in a chart. Data labels can be applied to a single marker, an entire data series, or all data markers in a chart. Depending on the chart type, data labels can show values, names of data series (or categories), percentages, or a combination of these. They may be formatted and moved, but not sized.

Data Marker A bar, area, dot, slice, or other symbol in a chart that represents a single data point or value originating from a worksheet cell. Related data markers in a chart comprise a data series.

Data Point An individual value plotted in a chart that originates from a single cell in a worksheet. Data points are represented by bars, columns, lines, pie or doughnut slices, dots, and various other shapes. These shapes are called data markers.

Data Region A range of cells containing data and bounded by empty cells.

Data Series A group of related data points in a chart that originate from a single worksheet row or column. Each data series in a chart is distinguished by a unique color or pattern. You can plot one or more data series in a chart (a pie chart is limited to one series).

Data Source A data source includes the data a user wants to access from any database, and the information needed to get to that data.

Database A range of cells containing data that is related to a particular subject or purpose. The first row in the database contains field names. Each additional row in the database is one record; each column in the database is one field. In Excel, a database is also referred to as a list.

Database Management System (DBMS) The software used to analyze, organize, search for, update and retrieve data.

Default Startup Workbook The new, unsaved workbook that is displayed when you start Excel. The default startup workbook is displayed only if you have not included other workbooks in the XLSTART directory.

Dependent Worksheet A worksheet that contains an external reference formula or a remote reference formula. When two Excel worksheets are linked, the dependent worksheet relies on a source worksheet for external reference values. When you link a worksheet to a document in another application, the dependent worksheet relies on that document for remote reference values.

Glossary

Ap.
D

Dependents Cells containing formulas that refer to the active cell.

Destination Area The range of cells you select to hold the summarized data when using the Consolidate command. The destination area can be on the same worksheet as the source data, or it can be on a different worksheet.

Dialog Box A dialog box appears when you choose a command that requires additional information. It may include areas in which you type text or numbers, and view or change settings for options related to the command. Every dialog box has a Help button, which you can choose when you do not understand a dialog box option.

Discontiguous Selection A selection of two or more cells or ranges that do not touch each other.

Drop-Down List Box A control composed of a single box with uneditable text and an arrow button, paired with a drop-down list that appears when the user selects the arrow.

Dynamic Data Exchange (DDE) A technology which allows data to be exchanged between different applications, such as Word and Excel. DDE is being replaced by OLE.

Edit Box A box in which the user can enter text, numbers, or cell references.

Embed The process of creating or copying an object into another document. Objects can be embedded between documents within the same application, or between documents in different applications if both applications support the embedding process. An embedded object maintains a connection to its original application, so that you can open the original application and edit the embedded object by double-clicking the object.

Embedded Chart A chart object that has been placed on a worksheet and that is saved on that worksheet when the workbook is saved. When it is selected, you can move and size it. When it is activated, you can select items and add data. You can also move, format, and size items in the chart, depending on the item. Embedded charts are linked to worksheet data and are updated when worksheet data changes.

Embedded Object An object which has links to a different document or application. For example, a paragraph from a Word document which is paste-linked into an Excel spreadsheet is an embedded object.

Empty Text Text without characters, or null text; for example, a pair of quotes with nothing between them ("").

End Mode An alternate method of navigating within and between adjacent blocks of values on a worksheet. To navigate in End mode, press End, then press an arrow key.

Enter Box A box in the formula bar with a check mark in it. When entering or editing data, you can click on the Enter box as an alternative to pressing Enter on the keyboard.

Error Bars Graphical bars that express potential error (or degree of uncertainty) relative to each data marker in a series. You can add Y error bars to data series in 2-D area, bar, column, line, and XY (scatter) chart type groups. XY charts can also display X error bars. Error bars can be selected and formatted as a group.

Extend Mode An alternate method of selecting adjacent cells on a sheet. Press F8, then press an arrow key to select adjacent cells.

External Reference In a formula, a reference to a cell, range, or named area on a different worksheet.

Field A column in a database. Each field (column) in a database contains a unique category of data, and each cell in a database shares a common characteristic with other cells in the same field (column).

Fill Handle The small black square in the lower right corner of the selected cell or range (only visible if Allow Cell Drag and Drop is turned on). When you position the mouse pointer over the fill handle, the pointer changes to a black cross. Drag the fill handle to copy contents to adjacent cells or to create a series. Holding down Control while you drag the fill handle displays a shortcut menu.

Filtering Extracting data that meets certain criteria from a database. Use the field names in the worksheet and comparison operators to filter data.

Floating Toolbar A toolbar that is not docked at the edges of the application window. A floating toolbar stays on top of other windows within the application window.

Font A collection of letters, numbers, and special characters that share a consistent and identifiable typeface, such as Courier or Times New Roman.

Formula A sequence of values, cell references, names, functions, or operators that is contained in a cell and produces a new value from existing values. A formula always begins with an equal sign (=).

Formula Bar A bar near the top of the Excel window that you use to enter or edit values and formulas in cells or charts. Displays the formula or constant value from the active cell or object. You can display or hide the formula bar with the View ▶ Formula Bar command.

Function A built-in formula that uses a series of values (arguments) to perform an operation and returns the result of that operation. You can use the Function Wizard to select a function and enter it into a cell.

General Number Format General is the default number format for all cells on a new worksheet. In the General format, Excel displays numbers using integer format (e.g., 125), decimal fraction format (e.g., 125.42), or scientific notation (e.g., 125E+07) if the number is longer than the width of the cell. The General format displays up to 11 digits, numbers are right-aligned, text is left-aligned, and logical and error values are centered. When you enter data into a cell formatted as General, Excel will assign another built-in format based on what you enter.

Goal Seek A tool for finding the input value a formula needs in order to return a specific result. You can enter your goal value, select the variable that you want to change, and then let Excel find the value that will return your goal.

Graphic Object A line or shape (button, text box, ellipse, rectangle, arc, picture) you draw using the tools on the toolbar, or a picture you paste into Excel.

Gridlines (chart) Lines you may add to your chart that extend from the tickmarks on an axis across the plot area. Gridlines come in various forms: horizontal, vertical, major, minor, and combinations. They make it easier to view and evaluate data in a chart.

Group In an outline or PivotTable, one or more detail rows or columns that are adjacent and subordinate to a summary row or column.

Group Box A control composed of a bordered area containing a group of option buttons, only one of which can be selected at a time.

Handles Small black squares located around the perimeter of selected graphic objects, chart items, or chart text. By dragging the handles, you can move, copy, or size the selected object, chart item, or chart text.

Insertion Point A flashing vertical line that shows the text entry point. Also referred to as the cursor.

Iteration Repeated calculation of the worksheet until a specific numeric condition is met. When iteration is turned on (the feature is found on the Tools ➤ Options, Calculation dialog tab) Excel can solve formulas containing circular references. Also, Solver uses iteration to solve multiple-variable problems.

Label Text you provide for the user, including names, instructions, and cautions.

Legend A box containing legend entries and keys that help to identify the data series or categories in a chart. The legend keys, to the left of each entry, show the patterns and colors assigned to the data series or categories in the chart.

Link A data connection between a dependent worksheet (the worksheet that will use the data) and a source worksheet (the worksheet in which the original data resides). The dependent worksheet is updated whenever the data changes in the source worksheet. You can link graphics, text, and other types of information between a source file and a dependent file.

List A range of cells containing data that is related to a particular subject or purpose. In Excel 5, the terms list and database are used interchangeably.

List Box A control composed of a box that contains a list of text strings from which you can select.

Macro A sequence of commands recorded on a module or macro sheet. You can record a macro, then run the macro to automate your work. A macro can be assigned to a shortcut key, button, object, or tool for easy use.

Macro Sheet A document similar to a worksheet that contains sets of instructions (macros) for accomplishing specific tasks.

Mixed Reference In a formula, a combination of a relative reference and an absolute reference. A mixed reference takes the form $A1 or A$1, where A is the column cell address and 1 is the row cell address. For example, the mixed reference $A1 always refers to column A, regardless of the position of the cell containing the formula. The row address 1 refers to the row in relation to the cell containing the formula. If the cell containing the formula is moved down one row, the mixed reference $A1 changes to $A2.

Module A workbook sheet that contains VBA instructions (macros) for accomplishing specific tasks.

Moving Average A sequence of averages computed from parts of a data series. In a chart, a moving average smoothes the fluctuations in data, thus showing the pattern or trend more clearly.

Name A unique identifier you create to refer to one or more cells, an array of values, a formula, or an object. When you use names in a formula, the formula is easier to read and maintain than a formula containing cell references.

Nested Subtotals Multiple levels of subtotals within a table that provide additional levels of detail.

Normal Style The style used by all cells on sheets until another style is applied.

OLE OLE (Object Linking and Embedding) is a technology for exchanging data between different applications. The exchanged data can be linked or embedded, but to embed an object, both applications must support OLE.

Open Database Connectivity (ODBC) A Driver Manager and a set of ODBC drivers that enable applications to use Structured Query Language (SQL) as a standard language to access data created and stored in another format, such as FoxPro or Access.

Open Database Connectivity (ODBC) Drivers Dynamic-link libraries (DLL) that an open database connectivity (ODBC)-enabled application such as Excel can use to gain access to a particular data source. Each database management system (DBMS), such as SQL Server or FoxPro, requires a different driver.

Option Button A button for selecting one of a group of mutually exclusive options. Place a series of option buttons in a Group Box to group them.

Outline A summary report of worksheet data which contains up to eight nested levels of detail data, and summary data for each level of detail. The user can change the view of the outline to show or hide as much detail as needed.

Pane Panes allow you to view different areas of a large worksheet simultaneously. You can horizontally or vertically split a window into two panes or split a window both vertically and horizontally to display four panes.

Password A secret word or expression which prevents access to a protected item by unauthorized users.

Paste Area The destination for data that has been cut or copied to the Clipboard.

Personal Macro Workbook A workbook that contains macros which are available every time you start Excel. When you record a macro, you can choose to record it into your personal macro workbook.

Picture A linked image of a range of cells. When the contents of the cells changes, the picture or image also changes. You can take a picture of a selected cell or range using the Camera tool the Edit ➤ Copy

Picture and Edit ➤ Paste Picture commands. To see the Edit commands, hold down Shift while selecting the Edit menu.

Pivot Area The worksheet area into which you drag PivotTable fields to change them from one field orientation to another. For example, you can change a row field to a column orientation by dragging it with the mouse to the pivot area for columns. The term Pivot Area also applies to the graphic representation of a PivotTable in step 3 of the PivotTable Wizard.

Pivot Table An interactive worksheet table that enables you to summarize and analyze data from existing databases, lists and tables. Use the PivotTable Wizard to specify the database, list or table you want to use and to define how you want to arrange the data in the PivotTable. Once you create a PivotTable, you can reorganize the data by dragging fields and items.

Pivot Table Block Totals Custom subtotals for the innermost column or row items in a PivotTable. Block totals are inserted above the grand totals for columns or to the left of the grand totals for rows.

Pivot Table Column Field A field that is assigned a column orientation in a PivotTable. Items associated with a column field are displayed as column labels.

Pivot Table Data In a PivotTable, the summarized data calculated from the data fields of a source list or table.

Pivot Table Data Area The part of a PivotTable that contains summary data. Values in each cell of the data area represent a summary of data from the source records or rows.

Pivot Table Data Area Label In a PivotTable, the cell that identifies the source field for the data area and the function used to calculate the values of cells. For example, a data label for a data area calculated using the default summary function in the Sales field reads "Sum of Sales".

Pivot Table Data Field A field in a source list or table that contains data you want summarized in a PivotTable. A data field usually contains numeric data, such as statistics or sales amounts, but it can also contain text. Data from a data field is summarized in the data area of a PivotTable.

Pivot Table Detail Item An item associated with an inner row or column field in a PivotTable.

Pivot Table Field A category of data that is derived from a field in a source list or table. For example, the Year field in a source list or database becomes the Year field in a PivotTable. Items from the source list or table, such as 1994, 1995, and so on, become subcategories in the PivotTable.

Pivot Table Grand Totals Total values for all cells in a row or all cells in a column of a PivotTable. Values in a grand total row or column are calculated using the same summary function used in the data area of the PivotTable.

Pivot Table Item A subcategory of a PivotTable field. Items in a Pivot-Table are derived from unique items in a database field or from unique cells in a list column. In a PivotTable, items appear as row, column, or page labels.

Pivot Table Page Field A field that is assigned to a page orientation in a PivotTable. Items in a page field are displayed one at a time in a PivotTable.

Pivot Table Row Field A field that is assigned a row orientation in a PivotTable. Items associated with a row field are displayed as row labels.

Pivot Table Subtotal A row or column that displays the total of detail items in a PivotTable field, using a summary function you choose.

Plot Area The area of a chart in which data is plotted. In 2-D charts, it is bounded by the axes and encompasses the data markers and gridlines. In 3-D charts, the plot area includes the chart's walls, axes, and tick-mark labels.

Precedents Cells that are referred to by the formula in the active cell.

Precision The number of digits Excel uses when calculating values. By default, Excel calculates with a maximum of 15 digits of a value (full precision). If Precision As Displayed is selected (on the Tools ➤ Options, Calculation tab), Excel rounds values to the number of digits displayed on the worksheet before calculating. Numbers in General format are always calculated with full precision, regardless of the Precision As Displayed setting.

Print Area An area of a worksheet which is specified to be printed.

Print Titles Rows or columns that you select to print at the top or left of every page. For example, if you select row 1 for a print title, row 1 is printed at the top of every page. If you select column A for a print title, column A is printed at the left of every page. Print titles are part of the sheet, not in the margin like headers and footers.

Query In Microsoft Query, a means of finding the records that answer a particular question you ask about the data stored in a data source.

Query Definition Information that Microsoft Query uses to connect to and determine which data to retrieve from a data source. A query definition can include table names, field names, and criteria. A query definition is sent to a data source for execution in the form of a Structured Query Language (SQL) statement.

R-squared value In regression analysis, a calculated value that indicates how valid a trendline is for forecasting.

Range Two or more cells on a sheet. Ranges can be contiguous or discontiguous.

Range Edit A range reference entered in a dialog edit box.

Record A single row in a database. The first row of a database usually contains field names, and each additional row in the database is a record. Each record in the database contains the same categories (fields) of data as every other record in the database.

Reference The location of a cell or range of cells on a worksheet, indicated by column letter and row number. For example, B2, C3:D4, and R[2]C[5] are all references.

Reference Style The method used to identify cells in a worksheet. In the A1 reference style, columns are lettered and rows are numbered. In the R1C1 reference style, R indicates row and C indicates column, and both rows and columns are numbered.

Reference Type The type of reference: absolute, relative, or mixed. A relative reference (e.g., A1) in a formula indicates the location of the referenced cell relative to the cell containing the formula. An absolute reference (e.g., $A$1) always refers to the exact location of the referenced cell. A mixed reference (e.g., $A1; A$1) is half relative and half absolute.

Refresh Update a pivot table or a query.

Regression Analysis A form of statistical analysis used for forecasting. Regression analysis estimates the relationship between variables so that one variable can be predicted from others.

Relative Reference Specifies the location of a referenced cell in relation to the cell containing the reference. A relative reference takes the form A4, C12, etc.

Result Cell A cell on the worksheet that is recalculated when a new scenario is applied.

Result Set The set of records that results from running a query. Microsoft Query displays the result set in a row-and-column format in the Data pane.

Row A horizontal set of cells. Each row is identified by a unique number.

Scale In a chart, the scale determines what value tick-mark labels are displayed on an axis, at what intervals the values occur, and where one axis crosses another. You can make changes to an axis scale on the Format ➤ Axis, Scale dialog tab.

Scenario A named set of input values that you can substitute in a worksheet model to perform what-if analysis.

Glossary

Ap.
D

Scenario Manager An add-in which allows you to create, view, merge, and summarize scenarios.

Scroll Bars The shaded bars along the right side and bottom of the Excel window. With the scroll bars, you can scroll from top to bottom in a long sheet, or from side to side in a wide sheet.

Scroll Lock With Scroll Lock on, the arrow keys move the active sheet rather than making a different cell active.

Secondary Axis In a chart with more than one series, a secondary axis allows you to plot a series or a chart type group along a different value axis, so that you can create two different value scales in the same chart.

Select To highlight a cell or a range of cells on a worksheet, or choose an object or a chart item. The selected cells, objects, or chart items will be affected by the next command or action.

Sheet Tab Shortcut Menu A shortcut menu containing commands relative to Excel sheets. To display the sheet tab shortcut menu, hold down Control while clicking a sheet tab.

Shortcut Menu A menu that shows a list of commands relative to a selected item. You can display shortcut menus for rows, columns, cells, worksheet buttons and text boxes, toolbars, charts and chart items, drawing objects, PivotTables, and workbook sheet tabs. To display the shortcut menu for an item, hold down Control while clicking the item.

Solver An add-in which calculates solutions to what-if scenarios based on adjustable cells, constraint cells, and, optionally, cells that must be maximized or minimized. You must select the Solver option during Setup if you want to use Solver.

Sort Key The field name or criteria by which you want to sort data.

Sort Order A way to arrange data based on value or data type. An ascending sort order sorts text from A to Z, numbers from the smallest negative number to the largest positive number, and dates and times from the earliest to the latest. A descending sort order is the opposite of an ascending sort order, except for blanks, which are always sorted last. If you choose a custom sort order, an ascending sort order is the order in which the items appear in the Sort Options dialog box.

Source Data for Pivot Tables The list, database, or table used to create a PivotTable. Source data can be an Excel list or database, an external data source such as a dBase or Microsoft Access file, Excel worksheet ranges with labeled rows and columns, or another PivotTable.

Source Worksheet The worksheet referred to by an external reference formula or a remote reference formula. The source worksheet contains the value used by the external reference or remote reference formula.

Spinner A control composed of a pair of arrow buttons for increasing or decreasing a displayed value.

Split Bar The horizontal or vertical line dividing a split worksheet. You can change the position of the split bar by dragging it, or remove the split bar by double-clicking it.

Standard Font The default text font for worksheets. The standard font determines the default font for the Normal cell style. You can change the standard font on the Tools ➤ Options, General dialog tab.

Startup Directory A directory named XLSTART in which you save workbooks or other files which you want to open automatically when you start Excel. Templates placed in this directory are not opened automatically, but are listed in the New dialog box (displayed by choosing the File ➤ New command).

Status Bar The bar at the bottom of the screen that displays information about the selected command or tool, or an operation in progress. You can display or hide the Status Bar with the View ➤ Status Bar command.

Structured Query Language (SQL) A language used for retrieving, updating, and managing data.

Style A named combination of formats which can be applied to a cell or range. If you redefine the style to be a different combination of formats, all cells to which the style was applied will automatically change to reflect the new formats. A style can include (or exclude) formats for

Glossary

Ap.
D

number, font, alignment, borders, patterns, and protection. You can define or modify a style definition using the Format ➤ Style command.

Subtotal Row A row that displays one or more subtotals for columns in an Excel list. A list can contain multiple, nested subtotal rows.

Summary Data For automatic subtotals and worksheet outlines, the total rows or columns that summarize detail data. Summary data is usually adjacent to and below the detail data.

Summary Function A type of calculation that you direct Excel to use when combining source data in a PivotTable or a consolidation table, or when inserting automatic subtotals in a list or database. Examples of summary functions include Sum, Count, and Average.

Tab Dialog Box A dialog box that is divided into sections that have the appearance of file-folder tabs. To display another tab, click the tab name, or press Control+Tab.

Table Data about a specific topic that is stored in records (rows) and fields (columns).

Target Cell The cell that you want Solver to set to a minimum, maximum, or specific value by adjusting the changing cells defined in the problem. The target cell should contain a formula that depends, directly or indirectly, on the changing cells.

Template A workbook that you create and then use as the basis for other, similar workbooks. You can create templates for workbooks, worksheets, chart sheets, macro sheets. modules, and dialog sheets.

Text Box A rectangular object on a sheet in which you can type text.

Tick Marks In a chart, small lines that intersect an axis like divisions on a ruler. Tick marks are part of and can be formatted with an axis.

Tick-Mark Labels Labels that identify the categories, values, and series in a chart. They come from and are automatically linked to cells in the worksheet selection. They can be formatted like other chart text.

Title Bar The bar across the top of the main application window which contains the program name, "Microsoft Excel".

Tool A button that you click to perform an action quickly. Tools that perform related actions are grouped together on toolbars. You can change or reset any of the built-in toolfaces, and create or delete custom toolfaces.

Toolbar The bar on which tools reside. You can change any toolbar or create new toolbars by adding, deleting, or rearranging tools.

Toolbar Dock The region between the menu bar and the formula bar, or on the left, right, and bottom of the application window, where non-floating toolbars can reside. Toolbars that contain drop-down listboxes or tools with tear-off palettes cannot be docked at the sides of the application window.

Trendline A graphical representation of a trend in a data series. Trendlines are used to study problems of prediction, also called regression analysis. Trendlines can be added to data series in 2-D area, bar, column, line, and XY (scatter) chart type groups, and can be formatted.

Trendline Label Optional text for a trendline, including either the regression equation or the R-squared value, or both. A trendline label may be formatted and moved; it cannot be sized.

Unattached Text Text that is not linked to a chart object and can be moved anywhere on the chart. A text box is an example of unattached text.

View You can save different display and print settings of a worksheet as a named view. You can create several different views of the same worksheet without having to save separate versions of the worksheet.

VBA Visual Basic Programming System, Applications Edition. VBA is the macro language for Excel 5, replacing the old macro language XLM. VBA is both a subset and superset of the Visual Basic programming language.

Visual Basic Module A sheet in an Excel workbook in which you store Visual Basic macros and user-defined functions.

Wildcard Character A character (? or *) that stands for one or more other characters in search criteria. Used to find or filter data on a worksheet. An asterisk (*) represents any number of characters. A question mark (?) represents any single character in the same position as the question mark. To search for a literal question mark or asterisk, precede it with a tilde (~). For example, to search for asterisk, search for ~*.

Workbook An Excel file which contains at least one sheet. A workbook can contain multiple worksheets, modules, macro sheets, dialog sheets, and chart sheets.

Working Directory The directory that Excel first makes available to you when you choose the File ▶ Save As command or the File ▶ Open command.

Worksheet The primary document you use in Excel to store and manipulate data. A worksheet consists of cells organized into columns and rows, and is always part of a workbook.

X Axis On most charts, categories are plotted along the X axis. On a typical column chart, the X axis is the horizontal axis.

XLM The macro language used in Excel 4 and on macro sheets.

XY (scatter) chart A 2-D chart that has numeric values plotted along both axes, rather than values along one axis and categories along the other axis. This type of chart is typically used to analyze scientific data to see whether one set of values is related to another set of values.

Y Axis On most charts, data values are plotted along the Y axis. On a typical column chart, the Y axis is the vertical axis. When a secondary axis is added, it is a secondary Y axis.

Y-Intercept In a chart, the point at which a trendline meets the Y-axis. Setting the Y-intercept enables you to change the way data appears in a chart without actually changing the scale of the axis.

What's New in Excel 5.0c

Excel 5.0c is a *maintenance release*. It fixes several bugs in the original version 5.0; however, the bugs in the original version may or may not be apparent to you, depending on how you use Excel. This appendix will help you decide whether you want to upgrade to Excel 5.0c, particularly if you:

- Use Excel 4 files in Excel 5.0
- Experience problems with MS Query
- Use VBA and/or XLM

The information presented here is arranged by topic, to make it easy for you to locate specific problems. For example, if you are having a problem with Excel 4 files, check the Excel 4 Backwards Compatibility section; if you are having a problem with names, check the Names section, and so forth. Bugs that have been fixed are divided into the following sections:

- Miscellaneous worksheet bugs
- File ➤ Save bugs
- Charting bugs
- Names bugs
- Printing bugs
- Bugs exchanging data with other applications
- MS Query bugs
- Bugs with Excel 4 Backwards Compatibility
- VBA and/or XLM bugs

The last section in the appendix ("Known Bugs Which Have *Not* Been Fixed in Excel 5.0c") covers bugs which have not been fixed in

Excel 5.0c and workarounds (if any) to help you avoid or solve problems related to those bugs.

▶▶ *Miscellaneous Worksheet Bugs*

The following miscellaneous worksheet problems are bugs in Excel 5.0 which have been corrected in the Excel 5.0c maintenance release. If you experience any of these problems, you may want to install Excel 5.0c.

▶ *Can't Use Edit ➤ Replace Command to Search for Blank Cells (Fixed in Excel 5.0c)*

If you choose the Edit ➤ Replace command, then leave the Find What box blank and choose Find Next, Replace, or Replace All to fill blank cells on a worksheet, you may receive the error message "Search string must be specified."

▶ *GP Fault When Scrolling in Text Import Wizard Preview Window (Fixed in Excel 5.0c)*

When you open a text file, then scroll the columns in the file using the horizontal scroll bar under the Text Import Wizard preview window, you may receive a general protection (GP) fault.

▶ *GP Fault When Checking Spelling in a Worksheet (Fixed in Excel 5.0c)*

You may receive a general protection (GP) fault when you check the spelling in a worksheet if a cell on the worksheet contains:

- A recognized word followed by a period, then a space, then an unrecognized word (e.g. Mr. Shostokovitch)
- A recognized word followed by a space, then an unrecognized word (e.g. Mr Shostokovitch).

► GP Fault When Pasting Multiple Grouped Drawing Objects (Fixed in Excel 5.0c)

If you create several groups of drawing objects on a worksheet, then group the multiple object groups into a larger group, you may receive a general protection (GP) fault when you copy and paste the larger group.

► Errors When Consolidating Data Using a Wildcard in Sheet Name (Fixed in Excel 5.0c)

When you use a wildcard character in a sheet name in the Data ➤ Consolidate dialog box, you may receive the following error messages(BOOK1.XLS is the name of the workbook that contains the worksheets you want to consolidate, and SHEET* is the reference entered to consolidate all of the worksheets that begin with the word SHEET):

- Cannot open consolidation source file '[BOOK1.XLS]sheet*'
- Cannot find 'SHEET*'
- Cannot open consolidation source file 'SHEET*'
- No data was consolidated

Also, when you choose Data ➤ Consolidate again, the reference may be listed twice in the All References list; once with the worksheet name in capitals, and once in lowercase, like this:

- 'sheet*'!$A$1
- 'SHEET*'!$A$1

► Reference to Remote Link Not Updated (Fixed in Excel 5.0c)

A reference to a cell that contains a remote link may not be updated if these conditions are met:

- The cell containing the reference refers to a cell on another worksheet in the same workbook, and

- The worksheet referred to is linked to an external workbook, and
- The external workbook is not open when you open the linked workbook.

▶ GP Fault When Pasting an Object into a Protected Workbook (Fixed in Excel 5.0c)

When you paste an object into a password-protected workbook, you may receive a general protection (GP) fault.

▶ Copied Worksheet Reverts to Standard Row Height (Fixed in Excel 5.0c)

If you copy an empty worksheet to a new or existing workbook, and you have changed the row height on the worksheet before copying, the worksheet rows may revert to the standard row height in the copy of the worksheet. Additionally, even if the worksheet contains information, certain rows on the worksheet may revert to the standard row height when you copy the sheet.

▶ No Label Added to Subtotal in List (Fixed in Excel 5.0c)

When you use the Data ➤ Subtotals command to create subtotals in a list of data, there may be no Total and Grand Total labels describing the subtotal values in the list.

▶ Currency Number Format Lost When Entering Fraction (Fixed in Excel 5.0c)

If you enter a fraction (e.g. $^1/_2$) in a cell formatted with a currency number format, the number format changes from currency to fraction.

▶ GP Fault Using a Shared Formula as Computed Criteria (Fixed in Excel 5.0c)

When you filter a list using computed criteria, and the following conditions are met, you may receive a general protection (GP) fault when the named cell changes:

- The computed criteria contains a shared formula, and
- The criteria is on a different worksheet from your list, and
- The formula contains a defined name

▶▶ File ▶ Save Bugs

The following file-saving problems are bugs in Excel 5.0 which have been corrected in the Excel 5.0c maintenance release. If you experience any of these problems, you may want to install Excel 5.0c.

▶ Formulas Incorrect When File Saved in SYLK Format (Fixed in Excel 5.0c)

If you save a file in the SYMBOLIC LINK (SYLK) file format and close the file, then open the file again, groups of similar formulas may be converted into a single array formula that displays incorrect results.

▶ Hidden Column/Row Not Saved in Text or CSV File Format (Fixed in Excel 5.0c)

When you hide a column or row in your worksheet, then save the file in Text or CSV file format, the hidden column or row may not be saved.

▶▶ Charting Bugs

The following charting problems are bugs in Excel 5.0 which have been corrected in the Excel 5.0c maintenance release. If you experience any of these problems, you may want to install Excel 5.0c.

▶ *Embedded Chart Shrinks After Print or Print Preview (Fixed in Excel 5.0c)*

If an embedded chart has label text (for example, labels for the x or y axis) and the label text wraps differently in print preview than it does on the screen, the chart may "shrink" each time it is printed or print previewed.

▶ *Pie Chart Shows Incorrect Percentage Value (Fixed in Excel 5.0c)*

When you display percentages in a pie chart, Excel may calculate incorrect percentages.

▶ *GP Fault Using Size Command with Chart Corners Selected (Fixed in Excel 5.0c)*

If you have Excel 4.0 menus displayed, then select the corners on a chart and choose the Format ▶ Size command, you may receive a general protection (GP) fault when you click on the chart.

▶▶ *Names Bugs*

The following names problems are bugs in Excel 5.0 which have been corrected in the Excel 5.0c maintenance release. If you experience any of these problems, you may want to install Excel 5.0c.

▶ *Name Value Not Updated If Worksheet Not Active (Fixed in Excel 5.0c)*

If you use a defined name in a formula on a worksheet, and then change the value of the name when the active sheet is other than a worksheet, the value of the defined name is not updated on the worksheet.

▶ Can't Define Global Name If Same Local Name Exists (Fixed in Excel 5.0c)

If a local name exists on the active worksheet, you cannot define a global name using the same name. For example, if the name Sheet1!Sales exists on Sheet1, you cannot define the global name Sales while Sheet1 is active.

▶ GP Fault Using Paste Name Dialog Box in Print Area (Fixed in Excel 5.0c)

If you use the Paste Name dialog box (By pressing F3) to enter a defined name in the Print Area box in the Page Setup dialog box, you may receive either a general protection (GP) fault, or the error message "Margins do not fit page size."

▶▶ Printing Bugs

The following printing problems are bugs in Excel 5.0 which have been corrected in the Excel 5.0c maintenance release. If you experience any of these problems, you may want to install Excel 5.0c.

▶ Sheets in Wrong Orientation with Print Entire Workbook (Fixed in Excel 5.0c)

When you print an entire workbook that contains worksheets with different page setup orientations (i.e., some worksheets are portrait, some are landscape), some of the worksheets may be printed with the wrong page orientation.

▶ Print Reports Not Using Continuous Page Numbers (Fixed in Excel 5.0c)

When you use the File ▶ Print Report command to print a report, the pages in your report may not be numbered consecutively.

▶▶ *Data Exchange Bugs*

The following data exchange problems are bugs in Excel 5.0 which
have been corrected in the Excel 5.0c maintenance release. If you experience any of these problems, you may want to install Excel 5.0c.

▶ *Unexpected Results with Second Paste Link to Item (Fixed in Excel 5.0c)*

If you link an object or picture from another application using the
Paste Link option in the Paste Special dialog box, and then link the
same information as text, the link as text may appear on the worksheet
as #VALUE!

▶ *DDE Poke Command Fails When Mouse Cursor Over Toolbar (Fixed in Excel 5.0c)*

When you send dynamic data exchange (DDE) messages to Excel
from another application using the DDE POKE command, you may
not receive an acknowledgment from Excel if the mouse cursor is positioned over the toolbar in Excel.

▶▶ *MS Query Bugs*

The following query problems are bugs in Excel 5.0 which have been
corrected in the Excel 5.0c maintenance release. If you experience any
of these problems, you may want to install Excel 5.0c.

▶ *Error Using Decimal Values with Custom Expressions (Fixed in Excel 5.0c)*

In MS Query version 1.0, you may receive the message "Syntax error"
when you try to enter a custom expression that contains a decimal
value but does not have a numeric value to the left of the decimal point.

▶ Negative Number in Query is Incorrect When Returned to Worksheet (Fixed in Excel 5.0c)

When you return data from MS Query to Excel 5.0, negative numbers may be returned as positive numbers. For example, the value −1 in Microsoft Query is returned as 65535, the value −2 is returned as 65534, and so on.

▶ Refresh Data Command May Not Update as Expected (Fixed in Excel 5.0c)

When you choose the Refresh Data command, the data in your worksheet may not be updated as expected.

▶ GP Fault Exiting MS Query After Canceling Get External Data (Fixed in Excel 5.0c)

When you use the Data ➤ Get External Data command in Excel, perform a query in MS Query, then cancel the query and exit Excel, you may receive a general protection (GP) fault when you exit MS Query.

▶ No Option to Save/Not Save Password with MS Query Add-in (Fixed in Excel 5.0c)

When you use the Data ➤ Get External Data command to perform a query in MS Query, the dialog box that appears when you return to Excel does not contain a password option (i.e., you do not have the option to save the password with your data).

▶ GP Fault When Deleting Column After Copying Data (Fixed in Excel 5.0c)

If you copy records in a query that contains a field with the Image data type, and you then delete one of the columns in the query, you may receive a general protection (GP) fault. Additionally, if you copy records in a query that contains only a field with the Image data type, and you delete that column, you may receive the error message "Out of memory."

▶ "Can't Group By..." Error When Adding Criteria (Fixed in Excel 5.0c)

When you add criteria to a query created using a SQL data source, you may receive either the error message "Can't Group By Bit Field" or "TEXT and IMAGE data types may not be used in a GROUP BY clause."

▶ "Invalid Path" When Using Access 2.0 Driver (Fixed in Excel 5.0c)

When you open a database using the Microsoft Access 2.0 ODBC Driver for Microsoft Office, you may receive the error message "Invalid Path."

▶▶ *Excel 4 Backwards Compatibility Bugs*

The following Excel 4 backwards compatibility problems are bugs in Excel 5.0 which have been corrected in the Excel 5.0c maintenance release. If you experience any of these problems, you may want to install Excel 5.0c.

▶ GP Fault If REFTEXT() Refers to Closed Workbook (Fixed in Excel 5.0c)

When you use the REFTEXT() function in an Excel 4.0 macro sheet, and the reference includes the name of a closed workbook, you may receive a general protection (GP) fault.

▶ Cannot Reopen Password-Protected File (Fixed in Excel 5.0c)

If you save a worksheet that contains an embedded chart as a password-protected Excel 4.0 worksheet, you may receive a general protection (GP) fault if you try to open the file in Excel 5.0.

▶ Unattached Text in Wrong Place on Zoomed Embedded Chart (Fixed in Excel 5.0c)

If you open a Microsoft Excel 4.0 worksheet that contains an embedded chart, and the worksheet is at a zoom magnification other than 100 percent, unattached text on the chart may appear in the wrong location when you view the worksheet at 100 percent.

▶ Can't Reference Name in Closed Excel 4.0 Workbook (Fixed in Excel 5.0c)

If you reference a name on a closed Excel 4.0 workbook, and the name is defined on a worksheet other than the first worksheet in the workbook, you may receive the error message "name on 'WORKBOOK' is not defined or is too complex" (where 'name' is the name you are referencing, and 'WORKBOOK' is the workbook that contains the name). This error message appears when you create the reference as well as when you update the reference.

▶ Chart Sheet Tab Contains Filename Extension When Opened (Fixed in Excel 5.0c)

When you open an Excel 4.0, 3.0, or 2.1 chart file, the chart sheet tab contains the filename extension as well as the filename (e.g., sales.xlc).

▶ *GET.CHART.ITEM() Returns #Value! If Chart Item Selected (Fixed in Excel 5.0c)*

If you use the GET.CHART.ITEM() function in an Excel 4.0 macro, the function may return the #VALUE! error value instead of the position of the selected chart item.

▶ *NAMES( ) Returns #N/A If Active Sheet Is Chart or Module (Fixed in Excel 5.0c)*

If you use the NAMES() function in an Excel 4.0 macro to return defined names on a workbook, the function returns the #N/A error value if the active sheet in the workbook is a chart or a module, even if the active workbook contains workbook-level (global) defined names.

▶ *GP Fault When Evaluating INDIRECT( ) in Defined Name on Chart (Fixed in Excel 5.0c)*

If you open an Excel 4.0 chart file in Excel 5.0, and the chart has a reference that contains the INDIRECT() function in a defined name, you may receive a general protection (GP) fault if you evaluate the reference in the formula bar.

▶▶ *VBA and/or XLM Bugs*

The following VBA/XLM problems are bugs in Excel 5.0 which have been corrected in the Excel 5.0c maintenance release. Although teaching programming is beyond the scope of this book, this information is presented for the benefit of users who are familiar with VBA and/or XLM. If you experience any of these problems, you may want to install Excel 5.0c.

► Methods Fail When Embedded Chart Is Edited (Fixed in Excel 5.0c)

The following methods may fail if the active sheet is an embedded chart that is currently being edited and if an object is not specified for the method:

- Charts Method (Syntax 2)
- DialogSheets Method (Syntax 2)
- Modules Method (Syntax 2)
- Sheets Method (Syntax 2)
- Worksheets Method (Syntax 2)

► Can't Get or Set Properties of X Axis in XY Scatter Chart (Fixed in Excel 5.0c)

You may receive one of the following error messages when you attempt to set or return the X axis scale properties for an XY (scatter) chart:

- Run-time error '1005': "Unable to set the <property> property of the axis class"
- Run-time error '1005': "Unable to get the <property> property of the axis class"

► Selection.Cells with Nonadjacent Selection Returns Single Cell (Fixed in Excel 5.0c)

When you use the Range method or the Selection property with the Cells method in a Visual Basic module to return a nonadjacent selection of cells on a worksheet, only the first cell in the selection is returned.

▶ *Cannot Set Chart Data Marker Color Using Macro (Fixed in Excel 5.0c)*

When the background or foreground color of a chart data marker is set to none, you cannot change the color of that data marker with a macro.

▶ *"Cannot Find Macro..." Using Run Method with Add-in Macro (Fixed in Excel 5.0c)*

In a Visual Basic module, if you use the Run method of the Application object to run a macro located in an add-in, you may receive the error message "Run-time error '1004': Cannot find macro '<ADDIN.XLA>! <Addin_Macro>'" (<ADDIN.XLA> is the name of the add-in that contains the macro, and <Addin_Macro> is the name of the macro you want to run.)

▶ *"Cannot Find Macro" Running Macro in Active Workbook (Fixed in Excel 5.0c)*

In a Visual Basic procedure, if you activate a sheet in another workbook, then use the Run method to run a macro in the activated workbook (such as SHEET1!Auto_Activate), you may receive the following message "Run-time error '1004':Cannot find macro 'SHEET1!Auto_Activate'."

▶ *Macro Error Using GET.DOCUMENT(1) with Text File (Fixed in Excel 5.0c)*

If you use the GET.DOCUMENT(1) function in a macro to return the name of the active document (for example, to parse or process information in the file), you may receive a macro error if the file is in the Text, CSV, SYLK, or PRN file format.

► *DOCUMENTS( ) and WINDOWS( ) Return XL5GALRY.XLS Filename (Fixed in Excel 5.0c)*

If you use the DOCUMENTS() or the WINDOWS() macro function to return a list of open documents or document windows, the filename XL5GALRY.XLS may be returned in the list.

► *GET.DOCUMENT(4) Returns FALSE After FOR.CELL Function (Fixed in Excel 5.0c)*

If you use the FOR.CELL() macro function, then use the GET.DOCUMENT(4) function without the name_text argument, or with a workbook name, to return a value indicating whether changes have been made to the workbook since you saved it last, the value returned by the GET.DOCUMENT(4) function is FALSE.

► *Custom Function Doesn't Recalculate with Calculate Method (Fixed in Excel 5.0c)*

If you use the Calculate method to recalculate a custom function in a specified range on a worksheet, and you have the Manual calculation option selected, the function may not be recalculated.

► *Text Import Wizard Is Displayed Using OPEN?( ) with Text File (Fixed in Excel 5.0c)*

When you use the OPEN?() macro function to display the Open dialog box, the Text Import Wizard dialog box may appear when you open a text file.

► *Caller Does Not Return Hierarchical Menu Information (Fixed in Excel 5.0c)*

When you use the Caller function, or the Caller property, and the macro currently running was started by choosing a menu command, the array of values returned does not include information about whether the command that ran the macro was located on a top level menu or on a submenu.

▶ *"Cannot Find" Using Analysis ToolPak Visual Basic Function (Fixed in Excel 5.0c)*

If you use one of the functions provided in the Analysis ToolPak-VBA add-in, (ATPVBAEN.XLA), such as EDATE(), you may receive the error message "Run-time error '1004': Cannot find macro '[ATPV-BAEN.XLA]REG!reg_EDATE' " (the name of the function you use appears in the place of EDATE in the error message).

▶ *"Argument Not Optional" Using Visual Basic ATP Functions (Fixed in Excel 5.0c)*

When you use any of these Analysis ToolPak functions in a Visual Basic module, you may receive the error message "Argument not optional".

- GCD()
- LCM()
- MULTINOMIAL()
- IMPRODUCT()

▶▶ *Known Bugs Which Have Not Been Fixed in Excel 5.0c*

The following problems are known bugs in Excel 5.0 which have *not* been fixed in the maintenance release, Excel 5.0c; workarounds are presented, where available, to help you avoid or solve many of the problems.

▶ Formatting and Charts Lost When File Saved to .WQ1 (Quattro Pro for DOS) Format

When you save a file in the .WQ1 (Quattro Pro/DOS) file format, most of the formatting and any chart sheets contained in the file will be lost. In addition, only one worksheet can be saved.

To work around this problem:

Save the file in the **WK1,FMT (1-2-3)** (.WK1) file format instead. The WK1/FMT (1-2-3) file format can handle more formatting information than the .WQ1 file format, and the latest versions of Quattro Pro can read the WK1/FMT format. To save the file, activate the worksheet you want to save (only the active worksheet can be saved), then choose File ➤ Save As. Enter a name in the File Name box, then select WK1/FMT (1-2-3) from the Save File As Type box and click OK.

▶ Functions Not Saved to Quattro Pro File Format

When you save a worksheet to the .WQ1 (Quattro Pro/DOS) file format, you may receive the error message "Cannot write record. (Cell: A1)" if the file contains any of the following functions:

- N()
- T()
- NPER()
- FV() (only if you use the optional arguments pv and type)
- PMT() (only if you use the optional arguments fv and type)
- PV() (only if you use the optional arguments fv and type)

The error message will reference the cell that contains one of the functions listed above. When you open the saved file, the cell that contained the function will contain the *value* of the function, but not the function itself.

To work around this problem:

As of this writing, there is no workaround for the problem.

► *Chart References to Pivot Table Are Not Updated Correctly*

If you create a chart from data in a pivot table, and you move either the chart or the pivot table to another workbook, changes you make to the pivot table fields while the workbook containing the chart is closed may not be updated in the chart.

To work around this problem:

Do either of the following to avoid incorrect references when you create a chart from a pivot table:

- Keep the pivot table and the chart that references it in the same workbook.

- Or, before you update the references in the chart, open the workbook that contains the pivot table. As long as the workbook that contains the pivot table is open when you update the references in the chart, the references will be correct.

► *Embedded Chart is Grouped with Drawing Objects*

If you create multiple drawing objects on a worksheet and group them, then create an embedded chart on the worksheet, the chart becomes part of the group when you close and reopen the file containing the objects. This problem occurs whether you group the drawing objects before or after you create the embedded chart.

To work around this problem:

You can avoid the problem by creating the embedded chart before you create the last of the drawing objects that you are going to group (if you create one of the drawing objects that you want to group *after* you create the embedded chart, the problem does not occur).

If an embedded chart has become grouped with drawing objects on your worksheet because of this problem, follow these steps to correct it:

1. Ungroup the objects.

2. Use the Drawing Selection tool to select the objects that you want to group (not including the chart).

3. Group the selected objects. With the group selected, choose Edit ➤ Cut.

4. Save and close the file.

5. Open the file. Choose Edit ➤ Paste, then drag the grouped object to reposition it on the worksheet.

▶ Custom Default Chart Format Is Not Applied to an Embedded Chart

When you create an embedded chart, the built-in default chart format may be applied, even if you have selected a custom chart format as the default (in the Tools ➤ Options, Chart dialog tab).

To work around this problem:

If Excel applies the built-in default chart format to an embedded chart instead of the custom default chart format you have selected, use the chart AutoFormat feature to apply the custom format you want. See Chapter 14, Advanced Charting, to learn how to use chart Autoformats.

▶ Problems Resizing an Excel Chart Object that is Embedded in Word 6

If you embed (rather than link) an Excel chart object in Word 6, then resize the chart object by dragging a border handle, you may have problems with the chart remaining in correct proportion. If the embedded chart object was a chart sheet in Excel, the chart text, chart legend, and object frame will not remain in proportion if you resize the chart frame. If the embedded chart object was an embedded chart in Excel, the chart will be displayed off-center in the object frame, and worksheet cells will be visible in the frame.

These symptoms do not occur if you create a linked object rather than an embedded object in Word (choose the Paste Link button instead of the Paste button in the Edit ➤ Paste Special dialog box); however, when you link the chart, it resizes in Word whenever you resize the original chart in Microsoft Excel.

To work around this problem:

If you use a chart that is located on a chart sheet instead of an embedded chart, size the chart in Microsoft Excel before embedding it in Word. In Word, use this procedure to embed chart objects from chart sheets:

1. Choose Insert ➤ Object, and select the Create From File tab.

2. Select the Excel workbook that contains the chart sheet you want to embed, then click OK.

3. If the chart you want to embed is not the active sheet in the workbook, double-click the object and click the sheet tab in Excel for the appropriate chart.

4. When the chart you want to embed is displayed, scale or crop it as desired, and then click anywhere outside the chart to return to Word.

If you use an embedded chart instead of a chart sheet, use this method to size the embedded Excel chart object in Word without distorting the chart object or displaying cells from a worksheet:

1. Select the embedded chart object.

2. Press Shift+F9 to display the field code instead of the object. The field code representing the chart object looks like this: {**EMBED Excel.Chart.5 \s**}

3. Edit the field code to delete the **\s** (so that it reads: {**EMBED Excel.Chart.5**}).

4. With the cursor in the field code, press F9 to update the change.

5. Select the chart object and size it by dragging its border handles.

► *GP Fault When Using Tab Scrolling Button in an Embedded Worksheet*

If you edit an embedded Excel worksheet object in a Word document, and the first sheet in the embedded workbook is hidden, you may receive a general protection (GP) fault when you click the first tab scrolling button on the worksheet.

To work around this problem:

To avoid receiving a GP fault when you edit an embedded Excel worksheet object in which the first worksheet in the embedded workbook is hidden, do one of the following:

* Unhide the worksheet in Excel, move the sheet so that it is not the first sheet in the workbook, then hide the sheet again.

* Avoid clicking any of the tab scrolling buttons at the bottom of the workbook window. (Clicking these buttons when you are editing an embedded worksheet has no effect, because these buttons are disabled in an embedded worksheet.)

* Edit the worksheet object using the Open command rather than the Edit command (this method works only if you have not previously edited the embedded worksheet object by double-clicking the object or by choosing Edit ➤ Spreadsheet Object):

    1. In Word, select the worksheet object you want to edit.

    2. Choose Edit ➤ Spreadsheet Object, then choose Open.

Additional information: When you *edit* an embedded worksheet object in Word by double-clicking the object, or by choosing Edit ➤ Spreadsheet Object and choosing the Edit command, you cannot hide or unhide worksheets in the workbook; however, when you *open* an embedded worksheet object in Word by choosing Edit ➤ Spreadsheet Object and choosing the Open command, you can hide or unhide worksheets in the workbook.

▶ Can't Link to Worksheet with Exclamation Point in Name

If you link information from an Excel worksheet to another application, and the worksheet name contains an exclamation point, you may have one of these problems: either an error message appears in the other application, or the information appears in the other application but the link cannot be edited or updated.

To work around this problem:

When you link information from an Excel worksheet to another application, be sure the worksheet name does not contain an exclamation point.

▶ Infinite Loop if OLE Automation Server Busy

If you use the CreateObject function in a Visual Basic procedure to create an OLE Automation object, then request information from the object (for example, to display a dialog box), then switch back to Microsoft Excel, you may receive the error message "Microsoft Excel is waiting for another application to complete an OLE action." The only available buttons are OK and Help. The error message continues to appear when you choose OK.

This happens because when you create an OLE Automation object (run a server application) in a Visual Basic procedure in Excel, then send that object a command, the server must finish processing the command before you can continue working in Excel.

To work around this problem:

To break out of the infinite loop (i.e., the dialog box that contains the error message won't disappear), cancel or complete the request in the server application. For example, if a dialog box is open in the server application, close the dialog box, then return to the client application. Then you can click OK in the dialog box that contains the error message and it will not reappear.

▶ GP Fault if Too Many Consecutive Line Continuation Characters in VB Procedure

You may receive a general protection (GP) fault if you copy lines in a Visual Basic procedure that contain the line-continuation character (_), and paste the lines in a procedure such that there are more than ten consecutive lines joined with line-continuation characters.

To work around this problem:

Do not copy and paste lines that end in line-continuation characters such that the resulting code will contain more than nine consecutive lines that end with the line-continuation character.

▶ OLE Automation Error Using Quit Method with GetObject

If you use the GetObject function with a file name in a Visual Basic 3.0 procedure to open an Excel workbook, then use the Quit method to quit Excel, the following error message appears: "OLE Automation error. Worksheet does not have Quit method."

This happens because when you use the GetObject function with a file name to open a file, the OLE Automation object that is created is a Worksheet object, not an application object. The error occurs when you use the Quit method with the Worksheet object because the Quit method does not apply to a Worksheet object.

To work around this problem:

To use the Quit method to quit Excel after creating an OLE Automation object in an application that uses Visual Basic, do either of the following:

- Use the Parent property to return the Application object and use the Quit method as in the following Visual Basic procedure:

' Dimension variable x as Object type

Dim x As Object

' Set x equal to Microsoft Excel Worksheet object

Set x = GetObject("C:\EXCEL\BOOK1.XLS")

' Quit Microsoft Excel

x.Application.Quit

- Use the class argument of the GetObject function to return the Application object as the OLE Automation object, then open the desired workbook file as in the following Visual Basic procedure:

' Dimension variable x as object type

Dim x As Object

' Set x equal to Microsoft Excel Application object

Set x = GetObject("", "Excel.Application.5")

' Open workbook BOOK1.XLS

x.Workbooks.Open "C:\EXCEL\BOOK1.XLS"

' Quit Microsoft Excel

x.Quit

▶ GP Fault in VBA.DLL on Exit After Saving to Floppy Drive

If you save a workbook that contains a Visual Basic module to a floppy disk, then remove the floppy disk from the disk drive and save the file with the same file name to another drive, you may receive these error messages: "File already exists" and "Document not saved." When you quit Microsoft Excel, you may receive a general protection (GP) fault in module VBA.DLL.

This happens because OLE objects, pivot tables, and Visual Basic modules require the use of data on the file that contains them. When you use these objects in a workbook, the file that contains the workbook must be available when you choose the File ➤ Save or File ➤ Save As commands. In general, when you work with a file containing one of these objects on a floppy drive, you should keep the floppy disk in the drive while the file is open.

To work around this problem:

To avoid receiving these error messages after you save a workbook that contains a Visual Basic module to a floppy drive, make sure the floppy disk that contains the workbook file is still in the drive before you save the file to another drive.

▶ Index

Note to the Reader: Throughout this index **boldfaced** page numbers indicate primary discussions of a topic. *Italicized* page numbers indicate illustrations.

▶ Symbols

& (ampersands)
    evaluation order of, 98
    in file searches, 371
    in headers and footers,
        189
    for joining text, 99–100
' (apostrophes)
    in macros, 687
    with SQL.REQUEST,
        626
    for text, 66, 217
    for worksheet refer-
        ences, 110
* (asterisks)
    in cell selection, 74
    in consolidating data,
        766
    in criteria, 533
    in field selection, 612
    in file filtering, 35
    in file searches, 370–371
    as formatting symbols,
        153
    for multiplication, 97–99
    for sound notes, 360
    in text searches,
        86–87, 305

@ (at signs), 153
\ (backslashes), 153
{} (braces), 870
[] (brackets)
    in external references,
        111
    for time codes, 156
^ (carets), 98
: (colons)
    in cell references, 62,
        109
    as formatting symbols,
        153
    in number entry, 65
, (commas)
    as array separators, 263
    in file searches, 371
    as formatting symbols,
        153
    in functions, 119
    in number entry, 65
    for print areas, 191
$ (dollar signs)
    for cell references,
        105–108
    in number entry, 65
" (double quotes)
    in file searches, 371
    as formatting
        symbols, 153

with SQL.REQUEST
    function, **625–626**
= (equal signs)
    in criteria, 532–533
    evaluation order of, 98
    in filters, 512
    in formatting numbers,
        153
    in formulas, 94, 119
! (exclamation points)
    bugs with, 1135
    in external references,
        110–111
/ (forward slashes)
    for division, 98–99
    evaluation order of, 98
    as formatting symbols,
        153
    in Lotus 1-2-3, 854
    in number entry, 65
> (greater than signs)
    in criteria, 532–533
    evaluation order of, 98
    in filters, 512
    in formatting numbers,
        153
< (less than signs)
    in criteria, 532–533
    evaluation order of, 98
    in filters, 512

Index

X

Y

YES, YOU *CAN* DO WINDOWS.

964 pp. ISBN:842-4.

Mastering *Windows 3.1* is the most comprehensive start-to-finish Windows tutorial available today. And this Special Edition includes a special section that includes tips, tricks, and troubleshooting advice that alone is worth the price of the book.

Plus full coverage of all of the basics of Windows. Find out how to set up your desktop for ease of use, manipulate multiple windows and applications and more. You'll also find out about supercharging your system, running both Windows and DOS applications on your Windows 3.1 system.

There is also extensive coverage of advanced techniques, including TrueType font management, Dynamic Data Exchange (DDE) and Object Linking and Embedding (OLE) and multimedia support.

SYBEX. Help Yourself.

2021 Challenger Drive
Alameda, CA 94501
1-800-227-2346

SYBEX

POCKET-SIZED PC EXPERTISE.

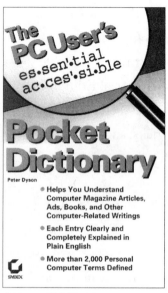

550 pp. ISBN: 756-8.

2021 Challenger Drive
Alameda, CA 94501
1-510-523-8233
1-800-227-2346

SYBEX

[1602] Mastering Excel 5 for Windows Special Edition

GET A FREE CATALOG JUST FOR EXPRESSING YOUR OPINION.

Help us improve our books and get a *FREE* full-color catalog in the bargain. Please complete this form, pull out this page and send it in today. The address is on the reverse side.

Name _____ **Company** _____

Address _____ **City** _____ **State** ____ **Zip** _____

Phone (___) _____

1. How would you rate the overall quality of this book?

❑ Excellent
❑ Very Good
❑ Good
❑ Fair
❑ Below Average
❑ Poor

2. What were the things you liked most about the book? (Check all that apply)

❑ Pace
❑ Format
❑ Writing Style
❑ Examples
❑ Table of Contents
❑ Index
❑ Price
❑ Illustrations
❑ Type Style
❑ Cover
❑ Depth of Coverage
❑ Fast Track Notes

3. What were the things you liked *least* about the book? (Check all that apply)

❑ Pace
❑ Format
❑ Writing Style
❑ Examples
❑ Table of Contents
❑ Index
❑ Price
❑ Illustrations
❑ Type Style
❑ Cover
❑ Depth of Coverage
❑ Fast Track Notes

4. Where did you buy this book?

❑ Bookstore chain
❑ Small independent bookstore
❑ Computer store
❑ Wholesale club
❑ College bookstore
❑ Technical bookstore
❑ Other _____

5. How did you decide to buy this particular book?

❑ Recommended by friend
❑ Recommended by store personnel
❑ Author's reputation
❑ Sybex's reputation
❑ Read book review in _____
❑ Other _____

6. How did you pay for this book?

❑ Used own funds
❑ Reimbursed by company
❑ Received book as a gift

7. What is your level of experience with the subject covered in this book?

❑ Beginner
❑ Intermediate
❑ Advanced

8. How long have you been using a computer?

years _____
months _____

9. Where do you most often use your computer?

❑ Home
❑ Work

❑ Both
❑ Other _____

10. What kind of computer equipment do you have? (Check all that apply)

❑ PC Compatible Desktop Computer
❑ PC Compatible Laptop Computer
❑ Apple/Mac Computer
❑ Apple/Mac Laptop Computer
❑ CD ROM
❑ Fax Modem
❑ Data Modem
❑ Scanner
❑ Sound Card
❑ Other _____

11. What other kinds of software packages do you ordinarily use?

❑ Accounting
❑ Databases
❑ Networks
❑ Apple/Mac
❑ Desktop Publishing
❑ Spreadsheets
❑ CAD
❑ Games
❑ Word Processing
❑ Communications
❑ Money Management
❑ Other _____

12. What operating systems do you ordinarily use?

❑ DOS
❑ OS/2
❑ Windows
❑ Apple/Mac
❑ Windows NT
❑ Other _____

13. On what computer-related subject(s) would you like to see more books?

_____

_____

_____

_____

14. Do you have any other comments about this book? (Please feel free to use a separate piece of paper if you need more room)

_____

_____

_____

_____

- - - - - - - - - - - - PLEASE FOLD, SEAL, AND MAIL TO SYBEX - - - - - - - - - - - - -

SYBEX INC.
Department M
2021 Challenger Drive
Alameda, CA
94501

SYBEX®

Function Key Shortcuts

F1	Display the Help Contents window
Shift+F1	Display context-sensitive help
F2	Activate the formula bar to edit the active cell
Shift+F2	Insert a cell note
Ctrl+F2	Display the Info window for a cell (shows formula and note)
F3	Display the Paste Name dialog box if there are names defined
Shift+F3	Display the Function Wizard
Ctrl+F3	Display the Define Name dialog box
Ctrl+Shift+F3	Display the Create Names dialog box
F4	Repeat the last action or, when you are editing a formula, convert a cell reference type (absolute, mixed, relative)
Shift+F4	Find the next occurrence of a search string
Ctrl+F4	Close the active window
Ctrl+Shift+F4	Find the previous occurrence of a search string
Alt+F4	Close Excel
F5	Display the Go To dialog box
Ctrl+F5	Restore the window's previous size
F6	Go to the next pane
Shift+F6	Go to the previous pane
Ctrl+F6	Go to the next window
Ctrl+Shift+F6	Go to the previous window
F7	Check spelling
Ctrl+F7	Move the window
F8	Turn Extend mode on or off (for selecting data)
Shift+F8	Turn Add mode on or off
Ctrl+F8	Size the window
F9	Calculate all sheets in all open workbooks
Shift+F9	Calculate the active sheet
Ctrl+F9	Minimize a workbook
F10	Activate the menu bar
Shift+F10	Activate the shortcut menu
Ctrl+F10	Maximize a workbook
F11	Insert a new chart sheet
Shift+F11	Insert a new worksheet
Ctrl+F11	Insert a new Excel 4.0 macro sheet
F12	Display the Save As dialog box
Shift+F12	Save a file (in Excel 5, Ctrl+S also works)
Ctrl+F12	Open a file (in Excel 5, Ctrl+0 also works)
Ctrl+Shift+F12	Print a file (in Excel 5, Ctrl+P also works)

For a complete list of keyboard shortcuts, organized by category, see Appendix C.